Excel® 2010 Bible

Excel® 2010 Bible

John Walkenbach

WILEY

John Wiley & Sons, Inc.

Excel® 2010 Bible

Published by
John Wiley & Sons, Inc.
10475 Crosspoint Boulevard
Indianapolis, IN 46256
www.wiley.com

Copyright © 2010 by John Wiley & Sons, Inc., Hoboken, New Jersey

Library of Congress Control Number: 2010922573

Published simultaneously in Canada

ISBN 978-0-470-47487-7 (pbk); ISBN 978-0-470-63474-5 (ebk); ISBN 978-0-470-63475-2 (ebk);
ISBN 978-0-470-63476-9 (ebk)

Manufactured in the United States of America

10 9

This book is dedicated to Wormpicker, a gentleman and a scholar who one day will be a fine old-time fiddler.

About the Author

John Walkenbach is a bestselling Excel author who has published more than 50 spreadsheet books. He lives amid the saguaros, javelinas, rattlesnakes, bobcats, and gila monsters in Southern Arizona — but the critters are mostly scared away by his clawhammer banjo playing. For more information, Google him.

About the Technical Editor

Niek Otten started in data processing in 1967 in an insurance company. He ran into VisiCalc in 1980 and has been addicted to spreadsheets ever since. His first acquaintance with Excel (version 1!) was in 1985 on a Macintosh. Since 2005, Niek has been self-employed. He answers questions about Excel in newsgroups and forums, reviews and edits Excel books, writes articles, and develops Excel-related software, such as a high-performance actuarial add-in. Niek has been a Microsoft Most Valuable Professional (MVP) for Excel since 2001.

Credits

Project Editor
Rebecca Senninger

Acquisitions Editor
Katie Mohr

Technical Editor
Niek Otten

Senior Copy Editor
Teresa Artman

Editorial Manager
Leah Cameron

Editorial Director
Mary C. Corder

**Vice President and Executive
Group Publisher**
Richard Swadley

Vice President and Publisher
Andy Cummings

Project Coordinator
Katie Crocker

Vertical Websites Project Manager
Laura Moss

**Vertical Websites Assistant
Project Manager**
Jenny Swisher

Vertical Websites Associate Producers
Josh Frank
Shawn Patrick
Doug Kuhn
Marilyn Hummel

Proofreading and Indexing
Linda Seifert
Broccoli Information Management

Contents

Acknowledgments xxxvii

Introduction xxxviii

Part I: Getting Started with Excel   1

Chapter 1: Introducing Excel 3

What Is Excel Good For? 3
What's New in Excel 2010? 4
Understanding Workbooks and Worksheets 5
Moving around a Worksheet 8
    Navigating with your keyboard 9
    Navigating with your mouse 10
Introducing the Ribbon 11
    Ribbon tabs 11
    Contextual tabs 13
    Types of commands on the Ribbon 13
    Accessing the Ribbon by using your keyboard 15
Using Shortcut Menus 16
Customizing Your Quick Access Toolbar 17
Working with Dialog Boxes 19
    Navigating dialog boxes 19
    Using tabbed dialog boxes 20
Using the Task Pane 22
Creating Your First Excel Worksheet 22
    Getting started on your worksheet 22
    Filling in the month names 23
    Entering the sales data 23
    Formatting the numbers 24
    Making your worksheet look a bit fancier .25
    Summing the values 25
    Creating a chart 26
    Printing your worksheet 27
    Saving your workbook 28

Contents

Chapter 2: Entering and Editing Worksheet Data **29**

Exploring the Types of Data You Can Use 29
  About numeric values 30
  About text entries 30
  About formulas 30
Entering Text and Values into Your Worksheets 32
Entering Dates and Times into Your Worksheets 33
  Entering date values 33
  Entering time values 34
Modifying Cell Contents 34
  Erasing the contents of a cell 35
  Replacing the contents of a cell 35
  Editing the contents of a cell 35
  Learning some handy data-entry techniques 37
      Automatically moving the cell pointer after entering data 37
      Using navigation keys instead of pressing Enter 37
      Selecting a range of input cells before entering data 38
      Using Ctrl+Enter to place information into multiple cells simultaneously 38
      Entering decimal points automatically 38
      Using AutoFill to enter a series of values 38
      Using AutoComplete to automate data entry 39
      Forcing text to appear on a new line within a cell 40
      Using AutoCorrect for shorthand data entry 40
      Entering numbers with fractions 40
      Simplifying data entry by using a form 40
      Entering the current date or time into a cell 42
Applying Number Formatting 42
  Using automatic number formatting 43
  Formatting numbers by using the Ribbon 44
  Using shortcut keys to format numbers 45
  Formatting numbers using the Format Cells dialog box 45
  Adding your own custom number formats 47

Chapter 3: Essential Worksheet Operations **49**

Learning the Fundamentals of Excel Worksheets 49
  Working with Excel windows 49
      Moving and resizing windows 51
      Switching among windows 52
      Closing windows 52
  Activating a worksheet 53
  Adding a new worksheet to your workbook 54
  Deleting a worksheet you no longer need 54
  Changing the name of a worksheet 55
  Changing a sheet tab color 56

Rearranging your worksheets 56
Hiding and unhiding a worksheet 57
Controlling the Worksheet View 58
Zooming in or out for a better view 59
Viewing a worksheet in multiple windows 60
Comparing sheets side by side..61
Splitting the worksheet window into panes 62
Keeping the titles in view by freezing panes 62
Monitoring cells with a Watch Window 64
Working with Rows and Columns 65
Inserting rows and columns 65
Deleting rows and columns 66
Hiding rows and columns 66
Changing column widths and row heights 67
Changing column widths 67
Changing row heights...68

Chapter 4: Working with Cells and Ranges **69**
Understanding Cells and Ranges...69
Selecting ranges..70
Selecting complete rows and columns 71
Selecting noncontiguous ranges..71
Selecting multisheet ranges 72
Selecting special types of cells 74
Selecting cells by searching 76
Copying or Moving Ranges 78
Copying by using Ribbon commands..79
Copying by using shortcut menu commands 80
Copying by using shortcut keys 81
Copying or moving by using drag-and-drop 81
Copying to adjacent cells..82
Copying a range to other sheets...83
Using the Office Clipboard to paste..84
Pasting in special ways 85
Using the Paste Special Dialog box 87
Performing mathematical operations without formulas....................88
Skipping blanks when pasting..89
Transposing a range 89
Using Names to Work with Ranges..89
Creating range names in your workbooks 90
Using the New Name dialog box 90
Using the Name box...91
Using the Create Names from Selection dialog box...........................91
Managing names 92

Contents

Adding Comments to Cells 94

    Formatting comments 95

    Changing a comment's shape 96

    Reading comments 96

    Printing comments 96

    Hiding and showing comments 97

    Selecting comments..97

    Editing comments 98

    Deleting comments 98

Chapter 5: Introducing Tables 99

What Is a Table? 99

Creating a Table...102

Changing the Look of a Table 103

Working with Tables 105

    Navigating in a table...105

    Selecting parts of a table 105

    Adding new rows or columns...105

    Deleting rows or columns..106

    Moving a table...106

    Setting table options..107

    Working with the Total Row 107

    Removing duplicate rows from a table...109

    Sorting and filtering a table 110

        Sorting a table 110

        Filtering a table 112

    Converting a table back to a range 113

Chapter 6: Worksheet Formatting 115

Getting to Know the Formatting Tools..115

    Using the formatting tools of the Home Tab......................................116

    Using the Mini toolbar 116

    Using the Format Cells dialog box..118

Using Different Fonts to Format Your Worksheet 119

Changing Text Alignment 122

    Choosing horizontal alignment options...122

    Choosing vertical alignment options 124

    Wrapping or shrinking text to fit the cell 124

    Merging worksheet cells to create additional text space......................124

    Displaying text at an angle..125

    Controlling the text direction 126

Using Colors and Shading...127

Adding Borders and Lines 128

Adding a Background Image to a Worksheet..130

Contents

Using Named Styles for Easier Formatting 131
    Applying styles 132
    Modifying an existing style 133
    Creating new styles 134
    Merging styles from other workbooks 134
    Controlling styles with templates 135
Understanding Document Themes 135
    Applying a theme 137
    Customizing a theme 138

Chapter 7: Understanding Excel Files 141

Creating a New Workbook 141
Opening an Existing Workbook 143
    Using the Favorite Links 146
    Filtering filenames 146
    Choosing your file display preferences 147
Saving a Workbook 147
Using AutoRecover 149
    Recovering versions of the current workbook 149
    Recovering unsaved work 149
Specifying a Password 150
Organizing Your Files 151
Other Workbook Info Options 153
    Security Warning section 153
    Compatibility Mode section 154
    Permissions section 154
    Prepare for Sharing section 155
    Versions section 156
Closing Workbooks 156
Safeguarding Your Work 157
Excel File Compatibility 157
    Checking compatibility 157
    Recognizing the Excel 2010 file formats 159
    Saving a file for use with an older version of Excel 159

Chapter 8: Using and Creating Templates 161

Exploring Excel Templates 161
    Viewing templates 161
    Creating a workbook from a template 162
    Modifying a template 164
Understanding Custom Excel Templates 165
    Working with the default templates 166
        Using the workbook template to change workbook defaults 166
        Using the worksheet template to change worksheet defaults 167

Contents

Editing your templates 168
Resetting the default workbook and worksheet settings 168
Creating custom templates 168
Saving your custom templates 170
Ideas for creating templates 170

Chapter 9: Printing Your Work 171

Printing with One Click 171
Changing Your Page View 172
Normal view 173
Page Layout view.. 174
Page Break Preview 175
Adjusting Common Page Setup Settings... 177
Choosing your printer 178
Specifying what you want to print... 178
Changing page orientation 179
Specifying paper size 179
Printing multiple copies of a report 180
Adjusting page margins 180
Understanding page breaks 181
Inserting a page break 181
Removing manual page breaks 182
Printing row and column titles 182
Scaling printed output 183
Printing cell gridlines 183
Printing row and column headers 185
Using a background image 185
Adding a Header or Footer to Your Reports 185
Selecting a predefined header or footer 186
Understanding header and footer element codes 186
Other header and footer options 187
Copying Page Setup Settings across Sheets... 188
Preventing Certain Cells from Being Printed 188
Preventing Objects from Being Printed.. 189
Creating Custom Views of Your Worksheet 190

Part II: Working with Formulas and Functions   193

Chapter 10: Introducing Formulas and Functions. 195

Understanding Formula Basics... 195
Using operators in formulas 196
Understanding operator precedence in formulas 197

Using functions in your formulas 199
    Examples of formulas that use functions.....................................200
    Function arguments 201
    More about functions 202
Entering Formulas into Your Worksheets 202
    Entering formulas manually 203
    Entering formulas by pointing...203
    Pasting range names into formulas 205
    Inserting functions into formulas..206
    Function entry tips 208
Editing Formulas 209
Using Cell References in Formulas 209
    Using relative, absolute, and mixed references 210
    Changing the types of your references 212
    Referencing cells outside the worksheet 212
        Referencing cells in other worksheets 213
        Referencing cells in other workbooks 213
Using Formulas in Tables...214
    Summarizing data in a table 214
    Using formulas within a table 216
    Referencing data in a table...217
Correcting Common Formula Errors 218
    Handling circular references...219
    Specifying when formulas are calculated 220
Using Advanced Naming Techniques 222
    Using names for constants..222
    Using names for formulas...223
    Using range intersections 224
    Applying names to existing references..226
Tips for Working with Formulas...227
    Don't hard-code values..227
    Using the Formula bar as a calculator.......................................227
    Making an exact copy of a formula 227
    Converting formulas to values..228

Chapter 11: Creating Formulas That Manipulate Text **229**
A Few Words about Text 229
Text Functions...230
    Working with character codes...231
        The CODE function..232
        The CHAR function...232
    Determining whether two strings are identical 233
    Joining two or more cells..234

Displaying formatted values as text 235
Displaying formatted currency values as text..236
Repeating a character or string 236
Creating a text histogram 237
Padding a number...238
Removing excess spaces and nonprinting characters 239
Counting characters in a string..239
Changing the case of text 239
Extracting characters from a string 240
Replacing text with other text..241
Finding and searching within a string 242
Searching and replacing within a string..242
Advanced Text Formulas 243
Counting specific characters in a cell..243
Counting the occurrences of a substring in a cell...243
Extracting a filename from a path specification 244
Extracting the first word of a string 244
Extracting the last word of a string..244
Extracting all but the first word of a string 245
Extracting first names, middle names, and last names 245
Removing titles from names 247
Creating an ordinal number 247
Counting the number of words in a cell 248

Chapter 12: Working with Dates and Times **249**
How Excel Handles Dates and Times 249
Understanding date serial numbers 249
Entering dates 250
Understanding time serial numbers..252
Entering times...253
Formatting dates and times 254
Problems with dates..255
Excel's leap year bug..255
Pre-1900 dates 256
Inconsistent date entries..257
Date-Related Worksheet Functions 258
Displaying the current date 259
Displaying any date 259
Generating a series of dates 260
Converting a nondate string to a date 261
Calculating the number of days between two dates 262
Calculating the number of work days between two dates 263
Offsetting a date using only work days..264
Calculating the number of years between two dates 265

Calculating a person's age..265
Determining the day of the year 266
Determining the day of the week..267
Determining the date of the most recent Sunday 267
Determining the first day of the week after a date..267
Determining the nth occurrence of a day of the week in a month 268
Calculating dates of holidays 268
New Year's Day...269
Martin Luther King, Jr. Day 269
Presidents' Day 269
Easter 270
Memorial Day...270
Independence Day 270
Labor Day...270
Columbus Day 270
Veterans Day 270
Thanksgiving Day...271
Christmas Day 271
Determining the last day of a month 271
Determining whether a year is a leap year 271
Determining a date's quarter 272
Time-Related Functions 272
Displaying the current time 272
Displaying any time...273
Calculating the difference between two times..274
Summing times that exceed 24 hours 275
Converting from military time 277
Converting decimal hours, minutes, or seconds to a time................................277
Adding hours, minutes, or seconds to a time..278
Rounding time values...279
Working with non–time-of-day values 279

Chapter 13: Creating Formulas That Count and Sum **281**
Counting and Summing Worksheet Cells 281
Basic Counting Formulas 283
Counting the total number of cells 283
Counting blank cells 284
Counting nonblank cells 285
Counting numeric cells 285
Counting text cells 285
Counting nontext cells 285
Counting logical values 286
Counting error values in a range 286

Contents

Advanced Counting Formulas...286

   Counting cells by using the COUNTIF function..287

   Counting cells based on multiple criteria 288

      Using And criteria 289

      Using Or criteria..290

      Combining And and Or criteria...290

   Counting the most frequently occurring entry..291

   Counting the occurrences of specific text 292

      Entire cell contents..292

      Partial cell contents 292

      Total occurrences in a range 293

   Counting the number of unique values 293

   Creating a frequency distribution 294

      The FREQUENCY function 294

      Using formulas to create a frequency distribution....................................296

      Using the Analysis ToolPak to create a frequency distribution 297

      Using a pivot table to create a frequency distribution 298

Summing Formulas...299

   Summing all cells in a range...299

   Computing a cumulative sum 300

   Summing the "top *n*" values 302

Conditional Sums Using a Single Criterion..303

   Summing only negative values 304

   Summing values based on a different range 304

   Summing values based on a text comparison 304

   Summing values based on a date comparison...305

Conditional Sums Using Multiple Criteria...305

   Using And criteria 305

   Using Or criteria 306

   Using And and Or criteria 307

Chapter 14: Creating Formulas That Look Up Values 309

Introducing Lookup Formulas 309

Functions Relevant to Lookups 310

Basic Lookup Formulas...312

   The VLOOKUP function 312

   The HLOOKUP function...313

   The LOOKUP function..314

   Combining the MATCH and INDEX functions...316

Specialized Lookup Formulas 318

   Looking up an exact value..318

   Looking up a value to the left...319

   Performing a case-sensitive lookup...320

   Looking up a value from multiple lookup tables 321

   Determining letter grades for test scores...322

Calculating a grade-point average..322
Performing a two-way lookup 323
Performing a two-column lookup...325
Determining the cell address of a value within a range 326
Looking up a value by using the closest match...327

Chapter 15: Creating Formulas for Financial Applications 329

The Time Value of Money 329
Loan Calculations 330
Worksheet functions for calculating loan information 331
PMT 331
PPMT 331
IPMT 332
RATE...332
NPER 333
PV 333
A loan calculation example..333
Credit card payments 334
Creating a loan amortization schedule...337
Summarizing loan options by using a data table...338
Creating a one-way data table 338
Creating a two-way data table 340
Calculating a loan with irregular payments...341
Investment Calculations...343
Future value of a single deposit...343
Calculating simple interest 343
Calculating compound interest..344
Calculating interest with continuous compounding.......................................346
Future value of a series of deposits 348
Depreciation Calculations 350

Chapter 16: Introducing Array Formulas. 355

Understanding Array Formulas...355
A multicell array formula...356
A single-cell array formula...357
Creating an array constant...358
Array constant elements 360
Understanding the Dimensions of an Array...360
One-dimensional horizontal arrays...360
One-dimensional vertical arrays...361
Two-dimensional arrays 361
Naming Array Constants...362
Working with Array Formulas 364
Entering an array formula...364
Selecting an array formula range 364

Contents

Editing an array formula..364
Expanding or contracting a multicell array formula................................365
Using Multicell Array Formulas..366
Creating an array from values in a range 366
Creating an array constant from values in a range 367
Performing operations on an array 368
Using functions with an array................................369
Transposing an array................................369
Generating an array of consecutive integers................................370
Using Single-Cell Array Formulas 371
Counting characters in a range 371
Summing the three smallest values in a range................................372
Counting text cells in a range 373
Eliminating intermediate formulas 374
Using an array in lieu of a range reference................................376

Chapter 17: Performing Magic with Array Formulas 379

Working with Single-Cell Array Formulas................................379
Summing a range that contains errors 379
Counting the number of error values in a range 380
Summing the *n* largest values in a range................................381
Computing an average that excludes zeros 381
Determining whether a particular value appears in a range 383
Counting the number of differences in two ranges 384
Returning the location of the maximum value in a range................................384
Finding the row of a value's *n*th occurrence in a range 385
Returning the longest text in a range 385
Determining whether a range contains valid values 386
Summing the digits of an integer................................386
Summing rounded values................................388
Summing every *n*th value in a range................................388
Removing non-numeric characters from a string................................390
Determining the closest value in a range 391
Returning the last value in a column 391
Returning the last value in a row 392
Ranking data with an array formula 392
Working with Multicell Array Formulas................................394
Returning only positive values from a range................................394
Returning nonblank cells from a range................................394
Reversing the order of cells in a range 395
Sorting a range of values dynamically................................396
Returning a list of unique items in a range 396
Displaying a calendar in a range................................398

Part III: Creating Charts and Graphics   401

Chapter 18: Getting Started Making Charts 403

What Is a Chart? 403
Understanding How Excel Handles Charts..404
    Embedded charts 405
    Chart sheets 406
Creating a Chart...408
Hands On: Creating and Customizing a Chart 408
    Selecting the data 408
    Choosing a chart type...409
    Experimenting with different layouts 409
    Trying another view of the data..411
    Trying other chart types 412
    Trying other chart styles 412
Working with Charts 413
    Resizing a chart 414
    Moving a chart 414
    Copying a chart..414
    Deleting a chart 414
    Adding chart elements...415
    Moving and deleting chart elements 415
    Formatting chart elements..415
    Printing charts..416
Understanding Chart Types 417
    Choosing a chart type...417
    Column..419
    Bar 422
    Line..423
    Pie..424
    XY (scatter) 426
    Area 427
    Doughnut...429
    Radar 430
    Surface 432
    Bubble..433
    Stock..433
Learning More 436

Chapter 19: Learning Advanced Charting 437

Selecting Chart Elements 437
    Selecting with the mouse...438
    Selecting with the keyboard 439
    Selecting with the Chart Element control 439

Contents

User Interface Choices for Modifying Chart Elements 441
    Using the Format dialog box 441
    Using the Ribbon 442
    Using the Mini toolbar 442
Modifying the Chart Area 443
Modifying the Plot Area 444
Working with Chart Titles 445
Working with a Legend 446
Working with Gridlines 448
Modifying the Axes 448
    Value axis 448
    Category axis 452
Working with Data Series 455
    Deleting a data series 456
    Adding a new data series to a chart 456
    Changing data used by a series 457
        Changing the data range by dragging the range outline 457
        Using the Edit Series dialog box 458
        Editing the Series formula 459
    Displaying data labels in a chart 460
    Handling missing data 461
    Adding error bars 461
    Adding a trendline 463
    Modifying 3-D charts 464
    Creating combination charts 465
    Displaying a data table 468
Creating Chart Templates 469
Learning Some Chart-Making Tricks 470
    Creating picture charts 470
    Creating a thermometer chart 472
    Creating a gauge chart 473
    Displaying conditional colors in a column chart 474
    Creating a comparative histogram 475
    Creating a Gantt chart 476
    Plotting mathematical functions with one variable 477
    Plotting mathematical functions with two variables 479

Chapter 20: Visualizing Data Using Conditional Formatting 481

About Conditional Formatting 481
Specifying Conditional Formatting 483
    Formatting types you can apply 483
    Making your own rules 484
Conditional Formats That Use Graphics 485
    Using data bars 485
        A simple data bar 486
        Using data bars in lieu of a chart 487

Using color scales 487

A color scale example 488

An extreme color scale example 489

Using icon sets 490

An icon set example 491

Another icon set example 492

Creating Formula-Based Rules 494

Understanding relative and absolute references 495

Conditional formatting formula examples 496

Identifying weekend days 496

Displaying alternate-row shading 497

Creating checkerboard shading 497

Shading groups of rows 497

Displaying a total only when all values are entered 498

Working with Conditional Formats 499

Managing rules 499

Copying cells that contain conditional formatting 500

Deleting conditional formatting 500

Locating cells that contain conditional formatting 501

Chapter 21: Creating Sparkline Graphics 503

Sparkline Types 504

Creating Sparklines 505

Customizing Sparklines 507

Sizing Sparkline cells 507

Handling hidden or missing data 508

Changing the Sparkline type 508

Changing Sparkline colors and line width 508

Highlighting certain data points 509

Adjusting Sparkline axis scaling 509

Faking a reference line 510

Specifying a Date Axis 512

Auto-Updating Sparklines 513

Displaying a Sparkline for a Dynamic Range 514

Chapter 22: Enhancing Your Work with Pictures and Drawings 517

Using Shapes 517

Inserting a Shape 518

Adding text to a Shape 520

Formatting Shapes 520

Grouping objects 522

Aligning and spacing objects 523

Reshaping Shapes 523

Printing objects 524

Contents

Using SmartArt 525

    Inserting SmartArt 525

    Customizing SmartArt 527

    Changing the layout 528

    Changing the style 528

    Learning more about SmartArt 529

Using WordArt 530

Working with Other Graphic Types 531

    About graphics files 531

    Using the Clip Art task pane 531

    Inserting graphics files 532

    Inserting screenshots 533

    Displaying a worksheet background image 535

Using the Equation Editor 535

Part IV: Using Advanced Excel Features   539

Chapter 23: Customizing the Excel User Interface 541

Customizing the Quick Access Toolbar 541

    About the Quick Access toolbar 542

    Adding new commands to the Quick Access toolbar 543

    Other Quick Access toolbar actions 545

Customizing the Ribbon 546

    Why customize the Ribbon? 546

    What can be customized 546

    How to customize the Ribbon 547

Chapter 24: Using Custom Number Formats 551

About Number Formatting 551

    Automatic number formatting 552

    Formatting numbers by using the Ribbon 552

    Using shortcut keys to format numbers 553

    Using the Format Cells dialog box to format numbers 554

Creating a Custom Number Format 555

    Parts of a number format string 557

    Custom number format codes 558

Custom Number Format Examples 560

    Scaling values 560

        Displaying values in thousands 560

        Displaying values in hundreds 561

        Displaying values in millions 562

        Adding zeros to a value 563

    Displaying leading zeros 564

    Displaying fractions 564

Displaying a negative sign on the right 565
Formatting dates and times 566
Displaying text with numbers... 566
Suppressing certain types of entries... 567
Filling a cell with a repeating character 568

Chapter 25: Using Data Validation 569
About Data Validation.. 569
Specifying Validation Criteria... 570
Types of Validation Criteria You Can Apply 571
Creating a Drop-Down List 573
Using Formulas for Data Validation Rules.. 574
Understanding Cell References.. 574
Data Validation Formula Examples 575
Accepting text only 576
Accepting a larger value than the previous cell 576
Accepting nonduplicate entries only... 576
Accepting text that begins with a specific character 577
Accepting dates by the day of the week 577
Accepting only values that don't exceed a total... 578
Creating a dependent list.. 578

Chapter 26: Creating and Using Worksheet Outlines. 581
Introducing Worksheet Outlines... 581
Creating an Outline 584
Preparing the data 584
Creating an outline automatically 585
Creating an outline manually 586
Working with Outlines 587
Displaying levels 587
Adding data to an outline 588
Removing an outline 588
Hiding the outline symbols 588

Chapter 27: Linking and Consolidating Worksheets. 589
Linking Workbooks.. 589
Creating External Reference Formulas.. 590
Understanding link formula syntax 590
Creating a link formula by pointing 591
Pasting links 591
Working with External Reference Formulas 592
Creating links to unsaved workbooks.. 592
Opening a workbook with external reference formulas 592
Changing the startup prompt 594
Updating links 594

Contents

Changing the link source 595
Severing links 595
Avoiding Potential Problems with External Reference Formulas 595
Renaming or moving a source workbook 596
Using the Save As command 596
Modifying a source workbook 596
Intermediary links 597
Consolidating Worksheets 597
Consolidating worksheets by using formulas 598
Consolidating worksheets by using Paste Special 599
Consolidating worksheets by using the Consolidate command 600
A workbook consolidation example 601
Refreshing a consolidation 604
More about consolidation 604

Chapter 28: Excel and the Internet 605

Understanding How Excel Uses HTML 605
Understanding the Different Web Formats 606
Creating an HTML file 607
Creating a single file Web page 607
Opening an HTML File 609
Working with Hyperlinks 610
Inserting a hyperlink 610
Using hyperlinks 611
Using Web Queries 612
Other Internet-Related Features 614

Chapter 29: Sharing Data with Other Office Applications 615

Copying and Pasting 615
Copying from Excel to Word 617
Pasting static information 617
Pasting a link 620
Embedding Objects in a Worksheet 622
Embedding Word documents 623
Embedding other types of documents 623
Embedding an Excel Workbook in a Word Document 624
Embedding a workbook in Word by copying 624
Embedding a saved workbook in Word 626
Creating a new Excel object in Word 626

Chapter 30: Using Excel in a Workgroup 627

Using Excel on a Network 627
Understanding File Reservations 628
Sharing Workbooks 629
Understanding shared workbooks 630
Designating a workbook as a shared workbook 631

Controlling the advanced sharing settings 632
    Tracking changes...632
    Updating changes 633
    Resolving conflicting changes between users 633
    Controlling the Include in Personal View settings....................633
Tracking Workbook Changes 633
  Turning Track Changes on and off 633
  Reviewing the changes 635

Chapter 31: Protecting Your Work 637
Types of Protection 637
Protecting a Worksheet..638
  Unlocking cells...639
  Sheet protection options...640
  Assigning user permissions...641
Protecting a Workbook 641
  Requiring a password to open a workbook..................................641
  Protecting a workbook's structure 643
  Protecting a workbook's windows 644
VB Project Protection 644
Related Topics 645
  Saving a worksheet as a PDF file 645
  Marking a workbook final 646
  Inspecting a workbook...646
  Using a digital signature 646
    Getting a digital ID 647
    Signing a workbook..647

Chapter 32: Making Your Worksheets Error-Free 649
Finding and Correcting Formula Errors 649
  Mismatched parentheses 650
  Cells are filled with hash marks...651
  Blank cells are not blank 651
  Extra space characters 652
  Formulas returning an error 653
    #DIV/0! errors 653
    #N/A errors 654
    #NAME? errors 655
    #NULL! errors 655
    #NUM! errors 655
    #REF! errors 656
    #VALUE! errors 656
  Absolute/relative reference problems..657
  Operator precedence problems 657
  Formulas are not calculated..658
  Actual versus displayed values..658

Contents

Floating point number errors 659

"Phantom link" errors..660

Using Excel Auditing Tools..661

Identifying cells of a particular type..661

Viewing formulas 662

Tracing cell relationships..663

Identifying precedents 664

Identifying dependents 665

Tracing error values 665

Fixing circular reference errors...665

Using background error-checking feature 665

Using the Excel Formula Evaluator 667

Searching and Replacing 668

Searching for information...669

Replacing information 670

Searching for formatting...670

Spell Checking Your Worksheets 671

Using AutoCorrect 672

Part V: Analyzing Data with Excel   675

Chapter 33: Getting Data from External Database Files. 677

Understanding External Database Files 677

Importing Access Tables 679

Retrieving Data with Query: An Example...680

The database file...681

The task 681

Selecting a data source 682

Using the Query Wizard...684

Query Wizard: Choosing the columns...684

Query Wizard: Filtering data 685

Query Wizard: Sort order..686

Query Wizard: Finish..686

Specifying a location for the data...687

Working with Data Returned by Query..688

Adjusting the external data range properties..688

Refreshing a query...689

Deleting a query 690

Changing your query 690

Using Query without the Wizard 690

Creating a query manually 690

Using multiple database tables 692

Contents

Adding and editing records in external database tables.........................693

Formatting data.........................693

Learning More about Query.........................693

Chapter 34: Introducing Pivot Tables 695

About Pivot Tables.........................695

A pivot table example.........................696

Data appropriate for a pivot table.........................698

Creating a Pivot Table.........................701

Specifying the data.........................701

Specifying the location for the pivot table.........................701

Laying out the pivot table.........................702

Formatting the pivot table.........................703

Modifying the pivot table.........................706

More Pivot Table Examples.........................708

Question 1.........................708

Question 2.........................709

Question 3.........................710

Question 4.........................710

Question 5.........................711

Question 6.........................712

Question 7.........................713

Learning More.........................714

Chapter 35: Analyzing Data with Pivot Tables. 715

Working with Non-Numeric Data.........................715

Grouping Pivot Table Items.........................717

A manual grouping example.........................717

Automatic grouping examples.........................719

Grouping by date.........................719

Grouping by time.........................722

Creating a Frequency Distribution.........................722

Creating a Calculated Field or Calculated Item.........................724

Creating a calculated field.........................726

Inserting a calculated item.........................728

Filtering Pivot Tables with Slicers.........................731

Referencing Cells within a Pivot Table.........................733

Creating Pivot Charts.........................735

A pivot chart example.........................736

More about pivot charts.........................738

Another Pivot Table Example.........................739

Producing a Report with a Pivot Table.........................742

Contents

Chapter 36: Performing Spreadsheet What-If Analysis 745

A What-If Example 745

Types of What-If Analyses...747

Manual What-If Analysis..747

Creating Data Tables...747

    Creating a one-input data table 748

    Creating a two-input data table 750

Using Scenario Manager...753

    Defining scenarios...754

    Displaying scenarios...757

    Modifying scenarios 758

    Merging scenarios 758

    Generating a scenario report..758

Chapter 37: Analyzing Data Using Goal Seeking and Solver 761

What-If Analysis, in Reverse..761

Single-Cell Goal Seeking...762

    A goal-seeking example 762

    More about goal seeking...763

Introducing Solver 764

    Appropriate problems for Solver 765

    A simple Solver example 765

    More about Solver 770

Solver Examples..771

    Solving simultaneous linear equations..771

    Minimizing shipping costs...773

    Allocating resources 776

    Optimizing an investment portfolio...778

Chapter 38: Analyzing Data with the Analysis ToolPak 781

The Analysis ToolPak: An Overview..781

Installing the Analysis ToolPak Add-in...782

Using the Analysis Tools 783

Introducing the Analysis ToolPak Tools 783

    Analysis of Variance 784

    Correlation..784

    Covariance 785

    Descriptive Statistics..785

    Exponential Smoothing...786

    F-Test (two-sample test for variance)...786

    Fourier Analysis 787

    Histogram 787

    Moving Average 788

    Random Number Generation 789

Rank and Percentile..790
Regression..790
Sampling..791
t-Test..792
z-Test (two-sample test for means) 792

Part VI: Programming Excel with VBA   793

Chapter 39: Introducing Visual Basic for Applications 795

Introducing VBA Macros..795
Displaying the Developer Tab 796
About Macro Security 797
Saving Workbooks That Contain Macros 798
Two Types of VBA Macros..799
　　VBA Sub procedures 799
　　VBA functions 800
Creating VBA Macros 802
　　Recording VBA macros..802
　　　　Recording your actions to create VBA code: The basics....................802
　　　　Recording a macro: A simple example 803
　　　　Examining the macro 804
　　　　Testing the macro 805
　　　　Editing the macro 805
　　　　Another example 806
　　　　Running the macro 806
　　　　Examining the macro 806
　　　　Re-recording the macro 807
　　　　Testing the macro 808
　　More about recording VBA macros..808
　　　　Absolute versus relative recording 808
　　　　Storing macros in your Personal Macro Workbook..............................809
　　　　Assigning a macro to a shortcut key 810
　　　　Assigning a macro to a button 810
　　Writing VBA code 811
　　　　The basics: Entering and editing code..812
　　　　How VBA works 812
　　　　Objects and collections..814
　　　　Properties 815
　　　　Methods 817
　　　　Variables..817
　　　　Controlling execution 818
　　　　A macro that can't be recorded 819
Learning More 821

Contents

Chapter 40: Creating Custom Worksheet Functions 823

Overview of VBA Functions 823
An Introductory Example...824
    A custom function...824
    Using the function in a worksheet 824
    Analyzing the custom function 825
About Function Procedures 826
Executing Function Procedures..827
    Calling custom functions from a procedure...827
    Using custom functions in a worksheet formula 828
Function Procedure Arguments 828
    A function with no argument 829
    A function with one argument...829
    Another function with one argument 830
    A function with two arguments 831
    A function with a range argument 832
Debugging Custom Functions..833
Inserting Custom Functions...834
Learning More 836

Chapter 41: Creating UserForms 837

Why Create UserForms? 837
UserForm Alternatives 838
    The InputBox function 838
    The MsgBox function 839
Creating UserForms: An Overview..842
    Working with UserForms...843
    Adding controls..843
    Changing the properties of a control 844
    Handling events 846
    Displaying a UserForm..846
A UserForm Example..846
    Creating the UserForm 847
    Testing the UserForm 848
    Creating an event-handler procedure 849
Another UserForm Example..850
    Creating the UserForm 850
    Testing the UserForm 852
    Creating event-handler procedures...853
    Testing the UserForm 854
    Making the macro available from a worksheet button 855
    Making the macro available on your Quick Access toolbar 855
More on Creating UserForms...856
    Adding accelerator keys...856
    Controlling tab order 856
Learning More 857

Contents

Chapter 42: Using UserForm Controls in a Worksheet 859

Why Use Controls on a Worksheet? 859
Using Controls 861
    Adding a control 862
    About design mode 862
    Adjusting properties 862
    Common properties 863
    Linking controls to cells 864
    Creating macros for controls 864
Reviewing the Available ActiveX Controls 866
    CheckBox 866
    ComboBox 867
    CommandButton 868
    Image 868
    Label 868
    ListBox 868
    OptionButton 869
    ScrollBar 869
    SpinButton 870
    TextBox 871
    ToggleButton 872

Chapter 43: Working with Excel Events. 873

Understanding Events 873
Entering Event-Handler VBA Code 874
Using Workbook-Level Events 875
    Using the Open event 876
    Using the SheetActivate event 878
    Using the NewSheet event 878
    Using the BeforeSave event 878
    Using the BeforeClose event 879
Working with Worksheet Events 879
    Using the Change event 880
    Monitoring a specific range for changes 881
    Using the SelectionChange event 882
    Using the BeforeRightClick event 883
Using Non-Object Events 883
    Using the OnTime event 883
    Using the OnKey event 884

Chapter 44: VBA Examples 887

Working with Ranges 887
    Copying a range 888
    Copying a variable-size range 889
    Selecting to the end of a row or column 890

Contents

Selecting a row or column...890
Moving a range..891
Looping through a range efficiently...891
Prompting for a cell value...893
Determining the type of selection...893
Identifying a multiple selection...895
Counting selected cells..895
Working with Workbooks..896
Saving all workbooks...896
Saving and closing all workbooks...896
Working with Charts...897
Modifying the chart type...898
Modifying chart properties..898
Applying chart formatting...899
VBA Speed Tips...899
Turning off screen updating..899
Preventing alert messages...900
Simplifying object references..900
Declaring variable types..901

Chapter 45: Creating Custom Excel Add-Ins 903

What Is an Add-In?..903
Working with Add-Ins..904
Why Create Add-Ins?..906
Creating Add-Ins...907
An Add-In Example..908
Setting up the workbook..908
Procedures in Module1...909
About the UserForm...909
Testing the workbook...910
Adding descriptive information...911
Protecting the project...911
Creating the add-in...912
Creating the user interface for your add-in macro 912
Installing the add-in..913

Part VII: Appendixes   915

Appendix A: Worksheet Function Reference 917

Appendix B: What's on the CD-ROM 933

System Requirements...933
Using the CD...933

Contents

What's on the CD 934
   Applications 934
   eBook version of *Excel 2010 Bible* 934
   Sample files for *Excel 2010 Bible*..934
      Chapter 01 935
      Chapter 02 935
      Chapter 04 935
      Chapter 05 935
      Chapter 06 935
      Chapter 10 936
      Chapter 11 936
      Chapter 12 936
      Chapter 13 936
      Chapter 14 937
      Chapter 15 937
      Chapter 16 937
      Chapter 17 937
      Chapter 18 938
      Chapter 19 938
      Chapter 20 939
      Chapter 21 939
      Chapter 22 939
      Chapter 24 939
      Chapter 25 939
      Chapter 26 939
      Chapter 27 939
      Chapter 28 940
      Chapter 33 940
      Chapter 34 940
      Chapter 35 940
      Chapter 36 940
      Chapter 37 941
      Chapter 38 941
      Chapter 39 941
      Chapter 40 941
      Chapter 41 941
      Chapter 42 941
      Chapter 43 942
      Chapter 44 942
      Chapter 45 942
Troubleshooting..942

Contents

Appendix C: Additional Excel Resources **943**

The Excel Help System 943
Microsoft Technical Support 944
   Support options 944
   Microsoft Knowledge Base 944
   Microsoft Excel Home Page 944
   Microsoft Office Home Page 944
Internet Newsgroups 945
   Accessing newsgroups by using a newsreader 945
   Accessing newsgroups by using a Web browser 945
   Searching newsgroups 946
Internet Web sites 947
   The Spreadsheet Page 947
   Daily Dose of Excel 948
   Jon Peltier's Excel Page 948
   Pearson Software Consulting 948
   Contextures 948
   David McRitchie's Excel Pages 948
   Pointy Haired Dilbert 948
   Mr. Excel 948

Appendix D: Excel Shortcut Keys **949**

Index **957**

End-User License Agreement **1007**

Acknowledgments

Thanks to everyone who bought the previous editions of this book. Your suggestions have helped make this edition the best one yet.

Introduction

Thanks for purchasing *Excel 2010 Bible*. If you're just starting with Excel, you'll be glad to know that Excel 2010 is the easiest version ever.

My goal in writing this book is to share with you some of what I know about Excel, and in the process, make you more efficient on the job. The book contains everything that you need to know to learn the basics of Excel and then move on to more advanced topics at your own pace. You'll find many useful examples and lots of tips and tricks that I've accumulated over the years.

Is This Book for You?

The *Bible* series from Wiley Publishing, Inc. is designed for beginning, intermediate, and advanced users. This book covers all the essential components of Excel and provides clear and practical examples that you can adapt to your own needs.

In this book, I've tried to maintain a good balance between the basics that every Excel user needs to know and the more complex topics that will appeal to power users. I've used Excel for more than 20 years, and I realize that almost everyone still has something to learn (including myself). My goal is to make that learning an enjoyable process.

Software Versions

This book was written for Excel 2010 for Windows. Much of the information also applies to Excel 2007, but if you're using an older version of Excel, I suggest that you put down this book immediately and find a book that's appropriate for your version of Excel. The user interface changes introduced in Excel 2007 are so extensive that you'll probably be hopelessly confused if you use an earlier version.

Conventions This Book Uses

Take a minute to scan this section to learn some of the typographical and organizational conventions that this book uses.

Excel commands

Excel 2010 (like Excel 2007) features a "menu-less" user interface. In place of a menu system, Excel uses a context-sensitive Ribbon system. The words along the top (such as File, Insert, Page Layout, and so on) are known as *tabs*. Click a tab, and the Ribbon displays the commands for the selected tab. Each command has a name, which is (usually) displayed next to or below the icon. The commands are arranged in groups, and the group name appears at the bottom of the Ribbon.

The convention I use is to indicate the tab name, followed by the group name, followed by the command name. So, the command used to toggle word wrap within a cell is indicated as:

Home ➪ Alignment ➪ Wrap Text

You'll learn more about using the Ribbon user interface in Chapter 1.

Filenames, named ranges, and your input

Input that you make from the keyboard appears in **bold**. Named ranges appear in a `monospace` font. Lengthy input usually appears on a separate line. For example, I may instruct you to enter a formula such as the following:

`="Part Name: " &VLOOKUP(PartNumber,PartList,2)`

Key names

Names of the keys on your keyboard appear in normal type. When two keys should be pressed simultaneously, they're connected with a plus sign, like this: "Press Ctrl+C to copy the selected cells." Here are the key names as I refer to them throughout the book:

Alt	down arrow	Num Lock	right arrow	End
Scroll Lock	Caps Lock	Home	PgDn	Shift
Ctrl	Insert	PgUp	Tab	Delete
left arrow	up arrow			

The four "arrow" keys are collectively known as the *navigation keys*.

Functions

Excel built-in worksheet functions appear in uppercase, like this: "Note the SUM formula in cell C20."

Mouse conventions

You'll come across some of the following mouse-related terms, all standard fare:

- **Mouse pointer:** The small graphic figure that moves onscreen when you move your mouse. The mouse pointer is usually an arrow, but it changes shape when you move to certain areas of the screen or when you're performing certain actions.

- **Point:** Move the mouse so that the mouse pointer is on a specific item: for example, "Point to the Save button on the toolbar."

- **Click:** Press the left mouse button once and release it immediately.

- **Right-click:** Press the right mouse button once and release it immediately. The right mouse button is used in Excel to pop up shortcut menus that are appropriate for whatever is currently selected.

- **Double-click:** Press the left mouse button twice in rapid succession.

- **Drag:** Press the left mouse button and keep it pressed while you move the mouse. Dragging is often used to select a range of cells or to change the size of an object.

What the Icons Mean

Throughout the book, you'll see special graphic symbols, or icons, in the left margin. These call your attention to points that are particularly important or relevant to a specific group of readers. The icons in this book are as follows:

Note

This icon signals the fact that something is important or worth noting. Notes may alert you to a concept that helps you master the task at hand, or they may denote something that is fundamental to understanding subsequent material. ■

Tip

This icon marks a more efficient way of doing something that may not be obvious. ■

Caution

I use this symbol when a possibility exists that the operation I'm describing may cause problems if you're not careful. ■

Cross-Reference

This icon indicates that a related topic is discussed elsewhere in the book. ■

On the CD
This icon indicates that a related example or file is available on the companion CD-ROM. ■

New Feature
This icon indicates a feature that is new to Excel 2010. ■

How This Book Is Organized

Notice that the book is divided into six main parts, followed by four appendixes.

Part I: Getting Started with Excel: This part consists of nine chapters that provide background about Excel. These chapters are considered required reading for Excel newcomers, but even experienced users will probably find some new information here.

Part II: Working with Formulas and Functions: The chapters in Part II cover everything that you need to know to become proficient with performing calculations in Excel.

Part III: Creating Charts and Graphics: The chapters in Part III describe how to create effective charts. In addition, you'll find a chapter on the conditional formatting visualization features, and a chapter on the new Sparkline graphics.

Part IV: Using Advanced Excel Features: This part consists of ten chapters that deal with topics that are sometimes considered advanced. However, many beginning and intermediate users may find this information useful as well.

Part V: Analyzing Data with Excel: Data analysis is the focus of the chapters in Part IV. Users of all levels will find some of these chapters of interest.

Part VI: Programming Excel with VBA: Part VI is for those who want to customize Excel for their own use or who are designing workbooks or add-ins that are to be used by others. It starts with an introduction to recording macros and VBA programming and then provides coverage of UserForms, add-ins, and events.

Appendixes: The book has four appendixes that cover Excel worksheet functions, the contents of the book's CD-ROM, other Excel resources, and Excel shortcut keys.

How to Use This Book

Although you're certainly free to do so, I didn't write this book with the intention that you would read it cover to cover. Rather, it's a reference book that you can consult when:

- You're stuck while trying to do something.
- You need to do something that you've never done.
- You have some time on your hands, and you're interested in learning something new about Excel.

The index is comprehensive, and each chapter typically focuses on a single broad topic. If you're just starting out with Excel, I recommend that you read the first few chapters to gain a basic understanding of the product and then do some experimenting on your own. After you become familiar with Excel's environment, you can refer to the chapters that interest you most. Some readers, however, may prefer to follow the chapters in order.

Don't be discouraged if some of the material is over your head. Most users get by just fine by using only a small subset of Excel's total capabilities. In fact, the 80/20 rule applies here: 80 percent of Excel users use only 20 percent of its features. However, using only 20 percent of Excel's features still gives you *lots* of power at your fingertips.

What's on the Companion CD

This book contains many examples, and the workbooks for those examples are available on the companion CD-ROM, arranged in directories that correspond to the chapters. Refer to Appendix B for a complete list of the files.

In addition, the CD-ROM contains an electronic version of this book. It's a searchable PDF file that's a perfect companion for your notebook computer when you take your next cross-country flight.

Part I

Getting Started with Excel

The chapters in this part are intended to provide essential background information for working with Excel. Here, you'll see how to make use of the basic features that are required for every Excel user. If you've used Excel (or even a different spreadsheet program) in the past, much of this information may seem like review. Even so, it's possible that you'll find quite a few tricks and techniques.

IN THIS PART

Chapter 1
Introducing Excel

Chapter 2
Entering and Editing Worksheet Data

Chapter 3
Essential Worksheet Operations

Chapter 4
Working with Cells and Ranges

Chapter 5
Introducing Tables

Chapter 6
Worksheet Formatting

Chapter 7
Understanding Excel Files

Chapter 8
Using and Creating Templates

Chapter 9
Printing Your Work

Introducing Excel

T his chapter serves as an introductory overview of Excel 2010. If you're already familiar with a previous version of Excel, reading this chapter is still a good idea. You'll find that Excel 2010 is very similar to Excel 2007. However, both Excel 2007 and Excel 2010 are different from every previous version — *very* different.

What Is Excel Good For?

Excel, as you probably know, is the world's most widely used spreadsheet program, and is part of the Microsoft Office suite. Other spreadsheet programs are available, but Excel is by far the most popular and has become the world standard.

Much of the appeal of Excel is due to the fact that it's so versatile. Excel's *forte,* of course, is performing numerical calculations, but Excel is also very useful for non-numeric applications. Here are just a few of the uses for Excel:

- **Number crunching:** Create budgets, analyze survey results, and perform just about any type of financial analysis you can think of.
- **Creating charts:** Create a wide variety of highly customizable charts.
- **Organizing lists:** Use the row-and-column layout to store lists efficiently.
- **Accessing other data:** Import data from a wide variety of sources.
- **Creating graphical dashboards:** Summarize a large amount of business information in a concise format.

IN THIS CHAPTER

Understanding what Excel is used for

What's new for Excel 2010

Learning the parts of Excel's window

Introducing the Ribbon user interface, shortcut menus, and dialog boxes

Navigating Excel worksheets

Introducing Excel with a quick hands-on session

- **Creating graphics and diagrams:** Use Shapes and the new SmartArt to create professional-looking diagrams.

- **Automating complex tasks:** Perform a tedious task with a single mouse click with Excel's macro capabilities.

What's New in Excel 2010?

When a new version of Microsoft Office is released, sometimes Excel gets lots of new features. And sometimes it gets very few new features. In the case of Office 2010, Excel got very few new features. Here's a quick summary of what's new in Excel 2010, relative to Excel 2007:

- **64-bit version:** If your hardware (and Windows version) supports it, you can install the 64-bit version, which lets you create larger workbooks. Most people do not require the 64-bit version, and using it might cause some add-ins to not function.

- **Sparkline charts:** Create small in-cell charts to summarize a range of data graphically. See Chapter 21.

- **Slicers:** A new way to filter and display data in pivot tables, by clicking buttons. See Chapter 35.

- **New pivot table formatting options:** You have more control over the appearance of pivot table reports. See Chapter 35.

- **Office button changes:** The big round Office button in Excel 2007 has been replaced by a File button/tab, displayed to the left of the tabs. Clicking it displays a screen that lets you perform various operations on your workbook. This view essentially replaces the traditional File and Print menus — plus quite a bit more.

- **Conditional formatting enhancements:** Data bar conditional formatting can display in a solid color, and the bars provide a more accurate display. See Chapter 20.

- **Function enhancements:** Some Excel worksheet financial and statistical functions have been improved in terms of numerical accuracy.

- **Image editing enhancements:** You have much more control over graphic images inserted into a workbook, including the ability to remove nonessential parts from the background of an image.

- **Screen capture tool:** You can easily capture a window from a different program and then insert the image on a worksheet.

- **Paste preview:** When you copy a range, the Paste command displays various options with a live preview so you can see how the paste operation will look.

- **Ribbon customization:** You can customize the Ribbon by adding new tabs and groups.

- **Equation editor:** Create and display (noncalculating) mathematical equations and embed them on a worksheet. See Chapter 22.

- **Faster:** Microsoft made some improvements to the calculation engine, and files load a bit faster.

- **New security features:** Workbooks downloaded from the Internet or from e-mail attachments are opened in Protected View mode. Workbooks can be designated as "trusted," and don't need to reside in special trusted folders.

- **Solver:** Excel 2010 includes a new version of the Solver add-in, which is useful for solving some complex problems.

- **Enhancements to VBA:** Operations that used to require old XLM macros can now be performed directly using VBA macro commands. In addition, macro recording now works for operations such as chart shape formatting.

Understanding Workbooks and Worksheets

The work you do in Excel is performed in a workbook file, which appears in its own window. You can have as many workbooks open as you need. By default, Excel 2010 workbooks use an `.xlsx` file extension.

Each *workbook* comprises one or more worksheets, and each *worksheet* is made up of individual *cells*. Each cell contains a value, a formula, or text. A worksheet also has an invisible *draw layer*, which holds charts, images, and diagrams. Each worksheet in a workbook is accessible by clicking the *tab* at the bottom of the workbook window. In addition, workbooks can store chart sheets. A *chart sheet* displays a single chart and is also accessible by clicking a tab.

Newcomers to Excel are often intimidated by all the different elements that appear within Excel's window. After you become familiar with the various parts, it all starts to make sense.

Figure 1.1 shows you the more important bits and pieces of Excel. As you look at the figure, refer to Table 1.1 for a brief explanation of the items shown in the figure.

FIGURE 1.1

The Excel screen has many useful elements that you will use often.

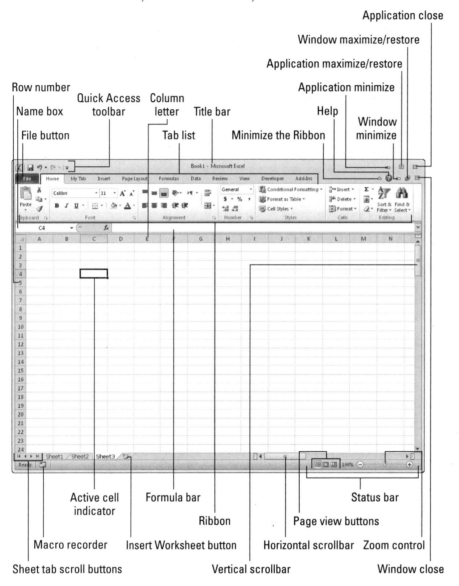

TABLE 1.1

Parts of the Excel Screen That You Need to Know

Name	Description
Active cell indicator	This dark outline indicates the currently active cell (one of the 17,179,869,184 cells on each worksheet).
Application Close button	Clicking this button closes Excel.
Application Minimize button	Clicking this button minimizes the Excel window.
Column letters	Letters range from A to XFD — one for each of the 16,384 columns in the worksheet. You can click a column heading to select an entire column of cells, or drag a column border to change its width.
File button	Click this button to open Back Stage view, which contains many options for working with your document (including printing), and setting Excel options.
Formula bar	When you enter information or formulas into a cell, it appears in this line.
Help button	Clicking this button displays the Excel Help system window.
Horizontal scrollbar	Use this tool to scroll the sheet horizontally.
Macro recorder indicator	Click to start recording a VBA macro. The icon changes while your actions are being recorded. Click again to stop recording.
Minimize Ribbon button	Clicking this button hides the Ribbon, giving you a bit more space onscreen. When you click a tab, the Ribbon reappears.
Name box	This field displays the active cell address or the name of the selected cell, range, or object.
Page View buttons	Change the way the worksheet is displayed by clicking one of these buttons.
Quick Access toolbar	This customizable toolbar holds commonly used commands. The Quick Access toolbar is always visible, regardless of which tab is selected.
Ribbon	This is the main location for Excel commands. Clicking an item in the tab list changes the Ribbon that displays.
Row numbers	Numbers range from 1 to 1,048,576 — one for each row in the worksheet. You can click a row number to select an entire row of cells.
Sheet tabs	Each of these notebook-like tabs represents a different sheet in the work-book. A workbook can have any number of sheets, and each sheet has its name displayed in a sheet tab.
Insert Sheet button	By default, each new workbook that you create contains three sheets. Add a new sheet by clicking the Insert Worksheet button (which is displayed after the last sheet tab).
Sheet tab scroll buttons	Use these buttons to scroll the sheet tabs to display tabs that aren't visible.

continued

TABLE 1.1	(continued)
Name	**Description**
Status bar	This bar displays various messages as well as the status of the Num Lock, Caps Lock, and Scroll Lock keys on your keyboard. It also shows summary information about the range of cells that is selected. Right-click the status bar to change the information that's displayed.
Tab list	Use these commands to display a different Ribbon, similar to a menu.
Title bar	This displays the name of the program and the name of the current workbook, and also holds some control buttons that you can use to modify the window.
Vertical scrollbar	Use this to scroll the sheet vertically.
Window Close button	Clicking this button closes the active workbook window.
Window Maximize/Restore button	Clicking this button increases the workbook window's size to fill Excel's complete workspace. If the window is already maximized, clicking this button "unmaximizes" Excel's window so that it no longer fills the entire screen.
Window Minimize button	Clicking this button minimizes the workbook window, and it displays as an icon.
Zoom control	Use this scroller to zoom your worksheet in and out.

Moving around a Worksheet

This section describes various ways to navigate through the cells in a worksheet. Every worksheet consists of rows (numbered 1 through 1,048,576) and columns (labeled A through XFD). After column Z comes column AA, which is followed by AB, AC, and so on. After column AZ comes BA, BB, and so on. After column ZZ is AAA, AAB, and so on.

The intersection of a row and a column is a single cell. At any given time, one cell is the *active cell.* You can identify the active cell by its darker border, as shown in Figure 1.2. Its *address* (its column letter and row number) appears in the Name box. Depending on the technique that you use to navigate through a workbook, you may or may not change the active cell when you navigate.

Notice that the row and column headings of the active cell appear in different colors to make it easier to identify the row and column of the active cell.

FIGURE 1.2

The active cell is the cell with the dark border — in this case, cell C8.

	A	B	C	D	E	F	G
1		Last Year	This Year				
2	January	89	98				
3	February	96	91				
4	March	121	103				
5	April	104	99				
6	May	121	96				
7	June	145	109				
8							
9							
10							
11							
12							

Sheet1

Navigating with your keyboard

Not surprisingly, you can use the standard navigational keys on your keyboard to move around a worksheet. These keys work just as you'd expect: The down arrow moves the active cell down one row, the right arrow moves it one column to the right, and so on. PgUp and PgDn move the active cell up or down one full window. (The actual number of rows moved depends on the number of rows displayed in the window.)

Tip

You can use the keyboard to scroll through the worksheet without changing the active cell by turning on Scroll Lock, which is useful if you need to view another area of your worksheet and then quickly return to your original location. Just press Scroll Lock and use the navigation keys to scroll through the worksheet. When you want to return to the original position (the active cell), press Ctrl+Backspace. Then, press Scroll Lock again to turn it off. When Scroll Lock is turned on, Excel displays `Scroll Lock` in the status bar at the bottom of the window. ■

The Num Lock key on your keyboard controls how the keys on the numeric keypad behave. When Num Lock is on, the keys on your numeric keypad generate numbers. Many keyboards have a separate set of navigation (arrow) keys located to the left of the numeric keypad. The state of the Num Lock key doesn't affect these keys.

Table 1.2 summarizes all the worksheet movement keys available in Excel.

TABLE 1.2

Excel Worksheet Movement Keys

Key	Action
Up arrow (↑)	Moves the active cell up one row.
Down arrow (↓)	Moves the active cell down one row.
Left arrow (←) or Shift+Tab	Moves the active cell one column to the left.
Right arrow (→) or Tab	Moves the active cell one column to the right.
PgUp	Moves the active cell up one screen.
PgDn	Moves the active cell down one screen.
Alt+PgDn	Moves the active cell right one screen.
Alt+PgUp	Moves the active cell left one screen.
Ctrl+Backspace	Scrolls the screen so that the active cell is visible.
↑*	Scrolls the screen up one row (active cell does not change).
↓*	Scrolls the screen down one row (active cell does not change).
←*	Scrolls the screen left one column (active cell does not change).
→*	Scrolls the screen right one column (active cell does not change).

* With Scroll Lock on

Navigating with your mouse

To change the active cell by using the mouse, click another cell; it becomes the active cell. If the cell that you want to activate isn't visible in the workbook window, you can use the scrollbars to scroll the window in any direction. To scroll one cell, click either of the arrows on the scrollbar. To scroll by a complete screen, click either side of the scrollbar's scroll box. You also can drag the scroll box for faster scrolling.

Tip

If your mouse has a wheel, you can use the mouse wheel to scroll vertically. Also, if you click the wheel and move the mouse in any direction, the worksheet scrolls automatically in that direction. The more you move the mouse, the faster the scrolling. ■

Press Ctrl while you use the mouse wheel to zoom the worksheet. If you prefer to use the mouse wheel to zoom the worksheet without pressing Ctrl, choose File ➪ Options and select the Advanced section. Place a check mark next to the Zoom on Roll with Intellimouse check box.

Using the scrollbars or scrolling with your mouse doesn't change the active cell. It simply scrolls the worksheet. To change the active cell, you must click a new cell after scrolling.

Introducing the Ribbon

The most dramatic change introduced in Office 2007 was the new user interface. In most Office 2007 applications, traditional menus and toolbars were replaced with the Ribbon. In Office 2010, all applications use the Ribbon interface. In addition, the Ribbon can be customized in Office 2010 (see Chapter 23).

Ribbon tabs

The commands available in the Ribbon vary, depending upon which tab is selected. The Ribbon is arranged into groups of related commands. Here's a quick overview of Excel's tabs.

- **Home:** You'll probably spend most of your time with the Home tab selected. This tab contains the basic Clipboard commands, formatting commands, style commands, commands to insert and delete rows or columns, plus an assortment of worksheet editing commands.

- **Insert:** Select this tab when you need to insert something in a worksheet — a table, a diagram, a chart, a symbol, and so on.

- **Page Layout:** This tab contains commands that affect the overall appearance of your worksheet, including some settings that deal with printing.

- **Formulas:** Use this tab to insert a formula, name a cell or a range, access the formula auditing tools, or control how Excel performs calculations.

- **Data:** Excel's data-related commands are on this tab.

- **Review:** This tab contains tools to check spelling, translate words, add comments, or protect sheets.

- **View:** The View tab contains commands that control various aspects of how a sheet is viewed. Some commands on this tab are also available in the status bar.

- **Developer:** This tab isn't visible by default. It contains commands that are useful for programmers. To display the Developer tab, choose File ➪ Options and then select Customize Ribbon. In the Customize the Ribbon section on the right, place a check mark next to Developer and then click OK.

- **Add-Ins:** This tab is visible only if you loaded an older workbook or add-in that customizes the menu or toolbars. Because menus and toolbars are no longer available in Excel 2010, these user interface customizations appear on the Add-Ins tab.

Note
Although the File button shares space with the tabs, it's not actually a tab. Clicking the File button displays the new Back Stage view, where you perform actions with your documents. ■

The appearance of the commands on the Ribbon varies, depending on the width of Excel window. When the window is too narrow to display everything, the commands adapt; some of them might seem to be missing, but the commands are still available. Figure 1.3 shows the Home tab of the Ribbon with all controls fully visible. Figure 1.4 shows the Ribbon when Excel's window is made more narrow. Notice that some of the descriptive text is gone, but the icons remain. Figure 1.5 shows the extreme case when the window is made very narrow. Some groups display a single icon. However, if you click the icon, all the group commands are available to you.

FIGURE 1.3

The Home tab of the Ribbon.

FIGURE 1.4

The Home tab when Excel's window is made narrower.

FIGURE 1.5

The Home tab when Excel's window is made very narrow.

Tip

If you would like to hide the Ribbon to increase your worksheet view, just double-click any tab. The Ribbon goes away, and you can see about five additional rows of your worksheet. When you need to use the Ribbon again, just click a tab, and it comes back temporarily. To keep the Ribbon turned on, double-click a tab. You can also press Ctrl+F1 to toggle the Ribbon display on and off. The Minimize the Ribbon button (to the left of the Help button) provides yet another way to toggle the Ribbon. ■

Contextual tabs

In addition to the standard tabs, Excel 2010 also includes *contextual tabs*. Whenever an object (such as a chart, a table, or a SmartArt diagram) is selected, specific tools for working with that object are made available in the Ribbon.

Figure 1.6 shows the contextual tab that appears when a chart is selected. In this case, it has three contextual tabs: Design, Layout, and Format. Notice that the contextual tabs contain a description (Chart Tools) in Excel's title bar. When contextual tabs appear, you can, of course, continue to use all the other tabs.

When you select an object, contextual tabs contain tools for working with that object.

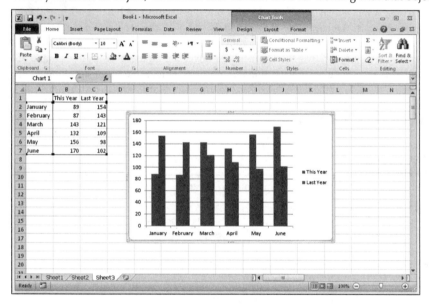

Types of commands on the Ribbon

When you hover your mouse pointer over a Ribbon command, you'll see a pop-up box that contains the command's name as well as a brief description. For the most part, the commands in the Ribbon work just as you would expect them to. You do encounter several different styles of commands on the Ribbon.

- **Simple buttons:** Click the button, and it does its thing. An example of a simple button is the Increase Font Size button in the Font group of the Home tab. Some buttons perform the action immediately; others display a dialog box so that you can enter additional information. Button controls may or may not be accompanied by a descriptive label.

- **Toggle buttons:** A toggle button is clickable and also conveys some type of information by displaying two different colors. An example is the Bold button in the Font group of the Home tab. If the active cell isn't bold, the Bold button displays in its normal color. If the active cell is already bold, though, the Bold button displays a different background color. If you click this button, it toggles the Bold attribute for the selection.

- **Simple drop-downs:** If the Ribbon command has a small down arrow, the command is a drop-down. Click it, and additional commands appear below it. An example of a simple drop-down is the Conditional Formatting command in the Styles group of the Home tab. When you click this control, you see several options related to conditional formatting.

- **Split buttons:** A *split button control* combines a one-click button with a drop-down. If you click the button part, the command is executed. If you click the drop-down part (a down arrow), you choose from a list of related commands. You can identify a split button command because it displays in two colors when you hover the mouse over it. An example of a split button is the Merge & Center command in the Alignment group of the Home tab (see Figure 1.7). Clicking the left part of this control merges and centers text in the selected cells. If you click the arrow part of the control (on the right), you get a list of commands related to merging cells.

FIGURE 1.7

The Merge & Center command is a split button control.

- **Check boxes:** A check box control turns something on or off. An example is the Gridlines control in the Show group of the View tab. When the Gridlines check box is checked, the sheet displays gridlines. When the control isn't checked, the sheet gridlines don't appear.

- **Spinners:** Excel's Ribbon has only one spinner control: the Scale To Fit group of the Page Layout tab. Click the top part of the spinner to increase the value; click the bottom part of the spinner to decrease the value.

Some of the Ribbon groups contain a small icon on the right side, known as a *dialog box launcher*. For example, if you examine the Home ⇨ Alignment group, you see this icon (see Figure 1.8). Click it, and Excel displays the Format Cells dialog box, with the Alignment tab preselected. The dialog launchers generally provide options that aren't available in the Ribbon.

FIGURE 1.8

Some Ribbon groups contain a small icon on the right side, known as a dialog box launcher.

Accessing the Ribbon by using your keyboard

At first glance, you may think that the Ribbon is completely mouse-centric. After all, none of the commands have the traditional underline letter to indicate the Alt+keystrokes. But in fact, the Ribbon is *very* keyboard friendly. The trick is to press the Alt key to display the pop-up *keytips*. Each Ribbon control has a letter (or series of letters) that you type to issue the command.

Tip
You don't need to hold down the Alt key while you type keytip letters. ∎

Figure 1.9 shows how the Home tab looks after I press the Alt key to display the keytips. If you press one of the keytips, the screen then displays more keytips. For example, to use the keyboard to align the cell contents to the left, press Alt, followed by H (for Home) and then AL (for Align Left). Nobody will memorize *all* these keys, but if you're a keyboard fan (like me), it takes just a few times before you memorize the keystrokes required for commands that you use frequently.

After you press Alt, you can also use the left- and right-arrow keys to scroll through the tabs. When you reach the proper tab, press the down arrow to enter the Ribbon. Then use left and right arrow keys to scroll through the Ribbon commands. When you reach the command you need, press Enter to execute it. This method isn't as efficient as using the keytips, but it's a quick way to take a look at the commands available.

FIGURE 1.9

Pressing Alt displays the keytips.

Using Shortcut Menus

In addition to the Ribbon, Excel features many shortcut menus, which you access by right-clicking just about anything within Excel. Shortcut menus don't contain every relevant command, just those that are most commonly used for whatever is selected.

As an example, Figure 1.10 shows the shortcut menu that appears when you right-click a cell. The shortcut menu appears at the mouse-pointer position, which makes selecting a command fast and efficient. The shortcut menu that appears depends on what you're doing at the time. For example, if you're working with a chart, the shortcut menu contains commands that are pertinent to the selected chart element.

FIGURE 1.10

Click the right mouse button to display a shortcut menu of commands you're most likely to use.

Mini Toolbar Be Gone

If you find the Mini toolbar annoying, you can search all day and not find an option to turn it off. The General tab of the Excel Options dialog box has an option labeled Show Mini Toolbar on Selection, but this option applies to selecting characters while editing a cell. The only way to turn off the Mini toolbar when you right-click is to execute a VBA macro:

```
Sub ZapMiniToolbar()
    Application.ShowMenuFloaties = True
End Sub
```

The statement might seem wrong, but it's actually correct. Setting that property to True turns off the Mini toolbar. It's a bug that appeared in Excel 2007 and was not fixed in Excel 2010 because correcting it would cause many macros to fail. (See Part VI for more information about VBA macros.)

The box above the shortcut menu — the Mini toolbar — contains commonly used tools from the Home tab. The Mini toolbar was designed to reduce the distance your mouse has to travel around the screen. Just right-click, and common formatting tools are within an inch from your mouse pointer. The Mini toolbar is particularly useful when a tab other than Home is displayed. If you use a tool on the Mini toolbar, the toolbar remains displayed in case you want to perform other formatting on the selection.

Customizing Your Quick Access Toolbar

The Ribbon is fairly efficient, but many users prefer to have some commands available at all times — without having to click a tab. The solution is to customize your Quick Access toolbar. Typically, the Quick Access toolbar appears on the left side of the title bar, above the Ribbon. Alternatively, you can display the Quick Access toolbar below the Ribbon; just right-click the Quick Access toolbar and choose Show Quick Access Toolbar below the Ribbon.

Displaying the Quick Access Toolbar below the Ribbon provides a bit more room for icons, but it also means that you see one less row of your worksheet.

By default, the Quick Access toolbar contains three tools: Save, Undo, and Repeat. You can customize the Quick Access toolbar by adding other commands that you use often. To add a command from the Ribbon to your Quick Access toolbar, right-click the command and choose Add to Quick Access Toolbar. If you click the down arrow to the right of the Quick Access toolbar, you see a drop-down menu with some additional commands that you might want to place in your Quick Access toolbar.

Excel has commands that aren't available on the Ribbon. In most cases, the only way to access these commands is to add them to your Quick Access toolbar. Right-click the Quick Access toolbar and choose Customize the Quick Access Toolbar. You see the dialog box shown in Figure 1.11. This section of the Excel Options dialog box is your one-stop shop for Quick Access toolbar customization.

FIGURE 1.11

Add new icons to your Quick Access toolbar by using the Quick Access Toolbar section of the Excel Options dialog box.

Cross-Reference

See Chapter 23 for more information about customizing your Quick Access toolbar. ■

Caution

You can't reverse every action, however. Generally, anything that you do using the File button can't be undone. For example, if you save a file and realize that you've overwritten a good copy with a bad one, Undo can't save the day. You're just out of luck. ■

The Repeat button, also on the Quick Access toolbar, performs the opposite of the Undo button: Repeat reissues commands that have been undone. If nothing has been undone, then you can use the Repeat button (or Ctrl+Y) to repeat the last command that you performed. For example, if you applied a particular style to a cell (by choosing Home ➪ Styles ➪ Cell Styles), you can activate another cell and press Ctrl+Y to repeat the command.

Changing Your Mind

You can reverse almost every action in Excel by using the Undo command, located on the Quick Access toolbar. Click Undo (or press Ctrl+Z) after issuing a command in error, and it's as if you never issued the command. You can reverse the effects of the past 100 actions that you performed by executing Undo more than once.

If you click the arrow on the right side of the Undo button, you see a list of the actions that you can reverse. Click an item in that list to undo that action and all the subsequent actions you performed.

Working with Dialog Boxes

Many Excel commands display a dialog box, which is simply a way of getting more information from you. For example, if you choose Review ⇨ Changes ⇨ Protect Sheet, Excel can't carry out the command until you tell it what parts of the sheet you want to protect. Therefore, it displays the Protect Sheet dialog box, shown in Figure 1.12.

FIGURE 1.12

Excel uses a dialog box to get additional information about a command.

Excel dialog boxes vary in how they work. You'll find two types of dialog boxes:

- **Typical dialog box:** A *modal* dialog box takes the focus away from the spreadsheet. When this type of dialog box is displayed, you can't do anything in the worksheet until you dismiss the dialog box. Clicking OK performs the specified actions, and clicking Cancel (or pressing Esc) closes the dialog box without taking any action. Most Excel dialog boxes are this type.

• **Stay-on-top dialog box:** A *modeless* dialog box works in a manner similar to a toolbar. When a modeless dialog box is displayed, you can continue working in Excel, and the dialog box remains open. Changes made in a modeless dialog box take effect immediately. For example, if you're applying formatting to a chart, changes you make in the Format dialog box appear in the chart as soon as you make them. A modeless dialog box has a Close button but no OK button.

Most people find working with dialog boxes to be quite straightforward and natural. If you've used other programs, you'll feel right at home. You can manipulate the controls either with your mouse or directly from the keyboard.

Navigating dialog boxes

Navigating dialog boxes is generally very easy — you simply click the control you want to activate.

Although dialog boxes were designed with mouse users in mind, you can also use the keyboard. Every dialog box control has text associated with it, and this text always has one underlined letter (a *hot key* or an *accelerator key*). You can access the control from the keyboard by pressing Alt and then the underlined letter. You also can press Tab to cycle through all the controls on a dialog box. Pressing Shift+Tab cycles through the controls in reverse order.

Tip
When a control is selected, it appears with a dotted outline. You can use the spacebar to activate a selected control. ∎

Using tabbed dialog boxes

Many Excel dialog boxes are "tabbed" dialog boxes: That is, they include notebook-like tabs, each of which is associated with a different panel.

When you click a tab, the dialog box changes to display a new panel containing a new set of controls. The Format Cells dialog box, shown in Figure 1.13, is a good example. It has six tabs, which makes it functionally equivalent to six different dialog boxes.

Tabbed dialog boxes are quite convenient because you can make several changes in a single dialog box. After you make all your setting changes, click OK or press Enter.

Tip
To select a tab by using the keyboard, press Ctrl+PgUp or Ctrl+PgDn, or simply press the first letter of the tab that you want to activate. ∎

Excel 2007 introduced a new style of modeless tabbed dialog box in which the tabs are on the left, rather than across the top. Excel 2010 also uses this style. Figure 1.14 shows the Format Shape dialog box, which is modeless tabbed. To select a tab using the keyboard, press the up- or down-arrow key and then Tab to access the controls.

Use the dialog box tabs to select different functional areas in the dialog box.

A tabbed dialog box with tabs on the left.

Using the Task Pane

The final user interface element that I discuss is the task pane. The task pane appears automatically in response to several commands. For example, to insert a clip art image, choose Insert ➪ Illustrations ➪ Clip Art. Excel responds by displaying the Clip Art task pane, shown in Figure 1.15. The task pane is similar to a dialog box except that you can keep it visible as long as you like. There's no OK button. When you're finished using a task pane, click the Close button in the upper-right corner.

By default, the task pane is docked on the right side of the Excel window, but you can move it anywhere you like by clicking its title bar and dragging. Excel remembers the last position, so the next time you use that task pane, it will be right where you left it.

FIGURE 1.15

The Clip Art task pane.

Creating Your First Excel Worksheet

This section presents an introductory hands-on session with Excel. If you haven't used Excel, you may want to follow along on your computer to get a feel for how this software works.

In this example, you create a simple monthly sales projection table along with a chart.

Getting started on your worksheet

Start Excel and make sure that you have an empty workbook displayed. To create a new, blank workbook, press Ctrl+N (the shortcut key for File ➪ New ➪ Blank Workbook ➪ Create).

The sales projection will consist of two columns of information. Column A will contain the month names, and column B will store the projected sales numbers. You start by entering some descriptive titles into the worksheet. Here's how to begin:

1. **Move the cell pointer to cell A1 (the upper-left cell in the worksheet) by using the navigation (arrow) keys.** The Name box displays the cell's address.

2. **Enter** Month **into cell A1 and press Enter.** Depending on your setup, Excel either moves the cell pointer to a different cell, or the pointer remains in cell A1.

3. **Move the cell pointer to B1, type** Projected Sales, **and press Enter.**

   The text extends beyond the cell width, but don't worry about that for now.

Filling in the month names

In this step, you enter the month names in column A.

1. **Move the cell pointer to A2 and type** Jan **(an abbreviation for January).** At this point, you can enter the other month name abbreviations manually, but you can let Excel do some of the work by taking advantage of the AutoFill feature.

2. **Make sure that cell A2 is selected.** Notice that the active cell is displayed with a heavy outline. At the bottom-right corner of the outline, you'll see a small square known as the *fill handle.* Move your mouse pointer over the fill handle, click, and drag down until you've highlighted from A2 down to A13.

3. **Release the mouse button, and Excel automatically fills in the month names.**

Your worksheet should resemble the one shown in Figure 1.16.

Entering the sales data

Next, you provide the sales projection numbers in column B. Assume that January's sales are projected to be $50,000, and that sales will increase by 3.5 percent in each subsequent month.

1. **Move the cell pointer to B2 and type** 50000, **the projected sales for January.** You could type a dollar sign and comma to make the number more legible, but you do the number formatting a bit later.

2. **To enter a formula to calculate the projected sales for February, move to cell B3 and enter the following:** =B2*103.5%. When you press Enter, the cell displays 51750. The formula returns the contents of cell B2, multiplied by 103.5%. In other words, February sales are projected to be 3.5% greater than January sales.

3. **The projected sales for subsequent months use a similar formula.** But rather than retype the formula for each cell in column B, once again take advantage of the AutoFill feature. Make sure that cell B3 is selected. Click the cell's fill handle, drag down to cell B13, and release the mouse button.

Your worksheet, after entering the column headings and month names.

At this point, your worksheet should resemble the one shown in Figure 1.17. Keep in mind that except for cell B2, the values in column B are calculated *with formulas*. To demonstrate, try changing the projected sales value for the initial month, January (in cell B2). You'll find that the formulas recalculate and return different values. These formulas all depend on the initial value in cell B2, though.

FIGURE 1.17

Your worksheet, after creating the formulas.

	A	B	C	D	E	F
1	Month	Projected Sales				
2	Jan	50000				
3	Feb	51750				
4	Mar	53561.25				
5	Apr	55435.89				
6	May	57376.15				
7	Jun	59384.32				
8	Jul	61462.77				
9	Aug	63613.96				
10	Sep	65840.45				
11	Oct	68144.87				
12	Nov	70529.94				
13	Dec	72998.49				
14						
15						

Formatting the numbers

The values in the worksheet are difficult to read because they aren't formatted. In this step, you apply a number format to make the numbers easier to read and more consistent in appearance:

1. **Select the numbers by clicking cell B2 and dragging down to cell B13.**

Tip
Don't drag the fill handle this time, though, because you're selecting cells, not filling a range. ∎

2. **Choose Home ➪ Number, click the drop-down Number Format control (it initially displays General), and select Currency from the list.** The numbers now display with a currency symbol and two decimal places. Much better!

Making your worksheet look a bit fancier

At this point, you have a functional worksheet, but it could use some help in the appearance department. Converting this range to an "official" (and attractive) Excel table is a snap:

1. **Move to any cell within the range.**

2. **Choose Insert ➪ Tables ➪ Table.** Excel displays its Create Table dialog box to make sure that it guessed the range properly.

3. **Click OK to close the Create Table dialog box.** Excel applies its default table formatting and also displays its Table Tools ➪ Design contextual tab. Your worksheet should look like Figure 1.18.

4. **If you don't like the default table style, just select another one from the Table Tools ➪ Design ➪ Table Styles group.** Notice that you can get a preview of different table styles by moving your mouse over the Ribbon. When you find one you like, click it, and style will be applied to your table.

FIGURE 1.18

Your worksheet, after converting the range to a table.

	A	B	C	D	E	F
1	Month	Projected Sales				
2	Jan	$50,000.00				
3	Feb	$51,750.00				
4	Mar	$53,561.25				
5	Apr	$55,435.89				
6	May	$57,376.15				
7	Jun	$59,384.32				
8	Jul	$61,462.77				
9	Aug	$63,613.96				
10	Sep	$65,840.45				
11	Oct	$68,144.87				
12	Nov	$70,529.94				
13	Dec	$72,998.49				
14						
15						
16						

Summing the values

The worksheet displays the monthly projected sales, but what about the total projected sales for the year? Because this range is a table, it's simple.

1. Activate any cell in the table

2. **Choose Table Tools ⇨ Design ⇨ Table Style Options ⇨ Total Row.** Excel automatically adds a new row to the bottom of your table, including a formula that calculated the total of the Projected Sales column.

3. **If you'd prefer to see a different summary formula (for example, average), click cell B14 and choose a different summary formula from the drop-down list.**

Creating a chart

How about a chart that shows the projected sales for each month?

1. **Activate any cell in the table.**

2. **Choose Insert ⇨ Charts ⇨ Column and then select one of the 2-D column chart types.** Excel inserts the chart in the center of your screen.

Tip

To move the chart to another location, click its border and drag it. To change the appearance and style of the chart, use the commands on the Chart Tools contextual tab. ∎

Figure 1.19 shows the worksheet with a column chart. Your chart may look different, depending on the chart layout or style you selected.

On the CD

This workbook is available on the companion CD-ROM. The filename is `table and chart.xlsx.`

FIGURE 1.19

The table and chart.

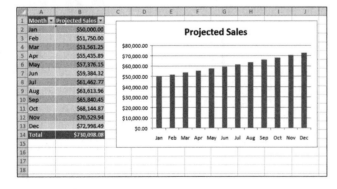

Printing your worksheet

Printing your worksheet is very easy (assuming that you have a printer attached and that it works properly).

1. **Make sure that the chart isn't selected.** If a chart is selected, it will print on a page by itself. To deselect the chart, just press Esc or click any cell.

2. **To make use of Excel's handy page layout view, click the Page Layout View button on the right side of the status bar.** Excel then displays the worksheet page by page so that you can easily see how your printed output will look. Figure 1.20 shows the worksheet zoomed out to show a complete page. In Page Layout view, you can tell immediately whether the chart is too wide to fit on one page. If the chart is too wide, click and drag a corner to resize it. Or, you can just move the chart below the table of numbers.

FIGURE 1.20

Viewing the worksheet in Page Layout mode.

3. **When you're ready to print, choose File ⇨ Print.**

   At this point, you can change some print settings. For example, you can choose to print in landscape rather than portrait orientation. Make the change, and you see the result in the preview window. When you're satisfied, click the Print button in the upper-left corner. The page is printed, and you're returned to your workbook.

Saving your workbook

Until now, everything that you've done has occurred in your computer's memory. If the power should fail, all may be lost — unless Excel's AutoRecover feature happened to kick in. It's time to save your work to a file on your hard drive.

1. **Click the Save button on the Quick Access toolbar.** (This button looks like an old-fashioned floppy disk, popular in the previous century.) Because the workbook hasn't been saved yet and still has its default name, Excel responds with the Save As dialog box.

2. **In the box labeled File Name, enter a name (such as Monthly Sales Projection), and then click Save or press Enter.** Excel saves the workbook as a file. The workbook remains open so that you can work with it some more.

Note

By default, Excel saves a backup copy of your work automatically every ten minutes. To adjust the AutoRecover setting (or turn if off), choose File ⇨ Options, and click the Save tab of the Excel Options dialog box. However, you should never rely on Excel's AutoRecover feature. Saving your work frequently is a good idea. ∎

If you've followed along, you may have realized that creating this workbook was not at all difficult. But, of course, you've barely scratched the surface. The remainder of this book covers these tasks (and many, many more) in much greater detail.

Entering and Editing Worksheet Data

This chapter describes what you need to know about entering, using, and modifying data in your worksheets. As you see, Excel doesn't treat all data equally. Therefore, you need to learn about the various types of data that you can use in an Excel worksheet.

Exploring the Types of Data You Can Use

An Excel workbook can hold any number of worksheets, and each worksheet is made up of more than 17 billion cells. A cell can hold any of three basic types of data:

- A numeric value
- Text
- A formula

A worksheet can also hold charts, diagrams, pictures, buttons, and other objects. These objects aren't contained in cells. Rather, they reside on the worksheet's *draw layer,* which is an invisible layer on top of each worksheet.

Cross-Reference

Chapter 22 discusses some of the items you can place on the draw layer. ∎

About numeric values

Numeric values represent a quantity of some type: sales amounts, number of employees, atomic weights, test scores, and so on. Values also can be dates (such as Feb-26-2011) or times (such as 3:24 a.m.).

Cross-Reference
Excel can display values in many different formats. Later in this chapter, you see how different format options can affect the display of numeric values (see "Applying Number Formatting"). ■

About text entries

Most worksheets also include text in their cells. You can insert text to serve as labels for values, headings for columns, or instructions about the worksheet. Text is often used to clarify what the values in a worksheet mean.

Text that begins with a number is still considered text. For example, if you type **12 Employees** into a cell, Excel considers the entry to be text rather than a value. Consequently, you can't use this cell for numeric calculations. If you need to indicate that the number 12 refers to employees, enter **12** into a cell and then type **Employees** into the cell to the right.

About formulas

Formulas are what make a spreadsheet a spreadsheet. Excel enables you to enter powerful *formulas* that use the values (or even text) in cells to calculate a result. When you enter a formula into a cell, the formula's result appears in the cell. If you change any of the values used by a formula, the formula recalculates and shows the new result.

Formulas can be simple mathematical expressions, or they can use some of the powerful functions that are built into Excel. Figure 2.1 shows an Excel worksheet set up to calculate a monthly loan payment. The worksheet contains values, text, and formulas. The cells in column A contain text. Column B contains four values and two formulas. The formulas are in cells B6 and B10. Column D, for reference, shows the actual contents of the cells in column B.

On the CD
This workbook, named `loan payment calculator.xlsx`, is available on the companion CD-ROM. ■

Cross-Reference
You can find out much more about formulas in Part II. ■

Excel's Numeric Limitations

You may be curious about the types of values that Excel can handle. In other words, how large can numbers be? And how accurate are large numbers?

Excel's numbers are precise up to 15 digits. For example, if you enter a large value, such as 123,456,789,123,456,789 (18 digits), Excel actually stores it with only 15 digits of precision. This 18-digit number displays as 123,456,789,123,456,000. This precision may seem quite limiting, but in practice, it rarely causes any problems.

One situation in which the 15-digit accuracy can cause a problem is when entering credit card numbers. Most credit card numbers are 16 digits, but Excel can handle only 15 digits, so it substitutes a zero for the last credit card digit. Even worse, you may not even realize that Excel made the card number invalid. The solution? Enter the credit card numbers as text. The easiest way is to preformat the cell as Text (choose Home ➪ Number and choose Text from the drop-down Number Format list). Or you can precede the credit card number with an apostrophe. Either method prevents Excel from interpreting the entry as a number.

Here are some of Excel's other numeric limits:

Largest positive number: 9.9E+307

Smallest negative number: –9.9E+307

Smallest positive number: 1E–307

Largest negative number: –1E–307

These numbers are expressed in scientific notation. For example, the largest positive number is "9.9 times 10 to the 307th power" — in other words, 99 followed by 306 zeros. Keep in mind, though, that this number has only 15 digits of accuracy.

FIGURE 2.1

You can use values, text, and formulas to create useful Excel worksheets.

	A	B	C	D	E
1	**Loan Payment Calculator**				
2					
3				Column B Contents	
4	Purchase Amount:	$475,000		475000	
5	Down Payment Pct:	20%		0.2	
6	Loan Amount:	$380,000		=B4*(1-B5)	
7	Term (months):	360		360	
8	Interest Rate (APR):	6.25%		0.0625	
9					
10	**Monthly Payment:**	$2,339.73		=PMT(B8/12,B7,-B6)	
11					
12					

Entering Text and Values into Your Worksheets

To enter a numeric value into a cell, move the cell pointer to the appropriate cell, type the value, and then press Enter or one of the navigation keys. The value is displayed in the cell and also appears in the Formula bar when the cell is selected. You can include decimal points and currency symbols when entering values, along with plus signs, minus signs, and commas (to separate thousands).

Note

If you precede a value with a minus sign or enclose it in parentheses, Excel considers it to be a negative number. ■

Entering text into a cell is just as easy as entering a value: Activate the cell, type the text, and then press Enter or a navigation key. A cell can contain a maximum of about 32,000 characters — more than enough to hold a typical chapter in this book. Even though a cell can hold a huge number of characters, you'll find that it's not possible to actually display all these characters.

Tip

If you type an exceptionally long text entry into a cell, the Formula bar may not show all the text. To display more of the text in the Formula bar, click the bottom of the Formula bar and drag down to increase the height (see Figure 2.2). Also useful is the Ctrl+Shift+U keyboard shortcut. Pressing this key combination toggles the height of the formula bar to show either one row, or the previous size. ■

What happens when you enter text that's longer than its column's current width? If the cells to the immediate right are blank, Excel displays the text in its entirety, appearing to spill the entry into adjacent cells. If an adjacent cell isn't blank, Excel displays as much of the text as possible. (The full text is contained in the cell; it's just not displayed.) If you need to display a long text string in a cell that's adjacent to a nonblank cell, you can take one of several actions:

- Edit your text to make it shorter.
- Increase the width of the column (drag the border in the column letter display).
- Use a smaller font.
- Wrap the text within the cell so that it occupies more than one line. Choose Home ➪ Alignment ➪ Wrap Text to toggle wrapping on and off for the selected cell or range.

FIGURE 2.2

The Formula bar, expanded in height to show more information in the cell.

Entering Dates and Times into Your Worksheets

Excel treats dates and times as special types of numeric values. Typically, these values are format-ted so that they appear as dates or times because we humans find it far easier to understand these values when they appear in the correct format. If you work with dates and times, you need to understand Excel's date and time system.

Entering date values

Excel handles dates by using a serial number system. The earliest date that Excel understands is January 1, 1900. This date has a serial number of 1. January 2, 1900, has a serial number of 2, and so on. This system makes it easy to deal with dates in formulas. For example, you can enter a for-mula to calculate the number of days between two dates.

Most of the time, you don't have to be concerned with Excel's serial number date system. You can simply enter a date in a familiar date format, and Excel takes care of the details behind the scenes. For example, if you need to enter June 1, 2001, you can simply enter the date by typing **June 1, 2001** (or use any of several different date formats). Excel interprets your entry and stores the value 39234, which is the serial number for that date.

Note
The date examples in this book use the U.S. English system. Depending on your Windows regional settings, entering a date in a format (such as June 1, 2011) may be interpreted as text rather than a date. In such a case, you need to enter the date in a format that corresponds to your regional date settings — for example, 1 June, 2011. ∎

Cross-Reference
For more information about working with dates, see Chapter 12. ∎

Entering time values

When you work with times, you simply extend Excel's date serial number system to include decimals. In other words, Excel works with times by using fractional days. For example, the date serial number for June 1, 2011, is 40695. Noon on June 1, 2011 (halfway through the day), is represented internally as 40695.5 because the time fraction is added to the date serial number to get the full date/time serial number.

Again, you normally don't have to be concerned with these serial numbers (or fractional serial numbers, for times). Just enter the time into a cell in a recognized format.

Cross-Reference
See Chapter 12 for more information about working with time values. ∎

Modifying Cell Contents

After you enter a value or text into a cell, you can modify it in several ways:

- Erase the cell's contents.
- Replace the cell's contents with something else.
- Edit the cell's contents.

Note
You can also modify a cell by changing its formatting. However, formatting a cell affects only a cell's appearance. Formatting does not affect its contents. Later sections in this chapter cover formatting. ∎

Erasing the contents of a cell

To erase the contents of a cell, just click the cell and press Delete. To erase more than one cell, select all the cells that you want to erase and then press Delete. Pressing Delete removes the cell's contents but doesn't remove any formatting (such as bold, italic, or a different number format) that you may have applied to the cell.

For more control over what gets deleted, you can choose Home ➪ Editing ➪ Clear. This command's drop-down list has five choices:

- **Clear All:** Clears everything from the cell — its contents, its formatting, and its cell comment (if it has one).
- **Clear Formats:** Clears only the formatting and leaves the value, text, or formula.
- **Clear Contents:** Clears only the cell's contents and leaves the formatting.
- **Clear Comments:** Clears the comment (if one exists) attached to the cell.
- **Clear Hyperlinks:** Removes hyperlinks contained in the selected cells. The text remains, but the cell no longer functions as a clickable hyperlink.

Note
Clearing formats doesn't clear the background colors in a range that has been designated as a table unless you replace the table style background colors manually. ■

Replacing the contents of a cell

To replace the contents of a cell with something else, just activate the cell and type your new entry, which replaces the previous contents. Any formatting applied to the cell remains in place and is applied to the new content.

Tip
You can also replace cell contents by dragging and dropping or by pasting data from the Clipboard. In both cases, the cell formatting will be replaced by the format of the new data. To avoid pasting formatting, choose Home ➪ Clipboard ➪ Paste ➪ Values (V), or Home ➪ Clipboard ➪ Paste ➪ Formulas (F). ■

Editing the contents of a cell

If the cell contains only a few characters, replacing its contents by typing new data usually is easiest. However, if the cell contains lengthy text or a complex formula and you need to make only a slight modification, you probably want to edit the cell rather than re-enter information.

When you want to edit the contents of a cell, you can use one of the following ways to enter cell-edit mode.

- **Double-click the cell** to edit the cell contents directly in the cell.

- **Select the cell and press F2** to edit the cell contents directly in the cell.

- **Select the cell that you want to edit and then click inside the Formula bar** to edit the cell contents in the Formula bar.

You can use whichever method you prefer. Some people find editing directly in the cell easier; others prefer to use the Formula bar to edit a cell.

Note

The Advanced tab of the Excel Options dialog box contains a section called Editing Options. These settings affect how editing works. (To access this dialog box, choose File ⇨ Options.) If the Allow Editing Directly in Cells option isn't enabled, you can't edit a cell by double-clicking. In addition, pressing F2 allows you to edit the cell in the Formula bar (not directly in the cell). ∎

All these methods cause Excel to go into *edit mode*. (The word Edit appears at the left side of the status bar at the bottom of the screen.) When Excel is in edit mode, the Formula bar displays two new icons: the X and the Check Mark (see Figure 2.3). Clicking the X icon cancels editing without changing the cell's contents. (Pressing Esc has the same effect.) Clicking the Check Mark icon completes the editing and enters the modified contents into the cell. (Pressing Enter has the same effect.)

FIGURE 2.3

While editing a cell, the Formula bar displays two new icons.

The X icon The Check Mark icon

When you begin editing a cell, the insertion point appears as a vertical bar, and you can perform the following tasks:

- **Add new characters at the location of the insertion point.** Move the insertion point by

  - Using the navigation keys to move within the cell

  - Pressing Home to move the insertion point to the beginning of the cell

  - Pressing End to move the insertion point to the end of the cell

- **Select multiple characters.** Press Shift while you use the navigation keys.
- **Select characters while you're editing a cell.** Use the mouse. Just click and drag the mouse pointer over the characters that you want to select.

Learning some handy data-entry techniques

You can simplify the process of entering information into your Excel worksheets and make your work go quite a bit faster by using a number of useful tricks, described in the following sections.

Automatically moving the cell pointer after entering data

By default, Excel automatically moves the cell pointer to the next cell down when you press the Enter key after entering data into a cell. To change this setting, choose File ➪ Options and click the Advanced tab (see Figure 2.4). The check box that controls this behavior is labeled After Pressing Enter, Move Selection. If you enable this option, you can choose the direction in which the cell pointer moves (down, left, up, or right).

Your choice is completely a matter of personal preference. I prefer to keep this option turned off. When entering data, I use the navigation keys rather than the Enter key (see the next section).

FIGURE 2.4

You can use the Advanced tab in Excel Options to select a number of helpful input option settings.

Using navigation keys instead of pressing Enter

Instead of pressing the Enter key when you're finished making a cell entry, you also can use any of the navigation keys to complete the entry. Not surprisingly, these navigation keys send you in the direction that you indicate. For example, if you're entering data in a row, press the right-arrow (→) key rather than Enter. The other arrow keys work as expected, and you can even use PgUp and PgDn.

Selecting a range of input cells before entering data

Here's a tip that most Excel users don't know about: When a range of cells is selected, Excel automatically moves the cell pointer to the next cell in the range when you press Enter. If the selection consists of multiple rows, Excel moves down the column; when it reaches the end of the selection in the column, it moves to the first selected cell in the next column.

To skip a cell, just press Enter without entering anything. To go backward, press Shift+Enter. If you prefer to enter the data by rows rather than by columns, press Tab rather than Enter. Excel continues to cycle through the selected range until you select a cell outside of the range.

Using Ctrl+Enter to place information into multiple cells simultaneously

If you need to enter the same data into multiple cells, Excel offers a handy shortcut. Select all the cells that you want to contain the data, enter the value, text, or formula, and then press Ctrl+Enter. The same information is inserted into each cell in the selection.

Entering decimal points automatically

If you need to enter lots of numbers with a fixed number of decimal places, Excel has a useful tool that works like some adding machines. Access the Excel Options dialog box and click the Advanced tab. Select the check box Automatically Insert a Decimal Point and make sure that the Places box is set for the correct number of decimal places for the data you need to enter.

When this option is set, Excel supplies the decimal points for you automatically. For example, if you specify two decimal places, entering **12345** into a cell is interpreted as 123.45. To restore things to normal, just clear the Automatically Insert a Decimal Point check box in the Excel Options dialog box. Changing this setting doesn't affect any values that you already entered.

Caution

The fixed decimal–places option is a global setting and applies to all workbooks (not just the active workbook). If you forget that this option is turned on, you can easily end up entering incorrect values — or cause some major confusion if someone else uses your computer. ∎

Using AutoFill to enter a series of values

The Excel AutoFill feature makes inserting a series of values or text items in a range of cells easy. It uses the AutoFill handle (the small box at the lower right of the active cell). You can drag the AutoFill handle to copy the cell or automatically complete a series.

Figure 2.5 shows an example. I entered **1** into cell A1 and **3** into cell A2. Then I selected both cells and dragged down the fill handle to create a linear series of odd numbers. The figure also shows a Smart Icon that, when clicked, displays some additional AutoFill options.

Tip

If you drag the AutoFill handle while you press and hold the right mouse button, Excel displays a shortcut menu with additional fill options. ∎

FIGURE 2.5

This series was created by using AutoFill.

Using AutoComplete to automate data entry

The Excel AutoComplete feature makes entering the same text into multiple cells easy. With AutoComplete, you type the first few letters of a text entry into a cell, and Excel automatically completes the entry based on other entries that you already made in the column. Besides reducing typing, this feature also ensures that your entries are spelled correctly and are consistent.

Here's how it works. Suppose that you're entering product information in a column. One of your products is named Widgets. The first time that you enter **Widgets** into a cell, Excel remembers it. Later, when you start typing **Widgets** in that same column, Excel recognizes it by the first few letters and finishes typing it for you. Just press Enter, and you're done. To override the suggestion, just keep typing.

AutoComplete also changes the case of letters for you automatically. If you start entering **widget** (with a lowercase w) in the second entry, Excel makes the w uppercase to be consistent with the previous entry in the column.

Tip

You also can access a mouse-oriented version of AutoComplete by right-clicking the cell and choosing Pick from Drop-Down List from the shortcut menu. Excel then displays a drop-down box that has all the entries in the current column, and you just click the one that you want. ■

Keep in mind that AutoComplete works only within a contiguous column of cells. If you have a blank row, for example, AutoComplete identifies only the cell contents below the blank row.

If you find the AutoComplete feature distracting, you can turn it off by using the Advanced tab of the Excel Options dialog box. Remove the check mark from the check box labeled Enable AutoComplete for Cell Values.

Forcing text to appear on a new line within a cell

If you have lengthy text in a cell, you can force Excel to display it in multiple lines within the cell: Press Alt+Enter to start a new line in a cell.

Note

When you add a line break, Excel automatically changes the cell's format to Wrap Text. But unlike normal text wrap, your manual line break forces Excel to break the text at a specific place within the text, which gives you more precise control over the appearance of the text than if you rely on automatic text wrapping. ■

Tip

To remove a manual line break, edit the cell and press Delete when the insertion point is located at the end of the line that contains the manual line break. You won't see any symbol to indicate the position of the manual line break, but the text that follows it will move up when the line break is deleted. ■

Using AutoCorrect for shorthand data entry

You can use the AutoCorrect feature to create shortcuts for commonly used words or phrases. For example, if you work for a company named Consolidated Data Processing Corporation, you can create an AutoCorrect entry for an abbreviation, such as *cdp*. Then, whenever you type **cdp**, Excel automatically changes it to Consolidated Data Processing Corporation.

Excel includes quite a few built-in AutoCorrect terms (mostly common misspellings), and you can add your own. To set up your custom AutoCorrect entries, access the Excel Options dialog box (choose File ➪ Options) and click the Proofing tab. Then click the AutoCorrect Options button to display the AutoCorrect dialog box. In the dialog box, click the AutoCorrect tab, check the option labeled Replace Text as You Type, and then enter your custom entries. (Figure 2.6 shows an example.) You can set up as many custom entries as you like. Just be careful not to use an abbreviation that might appear normally in your text.

Tip

Excel shares your AutoCorrect list with other Office applications. For example, any AutoCorrect entries you created in Word also work in Excel. ■

Entering numbers with fractions

To enter a fractional value into a cell, leave a space between the whole number and the fraction. For example, to enter 6⅞, enter **6 7/8** and then press Enter. When you select the cell, 6.875 appears in the Formula bar, and the cell entry appears as a fraction. If you have a fraction only (for example, ⅛), you must enter a zero first, like this — **0 1/8** — or Excel will likely assume that you're entering a date. When you select the cell and look at the Formula bar, you see 0.125. In the cell, you see ⅛.

Simplifying data entry by using a form

Many people use Excel to manage lists in which the information is arranged in rows. Excel offers a simple way to work with this type of data through the use of a data entry form that Excel can create automatically. This data form works with either a normal range of data, or with a range that has been designated as a table (choose Insert ➪ Tables ➪ Table). Figure 2.7 shows an example.

FIGURE 2.6

AutoCorrect allows you to create shorthand abbreviations for text you enter often.

Unfortunately, the command to access the data form is not on the Ribbon. To use the data form, you must add it to your Quick Access toolbar or add it to the Ribbon. The instructions that follow describe how to add this command to your Quick Access toolbar:

1. **Right-click the Quick Access toolbar and choose Customize Quick Access Toolbar.** The Quick Access Toolbar panel of the Excel Options dialog box appears.

2. **In the Choose Commands From drop-down list, choose Commands Not in the Ribbon.**

3. **In the list box on the left, select Form.**

4. **Click the Add button to add the selected command to your Quick Access toolbar.**

5. **Click OK to close the Excel Options dialog box.**

FIGURE 2.7

Excel's built-in data form can simplify many data-entry tasks.

After performing these steps, a new icon appears on your Quick Access toolbar.

To use a data entry form, follow these steps:

1. **Arrange your data so that Excel can recognize it as a table by entering headings for the columns in the first row of your data entry range.**

2. **Select any cell in the table and click the Form button on your Quick Access toolbar.**

   Excel displays a dialog box customized to your data (refer to Figure 2-7).

3. **Fill in the information.**

   Press Tab to move between the text boxes. If a cell contains a formula, the formula result appears as text (not as an edit box). In other words, you can't modify formulas using the data entry form.

4. **When you complete the data form, click the New button.**

   Excel enters the data into a row in the worksheet and clears the dialog box for the next row of data.

Entering the current date or time into a cell

If you need to date-stamp or time-stamp your worksheet, Excel provides two shortcut keys that do this task for you:

- **Current date:** Ctrl+; (semicolon)
- **Current time:** Ctrl+Shift+; (semicolon)

The date and time are from the system time in your computer. If the date or time is not correct in Excel, use the Windows Control Panel to make the adjustment.

Note

When you use either of these shortcuts to enter a date or time into your worksheet, Excel enters a static value into the worksheet. In other words, the date or time entered doesn't change when the worksheet is recalculated. In most cases, this setup is probably what you want, but you should be aware of this limitation. If you want the date or time display to update, use one of these formulas:

```
=TODAY()
=NOW()
```

Applying Number Formatting

Number formatting refers to the process of changing the appearance of values contained in cells. Excel provides a wide variety of number formatting options. In the following sections, you see how to use many of Excel's formatting options to quickly improve the appearance of your worksheets.

Tip

The formatting that you apply works with the selected cell or cells. Therefore, you need to select the cell (or range of cells) before applying the formatting. Also remember that changing the number format does not affect the underlying value. Number formatting affects only the appearance. ■

Values that you enter into cells normally are unformatted. In other words, they simply consist of a string of numerals. Typically, you want to format the numbers so that they're easier to read or are more consistent in terms of the number of decimal places shown.

Figure 2.8 shows a worksheet that has two columns of values. The first column consists of unformatted values. The cells in the second column are formatted to make the values easier to read. The third column describes the type of formatting applied.

On the CD

This workbook is available on the companion CD-ROM. The file is named number formatting.xlsx.

FIGURE 2.8

Use numeric formatting to make it easier to understand what the values in the worksheet represent.

	A	B	C	D
1				
2	Unformatted	Formatted	Type	
3	1200	$1,200.00	Currency	
4	0.231	23.1%	Percentage	
5	2/3/2010	2/3/2008	Short Date	
6	2/3/2010	Sunday, February 03, 2008	Long Date	
7	123439832	123,439,832.00	Accounting	
8	5559832	555-9832	Phone Number	
9	434988723	434-98-8723	Social Security Number	
10	0.552	1:14:53 PM	Time	
11	0.25	1/4	Fraction	
12	12332354090	1.23E+10	Scientific	
13				

Tip

If you move the cell pointer to a cell that has a formatted value, the Formula bar displays the value in its unformatted state because the formatting affects only how the value appears in the cell — not the actual value contained in the cell. ■

Using automatic number formatting

Excel is smart enough to perform some formatting for you automatically. For example, if you enter **12.2%** into a cell, Excel knows that you want to use a percentage format and applies it for you automatically. If you use commas to separate thousands (such as 123,456), Excel applies comma formatting for you. And if you precede your value with a dollar sign, the cell is formatted for currency (assuming that the dollar sign is your system currency symbol).

Tip

A handy default feature in Excel makes entering percentage values into cells easier. If a cell is formatted to display as a percent, you can simply enter a normal value (for example, 12.5 for 12.5%). To enter values less than 1%, precede the value with a zero (for example, 0.52 for 0.52%). If this automatic percent–entry feature isn't working (or if you prefer to enter the actual value for percents), access the Excel Options dialog box and click the Advanced tab. In the Editing Options section, locate the Enable Automatic Percent Entry check box and remove the check mark. ■

Formatting numbers by using the Ribbon

The Home ➭ Number group in the Ribbon contains controls that let you quickly apply common number formats (see Figure 2.9).

FIGURE 2.9

You can find number formatting commands in the Number group of the Home tab.

Comma Style

Decrease
Number | Decimal
Format | Places

Percent Increase
Style   Decimal
         Places

Accounting
Number
Format

The Number Format drop-down list contains 11 common number formats. Additional options include an Accounting Number Format drop-down list (to select a currency format), a Percent Style, and a Comma Style button. The group also contains a button to increase the number of decimal places, and another to decrease the number of decimal places.

When you select one of these controls, the active cell takes on the specified number format. You also can select a range of cells (or even an entire row or column) before clicking these buttons. If you select more than one cell, Excel applies the number format to all the selected cells.

Using shortcut keys to format numbers

Another way to apply number formatting is to use shortcut keys. Table 2.1 summarizes the short-cut-key combinations that you can use to apply common number formatting to the selected cells or range. Notice that these Ctrl+Shift characters are all located together, in the upper left of your keyboard.

TABLE 2.1

Number-Formatting Keyboard Shortcuts

Key Combination	Formatting Applied
Ctrl+Shift+~	General number format (that is, unformatted values)
Ctrl+Shift+$	Currency format with two decimal places (negative numbers appear in parentheses)
Ctrl+Shift+%	Percentage format, with no decimal places
Ctrl+Shift+^	Scientific notation number format, with two decimal places
Ctrl+Shift+#	Date format with the day, month, and year
Ctrl+Shift+@	Time format with the hour, minute, and AM or PM
Ctrl+Shift+!	Two decimal places, thousands separator, and a hyphen for negative values

Formatting numbers using the Format Cells dialog box

In most cases, the number formats that are accessible from the Number group on the Home tab are just fine. Sometimes, however, you want more control over how your values appear. Excel offers a great deal of control over number formats through the use of the Format Cells dialog box, shown in Figure 2.10. For formatting numbers, you need to use the Number tab.

You can bring up the Format Cells dialog box in several ways. Start by selecting the cell or cells that you want to format and then do one of the following:

- Choose Home ➪ Number and click the small dialog box launcher icon (in the lower-right corner of the Number group).

- Choose Home ➪ Number, click the Number Format drop-down list, and choose More Number Formats from the drop-down list.

- Right-click the cell and choose Format Cells from the shortcut menu.

- Press Ctrl+1.

FIGURE 2.10

When you need more control over number formats, use the Number tab of the Format Cells dialog box.

The Number tab of the Format Cells dialog box displays 12 categories of number formats from which to choose. When you select a category from the list box, the right side of the tab changes to display the appropriate options.

The Number category has three options that you can control: the number of decimal places displayed, whether to use a thousands separator, and how you want negative numbers displayed. Notice that the Negative Numbers list box has four choices (two of which display negative values in red), and the choices change depending on the number of decimal places and whether you choose to separate thousands.

The top of the tab displays a sample of how the active cell will appear with the selected number format (visible only if a cell with a value is selected). After you make your choices, click OK to apply the number format to all the selected cells.

Cross-Reference

Chapter 10 discusses ROUND and other built-in functions. ∎

The following are the number-format categories, along with some general comments:

- **General:** The default format; it displays numbers as integers, as decimals, or in scientific notation if the value is too wide to fit in the cell.

- **Number:** Enables you to specify the number of decimal places, whether to use a comma to separate thousands, and how to display negative numbers (with a minus sign, in red, in parentheses, or in red and in parentheses).

- **Currency:** Enables you to specify the number of decimal places, whether to use a currency symbol, and how to display negative numbers (with a minus sign, in red, in parentheses, or in red and in parentheses). This format always uses a comma to separate thousands.

- **Accounting:** Differs from the Currency format in that the currency symbols always align vertically.

- **Date:** Enables you to choose from several different date formats.

- **Time:** Enables you to choose from several different time formats.

- **Percentage:** Enables you to choose the number of decimal places and always displays a percent sign.

- **Fraction:** Enables you to choose from among nine fraction formats.

- **Scientific:** Displays numbers in exponential notation (with an E): 2.00E+05 = 200,000; 2.05E+05 = 205,000. You can choose the number of decimal places to display to the left of E.

- **Text:** When applied to a value, causes Excel to treat the value as text (even if it looks like a number). This feature is useful for such items as part numbers.

- **Special:** Contains additional number formats. In the U.S. version of Excel, the additional number formats are Zip Code, Zip Code +4, Phone Number, and Social Security Number.

- **Custom:** Enables you to define custom number formats that aren't included in any other category.

Tip

If a cell displays a series of hash marks (such as # # # # # # # #), it usually means that the column isn't wide enough to display the value in the number format that you selected. Either make the column wider or change the number format. ∎

Adding your own custom number formats

Sometimes you may want to display numerical values in a format that isn't included in any of the other categories. If so, the answer is to create your own custom format.

Cross-Reference

Excel provides you with a great deal of flexibility in creating number formats — so much so that I've devoted an entire chapter (Chapter 24) to this topic. ∎

When Numbers Appear to Add Incorrectly

Applying a number format to a cell doesn't change the value — only how the value appears in the worksheet. For example, if a cell contains 0.874543, you may format it to appear as 87%. If that cell is used in a formula, the formula uses the full value (0.874543), not the displayed value (87%).

In some situations, formatting may cause Excel to display calculation results that appear incorrect, such as when totaling numbers with decimal places. For example, if values are formatted to display two decimal places, you may not see the actual numbers used in the calculations. But because Excel uses the full precision of the values in its formula, the sum of the two values may appear to be incorrect.

Several solutions to this problem are available. You can format the cells to display more decimal places. You can use the ROUND function on individual numbers and specify the number of decimal places Excel should round to. Or you can instruct Excel to change the worksheet values to match their displayed format. To do so, access the Excel Options dialog box and click the Advanced tab. Check the Set Precision as Displayed check box (is located in the When Calculating This Workbook section).

Caution

Selecting the Precision as Displayed option changes the numbers in your worksheets to permanently match their appearance onscreen. This setting applies to all sheets in the active workbook. Most of the time, this option is not what you want. Make sure that you understand the consequences of using the Set Precision as Displayed option. ∎

Essential Worksheet Operations

This chapter covers some basic information regarding workbooks, worksheets, and windows. You discover tips and techniques to help you take control of your worksheets. The result? You'll be a more efficient Excel user.

IN THIS CHAPTER

Understanding Excel worksheet essentials

Controlling your views

Manipulating the rows and columns

Learning the Fundamentals of Excel Worksheets

In Excel, each file is called a *workbook,* and each workbook can contain one or more *worksheets.* You may find it helpful to think of an Excel workbook as a notebook and worksheets as pages in the notebook. As with a notebook, you can view a particular sheet, add new sheets, remove sheets, and copy sheets.

The following sections describe the operations that you can perform with worksheets.

Working with Excel windows

Each Excel workbook file is displayed in a window. A workbook can hold any number of sheets, and these sheets can be either worksheets (sheets consisting of rows and columns) or *chart sheets* (sheets that hold a single chart). A worksheet is what people usually think of when they think of a spreadsheet. You can open as many Excel workbooks as necessary at the same time.

Figure 3.1 shows Excel with four workbooks open, each in a separate window. One of the windows is minimized and appears near the lower-left corner of the screen. (When a workbook is minimized, only its title bar is visible.) Worksheet windows can overlap, and the title bar of one window is a different color. That's the window that contains the active workbook.

FIGURE 3.1

You can open several Excel workbooks at the same time.

The workbook windows that Excel uses work much like the windows in any other Windows program. Each window has three buttons at the right side of its title bar. From left to right, they are Minimize, Maximize (or Restore), and Close. When a workbook window is maximized, the three buttons appear directly below the Excel title bar.

Workbook windows can be in one of the following states:

- **Maximized:** Fills the entire Excel workspace. A maximized window doesn't have a title bar, and the workbook's name appears in the title bar for Excel. To maximize a window, click its Maximize button.

- **Minimized:** Appears as a small window with only a title bar. To minimize a window, click its Minimize button.

- **Restored:** A nonmaximized size. To restore a maximized or minimized window, click its Restore button.

If you work with more than one workbook simultaneously (which is quite common), you need to know how to move, resize, and switch among the workbook windows.

Moving and resizing windows

To move a window, make sure that it's not maximized. Then click and drag its title bar with your mouse.

To resize a window, click and drag any of its borders until it's the size that you want it to be. When you position the mouse pointer on a window's border, the mouse pointer changes to a double-sided arrow, which lets you know that you can now click and drag to resize the window. To resize a window horizontally and vertically at the same time, click and drag any of its corners.

Note

You can't move or resize a workbook window if it's maximized. You can move a minimized window, but doing so has no effect on its position when it's subsequently restored. ■

If you want all your workbook windows to be visible (that is, not obscured by another window), you can move and resize the windows manually, or you can let Excel do it for you. Choosing View ➪ Window ➪ Arrange All displays the Arrange Windows dialog box, shown in Figure 3.2. This dialog box has four window-arrangement options. Just select the one that you want and click OK. Windows that are minimized aren't affected by this command.

FIGURE 3.2

Use the Arrange Windows dialog box to quickly arrange all open non-minimized workbook windows.

Switching among windows

At any given time, one (and only one) workbook window is the active window. The active window accepts your input and is the window on which your commands work. The active window's title bar is a different color, and the window appears at the top of the stack of windows. To work in a different window, you need to make that window active. You can make a different window the active workbook in several ways:

- **Click another window, if it's visible.** The window you click moves to the top and becomes the active window. This method isn't possible if the current window is maximized.

- **Press Ctrl+Tab (or Ctrl+F6) to cycle through all open windows until the window that you want to work with appears on top as the active window.** Pressing Shift+Ctrl+Tab (or Shift+Ctrl+F6) cycles through the windows in the opposite direction.

- **Choose View ⇨ Window ⇨ Switch Windows and select the window that you want from the drop-down list (the active window has a check mark next to it).** This menu can display as many as nine windows. If you have more than nine workbook windows open, choose More Windows (which appears below the nine window names).

- **Click the icon for the window in the Windows taskbar.** This technique is available only if the Show All Windows in the Taskbar option is turned on. You can control this setting from the Advanced tab of the Excel Options dialog box (in the Display section).

Tip

Most people prefer to do most of their work with maximized workbook windows, which enables you to see more cells and eliminates the distraction of other workbook windows getting in the way. At times, however, viewing multiple windows is preferred. For example, displaying two windows is more efficient if you need to compare information in two workbooks or if you need to copy data from one workbook to another. ■

When you maximize one window, all the other windows are maximized, too (even though you don't see them). Therefore, if the active window is maximized and you activate a different window, the new active window is also maximized.

Tip

You also can display a single workbook in more than one window. For example, if you have a workbook with two worksheets, you may want to display each worksheet in a separate window to compare the two sheets. All the window-manipulation procedures described previously still apply. Choose View ⇨ Window ⇨ New Window to open an additional window in the active workbook. ■

Closing windows

If you have multiple windows open, you may want to close those windows that you no longer need. Excel offers several ways to close the active window:

- Choose File ⇨ Close.
- Click the Close button (the X icon) on the workbook window's title bar. If the workbook window is maximized, its title bar is not visible, so its Close button appears directly below the Excel Close button.
- Press Ctrl+W.

When you close a workbook window, Excel checks whether you made any changes since the last time you saved the file. If you have made changes, Excel prompts you to save the file before it closes the window. If not, the window closes without a prompt from Excel.

Activating a worksheet

At any given time, one workbook is the active workbook, and one sheet is the active sheet in the active workbook. To activate a different sheet, just click its sheet tab, located at the bottom of the workbook window. You also can use the following shortcut keys to activate a different sheet:

- **Ctrl+PgUp:** Activates the previous sheet, if one exists
- **Ctrl+PgDn:** Activates the next sheet, if one exists

If your workbook has many sheets, all its tabs may not be visible. Use the tab scrolling controls (see Figure 3.3) to scroll the sheet tabs. The sheet tabs share space with the worksheet's horizontal scroll bar. You also can drag the tab split control to display more or fewer tabs. Dragging the tab split control simultaneously changes the number of tabs and the size of the horizontal scroll bar.

Tip

When you right-click any of the tab scrolling controls, Excel displays a list of all sheets in the workbook. You can quickly activate a sheet by selecting it from the list. ■

FIGURE 3.3

Use the tab controls to activate a different worksheet or to see additional worksheet tabs.

Tab scrolling controls   Tab split control

Adding a new worksheet to your workbook

Worksheets can be an excellent organizational tool. Instead of placing everything on a single worksheet, you can use additional worksheets in a workbook to separate various workbook elements logically. For example, if you have several products whose sales you track individually, you may want to assign each product to its own worksheet and then use another worksheet to consolidate your results.

The following are three ways to add a new worksheet to a workbook:

- Click the Insert Worksheet control, which is located to the right of the last sheet tab. This method inserts the new sheet *after* the last sheet in the workbook.
- Press Shift+F11. This method inserts the new sheet *before* the active sheet.
- Right-click a sheet tab, choose Insert from the shortcut menu, and click the General tab of the Insert dialog box that appears. Then select the Worksheet icon and click OK. This method inserts the new sheet *before* the active sheet.

Deleting a worksheet you no longer need

If you no longer need a worksheet, or if you want to get rid of an empty worksheet in a workbook, you can delete it in either of two ways:

- Right-click its sheet tab and choose Delete from the shortcut menu.
- Activate the unwanted worksheet and choose Home ➪ Cells ➪ Delete ➪ Delete Sheet. If the worksheet contains any data, Excel asks you to confirm that you want to delete the sheet. If you've never used the worksheet, Excel deletes it immediately without asking for confirmation.

Tip
You can delete multiple sheets with a single command by selecting the sheets that you want to delete. To select multiple sheets, press Ctrl while you click the sheet tabs that you want to delete. To select a group of contiguous sheets, click the first sheet tab, press Shift, and then click the last sheet tab. Then use either method to delete the selected sheets. ■

Caution
When you delete a worksheet, it's gone for good. Deleting a worksheet is one of the few operations in Excel that can't be undone. ■

Changing the name of a worksheet

The default names that Excel uses for worksheets — Sheet1, Sheet2, and so on — aren't very descriptive. If you don't change the worksheet names, remembering where to find things in multiple-sheet workbooks can be a bit difficult. That's why providing more meaningful names for your worksheets is often a good idea.

Changing the Default Number of Sheets in Your Workbooks

By default, Excel automatically creates three worksheets in each new workbook. You can change this default behavior. For example, I prefer to start each new workbook with a single worksheet. After all, you can easily add new sheets if and when they're needed. To change the default number of worksheets:

1. **Choose File ➪ Excel Options to display the Excel Options window.**
2. **Click the General tab.**
3. **Change the value for the Include This Many Sheets setting and then click OK.**

Making this change affects all new workbooks but has no effect on existing workbooks.

To change a sheet's name, double-click the sheet tab. Excel highlights the name on the sheet tab so that you can edit the name or replace it with a new name.

Sheet names can be up to 31 characters, and spaces are allowed. However, you can't use the following characters in sheet names:

:   colon

/   slash

\   backslash

[ ] square brackets

< > angle brackets

.   period

?   question mark

'   apostrophe

*   asterisk

Keep in mind that a longer worksheet name results in a wider tab, which takes up more space onscreen. Therefore, if you use lengthy sheet names, you won't be able to see very many sheet tabs without scrolling the tab list.

Changing a sheet tab color

Excel allows you to change the color of your worksheet tabs. For example, you may prefer to color-code the sheet tabs to make identifying the worksheet's contents easier.

To change the color of a sheet tab, right-click the tab and choose Tab Color from the shortcut menu. Then select the color from the color selector box.

Rearranging your worksheets

You may want to rearrange the order of worksheets in a workbook. If you have a separate worksheet for each sales region, for example, arranging the worksheets in alphabetical order may be helpful. You may want to move a worksheet from one workbook to another. (To move a worksheet to a different workbook, both workbooks must be open.) You can also create copies of worksheets.

You can move or copy a worksheet in the following ways:

- Right-click the sheet tab and choose Move or Copy to display the Move or Copy dialog box (see Figure 3.4). Use this dialog box to specify the operation and the location for the sheet.

FIGURE 3.4

Use the Move or Copy dialog box to move or copy worksheets in the same or another workbook.

- To move a worksheet, click the worksheet tab and drag it to its desired location (either in the same workbook or in a different workbook). When you drag, the mouse pointer changes to a small sheet, and a small arrow guides you.
- To copy a worksheet, click the worksheet tab, and press Ctrl while dragging the tab to its desired location (either in the same workbook or in a different workbook). When you drag, the mouse pointer changes to a small sheet with a plus sign on it.

Tip

You can move or copy multiple sheets simultaneously. First select the sheets by clicking their sheet tabs while holding down the Ctrl key. Then you can move or copy the set of sheets by using the preceding methods. ■

If you move or copy a worksheet to a workbook that already has a sheet with the same name, Excel changes the name to make it unique. For example, Sheet1 becomes Sheet1 (2). You probably want to rename the copied sheet to give it a more meaningful. See "Changing the name of a worksheet," earlier in this chapter.

Note
When you move or copy a worksheet to a different workbook, any defined names and custom formats also get copied to the new workbook. ■

Hiding and unhiding a worksheet

In some situations, you may want to hide one or more worksheets. Hiding a sheet may be useful if you don't want others to see it or if you just want to get it out of the way. When a sheet is hidden, its sheet tab is also hidden. You can't hide all the sheets in a workbook; at least one sheet must remain visible.

To hide a worksheet, right-click its sheet tab and choose Hide Sheet. The active worksheet (or selected worksheets) will be hidden from view.

Preventing Sheet Actions

To prevent others from unhiding hidden sheets, inserting new sheets, renaming sheets, copying sheets, or deleting sheets, protect the workbook's structure:

1. **Choose Review ⇨ Changes ⇨ Protect Workbook.**
2. **In the Protect Workbook dialog box, click the Structure option.**
3. **(Optional) Provide a password.**

After performing these steps, several commands will no longer be available when you right-click a sheet tab: Insert, Delete Sheet, Rename Sheet, Move or Copy Sheet, Tab Color, Hide Sheet, and Unhide Sheet. Be aware, however, that this is a very weak security measure. Cracking Excel's protection features is relatively easy.

You can also make a sheet "very hidden." A sheet that is very hidden doesn't appear in the Unhide dialog box. To make a sheet very hidden:

1. **Activate the worksheet.**
2. **Choose Developer ⇨ Controls ⇨ Properties.** The Properties dialog box, shown in the following figure, appears. (If the Developer tab isn't available, you can turn it on using the Customize Ribbon tab of the Excel Options dialog box.)
3. **In the Properties box, select the Visible option and choose 2 - xlSheetVeryHidden.**

continued

continued

After performing these steps, the worksheet is hidden and doesn't appear in the Unhide dialog box.

Caution

Be careful! After you make a sheet very hidden, you can't use the Properties box to unhide it because you aren't able to select the sheet! To unhide such a sheet, press Alt+F11 to activate the Visual Basic Editor. Locate the workbook in the Projects window and select the name of the sheet that is very hidden. Press F4 to display the Properties box, in which you can change the Visible property back to –1 - xlSheetVisible ■

To unhide a hidden worksheet, right-click any sheet tab and choose Unhide Sheet. Excel opens its Unhide dialog box that lists all hidden sheets. Choose the sheet that you want to redisplay and click OK. For reasons known only to a Microsoft programmer who is probably retired by now, you can't select multiple sheets from this dialog box, so you need to repeat the command for each sheet that you want to unhide. When you unhide a sheet, it appears in its previous position among the sheet tabs.

Controlling the Worksheet View

As you add more information to a worksheet, you may find that navigating and locating what you want gets more difficult. Excel includes a few options that enable you to view your sheet, and sometimes multiple sheets, more efficiently. This section discusses a few additional worksheet options at your disposal.

Zooming in or out for a better view

Normally, everything you see onscreen is displayed at 100%. You can change the *zoom percentage* from 10% (very tiny) to 400% (huge). Using a small zoom percentage can help you to get a bird's-eye view of your worksheet to see how it's laid out. Zooming in is useful if your eyesight isn't quite what it used to be and you have trouble deciphering tiny type. Zooming doesn't change the font size, so it has no effect on printed output.

Cross-Reference

Excel contains separate options for changing the size of your printed output. (Use the controls in the Page Layout ⇨ Scale to Fit ribbon group.) See Chapter 9 for details. ∎

Figure 3.5 shows a window zoomed to 10% and a window zoomed to 400%.

FIGURE 3.5

You can zoom in or out for a different view of your worksheets.

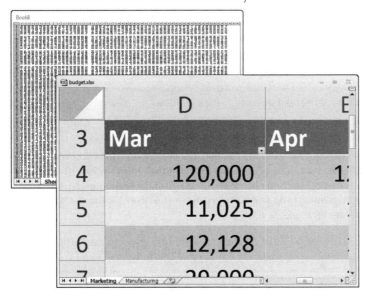

You can easily change the zoom factor of the active worksheet by using the Zoom slider located on the right side of the status bar. Click and drag the slider, and your screen transforms instantly.

Another way to zoom is to choose View ⇨ Zoom ⇨ Zoom, which displays a dialog box. Choosing View ⇨ Zoom ⇨ Zoom to Selection zooms the worksheet to display only the selected cells (useful if you want a particular range of cells to fill the workbook window).

Tip

Zooming affects only the active worksheet, so you can use different zoom factors for different worksheets. Also, if you have a worksheet displayed in two different windows, you can set a different zoom factor for each of the windows. ■

Cross-Reference

If your worksheet uses named ranges (see Chapter 4), zooming your worksheet to 39% or less displays the name of the range overlaid on the cells. Viewing named ranges in this manner is useful for getting an overview of how a worksheet is laid out. ■

Viewing a worksheet in multiple windows

Sometimes, you may want to view two different parts of a worksheet simultaneously — perhaps to make referencing a distant cell in a formula easier. Or you may want to examine more than one sheet in the same workbook simultaneously. You can accomplish either of these actions by opening a new view to the workbook, using one or more additional windows.

To create and display a new view of the active workbook, choose View ➪ Window ➪ New Window.

Excel displays a new window for the active workbook, similar to the one shown in Figure 3.6. In this case, each window shows a different worksheet in the workbook. Notice the text in the windows' title bars: `climate data.xlsx:1` and `climate data.xlsx:2`. To help you keep track of the windows, Excel appends a colon and a number to each window.

Tip

If the workbook is maximized when you create a new window, you may not even notice that Excel created the new window. If you look at the Excel title bar, though, you'll see that the workbook title now has `:2` appended to the name. Choose View ➪ Window ➪ Arrange All and choose one of the Arrange options in the Arrange Windows dialog box to display the open windows. If you select the Windows of Active Workbook check box, only the windows of the active workbook are arranged. ■

A single workbook can have as many views (that is, separate windows) as you want. Each window is independent. In other words, scrolling to a new location in one window doesn't cause scrolling in the other window(s). However, if you make changes to the worksheet shown in a particular window, those changes are also made in all views of that worksheet.

You can close these additional windows when you no longer need them. For example, clicking the Close button on the active window's title bar closes the active window but doesn't close the other windows for the workbook.

Tip

Multiple windows make copying or moving information from one worksheet to another easier. You can use Excel's drag-and-drop procedures to copy or move ranges. ■

FIGURE 3.6

Use multiple windows to view different sections of a workbook at the same time.

Comparing sheets side by side

In some situations, you may want to compare two worksheets that are in different windows. The View Side by Side feature makes this task a bit easier.

First, make sure that the two sheets are displayed in separate windows. (The sheets can be in the same workbook or in different workbooks.) If you want to compare two sheets in the same work-book, choose View ➪ Window ➪ New Window to create a new window for the active workbook. Activate the first window; then choose View ➪ Window ➪ View Side by Side. If more than two windows are open, you see a dialog box that lets you select the window for the comparison. The two windows appear next to each other.

When using the Compare Side by Side feature, scrolling in one of the windows also scrolls the other window. If you don't want this simultaneous scrolling, choose View ➪ Window ➪ Synchronous Scrolling (which is a toggle). If you have rearranged or moved the windows, choose View ➪ Window ➪ Reset Window Position to restore the windows to the initial side-by-side arrangement. To turn off the side-by-side viewing, choose View ➪ Window ➪ View Side by Side again.

Keep in mind that this feature is for manual comparison only. Unfortunately, Excel doesn't provide a way to actually point out the differences between two sheets.

Splitting the worksheet window into panes

If you prefer not to clutter your screen with additional windows, Excel provides another option for viewing multiple parts of the same worksheet. Choosing View ➪ Window ➪ Split splits the active worksheet into two or four separate panes. The split occurs at the location of the cell pointer. If the cell pointer is in row 1 or column A, this command results in a two-pane split. Otherwise, it gives you four panes. You can use the mouse to drag the individual panes to resize them.

Figure 3.7 shows a worksheet split into two panes. Notice that row numbers aren't continuous. The top pane shows rows 8 through 21, and the bottom pane shows rows 1020 through 1029. In other words, splitting panes enables you to display in a single window widely separated areas of a worksheet. To remove the split panes, choose View ➪ Window ➪ Split again.

FIGURE 3.7

You can split the worksheet window into two or four panes to view different areas of the worksheet at the same time.

Keeping the titles in view by freezing panes

If you set up a worksheet with row or column headings, these headings will not be visible when you scroll down or to the right. Excel provides a handy solution to this problem: freezing panes. Freezing panes keeps the headings visible while you're scrolling through the worksheet.

To freeze panes, start by moving the cell pointer to the cell below the row that you want to remain visible while you scroll vertically, and to the right of the column that you want to remain visible while you scroll horizontally. Then, choose View ⇨ Window ⇨ Freeze Panes and select the Freeze Panes option from the drop-down list. Excel inserts dark lines to indicate the frozen rows and columns. The frozen row and column remain visible while you scroll throughout the worksheet. To remove the frozen panes, choose View ⇨ Window ⇨ Freeze Panes, and select the Unfreeze Panes option from the drop-down list.

Figure 3.8 shows a worksheet with frozen panes. In this case, rows 1:4 and column A are frozen in place. This technique allows you to scroll down and to the right to locate some information while keeping the column titles and the column A entries visible.

FIGURE 3.8

Freeze certain columns and rows to make them remain visible while you scroll the worksheet.

The vast majority of the time, you'll want to freeze either the first row or the first column. The View ⇨ Window ⇨ Freeze Panes drop-down list has two additional options: Freeze Top Row and Freeze First Column. Using these commands eliminates the need to position the cell pointer before freezing panes.

Tip

If you designated a range to be a table (by choosing Insert ⇨ Tables ⇨ Table), you may not even need to freeze panes. When you scroll down, Excel displays the table column headings in place of the column letters. Figure 3.9 shows an example. The table headings replace the column letters only when a cell within the table is selected. ∎

FIGURE 3.9

When using a table, scrolling down displays the table headings where the column letters normally appear.

City	JAN	FEB	MAR	APR	MAY	JUN	JUL	AUG
16 ATHENS, GA	4.69	4.39	4.99	3.35	3.86	3.94	4.41	3.
17 ATLANTA, GA	5.02	4.68	5.38	3.62	3.95	3.63	5.12	3.
18 ATLANTIC CITY AP, NJ	3.6	2.85	4.06	3.45	3.38	2.66	3.86	4.
19 ATLANTIC CITY C.O.,NJ	3.44	2.88	3.79	3.25	3.16	2.46	3.36	4.
20 AUGUSTA,GA	4.5	4.11	4.61	2.94	3.07	4.19	4.07	4.
21 AUSTIN/BERGSTROM, TX	2.2	1.73	1.98	2.77	5.87	3.38	1.61	1.
22 AUSTIN/CITY, TX	1.89	1.99	2.14	2.51	5.03	3.81	1.97	2.
23 AVOCA, PA	2.46	2.08	2.69	3.28	3.69	3.97	3.74	
24 BAKERSFIELD, CA	1.18	1.21	1.41	0.45	0.24	0.12	0	0.
25 BALTIMORE, MD	3.47	3.02	3.93	3	3.89	3.43	3.85	3.
26 BARROW, AK	0.12	0.12	0.09	0.12	0.12	0.32	0.87	1.
27 BATON ROUGE, LA	6.19	5.1	5.07	5.56	5.34	5.33	5.96	5.
28 BECKLEY, WV	3.23	2.96	3.63	3.42	4.39	3.92	4.78	3.
29 BETHEL, AK	0.62	0.51	0.67	0.65	0.85	1.6	2.03	3.
30 BETTLES,AK	0.84	0.61	0.55	0.38	0.85	1.43	2.1	2.
31 BIG DELTA,AK	0.34	0.41	0.22	0.2	0.77	2.38	2.77	2.
32 BILLINGS, MT	0.81	0.57	1.12	1.74	2.48	1.89	1.28	0.
33 BINGHAMTON, NY	2.58	2.46	2.97	3.49	3.55	3.8	3.49	3.
34 BIRMINGHAM AP,AL	5.45	4.21	6.1	4.67	4.83	3.78	5.09	3.
35 BISHOP, CA	0.88	0.97	0.62	0.24	0.26	0.21	0.17	0.

Sheet1 | Data

Monitoring cells with a Watch Window

In some situations, you may want to monitor the value in a particular cell as you work. As you scroll throughout the worksheet, that cell may disappear from view. A feature known as Watch Window can help. A *Watch Window* displays the value of any number of cells in a handy window that's always visible.

To display the Watch Window, choose Formulas ➪ Formula Auditing ➪ Watch Window. The Watch Window appears in the task pane, but you can also drag it and make it float over the worksheet.

To add a cell to watch, click Add Watch and specify the cell that you want to watch. The Watch Window displays the value in that cell. You can add any number of cells to the Watch Window, and you can move the window to any convenient location. Figure 3.10 shows the Watch Window monitoring four cells.

FIGURE 3.10

Use the Watch Window to monitor the value in one or more cells.

Book	Sheet	Name	Cell	Value	Formula
budget.xlsx	Marketing		E8	173,310	=SUBTOTAL(109,[Ap
budget.xlsx	Manufacturing		F9	1,423,601.13	=SUM(F4:F8)
budget.xlsx	Sheet1	grandtotal	C9	78984	=SUM(C1:C8)

Tip

Double-click a cell in the Watch Window to immediately select that cell. ■

Working with Rows and Columns

This section discusses worksheet operations that involve complete rows and columns (rather than individual cells). Every worksheet has exactly 1,048,576 rows and 16,384 columns, and these values can't be changed.

Note

If you open a workbook that was created in a version of Excel prior to Excel 2007, the workbook is opened in Compatibility Mode. These workbooks have 65,536 rows and 256 columns. To increase the number of rows and columns, save the workbook as an Excel 2010 `.xlsx` file and then reopen it. ■

Inserting rows and columns

Although the number of rows and columns in a worksheet is fixed, you can still insert and delete rows and columns if you need to make room for additional information. These operations don't change the number of rows or columns. Rather, inserting a new row moves down the other rows to accommodate the new row. The last row is simply removed from the worksheet if it's empty. Inserting a new column shifts the columns to the right, and the last column is removed if it's empty.

Note

If the last row isn't empty, you can't insert a new row. Similarly, if the last column contains information, Excel doesn't let you insert a new column. Attempting to add a row or column displays the dialog box shown in Figure 3.11. ■

To insert a new row or rows, you can use any of these techniques:

- Select an entire row or multiple rows by clicking the row numbers in the worksheet border. Right-click and choose Insert from the shortcut menu.
- Move the cell pointer to the row that you want to insert and then choose Home ⇨ Cells ⇨ Insert ⇨ Insert Sheet Rows. If you select multiple cells in the column, Excel inserts additional rows that correspond to the number of cells selected in the column and moves the rows below the insertion down.

The procedures for inserting a new column or columns is similar, but you choose Home ⇨ Cells ⇨ Insert ⇨ Insert Sheet Columns.

You also can insert cells, rather than just rows or columns. Select the range into which you want to add new cells and then choose Home ⇨ Cells ⇨ Insert ⇨ Insert Cells (or right-click the selection and choose Insert). To insert cells, the existing cells must be shifted to the right or shifted down. Therefore, Excel displays the Insert dialog box shown in Figure 3.12 so that you can specify the direction in which you want to shift the cells.

You can't add a new row or column if it causes nonblank cells to move off the worksheet.

You can insert partial rows or columns by using the Insert dialog box.

Deleting rows and columns

You may also want to delete rows or columns in a worksheet. For example, your sheet may contain old data that is no longer needed.

To delete a row or rows, use either of these methods:

- Select an entire row or multiple rows by clicking the row numbers in the worksheet border. Right-click and choose Delete from the shortcut menu.
- Move the cell pointer to the row that you want to delete and then choose Home ➪ Cells ➪ Delete Sheet Rows. If you select multiple cells in the column, Excel deletes all rows in the selection.

Deleting columns works in a similar way. If you discover that you accidentally deleted a row or column, select Undo from the Quick Access toolbar (or press Ctrl+Z) to undo the action.

Hiding rows and columns

In some cases, you may want to hide particular rows or columns. Hiding rows and columns may be useful if you don't want users to see particular information, or if you need to print a report that summarizes the information in the worksheet without showing all the details.

Cross-Reference
Chapter 26 discusses another way to summarize worksheet data without showing all the details — outlining. ■

To hide rows or columns in your worksheet, select the row or rows that you want to hide by clicking in the row or column header. Then right-click and choose Hide from the shortcut menu. Or, you can use the commands on the Home ➪ Cells ➪ Format ➪ Hide & Unhide drop-down list.

Tip

You also can drag the row or column's border to hide the row or column. You must drag the border in the row or column heading. Drag the bottom border of a row upward or the border of a column to the left. ■

A hidden row is actually a row with its height set to zero. Similarly, a hidden column has a column width of zero. When you use the navigation keys to move the cell pointer, cells in hidden rows or columns are skipped. In other words, you can't use the navigation keys to move to a cell in a hidden row or column.

Unhiding a hidden row or column can be a bit tricky because selecting a row or column that's hidden is difficult. The solution is to select the columns or rows that are adjacent to the hidden column or row. (Select at least one column or row on either side.) Then right-click and choose Unhide. For example, if column G is hidden, select columns F and H.

Another method is to choose Home ➪ Find & Select ➪ Go To (or its F5 equivalent) to select a cell in a hidden row or column. For example, if column A is hidden, you can press F5 and specify cell A1 (or any other cell in column A) to move the cell pointer to the hidden column. Then you can choose Home ➪ Cells ➪ Format ➪ Hide & Unhide ➪ Unhide Columns.

Changing column widths and row heights

Often, you'll want to change the width of a column or the height of a row. For example, you can make columns narrower to accommodate more information on a printed page. Or you may want to increase row height to create a "double-spaced" effect.

Excel provides several different ways to change the widths of columns and the height of rows.

Changing column widths

Column width is measured in terms of the number of characters of a *fixed pitch font* that will fit into the cell's width. By default, each column's width is 8.43 units, which equates to 64 pixels (px).

Tip

If hash symbols (#) fill a cell that contains a numerical value, the column isn't wide enough to accommodate the information in the cell. Widen the column to solve the problem. ■

Before you change the column width, you can select multiple columns so that the width will be the same for all selected columns. To select multiple columns, either click and drag in the column border or press Ctrl while you select individual columns. To select all columns, click the button where the row and column headers intersect. You can change columns widths by using any of the following techniques.

- Drag the right-column border with the mouse until the column is the desired width.

- Choose Home ⇨ Cells ⇨ Format ⇨ Column Width and enter a value in the Column Width dialog box.

- Choose Home ⇨ Cells ⇨ Format ⇨ AutoFit Column Width to adjust the width of the selected column so that the widest entry in the column fits. Rather than selecting an entire column, you can just select cells in the column, and the column is adjusted based on the widest entry in your selection.

- Double-click the right border of a column header to set the column width automatically to the widest entry in the column.

Tip

To change the default width of all columns, choose Home ⇨ Cells ⇨ Format ⇨ Column ⇨ Default Width. This command displays a dialog box into which you enter the new default column width. All columns that haven't been previously adjusted take on the new column width. ∎

Caution

After you manually adjust a column's width, Excel will no longer automatically adjust the column to accommodate longer numerical entries. You need to change the column width manually. ∎

Changing row heights

Row height is measured in points (pt; a standard unit of measurement in the printing trade — 72 pt is equal to 1 inch). The default row height using the default font is 15 pt, or 20 px.

The default row height can vary, depending on the font defined in the Normal style. In addition, Excel automatically adjusts row heights to accommodate the tallest font in the row. So, if you change the font size of a cell to 20 pt, for example, Excel makes the row taller so that the entire text is visible.

You can set the row height manually, however, by using any of the following techniques. As with columns, you can select multiple rows.

- Drag the lower row border with the mouse until the row is the desired height.

- Choose Home ⇨ Cells ⇨ Format ⇨ Row Height and enter a value (in points) in the Row Height dialog box.

- Double-click the bottom border of a row to set the row height automatically to the tallest entry in the row. You also can choose Home ⇨ Cells ⇨ Format ⇨ Autofit Row Height for this task.

Changing the row height is useful for spacing out rows and is almost always preferable to inserting empty rows between lines of data.

Working with Cells and Ranges

M ost of the work you do in Excel involves cells and ranges. Understanding how best to manipulate cells and ranges will save you time and effort. This chapter discusses a variety of techniques that you can use to help increase your efficiency.

IN THIS CHAPTER

Understanding Excel cells and ranges

Selecting cells and ranges

Copying or moving ranges

Using names to work with ranges

Adding comments to cells

Understanding Cells and Ranges

A *cell* is a single element in a worksheet that can hold a value, some text, or a formula. A cell is identified by its *address,* which consists of its column letter and row number. For example, cell D12 is the cell in the fourth column and the twelfth row.

A group of cells is called a *range.* You designate a range address by specifying its upper-left cell address and its lower-right cell address, separated by a colon.

Here are some examples of range addresses:

C24	A range that consists of a single cell.
A1:B1	Two cells that occupy one row and two columns.
A1:A100	100 cells in column A.
A1:D4	16 cells (four rows by four columns).
C1:C1048576	An entire column of cells; this range also can be expressed as C:C.
A6:XFD6	An entire row of cells; this range also can be expressed as 6:6.
A1:XFD1048576	All cells in a worksheet. This range also can be expressed as either A:XFD or 1:1048576.

Selecting ranges

To perform an operation on a range of cells in a worksheet, you must first select the range. For example, if you want to make the text bold for a range of cells, you must select the range and then choose Home ⇨ Font ⇨ Bold (or press Ctrl+B).

When you select a range, the cells appear highlighted. The exception is the active cell, which remains its normal color. Figure 4.1 shows an example of a selected range (B5:C8) in a worksheet. Cell B5, the active cell, is selected but not highlighted.

When you select a range, it appears highlighted, but the active cell within the range is not highlighted.

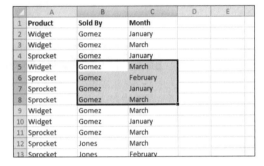

You can select a range in several ways:

- Press the left mouse button and drag, highlighting the range. Then release the mouse button. If you drag to the end of the screen, the worksheet will scroll.

- Press the Shift key while you use the navigation keys to select a range.

- Press F8 and then move the cell pointer with the navigation keys to highlight the range. Press F8 again to return the navigation keys to normal movement.

- Type the cell or range address into the Name box and press Enter. Excel selects the cell or range that you specified.

- Choose Home ⇨ Editing ⇨ Find & Select ⇨ Go To (or press F5) and enter a range's address manually into the Go To dialog box. When you click OK, Excel selects the cells in the range that you specified.

Tip

While you're selecting a range, Excel displays the number of rows and columns in your selection in the Name box (located on the left side of the Formula bar). As soon as you finish the selection, the Name box reverts to showing the address of the active cell. ■

Selecting complete rows and columns

Often, you'll need to select an entire row or column. For example, you may want to apply the same numeric format or the same alignment options to an entire row or column. You can select entire rows and columns in much the same manner as you select ranges:

- Click the row or column border to select a single row or column.
- To select multiple adjacent rows or columns, click a row or column border and drag to highlight additional rows or columns.
- To select multiple (nonadjacent) rows or columns, press Ctrl while you click the row or column borders that you want.
- Press Ctrl+spacebar to select a column. The column of the active cell (or columns of the selected cells) is highlighted.
- Press Shift+spacebar to select a row. The row of the active cell (or rows of the selected cells) is highlighted.

Tip

Press Ctrl+A to select all cells in the worksheet, which is the same as selecting all rows and all columns. If the active cell is within a table, you may need to press Ctrl+A two or even three times to select all cells in the worksheet. You can also click the area at the intersection of the row and column borders to select all cells. ■

Selecting noncontiguous ranges

Most of the time, the ranges that you select are *contiguous* — a single rectangle of cells. Excel also enables you to work with *noncontiguous ranges,* which consist of two or more ranges (or single cells) that aren't next to each other. Selecting noncontiguous ranges is also known as a *multiple selection*. If you want to apply the same formatting to cells in different areas of your worksheet, one approach is to make a multiple selection. When the appropriate cells or ranges are selected, the formatting that you select is applied to them all. Figure 4.2 shows a noncontiguous range selected in a worksheet. Three ranges are selected: A2:C3, A5:C5, and A9:C10.

You can select a noncontiguous range in several ways:

- Select the first range (or cell). Then press and hold Ctrl as you click and drag the mouse to highlight additional cells or ranges.
- From the keyboard, select a range as described previously (using F8 or the Shift key). Then press Shift+F8 to select another range without canceling the previous range selections.
- Enter the range (or cell) address in the Name box and press Enter. Separate each range address with a comma.
- Choose Home ➪ Editing ➪ Find & Select ➪ Go To (or press F5) to display the Go To dialog box. Enter the range (or cell) address in the Reference box and separate each range address with a comma. Click OK, and Excel selects the ranges.

FIGURE 4.2

Excel enables you to select noncontiguous ranges.

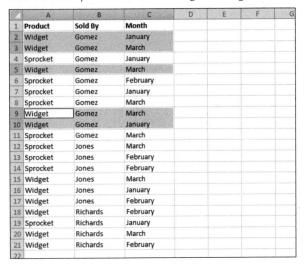

Note

Noncontiguous ranges differ from contiguous ranges in several important ways. One obvious difference is that you can't use drag-and-drop methods (described later) to move or copy noncontiguous ranges. ■

Selecting multisheet ranges

In addition to two-dimensional ranges on a single worksheet, ranges can extend across multiple worksheets to be three-dimensional ranges.

Suppose that you have a workbook set up to track budgets. A common approach is to use a separate worksheet for each department, making it easy to organize the data. You can click a sheet tab to view the information for a particular department.

Figure 4.3 shows a simplified example. The workbook has four sheets: Totals, Operations, Marketing, and Manufacturing. The sheets are laid out identically. The only difference is the values. The Totals sheet contains formulas that compute the sum of the corresponding items in the three departmental worksheets.

On the CD

This workbook, named `budget.xlsx`, is available on the companion CD-ROM. ■

FIGURE 4.3

The worksheets in this workbook are laid out identically.

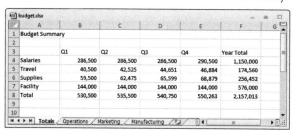

Assume that you want to apply formatting to the sheets — for example, make the column headings bold with background shading. One (albeit not-so-efficient) approach is to format the cells in each worksheet separately. A better technique is to select a multisheet range and format the cells in all the sheets simultaneously. The following is a step-by-step example of multisheet formatting, using the workbook shown in Figure 4.3.

1. **Activate the Totals worksheet by clicking its tab.**

2. **Select the range B3:F3.**

3. **Press Shift and click the Manufacturing sheet tab.** This step selects all worksheets between the active worksheet (Totals) and the sheet tab that you click — in essence, a three-dimensional range of cells (see Figure 4.4). Notice that the workbook window's title bar displays [Group] to remind you that you've selected a group of sheets and that you're in Group mode.

FIGURE 4.4

In Group mode, you can work with a three-dimensional range of cells that extend across multiple worksheets.

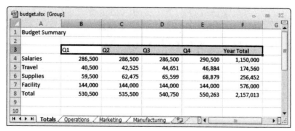

4. **Choose Home ➪ Font ➪ Bold and then choose Home ➪ Font ➪ Fill Color to apply a colored background.** Excel applies the formatting to the selected range across the selected sheets.

5. **Click one of the other sheet tabs.** This step selects the sheet and also cancels Group mode; [Group] is no longer displayed in the title bar.

When a workbook is in Group mode, any changes that you make to cells in one worksheet also apply to all the other grouped worksheets. You can use this to your advantage when you want to set up a group of identical worksheets because any labels, data, formatting, or formulas you enter are automatically added to the same cells in all the grouped worksheets.

Note

When Excel is in Group mode, some commands are disabled and can't be used. In the preceding example, you can't convert all these ranges to tables by choosing Insert ➪ Tables ➪ Table. ∎

In general, selecting a multisheet range is a simple two-step process: Select the range in one sheet and then select the worksheets to include in the range. To select a group of contiguous worksheets, you can press Shift and click the sheet tab of the last worksheet that you want to include in the selection. To select individual worksheets, press Ctrl and click the sheet tab of each worksheet that you want to select. If all the worksheets in a workbook aren't laid out the same, you can skip the sheets that you don't want to format. When you make the selection, the sheet tabs of the selected sheets appear with a white background, and Excel displays [Group] in the title bar.

Tip

To select all sheets in a workbook, right-click any sheet tab and choose Select All Sheets from the shortcut menu. ∎

Selecting special types of cells

As you use Excel, you may need to locate specific types of cells in your worksheets. For example, wouldn't it be handy to be able to locate every cell that contains a formula — or perhaps all the cells whose value depends on the current cell? Excel provides an easy way to locate these and many other special types of cells. Simply choose Home ➪ Editing ➪ Find & Select ➪ Go to Special to display the Go to Special dialog box, shown in Figure 4.5.

After you make your choice in the dialog box, Excel selects the qualifying subset of cells in the current selection. Often, this subset of cells is a multiple selection. If no cells qualify, Excel lets you know with the message No cells were found.

Tip

If you bring up the Go to Special dialog box with only one cell selected, Excel bases its selection on the entire used area of the worksheet. Otherwise, the selection is based on the selected range. ∎

FIGURE 4.5

Use the Go to Special dialog box to select specific types of cells.

Table 4.1 offers a description of the options available in the Go to Special dialog box. Some of the options are very useful.

TABLE 4.1

Go to Special Options

Option	What It Does
Comments	Selects only the cells that contain a cell comment.
Constants	Selects all nonempty cells that don't contain formulas. Use the check boxes under the Formulas option to choose which types of nonformula cells to include.
Formulas	Selects cells that contain formulas. Qualify this by selecting the type of result: numbers, text, logical values (TRUE or FALSE), or errors.
Blanks	Selects all empty cells.
Current Region	Selects a rectangular range of cells around the active cell. This range is determined by surrounding blank rows and columns. You can also press Ctrl+Shift+*.
Current Array	Selects the entire array. See Chapter 16 for more information about arrays.
Objects	Selects all graphic objects on the worksheet.
Row Differences	Analyzes the selection and selects cells that are different from other cells in each row.
Column Differences	Analyzes the selection and selects the cells that are different from other cells in each column.

continued

TABLE 4.1	*(continued)*
Option	**What It Does**
Precedents	Selects cells that are referred to in the formulas in the active cell or selection (limited to the active sheet). You can select either direct precedents or precedents at any level. See Chapter 32 for more information.
Dependents	Selects cells with formulas that refer to the active cell or selection (limited to the active sheet). You can select either direct dependents or dependents at any level. See Chapter 32 for more information.
Last Cell	Selects the bottom-right cell in the worksheet that contains data or formatting.
Visible Cells Only	Selects only visible cells in the selection. This option is useful when dealing with outlines or a filtered table.
Conditional Formats	Selects cells that have a conditional format applied (by choosing Home ➪ Styles ➪ Conditional Formatting). The Same option selects only the cells that have the same conditional formatting as the active cell.
Data Validation	Selects cells that are set up for data-entry validation (by choosing Data ➪ Date Tools ➪ Data Validation). The All option selects all such cells. The Same option selects only the cells that have the same validation rules as the active cell.

Tip

When you select an option in the Go to Special dialog box, be sure to note which suboptions become available. For example, when you select Constants, the suboptions under Formulas become available to help you further refine the results. Likewise, the suboptions under Dependents also apply to Precedents, and those under Data Validation also apply to Conditional Formats. ■

Selecting cells by searching

Another way to select cells is to use the Excel Home ➪ Editing ➪ Find & Select ➪ Find, command (or press Ctrl+F), which allows you to select cells by their contents. The Find and Replace dialog box is shown in Figure 4.6. This figure shows additional options that are available when you click the Options button.

Enter the text that you're looking for; then click Find All. The dialog box expands to display all the cells that match your search criteria. For example, Figure 4.7 shows the dialog box after Excel has located all cells that contain the text *March*. You can click an item in the list, and the screen will scroll so that you can view the cell in context. To select all the cells in the list, first select any single item in the list. Then press Ctrl+A to select them all.

FIGURE 4.6

The Find and Replace dialog box, with its options displayed.

FIGURE 4.7

The Find and Replace dialog box, with its results listed.

Note

The Find and Replace dialog box allows you to return to the worksheet without dismissing the dialog box. ■

The Find and Replace dialog box supports two wildcard characters:

- ? matches any single character.
- * matches any number of characters.

Wildcard characters also work with values. For example, searching for 3* locates all cells that contain a value that begins with 3. Searching for 1?9 locates all three-digit entries that begin with 1 and end with 9.

Tip

To search for a question mark or an asterisk, precede the character with a tilde character (~). For example, the following search string finds the text *NONE*:

~*NONE~*

If you need to search for the tilde character, use two tildes. ■

If your searches don't seem to be working correctly, double-check these three options (which sometimes have a way of changing on their own):

- **Match Case:** If this check box is selected, the case of the text must match exactly. For example, searching for smith does not locate Smith.
- **Match Entire Cell Contents:** If this check box is selected, a match occurs if the cell contains only the search string (and nothing else). For example, searching for Excel doesn't locate a cell that contains Microsoft Excel.
- **Look In:** This drop-down list has three options: Values, Formulas, and Comments. If, for example, Values is selected, searching for 900 doesn't find a cell that contains 900 if that value is generated by a formula.

Copying or Moving Ranges

As you create a worksheet, you may find it necessary to copy or move information from one location to another. Excel makes copying or moving ranges of cells easy. Here are some common things you might do:

- Copy a cell to another cell.
- Copy a cell to a range of cells. The source cell is copied to every cell in the destination range.
- Copy a range to another range. Both ranges must be the same size.
- Move a range of cells to another location.

The primary difference between copying and moving a range is the effect of the operation on the source range. When you copy a range, the source range is unaffected. When you move a range, the contents are removed from the source range.

Note

Copying a cell normally copies the cell's contents, any formatting that is applied to the original cell (including conditional formatting and data validation), and the cell comment (if it has one). When you copy a cell that contains a formula, the cell references in the copied formulas are changed automatically to be relative to their new destination. ∎

Copying or moving consists of two steps (although shortcut methods do exist):

1. Select the cell or range to copy (the source range) and copy it to the Clipboard. To move the range instead of copying it, cut the range rather than copying it.

2. Move the cell pointer to the range that will hold the copy (the destination range) and paste the Clipboard contents.

Caution

When you paste information, Excel overwrites any cells that get in the way without warning you. If you find that pasting overwrote some essential cells, choose Undo from the Quick Access toolbar (or press Ctrl+Z). ∎

Note

When you copy a cell or range, Excel surrounds the copied area with an animated border (sometimes referred to as "marching ants"). As long as that border remains animated, the copied information is available for pasting. If you press Esc to cancel the animated border, Excel removes the information from the Clipboard. ∎

Because copying (or moving) is used so often, Excel provides many different methods. I discuss each method in the following sections. Copying and moving are similar operations, so I point out only important differences between the two.

Copying by using Ribbon commands

Choosing Home ➪ Clipboard ➪ Copy transfers a copy of the selected cell or range to the Windows Clipboard and the Office Clipboard. After performing the copy part of this operation, select the cell that will hold the copy and choose Home ➪ Clipboard ➪ Paste.

Rather than choosing Home ➪ Clipboard ➪ Paste, you can just activate the destination cell and press Enter. If you use this technique, Excel removes the copied information from the Clipboard so that it can't be pasted again.

Note

If you click the Copy button more than once before you click the Paste button, Excel may automatically display the Office Clipboard task bar. To prevent this task bar from appearing, click the Options button at the bottom and then remove the check mark from Show Office Clipboard Automatically. ∎

If you're copying a range, you don't need to select an entire same-sized range before you click the Paste button. You need only activate the upper-left cell in the destination range.

Understanding the Office Clipboard

Whenever you cut or copy information from a Windows program, Windows stores the information on the Windows Clipboard, which is an area of your computer's memory. Each time that you cut or copy information, Windows replaces the information previously stored on the Clipboard with the new information that you cut or copied. The Windows Clipboard can store data in a variety of formats. Because Windows manages information on the Clipboard, it can be pasted to other Windows applications, regardless of where it originated.

Office has its own Clipboard (the Office Clipboard), which is available only in Office programs. To view or hide the Office Clipboard, click the dialog launcher icon in the bottom-right corner of the Home ⇨ Clipboard group.

Whenever you cut or copy information in an Office program, such as Excel or Word, the program places the information on both the Windows Clipboard and the Office Clipboard. However, the program treats information on the Office Clipboard differently than it treats information on the Windows Clipboard. Instead of replacing information on the Office Clipboard, the program appends the information to the Office Clipboard. With multiple items stored on the Clipboard, you can then paste the items either individually or as a group.

Find out more about this feature in "Using the Office Clipboard to paste," later in this chapter.

New Feature

The Home ⇨ Clipboard ⇨ Paste control contains a drop-down arrow that, when clicked, gives you additional paste option icons. The paste preview icons are new to Excel 2010. These icons are explained later in this chapter (see "Pasting in Special Ways"). The difference is that you can preview how the pasted information will appear. ■

Copying by using shortcut menu commands

If you prefer, you can use the following shortcut menu commands for copying and pasting:

- Right-click the range and choose Copy (or Cut) from the shortcut menu to copy the selected cells to the Clipboard.
- Right-click and choose Paste from the shortcut menu that appears to paste the Clipboard contents to the selected cell or range.

For more control over how the pasted information appears, use one of the paste icons in the shortcut menu (see Figure 4.8).

Rather than using Paste, you can just activate the destination cell and press Enter. If you use this technique, Excel removes the copied information from the Clipboard so that it can't be pasted again.

FIGURE 4.8

The paste icons on the shortcut menu provide more control over how the pasted information appears.

Copying by using shortcut keys

The copy and paste operations also have shortcut keys associated with them:

- Ctrl+C copies the selected cells to both the Windows and Office Clipboards.
- Ctrl+X cuts the selected cells to both the Windows and Office Clipboards.
- Ctrl+V pastes the Windows Clipboard contents to the selected cell or range.

Tip
Most other Windows applications also use these shortcut keys. ■

Copying or moving by using drag-and-drop

Excel also enables you to copy or move a cell or range by dragging. Be aware, however, that dragging and dropping does not place any information on either the Windows Clipboard or the Office Clipboard.

Caution
The drag-and-drop method of moving does offer one advantage over the cut-and-paste method — Excel warns you if a drag-and-drop move operation will overwrite existing cell contents. However, you do not get a warning if a drag-and-drop copy operation will overwrite existing cell contents. ■

To copy using drag-and-drop, select the cell or range that you want to copy and then press Ctrl and move the mouse to one of the selection's borders (the mouse pointer is augmented with a small plus sign). Then, simply drag the selection to its new location while you continue to press the Ctrl key. The original selection remains behind, and Excel makes a new copy when you release the mouse button. To move a range using drag-and-drop, don't press Ctrl while dragging the border.

Using Smart Tags When Inserting and Pasting

Some cell and range operations — specifically inserting, pasting, and filling cells by dragging — result in the display of a Smart Tag. A *Smart Tag* is a small square that when clicked, presents you with options. For example, if you copy a range and then paste it to a different location, a Smart Tag appears at the lower-right of the pasted range. Click the Smart Tag (or press Ctrl), and you see the options shown in the figure here. These options enable you to specify how the data should be pasted, such as values only or formatting only. In this case, using the Smart Tag is an alternative to using options in the Paste Special dialog box. (Read more about Paste Special in the upcoming section, "Using the Paste Special Dialog box.")

Some users find these Smart Tags helpful, and others think that they're annoying. (Count me in the latter group.) To turn off these Smart Tags, choose File ➪ Options and click the Advanced tab. Remove the check mark from the two options labeled Show Paste Options Buttons and Show Insert Options Buttons.

Tip

If the mouse pointer doesn't turn into an arrow when you point to the border of a cell or range, you need to make a change to your settings. Access the Excel Options dialog box, click the Advanced tab, and place a check mark on the option labeled Enable Fill Handle and Cell Drag-and-Drop. ■

Copying to adjacent cells

Often, you need to copy a cell to an adjacent cell or range. This type of copying is quite common when working with formulas. For example, if you're working on a budget, you might create a formula to add the values in column B. You can use the same formula to add the values in the other columns. Rather than re-enter the formula, you can copy it to the adjacent cells.

Excel provides additional options for copying to adjacent cells. To use these commands, activate the cell that you're copying *and* extend the cell selection to include the cells that you're copying to. Then issue the appropriate command from the following list for one-step copying:

- Home ⇨ Editing ⇨ Fill ⇨ Down (or Ctrl+D) copies the cell to the selected range below.
- Home ⇨ Editing ⇨ Fill ⇨ Right (or Ctrl+R) copies the cell to the selected range to the right.
- Home ⇨ Editing ⇨ Fill ⇨ Up copies the cell to the selected range above.
- Home ⇨ Editing ⇨ Fill ⇨ Left copies the cell to the selected range to the left.

None of these commands places information on either the Windows Clipboard or the Office Clipboard.

Tip

You also can use AutoFill to copy to adjacent cells by dragging the selection's fill handle (the small square in the bottom-right corner of the selected cell or range). Excel copies the original selection to the cells that you highlight while dragging. For more control over the AutoFill operation, drag the fill handle with the right mouse button, and you'll get a shortcut menu with additional options. ∎

Copying a range to other sheets

You can use the copy procedures described previously to copy a cell or range to another worksheet, even if the worksheet is in a different workbook. You must, of course, activate the other worksheet before you select the location to which you want to copy.

Excel offers a quicker way to copy a cell or range and paste it to other worksheets in the same workbook.

1. **Select the range to copy.**
2. **Press Ctrl and click the sheet tabs for the worksheets to which you want to copy the information.** Excel displays [Group] in the workbook's title bar.
3. **Choose Home ⇨ Editing ⇨ Fill ⇨ Across Worksheets.** A dialog box appears to ask you what you want to copy (All, Contents, or Formats).
4. **Make your choice and then click OK.** Excel copies the selected range to the selected worksheets; the new copy occupies the same cells in the selected worksheets as the original occupies in the initial worksheet.

Caution

Be careful with the Home ⇨ Editing ⇨ Fill ⇨ Across Worksheets command because Excel doesn't warn you when the destination cells contain information. You can quickly overwrite lots of cells with this command and not even realize it. So make sure you check your work, and use Undo if the result isn't what you expected. ∎

Using the Office Clipboard to paste

Whenever you cut or copy information in an Office program, such as Excel, you can place the data on both the Windows Clipboard and the Office Clipboard. When you copy information to the Office Clipboard, you append the information to the Office Clipboard instead of replacing what is already there. With multiple items stored on the Office Clipboard, you can then paste the items either individually or as a group.

To use the Office Clipboard, you first need to open it. Use the dialog launcher on the bottom right of the Home ➪ Clipboard group to toggle the Clipboard task pane on and off.

Tip

To make the Clipboard task pane open automatically, click the Options button near the bottom of the task pane and choose the Show Office Clipboard Automatically option. ∎

After you open the Clipboard task pane, select the first cell or range that you want to copy to the Office Clipboard and copy it by using any of the preceding techniques. Repeat this process, selecting the next cell or range that you want to copy. As soon as you copy the information, the Office Clipboard task pane shows you the number of items that you've copied and a brief description (it will hold up to 24 items). Figure 4.9 shows the Office Clipboard with four copied items.

FIGURE 4.9

Use the Clipboard task pane to copy and paste multiple items.

When you're ready to paste information, select the cell into which you want to paste information. To paste an individual item, click it in the Clipboard task pane. To paste all the items that you've copied, click the Paste All button (which is at the top of the Clipboard task pane). The items are pasted, one after the other. The Paste All button is probably more useful in Word, for situations in which you copy text from various sources, and then paste it all at once.

You can clear the contents of the Office Clipboard by clicking the Clear All button.

The following items about the Office Clipboard and its functioning are worth noting:

- Excel pastes the contents of the Windows Clipboard (the last item you copied to the Office Clipboard) when you paste by choosing Home ⇨ Clipboard ⇨ Paste, by pressing Ctrl+V, or by right-clicking and choosing Paste from the shortcut menu.

- The last item that you cut or copied appears on both the Office Clipboard and the Windows Clipboard.

- Pasting from the Office Clipboard also places that item on the Windows Clipboard. If you choose Paste All from the Office Clipboard toolbar, you paste all items stored on the Office Clipboard onto the Windows Clipboard as a single item.

- Clearing the Office Clipboard also clears the Windows Clipboard.

Caution

The Office Clipboard has a serious problem that makes it virtually worthless for Excel users: If you copy a range that contains formulas, the formulas are not transferred when you paste to a different range. Only the values are pasted. Furthermore, Excel doesn't even warn you about this fact. ■

Pasting in special ways

You may not always want to copy everything from the source range to the destination range. For example, you may want to copy only the formula results rather than the formulas themselves. Or you may want to copy the number formats from one range to another without overwriting any existing data or formulas.

To control what is copied into the destination range, choose Home ⇨ Clipboard ⇨ Paste and use the drop-down menu shown in Figure 4.10. When you hover your mouse pointer over an icon, you'll see a preview of the pasted information in the destination range. Click the icon to use the selected paste option.

The paste options are

- **Paste (P):** Pastes the cell's contents, formats, and data validation from the Windows Clipboard.

- **Formulas (F):** Pastes formulas, but not formatting.

- **Formulas & Number Formatting (O):** Pastes formulas and number formatting only.

- **Keep Source Formatting (K):** Pastes formulas, and all formatting.

- **No Borders (B):** Pastes everything except borders that appear in the source range.

- **Keep Source Column Width (W):** Pastes formulas, and also duplicates the column width of the copied cells.

- **Transpose (T):** Changes the orientation of the copied range. Rows become columns, and columns become rows. Any formulas in the copied range are adjusted so that they work properly when transposed.

- **Merge Conditional Formatting (G):** This icon is displayed only when the copied cells contain conditional formatting. When clicked, it merges the copied conditional formatting with any conditional formatting in the destination range.

- **Values (V):** Pastes the results of formulas. The destination for the copy can be a new range or the original range. In the latter case, Excel replaces the original formulas with their current values.

- **Values & Number Formatting (A):** Pastes the results of formulas, plus the number formatting.

- **Values & Source Formatting (E):** Pastes the results of formulas, plus all formatting.

- **Formatting (R):** Pastes only the formatting of the source range.

- **Paste Link (N):** Creates formulas in the destination range that refer to the cells in the copied range.

- **Picture (U):** Pastes the copied information as a picture.

- **Linked Picture (I):** Pastes the copied information as a "live" picture that is updated if the source range is changed.

- **Paste Special:** Displays the Paste Special dialog box (described in the next section).

FIGURE 4.10

Excel offers several pasting options, with preview. Here, the information is copied from D2:E5, and is being pasted beginning at cell D10.

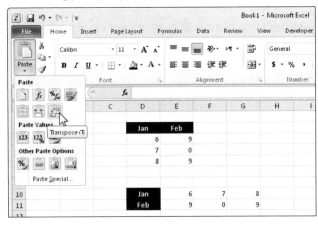

Note

After you paste, you're offered another chance to change your mind. A Smart Tag appears at the lower right of the pasted range. Click the Smart Tag (or press Ctrl), and you see the paste option icons again. ■

Using the Paste Special Dialog box

For yet another pasting method, choose Home ➪ Clipboard ➪ Paste ➪ Paste Special to display the Paste Special dialog box (see Figure 4.11). You can also right-click and choose Paste Special from the shortcut menu to display this dialog box. This dialog box has several options, which I explain in the following list.

Note

Excel actually has several different Paste Special dialog boxes, each with different options. The one displayed depends on what's copied. This section describes the Paste Special dialog box that appears when a range or cell has been copied. ■

FIGURE 4.11

The Paste Special dialog box.

Tip

For the Paste Special command to be available, you need to copy a cell or range. (Choosing Home ➪ Clipboard ➪ Cut doesn't work.) ■

- **All:** Pastes the cell's contents, formats, and data validation from the Windows Clipboard.

- **Formulas:** Pastes values and formulas, with no formatting.

- **Values:** Pastes values and the results of formulas (no formatting). The destination for the copy can be a new range or the original range. In the latter case, Excel replaces the original formulas with their current values.

- **Formats:** Copies only the formatting.

- **Comments:** Copies only the cell comments from a cell or range. This option doesn't copy cell contents or formatting.

- **Validation:** Copies the validation criteria so the same data validation will apply. Data validation is applied by choosing Data ➪ Data Tools ➪ Data Validation.

- **All Using Source Theme:** Pastes everything, but uses the formatting from the document theme of the source. This option is relevant only if you're pasting information from a different workbook, and the workbook uses a different document theme than the active workbook.

- **All Except Borders:** Pastes everything except borders that appear in the source range.

- **Column Widths:** Pastes only column width information.

- **Formulas and Number Formats:** Pastes all values, formulas and number formats (but no other formatting).

- **Values and Number Formats:** Pastes all values and numeric formats, but not the formulas themselves.

- **All merging conditional formats:** Merges the copied conditional formatting with any conditional formatting in the destination range. This option is enabled only when you are copying a range that contains conditional formatting.

In addition, the Paste Special dialog box enables you to perform other operations, described in the following sections.

Performing mathematical operations without formulas

The option buttons in the Operation section of the Paste Special dialog box let you perform an arithmetic operation on values and formulas in the destination range. For example, you can copy a range to another range and select the Multiply operation. Excel multiplies the corresponding values in the source range and the destination range and replaces the destination range with the new values.

This feature also works with a single copied cell, pasted to a multi-cell range. Assume that you have a range of values, and you want to increase each value by 5 percent. Enter **105%** into any blank cell and copy that cell to the Clipboard. Then select the range of values and bring up the Paste Special dialog box. Select the Multiply option, and each value in the range is multiplied by 105 percent.

Warning
If the destination range contains formulas, the formulas are also modified. In many cases, this is not what you want. ■

Skipping blanks when pasting

The Skip Blanks option in the Paste Special dialog box prevents Excel from overwriting cell contents in your paste area with blank cells from the copied range. This option is useful if you're copying a range to another area but don't want the blank cells in the copied range to overwrite existing data.

Transposing a range

The Transpose option in the Paste Special dialog box changes the orientation of the copied range. Rows become columns, and columns become rows. Any formulas in the copied range are adjusted so that they work properly when transposed. Note that you can use this check box with the other options in the Paste Special dialog box. Figure 4.12 shows an example of a horizontal range (A1:D5) that was transposed to a different range (A9:E12).

FIGURE 4.12

Transposing a range changes the orientation as the information is pasted into the worksheet.

	A	B	C	D	E	F	G
1		Jan	Feb	Mar			
2	Region 1	12	32	55			
3	Region 2	34	36	68			
4	Region 3	45	64	96			
5	Region 5	17	21	27			
6							
7							
8							
9		Region 1	Region 2	Region 3	Region 5		
10	Jan	12	34	45	17		
11	Feb	32	36	64	21		
12	Mar	55	68	96	27		
13							
14							

Tip

If you click the Paste Link button in the Paste Special dialog box, you create formulas that link to the source range. As a result, the destination range automatically reflects changes in the source range. ■

Using Names to Work with Ranges

Dealing with cryptic cell and range addresses can sometimes be confusing. (This confusion becomes even more apparent when you deal with formulas, which I cover in Chapter 10.) Fortunately, Excel allows you to assign descriptive names to cells and ranges. For example, you can give a cell a name such as Interest_Rate, or you can name a range JulySales. Working with these names (rather than cell or range addresses) has several advantages:

- A meaningful range name (such as Total_Income) is much easier to remember than a cell address (such as AC21).

- Entering a name is less error-prone than entering a cell or range address.

- You can quickly move to areas of your worksheet either by using the Name box, located at the left side of the Formula bar (click the arrow to drop down a list of defined names) or by choosing Home ➪ Editing ➪ Find & Select ➪ Go To (or F5) and specifying the range name.

- Creating formulas is easier. You can paste a cell or range name into a formula by using Formula Autocomplete.

- Names make your formulas more understandable and easier to use. A formula such as =Income−Taxes is more intuitive than =D20−D40.

Creating range names in your workbooks

Excel provides several different methods that you can use to create range names. Before you begin, however, you should be aware of some important rules about what is acceptable:

- Names can't contain any spaces. You may want to use an underscore character to simulate a space (such as Annual_Total).

- You can use any combination of letters and numbers, but the name must begin with a letter. A name can't begin with a number (such as 3rdQuarter) or look like a cell reference (such as QTR3). If these are desirable names, though, you can precede the name with an underscore: for example, _3rd Quarter and _QTR3.

- Symbols, except for underscores and periods, aren't allowed.

- Names are limited to 255 characters, but it's a good practice to keep names as short as possible yet still meaningful and understandable.

Caution

Excel also uses a few names internally for its own use. Although you can create names that override Excel's internal names, you should avoid doing so. To be on the safe side, avoid using the following for names: Print_ Area, Print_Titles, Consolidate_Area, and Sheet_Title. To delete a range name or rename a range, see "Managing Names," later in this chapter. ∎

Using the New Name dialog box

To create a range name, start by selecting the cell or range that you want to name. Then, choose Formulas ➪ Defined Names ➪ Define Name. Excel displays the New Name dialog box, shown in Figure 4.13. Note that this is a resizable dialog box. Click and drag a border to change the dimensions.

FIGURE 4.13

Create names for cells or ranges by using the New Name dialog box.

Type a name in the Name text field (or use the name that Excel proposes, if any). The selected cell or range address appears in the Refers To text field. Use the Scope drop-down list to indicate the scope for the name. The *scope* indicates where the name will be valid, and it's either the entire workbook or a particular sheet. If you like, you can add a comment that describes the named range or cell. Click OK to add the name to your workbook and close the dialog box.

Using the Name box

A faster way to create a name is to use the Name box (to the left of the Formula bar). Select the cell or range to name, click the Name box, and type the name. Press Enter to create the name. (You must press Enter to actually record the name; if you type a name and then click in the worksheet, Excel doesn't create the name.) If a name already exists, you can't use the Name box to change the range to which that name refers. Attempting to do so simply selects the range.

The Name box is a drop-down list and shows all names in the workbook. To choose a named cell or range, click the Name box and choose the name. The name appears in the Name box, and Excel selects the named cell or range in the worksheet.

Using the Create Names from Selection dialog box

You may have a worksheet that contains text that you want to use for names for adjacent cells or ranges. For example, you may want to use the text in column A to create names for the corresponding values in column B. Excel makes this task easy to do.

To create names by using adjacent text, start by selecting the name text and the cells that you want to name. (These items can be individual cells or ranges of cells.) The names must be adjacent to the cells that you're naming. (A multiple selection is allowed.) Then, choose Formulas ➪ Defined Names ➪ Create from Selection. Excel displays the Create Names from Selection dialog box, shown in Figure 4.14. The check marks in this dialog box are based on Excel's analysis of the selected range. For example, if Excel finds text in the first row of the selection, it proposes that you create names based on the top row. If Excel didn't guess correctly, you can change the check boxes. Click OK, and Excel creates the names. Using the data in Figure 4.14, Excel creates six names: January for cell B1, February for cell B2, and so on.

FIGURE 4.14

Use the Create Names from Selection dialog box to name cells using labels that appear in the worksheet.

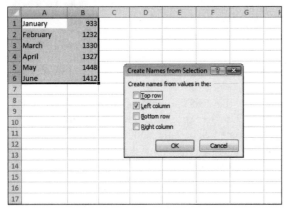

Note

If the text contained in a cell would result in an invalid name, Excel modifies the name to make it valid. For example, if a cell contains the text Net Income (which is invalid for a name because it contains a space), Excel converts the space to an underscore character. If Excel encounters a value or a numeric formula where text should be, however, it doesn't convert it to a valid name. It simply doesn't create a name — and does not inform you of that fact. ■

Caution

If the upper-left cell of the selection contains text and you choose the Top Row and Left Column options, Excel uses that text for the name of the entire data, excluding the top row and left column. So, after Excel creates the names, take a minute to make sure that they refer to the correct ranges. If Excel creates a name that is incorrect, you can delete or modify it by using the Name Manager (described next). ■

Managing names

A workbook can have any number of names. If you have many names, you should know about the Name Manager, shown in Figure 4.15.

FIGURE 4.15

Use the Name Manager to work with range names.

The Name Manager appears when you choose Formulas ➪ Defined Names ➪ Name Manager (or press Ctrl+F3). The Name Manager has the following features:

- **Displays information about each name in the workbook.** You can resize the Name Manager dialog box and widen the columns to show more information. You can also click a column heading to sort the information by the column.

- **Allows you to filter the displayed names.** Clicking the Filter button lets you show only those names that meet a certain criteria. For example, you can view only the worksheet level names.

- **Provides quick access to the New Name dialog box.** Click the New button to create a new name without closing the Name Manager.

- **Lets you edit names.** To edit a name, select it in the list and then click the Edit button. You can change the name itself, modify the Refers To range, or edit the comment.

- **Lets you quickly delete unneeded names.** To delete a name, select it in the list and click Delete.

Caution

Be extra careful when deleting names. If the name is used in a formula, deleting the name causes the formula to become invalid. (It displays #NAME?.) However, deleting a name can be undone, so if you find that formulas return #NAME? after you delete a name, choose Undo from the Quick Access toolbar (or press Ctrl+Z) to get the name back. ■

If you delete the rows or columns that contain named cells or ranges, the names contain an invalid reference. For example, if cell A1 on Sheet1 is named Interest and you delete row 1 or column A, the name Interest then refers to =Sheet1!#REF! (that is, to an erroneous reference). If you use Interest in a formula, the formula displays #REF.

Tip

The Name Manager is useful, but it has a shortcoming: It doesn't let you display the list of names in a worksheet range so you can view or print them. Such a feat is possible, but you need to look beyond the Name Manager.

To create a list of names in a worksheet, first move the cell pointer to an empty area of your worksheet — the list is created at the active cell position and overwrites any information at that location. Press F3 to display the Paste Name dialog box, which lists all the defined names. Then click the Paste List button. Excel creates a list of all names in the workbook and their corresponding addresses. ■

Adding Comments to Cells

Documentation that explains certain elements in the worksheet can often be helpful. One way to document your work is to add comments to cells. This feature is useful when you need to describe a particular value or explain how a formula works.

To add a comment to a cell, select the cell and use any of these actions:

- Choose Review ➪ Comments ➪ New Comment.
- Right-click the cell and choose Insert Comment from the shortcut menu.
- Press Shift+F2.

Excel inserts a comment that points to the active cell. Initially, the comment consists of your name, as specified in the Excel Options dialog box (you can delete your name, if you like). Enter the text for the cell comment and then click anywhere in the worksheet to hide the comment. You can change the size of the comment by clicking and dragging any of its borders. Figure 4.16 shows a cell with a comment.

FIGURE 4.16

You can add comments to cells to help clarify important items in your worksheets.

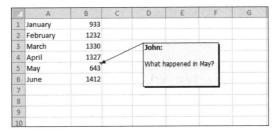

Cells that have a comment display a small red triangle in the upper-right corner. When you move the mouse pointer over a cell that contains a comment, the comment becomes visible.

You can force a comment to be displayed even when its cell is not activated. Right-click the cell and choose Show/Hide Comments. Although this command refers to "comments" (plural), it affects only the comment in the active cell. To return to normal (make the comment appear only when its cell is activated), right-click the cell and choose Hide Comment.

Tip

You can control how comments are displayed. Access the Advanced tab of the Excel Options dialog box. In the Display section, select the No Comments or Indicators option from the For Cells with Comments, Show list. ■

Formatting comments

If you don't like the default look of cell comments, you can make some changes. Right-click the cell and choose Edit Comment. Select the text in the comment and use the commands of the Font and the Alignment groups (on the Home tab) to make changes to the comment's appearance.

For even more formatting options, right-click the comment's border and choose Format Comment from the shortcut menu. Excel responds by displaying the Format Comment dialog box, which allows you to change many aspects of its appearance, including color, border, and margins.

Tip

You can also display an image inside a comment. Right-click the cell and choose Edit Comment. Then right-click the comment's border and choose Format Comment. Select the Colors and Lines tab in the Format Comment dialog box. Click the Color drop-down list and select Fill Effects. In the Fill Effects dialog box, click the Picture tab and then click the Select Picture button to specify a graphics file. Figure 4.17 shows a comment that contains a picture. ■

FIGURE 4.17

This comment contains a graphics image.

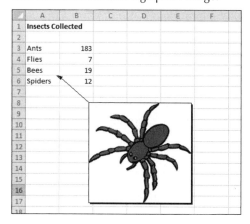

Changing a comment's shape

Normally, a cell comment is rectangular, but they don't have to be. To change the shape of a cell comment, add a command to your Quick Access toolbar:

1. **Right-click the Quick Access toolbar and choose Customize Quick Access Toolbar.** The Quick Access Toolbar section of the Excel Options dialog box appears.

2. **From the Choose Commands From drop-down list, select Drawing Tools | Format Tab.**

3. **From the list on the left, select Change Shape and then click Add.**

4. **Click OK to close the Excel Options dialog box.**

After performing these steps, your Quick Access toolbar has a new Change Shape icon.

To change the shape of a comment, make sure that it's visible (right-click the cell and select Show/Hide Comments). Then click the comment's border to select it as a Shape (or, Ctrl-click the comment to select it as a Shape). Click the Change Shape button on the Quick Access toolbar and choose a new shape for the comment. Figure 4.18 shows a cell comment with a nonstandard shape.

FIGURE 4.18

Cell comments don't have to be rectangles.

Reading comments

To read all comments in a workbook, choose Review ➪ Comments ➪ Next. Keep clicking Next to cycle through all the comments in a workbook. Choose Review ➪ Comments ➪ Previous to view the comments in reverse order.

Printing comments

Normally, when you print a worksheet that contains cell comments, the comments are not printed. If you would like to print the comments, though, here's how:

1. **Click the dialog box launcher in the Page Layout ⇨ Page Setup group.** This is the small icon to the right of the Page Setup group name. Clicking this icon displays the Page Setup dialog box.

2. **In the Page Setup dialog box, click the Sheet tab.**

3. **Make your choice from the Comments drop-down control: At End of Sheet, or As Displayed on Sheet (see Figure 4.19).**

FIGURE 4.19

Specifying how to print cell comments.

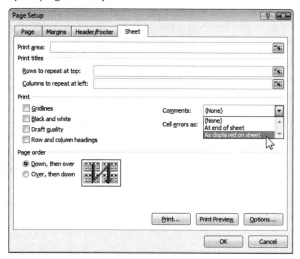

4. **Click OK to close the Page Setup dialog box.** Or, click the Print button to print the worksheet.

Hiding and showing comments

If you want all cell comments to be visible (regardless of the location of the cell pointer), choose Review ⇨ Comments ⇨ Show All Comments. This command is a toggle; select it again to hide all cell comments. To toggle the display of an individual comments, select its cell and then choose Review ⇨ Comments ⇨ Show/Hide Comment.

Selecting comments

To quickly select all cells in a worksheet that contain a comment, choose Home ⇨ Editing ⇨ Find & Select ⇨ Go to Special. Then choose the Comments option and click OK.

An Alternative to Cell Comments

You can make use of Excel's Data Validation (covered in Chapter 25) feature to add a different type of comment to a cell. This type of comment appears automatically when the cell is selected. Follow these steps:

1. **Select the cell that will contain the comment.**
2. **Choose Data ⇨ Data Tools ⇨ Data Validation to display the Data Validation dialog box.**
3. **Click the Input Message tab.**
4. **Make sure that the Show Input Message When Cell Is Selected check box is selected.**
5. **Type your comment in the Input Message box.**
6. **As an option, type a title in the Title box. (This text will appear in bold at the top of the message.)**
7. **Click OK to close the Data Validation dialog box.**

After performing these steps, the message appears when the cell is activated, and it disappears when any other cell is activated.

Note that this message isn't a "real" comment. For example, a cell that contains this type of message doesn't display a comment indicator, and it's not affected by any of the commands used to work with cell comments. In addition, you can't format these messages in any way.

Editing comments

To edit a comment, activate the cell, right-click, and then choose Edit Comment from the shortcut menu. Or, select the cell and press Shift+F2. After you make your changes, click any cell.

Deleting comments

To delete a cell comment, activate the cell that contains the comment and then choose Review ⇨ Comments ⇨ Delete. Or, right-click and then choose Delete Comment from the shortcut menu.

Introducing Tables

M any worksheets are designed to store data in a table. A *table* is a rectangular range of data that usually has a row of text headings to describe the contents of each column. Excel's table feature (introduced in Excel 2007) makes common tasks much easier — and a lot better looking. More importantly, the table features may help eliminate some common errors.

This chapter is a basic introduction to Excel table features. As always, I urge you to just dig in and experiment with the various table-related commands. You may be surprised at what you can accomplish with just a few mouse clicks.

IN THIS CHAPTER

Understanding how a table differs from a normal range

Working with tables

Using the Total Row

Removing duplicate rows from a table

Sorting and filtering a table

What Is a Table?

A *table* is simply a rectangular range of structured data. Each row in the table corresponds to a single entity. For example, a row can contain information about a customer, a bank transaction, an employee, a product, and so on. Each column contains a specific piece of information. For example, if each row contains information about an employee, the columns can contain data such as name, employee number, hire date, salary, department, and so on. Tables typically have a header row at the top that describes the information contained in each column.

Setting up data like this in a range of cells is very straightforward. The magic happens when you tell Excel to convert a range of data into an "official" table. You do this by selecting any cell within the range and then choosing Insert ➪ Tables ➪ Table.

When you explicitly identify a range as a table, Excel can respond more intelligently to the actions you perform with that range. For example, if you create a chart from a table, the chart will expand automatically as you add new rows to the table.

Figure 5.1 shows a range of data that has not yet been converted to a table. Notice that this range corresponds to the description I provide earlier: It's a range of structured data with column headers. In this example, each row contains information about a single real estate listing. The range has 10 columns and 125 rows of data (plus a descriptive header row).

FIGURE 5.1

This range of data is a good candidate for a table.

	A	B	C	D	E	F	G	H	I	J
1	Agent	Date Listed	Area	List Price	Bedrooms	Baths	SqFt	Type	Pool	Sold
2	Shasta	2/9/2009	Central	$350,000	3	2	2,275	Single Family	TRUE	FALSE
3	Daily	2/19/2009	Central	$354,000	4	2	2,088	Single Family	FALSE	FALSE
4	Hamilton	2/23/2009	N. County	$425,900	5	3	2,414	Single Family	TRUE	FALSE
5	Daily	2/24/2009	S. County	$204,900	3	2.5	1,630	Single Family	FALSE	TRUE
6	Lang	2/25/2009	Central	$239,900	2	2	1,248	Condo	FALSE	FALSE
7	Peterson	2/26/2009	S. County	$269,900	4	2.5	1,911	Single Family	FALSE	FALSE
8	Jenkins	3/2/2009	S. County	$338,876	4	2.5	2,612	Single Family	FALSE	FALSE
9	Barnes	3/6/2009	N. County	$299,000	3	2	2,050	Condo	FALSE	FALSE
10	Lang	3/7/2009	Central	$229,900	4	3	2,006	Single Family	FALSE	FALSE
11	Peterson	3/13/2009	Central	$364,900	4	2.5	2,507	Single Family	FALSE	FALSE
12	Barnes	3/13/2009	N. County	$264,900	3	3	2,495	Condo	FALSE	FALSE
13	Romero	3/15/2009	Central	$235,910	4	3	2,285	Single Family	TRUE	TRUE
14	Chung	3/21/2009	S. County	$205,000	3	2.5	2,001	Single Family	TRUE	FALSE
15	Barnes	3/21/2009	N. County	$350,000	3	2.5	1,991	Condo	FALSE	TRUE
16	Lang	3/22/2009	S. County	$325,000	4	3	2,770	Single Family	FALSE	FALSE
17	Shasta	3/23/2009	N. County	$398,000	4	2.5	2,620	Single Family	FALSE	FALSE
18	Shasta	3/23/2009	Central	$215,000	3	1.75	2,157	Single Family	TRUE	TRUE
19	Jenkins	3/25/2009	S. County	$247,500	4	3	2,000	Single Family	FALSE	TRUE
20	Robinson	3/25/2009	S. County	$215,000	1	2	1,552	Condo	FALSE	TRUE
21	Robinson	3/29/2009	N. County	$379,000	4	3	3,000	Single Family	FALSE	TRUE
22	Romero	4/3/2009	N. County	$799,000	6	5	4,800	Single Family	FALSE	FALSE
23	Peterson	4/6/2009	N. County	$309,900	5	3	2,447	Condo	TRUE	FALSE
24	Shasta	4/6/2009	Central	$365,000	3	2.5	1,871	Single Family	FALSE	FALSE
25	Jenkins	4/8/2009	N. County	$248,500	4	2.5	2,101	Single Family	TRUE	TRUE

Figure 5.2 shows the range after I converted it to a table by choosing Insert ➪ Tables ➪ Table.

On the CD

If you'd like to practice working with tables, the workbook shown here is available on the CD-ROM. The file is named `real estate table.xlsx`.

FIGURE 5.2

An Excel table.

Agent	Date Listed	Area	List Price	Bedrooms	Baths	SqFt	Type	Pool	Sold
Shasta	2/9/2009	Central	$350,000	3	2	2,275	Single Family	TRUE	FALSE
Daily	2/19/2009	Central	$354,000	4	2	2,088	Single Family	FALSE	FALSE
Hamilton	2/23/2009	N. County	$425,900	5	3	2,414	Single Family	TRUE	FALSE
Daily	2/24/2009	S. County	$204,900	3	2.5	1,630	Single Family	FALSE	TRUE
Lang	2/25/2009	Central	$239,900	2	2	1,248	Condo	FALSE	FALSE
Peterson	2/26/2009	S. County	$269,900	4	2.5	1,911	Single Family	FALSE	FALSE
Jenkins	3/2/2009	S. County	$338,876	4	2.5	2,612	Single Family	FALSE	FALSE
Barnes	3/6/2009	N. County	$299,000	3	2	2,050	Condo	FALSE	FALSE
Lang	3/7/2009	Central	$229,900	4	3	2,006	Single Family	FALSE	FALSE
Peterson	3/13/2009	Central	$364,900	4	2.5	2,507	Single Family	FALSE	FALSE
Barnes	3/13/2009	N. County	$264,900	3	3	2,495	Condo	FALSE	FALSE
Romero	3/15/2009	Central	$235,910	4	3	2,285	Single Family	TRUE	TRUE
Chung	3/21/2009	S. County	$205,000	3	2.5	2,001	Single Family	TRUE	FALSE
Barnes	3/21/2009	N. County	$350,000	3	2.5	1,991	Condo	FALSE	TRUE
Lang	3/22/2009	S. County	$325,000	4	3	2,770	Single Family	FALSE	FALSE
Shasta	3/23/2009	N. County	$398,000	4	2.5	2,620	Single Family	FALSE	FALSE
Shasta	3/23/2009	Central	$215,000	3	1.75	2,157	Single Family	TRUE	TRUE
Jenkins	3/25/2009	S. County	$247,500	4	3	2,000	Single Family	FALSE	FALSE
Robinson	3/25/2009	S. County	$215,000	1	2	1,552	Condo	FALSE	TRUE
Robinson	3/29/2009	N. County	$379,000	4	3	3,000	Single Family	FALSE	TRUE
Romero	4/3/2009	N. County	$799,000	6	5	4,800	Single Family	FALSE	FALSE
Peterson	4/6/2009	N. County	$309,900	5	3	2,447	Condo	TRUE	FALSE
Shasta	4/6/2009	Central	$365,000	3	2.5	1,871	Single Family	FALSE	FALSE
Jenkins	4/8/2009	N. County	$248,500	4	2.5	2,101	Single Family	TRUE	TRUE

What's the difference between a standard range and table?

- Activating any cell in the table gives you access to the Table Tools contextual tab on the Ribbon (see Figure 5.3).

- The cells contain background color and text color formatting. This formatting is optional.

- Each column header contains a drop-down list, which you can use to sort the data or filter the table to hide specific rows.

- If the active cell is within the table, when you scroll the sheet down so that the header row disappears, the table headers replace the column letters in the worksheet header.

- Tables support calculated columns. A single formula in a column is automatically propagated to all cells in the column. (See Chapter 10.)

- Tables support structured references. Rather than using cell references, formulas can use table names and column headers. (See Chapter 10.)

- The lower-right corner of the lower-right cell contains a small control that you can click and drag to extend the table's size, either horizontally (add more columns) or vertically (add more rows).

- Excel can remove duplicate rows automatically.

- Selecting rows and columns within the table is simplified.

When you select a cell in a table, you can use the commands located on the Table Tools ⇨ Design tab.

Creating a Table

Most of the time, you'll create a table from an existing range of data. However, Excel also allows you to create a table from an empty range so that you can fill in the details later. The following instructions assume that you already have a range of data that's suitable for a table.

1. **Make sure that the range doesn't contain any completely blank rows or columns; otherwise, Excel will not guess the table range correctly.**

2. **Select any cell within the range.**

3. **Choose Insert ⇨ Tables ⇨ Table (or press Ctrl+T).** Excel responds with its Create Table dialog box, shown in Figure 5.4. Excel tries to guess the range as well as whether the table has a header row. Most of the time, it guesses correctly. If not, make your corrections before you click OK.

Use the Create Table dialog box to verify that Excel guessed the table dimensions correctly.

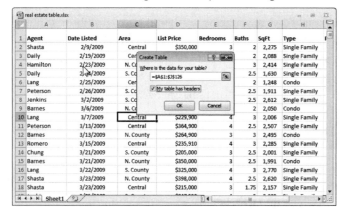

The range is converted to a table (using the default table style), and the Table Tools ⇨ Design tab of the Ribbon appears.

Note

Excel may guess the table's dimensions incorrectly if the table isn't separated from other information by at least one empty row or column. If Excel guesses incorrectly, just specify the exact range for the table in the Create Table dialog box. Better yet, click Cancel and rearrange your worksheet such that the table is separated from your other data by at least one blank row or column. ∎

To create a table from an empty range, just select the range and choose Insert ⇨ Tables ⇨ Table. Excel creates the table, adds generic column headers (such as Column1 and Column2), and applies table formatting to the range.

Changing the Look of a Table

When you create a table, Excel applies the default table style. The actual appearance depends on which document theme is used in the workbook. If you prefer a different look, you can easily change the entire look of the table.

Select any cell in the table and choose Table Tools ⇨ Design ⇨ Table Styles. The Ribbon shows one row of styles, but if you click the bottom of the scrollbar to the right, the table styles group expands, as shown in Figure 5.5. The styles are grouped into three categories: Light, Medium, and Dark. Notice that you get a "live" preview as you move your mouse among the styles. When you see one you like, just click to make it permanent. And yes, some are really ugly and practically illegible.

For a different set of color choices, choose Page Layout ⇨ Themes ⇨ Themes to select a different document theme. For more information about themes, see Chapter 6.

Tip

If applying table styles isn't working, it's probably because the range was already formatted before you converted it to a table. Table formatting doesn't override normal formatting. To clear existing background fill colors, select the entire table and choose Home ⇨ Font ⇨ Fill Color ⇨ No Fill. To clear existing font colors, choose Home ⇨ Font ⇨ Font Color ⇨ Automatic. To clear existing borders, choose Home ⇨ Font ⇨ Borders ⇨ No Borders. After you issue these commands, the table styles should work as expected. ∎

If you'd like to create a custom table style, choose Table Tools ⇨ Design ⇨ Table Styles ⇨ New Table Style to display the New Table Quick Style dialog box shown in Figure 5.6. You can customize any or all of the 12 table elements. Select an element from the list, click Format, and specify the formatting for that element. When you're finished, give the new style a name and click OK. Your custom table style will appear in the Table Styles gallery in the Custom category. Unfortunately, custom table styles are available only in the workbook in which they were created.

Excel offers many different table styles.

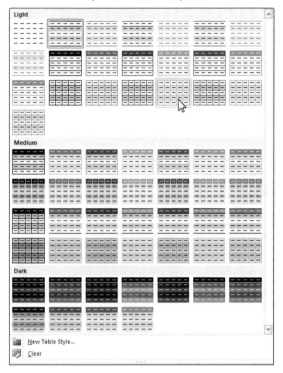

Use this dialog box to create a new table style.

Tip

If you would like to make changes to an existing table style, locate it in the Ribbon and right-click. Choose Duplicate from the shortcut menu. Excel displays the Modify Table Quick Style dialog box with all the settings from the specified table style. Make your changes, give the style a new name, and click OK to save it as a custom table style. ∎

Working with Tables

This section describes some common actions you'll take with tables.

Navigating in a table

Selecting cells in a table works just like selecting cells in a normal range. One difference is when you use the Tab key. Pressing Tab moves to the cell to the right, and when you reach the last column, pressing Tab again moves to the first cell in the next row.

Selecting parts of a table

When you move your mouse around in a table, you may notice that the pointer changes shapes. These shapes help you select various parts of the table.

- **To select an entire column:** Move the mouse to the top of a cell in the header row, and the mouse pointer changes to a down-pointing arrow. Click to select the data in the column. Click a second time to select the entire table column (including the Header Row and the Total Row, if it has one). You can also press Ctrl+spacebar (once or twice) to select a column.

- **To select an entire row:** Move the mouse to the left of a cell in the first column, and the mouse pointer changes to a right-pointing arrow. Click to select the entire table row. You can also press Shift+spacebar to select a table row.

- **To select the entire table:** Move the mouse to the upper-left part of the upper-left cell. When the mouse pointer turns into a diagonal arrow, click to select the data area of the table. Click a second time to select the entire table (including the Header Row and the Total Row). You can also press Ctrl+A (once or twice) to select the entire table.

Tip

Right-clicking a cell in a table displays several selection options in the shortcut menu. ∎

Adding new rows or columns

To add a new column to the end of a table, select a cell in the column to the right of the table and start entering the data. Excel automatically extends the table horizontally.

Similarly, if you enter data in the row below a table, Excel extends the table vertically to include the new row.

Note

An exception to automatically extending tables is when the table is displaying a Total Row. If you enter data below the Total Row, the table will not be extended. and the data will not be part of the table. ■

To add rows or columns within the table, right-click and choose Insert from the shortcut menu. The Insert shortcut menu command displays additional menu items:

- Table Columns to the Left
- Table Columns to the Right
- Table Rows Above
- Table Rows Below

Tip

When the cell pointer is in the bottom-right cell of a table, pressing Tab inserts a new row at the bottom of the table, above the Total Row (if the table has one). ■

When you move your mouse to the resize handle at bottom-right cell of a table, the mouse pointer turns into a diagonal line with two arrow heads. Click and drag down to add more rows to the table. Click and drag to the right to add more columns.

When you insert a new column, the Header Row displays a generic description, such as Column1, Column2, and so on. Typically, you'll want to change these names to more descriptive labels. Just select the cell and overwrite the generic text with your new text.

Deleting rows or columns

To delete a row (or column) in a table, select any cell in the row (or column) to be deleted. To delete multiple rows or columns, select a range of cells. Then right-click and choose Delete ⇨ Table Rows (or Delete ⇨ Table Columns).

Moving a table

To move a table to a new location in the same worksheet, move the mouse pointer to any of its borders. When the mouse pointer turns into a cross with four arrows, click and drag the table to its new location.

To move a table to a different worksheet (which could be in a different workbook), you can drag and drop it as well — as long as the destination worksheet is visible onscreen.

Excel Remembers

When you do something with a complete column in a table, Excel remembers that and extends that "something" to all new entries added to that column. For example, if you apply currency formatting to a column and then add a new row, Excel applies currency formatting to the new value in that column.

The same thing applies to other operations, such as conditional formatting, cell protection, data validation, and so on. And if you create a chart using the data in a table, the chart will be extended automatically if you add new data to the table. Those who have used versions prior to Excel 2007 will appreciate this feature the most.

Or, you can use these steps to move a table to different worksheet or workbook:

1. Press Ctrl+A *twice* to select the entire table.
2. Press Ctrl+X to cut the selected cells.
3. Activate the new worksheet and select the upper-left cell for the table.
4. Press Ctrl+V to paste the table.

Setting table options

The Table Style Options group of the Table Tools ⇨ Design tab contains several check boxes that determine whether various elements of the table are displayed, and whether some formatting options are in effect:

- **Header Row:** Toggles the display of the Header Row.
- **Total Row:** Toggles the display of the Total Row.
- **First Column:** Toggles special formatting for the first column. Depending on the table style used, this command might have no effect.
- **Last Column:** Toggles special formatting for the last column. Depending on the table style used, this command might have no effect.
- **Banded Rows:** Toggles the display of *banded* (alternating color) rows.
- **Banded Columns:** Toggles the display of banded columns.

Working with the Total Row

The Total Row in a table contains formulas that summarize the information in the columns. When you create a table, the Total Row isn't turned on. To display the Total Row, choose Table Tools ⇨ Design ⇨ Table Style Options and put a check mark next to Total Row.

By default, a Total Row displays the sum of the values in a column of numbers. In many cases, you'll want a different type of summary formula. When you select a cell in the Total Row, a drop-down arrow appears in the cell. Click the arrow, and you can select from a number of other summary formulas (see Figure 5.7):

- **None:** No formula

- **Average:** Displays the average of the numbers in the column

- **Count:** Displays the number of entries in the column (blank cells are not counted)

- **Count Numbers:** Displays the number of numeric values in the column (blank cells, text cells, and error cells are not counted)

- **Max:** Displays the maximum value in the column

- **Min:** Displays the minimum value in the column

- **Sum:** Displays the sum of the values in the column

- **StdDev:** Displays the standard deviation of the values in the column. Standard deviation is a statistical measure of how "spread out" the values are.

- **Var:** Displays the variance of the values in the column. Variance is another statistical measure of how "spread out" the values are.

- **More Functions:** Displays the Insert Function dialog box so that you can select a function that isn't in the list.

FIGURE 5.7

Several types of summary formulas are available for the Total Row.

Caution

If you have a formula that refers to a value in the Total Row of a table, the formula returns an error if you hide the Total Row. But if you make the Total Row visible again, the formula works as it should. ■

Cross-Reference

For more information about formulas, including the use of formulas in a table column, see Chapter 10. ∎

Removing duplicate rows from a table

If data in a table was obtained from multiple sources, the table may contain duplicate items. Most of the time, you want to eliminate the duplicates. In the past, removing duplicate data was essentially a manual task, but it's very easy if the data is in a table.

Start by selecting any cell in your table. Then choose Table Tools ➪ Design ➪ Tools ➪ Remove Duplicates. Excel responds with Remove Duplicates dialog box shown in Figure 5.8. The dialog box lists all the columns in your table. Place a check mark next to the columns that you want to be included in the duplicate search. Most of the time, you'll want to select all the columns, which is the default. Click OK, and Excel weeds out the duplicate rows and displays a message that tells you how many duplicates it removed.

When you select all columns in the Remove Duplicates dialog box, Excel will delete a row only if the content of every column is duplicated. In some situations, you may not care about matching some columns, so you would deselect those columns in the Remove Duplicates dialog box. In the example shown in Figure 5.8, removing the check mark from all columns except Agent would result in a table that showed one row per agent — an unduplicated list of all agents.

FIGURE 5.8

Removing duplicate rows from a table is easy.

Caution

It's important to understand that duplicate values are determined by the value displayed in the cell — not necessarily the value stored in the cell. For example, assume that two cells contain the same date. One of the dates is formatted to display as 5/15/2011, and the other is formatted to display as May 15, 2011. When removing duplicates, Excel considers these dates to be different. ∎

Sorting and filtering a table

The Header Row of a table contains a drop-down arrow that, when clicked, displays sorting and filtering options (see Figure 5.9).

Each column in a table contains sorting and filtering option.

Sorting a table

Sorting a table rearranges the rows based on the contents of a particular column. You may want to sort a table to put names in alphabetical order. Or, maybe you want to sort your sales staff by the totals sales made.

To sort a table by a particular column, click the drop-down in the column header and choose one of the sort commands. The exact command varies, depending on the type of data in the column.

You can also select Sort by Color to sort the rows based on the background or text color of the data. This option is relevant only if you've overridden the table style colors with custom formatting.

You can sort on any number of columns. The trick is to sort the least significant column first and then proceed until the most significant column is sorted lasted. For example, in the real estate table, you may want to sort the list by agent. And within each agent's group, sort the rows by area.

And within each area, sort the rows by list price. For this type of sort, first sort by the List Price column, then sort by the Area column, and then sort by the Agent column. Figure 5.10 shows the table sorted in this manner.

Note

When a column is sorted, the drop-down list in the header row displays a different graphic to remind you that the table is sorted by that column. ∎

FIGURE 5.10

A table, after performing a three-column sort.

	A	B	C	D	E	F	G	H
1	Agent	Date Listed	Area	List Price	Bedrooms	Baths	SqFt	Type
2	Adams	10/8/2009	Central	$199,000	3	2.5	1,510	Condo
3	Adams	8/18/2009	Central	$214,500	4	2.5	1,862	Single Famil
4	Adams	4/27/2009	Central	$265,000	4	3	1,905	Single Famil
5	Adams	7/18/2009	Central	$268,500	4	2.5	1,911	Single Famil
6	Adams	12/5/2009	Central	$273,500	2	2	1,552	Single Famil
7	Adams	7/31/2009	Central	$309,950	4	3	2,800	Single Famil
8	Adams	6/14/2009	Central	$325,000	3	2.5	1,752	Single Famil
9	Adams	4/14/2009	N. County	$339,900	3	2	1,828	Single Famil
10	Adams	5/23/2009	N. County	$349,000	4	2.5	2,730	Condo
11	Adams	8/7/2009	N. County	$379,000	3	3	2,354	Condo
12	Adams	6/5/2009	N. County	$379,900	3	2.5	2,468	Condo
13	Adams	4/20/2009	S. County	$208,750	4	3	2,207	Single Famil
14	Barnes	9/26/2009	N. County	$239,900	4	3	2,041	Condo
15	Barnes	3/13/2009	N. County	$264,900	3	3	2,495	Condo
16	Barnes	3/6/2009	N. County	$299,000	3	2	2,050	Condo
17	Barnes	8/9/2009	N. County	$345,000	4	3	2,388	Condo
18	Barnes	3/21/2009	N. County	$350,000	3	2.5	1,991	Condo
19	Barnes	6/25/2009	N. County	$355,000	4	2.5	2,647	Condo
20	Barnes	6/25/2009	S. County	$208,750	4	2	1,800	Single Famil
21	Bennet	5/11/2009	Central	$229,500	4	3	2,041	Single Famil
22	Bennet	5/8/2009	Central	$549,000	4	3	1,940	Single Famil
23	Bennet	6/30/2009	N. County	$229,500	6	3	2,700	Single Famil
24	Bennet	4/20/2009	N. County	$229,900	3	3	2,266	Condo
25	Bennet	5/26/2009	N. County	$229,900	4	3	2,041	Condo
26	Bennet	6/25/2009	S. County	$229,900	3	2.5	1,580	Single Famil
27	Chung	7/7/2009	Central	$236,900	3	2	1,700	Single Famil
28	Chung	8/26/2009	Central	$339,900	4	2	2,238	Single Famil
29	Chung	4/20/2009	Central	$375,000	4	3	2,467	Single Famil
30	Chung	3/21/2009	S. County	$205,000	3	2.5	2,001	Single Famil

Another way of performing a multiple-column sort is to use the Sort dialog box (choose Home ➪ Editing ➪ Sort & Filter ➪ Custom Sort). Or, right-click any cell in the table and choose Sort ➪ Custom Sort from the shortcut menu.

In the Sort dialog box, use the drop-down lists to specify the sort specifications. In this example, you start with Agent. Then, click the Add Level button to insert another set of search controls. In this new set of controls, specify the sort specifications for the Area column. Then, add another level and enter the specifications for the List Price column. Figure 5.11 shows the dialog box after entering the specifications for the three-column sort. This technique produces exactly the same sort as described in the previous paragraph.

Using the Sort dialog box to specify a three-column sort.

Filtering a table

Filtering a table refers to displaying only the rows that meet certain conditions. (The other rows are hidden.)

Using the real estate table, assume that you're only interested in the data for the N. County area. Click the drop-down arrow in the Area Row Header and remove the check mark from Select All, which unselects everything. Then, place a check mark next to N. County and click OK. The table, shown in Figure 5.12, is now filtered to display only the listings in the N. County area. Notice that some of the row numbers are missing; these rows contain the filtered (hidden) data.

Also notice that the drop-down arrow in the Area column now shows a different graphic — an icon that indicates the column is filtered.

This table is filtered to show only the information for N. County.

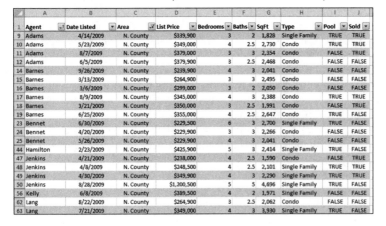

	Agent	Date Listed	Area	List Price	Bedrooms	Baths	SqFt	Type	Pool	Sold
9	Adams	4/14/2009	N. County	$339,900	3	2	1,828	Single Family	TRUE	TRUE
10	Adams	5/23/2009	N. County	$349,000	4	2.5	2,730	Condo	TRUE	TRUE
11	Adams	8/7/2009	N. County	$379,000	3	3	2,354	Condo	FALSE	TRUE
12	Adams	6/5/2009	N. County	$379,900	3	2.5	2,468	Condo	FALSE	FALSE
14	Barnes	9/26/2009	N. County	$239,900	4	3	2,041	Condo	FALSE	FALSE
15	Barnes	3/13/2009	N. County	$264,900	3	3	2,495	Condo	FALSE	FALSE
16	Barnes	3/6/2009	N. County	$299,000	3	2	2,050	Condo	FALSE	FALSE
17	Barnes	8/9/2009	N. County	$345,000	4	3	2,388	Condo	TRUE	TRUE
18	Barnes	3/21/2009	N. County	$350,000	3	2.5	1,991	Condo	FALSE	TRUE
19	Barnes	6/25/2009	N. County	$355,000	4	2.5	2,647	Condo	TRUE	FALSE
23	Bennet	6/30/2009	N. County	$229,500	6	3	2,700	Single Family	TRUE	FALSE
24	Bennet	4/20/2009	N. County	$229,900	3	3	2,266	Condo	FALSE	FALSE
25	Bennet	5/26/2009	N. County	$229,900	4	3	2,041	Condo	FALSE	FALSE
44	Hamilton	2/23/2009	N. County	$425,900	5	3	2,414	Single Family	TRUE	FALSE
47	Jenkins	4/21/2009	N. County	$238,000	4	2.5	1,590	Condo	FALSE	TRUE
48	Jenkins	4/8/2009	N. County	$248,500	4	2.5	2,101	Single Family	TRUE	TRUE
49	Jenkins	4/30/2009	N. County	$349,900	4	3	2,290	Single Family	TRUE	TRUE
50	Jenkins	8/28/2009	N. County	$1,200,500	5	5	4,696	Single Family	TRUE	FALSE
56	Kelly	6/8/2009	N. County	$389,500	4	2	1,971	Single Family	FALSE	FALSE
62	Lang	8/22/2009	N. County	$264,900	3	2.5	2,062	Condo	FALSE	FALSE
63	Lang	7/21/2009	N. County	$349,000	4	3	3,930	Single Family	TRUE	FALSE

You can filter by multiple values in a column by using multiple check marks. For example, to filter the table to show only N. County and Central, place a check mark next to both values in the drop-down list in the Area Row Header.

You can filter a table using any number of columns. For example, you may want to see only the N. County listings in which the Type is Single Family. Just repeat the operation using the Type column. All tables then display only the rows in which the Area is N. County and the Type is Single Family.

For additional filtering options, select Text Filters (or Number Filters, if the column contains values). The options are fairly self-explanatory, and you have a great deal of flexibility in displaying only the rows that you're interested in.

In addition, you can right-click a cell and use the Filter command on the shortcut menu. This menu item leads to several additional filtering options.

Note

As you may expect, the Total Row is updated to show the total only for the visible rows. ■

When you copy data from a filtered table, only the visible data is copied. In other words, rows that are hidden by filtering don't get copied. This filtering makes it very easy to copy a subset of a larger table and paste it to another area of your worksheet. Keep in mind, though, that the pasted data is not a table — it's just a normal range. You can, however, convert the copied range to a table.

To remove filtering for a column, click the drop-down in the Row Header and select Clear Filter. If you've filtered using multiple columns, it may be faster to remove all filters by choosing Home ➪ Editing ➪ Sort & Filter ➪ Clear.

Converting a table back to a range

If you need to convert a table back to a normal range, just select a cell in the table and choose Table Tools ➪ Design ➪ Tools ➪ Convert to Range. The table style formatting remains intact, but the range no longer functions as a table.

Worksheet Formatting

Formatting your worksheet is like the icing on a cake — it may not be absolutely necessary, but it can make the end product a lot more attractive. In an Excel worksheet, formatting can also make it easier for others to understand the worksheet's purpose.

Stylistic formatting isn't essential for every workbook that you develop — especially if it is for your own use only. On the other hand, it takes only a few moments to apply some simple formatting; and, after you apply it, the formatting will remain in place without further effort on your part.

In Chapter 5, I show how easy it is to apply formatting to a table. The information in this chapter applies to normal ranges. I show you how to work with the Excel formatting tools: fonts; colors; and styles, such as bold and italic. I also cover custom styles that you can create to make formatting large amounts of material in a similar way easier.

IN THIS CHAPTER

Understanding how formatting can improve your worksheets

Getting to know the formatting tools

Using formatting in your worksheets

Using named styles for easier formatting

Understanding document themes

Getting to Know the Formatting Tools

Figure 6.1 shows how even simple formatting can significantly improve a worksheet's readability. The unformatted worksheet (on the left) is perfectly functional but not very readable compared with the formatted worksheet (on the right).

On the CD

This workbook is available on the companion CD-ROM. The file is named loan payments.xlsx.

FIGURE 6.1

In just a few minutes, some simple formatting can greatly improve the appearance of your worksheets.

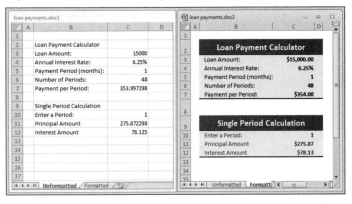

The Excel formatting tools are available in three locations:

- On the Home tab of the Ribbon
- On the Mini toolbar that appears when you right-click a range or a cell
- From the Format Cells dialog box

In addition, many common formatting commands have keyboard shortcuts that you can use.

Cross-Reference
Excel also enables you to format cells based on the cell's contents. Chapter 20 discusses conditional formatting. ■

Using the formatting tools of the Home Tab

The Home tab of the Ribbon provides quick access to the most commonly used formatting options. Start by selecting the cell or range; then use the appropriate tool in the Font, Alignment, or Number groups.

Using these tools is very intuitive, and the best way to familiarize yourself with them is to experiment. Enter some data, select some cells, and then click the controls to change the appearance. Note that some of these controls are actually drop-down lists. Click the small arrow on the button, and the button expands to display your choices.

Using the Mini toolbar

When you right-click a cell or a range selection, you get a shortcut menu. In addition, the Mini toolbar appears above the shortcut menu. Figure 6.2 shows how this toolbar looks.

FIGURE 6.2

The Mini toolbar appears above the right-click shortcut menu.

The Mini toolbar contains controls for common formatting:

- Font
- Font Size
- Increase Font
- Decrease Font
- Accounting Number Format
- Percent Style
- Comma Style
- Format Painter
- Bold
- Italic
- Center
- Borders
- Fill Color
- Font Color
- Increase Decimal
- Decrease Decimal
- Merge & Center

If you use a tool on the Mini toolbar, the shortcut menu disappears, but the toolbar remains visible so you can apply other formatting if you like. Also, notice that after you use it, the Mini toolbar gradually fades away if you move the mouse pointer away from it. To hide the Mini toolbar, just click in any cell.

Some people find the Mini toolbar distracting. Unfortunately, Excel does not provide an option to turn it off. The Excel Options dialog box does offer the Show Mini Toolbar on Selection option, but this option applies only to selecting text while editing a cell.

Tip

If you really want to disable the Mini toolbar, you can execute this VBA statement in the Immediate window of the Visual Basic Editor (VBE):

```
Application.ShowMenuFloaties = True
```

Yes, setting the property to `True` is completely counter-intuitive! But it works. You need to execute this statement only one time, and Excel remembers the setting between sessions. If you change your mind, execute that statement again, but change `True` to `False`.

Using the Format Cells dialog box

The formatting controls available on the Home tab of the Ribbon are sufficient most of the time, but some types of formatting require that you use the Format Cells dialog box. This tabbed dialog box lets you apply nearly any type of stylistic formatting, as well as number formatting. The formats that you choose in the Format Cells dialog box apply to the cells that you have selected at the time. Later sections in this chapter cover the tabs of the Format Cells dialog box.

Note

When you use the Format Cells dialog box, you don't see the effects of your formatting choices until you click OK. ■

After selecting the cell or range to format, you can display the Format Cells dialog box by using any of the following methods:

- Press Ctrl+1.
- Click the dialog box launcher in Home ➪ Font, Home ➪ Alignment, or Home ➪ Number. (The dialog box launcher is the small downward-pointing arrow icon displayed to the right of the group name in the Ribbon.) When you display the Format Cells dialog box using a dialog box launcher, the dialog box is displayed with the appropriate tab visible.
- Right-click the selected cell or range and choose Format Cells from the shortcut menu.
- Click the More command in some of the drop-down controls in the Ribbon. For example, the Home ➪ Font ➪ Border ➪ More Borders drop-down includes an item named More Borders.

The Format Cells dialog box contains six tabs: Number, Alignment, Font, Border, Patterns, and Protection. The following sections contain more information about the formatting options available in this dialog box.

Using Different Fonts to Format Your Worksheet

You can use different fonts, sizes, or text attributes in your worksheets to make various parts — such as the headers for a table — stand out. You also can adjust the font size. For example, using a smaller font allows for more information on a single page.

By default, Excel uses 11 point (pt) Calibri font. A *font* is described by its typeface (Calibri, Cambria, Arial, Times New Roman, Courier New, and so on), as well as by its size, measured in points. (Seventy-two pt equal one inch.) Excel's row height, by default, is 15 pt. Therefore, 11 pt type entered into 15 pt rows leaves a small amount of blank space between the characters in adjacent rows.

Tip
If you've not manually changed a row's height, Excel automatically adjusts the row height based on the tallest text that you enter into the row. ■

Updating Old Fonts

Office 2007 introduced several new fonts, and the default font has been changed for all the Office applications. In versions prior to Excel 2007, the default font was 10 pt Arial. In Excel 2007 and Excel 2010, the default font for the Office theme is 11 pt Calibri. Most people will agree that Calibri is much easier to read, and it gives the worksheet a more modern appearance.

If you open a workbook created in a pre-Excel 2007 version, the default font will not be changed, even if you apply a document style (by choosing Page Layout ⇨ Themes ⇨ Themes). But here's an easy way to update the fonts in a workbook that was created using an older version of Excel:

1. **Press Ctrl+N to open a new, empty workbook.** The new workbook will use the default document theme.

2. **Open your old workbook file.**

3. **Choose Home ⇨ Styles ⇨ Cell Styles ⇨ Merge Styles.** Excel displays its Merge Styles dialog box.

4. **In the Merge Styles dialog box, select the new workbook that you created in Step 1.**

5. **Click OK.**

6. **Click Yes in response to Excel's question regarding merging styles that have the same name.**

This technique changes the font and size for all unformatted cells. If you've applied font formatting to some cells (for example, made them bold), the font for those cells will not be changed (but you can change the font manually). If you don't like the new look of your workbook, just close the workbook without saving the changes.

Tip

If you plan to distribute a workbook to other users, you should stick with the standard fonts that are included with Windows or Microsoft Office. If you open a workbook and your system doesn't have the font with which the workbook was created, Windows attempts to use a similar font. Sometimes this attempt works okay, and sometimes it doesn't. ■

Use the Font and Font Size tools on the Home tab of the Ribbon (or on the Mini toolbar) to change the font or size for selected cells.

You also can use the Font tab in the Format Cells dialog box to choose fonts, as shown in Figure 6.3. This tab enables you to control several other font attributes that aren't available elsewhere. Besides choosing the font, you can change the font style (bold, italic), underlining, color, and effects (strikethrough, superscript, or subscript). If you select the Normal Font check box, Excel displays the selections for the font defined for the Normal style. I discuss styles later in this chapter. See "Using Named Styles for Easier Formatting."

FIGURE 6.3

The Font tab of the Format Cells dialog box gives you many additional font attribute options.

Figure 6.4 shows several different examples of font formatting. In this figure, gridlines were turned off to make the underlining more visible. Notice, in the figure, that Excel provides four different underlining styles. In the two non-accounting underline styles, only the cell contents are underlined. In the two accounting underline styles, the entire width of the cells is always underlined.

FIGURE 6.4

You can choose many different font-formatting options for your worksheets.

If you prefer to keep your hands on the keyboard, you can use the following shortcut keys to format a selected range quickly:

- **Ctrl+B**: Bold
- **Ctrl+I**: Italic
- **Ctrl+U**: Underline
- **Ctrl+5**: Strikethrough

These shortcut keys act as a toggle. For example, you can turn bold on and off by repeatedly pressing Ctrl+B.

Note

Beginning with Excel 2007, the Document Themes feature attempts to assist nondesigners in creating attractive worksheets. I discuss document themes later in this chapter. See "Understanding Document Themes." ■

Using Multiple Formatting Styles in a Single Cell

If a cell contains text (as opposed to a value or a formula), Excel also enables you to format individual characters in the cell. To do so, switch to Edit mode (press F2, or double-click the cell) and then select the characters that you want to format. You can select characters either by dragging the mouse over them or by pressing the Shift key as you press the left- or right-arrow key.

After you select the characters for format, use any of the standard formatting techniques. The changes apply only to the selected characters in the cell. This technique doesn't work with cells that contain values or formulas.

Changing Text Alignment

The contents of a cell can be aligned horizontally and vertically. By default, Excel aligns numbers to the right and text to the left. All cells use bottom alignment, by default.

Overriding these defaults is a simple matter. The most commonly used alignment commands are in the Alignment group on the Home tab of the Ribbon. Use the Alignment tab of the Format Cells dialog box for even more options (see Figure 6.5).

FIGURE 6.5

The full range of alignment options are available on the Alignment tab of the Format Cells dialog box.

Choosing horizontal alignment options

Horizontal alignment options, which control how cell contents are distributed across the width of the cell (or cells), are available from the Format Cells dialog box:

- **General:** Aligns numbers to the right, aligns text to the left, and centers logical and error values. This option is the default alignment.

- **Left:** Aligns the cell contents to the left side of the cell. If the text is wider than the cell, the text spills over to the cell on the right. If the cell on the right isn't empty, the text is truncated and not completely visible. Also available on the Ribbon.

- **Center:** Centers the cell contents in the cell. If the text is wider than the cell, the text spills over to cells on either side if they're empty. If the adjacent cells aren't empty, the text is truncated and not completely visible. Also available on the Ribbon.

- **Right:** Aligns the cell contents to the right side of the cell. If the text is wider than the cell, the text spills over to the cell on the left. If the cell on the left isn't empty, the text is truncated and not completely visible. Also available on the Ribbon.

- **Fill:** Repeats the contents of the cell until the cell's width is filled. If cells to the right also are formatted with Fill alignment, they also are filled.

- **Justify:** Justifies the text to the left and right of the cell. This option is applicable only if the cell is formatted as wrapped text and uses more than one line.

- **Center across Selection:** Centers the text over the selected columns. This option is useful for precisely centering a heading over a number of columns.

- **Distributed:** Distributes the text evenly across the selected column.

Note

If you choose Left, Right, or Distributed, you can also adjust the Indent setting, which adds space between the cell border and the text. ■

Figure 6.6 shows examples of text that uses three types of horizontal alignment: Left, Justify, and Distributed (with an indent).

On the CD

If you would like to experiment with text alignment settings, this workbook is available on the companion CD-ROM. The file is named `text alignment.xlsx.`

FIGURE 6.6

The same text, displayed with three types of horizontal alignment.

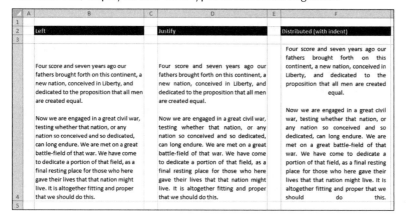

Choosing vertical alignment options

Vertical alignment options typically aren't used as often as the horizontal alignment options. In fact, these settings are useful only if you've adjusted row heights so that they're considerably taller than normal.

Vertical alignment options available in the Format Cells dialog box are

- **Top:** Aligns the cell contents to the top of the cell. Also available on the Ribbon.
- **Center:** Centers the cell contents vertically in the cell. Also available on the Ribbon.
- **Bottom:** Aligns the cell contents to the bottom of the cell. Also available on the Ribbon.
- **Justify:** Justifies the text vertically in the cell; this option is applicable only if the cell is formatted as wrapped text and uses more than one line. This setting can be used to increase the line spacing.
- **Distributed:** Distributes the text evenly vertically in the cell. This setting seems to have the same effect as Justify.

Wrapping or shrinking text to fit the cell

If you have text too wide to fit the column width but don't want that text to spill over into adjacent cells, you can use either the Wrap Text option or the Shrink to Fit option to accommodate that text. The Wrap Text control is also available on the Ribbon.

The Wrap Text option displays the text on multiple lines in the cell, if necessary. Use this option to display lengthy headings without having to make the columns too wide, and without reducing the size of the text.

The Shrink to Fit option reduces the size of the text so that it fits into the cell without spilling over to the next cell. Usually, it's easier to make this adjustment manually.

Note
If you apply Wrap Text formatting to a cell, you can't use the Shrink to Fit formatting. ■

Merging worksheet cells to create additional text space

Excel also enables you to merge two or more cells. When you merge cells, you don't combine the contents of cells. Rather, you combine a group of cells into a single cell that occupies the same space. The worksheet shown in Figure 6.7 contains four sets of merged cells. For example, range C2:I2 has been merged into a single cell, and so has range J2:P2. In addition, ranges B4:B8 and B9:B13 have also been merged. In the latter two cases, the text direction has been changed (see "Displaying text at an angle," later in this chapter).

FIGURE 6.7

Merge worksheet cells to make them act as if they were a single cell.

You can merge any number of cells occupying any number of rows and columns. In fact, you can merge all 17,179,869,184 cells in a worksheet into a single cell — although I can't think of any good reason to do so, except maybe to play a trick on a co-worker.

The range that you intend to merge should be empty, except for the upper-left cell. If any of the other cells that you intend to merge are not empty, Excel displays a warning. If you continue, all the data (except in the upper-left cell) will be deleted. To avoid deleting data, click Cancel in response to the warning.

You can use the Alignment tab of the Format Cells dialog box to merge cells, but using the Merge & Center control on the Ribbon (or on the Mini toolbar) is simpler. To merge cells, select the cells that you want to merge and then click the Merge & Center button. The cells will be merged, and the content in the upper-left cells will be centered horizontally. The Merge & Center button acts as a toggle. To unmerge cells, select the merged cells and click the Merge & Center button again.

After you merge cells, you can change the alignment to something other than Center.

The Home ⇨ Alignment ⇨ Merge & Center control contains a drop-down list with these additional options:

- **Merge Across:** When a multirow range is selected, this command creates multiple merged cells — one for each row.
- **Merge Cells:** Merges the selected cells without applying the Center attribute.
- **Unmerge Cells:** Unmerges the selected cells.

Displaying text at an angle

In some cases, you may want to create more visual impact by displaying text at an angle within a cell. You can display text horizontally, vertically, or at an angle between 90 degrees up and 90 degrees down.

From the Home ➪ Alignment ➪ Orientation drop-down list, you can apply the most common text angles. For more control, use the Alignment tab of the Format Cells dialog box. In the Format Cells dialog box (refer to Figure 6-5), use the Degrees spinner control — or just drag the pointer in the gauge. You can specify a text angle between –90 and +90 degrees.

Figure 6.8 shows an example of text displayed at a 45-degree angle.

Note

Rotated text may look a bit distorted onscreen, but the printed output is usually of much better quality. ■

FIGURE 6.8

Rotate text for additional visual impact.

Controlling the text direction

Not all languages use the same character direction. Although most Western languages are read left to right, other languages are read right to left. You can use the Text Direction option to select the appropriate setting for the language you use. This command is available only in the Alignment tab of the Format Cells dialog box.

Don't confuse the Text Direction setting with the Orientation setting (discussed in the previous section). Changing the text orientation is common. Changing the text direction is used only in very specific situations.

Note

Changing the Text Direction setting won't have any effect unless you have the proper language drivers installed on your system. For example, you must install Japanese language support from the Office CD-ROM to use right-to-left text direction Japanese characters. ■

New Feature

Use the Language tab of the Excel Options dialog box to determine which languages are installed. ■

Using Colors and Shading

Excel provides the tools to create some very colorful worksheets. You can change the color of the text or add colors to the backgrounds of the worksheet cells.

Note

Prior to Excel 2007, workbooks were limited to a palette of 56 colors. Excel 2010 allows a virtually unlimited number of colors. ■

You control the color of the cell's text by choosing Home ⇨ Font ⇨ Font Color. Control the cell's background color by choosing Home ⇨ Font ⇨ Fill Color. Both of these color controls are also available on the Mini toolbar, which appears when you right-click a cell or range.

Tip

To hide the contents of a cell, make the background color the same as the font text color. The cell contents are still visible in the Formula bar when you select the cell. Keep in mind, however, that some printers may override this setting, and the text may be visible when printed. ■

Even though you have access to an unlimited number of colors, you might want to stick with the ten theme colors (and their light/dark variations) displayed in the various color selection controls. In other words, avoid using the More Color option, which lets you select a color. Why? First of all, those ten colors were chosen because they "go together" (well, at least *somebody* thought they did). Another reason involves document themes. If you switch to a different document theme for your workbook, nontheme colors aren't changed. In some cases, the result may be less than pleasing, aesthetically. See "Understanding Document Themes," later in this chapter, for more information about themes.

Using Colors with Table Styles

In Chapter 5, I discuss the handy Table feature. One advantage to using tables is that it's very easy to apply table styles. You can change the look of your table with a single mouse click.

It's important to understand how table styles work with existing formatting. A simple rule is that applying a style to a table doesn't override existing formatting. For example, assume that you have a range of data that uses yellow as the background color for the cells. When you convert that range to a table (by choosing Insert ⇨ Tables ⇨ Table), the default table style (alternating row colors) isn't visible. Rather, the table will display the previously applied yellow background.

To make table styles visible with this table, you need to remove the manually applied background cell colors. Select the entire table and then choose Home ⇨ Font ⇨ Fill Color ⇨ No Fill.

You can apply any type of formatting to a table, and that formatting will override the table style formatting. For example, you may want to make a particular cell stand out by using a different fill color.

Adding Borders and Lines

Borders (and lines within the borders) are another visual enhancement that you can add around groups of cells. Borders are often used to group a range of similar cells or to delineate rows or columns. Excel offers 13 preset styles of borders, as you can see in the Home ➪ Font ➪ Borders drop-down list shown in Figure 6.9. This control works with the selected cell or range and enables you to specify which, if any, border style to use for each border of the selection.

Use the Borders drop-down list to add lines around worksheet cells.

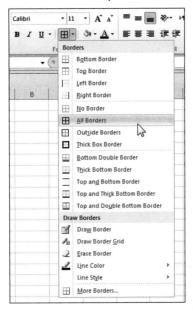

You may prefer to draw borders rather than select a preset border style. To do so, use the Draw Border or Draw Border Grid command from the Home ➪ Font ➪ Borders drop-down list. Selecting either command lets you create borders by dragging your mouse. Use the Line Color or Line Style commands to change the color or style. When you're finished drawing borders, press Esc to cancel the border-drawing mode.

Another way to apply borders is to use the Border tab of the Format Cells dialog box, which is shown in Figure 6.10. One way to display this dialog box is to select More Borders from the Borders drop-down list.

Use the Border tab of the Format Cells dialog box for more control over cell borders.

Before you display the Format Cells dialog box, select the cell or range to which you want to add borders. First, choose a line style and then choose the border position for the line style by clicking one of the Border icons (these icons are toggles).

Notice that the Border tab has three preset icons, which can save you some clicking. If you want to remove all borders from the selection, click None. To put an outline around the selection, click Outline. To put borders inside the selection, click Inside.

Excel displays the selected border style in the dialog box; there is no live preview. You can choose different styles for different border positions; you can also choose a color for the border. Using this dialog box may require some experimentation, but you'll get the hang of it.

When you apply diagonal lines to a cell or range, the selection looks like it has been crossed out.

Tip

If you use border formatting in your worksheet, you may want to turn off the grid display to make the borders more pronounced. Choose View ⇨ Show ⇨ Gridlines to toggle the gridline display. ■

Adding a Background Image to a Worksheet

Excel also enables you to choose a graphics file to serve as a background for a worksheet. This effect is similar to the wallpaper that you may display on your Windows desktop or as a background for a Web page.

To add a background to a worksheet, choose Page Layout ➪ Page Setup ➪ Background. Excel displays a dialog box that enables you to select a graphics file; all common graphic file formats are supported. When you locate a file, click Insert. Excel tiles the graphic across your worksheet. Some images are specifically designed to be tiled, such as the one shown in Figure 6.11. This type of image is often used for Web page backgrounds, and it creates a seamless background.

FIGURE 6.11

You can add almost any image file as a worksheet background image.

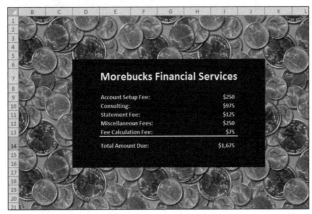

On the CD

This workbook, named `background image.xlsx,` **is available on the companion CD-ROM.** ∎

You also want to turn off the gridline display because the gridlines show through the graphic. Some backgrounds make viewing text difficult, so you may want to use a solid background color for cells that contain text.

Keep in mind that using a background image will increase the size of your workbook. This may be a consideration if you plan to e-mail the workbook to others.

Note

The graphic background on a worksheet is for onscreen display only — it isn't printed when you print the worksheet. ■

Copying Formats by Painting

Perhaps the quickest way to copy the formats from one cell to another cell or range is to use the Format Painter button (the button with the paintbrush image) of the Home ➪ Clipboard group.

1. **Select the cell or range that has the formatting attributes you want to copy.**
2. **Click the Format Painter button.** The mouse pointer changes to include a paintbrush.
3. **Select the cells to which you want to apply the formats.**
4. **Release the mouse button, and Excel applies the same set of formatting options that were in the original range.**

If you double-click the Format Painter button, you can paint multiple areas of the worksheet with the same formats. Excel applies the formats that you copy to each cell or range that you select. To get out of Paint mode, click the Format Painter button again (or press Esc).

Using Named Styles for Easier Formatting

One of the most underutilized features in Excel is named styles. Named styles make it very easy to apply a set of predefined formatting options to a cell or range. In addition to saving time, using named styles also helps to ensure a consistent look.

A style can consist of settings for up to six different attributes:

- Number format
- Font (type, size, and color)
- Alignment (vertical and horizontal)
- Borders
- Pattern
- Protection (locked and hidden)

The real power of styles is apparent when you change a component of a style. All cells which use that named style automatically incorporate the change. Suppose that you apply a particular style to a dozen cells scattered throughout your worksheet. Later, you realize that these cells should have a font size of 14 pt rather than 12 pt. Rather than change each cell, simply edit the style. All cells with that particular style change automatically.

Applying styles

Beginning with Excel 2007, the style feature has been revamped significantly, and Excel now includes a good selection of predefined named styles that work in conjunction with document themes. Figure 6.12 shows the effect of choosing Home ⇨ Styles ⇨ Cell Styles. Note that this display is a *live preview:* that is, as you move your mouse over the style choices, the selected cell or range temporarily displays the style. When you see a style you like, click it to apply the style to the selection.

Note

If Excel's window is wide enough, you won't see the Cell Styles command in the Ribbon. Rather, you will see four or more formatted style boxes. Click the drop-down arrow to the right of these boxes to display all the defined styles. ■

FIGURE 6.12

Excel displays samples of available cell styles.

Note

By default, all cells use the Normal style. If you modify the Normal style, all cells that haven't been assigned a different style will reflect the new formatting. ■

After you apply a style to a cell, you can apply additional formatting to it by using any formatting method discussed in this chapter. Formatting modifications that you make to the cell don't affect other cells that use the same style.

You have quite a bit of control over styles. In fact, you can do any of the following:

- Modify an existing style.
- Create a new style.
- Merge styles from another workbook into the active workbook.

The following sections describe these procedures.

Modifying an existing style

To change an existing style, choose Home ➪ Styles ➪ Cell Styles. Right-click the style you want to modify and choose Modify from the shortcut menu. Excel displays the Style dialog box, shown in Figure 6.13. In this example, the Style dialog box shows the settings for the Office theme Normal style — which is the default style for all cells. The style definitions vary, depending on which document theme is active.

FIGURE 6.13

Use the Style dialog box to modify named styles.

Here's a quick example of how you can use styles to change the default font used throughout your workbook.

1. **Choose Home ➪ Styles ➪ Cell Styles.** Excels displays the list of styles for the active workbook.

2. **Right-click Normal and choose Modify.** Excel displays the Style dialog box (Figure 6-13), with the current settings for the Normal style.

3. **Click the Format button.** Excel displays the Format Cells dialog box.

4. **Click the Font tab and choose the font and size that you want as the default.**

5. **Click OK to return to the Style dialog box.**

6. **Click OK again to close the Style dialog box.**

The font for all cells that use the Normal style changes to the font that you specified. You can change any formatting attributes for any style.

Creating new styles

In addition to using Excel's built-in styles, you can create your own styles. This flexibility can be quite handy because it enables you to apply your favorite formatting options very quickly and consistently.

To create a new style, follow these steps:

1. **Select a cell and apply all the formatting that you want to include in the new style.** You can use any of the formatting that is available in the Format Cells dialog box (refer to Figures 6-3 and 6-5).

2. **After you format the cell to your liking, choose Home ⇨ Styles ⇨ Cell Styles, and choose New Cell Style.** Excel displays its Style dialog box (refer to Figure 6-13), along with a proposed generic name for the style. Note that Excel displays the words By Example to indicate that it's basing the style on the current cell.

3. **Enter a new style name in the Style Name field.** The check boxes display the current formats for the cell. By default, all check boxes are selected.

4. **(Optional) If you don't want the style to include one or more format categories, remove the check(s) from the appropriate check box(es).**

5. **Click OK to create the style and to close the dialog box.**

After you perform these steps, the new custom style is available when you choose Home ⇨ Styles ⇨ Cell Styles. Custom styles are available only in the workbook in which they were created. To copy your custom styles to another workbook, see the section that follows.

Note
The Protection option in the Style dialog box controls whether users will be able to modify cells for the selected style. This option is effective only if you've also turned on worksheet protection, by choosing Review ⇨ Changes ⇨ Protect Sheet. ∎

Merging styles from other workbooks

Custom styles are stored with the workbook in which they were created. If you've created some custom styles, you probably don't want to go through all the work to create copies of those styles in each new Excel workbook. A better approach is to merge the styles from a workbook in which you previously created them.

To merge styles from another workbook, open both the workbook that contains the styles that you want to merge and the workbook into which you want to merge styles. From the workbook into which you want to merge styles, choose Home ⇨ Styles ⇨ Cell Styles and choose Merge Styles. Excel displays the Merge Styles dialog box that shows a list of all open workbooks. Select the workbook that contains the styles you want to merge and click OK. Excel copies styles from the workbook that you selected into the active workbook.

Tip

You may want to create a master workbook that contains all your custom styles so that you always know which workbook to merge styles from. ∎

Controlling styles with templates

When you start Excel, it loads with several default settings, including the settings for stylistic formatting. If you spend a lot of time changing the default elements, you should know about templates.

Here's an example. You may prefer that gridlines aren't displayed in worksheets. And maybe you prefer Wrap Text to be the default setting for alignment. Templates provide an easy way to change defaults.

The trick is to create a workbook with the Normal style modified to the way that you want it. Then, save the workbook as a template in your XLStart folder. After doing so, you choose Office ➪ New to display a dialog box from which you can choose the template for the new workbook. Template files also can store other named styles, providing you with an excellent way to give your workbooks a consistent look.

Cross-Reference

Chapter 8 discusses templates in detail. ∎

Understanding Document Themes

To help users create more professional-looking documents, the Office designers incorporated a concept known as *document themes*. Using themes is an easy (and almost foolproof) way to specify the colors, fonts, and a variety of graphic effects in a document. And best of all, changing the entire look of your document is a breeze. A few mouse clicks is all it takes to apply a different theme and change the look of your workbook.

Importantly, the concept of themes is incorporated into other Office 2010 (and Office 2007) applications. Therefore, a company can easily create a standard look and feel for all its documents.

Note

Themes don't override specific formatting that you apply. For example, assume that you apply the Accent 1–named style to a range. Then you use the Fill Color control to change the background color of that range. If you change to a different theme, the manually applied fill color will not be modified. Bottom line? If you plan to take advantage of themes, stick with default formatting choices. ∎

Figure 6.14 shows a worksheet that contains a SmartArt diagram, a table, a chart, and range formatted with the Heading 1–named style. These items all use the default theme, which is the Office Theme.

FIGURE 6.14

The elements in this worksheet use the default theme.

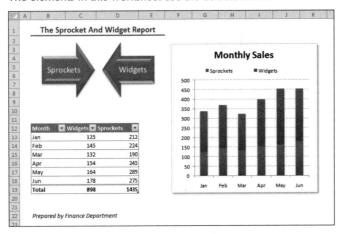

Figure 6.15 shows the same worksheet after applying a different document theme. The different theme changed the fonts, colors (which may not be apparent in the figure), and the graphic effects for the SmartArt diagram.

On the CD

If you'd like to experiment with using various themes, the workbook shown in Figures 6.14 and 6.15 is available on the companion CD-ROM. The file is named theme examples.xlsx.

FIGURE 6.15

The worksheet, after applying a different theme.

Applying a theme

Figure 6.16 shows the theme choices that appear when you choose Page ⇨ Layout ⇨ Themes ⇨ Themes. This display is a live preview. (While you move your mouse over the theme choices, the active worksheet displays the theme.) When you see a theme you like, click it to apply the theme to all worksheets in the workbook.

Note

A theme applies to the entire workbook. You can't use different themes on different worksheets within a workbook. ■

Built-in Excel theme choices.

When you specify a particular theme, the gallery choices for various elements reflect the new theme. For example, the chart styles that you can choose from vary, depending on which theme is active.

Because themes use different fonts and font sizes, changing to a different theme may affect the layout of your worksheet. For example, after applying a new theme, a worksheet that printed on a single page may spill over to a second page. Therefore, you may need to make some adjustments after you apply a new theme.

Customizing a theme

Notice that the Themes group on the Page Layout tab contains three other controls: Colors, Fonts, and Effects. You can use these controls to change just one of the three components of a theme. For example, if you like the Urban theme but would prefer different fonts, apply the Urban theme and then specify your preferred font set by choosing Page Layout ⇨ Themes ⇨ Font.

Each theme uses two fonts (one for headers, and one for the body), and in some cases, these two fonts are the same. If none of the theme choices is suitable, choose Page Layout ⇨ Themes ⇨ Font ⇨ Create New Theme Fonts to specify the two fonts you prefer (see Figure 6.17).

FIGURE 6.17

Use this dialog box to specify two fonts for a theme.

Tip

When you choose Home ⇨ Fonts ⇨ Font, the two fonts for the current theme are listed first in the drop-down list. ■

Choose Page Layout ⇨ Themes ⇨ Colors to select a different set of colors. And, if you're so inclined, you can even create a custom set of colors by choosing Page Layout ⇨ Themes ⇨ Colors ⇨ Create New Theme Colors. This command displays the Create New Theme Colors dialog box, shown in Figure 6.18. Note that each theme consists of 12 colors. Four of the colors are for text and backgrounds, six are for accents, and two are for hyperlinks. As you specify different colors, the preview panel in the dialog box updates.

FIGURE 6.18

If you're feeling creative, you can specify a set of custom colors for a theme.

Note

Theme effects operate on graphic elements, such as SmartArt, Shapes, and charts. You can't customize theme effects. ■

If you've customized a theme using different fonts or colors, you can save the new theme by choosing Page Layout ⟳ Themes ⟳ Save Current Theme. Your customized themes appear in the theme list in the Custom category. Other Office applications, such as Word and PowerPoint, can use these theme files.

Understanding Excel Files

E xcel, of course, uses files to store its workbooks. This chapter describes the operations that you perform with workbook files: opening, saving, closing, deleting, and so on. It discusses how Excel uses files and provides an overview of the various types of files. Most of the file operations discussed here occur in the new *Backstage View,* the screen that you see when you click File on the Excel Ribbon.

This chapter also discusses the Excel 2007 and Excel 2010 file formats and describes how to determine what (if anything) will be lost if you save your workbook in an earlier file format.

As you read through this chapter, remember that you can have any number of workbooks open simultaneously, and that only one workbook is the active workbook at any given time. The workbook's name appears in its title bar (or in the Excel title bar if the workbook is maximized).

IN THIS CHAPTER

Creating a new workbook

Opening an existing workbook

Saving and closing workbooks

Sharing workbooks with those who use an older version of Excel

Creating a New Workbook

When you start Excel normally, it automatically creates a new (empty) workbook called Book1. This workbook exists only in memory and has not been saved to disk. By default, this workbook consists of three worksheets named Sheet1, Sheet2, and Sheet3. If you're starting a project from scratch, you can use this blank workbook.

While you're working in Excel, you can create a new (empty) workbook at any time. Excel provides two ways to create a new workbook:

- Choose File ➪ New, which displays a screen like the one shown see Figure 7.1. This screen lets you create a blank workbook, a workbook based on a template, or a workbook based on an existing workbook. To create a new blank workbook, select Blank Workbook and then click the Create button.
- Press Ctrl+N. This shortcut is the fastest way to start a new workbook if you're not using a template.

FIGURE 7.1

Choosing File ➪ New presents you with options for creating a new workbook.

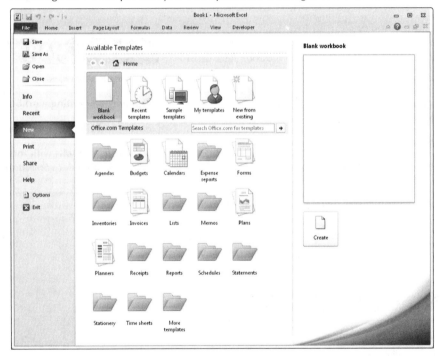

Cross-Reference

See Chapter 8 for more information about using and creating templates. ■

Starting Excel without an Empty Workbook

If you prefer to avoid the empty workbook displayed when Excel starts up, edit the command line used to start Excel. You need to create a new shortcut to `excel.exe` and then modify the properties:

1. **Use Windows Explorer and locate the `excel.exe` program.** The default location is

   `C:\Program Files\Microsoft Office\Office14\`

2. **Pressing and holding the right mouse button, drag the `excel.exe` filename (or icon) to your desktop and then release the mouse button.**

3. **From the shortcut menu that appears, choose Create Shortcuts Here.** Windows creates a new shortcut icon on your desktop.

4. **Right-click the shortcut icon and choose Properties.**

5. **In the Properties dialog box that appears, click the Shortcut tab.**

6. **Edit the Target field by adding a space, followed by /e, to the end.** For example:

   `"C:\Program Files\Microsoft Office\Office14\EXCEL.EXE" /e`

7. **(Optional) Specify a shortcut key.** If you provide a shortcut key, you can use that keystroke combination to start or active Excel.

8. **Click OK.**

After making that change, Excel doesn't display an empty workbook when you start it by clicking that shortcut icon. In addition, you won't see the normal "splash" screen.

Opening an Existing Workbook

Following are some of the ways to open a workbook saved on your hard drive:

- Choose File ➪ Recent and then select the file you want from the Recent Workbooks list. Only the most recently used files are listed. You can specify the number of files to display (maximum of 50) in the Advanced section of the Excel Options dialog box.

- Locate the Excel workbook file via a Windows Explorer file list. Just double-click the filename (or icon), and the workbook opens in Excel. If Excel is not running, Windows automatically starts Excel and loads the workbook file.

- Use either of the following methods to display the Open dialog box:

  - Choose File ➪ Open.

  - Press Ctrl+O.

  From this dialog box, you can browse your computer for workbooks.

Tip

When you choose File ⇨ Recent, each file in the recent workbooks list displays a pushpin icon on the right. Click the pushpin icon, and that file becomes "pinned" to the list and will always appear at the top of the list. This handy feature ensures that important files always appear on the recent workbooks list — even if you haven't opened the file recently.

Also, notice that you can right-click a workbook in the list and choose Remove from List. Or, choose Clear Unpinned Items to clear the list and start fresh. ■

The Open dialog box, shown in Figure 7.2, is resizable. To make it larger or smaller, click the lower-right corner and drag. Also, notice that it's virtually identical to a Windows Explorer window. The only difference is that it includes additional controls at the bottom.

Note

The appearance of the Open dialog box varies, depending on the version of Windows you use. The dialog box in Figure 7.2 shows the Open dialog box when running Windows Vista. ■

FIGURE 7.2

Use the Open dialog box to open any of your Excel workbook files.

To open a workbook from the Open dialog box, use the folder tree display on the left to locate the folder that contains the file, and then select the workbook file from the list on the right. After you locate and select the file, click Open, and the file opens. Or, just double-click the filename to open it.

About Protected View

New Feature

Protected View is a new feature in Excel 2010. ■

One of the new features in Excel 2010 is Protected View. Although it might seem like Excel is trying to keep you from opening your own files, protected view is all about protecting you from malware. *Malware* refers to something that can harm your system. Hackers have figured out several way to manipulate Excel files in a way that harmful code can be executed. Protected View essentially prevents these types of attacks by opening a file in a protected environment (a "sandbox").

If you use Excel 2010 to open an Excel workbook that you downloaded from the Web, you'll see a colorful message above the Formula bar. In addition, the Excel title bar displays [Protected View].

If you are certain that the file is safe, click Enable Editing. If you don't enable editing, you will be able to view the contents of the workbook, but you won't be able to make any changes to it.

If the workbook contains macros, you'll see another message after you enable editing: Security Warning. Macros have been disabled. If you are sure that the macros are harmless, click Enable Content.

Protected View kicks in for the following:

- Files downloaded from the Internet
- Attachments opened from Outlook 2010
- Files open from potentially unsafe locations, such as your Temporary Internet Files folder
- File that are blocked by File Block Policy (a feature that allows administrators to define potentially dangerous files)
- Files that were digitally signed, but the signature has expired

In some situations, you don't care about working with the document. You just want to print it. In that case, choose File ⇨ Print, and then click the Enable Printing button.

It would be nice if copying were allowed in Protected View — but it's not. The only way to copy information from a workbook in Protected View is to enable editing.

You have some control over how Protected View works. To change the settings, choose File ⇨ Options, and click Trust Center. Then click the Trust Center Settings button and click the Protected View tab in the Trust Center dialog box.

Notice that the Open button is actually a drop-down list. Click the arrow, and you see the additional options:

- **Open:** Opens the file normally.
- **Open Read-Only:** Opens the selected file in read-only mode. When a file is opened in this mode, you can't save changes with the original filename.

- **Open as Copy:** Opens a copy of the selected file. If the file is named `budget.xlsx`, the workbook that opens is named `Copy(1)budget.xlsx`.

- **Open in Browser:** Opens the file in your default Web browser. If the file can't be opened in a browser, this option is disabled.

- **Open in Protected View:** Opens the file in a special mode that does not allow editing. In this view, most of the Excel Ribbon commands are disabled. Read more about this new feature in the sidebar, "About Protected View."

- **Open and Repair:** Attempts to open a file that may be damaged and recover information contained in it.

Tip

You can hold down the Ctrl key and select multiple workbooks. When you click Open, all the selected workbook files open. ∎

Right-clicking a filename in the Open dialog box displays a shortcut menu with many extra Windows commands. For example, you can copy, delete, or rename the file, modify its properties, and so on.

Using the Favorite Links

Your Favorite Links list appears at the top of the left panel of the Open dialog box. It contains a list of shortcuts to folders on your system. Initially, it's just a partial list of folders, but you can click More to expand the list.

To add a new folder to the Favorite Links section, click the folder in the Open dialog box and drag it into the Favorite Links area. Customizing the Favorite Links section by adding shortcuts to folders that you use frequently can save you lots of clicking.

Filtering filenames

At the bottom of the Open dialog box is a button with a drop-down list. When the Open dialog box is displayed, this button shows All Excel Files (and a long list of file extensions). The Open dialog box displays only those files that match the extensions. In other words, you see only standard Excel files.

If you want to open a file of a different type, click the arrow in the drop-down list and select the file type that you want to open. This changes the filtering and displays only files of the type that you specify.

You can also type a filter directly in the File Name box. For example, typing the following will display only files that have an `.xlsx` extension (press Enter after typing the filter): ***.xlsx**.

Opening Workbooks Automatically

Many people work on the same workbooks each day. If this describes you, you'll be happy to know that Excel can open specific workbook files automatically whenever you start Excel. Any workbooks placed in the XLStart folder open automatically.

The location of the XLStart folder varies, depending on your Windows version. To determine the location of the XLStart folder on your system

1. **Choose File ⇨ Options and click Trust Center.**
2. **Click the Trust Center Settings button.**
3. **In the Trust Center dialog box, click the Trusted Locations tab.** You'll see a list of trusted locations.
4. **Look for the path for the location described as User Startup.** The path might look something like this:

```
C:\Users\<username>\AppData\Roaming\Microsoft\Excel\XLSTART\
```

Another XLStart folder may be located here:

```
C:\Program Files\Microsoft Office\Office14\XLStart\
```

Any workbook files (excluding template files) stored in either of these XLStart folders open automatically when Excel starts. If one or more files open automatically from an XLStart folder, Excel won't start with a blank workbook.

You can specify an alternate startup folder in addition to the XLStart folder. Choose File ⇨ Options and select the Advanced tab. Scroll down to the General section and enter a new folder name in the At Startup, Open All Files In field. Then, when you start Excel, it automatically opens all workbook files in both the XLStart folders and the alternate folder that you specified.

Choosing your file display preferences

The Open dialog box can display your workbook filenames in several different styles: as a list, with complete details, as icons, and so on. You control the style by clicking the Views icon and then selecting from the drop-down list. The style that you choose is entirely up to you.

Saving a Workbook

When you're working in Excel, your workbook is vulnerable to day-ruining events such as power failures and system crashes. Therefore, you should save your work often. Saving a file takes only a few seconds, but re-creating hours of lost work takes many hours.

Excel provides four ways to save your workbook:

- Click the Save icon on the Quick Access toolbar.
- Press Ctrl+S.
- Press Shift+F12.
- Choose File ⇨ Save.

Caution

Saving a file overwrites the previous version of the file on your hard drive. If you open a workbook and then completely mess it up, don't save the file! Instead, close the workbook without saving it and then reopen the good copy on your hard drive. ∎

If your workbook has already been saved, it's saved again using the same filename. If you want to save the workbook to a new file, choose File ⇨ Save As (or press F12).

If your workbook has never been saved, its title bar displays a default name, such as Book1 or Book2. Although Excel allows you to use these generic workbook names for filenames, you'll be better off using more descriptive filenames. Therefore, the first time that you save a new workbook, Excel displays the Save As dialog box to let you provide a more meaningful name.

The Save As dialog box is similar to the Open dialog box. Select the desired folder in the folder list on the left. After you select the folder, enter the filename in the File Name field. You don't need to specify a file extension — Excel adds it automatically, based on the file type specified in the Save as Type field. By default, files are saved in the standard Excel file format, which uses an .xlsx file extension.

Tip

To change the default file format for saving files, access the Excel Options dialog box. Click the Save tab and change the setting for the Save Files in This Format option. For example, if your workbooks must be compatible with older versions of Excel, you can change the default format to Excel 97-2003 Workbook (*.xls). Doing so eliminates the need to select the older file type every time you save a new workbook. ∎

Caution

If your workbook contains VBA macros, saving it with an .xlsx file extension will erase all the macros. It must be saved with an .xlsm extension (or saved in the XLS or XLSB format)). If your workbook has macros, Excel will still propose to save it as an XLSX file. It other words, Excel suggests a file format that will destroy your macros! It will, however, warn you that the macros will be lost. ∎

If a file with the same name already exists in the folder that you specify, Excel asks whether you want to overwrite that file with the new file. *Be careful:* You can't recover the previous file after you overwrite it.

Using AutoRecover

If you've used computers for any length of time, you've probably lost some work. You forgot to save a file, or maybe the power went out and your unsaved work was lost. Or maybe you were working on something and didn't think it was important, so you closed it without saving — and later realized that it *was* important. A new feature in Excel 2010 called Versions might make these types of "D'oh!" moments less frequent.

As you work in Excel, your work is periodically saved, automatically. It happens in the background so you don't even know that it's happening. What's new in Excel 2010 is that you can access these autosaved versions of your work. And this even applies to workbooks that you never explicitly saved.

The Versions feature consists of two components:

- Versions of a workbook are saved automatically, and you can view them.
- Workbooks that you closed without saving are saved as draft versions.

Recovering versions of the current workbook

To see whether any previous versions of the current workbook are available, choose File ⇨ Info. The Versions section Versions lists the available old versions (if any) of the current workbook. In some cases, more than one autosaved version will be listed. In other cases, no autosaved versions will be available.

You can open an autosaved version by clicking its name. Remember that opening an autosaved version *won't* automatically replace the current version of your workbook. Therefore, you can decide whether the autosaved version is preferable to the current version. Or, you can just copy some information that may have been accidentally deleted, and paste it to your current workbook.

When you close the workbook, the autosaved versions are deleted.

Recovering unsaved work

When you close a workbook without saving your changes, Excel asks whether you're sure. If that unsaved workbook has an autosaved version, the "Are you sure?" dialog box informs you of that fact.

To recover a workbook that you closed without saving, choose File ⇨ Info ⇨ Versions, and choose Recover Draft Versions. You'll see a list of all draft versions of your workbooks. You can open them and (hopefully) recover something that you needed. These drafts are also listed in the recent file list, displayed when you choose File ⇨ Recent.

Draft versions are deleted after four days, or until you edit the file.

Filenaming Rules

Excel workbook files are subject to the same rules that apply to other Windows files. A filename can be up to 255 characters, including spaces. This length enables you to give meaningful names to your files. You can't, however, use any of the following characters in your filenames:

\ (slash)	? (question mark)
: (colon)	* (asterisk)
" (quote)	< (less than)
> (greater than)	| (vertical bar)

You can use uppercase and lowercase letters in your names to improve readability. The filenames aren't case sensitive. For example, My 2011 Budget.xlsx and MY 2011 BUDGET.xlsx are equivalent names.

Note

You can adjust the Versions feature in the Save tab of the Excel Options dialog box. For example, you can change the autosave time interval (the default is 10 minutes), turn off autosave for a particular workbook, or disable this feature for all workbooks. ■

Specifying a Password

In some cases, you may want to specify a password for your workbook. When a user attempts to open a password-protected workbook, a password must be entered before the file is opened.

To set a password for a workbook, choose File ➪ Info, and click the Protect Workbook button. This button displays some additional options. Choose Encrypt With Password. Excel displays the Encrypt Document dialog box, shown in Figure 7.3. Enter the password, and then enter it again. Click OK, and save the workbook.

When you re-open the workbook, you will be prompted for a password.

FIGURE 7.3

The Encrypt Document dialog box is where you specify a password for your workbook.

Caution

Passwords are case sensitive. Be careful with this option because it is impossible to open the workbook (using normal methods) if you forget the password. Also, remember that Excel passwords can be cracked, so it's not a perfect security measure. ■

Organizing Your Files

If you have hundreds of Excel files, you might have a problem locating the workbook that you need. Using descriptive filenames can help, and using folders and subfolders (with descriptive names) also makes it easier to find the particular file you need. In some cases, though, that's not enough.

Fortunately, Excel lets you assign a variety of descriptive information (sometimes known as *metadata*) to a workbook. These are known as document properties. This information includes such items as the author, title, subject, and so on.

When you choose File ⇨ Info you can view (or modify) the document properties for the active workbook. This information is shown on the right side of the screen (see Figure 7.4).

Tip

If you aren't seeing all the properties for your workbook, click the down-arrow on Properties and select Show All Properties Another option on the Document Properties drop-down list is Show Document Panel. Choosing this command displays the properties in a panel below the Ribbon. ■

When you use the Open dialog box, you can specify additional columns to display. Start by clicking Views (at the top of the Open dialog box) and then choose Details. Right-click the column header to see a list of other properties to include. Click the More option for a longer list of properties (see Figure 7.5).

You can sort the file list in the Open dialog box by a particular column by clicking the column heading. Also, notice that each heading is actually a drop-down list. Click the drop-down arrow, and you can filter the list to show only files that match the selected properties.

Using document properties lets you work with files as if they were in a database. The key, of course, is taking the time to ensure that the document properties are actually assigned, and are accurate.

Tip

If you would like to be prompted to ensure that the document properties are correct, choose Developer ⇨ Modify ⇨ Document Panel. In the Document Information Panel dialog box, select the Always Show Document Information Panel on Document Open and Initial Save check box. If the Developer tab isn't visible, use the Customize Ribbon panel in the Excel Options dialog box to display it. ■

FIGURE 7.4

Use Properties to store additional information about your workbook.

FIGURE 7.5

The Choose Details dialog box, where you choose additional properties to display in the file list.

Using Workspace Files

If you have a project that uses multiple workbooks, you probably get tired of opening the same files every time you work on the project. The solution? Create a workspace file:

1. **Open all the workbooks used for your project.**

2. **Arrange the workbook windows the way you like them.**

3. **Choose View ⇨ Window ⇨ Save Workspace to display the Save Workspace dialog box.**

4. **Excel proposes the name resume.xlw, but you can specify any name you like. Just make sure that you use the XLW extension.**

5. **Click Save.** The workspace file is created.

After creating a workspace file, you can open it by choosing File ⇨ Open. In the Open dialog box, specify Workspaces (*.xlw) from the Files of Type drop-down list. Better yet, pin it to the top of the recent files list so it will always be easily accessible.

Note

A workspace file contains only the filenames and window position information — not the workbooks. Make sure that you save the workbooks that comprise the workspace. ■

Note

This discussion of document properties just barely scratches the surface. For example, you can display additional properties and even specify a custom document information panel template that contains information specific to your needs. A complete discussion is beyond the scope of this book. ■

Other Workbook Info Options

The Info pane of Backstage View displays more file-related options, as shown in Figure 7.6. To display this pane, choose File ⇨ Info. These options, described in the following sections, may be useful if you plan to distribute your workbook to others. Note that not all workbooks display all the options shown in Figure 7.6. Only the relevant options are shown.

Security Warning section

If the active workbook displayed a security warning when you opened it, the Info pane will display a Security Warning section, with an Enable Content button. Use this panel to find out more about why Excel triggered the security warning, and to enable the content if you're sure that it's safe to do so.

FIGURE 7.6

Choose File ➪ Info for additional options.

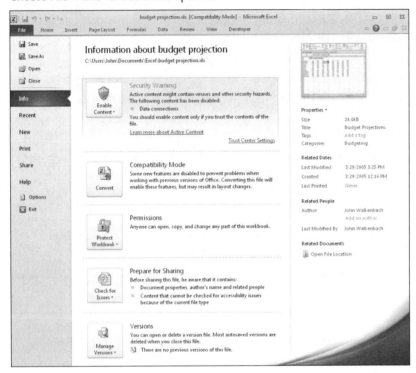

Compatibility Mode section

If the active workbook is an old workbook opened in compatibility mode, you'll see the Compatibility Mode section in the Info pane. To convert the workbook to the Excel 2007/2010 format, click the Convert button.

Caution

Be aware that this command deletes the original version of the file — which seems like a rather drastic measure. It's probably wise to make a copy of your workbook before you use this command. ■

Permissions section

In the Permissions section of the Info pane, click the Protect Workbook button to display the following options:

- **Mark as Final**

  Use this option to designate the workbook as "final." The document is saved as a read-only file to prevent changes. This isn't a security feature. Rather, the Mark as Final command is useful to let others know that you are sharing a completed version of a workbook.

- **Encrypt with Password**

  Use this command to specify a password that is required to open the workbook. See "Specifying a password," earlier in this chapter.

- **Protect Current Sheet**

  This command lets you protect various elements of a worksheet. It displays the same dialog box as the Review ⇨ Changes ⇨ Protect Sheet command. See Chapter 31 for more information about protecting worksheets.

- **Protect Workbook Structure**

  This command lets you protect the structure of a workbook. It displays the same dialog box as Review ⇨ Changes ⇨ Protect Workbook. See Chapter 31 for more information for more information about protecting the structure of a workbook.

- **Restrict Permission by People**

  Use this option to specify those who may open the document. This feature requires a fee-based service called *Information Rights Management*.

- **Add a Digital Signature**

  This command allows you to "sign" a workbook digitally. See Chapter 31 for more information about digital signatures.

Prepare for Sharing section

The Prepare for Sharing section of the Info pane contains a Check for Issues button. When clicked, the button displays three options:

- **Inspect Document**

  This command displays the Document Inspector dialog box. This feature can alert you to some potentially private information that may be contained in your workbook — perhaps information that's contained in hidden rows or columns or hidden worksheets. If you plan on making a workbook available to a large audience, it's an excellent idea to use the Document Inspector for a final check.

- **Check Accessibility**

  This command checks the workbook for potential problems that might occur for people with disabilities. The results of the check are displayed in a task pane in the workbook. This feature works only with Excel 2007/2010 workbooks.

- **Check Compatibility**

  This command is useful if you need to save your workbook in an older file format. It displays a very helpful Compatibility Checker dialog box that lists potential compatibility problems. This dialog box also appears when you save a workbook using an older file format. For more information, see "Excel File Compatibility," later in this chapter.

Versions section

Clicking the Manage Versions button of the Versions section of the Info pane displays two options:

- **Recover Draft Versions**

  This command displays the Open dialog box, pointed to the folder where Excel displays AutoRecover versions of workbooks that were not saved. If you accidentally forget to save a file, this command may help you out.

- **Delete All Draft Versions**

  This command simply deletes all unsaved files on your drive. Alternatively, you can delete the files manually.

Closing Workbooks

After you're finished with a workbook, you can close it to free the memory that it uses. You can close a workbook by using any of the following methods:

- Choose File ⇨ Close.
- Click the Close button (the X) in the workbook's title bar.
- Double-click the Excel icon on the left side of the workbook's title bar. This icon is visible only if the workbook window is not maximized.
- Press Ctrl+F4.
- Press Ctrl+W.

If you've made any changes to your workbook since it was last saved, Excel asks whether you want to save the changes to the workbook before closing it.

Tip

When you close Excel, you are prompted to save each workbook that hasn't been saved. The dialog box has a Save All button, but it doesn't have a Don't Save Anything button. If you'd like a quick exit, without saving any workbooks, press Shift while you click the Don't Save button. Excel shuts down immediately. ∎

Safeguarding Your Work

Nothing is more frustrating than spending hours creating a complicated Excel workbook only to have it destroyed by a power failure, a hard drive crash, or even human error. Fortunately, protecting yourself from these disasters is not a difficult task.

Earlier in the chapter, I discuss the AutoRecover feature that makes Excel save a backup copy of your workbook at regular intervals (see "Using AutoRecover"). AutoRecover is a good idea, but it certainly isn't the only backup protection you should use. If a workbook is important, you need to take extra steps to ensure its safety. The following backup options help ensure the safety of individual files:

- **Keep a backup copy of the file on the same drive.** Although this option offers some protection if you make a mess of the workbook, it won't do you any good if the entire hard drive crashes.

- **Keep a backup copy on a different hard drive.** This method assumes, of course, that your system has more than one hard drive. This option offers more protection than the preceding method, because the likelihood that both hard drives will fail is remote. If the entire system is destroyed or stolen, however, you're out of luck.

- **Keep a backup copy on a network server.** This method assumes that your system is connected to a server on which you can write files. This method is fairly safe. If the network server is located in the same building, however, you're at risk if the entire building burns down or is otherwise destroyed.

- **Keep a backup copy on an Internet backup site.** Several Web sites specialize in storing backup files. This is a safe method, as long as the company doesn't go out of business.

- **Keep a backup copy on a removable medium.** This is the safest method. Using a removable medium, such as a USB drive enables you to physically take the backup to another location. So, if your system (or the entire building) is damaged, your backup copy remains intact.

Excel File Compatibility

It's important to understand the limitations regarding version compatibility. Even though your colleague is able to open your file, there is no guarantee that everything will function correctly or look the same.

Checking compatibility

If you save your workbook to an older file format (such as XLS, for versions prior to Excel 2007), Excel automatically runs the Compatibility Checker. The Compatibility Checker identifies the elements of your workbook that will result in loss of functionality or fidelity (cosmetics).

Figure 7.7 shows the Compatibility Checker dialog box. Use the Select Versions to Show button to limit the compatibility checking to a specific version of Excel.

The Compatibility Checker is a useful tool for those who share workbooks with others.

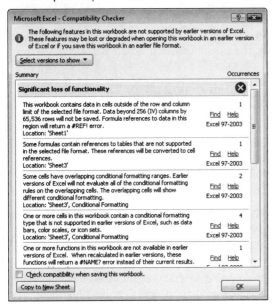

The bottom part of the Compatibility Checker lists the potential compatibility problems. To display the results in a more readable format, click the Copy to New Sheet button.

Keep in mind that compatibility problems can also occur with Excel 2007 even though that version uses the same file format as Excel 2010. You can't expect features that are new to Excel 2010 to work in earlier versions. For example, if you create a workbook with Sparkline charts (a new feature in Excel 2010) and send it to a colleague who uses Excel 2007, the cells that contain the Sparklines will be empty. In addition, formulas that use any of the new worksheet functions will return an error. The Compatibility Checker identifies these types of problems.

Perhaps one of the most confusing aspects of Excel is the nearly overwhelming number of file formats that it can read and write. With the introduction of Excel 2007, things got even more confusing because it has quite a few new file formats.

Note
Excel 2010 can open all files created with earlier versions of Excel. ∎

Recognizing the Excel 2010 file formats

Excel file formats (which were introduced in Excel 2007) are

- XLSX: A workbook file that does not contain macros
- XLSM: A workbook file that contains macros
- XLTX: A workbook template file that does not contain macros
- XLTM: A workbook template file that contains macros
- XLSA: An add-in file
- XLSB: A binary file similar to the old XLS format but able to accommodate the new features
- XLSK: A backup file

With the exception of XLSB, these are all "open" XML files, which means that other applications are able to read and write these types of files.

Tip

XML files are actually Zip-compressed text files. If you rename one of these files to have a ZIP extension, you'll be able to examine the contents using any of several zip file utilities — including the Zip file support built into Windows. Taking a look at the innards of an Excel workbook is an interesting exercise for curious-minded users. ■

Saving a file for use with an older version of Excel

To save a file for use with an older version of Excel, choose File ➪ Save As. In the Save As dialog box, select one of the following from the Save as Type drop-down:

- **Excel 97-2003 Workbook (*.xls):** If the file will be used by someone who has Excel 97, Excel 2000, Excel 2002, or Excel 2003.
- **Microsoft Excel 5.0/95 Workbook (*.xls):** If the file will be used by someone who has Excel 5 or Excel 95.

The Office Compatibility Pack

Normally, those who use an earlier version of Excel can't open workbooks saved in the new Excel file formats. But, fortunately, Microsoft has released a free Compatibility Pack for Office 2003 and Office XP.

If an Office 2003 or Office XP user installs the Compatibility Pack, they can open files created in Office 2007 or Office 2010 and also save files in the new format. The Office programs that are affected are Excel, Word, and PowerPoint. This software doesn't endow the older versions with any new features: It just gives them the capability to open and save files in the new format.

To download the Compatibility Pack, search the Web for *Office Compatibility Pack*.

Using and Creating Templates

A template is essentially a model that serves as the basis for something else. An Excel template is a workbook that's used to create other workbooks. This chapter discusses some of the templates included with Excel and also describes how to create your own template files. Creating a template takes some time, but in the long run, doing so may save you a lot of work.

IN THIS CHAPTER

Understanding Excel templates

Working with the default templates

Creating custom templates

Exploring Excel Templates

The best way to become familiar with Excel template files is to jump in and try a few. Excel 2010 gives you quick access to hundreds of template files.

Viewing templates

To explore the Excel templates, choose File ⇨ New to display the Available Templates screen in Backstage View. You can select a template stored on your hard drive, or a template from Microsoft Office Online. If you choose a template from Microsoft Office Online, you must be connected to the Internet to download it.

The Office Online Templates section contains a number of icons, which represent various categories of templates (see Figure 8.1). Click an icon, and you'll see the available templates. When you select a template thumbnail, you see a preview in the right panel.

FIGURE 8.1

The New page in Backstage View displays template categories.

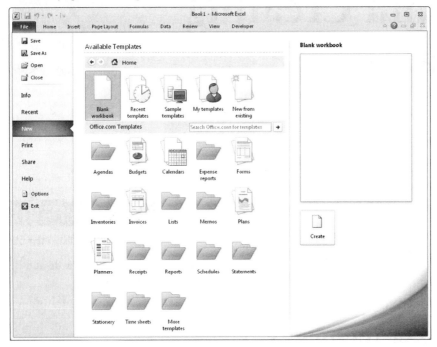

Note

Microsoft Office Online has a wide variety of templates, and some are better than others. If you download a few duds, don't give up. Even though a template may not be perfect, you can often modify a template to meet your needs. Modifying an existing template is often easier than creating a workbook from scratch. ■

Creating a workbook from a template

To create a workbook based on a template, just locate the template and click the Create button on the right. If the template is on Microsoft Office Online, the Create button is replaced with a Download button.

What you do next depends on the template. Every template is different, but most are self-explanatory. Some workbooks require customization. Just replace the generic information with your own information.

Figure 8.2 shows a workbook based on an invoice template. This particular workbook has a few simple formulas that perform calculations using the data that you enter. Figure 8.3 shows the workbook after it has been customized a bit, and some items added. Notice that formulas calculate the subtotal, sales tax, and total.

Note

It's important to understand that you're not working with the template file. Rather, you're working with a workbook that was created from the template file. If you make any changes, you're not changing the template — you're changing the workbook that's based on the template. After you download a template from Microsoft Office Online, that template is available in the My Templates category (in the Available Templates screen) so you don't need to redownload it if you want to re-use the template. ■

A workbook created from an invoice template downloaded from Microsoft Office Online.

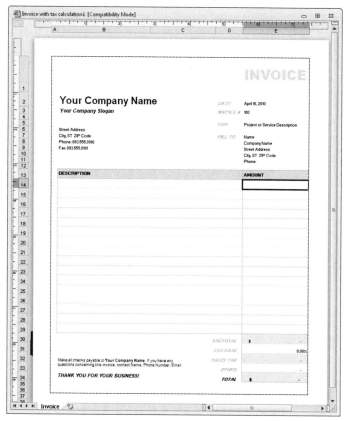

If you want to save the workbook, click the Save button. Excel proposes a named based on the template's name, but you can use any name you like.

FIGURE 8.3

The workbook, after customizing it and entering some information.

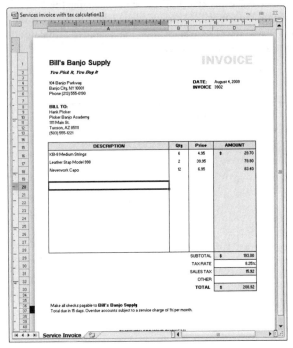

Modifying a template

A template file is just like a workbook file. As such, you can open a template file, make changes to it, and then resave the template file. Looking at the invoice template shown earlier in this chapter, you may want to modify it so that it shows your company information and uses your actual sales tax rate. Then, when you use that template in the future, the workbook created from it will already be customized.

To open a template, choose File ➪ Open (not File ➪ New) and locate the template file (it will have an .xltx or .xlt extension).

Tip

The location for template files varies. To find out where Excel stores template files, open a new workbook and choose File ➪ Save As. In the Save As dialog box, choose Excel Template (*.xltx) from the Save as Type drop-down list. Excel will activate your template folder. Make a note of this location, and click Cancel to close the Save As dialog box. On my system, templates are stored here:

```
C:\Users\<username>\AppData\Roaming\Microsoft\Templates
```

When you open a XLST (or *.XLT) template file, you are opening the actual file — you are *not* creating a workbook from the template file.

Note

To create a workbook from a modified template, you must select the template from the My Templates icon in the Available Template screen. Clicking My Templates displays the New dialog box shown in Figure 8.4. Just select the template and click OK. ■

FIGURE 8.4

The New dialog box displays downloaded and custom templates stored on your hard drive.

Understanding Custom Excel Templates

So far, this chapter has focused on templates that were created by others. The remainder of the chapter deals with *custom templates* — templates that you create.

Why create custom templates? The main reason is to make your job easier. For example, you may always like to use a particular header or footer on your printouts. Consequently, the first time that you print a worksheet, you need to spend time entering the header and footer information. Although it isn't a lot of work, wouldn't it be easier if Excel simply remembered your favorite page settings and used them automatically?

The solution is to modify the template that Excel uses to create new workbooks. In this case, the modification consists of inserting your header into the template. Save the template file using a special name, and then every new workbook that you create (including the workbook created when Excel starts) has your customized page settings.

Excel supports three types of templates, which I discuss in the following sections:

- **The default workbook template:** Used as the basis for new workbooks.

- **The default worksheet template:** Used as the basis for new worksheets inserted into a workbook.

- **Custom workbook templates:** Usually, these ready-to-run workbooks include formulas, but they can be as simple or as complex as you like. Typically, these templates are set up so that a user can simply plug in values and get immediate results. The Microsoft Office Online templates (discussed earlier in this chapter) are examples of this type of template.

Working with the default templates

The term *default template* may be a little misleading. If you haven't created your own template files to control the default settings, Excel uses its own internal settings — not an actual template file. In other words, Excel uses your template files to set the defaults for new workbooks or worksheets, if these files exist. But if you haven't created these files, Excel is perfectly happy to use its own settings.

Using the workbook template to change workbook defaults

Every new workbook that you create starts out with some default settings. For example, the workbook has three worksheets, the worksheets have gridlines, the page header and footer are blank, and text appears in the fonts specified by the default document template. Columns are 8.43 units wide, and so on. If you're not happy with any of the default workbook settings, you can change them by creating a workbook template.

Making changes to Excel's default workbook is fairly easy to do, and it can save you lots of time in the long run. Here's how you change Excel's workbook defaults:

1. **Open a new workbook.**

2. **Add or delete sheets to give the workbook the number of worksheets that you want.**

3. **Make any other changes that you want to make, which can include column widths, named styles, page setup options, and many of the settings that are available in the Excel Options dialog box.** To change the default formatting for cells, choose Home ➪ Styles ➪ Cell Styles and then modify the settings for the Normal style. For example, you can change the default font, size, or number format.

4. **When your workbook is set up to your liking, choose File ➪ Save As.**

5. **In the Save As dialog box, select Excel Template (*.xltx) from the Save As Type list.** If your template contains any VBA macros, select Excel Macro-Enabled Template (*.xltm).

6. **Enter** book **for the filename.**

Caution

Excel will offer a name, such as `Book1.xlt`. You must change this name to `book.xlt` (or `book.xltm`) if you want Excel to use your template to set the workbook defaults. ∎

7. Save the file in your XLStart folder (not in your Templates folder).

Tip

The location of the XLStart folder varies, but it is probably located here:

```
C:\Program Files\Microsoft Office\Office14\XLStart
```

8. Close the file.

After you perform the preceding steps, the new default workbook is based on the `book.xltx` (or `book.xltm`) workbook template. You can create a workbook based on your template by using any of these methods:

- Press Ctrl+N.

- Open Excel without first selecting a workbook to open.

Note

For some reason, the `book.xltx` template is not used if you choose File ⇨ New and choose Blank Workbook. That command results in a default workbook. I'm not sure whether this is a bug or whether it's by design. In any case, it provides a way to override the custom `book.xltx` template if you need to. ∎

Caution

If you insert a new worksheet into a workbook that's based on the `book.xlxt` template, the new worksheet will not use any customized worksheet settings specified in the template (for example, a different column width). Therefore, you may also want to create a `sheet.xltx` template (described in the next section), which controls the settings for new worksheets. ∎

If you ever want to revert to the standard default workbook, just delete the `book.xltx` file.

Using the worksheet template to change worksheet defaults

When you insert a new worksheet into a workbook, Excel uses its built-in worksheet defaults for the worksheet. These default settings include items such as column width, row height, and so on.

If you don't like the default settings for a new worksheet, you can change them by following these steps:

1. Start with a new workbook and delete all the sheets except one.

2. Make any changes that you want to make, which can include column widths, named styles, page setup options, and many settings available in the Excel Options dialog box.

3. When your workbook is set up to your liking, choose File ⇨ Save As.

4. In the Save As dialog box, select Template (*.xltx) from the Save As Type list.

5. Enter sheet.xltx for the filename.

6. Save the file in your \XLStart folder (*not* in your \Templates folder).

7. Close the file.

8. Close and restart Excel.

After performing these steps, all new worksheets that you insert by using any of these methods will be formatted like your `sheet.xltx` template:

- Click the Insert Worksheet button (next to the last sheet tab).
- Choose Home ⇨ Cells ⇨ Insert ⇨ Insert Sheet.
- Press Shift+F11.
- Right-click a sheet tab, choose Insert from the shortcut menu, and choose the Worksheet icon in the Insert dialog box.

Editing your templates

After you create your `book.xltx` or `sheet.xltx` templates, you may discover that you need to change them. You can open the template files and edit them just like any other workbook. After you make your changes, save the file to its original location, and close it.

Resetting the default workbook and worksheet settings

If you create a `book.xltx` or `sheet.xltx` file and then decide that you would rather use the standard default settings, simply delete the `book.xltx` or `sheet.xltx` template file — depending on whether you want to use the standard workbook or worksheet defaults — from the XLStart folder. Excel then uses its built-in default settings for new workbooks or worksheets.

Tip
You can also rename or move the template files if you'd like to keep them for future use. ■

Creating custom templates

The `book.xltx` and `sheet.xltx` templates discussed in the preceding section are two special types of templates that determine default settings for new workbooks and new worksheets. This section discusses other types of templates, referred to as *workbook templates,* which are simply workbooks that you set up as the basis for new workbooks or worksheets.

Creating a workbook template can eliminate repeating work. Assume that you create a monthly sales report that consists of your company's sales by region, plus several summary calculations and charts. You can create a template file that consists of everything except the input values. Then, when it's time to create your report, you can open a workbook based on the template, fill in the blanks, and be finished.

Note

You could, of course, just use the previous month's workbook and save it with a different name. This is prone to errors, however, because you easily can forget to use the Save As command and accidentally overwrite the previous month's file. Another option is to use File ⇨ New, and choose the New from Existing option in the Available Templates screen. This command creates a new workbook from an existing one, but gives a different name to ensure that the old file is not overwritten. ■

When you create a workbook that's based on a template, the default workbook name is the template name with a number appended. For example, if you create a new workbook based on a template named `Sales Report.xltx`, the workbook's default name is `Sales Report1.xlsx`. The first time that you save a workbook that is created from a template, Excel displays its Save As dialog box so that you can give the template a new name if you want to.

A *custom template* is essentially a normal workbook, and it can use any Excel feature, such as charts, formulas, and macros. Usually, a template is set up so that the user can enter values and get immediate results. In other words, most templates include everything but the data, which is entered by the user.

Note

If your template contains macros, it must be saved as an Excel Macro-Enabled Template, with an XLTM extension. ■

Locking Formula Cells in a Template File

If novices will use the template, you might consider locking all the formula cells to make sure that the formulas aren't deleted or modified. By default, all cells are locked and cannot be changed when the worksheet is protected. The following steps describe how to unlock the nonformula cells:

1. **Choose Home ⇨ Editing ⇨ Find & Select ⇨ Go to Special to display the Go To Special dialog box.**

2. **Select Constants and click OK.** This step selects all nonformula cells.

3. **Press Ctrl+1 to display the Format Cells dialog box.**

4. **In the Format Cells dialog box, click the Protection tab.**

5. **Remove the check mark from the Locked check box.**

6. **Click OK to close the Format Cells dialog box.**

7. **Choose Review ⇨ Changes ⇨ Protect Sheet to display the Protect Sheet dialog box.**

8. **Specify a password (optional) and then click OK.**

After you perform these steps, you can't modify the formula cells — unless the sheet is unprotected.

Saving your custom templates

To save a workbook as a template, choose File ⇨ Save As and select Template (*.xltx) from the Save as Type drop-down list. If the workbook contains any VBA macros, select Excel Macro-Enabled Template (*.xltm). Save the template in your Templates folder — which Excel automatically suggests — or a folder within that Templates folder.

If you later discover that you want to modify the template, choose File ⇨ Open to open and edit the template.

Ideas for creating templates

This section provides a few ideas that may spark your imagination for creating templates. The following is a partial list of the settings that you can adjust and use in your custom templates:

- **Multiple formatted worksheets:** You can, for example, create a workbook template that has two worksheets — one formatted to print in landscape mode and one formatted to print in portrait mode.
- **Style:** The best approach is to choose Home ⇨ Styles ⇨ Cell Styles and modify the attributes of the Normal style. For example, you can change the font or size, the alignment, and so on.
- **Custom number formats:** If you create number formats that you use frequently, you can store them in a template.
- **Column widths and row heights:** You may prefer that columns be wider or narrower, or you may want the rows to be taller.
- **Print settings:** Change these settings in the Page Layout tab. You can adjust the page orientation, paper size, margins, and several other attributes.
- **Header and footer:** You enter custom headers or footers in Page Layout view (choose View ⇨ Workbook Views ⇨ Page Layout).
- **Sheet settings:** These options are in the Show group on the View tab, and also on the Advanced tab of the Excel Options dialog box (in the Display Options for This Worksheet section). Options include row and column header, page break display, gridlines, and others.

You can, of course, also create complete workbooks and save them as templates. For example, if you frequently need to produce a specific report, you may want to create a template that has everything for the report except for the data you need to enter. By saving your master copy as a template, you're less likely to overwrite the original file when you save the file after entering your data.

Printing Your Work

Despite predictions of the "paperless office," reports printed on paper remain commonplace, and they will be around for a long time. Many worksheets that you develop with Excel can probably serve as printed reports. You'll find that printing from Excel is quite easy and that you can generate attractive, well-formatted reports with minimal effort. In addition, Excel has many options that provide you with a great deal of control over the printed page so that you can make your printed reports even better. These options are explained in this chapter.

Printing with One Click

If you want to print a copy of a worksheet with no fuss and bother, use the Quick Print option. One way to access this command is to choose File ⇨ Print (which displays the Print pane of Backstage View), and then click the Print button.

Issuing that command with a mouse takes three clicks, though. A slightly more efficient method is to press Ctrl+P and then click the Print button (or press Enter).

But if you like the idea of one-click printing, take a few seconds to add a new button to your Quick Access toolbar: Click the downward-pointing arrow on the right of the Quick Access toolbar and then choose Quick Print from the drop-down list. Excel adds the Quick Print icon (looks like a desktop printer) to your Quick Access toolbar.

Clicking the Quick Print button prints the current worksheet on the currently selected printer, using the default print settings. If you've changed any

IN THIS CHAPTER
One-click printing
Changing your worksheet view
Adjusting your print settings for better results
Preventing some cells from being printed
Using Custom Views

of the default print settings (by using the Page Layout tab), Excel uses the new settings; otherwise, it uses the following default settings:

- Prints the active worksheet (or all selected worksheets), including any embedded charts or objects
- Prints one copy
- Prints the entire active worksheet
- Prints in portrait mode
- Doesn't scale the printed output
- Uses letter-size paper with .75" margins for the top and bottom and .70" margins for the left and right margins (for the U.S. version)
- Prints with no headers or footers
- Doesn't print cell comments
- Prints with no cell gridlines
- For wide worksheets that span multiple pages, prints down and then over

When you print a worksheet, Excel prints only the active area of the worksheet. In other words, it won't print all 17 billion cells — just those that have data in them. If the worksheet contains any embedded charts or other graphic objects (such as SmartArt or Shapes), they're also printed.

Tip

To quickly determine the active area of the worksheet, press Ctrl+End to move to the last active cell in the worksheet. The active area is between cell A1 and the last active cell. You may notice that Ctrl+End isn't always accurate. For example, if you've deleted some rows, Ctrl+End will take you to the last row that you deleted. However, when the sheet is printed, the active area is reset, so the empty rows are not printed. ∎

Changing Your Page View

Page Layout view, a feature introduced in Excel 2007, shows your worksheet divided up into pages. In other words, you can visualize your printed output while you work.

Page Layout view is one of three worksheet views, which are controlled by the three icons on the right side of the status bar. You could also use the commands in the View ➪ Workbook Views group on the Ribbon to switch views. The three view options are

- **Normal:** The default view of the worksheet. This view may or may not show page breaks.
- **Page Layout:** Shows individual pages.
- **Page Break Preview:** Allows you to manually adjust page breaks.

Using Print Preview

When you choose File ➪ Print, Backstage View displays a preview of your printed output, exactly as it will be printed. Initially, Excel displays the first page of your printed output. To view subsequent pages, use the page controls along the bottom of the preview pane (or, use the vertical scrollbar along the right side of the screen).

For one-click access to the Print Preview display, add a button to your Quick Access toolbar: Click the downward-pointing arrow on the right of the Quick Access toolbar, and choose Print Preview from the drop-down list. Excel adds the Print Preview icon (a dog-eared piece of paper with a magnifying glass) to your Quick Access toolbar.

The Print Preview window has a few other commands (at the bottom) that you can use while previewing your output. For multipage printout, use the page number controls to quickly jump to a particular page. The Show Margins button toggles the display of margins, and the Zoom to Page ensures that a complete page is displayed.

When the Show Margins option is in effect, Excel adds markers to the preview that indicate column borders and margins. You can drag the column or margin markers to make changes that appear onscreen. Changes that you make to column widths in preview mode are also made in the actual worksheet.

Print Preview is certainly useful, but you may prefer to use Page Layout view to preview your output (see "Changing Your Page View").

Just click one of the icons to change the view. You can also use the Zoom slider to change the magnification from 10% (a very tiny, bird's-eye view) to 400% (very large, for showing fine detail).

The following sections describe how these views can help with printing.

Normal view

Most of the time when you work in Excel, you use Normal view. Normal view can display page breaks in the worksheet. The page breaks are indicated by horizontal and vertical dotted lines. These page break lines adjust automatically if you change the page orientation, add or delete rows or columns, change row heights, change column widths, and so on. For example, if you find that your printed output is too wide to fit on a single page, you can adjust the column widths (keeping an eye on the page-break display) until the columns are narrow enough to print on one page.

Note

Page breaks aren't displayed until you print (or preview) the worksheet at least one time. Page breaks are also displayed if you set a print area by choosing Page Layout ➪ Page Setup ➪ Print Area. ■

Tip

If you'd prefer to not see the page break display in Normal view, choose FIle ⇨ Options and select the Advanced tab. Scroll down to the Display Options for This Worksheet section and remove the check mark from Show Page Breaks. This setting applies only to the active worksheet. Unfortunately, the option to turn off page break display is not on the Ribbon, and it's not even available for inclusion on the Quick Access toolbar. ■

Figure 9.1 shows a worksheet in Normal view, zoomed out to show multiple pages. Notice the dotted lines that indicate page breaks.

FIGURE 9.1

In Normal view, dotted lines indicate page breaks.

Page Layout view

Page Layout view is the ultimate print preview. Unlike the preview in Backstage View (choose File ⇨ Print), this mode is not a view-only mode. You have complete access to all Excel commands. In fact, you can use Page Layout view all the time if you like.

Figure 9.2 shows a worksheet in Page Layout view, zoomed out to show multiple pages. Notice that the page header and footer (if any) appear on each page, giving you a true preview of the printed output.

Tip

If you move the mouse to the corner of a page while in Page Layout view, you can click to hide the white space in the margins. Doing so gives you all the advantages of Page Layout view, but you can see more information onscreen because the unused margin space is hidden. ∎

In Page Layout view, the worksheet resembles printed pages.

Page Break Preview

Page Break Preview displays the worksheet and shows where the page breaks occur. Figure 9.3 shows an example. This view mode is different from Normal view mode with page breaks turned on: The key difference is that you can drag the page breaks. Unlike Page Layout view, Page Break Preview does not display headers and footers.

When you enter Page Break Preview, Excel performs the following:

- Changes the zoom factor so that you can see more of the worksheet.
- Displays the page numbers overlaid on the pages.

- Displays the current print range with a white background; nonprinting data appears with a gray background.
- Displays all page breaks as draggable dashed lines.

When you change the page breaks by dragging, Excel automatically adjusts the scaling so that the information fits on the pages, per your specifications.

Tip

In Page Break Preview, you still have access to all Excel commands. You can change the zoom factor if you find the text to be too small. ■

To exit Page Break Preview, just click one of the other View icons on the status bar.

FIGURE 9.3

Page Break Preview mode gives you a bird's-eye view of your worksheet and shows exactly where the page breaks occur.

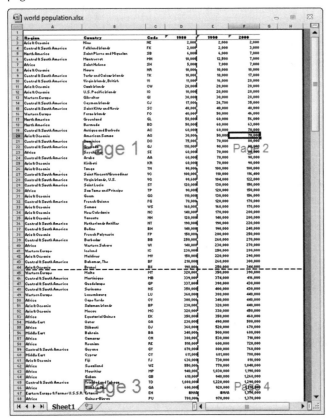

Adjusting Common Page Setup Settings

Clicking the Quick Print button (or choosing File ⇨ Print ⇨ Print) may produce acceptable results in many cases, but a little tweaking of the print settings can often improve your printed reports. You can adjust print settings in three places:

- The Print screen in Backstage View, displayed when you choose File ⇨ Print
- The Page Layout tab of the Ribbon
- The Page Setup dialog box, displayed when you click the dialog launcher in the bottom-right corner of the Page Layout ⇨ Page Setup group on the Ribbon

Table 9.1 summarizes the locations where you can make various types of print adjustments in Excel 2010.

TABLE 9.1

Where to Change Printer Settings

Setting	Print Settings Screen	Page Layout Tab of Ribbon	Page Setup Dialog Box
Number of copies	X		
Printer to use	X		
What to print	X		
Specify worksheet print area		X	X
1-sided or 2-sided	X		
Collated	X		
Orientation	X	X	X
Paper size	X	X	X
Adjust margins	X	X	X
Specify manual page breaks		X	
Specify repeating rows and/or columns			X
Set print scaling		X	X
Print or hide gridlines		X	X
Print or hide row and column headings		X	X
Specify the first page number			X
Center output on page			X
Specify header/footers and options			X
Specify how to print cell comments			X

continued

TABLE 9.1	(continued)		
Setting	Print Settings Screen	Page Layout Tab of Ribbon	Page Setup Dialog Box
Specify page order			X
Specify black-and-white output			X
Specify how to print error cells			X
Launch dialog box for printer-specific settings	X		X

Choosing your printer

To switch to a different printer, choose File ➪ Print, and use the drop-down control in the Printer section to select a different installed printer.

Note

To adjust printer settings, click the Printer Properties link to display a property box for the selected printer. The exact dialog box that you see depends on the printer. The Properties dialog box lets you adjust printer-specific settings, such as the print quality and the paper source. In most cases, you won't have to change any of these settings, but if you're having print-related problems, you may want to check the settings. ■

Specifying what you want to print

Sometimes you may want to print only a part of the worksheet rather than the entire active area. Or you may want to reprint selected pages of a report without printing all the pages. Choose File ➪ Print, and use the controls in the Settings section to specify what to print.

You have several options:

- **Active Sheets:** Prints the active sheet or sheets that you selected. (This option is the default.) You can select multiple sheets to print by pressing Ctrl and clicking the sheet tabs. If you select multiple sheets, Excel begins printing each sheet on a new page.

- **Entire Workbook:** Prints the entire workbook, including chart sheets.

- **Selection:** Prints only the range that you selected before choosing File ➪ Print.

- **Selected Table:** Appears only if the cell pointer is within a table (created with Insert ➪ Tables ➪ Table) when the Print Setting screen is displayed. If selected, only the table will be printed.

Tip

You can also choose Page Layout ➪ Page Setup ➪ Print Area ➪ Set Print Area to specify the range or ranges to print. Before you choose this command, select the range or ranges that you want to print. To clear the print area, choose Page Layout ➪ Page Setup ➪ Print Area ➪ Clear Print Area. To override the print area, select the Ignore Print Areas check box in the list of Print What options. ■

Is Printing Getting More Complicated?

If you're new to Excel, the information in Table 9.1 might be a bit overwhelming. Why does Excel provide three ways to adjust printing options? After all, before Excel 2007, Excel provided the Page Setup dialog box, plus a Print dialog box. Everything you needed was in these two dialog boxes. It was fairly simple.

With the introduction of the Ribbon in Excel 2007, though, things got a bit more complicated. Some of the more common print settings were in the Page Layout ➪ Page Setup Ribbon group, where they are easily seen. These are also the settings that determine how the Page Layout View is displayed. The Page Setup and Print dialog boxes were still used.

New Feature

In Excel 2010, the Print tab in Backstage View replaces the Print dialog box. The Page Layout ➪ Page Setup Ribbon group remains unchanged. And users still need to use the Page Setup dialog box to make some changes. ■

Table 9.1 might make printing seem more complicated than it really is. The key point to remember is this: If you can't find a way to make a particular adjustment, it's probably available from the Page Setup dialog box.

Note

The print area does not have to be a single range. You make a multiple selection before you set the print area. Each area will print on a separate page. ■

If your printed output uses multiple pages, you can select which pages to print by indicating the number of the first and last pages to print by using Pages controls in the Settings section. You can either use the spinner controls or type the page numbers in the edit boxes.

Changing page orientation

Page orientation refers to how output is printed on the page. Choose Page Layout ➪ Page Setup ➪ Orientation ➪ Portrait to print tall pages (the default) or Page Layout ➪ Page Setup ➪ Orientation ➪ Landscape to print wide pages. Landscape orientation is useful when you have a wide range that doesn't fit on a vertically oriented page.

If you change the orientation, the onscreen page breaks adjust automatically to accommodate the new paper orientation.

Page orientation settings are also available when you choose File ➪ Print.

Specifying paper size

Choose Page Layout ➪ Page Setup ➪ Size to specify the paper size you're using. The paper size settings are also available when you choose File ➪ Print.

Note

Even though Excel displays a variety of paper sizes, your printer may not be capable of using them. ■

Printing multiple copies of a report

Use the Copies control at the top of the Print tab in Backstage View to specify the number of copies to print. Just enter the number of copies you want and then click Print.

Tip

If you're printing multiple copies of a report, make certain that the Collated option is selected so that Excel prints the pages in order for each set of output. If you're printing only one page, Excel ignores the Collated setting. ■

Adjusting page margins

Margins are the unprinted areas along the sides, top, and bottom of a printed page. Excel provides four "quick margin" settings, and you can also specify the exact margin size you require. All printed pages have the same margins. You can't specify different margins for different pages.

In Page Layout view, a ruler is displayed above the column header and to the left of the row header. Use your mouse to drag the margins in the ruler. Excel adjusts the page display immediately. Use the horizontal ruler to adjust the left and right margins, and use the vertical ruler to adjust the top and bottom margins.

From the Page Layout ➪ Page Setup ➪ Margins drop-down list, you can select Normal, Wide, Narrow, or the Last custom Setting. These options are also available when you choose File ➪ Print. If none of these settings does the job, choose Custom Margins to display the Margins tab of the Page Setup dialog box, shown in Figure 9.4.

To change a margin, click the appropriate spinner (or you can enter a value directly). The margin settings that you specify in the Page Setup dialog box will then be available in the Page Layout ➪ Page Setup ➪ Margins drop-down list, referred to as Last Custom Setting.

Note

The Preview box in the center of the Page Setup dialog box is a bit deceiving because it doesn't really show you how your changes look in relation to the page; rather, it displays a darker line to let you know which margin you're adjusting. ■

In addition to the page margins, you can adjust the distance of the header from the top of the page and the distance of the footer from the bottom of the page. These settings should be less than the corresponding margin; otherwise, the header or footer may overlap with the printed output.

By default, Excel aligns the printed page at the top and left margins. If you want the output to be centered vertically or horizontally, select the appropriate check box in the Center on Page section of the Margins tab.

FIGURE 9.4

The Margins tab of the Page Setup dialog box.

Understanding page breaks

When printing lengthy reports, controlling where pages break is often important. For example, you probably don't want a row to print on a page by itself, nor do you want a table header row to be the last line on a page. Fortunately, Excel gives you precise control over page breaks.

Excel handles page breaks automatically, but sometimes you may want to force a page break — either a vertical or a horizontal one — so that the report prints the way you want. For example, if your worksheet consists of several distinct sections, you may want to print each section on a separate sheet of paper.

Inserting a page break

To insert a horizontal page-break line, move the cell pointer to the cell that will begin the new page. Just make sure that you place the pointer in column A, though; otherwise, you'll insert a vertical page break *and* a horizontal page break. For example, if you want row 14 to be the first row of a new page, select cell A14. Then choose Page Layout ➪ Page Setup ➪ Breaks ➪ Insert Page Break.

Note

Page breaks are visualized differently, depending on which view mode you're using. See "Changing Your Page View," earlier in this chapter. ■

To insert a vertical page-break line, move the cell pointer to the cell that will begin the new page. In this case, though, make sure to place the pointer in row 1. Choose Page Layout ➪ Page Setup ➪ Breaks ➪ Insert Page Break to create the page break.

Removing manual page breaks

To remove a page break you've added, move the cell pointer to the first row beneath (or the first column to the right) of the manual page break and then choose Page Layout ➪ Page Setup ➪ Breaks ➪ Remove Page Break.

To remove all manual page breaks in the worksheet, choose Page Layout ➪ Page Setup ➪ Breaks ➪ Reset All Page Breaks.

Printing row and column titles

If your worksheet is set up with titles in the first row and descriptive names in the first column, it can be difficult to identify data that appears on printed pages where those titles do not appear. To resolve this problem, you can choose to print selected rows or columns as titles on each page of the printout.

Cross-Reference

Row and column titles serve pretty much the same purpose on a printout as frozen panes do in navigating within a worksheet. See Chapter 3 for more information on freezing panes. Keep in mind, however, that these features are independent of each other. In other words, freezing panes does not affect the printed output. ■

Caution

Don't confuse print titles with headers; these are two different concepts. Headers appear at the top of each page and contain information, such as the worksheet name, date, or page number. Row and column titles describe the data being printed, such as field names in a database table or list. ■

You can specify particular rows to repeat at the top of every printed page or particular columns to repeat at the left of every printed page. To do so, choose Page Layout ➪ Page Setup ➪ Print Titles. Excel displays the Sheet tab of the Page Setup dialog box, shown in Figure 9.5.

Activate the appropriate box (either Rows To Repeat At Top or Columns To Repeat At Left) and then select the rows or columns in the worksheet. Or you can enter these references manually. For example, to specify rows 1 and 2 as repeating rows, enter **1:2**.

Note

When you specify row and column titles and use Page Layout view, these titles will repeat on every page (just as when the document is printed). However, the cells used in the title can be selected only on the page in which they first appear. ■

FIGURE 9.5

Use the Sheet tab of the Page Setup dialog box to specify rows or columns that will appear on each printed page.

Scaling printed output

In some cases, you may need to force your printed output to fit on a specific number of pages. You can do so by enlarging or reducing the size. To enter a scaling factor, choose Page Layout ⇨ Scale to Fit ⇨ Scale. You can scale the output from 10% up to 400%. To return to normal scaling, enter **100%**.

To force Excel to print using a specific number of pages, choose Page Layout ⇨ Scale to Fit ⇨ Width and Page Layout ⇨ Scale to Fit ⇨ Height. When you change either one of these settings, the corresponding scale factor is displayed in the Scale control.

Caution
Excel doesn't care about legibility, however. It will gladly scale your output to be so small that no one can read it. ■

Printing cell gridlines

Typically, cell gridlines aren't printed. If you want your printout to include the gridlines, choose Page Layout ⇨ Sheet Options ⇨ Gridlines ⇨ Print.

Alternatively, you can insert borders around some cells to simulate gridlines. See Chapter 6 for information about borders.

Inserting a Watermark

A *watermark* is an image (or text) that appears on each printed page. A watermark can be a faint company logo, or a word such as DRAFT. Excel doesn't have an official command to print a watermark, but you can add a watermark by inserting a picture in the page header or footer. Here's how:

1. **Locate an image on your hard drive that you want to use for the watermark.**

2. **Choose View ⇨ Workbook Views ⇨ Page Layout View.**

3. **Click the center section of the header.**

4. **Choose Header & Footer Tools ⇨ Header & Footer Elements ⇨ Picture.**

5. **Using the Insert Picture dialog box, locate the image from Step 1.**

6. **Click outside the header to see your image.**

7. **To center the image in the middle of the page, click the center section of the header and add some carriage returns before the** `&[Picture]` **code.** You'll need to experiment to determine the number of carriage returns required to push the image into the body of the document.

8. **If you need to adjust the image (for example, make it lighter), click the center section of the header and then choose Header & Footer Tools ⇨ Header & Footer Elements ⇨ Format Picture. Use the Image controls in the Picture tab of the Format Picture dialog box to adjust the image.** You may need to experiment with the settings to make sure that the worksheet text is legible.

The accompanying figure shows an example of a header image (a globe) used as a watermark. You can do a similar thing with text, of course.

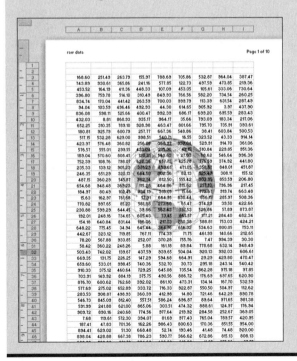

Printing row and column headers

By default, row and column headers for a worksheet are not printed. If you want your printout to include these items, choose Page Layout ⇨ Sheet Options ⇨ Headings ⇨ Print.

Using a background image

Would you like to have a background image on your printouts? Unfortunately, you can't. You may have noticed the Page Layout ⇨ Page Setup ⇨ Background command. This button displays a dialog box that lets you select an image to display as a background. Placing this control among the other print-related commands is very misleading. Background images placed on a worksheet are never printed.

Tip

In lieu of a true background image, you can insert a Shape, WordArt, or a picture on your worksheet and then adjust its transparency. Then copy the image to all printed pages. Alternatively, you can insert an object in a page header or footer. See the sidebar titled, "Inserting a Watermark." ■

Adding a Header or Footer to Your Reports

A *header* is information that appears at the top of each printed page. A *footer* is information that appears at the bottom of each printed page. By default, new workbooks do not have headers or footers.

You can specify headers and footers by using the Header/Footer tab of the Page Setup dialog box. This task is much easier if you switch to Page Layout view, though, where you can click the section labeled Click to Add Header or Click to Add Footer.

Note

If you're working in Normal view, you can choose Insert ⇨ Text ⇨ Header & Footer. Excel switches to Page Layout view and activates the center section of the page header. ■

You can then type the information and apply any type of formatting you like. Note that headers and footers consist of three sections: left, center, and right. For example, you can create a header that prints your name at the left margin, the worksheet name centered in the header, and the page number at the right margin.

Tip

If you would like a consistent header or footer for all your documents, create a `book.xlt` with your headers or footers specified. A `book.xlt` template is used as the basis for new workbooks. See Chapter 8 for details. ■

When you activate the header or footer section in Page Layout view, the Ribbon displays a new contextual tab: Header & Footer Tools ⇨ Design. Use the controls on this tab to work with headers and footers.

Selecting a predefined header or footer

You can choose from a number of predefined headers or footers by using either of the two drop-down lists in the Header & Footer Tools ⇨ Design ⇨ Header & Footer group. Notice that some items in these lists consist of multiple parts, separated by a comma. Each part goes into one of the three header or footer sections (left, center, or right). Figure 9.6 shows an example of a header that uses all three sections.

FIGURE 9.6

This three-part header is one of Excel's predefined headers.

Understanding header and footer element codes

When a header or footer section is activated, you can type whatever text you like into the section. Or, to insert variable information, you can insert any of several element codes by clicking a button in the Header & Footer Tools ⇨ Design ⇨ Header & Footer Elements group. Each button inserts a code into the selected section. For example, to insert the current date, click the Current Date button. Table 9.2 lists the buttons and their functions.

TABLE 9.2

Header & Footer Buttons and Their Functions

Button	Code	Function
Page Number	&[Page]	Displays the page number
Number of Pages	&[Pages]	Displays the total number of pages to be printed
Current Date	&[Date]	Displays the current date
Current Time	&[Time]	Displays the current time

Button	Code	Function
File Path	&[Path]&[File]	Displays the workbook's complete path and filename
File Name	&[File]	Displays the workbook name
Sheet Name	&[Tab]	Displays the sheet's name
Picture	Not applicable	Enables you to add a picture
Format Picture	Not applicable	Enables you to change an added picture's settings

You can combine text and codes and insert as many codes as you like into each section.

Note

If the text that you enter uses an ampersand (&), you must enter the ampersand twice (because Excel uses an ampersand to signal a code). For example, to enter the text Research & Development into a section of a header or footer, enter Research && Development. ∎

You can also use different fonts and sizes in your headers and footers. Just select the text that you want to change and then use the formatting tools in the Home ➪ Font group. Or use the controls on the Mini toolbar, which appears automatically when you select the text. If you don't change the font, Excel uses the font defined for the Normal style.

Tip

You can use as many lines as you like. Press Enter to force a line break for multiline headers or footers. If you use multiline headers or footers, you may need to adjust the top or bottom margin so the text won't overlap with the worksheet data. See "Adjusting the page margins," earlier in this chapter. ∎

Unfortunately, you can't print the contents of a specific cell in a header or footer. For example, you may want Excel to use the contents of cell A1 as part of a header. To do so, you need to enter the cell's contents manually — or write a VBA macro to perform this operation before the sheet is printed.

Other header and footer options

When a header or footer is selected in Page Layout view, the Header & Footer ➪ Design ➪ Options group contains controls that let you specify other options:

- **Different First Page:** If checked, you can specify a different header/footer for the first printed page.

- **Different Odd & Even Pages:** If checked, you can specify a different header/footer for odd and even pages.

- **Scale with Document:** If checked, the font size in the header and footer will be sized accordingly if the document is scaled when printed. This option is enabled, by default.

- **Align with Page Margins:** If checked, the left header and footer will be aligned with the left margin, and the right header and footer will be aligned with the right margin. This option is enabled, by default.

Copying Page Setup Settings across Sheets

Each Excel worksheet has its own print setup options (orientation, margins, headers and footers, and so on). These options are specified in the Page Setup group of the Page Layout tab.

When you add a new sheet to a workbook, it contains the default page setup settings. Here's an easy way to transfer the settings from one worksheet to additional worksheets:

1. **Activate the sheet that contains the desired setup information.** This is the source sheet.

2. **Select the target sheets.** Ctrl-click the sheet tabs of the sheets you want to update with the settings from the source sheet.

3. **Click the dialog box launcher in the lower-right corner of the Page Layout ⇨ Page Setup group.**

4. **When the Page Setup dialog box appears, click OK to close it.**

5. **Ungroup the sheets by right-clicking any selected sheet and choosing Ungroup Sheets from the shortcut menu.** Because multiple sheets are selected when you close the Page Setup dialog box, the settings of the source sheet will be transferred to all target sheets.

Note
Two settings located on the Sheet tab of the Page Setup dialog box are not transferred: Print Area and Print Titles. In addition, pictures in the header or footer are not transferred. ■

Preventing Certain Cells from Being Printed

If your worksheet contains confidential information, you may want to print the worksheet but not the confidential parts. You can use several techniques to prevent certain parts of a worksheet from printing:

- **Hide rows or columns.** When you hide rows or columns, the hidden rows or columns aren't printed. Use the Home ⇨ Cells ⇨ Format drop-down list to hide the selected rows or columns.

- **Hide cells or ranges.**
  - You can hide cells or ranges by making the text color the same color as the background color. Be aware, however, that this method may not work for all printers.
  - You can hide cells by using a custom number format that consists of three semicolons (; ; ;). See Chapter 24 for more information about using custom number formats.

- **Mask an area.** You can mask a confidential area of a worksheet by covering it with a rectangle Shape. Choose Insert ⇨ Illustrations ⇨ Shapes and click the Rectangle Shape. You'll probably want to adjust the fill color to match the cell background and remove the border.

If you find that you must regularly hide data before you print certain reports, consider using the Custom Views feature, discussed later in this chapter (see "Creating Custom Views of Your Worksheet"). This feature allows you to create a named view that doesn't show the confidential information.

Preventing Objects from Being Printed

To prevent objects on the worksheet (such as charts, Shapes, and SmartArt) from being printed, you need to access the Properties tab of the object's Format dialog box (see Figure 9.7):

1. **Right-click the object and choose Format *xxxx* from the shortcut menu.** (*xxxx* varies, depending on the object.)
2. **In the Format dialog box that opens for the object, click the Properties tab.**
3. **Remove the check mark for Print Object.**

Note

For a chart, you must right-click the chart's Chart Area (the background of the chart). Or, double-click the chart's border to display the Format Chart Area dialog box. Then click the Properties tab and remove the check mark from Print Object. ■

FIGURE 9.7

Use the Properties tab of the object's Format dialog box to prevent objects from printing.

Creating Custom Views of Your Worksheet

If you need to create several different printed reports from the same Excel workbook, setting up the specific settings for each report can be a tedious job. For example, you may need to print a full report in landscape mode for your boss. Another department may require a simplified report using the same data, but with some hidden columns in portrait mode. You can simplify the process by creating custom named views of your worksheets that include the proper settings for each report.

The Custom Views feature enables you to give names to various views of your worksheet, and you can quickly switch among these named views. A *view* includes settings for the following:

- Print settings, as specified in the Page Layout ⇨ Page Setup, Page Layout ⇨ Scale to Fit, and Page ⇨ Page Setup ⇨ Sheet Options groups
- Hidden rows and columns
- The worksheet view (Normal, Page Layout, Page Break preview)
- Selected cells and ranges
- The active cell
- The zoom factor
- Window sizes and positions
- Frozen panes

If you find that you're constantly fiddling with these settings before printing and then changing them back, using named views can save you lots of effort.

Caution

Unfortunately, the Custom Views feature does not work if the workbook (not just the worksheet) contains at least one table. When a workbook that contains a table is active, the Custom View command is disabled. This limitation severely limits the usefulness of the Custom Views feature. ∎

To create a named view

1. **Set up the view settings the way you want them.** For example, hide some columns.
2. **Choose View ⇨ Workbook Views ⇨ Custom Views to display the Custom Views dialog box.**
3. **Click the Add button and provide a descriptive name in the Add View dialog box that appears (see Figure 9.8).** You can also specify what to include in the view by using the two check boxes. For example, if you don't want the view to include print settings, remove the check mark from Print Settings.
4. **Click OK to save the named view.**

FIGURE 9.8

Use the Add View dialog box to create a named view.

Then, when you're ready to print, open the Custom Views dialog box to see all named views. To select a particular view, just select it from the list and click the Show button. To delete a named view from the list, click the Delete button.

Part II

Working with Formulas and Functions

Formulas and worksheet functions are essential to manipulating data and obtaining useful information from your Excel workbooks. The chapters in this part present a wide variety of formula examples that use many Excel functions. Two of the chapters are devoted to array formulas. These chapters are intended primarily for advanced users who need to perform calculations that may otherwise be impossible.

IN THIS PART

Chapter 10
Introducing Formulas and Functions

Chapter 11
Creating Formulas That Manipulate Text

Chapter 12
Working with Dates and Times

Chapter 13
Creating Formulas That Count and Sum

Chapter 14
Creating Formulas That Look Up Values

Chapter 15
Creating Formulas for Financial Applications

Chapter 16
Introducing Array Formulas

Chapter 17
Performing Magic with Array Formulas

Introducing Formulas and Functions

Formulas are what make a spreadsheet program so useful. If it weren't for formulas, a spreadsheet would simply be a glorified word-processing document that has great support for tabular information. You use formulas in your Excel worksheets to calculate results from the data stored in the worksheet. When data changes, the formulas calculate updated results with no extra effort on your part. This chapter introduces formulas and functions and helps you get up to speed with this important element.

Understanding Formula Basics

A *formula* consists of special code entered into a cell. It performs a calculation of some type and returns a result, which is displayed in the cell. Formulas use a variety of operators and worksheet functions to work with values and text. The values and text used in formulas can be located in other cells, which makes changing data easy and gives worksheets their dynamic nature. For example, you can see multiple scenarios quickly by changing the data in a worksheet and letting your formulas do the work.

A formula can consist of any of these elements:

- Mathematical operators, such as + (for addition) and * (for multiplication)
- Cell references (including named cells and ranges)
- Values or text
- Worksheet functions (such as SUM or AVERAGE)

IN THIS CHAPTER

Understanding formula basics

Entering formulas and functions into your worksheets

Understanding how to use references in formulas

Correcting common formula errors

Using advanced naming techniques

Tips for working with formulas

Note

When you're working with a table, a feature introduced in Excel 2007 enables you to create formulas that use column names from the table — which can make your formulas much easier to read. I discuss table formulas later in this chapter. (See "Using Formulas In Tables.") ∎

After you enter a formula, the cell displays the calculated result of the formula. The formula itself appears in the Formula bar when you select the cell, however.

Here are a few examples of formulas:

`=150*.05`	Multiplies 150 times 0.05. This formula uses only values, and it always returns the same result. You could just enter the value 7.5 into the cell.
`=A1+A2`	Adds the values in cells A1 and A2.
`=Income-Expenses`	Subtracts the value in the cell named `Expenses` from the value in the cell named `Income`.
`=SUM(A1:A12)`	Adds the values in the range A1:A12.
`=A1=C12`	Compares cell A1 with cell C12. If the cells are identical, the formula returns `TRUE`; otherwise, it returns `FALSE`.

Tip

Formulas always begin with an equal sign so that Excel can distinguish them from text. ∎

Using operators in formulas

Excel lets you use a variety of operators in your formulas. *Operators* are symbols that indicate what mathematical operation you want the formula to perform. Table 10.1 lists the operators that Excel recognizes. In addition to these, Excel has many built-in functions that enable you to perform additional calculations.

TABLE 10.1

Operators Used in Formulas

Operator	Name
+	Addition
−	Subtraction
*	Multiplication
/	Division
^	Exponentiation
&	Concatenation

Operator	Name
=	Logical comparison (equal to)
>	Logical comparison (greater than)
<	Logical comparison (less than)
>=	Logical comparison (greater than or equal to)
<=	Logical comparison (less than or equal to)
<>	Logical comparison (not equal to)

You can, of course, use as many operators as you need to perform the desired calculation.

Here are some examples of formulas that use various operators.

Formula	What It Does
="Part-"&"23A"	Joins (concatenates) the two text strings to produce Part-23A.
=A1&A2	Concatenates the contents of cell A1 with cell A2. Concatenation works with values as well as text. If cell A1 contains 123 and cell A2 contains 456, this formula would return the text 123456.
=6^3	Raises 6 to the third power (216).
=216^(1/3)	Raises 216 to the 1/3 power. This is mathematically equivalent to calculating the cube root of 216, which is 6.
=A1<A2	Returns TRUE if the value in cell A1 is less than the value in cell A2. Otherwise, it returns FALSE. Logical-comparison operators also work with text. If A1 contains Bill and A2 contains Julia, the formula would return TRUE because Bill comes before Julia in alphabetical order.
=A1<=A2	Returns TRUE if the value in cell A1 is less than or equal to the value in cell A2. Otherwise, it returns FALSE.
=A1<>A2	Returns TRUE if the value in cell A1 isn't equal to the value in cell A2. Otherwise, it returns FALSE.

Understanding operator precedence in formulas

When Excel calculates the value of a formula, it uses certain rules to determine the order in which the various parts of the formula are calculated. You need to understand these rules if you want your formulas to produce the desired results.

Table 10.2 lists the Excel operator precedence. This table shows that exponentiation has the highest precedence (performed first) and logical comparisons have the lowest precedence (performed last).

TABLE 10.2

Operator Precedence in Excel Formulas

Symbol	Operator	Precedence
^	Exponentiation	1
*	Multiplication	2
/	Division	2
+	Addition	3
−	Subtraction	3
&	Concatenation	4
=	Equal to	5
<	Less than	5
>	Greater than	5

You can use parentheses to override the Excel's built-in order of precedence. Expressions within parentheses are always evaluated first. For example, the following formula uses parentheses to control the order in which the calculations occur. In this case, cell B3 is subtracted from cell B2, and the result is multiplied by cell B4:

```
=(B2-B3)*B4
```

If you enter the formula without the parentheses, Excel computes a different answer. Because multiplication has a higher precedence, cell B3 is multiplied by cell B4. Then this result is subtracted from cell B2, which isn't what was intended.

The formula without parentheses looks like this:

```
=B2-B3*B4
```

It's a good idea to use parentheses even when they aren't strictly necessary. Doing so helps to clarify what the formula is intended to do. For example, the following formula makes it perfectly clear that B3 should be multiplied by B4, and the result subtracted from cell B2. Without the parentheses, you would need to remember Excel's order of precedence.

```
=B2-(B3*B4)
```

You can also *nest* parentheses within formulas — that is, put them inside other parentheses. If you do so, Excel evaluates the most deeply nested expressions first — and then works its way out. Here's an example of a formula that uses nested parentheses:

```
=((B2*C2)+(B3*C3)+(B4*C4))*B6
```

This formula has four sets of parentheses — three sets are nested inside the fourth set. Excel evaluates each nested set of parentheses and then sums the three results. This result is then multiplied by the value in cell B6.

Although the preceding formula uses four sets of parentheses, only the outer set is really necessary. If you understand operator precedence, it should be clear that you can rewrite this formula as:

```
=(B2*C2+B3*C3+B4*C4)*B6
```

But most would agree that using the extra parentheses makes the calculation much clearer.

Every left parenthesis, of course, must have a matching right parenthesis. If you have many levels of nested parentheses, keeping them straight can sometimes be difficult. If the parentheses don't match, Excel displays a message explaining the problem — and won't let you enter the formula.

Caution

In some cases, if your formula contains mismatched parentheses, Excel may propose a correction to your formula. Figure 10.1 shows an example of the Formula AutoCorrect feature. You may be tempted simply to accept the proposed correction, but be careful — in many cases, the proposed formula, although syntactically correct, isn't the formula you intended, and it will produce an incorrect result. ∎

FIGURE 10.1

The Excel Formula AutoCorrect feature sometimes suggests a syntactically correct formula, but not the formula you had in mind.

Tip

Excel lends a hand in helping you match parentheses. When the insertion point moves over a parenthesis while you're editing a cell, Excel momentarily makes the parenthesis character bold and displays it in a different color — and does the same with its matching parenthesis. ∎

Using functions in your formulas

Many formulas you create use worksheet functions. These functions enable you to greatly enhance the power of your formulas and perform calculations that are difficult (or even impossible) if you use only the operators discussed previously. For example, you can use the TAN function to calculate the tangent of an angle. You can't do this complicated calculation by using the mathematical operators alone.

Examples of formulas that use functions

A worksheet function can simplify a formula significantly.

Here's an example. To calculate the average of the values in 10 cells (A1:A10) without using a function, you'd have to construct a formula like this:

```
=(A1+A2+A3+A4+A5+A6+A7+A8+A9+A10)/10
```

Not very pretty, is it? Even worse, you would need to edit this formula if you added another cell to the range. Fortunately, you can replace this formula with a much simpler one that uses one of Excel's built-in worksheet functions, AVERAGE:

```
=AVERAGE(A1:A10)
```

The following formula demonstrates how using a function can enable you to perform calculations that are not otherwise possible. Say you need to determine the largest value in a range. A formula can't tell you the answer without using a function. Here's a formula that uses the MAX function to return the largest value in the range A1:D100:

```
=MAX(A1:D100)
```

Functions also can sometimes eliminate manual editing. Assume that you have a worksheet that contains 1,000 names in cells A1:A1000, and the names appear in all-capital letters. Your boss sees the listing and informs you that the names will be mail-merged with a form letter. All-uppercase letters is not acceptable; for example, JOHN F. SMITH must now appear as John F. Smith. You *could* spend the next several hours re-entering the list — ugh — or you could use a formula, such as the following, which uses the PROPER function to convert the text in cell A1 to the proper case:

```
=PROPER(A1)
```

Enter this formula once in cell B1 and then copy it down to the next 999 rows. Then select B1:B1000 and choose Home ⇨ Clipboard ⇨ Copy to copy the range. Next, with B1:B1000 still selected, choose Home ⇨ Clipboard ⇨ Paste Values (V) to convert the formulas to values. Delete the original column, and you've just accomplished several hours of work in less than a minute.

One last example should convince you of the power of functions. Suppose you have a worksheet that calculates sales commissions. If the salesperson sold more than $100,000 of product, the commission rate is 7.5 percent; otherwise, the commission rate is 5.0 percent. Without using a function, you would have to create two different formulas and make sure that you use the correct formula for each sales amount. A better solution is to write a formula that uses the IF function to ensure that you calculate the correct commission, regardless of sales amount:

```
=IF(A1<100000,A1*5%,A1*7.5%)
```

This formula performs some simple decision-making. The formula checks the value of cell A1. If this value is less than 100,000, the formula returns cell A1 multiplied by 5 percent. Otherwise, it returns what's in cell A1, multiplied by 7.5 percent. This example uses three arguments, separated by commas. I discuss this in the upcoming section, "Function arguments."

New Functions in Excel 2010

New Feature
Excel 2010 contains more than 50 new worksheet functions. ∎

But, before you get too excited, understand that nearly all the new functions are simply improved versions of existing statistical functions. For example, you'll find five new functions that deal with the Chi Square distribution: CHISQ.DIST, CHISQ.DIST.RT, CHISQ.INV, CHISQ.INV.RT, and CHISQ.TEST. These are very specialized functions, and the average Excel user will have no need for them.

Excel 2010 offers only three new functions that might appeal to a more general audience:

- AGGREGATE: A function that calculates sums, averages, and so on, with the ability to ignore errors and/or hidden rows.

- NETWORKDAYS.INTL: An international version of the NETWORKDAYS function, which returns the number of workdays between two dates.

- WORKDAY.INTL: An international version of the WORKDAY function, which returns a date before or after a specified number of workdays.

Keep in mind that if you use any of these new functions, you can't share your workbook with someone who uses an earlier version of Excel.

Function arguments

In the preceding examples, you may have noticed that all the functions used parentheses. The information inside the parentheses is the *list of arguments*.

Functions vary in how they use arguments. Depending on what it has to do, a function may use

- No arguments
- One argument
- A fixed number of arguments
- An indeterminate number of arguments
- Optional arguments

An example of a function that doesn't use an argument is the NOW function, which returns the current date and time. Even if a function doesn't use an argument, you must still provide a set of empty parentheses, like this:

```
=NOW()
```

If a function uses more than one argument, you must separate each argument with a comma. The examples at the beginning of the chapter used cell references for arguments. Excel is quite flexible when it comes to function arguments, however. An argument can consist of a cell reference, literal values, literal text strings, expressions, and even other functions. Here are some examples of functions that use various types of arguments:

- **Cell reference:** =SUM(A1:A24)
- **Literal value:** =SQRT(121)
- **Literal text string:** =PROPER("john smith")
- **Expression:** =SQRT(183+12)
- **Other functions:** =SQRT(SUM(A1:A24))

Note

A comma is the list-separator character for the U.S. version of Excel. Some other versions may use a semicolon. The list separator is a Windows setting, which can be adjusted in the Windows Control Panel (the Regional and Language Options dialog box). ■

More about functions

All told, Excel includes more than 400 functions. And if that's not enough, you can purchase additional specialized functions from third-party suppliers — and even create your own custom functions (by using VBA) if you're so inclined.

Some users feel a bit overwhelmed by the sheer number of functions, but you'll probably find that you use only a dozen or so on a regular basis. And as you'll see, the Excel Insert Function dialog box (described later in this chapter) makes it easy to locate and insert a function, even if it's not one that you use frequently.

Cross-Reference

You'll find many examples of Excel's built-in functions in Chapters 11 through 17. Appendix A contains a complete listing of Excel's worksheet functions, with a brief description of each. Chapter 40 covers the basics of creating custom functions with VBA. ■

Entering Formulas into Your Worksheets

As I mention earlier, a formula must begin with an equal sign to inform Excel that the cell contains a formula rather than text. Excel provides two ways to enter a formula into a cell: manually or by pointing to cell references. The following sections discuss each way in detail.

Excel provides additional assistance when you create formulas by displaying a drop-down list that contains function names and range names. The items displayed in the list are determined by what you've already typed. For example, if you're entering a formula and then type the letter L, you'll see the drop-down list shown in Figure 10.2. If you type an additional letter, the list is shortened to show only the matching functions. To have Excel autocomplete an entry in that list, use the navigation keys to highlight the entry, and then press Tab. Notice that highlighting a function in the list also displays a brief description of the function. See the sidebar "Using Formula Autocomplete" for an example of how this feature works.

FIGURE 10.2

Excel displays a drop-down list when you enter a formula.

Entering formulas manually

Entering a formula manually involves, well, entering a formula manually. In a selected cell, you simply type an equal sign (=) followed by the formula. As you type, the characters appear in the cell and in the Formula bar. You can, of course, use all the normal editing keys when entering a formula.

Entering formulas by pointing

Even though you can enter formulas by typing in the entire formula, Excel provides another method of entering formulas that is generally easier, faster, and less error-prone. This method still involves some manual typing, but you can simply *point* to the cell references instead of typing their values manually. For example, to enter the formula =A1+A2 into cell A3, follow these steps:

1. **Move the cell pointer to cell A3.**

2. **Type an equal sign (=) to begin the formula.** Notice that Excel displays Enter in the status bar (bottom left of your screen).

3. **Press the up arrow twice.** As you press this key, Excel displays a faint moving border around cell A1, and the cell reference appears in cell A3 and in the Formula bar. In addition, Excel displays Point in the status bar.

4. **Type a plus sign (+).** A solid-color border replaces the faint border, and Enter reappears in the status bar.

5. **Press the up arrow again.** The moving border encompasses cell A2, and adds that cell address to the formula.

6. **Press Enter to end the formula.**

Tip

You can also point to the data cells by using your mouse. ∎

Using Formula Autocomplete

The Formula Autocomplete feature (introduced in Excel 2007) makes entering formulas easier than ever. Here's a quick walk-through that demonstrates how it works. The goal is to create a formula that uses the AGGREGATE function to calculate the average value in a range that I named TestScores. The AVERAGE function will not work in this situation because the range contains an error value.

1. **Select the cell that will hold the formula, and type an equal sign (=) to signal the start of a formula.**

2. **Type the letter A. You get a list of functions and names that begin with A (see the figure here).** This feature is not case sensitive, so you can use either uppercase or lowercase characters.

3. **Scroll through the list, or type another letter to narrow down the choices.**

4. **When AGGREGATE is highlighted, press Tab to select it.** Excel adds the opening parenthesis and displays another list that contains options for the first argument for AGGREGATE, as shown in the figure here.

5. **Select** 1 - AVERAGE **and then press Tab.** Excel inserts 1, which is the code for calculating the average.

6. **Type a comma to separate the next argument.**

7. **When Excel displays a list of items for the** AGGREGATE **function's second argument, select** 2 - Ignore Error Values **and then press Tab.**

8. **Type a comma to separate the third argument (the range of test scores).**

9. **Type a T to get a list of functions and names that begin with** *T*. **You're looking for** TestScores, **so narrow it down a bit by typing the second character (e).**

10. **Highlight** TestScores **and then press Tab.**

11. **Type a closing parenthesis and then press Enter.**

The completed formula is

```
=AGGREGATE(1,2,TestScores)
```

Formula Autocomplete includes the following items (and each type is identified by a separate icon):

- Excel built-in functions
- User-defined functions (functions defined by the user through VBA or other methods)
- Defined names (named using the Formulas ⇨ Defined Names ⇨ Define Name command)
- Enumerated arguments that use a value to represent an option (only a few functions use such arguments, and AGGREGATE is one of them)
- Table structure references (used to identify portions of a table)

Pasting range names into formulas

If your formula uses named cells or ranges, you can either type the name in place of the address, or choose the name from a list and have Excel insert the name for you automatically. Two ways to insert a name into a formula are available:

- **Select the name from the drop-down list.** To use this method, you must know at least the first character of the name. When you're entering the formula, type the first character and then select the name from the drop-down list.

- **Press F3.** This action displays the Paste Name dialog box. Select the name from the list and then click OK (or just double-click the name). Excel will enter the name into your formula. If no names are defined, pressing F3 has no effect.

Figure 10.3 shows an example. The worksheet contains two defined names: Expenses and Sales. The Paste Name dialog box is being used to insert a name (Sales) into the formula being entered in cell B10.

Cross-Reference

See Chapter 4 for information about defining names. ■

FIGURE 10.3

Use the Paste Name dialog box to quickly enter a defined name into a formula.

Inserting functions into formulas

The easiest way to enter a function into a formula is to use Formula AutoComplete (the drop-down list that Excel displays while you type a formula). To use this method, however, you must know at least the first character of the function's name.

Another way to insert a function is to use the Function Library group on the Formulas tab (see Figure 10.4). This method is especially useful if you can't remember which function you need. When entering a formula, click the function category (Financial, Logical, Text, and so on) to get a list of the functions in that category. Click the function you want, and Excel displays its Function Arguments dialog box. This is where you enter the function's arguments. In addition, you can click the Help on This Function link to learn more about the selected function.

FIGURE 10.4

You can insert a function by selecting it from one of the function categories.

Yet another way to insert a function into a formula is to use the Insert Function dialog box (see Figure 10.5). You can access this dialog box in several ways:

- Choose Formulas ➪ Function Library ➪ Insert Function.
- Use the Insert Function command, which appears at the bottom of each drop-down list in the Formulas ➪ Function Library group.
- Click the Insert Function icon, which is directly to the left of the Formula bar. This button displays fx.
- Press Shift+F3.

FIGURE 10.5

The Insert Function dialog box.

The Insert Function dialog box shows a drop-down list of function categories. Select a category, and the functions in that category are displayed in the list box. To access a function that you recently used, select Most Recently Used from the drop-down list.

If you're not sure which function you need, you can search for the appropriate function by using the Search for a Function field at the top of the dialog box.

1. **Enter your search terms and click Go.** You get a list of relevant functions. When you select a function from the Select a Function list, Excel displays the function (and its argument names) in the dialog box along with a brief description of what the function does.

2. **When you locate the function you want to use, highlight it and click OK.** Excel then displays its Function Arguments dialog box, as shown in Figure 10.6.

3. **Specify the arguments for the function.** The Function Arguments dialog box will vary, depending on the function you're inserting, and it will show one text box for each of the function's arguments. To use a cell or range reference as an argument, you can enter the address manually or click inside the argument box and then select (that is, point to) the cell or range in the sheet.

4. **After you specify all the function arguments, click OK.**

FIGURE 10.6

The Function Arguments dialog box.

Tip

Yet another way to insert a function while you're entering a formula is to use the Function List to the left of the Formula bar. When you're entering or editing a formula, the space typically occupied by the Name box displays a list of the functions you've used most recently. After you select a function from this list, Excel displays the Function Arguments dialog box. ■

Function entry tips

Here are some additional tips to keep in mind when you use the Insert Function dialog box to enter functions:

- You can use the Insert Function dialog box to insert a function into an existing formula. Just edit the formula and move the insertion point to the location at which you want to insert the function. Then open the Insert Function dialog box (using any of the methods described earlier) and select the function.

- You can also use the Function Arguments dialog box to modify the arguments for a function in an existing formula. Click the function in the Formula bar and then click the Insert Function button (the *fx* button, to the left of the Formula bar).

- If you change your mind about entering a function, click the Cancel button.

- How many boxes you see in the Function Arguments dialog box depends on the number of arguments used in the function you selected. If a function uses no arguments, you won't see any boxes. If the function uses a variable number of arguments (such as the AVERAGE function), Excel adds a new box every time you enter an optional argument.

- As you provide arguments in the Function Argument dialog box, the value of each argument is displayed to the right of each box.

- A few functions, such as INDEX, have more than one form. If you choose such a function, Excel displays another dialog box that lets you choose which form you want to use.

- As you become familiar with the functions, you can bypass the Insert Function dialog box and type the function name directly. Excel prompts you with argument names as you enter the function.

Editing Formulas

After you enter a formula, you can (of course) edit that formula. You may need to edit a formula if you make some changes to your worksheet and then have to adjust the formula to accommodate the changes. Or the formula may return an error value, in which case you have to edit the formula to correct the error.

The following are some of the ways to get into cell edit mode:

- Double-click the cell, which enables you to edit the cell contents directly in the cell.

- Press F2, which enables you to edit the cell contents directly in the cell.

- Select the cell that you want to edit, and then click in the Formula bar. This enables you to edit the cell contents in the Formula bar.

- If the cell contains a formula that returns an error, Excel will display a small triangle in the upper-left corner of the cell. Activate the cell, and you'll see a Smart Tag. Click the Smart Tag, and you can choose one of the options for correcting the error. (The options will vary according to the type of error in the cell.)

Tip

You can control whether Excel displays these formula-error–checking Smart Tags in the Formulas section of the Excel Options dialog box. To display this dialog box, choose File ➪ Options. If you remove the check mark from Enable Background Error Checking, Excel no longer displays these Smart Tags. ■

While you're editing a formula, you can select multiple characters either by dragging the mouse cursor over them or by pressing Shift while you use the navigation keys.

Tip

If you have a formula that you can't seem to edit correctly, you can convert the formula to text and tackle it again later. To convert a formula to text, just remove the initial equal sign (=). When you're ready to try again, type the initial equal sign to convert the cell contents back to a formula. ■

Using Cell References in Formulas

Most formulas you create include references to cells or ranges. These references enable your formulas to work dynamically with the data contained in those cells or ranges. For example, if your formula refers to cell A1 and you change the value contained in A1, the formula result changes to reflect the new value. If you didn't use references in your formulas, you would need to edit the formulas themselves in order to change the values used in the formulas.

Using relative, absolute, and mixed references

When you use a cell (or range) reference in a formula, you can use three types of references:

- **Relative:** The row and column references can change when you copy the formula to another cell because the references are actually offsets from the current row and column. By default, Excel creates relative cell references in formulas.

- **Absolute:** The row and column references do not change when you copy the formula because the reference is to an actual cell address. An absolute reference uses two dollar signs in its address: one for the column letter and one for the row number (for example, $A$5).

- **Mixed:** Either the row or column reference is relative, and the other is absolute. Only one of the address parts is absolute (for example, $A4 or A$4).

The type of cell reference is important only if you plan to copy the formula to other cells. The following examples illustrate this point.

Figure 10.7 shows a simple worksheet. The formula in cell D2, which multiplies the quantity by the price, is

    =B2*C2

This formula uses relative cell references. Therefore, when the formula is copied to the cells below it, the references adjust in a relative manner. For example, the formula in cell D3 is

    =B3*C3

FIGURE 10.7

Copying a formula that contains relative references.

	A	B	C	D	E	F
1	Item	Quantity	Price	Total		
2	Chair	4	$125.00	$500.00		
3	Desk	4	$695.00	$2,780.00		
4	Lamp	3	$39.95	$119.85		
5						
6						
7						
8						
9						

But what if the cell references in D2 contained absolute references, like this?

    =$B$2*$C$2

In this case, copying the formula to the cells below would produce incorrect results. The formula in cell D3 would be exactly the same as the formula in cell D2.

Now I'll extend the example to calculate sales tax, which is stored in cell B7 (see Figure 10.8). In this situation, the formula in cell D2 is

    =(B2*C2)*$B$7

The quantity is multiplied by the price, and the result is multiplied by the sales-tax rate stored in cell B7. Notice that the reference to B7 is an absolute reference. When the formula in D2 is copied to the cells below it, cell D3 will contain this formula:

    =(B3*C3)*$B$7

Here, the references to cells B2 and C2 were adjusted, but the reference to cell B7 was not — which is exactly what I want because the cell that contains the sales tax never changes.

FIGURE 10.8

Formula references to the sales tax cell should be absolute.

	A	B	C	D	E	F
1	Item	Quantity	Price	Sales Tax	Total	
2	Chair	4	$125.00	$37.50		
3	Desk	4	$695.00			
4	Lamp	3	$39.95			
5						
6						
7	Sales Tax:	7.50%				
8						

Figure 10.9 demonstrates the use of mixed references. The formulas in the C3:F7 range calculate the area for various lengths and widths. The formula in cell C3 is

    =$B3*C$2

FIGURE 10.9

Using mixed cell references.

	A	B	C	D	E	F	G
1				Width			
2			1.0	1.5	2.0	2.5	
3		1.0	1.0	1.5	2.0	2.5	
4	Length	1.5	1.5	2.3	3.0	3.8	
5		2.0	2.0	3.0	4.0	5.0	
6		2.5	2.5	3.8	5.0	6.3	
7		3.0	3.0	4.5	6.0	7.5	
8							
9							

Notice that both cell references are mixed. The reference to cell B3 uses an absolute reference for the column ($B), and the reference to cell C2 uses an absolute reference for the row ($2). As a result, this formula can be copied down and across, and the calculations will be correct. For example, the formula in cell F7 is

```
=$B7*F$2
```

If C3 used either absolute or relative references, copying the formula would produce incorrect results.

On the CD

The workbook that demonstrates the various types of references is available on the companion CD-ROM. The file is named `cell references.xlsx`**.**

Note

When you cut and paste a formula (move it to another location), the cell references in the formula aren't adjusted. Again, this is usually what you want to happen. When you move a formula, you generally want it to continue to refer to the original cells. ■

Changing the types of your references

You can enter *nonrelative* references (that is, absolute or mixed) manually by inserting dollar signs in the appropriate positions of the cell address. Or you can use a handy shortcut: the F4 key. When you've entered a cell reference (by typing it or by pointing), you can press F4 repeatedly to have Excel cycle through all four reference types.

For example, if you enter **=A1** to start a formula, pressing F4 converts the cell reference to =$A$1. Pressing F4 again converts it to =A$1. Pressing it again displays =$A1. Pressing it one more time returns to the original =A1. Keep pressing F4 until Excel displays the type of reference that you want.

Note

When you name a cell or range, Excel (by default) uses an absolute reference for the name. For example, if you give the name `SalesForecast` **to B1:B12, the Refers To box in the New Name dialog box lists the reference as** `$B$1:$B$12`**. This is almost always what you want. If you copy a cell that has a named reference in its formula, the copied formula contains a reference to the original name. ■**

Referencing cells outside the worksheet

Formulas can also refer to cells in other worksheets — and the worksheets don't even have to be in the same workbook. Excel uses a special type of notation to handle these types of references.

Referencing cells in other worksheets

To use a reference to a cell in another worksheet in the same workbook, use this format:

```
SheetName!CellAddress
```

In other words, precede the cell address with the worksheet name, followed by an exclamation point. Here's an example of a formula that uses a cell on the Sheet2 worksheet:

```
=A1*Sheet2!A1
```

This formula multiplies the value in cell A1 on the current worksheet by the value in cell A1 on Sheet2.

Tip

If the worksheet name in the reference includes one or more spaces, you must enclose it in single quotation marks. (Excel does that automatically if you use the point-and-click method.) For example, here's a formula that refers to a cell on a sheet named All Depts:

```
=A1*'All Depts'! A1
```

Referencing cells in other workbooks

To refer to a cell in a different workbook, use this format:

```
=[WorkbookName]SheetName!CellAddress
```

In this case, the workbook name (in square brackets), the worksheet name, and an exclamation point precede the cell address. The following is an example of a formula that uses a cell reference in the Sheet1 worksheet in a workbook named Budget:

```
=[Budget.xlsx]Sheet1!A1
```

If the workbook name in the reference includes one or more spaces, you must enclose it (and the sheet name) in single quotation marks. For example, here's a formula that refers to a cell on Sheet1 in a workbook named Budget For 2011:

```
=A1*'[Budget For 2011.xlsx]Sheet1'!A1
```

When a formula refers to cells in a different workbook, the other workbook doesn't have to be open. If the workbook is closed, however, you must add the complete path to the reference so that Excel can find it. Here's an example:

```
=A1*'C:\My Documents\[Budget For 2011.xlsx]Sheet1'!A1
```

A linked file can also reside on another system that's accessible on your corporate network. The following formula refers to a cell in a workbook in the files directory of a computer named DataServer.

```
='\\DataServer\files\[budget.xlsx]Sheet1'!$D$7
```

Cross-Reference

See Chapter 27 for more information about linking workbooks. ∎

Tip

To create formulas that refer to cells not in the current worksheet, point to the cells rather than entering their references manually. Excel takes care of the details regarding the workbook and worksheet references. The workbook you're referencing in your formula must be open if you're going to use the pointing method. ∎

Note

If you point to a different worksheet or workbook when creating a formula, you'll notice that Excel always inserts absolute cell references. Therefore, if you plan to copy the formula to other cells, make sure that you change the cell references to relative before you copy. ∎

Using Formulas in Tables

A table is a specially designated range of cells, set up with column headers. In this section, I describe how formulas work with tables.

Cross-Reference

See Chapter 5 for an introduction to the Excel table features. ∎

Summarizing data in a table

Figure 10.10 shows a simple table with three columns. I entered the data, and then converted the range to a table by choosing Insert ➪ Tables ➪ Table. Note that I didn't define any names, but the table is named `Table1` by default.

FIGURE 10.10

A simple table with three columns of information.

	A	B	C	D	E	F
1						
2		Month	Projected	Actual		
3		Jan	4,000	3,255		
4		Feb	4,000	4,102		
5		Mar	4,000	3,982		
6		Apr	5,000	4,598		
7		May	5,000	5,873		
8		Jun	5,000	4,783		
9		Jul	5,000	5,109		
10		Aug	6,000	5,982		
11		Sep	6,000	6,201		
12		Oct	7,000	6,833		
13		Nov	8,000	7,983		
14		Dec	9,000	9,821		
15						

On the CD

This workbook is available on the companion CD-ROM. It is named `table formulas.xlsx`.

If you'd like to calculate the total projected and total actual sales, you don't even need to write a formula. Simply click a button to add a row of summary formulas to the table:

1. **Activate any cell in the table.**

2. **Place a check mark next to Table Tools ⇨ Design ⇨ Table Style Options ⇨ Total Row.**

3. **Activate a cell in the Total Row and use the drop-down list to select the type of summary formula to use (see Figure 10.11).** For example, to calculate the sum of the Actual column, select SUM from the drop-down list in cell D15. Excel creates this formula:

   `=SUBTOTAL(109,[Actual])`

For the SUBTOTAL function, 109 is an enumerated argument that represents SUM. The second argument for the SUBTOTAL function is the column name, in square brackets. Using the column name within brackets creates "structured" references within a table. (I discuss this further in the upcoming section, "Referencing data in a table.")

FIGURE 10.11

A drop-down list enables you to select a summary formula for a table column.

Note

You can toggle the Total Row display via Table Tools ⇨ Design ⇨ Table Style Options ⇨ Total Row. If you turn it off, the summary options you selected will be displayed again when you turn it back on. ■

Using formulas within a table

In many cases, you'll want to use formulas within a table to perform calculations that use other columns. For example, in the table shown in Figure 10.11, you may want a column that shows the difference between the Actual and Projected amounts. To add this formula:

1. **Activate cell E2 and type** Difference **for the column header.** Excel automatically expands the table for you to include the new column.

2. **Move to cell E3 and type an equal sign to signify the beginning of a formula.**

3. **Press the left arrow key.** Excel displays [@Actual], which is the column heading, in the Formula bar.

4. **Type a minus sign and then press left arrow twice.** Excel displays [@Projected] in your formula.

5. **Press Enter to end the formula.** Excel copies the formula to all rows in the table.

Figure 10.12 shows the table with the new column.

FIGURE 10.12

The Difference column contains a formula.

	A	B	C	D	E	F
1						
2		Month	Projected	Actual	Difference	
3		Jan	4,000	3,255	-745	
4		Feb	4,000	4,102	102	
5		Mar	4,000	3,982	-18	
6		Apr	5,000	4,598	-402	
7		May	5,000	5,873	873	
8		Jun	5,000	4,783	-217	
9		Jul	5,000	5,109	109	
10		Aug	6,000	5,982	-18	
11		Sep	6,000	6,201	201	
12		Oct	7,000	6,833	-167	
13		Nov	8,000	7,983	-17	
14		Dec	9,000	9,821	821	
15		Total	68,000	68,522		
16						
17						

Examine the table, and you find this formula for all cells in the Difference column:

```
=[@Actual]-[@Projected]
```

Although the formula was entered into the first row of the table, that's not necessary. Any time a formula is entered into an empty table column, it will automatically fill all the cells in that column. And if you need to edit the formula, Excel will automatically copy the edited formula to the other cells in the column.

Note

The "at" (@) symbol that precedes the column header represents "this row." ■

These steps use the pointing technique to create the formula. Alternatively, you could have entered the formula manually using standard cell references rather than column headers. For example, you could have entered the following formula in cell E3:

```
=D3-C3
```

If you type the cell references, Excel will still copy the formula to the other cells automatically.

One thing should be clear, however, about formulas that use the column headers instead of cell references: They are much easier to understand.

Tip

When you add a formula to a column in a table, Excel displays a SmartTag. To override the automatic column formulas, click the SmartTag and choose Stop Automatically Creating Calculated Columns. Use this option if you need different formulas for different rows within the table. ■

Referencing data in a table

Excel offers some other ways to refer to data that's contained in a table by using the table name and column headers.

Note

Remember that you don't need to create names for tables and columns. The table itself has a range name, which is provided when you create the table (for example, `Table1`), and you can refer to data within the table by using the column headers — which are not range names. ■

You can, of course, use standard cell references to refer to data in a table, but using the table name and column headers has a distinct advantage: The names adjust automatically if the table size changes by adding or deleting rows. In addition, formulas the use table names and column headers will adjust automatically if you change the name of the table or give a new name to a column.

Refer to the table (`Table1`) shown in Figure 10.11. To calculate the sum of all the data in the table, use this formula:

```
=SUM(Table1)
```

This formula will always return the sum of all the data (excluding calculated Total Row values, if any), even if rows or columns are added or deleted. And if you change the name of Table1, Excel will adjust formulas that refer to that table automatically. For example, if you renamed Table1 to AnnualData (by using the Name Manager, or by using Table Tools ⇨ Design ⇨ Properties ⇨ Table Name), the preceding formula would change to

=SUM(AnnualData)

Most of the time, you want to refer to a specific column in the table. The following formula returns the sum of the data in the Actual column:

=SUM(Table1[Actual])

Notice that the column name is enclosed in square brackets. Again, the formula adjusts automatically if you change the text in the column heading.

Even better, Excel provides some helpful assistance when you create a formula that refers to data within a table. Figure 10.13 shows the formula Autocomplete helping to create a formula by showing a list of the elements in the table. Notice that, in addition to the column headers in the table, Excel lists other table elements that you can reference: #All, #Data, #Headers, #Totals, and @ - This Row.

FIGURE 10.13

The formula Autocomplete feature is useful when creating a formula that refers to data in a table.

Correcting Common Formula Errors

Sometimes, when you enter a formula, Excel displays a value that begins with a hash mark (#). This is a signal that the formula is returning an error value. You have to correct the formula (or correct a cell that the formula references) to get rid of the error display.

Tip

If the entire cell is filled with hash-mark characters, the column isn't wide enough to display the value. You can either widen the column or change the number format of the cell. ■

In some cases, Excel won't even let you enter an erroneous formula. For example, the following formula is missing the closing parenthesis:

```
=A1*(B1+C2
```

If you attempt to enter this formula, Excel informs you that you have unmatched parentheses, and it proposes a correction. Often, the proposed correction is accurate, but you can't count on it.

Table 10.3 lists the types of error values that may appear in a cell that has a formula. Formulas may return an error value if a cell to which they refer has an error value. This is known as the *ripple effect* — a single error value can make its way into lots of other cells that contain formulas that depend on that one cell.

TABLE 10.3

Excel Error Values

Error Value	Explanation
#DIV/0!	The formula is trying to divide by zero. This also occurs when the formula attempts to divide by what's in a cell that is empty (that is, by nothing).
#NAME?	The formula uses a name that Excel doesn't recognize. This can happen if you delete a name that's used in the formula or if you have unmatched quotes when using text.
#N/A	The formula is referring (directly or indirectly) to a cell that uses the NA function to signal that data is not available. Some functions (for example, VLOOKUP) can also return #N/A.
#NULL!	The formula uses an intersection of two ranges that don't intersect. (This concept is described later in the chapter.)
#NUM!	A problem with a value exists; for example, you specified a negative number where a positive number is expected.
#REF!	The formula refers to a cell that isn't valid. This can happen if the cell has been deleted from the worksheet.
#VALUE!	The formula includes an argument or operand of the wrong type. An *operand* is a value or cell reference that a formula uses to calculate a result.

Handling circular references

When you're entering formulas, you may occasionally see a Circular Reference Warning message, shown in Figure 10.14, indicating that the formula you just entered will result in a *circular reference*. A circular reference occurs when a formula refers to its own value — either directly or indirectly. For example, you create a circular reference if you enter **=A1+A2+A3** into cell A3 because the formula in cell A3 refers to cell A3. Every time the formula in A3 is calculated, it must be calculated again because A3 has changed. The calculation could go on forever.

FIGURE 10.14

If you see this warning, you know that the formula you entered will result in a circular reference.

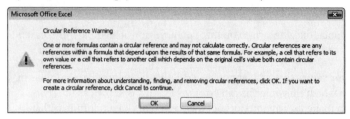

When you get the circular reference message after entering a formula, Excel gives you two options:

- Click OK, and Excel displays a Help screen that tells you more about circular references.
- Click Cancel to enter the formula as is.

Regardless of which option you choose, Excel displays a message in the left side of the status bar to remind you that a circular reference exists.

Warning

Excel won't tell you about a circular reference if the Enable Iterative Calculation setting is in effect. You can check this setting in the Formulas section of the Excel Options dialog box. If Enable Iterative Calculation is turned on, Excel performs the circular calculation exactly the number of times specified in the Maximum Iterations field (or until the value changes by less than 0.001 or whatever value is in the Maximum Change field). In a few situations, you may use a circular reference intentionally. In these cases, the Enable Iterative Calculation setting must be on. However, it's best to keep this setting turned off so that you're warned of circular references. Usually a circular reference indicates an error that you must correct. ■

Usually, a circular reference is quite obvious and easy to identify and correct. But when a circular reference is indirect (as when a formula refers to another formula that refers to yet another formula that refers back to the original formula), it may require a bit of detective work to get to the problem.

On the CD

The companion CD-ROM contains a workbook that demonstrates an intentional circular reference. This file is named circular reference.xlsx.

Specifying when formulas are calculated

You've probably noticed that Excel calculates the formulas in your worksheet immediately. If you change any cells that the formula uses, Excel displays the formula's new result with no effort on your part. All this happens when Excel's Calculation mode is set to Automatic. In Automatic Calculation mode (which is the default mode), Excel follows these rules when it calculates your worksheet:

- When you make a change — enter or edit data or formulas, for example — Excel calculates immediately those formulas that depend on new or edited data.

- If Excel is in the middle of a lengthy calculation, it temporarily suspends the calculation when you need to perform other worksheet tasks; it resumes calculating when you're finished with your other worksheet tasks.

- Formulas are evaluated in a natural sequence. In other words, if a formula in cell D12 depends on the result of a formula in cell D11, Excel calculates cell D11 before calculating D12.

Sometimes, however, you may want to control when Excel calculates formulas. For example, if you create a worksheet with thousands of complex formulas, you'll find that processing can slow to a snail's pace while Excel does its thing. In such a case, set Excel's calculation mode to Manual — which you can do by choosing Formulas ➪ Calculation ➪ Calculation Options ➪ Manual (see Figure 10.15).

You can control when Excel calculates formulas.

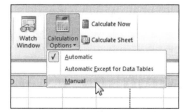

Intentional Circular References

You can sometimes use a circular reference to your advantage. For example, suppose your company has a policy of contributing 5 percent of its net profit to charity. The contribution itself, however, is considered an expense — and is therefore subtracted from the net profit figure. This produces a circular reference (see the accompanying figure).

The `Contributions` cell contains the following formula:

```
=5%*Net_Profit
```

The `Net Profit` cell contains the following formula:

```
=Gross_Income-Expenses-Contributions
```

	A	B	C	D	E	F
1	Gross Income	600,000				
2	Expenses	225,000				
3	Contributions	17,857	Should be 5% of Net Profits			
4	Net Profit	357,143	Gross Profits - Expenses - Contributions			
5						

These formulas produce a resolvable circular reference. If the Enable Iterative Calculation setting is on, Excel keeps calculating until the `Contributions` value is, indeed, 5 percent of `Net Profit`. In other words, the result becomes increasingly accurate until it converges on the final solution.

Tip

If your worksheet uses any data tables (described in Chapter 36), you may want to select the Automatically Except for Data Tables option. Large data tables calculate notoriously slowly. Note: A data table is not the same as a table created by choosing Insert ⇨ Tables ⇨ Table. ∎

When you're working in Manual Calculation mode, Excel displays `Calculate` in the status bar when you have any uncalculated formulas. You can use the following shortcut keys to recalculate the formulas:

- **F9**: Calculates the formulas in all open workbooks.
- **Shift+F9**: Calculates only the formulas in the active worksheet. Other worksheets in the same workbook aren't calculated.
- **Ctrl+Alt+F9**: Forces a complete recalculation of all formulas.

Note

Excel's Calculation mode isn't specific to a particular worksheet. When you change the Calculation mode, it affects all open workbooks, not just the active workbook. ∎

Using Advanced Naming Techniques

Using range names can make your formulas easier to understand, easier to modify, and even help prevent errors. It's much easier to deal with a meaningful name such as `AnnualSales` than with a range reference, such as AB12:AB68.

Cross-Reference

See Chapter 4 for basic information regarding working with names. ∎

Excel offers a number of advanced techniques that make using names even more useful. I discuss these techniques in the sections that follow.

Using names for constants

Many Excel users don't realize that you can give a name to an item that doesn't appear in a cell. For example, if formulas in your worksheet use a sales-tax rate, you would probably insert the tax-rate value into a cell and use this cell reference in your formulas. To make things easier, you would probably also name this cell something similar to `SalesTax`.

Here's how to provide a name for a value that doesn't appear in a cell:

1. **Choose Formulas ⇨ Defined Names ⇨ Define Name.** Excel displays the New Name dialog box.
2. **Enter the name (in this case, SalesTax) into the Name field.**

3. Select a scope in which the name will be valid (either the entire workbook or a specific worksheet).

4. Click the Refers To text box, delete its contents, and replace the old contents with a value (such as .075).

5. (Optional). Use the Comment box to provide a comment about the name.

6. Click OK to close the New Name dialog box and create the name.

You just created a name that refers to a constant rather than a cell or range. Now if you type =SalesTax into a cell that's within the scope of the name, this simple formula returns 0.075 — the constant that you defined. You also can use this constant in a formula, such as =A1*SalesTax.

Tip

A constant also can be text. For example, you can define a constant for your company's name. ∎

Note

Named constants don't appear in the Name box or in the Go To dialog box. This makes sense because these constants don't reside anywhere tangible. They do appear in the drop-down list that's displayed when you enter a formula — which is handy because you use these names in formulas. ∎

Using names for formulas

Just like you can create a named constant, you can also create named formulas. Like with named constants, named formulas don't appear in the worksheet.

You create named formulas the same way you create named constants — by using the New Name dialog box. For example, you might create a named formula that calculates the monthly interest rate from an annual rate; Figure 10.16 shows an example. In this case, the name MonthlyRate refers to the following formula:

=Sheet3!$B$1/12

FIGURE 10.16

Excel allows you to name a formula that doesn't exist in a worksheet cell.

When you use the name `MonthlyRate` in a formula, it uses the value in B1 divided by 12. Notice that the cell reference is an absolute reference.

Naming formulas gets more interesting when you use relative references rather than absolute references. When you use the pointing technique to create a formula in the Refers To field of the New Name dialog box, Excel always uses absolute cell references — which is unlike its behavior when you create a formula in a cell.

For example, activate cell B1 on `Sheet1` and create the name **Cubed** for the following formula:

```
=Sheet1!A1^3
```

In this example, the relative reference points to the cell to the left of the cell in which the name is used. Therefore, make certain that cell B1 is the active cell *before* you open the New Name dialog box; this is very important. The formula contains a relative reference; when you use this named formula in a worksheet, the cell reference is always relative to the cell that contains the formula. For example, if you enter **=Cubed** into cell D12, then cell D12 displays the contents of cell C12 raised to the third power (C12 is the cell directly to the left of D12).

Using range intersections

This section describes a concept known as *range intersections* — individual cells that two ranges have in common. Excel uses an *intersection operator* — a space character — to determine the overlapping references in two ranges. Figure 10.17 shows a simple example.

FIGURE 10.17

You can use a range-intersection formula to determine values.

	A	B	C	D	E	F	G	H
1	74	105	107	90	40			
2	176	33	32	68	130			
3	107	130	124	199	133			
4	162	62	57	106	69			
5	192	69	138	111	123			
6	167	133	141	87	63			
7								
8								
9		130						
10								
11								

The formula in cell B9 is

```
=B1:B6 A3:D3
```

This formula returns 130, the value in cell B3 — that is, the value at the intersection of the two ranges.

The intersection operator is one of three reference operators used with ranges. Table 10.4 lists these operators.

TABLE 10.4

Reference Operators for Ranges

Operator	What It Does
: (colon)	Specifies a range.
, (comma)	Specifies the union of two ranges. This operator combines multiple range references into a single reference.
(space)	Specifies the intersection of two ranges. This operator produces cells that are common to two ranges.

The real value of knowing about range intersections is apparent when you use names. Examine Figure 10.18, which shows a table of values. I selected the entire table and then used Formulas ➪ Defined Names ➪ Create from Selection to create names automatically by using the top row and left column.

FIGURE 10.18

When you use names, using a range-intersection formula to determine values is even more useful.

	A	B	C	D	E	F
1		Quarter1	Quarter2	Quarter3	Quarter4	
2	North	93	103	88	122	
3	South	43	40	45	56	
4	East	109	121	137	144	
5	West	214	198	254	291	
6						
7						
8						

Excel created the following names:

North	=Sheet1!$B$2:$E$2	Quarter1	=Sheet1!$B$2:$B$5
South	=Sheet1!$B$3:$E$3	Quarter2	=Sheet1!$C$2:$C$5
West	=Sheet1!$B$4:$E$4	Quarter3	=Sheet1!$D$2:$D$5
East	=Sheet1!$B$5:$E$5	Quarter4	=Sheet1!$E$2:$E$5

With these names defined, you can create formulas that are easy to read and use. For example, to calculate the total for Quarter 4, just use this formula:

```
=SUM(Quarter4)
```

To refer to a single cell, use the intersection operator. Move to any blank cell and enter the following formula:

    =Quarter1 West

This formula returns the value for the first quarter for the West region. In other words, it returns the value that exists where the Quarter1 range intersects with the West range. Naming ranges in this manner can help you create very readable formulas.

Applying names to existing references

When you create a name for a cell or a range, Excel doesn't automatically use the name in place of existing references in your formulas. For example, suppose you have the following formula in cell F10:

    =A1-A2

If you define a name Income for A1 and Expenses for A2, Excel won't automatically change your formula to =Income-Expenses. Replacing cell or range references with their corresponding names is fairly easy, however.

To apply names to cell references in formulas after the fact, start by selecting the range that you want to modify. Then choose Formulas ⇨ Defined Names ⇨ Define Name ⇨ Apply Names. Excel displays the Apply Names dialog box, as shown in Figure 10.19. Select the names that you want to apply by clicking them and then click OK. Excel replaces the range references with the names in the selected cells.

FIGURE 10.19

Use the Apply Names dialog box to replace cell or range references with defined names.

Tips for Working with Formulas

In this section, I offer a few additional tips and pointers relevant to formulas.

Don't hard-code values

When you create a formula, think twice before you use any specific value in the formula. For example, if your formula calculates sales tax (which is 6.5 percent), you may be tempted to enter a formula, such as the following:

```
=A1*.065
```

A better approach is to insert the sales tax rate in a cell — and use the cell reference. Or you can define the tax rate as a named constant, using the technique presented earlier in this chapter. Doing so makes modifying and maintaining your worksheet easier. For example, if the sales tax rate changed to 6.75 percent, you would have to modify every formula that used the old value. If you store the tax rate in a cell, however, you simply change that one cell — and Excel updates all the formulas.

Using the Formula bar as a calculator

If you need to perform a quick calculation, you can use the Formula bar as a calculator. For example, enter the following formula — but don't press Enter:

```
=(145*1.05)/12
```

If you press Enter, Excel enters the formula into the cell. But because this formula always returns the same result, you may prefer to store the formula's *result* rather than the formula itself. To do so, press F9 and watch the result appear in the Formula bar. Press Enter to store the result in the active cell. (This technique also works if the formula uses cell references or worksheet functions.)

Making an exact copy of a formula

When you copy a formula, Excel adjusts its cell references when you paste the formula to a different location. Sometimes, you may want to make an exact copy of the formula. One way to do this is to convert the cell references to absolute values, but this isn't always desirable. A better approach is to select the formula in Edit mode and then copy it to the Clipboard as text. You can do this in several ways. Here's a step-by-step example of how to make an exact copy of the formula in A1 and copy it to A2:

1. **Double-click A1 (or press F2) to get into Edit mode.**
2. **Drag the mouse to select the entire formula.** You can drag from left to right or from right to left. To select the entire formula with the keyboard, press Shift+Home.
3. **Choose Home ⇨ Clipboard ⇨ Copy (or press Ctrl+C).** This copies the selected text (which will become the copied formula) to the Clipboard.

4. Press Esc to leave Edit mode.

5. Select cell A2.

6. Choose Home ⇨ Clipboard ⇨ Paste (or press Ctrl+V) to paste the text into cell A2.

You also can use this technique to copy just *part* of a formula, if you want to use that part in another formula. Just select the part of the formula that you want to copy by dragging the mouse, and then use any of the available techniques to copy the selection to the Clipboard. You can then paste the text to another cell.

Formulas (or parts of formulas) copied in this manner won't have their cell references adjusted when they are pasted to a new cell. That's because the formulas are being copied as text, not as actual formulas.

Tip

You can also convert a formula to text by adding an apostrophe (') in front of the equal sign. Then, copy the formula as usual and paste it to its new location. Remove the apostrophe from the pasted formula, and it will be identical to the original formula. And don't forget to remove the apostrophe from the original formula as well. ■

Converting formulas to values

If you have a range of formulas that will always produce the same result (that is, *dead formulas*), you may want to convert them to values. If, say, range A1:A20 contains formulas that have calculated results that will never change — or that you don't want to change. For example, if you use the RANDBETWEEN function to create a set of random numbers and you don't want Excel to recalculate those random numbers each time you press Enter, you can convert the formulas to values. Just follow these steps:

1. Select A1:A20.

2. Choose Home ⇨ Clipboard ⇨ Copy (or press Ctrl+C).

3. Choose Home ⇨ Clipboard ⇨ Paste Values (V).

4. Press Esc to cancel Copy mode.

Creating Formulas That Manipulate Text

Excel is, of course, best known for its ability to crunch numbers. It's also quite versatile, however, with handling text. As you know, you can enter text for such things as row and column headings, customer names and addresses, part numbers, and just about anything else. In addition (as you may expect), you can use formulas to manipulate the text contained in cells.

This chapter contains many examples of formulas that use a variety of functions to manipulate text. Some of these formulas perform feats that you may not have thought possible.

IN THIS CHAPTER

How Excel handles text entered into cells

Excel worksheet functions that handle text

Examples of advanced text formulas

A Few Words about Text

When you enter data into a cell, Excel immediately goes to work and determines whether you're entering a formula, a number (including a date or time), or anything else. That "anything else" is considered text.

Note
You may hear the term string used instead of text. You can use these terms interchangeably. Sometimes they even appear together, as in text string. ■

A single cell can hold up to 32,000 characters — roughly equivalent to the number of characters in this chapter. But Excel is not a word processor, and I can't think of a reason why anyone would need to even come close to that number.

When a Number Isn't Treated as a Number

If you import data into Excel, you may be aware of a common problem: Sometimes the imported values are treated as text.

Depending on your error-checking settings (as specified on the Formula tab of the Excel Options dialog box), Excel may display a Smart Tag to identify numbers stored as text. If the cell contains a Smart Tag, you'll see a small rectangle in the upper-left corner of the cells. Activate the cell, and you can respond to the Smart Tag. To force the number to be treated as an actual number, select Convert to Number from the Smart Tag list of options.

If the Smart Tag isn't displayed, here's another way to convert these non-numbers to actual values. Activate any empty cell and choose Home ⇨ Clipboard ⇨ Copy (or press Ctrl+C). Then select the range that contains the values you need to fix. Choose Home ⇨ Clipboard ⇨ Paste Special. In the Paste Special dialog box, select the Add operation and then click OK. This procedure essentially adds zero to each cell — and, in the process, forces Excel to treat the non-numbers as actual values.

If you need to display lots of text in a worksheet, consider using a text box. Choose Insert ⇨ Text ⇨ Text Box, and start typing. Working with large amounts of text in a text box is easier than editing cells. In addition, you can easily move, resize, or change the dimensions of a text box. However, if you need to work with the text using formulas and functions, the text must reside in cells.

Text Functions

Excel has an excellent assortment of worksheet functions that can handle text. You can access these functions just where you'd expect: from the Text control in the Function Library group of the Formula tab.

A few other functions that are relevant to text manipulation appear in other function categories.

Cross-Reference

See Appendix A for a listing of the functions in the Text category. Or, you can peruse these functions in the Insert Function dialog box. Activate an empty cell, and choose Formulas ⇨ Function Library ⇨ Insert Function. In the Insert Function dialog box, select the Text category and scroll through the list. To find out more about a particular function, click the Help on This Function link. ∎

Most text functions are not limited to text: They can also operate with cells that contain values. You'll find that Excel is very accommodating when it comes to treating numbers as text and text as numbers.

The examples discussed in this section demonstrate some common (and useful) things you can do with text. You may need to adapt some of these examples for your own use.

Working with character codes

Every character you see on your screen has an associated code number. For Windows systems, Excel uses the standard ANSI character set. The ANSI character set consists of 255 characters, numbered (not surprisingly) from 1–255.

Figure 11.1 shows a portion of an Excel worksheet that displays all of the 255 characters. This example uses the Wingdings 3 font. (Other fonts may have different characters.)

On the CD

The companion CD-ROM includes a copy of this workbook, which also includes some simple VBA macros that enable you to display the character set for any font installed on your system. The file is named character set.xlsm.

FIGURE 11.1

The ANSI character set (for the Wingdings 3 font).

Two functions come into play when dealing with character codes: CODE and CHAR. These functions may not be very useful by themselves, but they can prove quite useful in conjunction with other functions. I discuss these functions in the following sections.

The CODE function

The Excel CODE function returns the character code for its argument. The formula that follows returns 65, the character code for uppercase *A*:

```
=CODE("A")
```

If the argument for CODE consists of more than one character, the function uses only the first character. Therefore, this formula also returns 65:

```
=CODE("Abbey Road")
```

The CHAR function

The CHAR function is essentially the opposite of the CODE function. Its argument should be a value between 1 and 255, and the function returns the corresponding character. The following formula, for example, returns the letter *A*:

```
=CHAR(65)
```

To demonstrate the opposing nature of the CODE and CHAR functions, try entering this formula:

```
=CHAR(CODE("A"))
```

This formula, which is illustrative rather than useful, returns the letter *A*. First, it converts the character to its code value (65), and then it converts this code back to the corresponding character.

Assume that cell A1 contains the letter *A* (uppercase). The following formula returns the letter *a* (lowercase):

```
=CHAR(CODE(A1)+32)
```

This formula takes advantage of the fact that the alphabetic characters all appear in alphabetical order within the character set; lowercase letters follow uppercase letters (with a few other characters tossed in between). Each lowercase letter is exactly 32 character positions higher than its corresponding uppercase letter.

Inserting Special Characters

If you need to insert special characters not found on your keyboard, you can use the Symbol dialog box (choose Insert ⇨ Symbols ⇨ Symbol). This dialog box simplifies inserting special characters (including Unicode characters) into cells. For example, you may want to display the Greek letter *pi* (π) in your worksheet. From the Symbol dialog box, select the Symbol font (see the accompanying figure). Examine the characters, locate the pi character, and click Insert. You'll see (in the Character Code area of the Symbol dialog box) that this character has a numerical code of 112.

In addition, Excel has several built-in AutoCorrect symbols. For example, if you type **(c)** followed by a space or the Enter key, Excel converts it to a copyright symbol.

To see the other symbols that you can enter this way, display the AutoCorrect dialog box. To display this dialog box, choose File ⇨ Options and select the Proofing tab in the Excel Options dialog box. Then click the AutoCorrect Options button. You can then scroll through the list to see which autocorrections are enabled (and delete those that you don't want).

If you find that Excel makes an autocorrection that you don't want, press Ctrl+Z immediately to undo the autocorrection.

Determining whether two strings are identical

You can create a simple logical formula to determine whether two cells contain the same entry. For example, use this formula to determine whether cell A1 has the same contents as cell A2:

    =A1=A2

This formula will return either TRUE or FALSE, depending on the contents of cells A1 and A2. However, Excel is a bit lax in its comparisons when text is involved. Consider the case in which A1 contains the word January (initial capitalization), and A2 contains JANUARY (all uppercase).

You'll find that the previous formula returns TRUE even though the contents of the two cells are not really the same — the comparison is not case-sensitive.

Often, you don't need to worry about the case of the text. If you need to make an exact, case-sensitive comparison, though, use the EXACT function. The following formula returns TRUE *only if* cells A1 and A2 contain *exactly* the same entry:

```
=EXACT(A1,A2)
```

When you compare text, be careful with trailing space characters, which are often difficult to identify. The following formula returns FALSE because the first string contains a trailing space:

```
=EXACT("Canada ","Canada")
```

Joining two or more cells

Excel uses an ampersand (&) as its concatenation operator. *Concatenation* is simply a fancy term that describes what happens when you join the contents of two or more cells. For example, if cell A1 contains the text Tucson and cell A2 contains the text Arizona, the following formula will return TucsonArizona:

```
=A1&A2
```

Notice that the two strings are joined together without an intervening space. To add a space between the two entries (to get Tucson Arizona), use a formula like this one:

```
=A1&" "&A2
```

Or, even better, use a comma and a space to produce Tucson, Arizona:

```
=A1&", "&A2
```

If you'd like to force the second string to be on a new line, concatenate the strings using CHAR(10), which inserts a line-break character. Also, make sure that you apply the Wrap Text format to the cell. The following example joins the text in cell A1 and the text in cell B1, with a line break in between:

```
=A1&CHAR(10)&B1
```

Tip
To apply Wrap Text formatting, select the cells and then choose Home ➪ Alignment ➪ Wrap Text. ∎

You can also concatenate characters returned by the CHAR function. The following formula returns the string Stop by concatenating four characters returned by the CHAR function:

```
=CHAR(83)&CHAR(116)&CHAR(111)&CHAR(112)
```

Here's a final example of using the & operator. In this case, the formula combines text with the result of an expression that returns the maximum value in column C:

```
="The largest value in Column C is " &MAX(C:C)
```

Note

Excel also has a CONCATENATE function, which takes up to 255 arguments. For example:

```
=CONCATENATE(A1,B1,C1,D1)
```

This function simply combines the arguments into a single string. You can use this function if you like, but using the & operator results in shorter formulas. ∎

Displaying formatted values as text

The TEXT function enables you to display a value in a specific number format. Figure 11.2 shows a simple worksheet. The formula in cell D3 is

```
="The net profit is " & B3
```

The formula in D3 doesn't display the formatted number.

	A	B	C	D
1	Gross	$354,234		
2	Expenses	$123,440		
3	Net	$230,794		The net profit is 230794
4				
5				

This formula essentially combines a text string with the contents of cell B3 and displays the result. Note, however, that the formula displays the contents of B3 as a raw value (no formatting). To improve readability, you might want to display the contents of B3 by using a Currency number format.

Note

Contrary to what you might expect, applying a number format to the cell that contains the formula has no effect. This is because the formula returns a string, not a value. ∎

Here's a revised formula that uses the TEXT function to apply formatting to the value in B3:

```
="The net profit is " & TEXT(B3," $#,##0")
```

This formula displays the text along with a nicely formatted value:

```
The net profit is $230,794
```

The second argument for the TEXT function consists of a standard Excel number format string. You can enter any valid number format code for this argument.

The preceding example uses a simple cell reference (B3). You can, of course, use an expression instead. Here's an example that combines text with a number resulting from a computation:

```
="Average Expenditure: "& TEXT(AVERAGE(A:A),"$#,##0.00")
```

This formula might return a string such as Average Expenditure: $7,794.57.

Here's another example that uses the NOW function (which returns the current date and time). The TEXT function displays the date and time, nicely formatted.

```
="Report printed on "&TEXT(NOW(),"mmmm d, yyyy at h:mm AM/PM")
```

The formula might display the following:

```
Report printed on March 22, 2010 at 3:23 PM
```

Cross-Reference
See Chapter 24 for details on Excel number formats. ∎

Displaying formatted currency values as text

The Excel DOLLAR function converts a number to text using the currency format. It takes two arguments: the number to convert, and the number of decimal places to display. The DOLLAR function uses the regional currency symbol (for example, a $).

You can sometimes use the DOLLAR function in place of the TEXT function. The TEXT function, however, is much more flexible because it doesn't limit you to a specific number format.

The following formula returns Total: $1,287.37 (the second argument for the DOLLAR function specifies the number of decimal places):

```
="Total: "&DOLLAR(1287.367, 2)
```

Note
If you're looking for a function that converts a number into spelled out text (such as "One hundred twelve and 32/100"), you won't find such a function. Well, Excel does have a function, BAHTTEXT — but it converts the number into the Thai language. The existence of this function in the English language version of Excel remains a mystery. ∎

Repeating a character or string

The REPT function repeats a text string (first argument) any number of times you specify (second argument). For example, this seasonal formula returns HoHoHo:

```
=REPT("Ho",3)
```

You can also use this function to create crude vertical dividers between cells. This example displays a squiggly line, 20 characters in length:

```
=REPT("~",20)
```

Creating a text histogram

A clever use for the REPT function is to create a simple *histogram* (or frequency-distribution chart) directly in a worksheet. Figure 11.3 shows an example of such a histogram. You'll find this type of graphical display especially useful when you need a visual summary of many values and a standard chart is unwieldy.

Cross-Reference

The Data Bars conditional formatting feature is a much better way to display a simple histogram directly in cells. See Chapter 20 for details. ■

FIGURE 11.3

Using the REPT function to create a histogram in a worksheet range.

	A	B	C	D	E
1	Month	Units Sold		Chart	
2	January	834		⊞⊞⊞⊞⊞⊞⊞⊞	
3	February	1,132		⊞⊞⊞⊞⊞⊞⊞⊞⊞⊞⊞	
4	March	1,243		⊞⊞⊞⊞⊞⊞⊞⊞⊞⊞⊞⊞	
5	April	1,094		⊞⊞⊞⊞⊞⊞⊞⊞⊞⊞	
6	May	902		⊞⊞⊞⊞⊞⊞⊞⊞⊞	
7	June	1,543		⊞⊞⊞⊞⊞⊞⊞⊞⊞⊞⊞⊞⊞⊞⊞	
8	July	1,654		⊞⊞⊞⊞⊞⊞⊞⊞⊞⊞⊞⊞⊞⊞⊞⊞	
9	August	2,123		⊞⊞⊞⊞⊞⊞⊞⊞⊞⊞⊞⊞⊞⊞⊞⊞⊞⊞⊞⊞⊞	
10	September	1,566		⊞⊞⊞⊞⊞⊞⊞⊞⊞⊞⊞⊞⊞⊞⊞	
11	October	1,434		⊞⊞⊞⊞⊞⊞⊞⊞⊞⊞⊞⊞⊞⊞	
12	November	1,321		⊞⊞⊞⊞⊞⊞⊞⊞⊞⊞⊞⊞⊞	
13	December	1,654		⊞⊞⊞⊞⊞⊞⊞⊞⊞⊞⊞⊞⊞⊞⊞⊞	
14					

The formulas in column D graphically depict the sales numbers in column B by displaying a series of characters in the Wingdings font. This example uses character code 61 (an equal sign), which appears onscreen as a small floppy disc in the Wingdings font. A formula using the REPT function determines the number of characters displayed. The formula in cell D2 is

```
=REPT("=",B2/100)
```

Assign the Wingdings font to cells D2, and then copy the formulas down the column to accommodate all the data. Depending on the numerical range of your data, you may need to change the scaling. Experiment by replacing the 100 value in the formulas. You can substitute any character you like for the equal sign character in the formula to produce a different character in the chart.

On the CD

The workbook shown in Figure 11.3 also appears on the companion CD-ROM. The file is named `text histogram.xlsx.`

Padding a number

You're probably familiar with a common security measure (frequently used on printed checks) in which numbers are padded with asterisks on the right. The following formula displays the value in cell A1, along with enough asterisks to make a total of 24 characters:

```
=(A1 & REPT("*",24-LEN(A1)))
```

If you'd prefer to pad the number with asterisks on the left instead, use this formula:

```
=REPT("*",24-LEN(A1))&A1
```

The following formula displays 12 asterisks on both sides of the number:

```
=REPT("*",12)&A1&REPT("*",12)
```

The preceding formulas are a bit deficient because they don't show any number formatting. This revised version displays the value in A1 (formatted), along with the asterisk padding on the right:

```
=(TEXT(A1,"$#,##0.00")&REPT("*",24-LEN(TEXT(A1,"$#,##0.00"))))
```

Figure 11.4 shows this formula in action.

FIGURE 11.4

Using a formula to pad a number with asterisks.

	A	B	C	D
1	$198.34	$198.34****************		
2	$9.00	$9.00*******************		
3	$0.98	$0.98*******************		
4	$1,093.00	$1,093.00***************		
5	$0.00	$0.00*******************		
6				
7				
8				

You can also pad a number by using a custom number format. To repeat the next character in that format until it fills the column width, include an asterisk (*) in the custom number format code. For example, use this number format to pad the number with dashes:

```
$#,##0.00*-
```

To pad the number with asterisks, use two asterisks in the number-format code, like this:

```
$#,##0.00**
```

Cross-Reference

See Chapter 24 for more information about custom number formats, including additional examples using the asterisk format code. ∎

Removing excess spaces and nonprinting characters

Often, data imported into an Excel worksheet contains excess spaces or strange (often unprintable) characters. Excel provides you with two functions to help whip your data into shape: TRIM and CLEAN:

- TRIM removes all leading and trailing spaces and replaces internal strings of multiple spaces by a single space.
- CLEAN removes all nonprinting characters from a string. These "garbage" characters often appear when you import certain types of data.

This example uses the TRIM function. The formula returns Fourth Quarter Earnings (with no excess spaces):

```
=TRIM("    Fourth    Quarter    Earnings    ")
```

Counting characters in a string

The LEN function takes one argument and returns the number of characters in the argument. For example, assume that the string September Sales is contained in cell A1. The following formula returns 15:

```
=LEN(A1)
```

Notice that space characters are included in the character count.

The following formula returns the total number of characters in the range A1:A3:

```
=LEN(A1)+LEN(A2)+LEN(A3)
```

Cross-Reference

You see example formulas that demonstrate how to count the number of specific characters within a string later in this chapter. Chapter 13 covers counting techniques further. ∎

Changing the case of text

Excel provides three handy functions to change the case of text:

- UPPER converts the text to ALL UPPERCASE.
- LOWER converts the text to all lowercase.
- PROPER converts the text to Proper Case (the first letter in each word is capitalized, as in a proper name).

Transforming Data with Formulas

Many of the examples in this chapter describe how to use functions to transform data in some way. For example, you can use the UPPER function to transform text into uppercase. Often, you'll want to replace the original data with the transformed data. Specifically, follow these steps:

1. **Insert a new temporary column for formulas to transform the original data.**

2. **Create your formulas in the temporary column.**

3. **Select the formula cells.**

4. **Choose Home ➪ Clipboard ➪ Copy (or press Ctrl+C).**

5. **Select the original data cells.**

6. **Choose Home ➪ Clipboard ➪ Paste ➪ Values (V).**

This procedure replaces the original data with the transformed data; then you can delete the temporary column that holds the formulas.

These functions are quite straightforward. The formula that follows, for example, converts the text in cell A1 to proper case.

```
=PROPER(A1)
```

If cell A1 contained the text MR. JOHN Q. PUBLIC, the formula would return Mr. John Q. Public.

These functions operate only on alphabetic characters; they simply ignore all other characters and return them unchanged.

These functions aren't perfect, and they sometimes produce undesired results. For example, this formula returns Don'T:

```
=PROPER("don't")
```

Apparently, the PROPER function is programmed to always capitalize the letter following an apostrophe. If the argument is "o'reilly", the function works perfectly.

Extracting characters from a string

Excel users often need to extract characters from a string. For example, you may have a list of employee names (first and last names) and need to extract the last name from each cell. Excel provides several useful functions for extracting characters:

- LEFT returns a specified number of characters from the beginning of a string.

- RIGHT returns a specified number of characters from the end of a string.

- MID returns a specified number of characters beginning at any position within a string.

The following formula returns the last 10 characters from cell A1; if A1 contains fewer than 10 characters, the formula returns all text in the cell:

```
=RIGHT(A1,10)
```

This next formula uses the MID function to return five characters from cell A1, beginning at character position 2. In other words, it returns characters 2–6.

```
=MID(A1,2,5)
```

The following example returns the text in cell A1 with only the first letter in uppercase. It uses the LEFT function to extract the first character and convert it to uppercase. This then concatenates to another string that uses the RIGHT function to extract all but the first character (converted to lowercase). Here's what it looks like:

```
=UPPER(LEFT(A1))&RIGHT(LOWER(A1),LEN(A1)-1)
```

If cell A1 contained the text FIRST QUARTER, the formula would return First quarter.

Note

This is different than the result obtained using the PROPER function. The PROPER function makes the first character in each word uppercase. ■

Replacing text with other text

In some situations, you may need a formula to replace a part of a text string with some other text. For example, you may import data that contains asterisks, and you need to convert the asterisks to some other character. You could use choose Home ➪ Editing ➪ Find & Select ➪ Replace to make the replacement. If you prefer a formula-based solution, you can take advantage of either of two functions:

- SUBSTITUTE replaces specific text in a string. Use this function when you know the character(s) to be replaced but not the position.

- REPLACE replaces text that occurs in a specific location within a string. Use this function when you know the position of the text to be replaced but not the actual text.

The following formula uses the SUBSTITUTE function to replace 2010 with 2011 in the string 2010 Budget. The formula returns 2011 Budget.

```
=SUBSTITUTE("2010 Budget","2010","2011")
```

The following formula uses the SUBSTITUTE function to remove all spaces from a string. In other words, it replaces all space characters with an empty string. The formula returns 2011OperatingBudget.

```
=SUBSTITUTE("2011 Operating Budget"," ","")
```

The following formula uses the REPLACE function to replace one character beginning at position 5 with nothing. In other words, it removes the fifth character (a hyphen) and returns Part544.

```
=REPLACE("Part-544",5,1,"")
```

Finding and searching within a string

The FIND and SEARCH functions enable you to locate the starting position of a particular substring within a string:

- FIND finds a substring within another text string and returns the starting position of the substring. You can specify the character position at which to begin searching. Use this function for case-sensitive text comparisons. Wildcard comparisons are not supported.

- SEARCH finds a substring within another text string and returns the starting position of the substring. You can specify the character position at which to begin searching. Use this function for non–case-sensitive text or when you need to use wildcard characters.

The following formula uses the FIND function and returns 7, the position of the first *m* in the string. Notice that this formula is case-sensitive.

```
=FIND("m","Big Mama Thornton",1)
```

The formula that follows, which uses the SEARCH function, returns 5, the position of the first *m* (either uppercase or lowercase):

```
=SEARCH("m","Big Mama Thornton",1)
```

You can use the following wildcard characters within the first argument for the SEARCH function:

- Question mark (?) matches any single character.
- Asterisk (*) matches any sequence of characters.

Tip
If you want to find an actual question mark or asterisk character, type a tilde (~) before the question mark or asterisk. ■

The next formula examines the text in cell A1 and returns the position of the first three-character sequence that has a hyphen in the middle of it. In other words, it looks for any character followed by a hyphen and any other character. If cell A1 contains the text Part-A90, the formula returns 4.

```
=SEARCH("?-?",A1,1)
```

Searching and replacing within a string

You can use the REPLACE function in conjunction with the SEARCH function to replace part of a text string with another string. In effect, you use the SEARCH function to find the starting location used by the REPLACE function.

For example, assume that cell A1 contains the text Annual Profit Figures. The following formula searches for the six-letter word Profit and replaces it with the word Loss:

```
=REPLACE(A1,SEARCH("Profit",A1),6,"Loss")
```

This next formula uses the SUBSTITUTE function to accomplish the same effect in a more efficient manner:

```
=SUBSTITUTE(A1,"Profit","Loss")
```

Advanced Text Formulas

The examples in this section appear more complex than the examples in the preceding section. As you can see, though, these examples can perform some very useful text manipulations. Space limitations prevent a detailed explanation of how these formulas work, but this section gives you a basic introduction.

On the CD
You can access all the examples in this section on the companion CD-ROM. The file is named text formula examples.xlsx.

Counting specific characters in a cell

This formula counts the number of Bs (uppercase only) in the string in cell A1:

```
=LEN(A1)-LEN(SUBSTITUTE(A1,"B",""))
```

This formula works by using the SUBSTITUTE function to create a new string (in memory) that has all the Bs removed. Then the length of this string is subtracted from the length of the original string. The result reveals the number of Bs in the original string.

The following formula is a bit more versatile: It counts the number of Bs (both uppercase and lowercase) in the string in cell A1. Using the UPPER function to convert the string makes this formula work with both uppercase and lowercase characters:

```
=LEN(A1)-LEN(SUBSTITUTE(UPPER(A1),"B",""))
```

Counting the occurrences of a substring in a cell

The formulas in the preceding section count the number of occurrences of a particular character in a string. The following formula works with more than one character. It returns the number of occurrences of a particular substring (contained in cell B1) within a string (contained in cell A1). The substring can consist of any number of characters.

```
=(LEN(A1)-LEN(SUBSTITUTE(A1,B1,"")))/LEN(B1)
```

For example, if cell A1 contains the text `Blonde On Blonde` and B1 contains the text `Blonde`, the formula returns 2.

The comparison is case sensitive, so if B1 contains the text `blonde`, the formula returns 0. The following formula is a modified version that performs a case-insensitive comparison by converting the characters to uppercase:

```
=(LEN(A1)-LEN(SUBSTITUTE(UPPER(A1),UPPER(B1),"")))/LEN(B1)
```

Extracting a filename from a path specification

The following formula returns the filename from a full path specification. For example, if cell A1 contains `c:\windows\important\myfile.xlsx`, the formula returns `myfile.xlsx`.

```
=MID(A1,FIND("*",SUBSTITUTE(A1,"\","*",LEN(A1)-LEN(SUBSTITUTE(A1,"\",
    ""))))+1,LEN(A1))
```

This formula assumes that the system path separator is a backslash (\). It essentially returns all text that follows the last backslash character. If cell A1 doesn't contain a backslash character, the formula returns an error.

Extracting the first word of a string

To extract the first word of a string, a formula must locate the position of the first space character and then use this information as an argument for the LEFT function. The following formula does just that:

```
=LEFT(A1,FIND(" ",A1)-1)
```

This formula returns all the text prior to the first space in cell A1. However, the formula has a slight problem: It returns an error if cell A1 consists of a single word. A slightly more complex formula that checks for the error using the IFERROR function solves that problem:

```
=IFERROR(LEFT(A1,FIND(" ",A1)-1),A1)
```

Caution
The preceding formula uses the IFERROR function, which was introduced in Excel 2007. If your workbook will be used with previous versions of Excel, use this formula:

```
=IF(ISERR(FIND(" ",A1)),A1,LEFT(A1,FIND(" ",A1)-1))
```

Extracting the last word of a string

Extracting the last word of a string is more complicated because the FIND function only works from left to right. Therefore the problem is locating the *last* space character. The formula that follows, however, solves this problem by returning the last word of a string (all text following the last space character):

```
=RIGHT(A1,LEN(A1)-FIND("*",SUBSTITUTE(A1," ","*",LEN(A1)-
    LEN(SUBSTITUTE(A1," ","")))))
```

This formula, however, has the same problem as the first formula in the preceding section: It fails if the string does not contain at least *one* space character. The following modified formula uses the IFERROR function to test for an error (that is, no spaces). If the first argument returns an error, the formula returns the complete contents of cell A1:

```
=IFERROR(RIGHT(A1,LEN(A1)-FIND("*",SUBSTITUTE(A1," ","*",LEN(A1)-
    LEN(SUBSTITUTE(A1," ","")))),A1)
```

Following is a modification that doesn't use the IFERROR function. This formula works for all versions of Excel:

```
=IF(ISERR(FIND(" ",A1)),A1,RIGHT(A1,LEN(A1)-FIND("*",SUBSTITUTE(A1,"
    ","*",LEN(A1)-LEN(SUBSTITUTE(A1," ","")))))))
```

Extracting all but the first word of a string

The following formula returns the contents of cell A1, except for the first word:

```
=RIGHT(A1,LEN(A1)-FIND(" ",A1,1))
```

If cell A1 contains 2010 Operating Budget, the formula returns Operating Budget.

The following formula, which uses the IFERROR function, returns the entire contents of cell A1 if the cell doesn't have a space character:

```
=IFERROR(RIGHT(A1,LEN(A1)-FIND(" ",A1,1)),A1)
```

A modification that works in all versions of Excel is

```
=IF(ISERR(FIND(" ",A1)),A1,RIGHT(A1,LEN(A1)-FIND(" ",A1,1)))
```

Extracting first names, middle names, and last names

Suppose you have a list consisting of people's names in a single column. You have to separate these names into three columns: one for the first name, one for the middle name or initial, and one for the last name. This task is more complicated than you may think because it must handle the situation for a missing middle initial. However, you can still do it.

Note
The task becomes a lot more complicated if the list contains names with titles (such as Mr. or Dr.) or names followed by additional details (such as Jr. or III). In fact, the following formulas will not handle these complex cases. However, they still give you a significant head start if you're willing to do a bit of manual editing to handle special cases. For a way to remove these titles, see the next section, "Removing titles from names." ■

The formulas that follow all assume that the name appears in cell A1.

You can easily construct a formula to return the first name:

```
=LEFT(A1,FIND(" ",A1)-1)
```

This formula returns the last name:

```
=RIGHT(A1,LEN(A1)-FIND("*",SUBSTITUTE(A1," ","*",LEN(A1)-
    LEN(SUBSTITUTE(A1," ","")))))
```

The next formula extracts the middle name and requires that you use the other formulas to extract the first name and the last name. It assumes that the first name is in B1 and the last name is in D1. Here's what it looks like:

```
=IF(LEN(B1&D1)+2>=LEN(A1),"",MID(A1,LEN(B1)+2,LEN(A1)-LEN(B1&D1)-2))
```

As you can see in Figure 11.5, the formulas work fairly well. There are a few problems, however, notably names that contain four "words." But, as I mentioned earlier, you can clean up these cases manually.

On the CD

This workbook, named `extract names.xlsx`, is available on the companion CD-ROM. ■

FIGURE 11.5

This worksheet uses formulas to extract the first name, last name, and middle name (or initial) from a list of names in column A.

	A	B	C	D	E
1	Full Name	First	Middle	Last	
2	John Q. Public	John	Q.	Public	
3	Lisa Smith	Lisa		Smith	
4	J. R. Robins	J.	R.	Robins	
5	Dr. Lester B. Jones	Dr.	Lester B.	Jones	
6	J. R. R. Tolkien	J.	R. R.	Tolkien	
7	Franklin H. Lee	Franklin	H.	Lee	
8	Melvina Pryce	Melvina		Pryce	
9	Suzette I. Thorson	Suzette	I.	Thorson	
10	J. Frank	J.		Frank	
11	Amanda M. Rowe	Amanda	M.	Rowe	
12	Melvin H. Hodges	Melvin	H.	Hodges	
13	Aaron E. Pacheco	Aaron	E.	Pacheco	
14	Dennis Michael Batie	Dennis	Michael	Batie	
15	Lloyd Benedict Arnold	Lloyd	Benedict	Arnold	
16	Agnes K. Saterfiel	Agnes	K.	Saterfiel	
17	Robert M. Simmons	Robert	M.	Simmons	
18	Joseph Q. Glenn	Joseph	Q.	Glenn	
19	Jeffrey George Bishop	Jeffrey	George	Bishop	
20	Henrietta D. Markowski	Henrietta	D.	Markowski	
21	William R. Gordon	William	R.	Gordon	
22	Khalilah Gorski	Khalilah		Gorski	
23	Tammy Faye. Lindsey	Tammy	Faye.	Lindsey	
24	Wilfred A. Moy	Wilfred	A.	Moy	

Splitting Text Strings without Using Formulas

In many cases, you can eliminate the use of formulas and use the Text to Columns command to parse strings into their component parts. This command is found in the Data Tools group of the Data tab. Text to Columns displays the Convert Text to Columns Wizard, which consists of a series of dialog boxes that walk you through the steps to convert a single column of data into multiple columns. Generally, you want to select the Delimited option (in Step 1) and use Space as the delimiter (in Step 2), as shown in the following figure.

Removing titles from names

You can use the formula that follows to remove three common titles (*Mr.*, *Ms.*, and *Mrs.*) from a name. For example, if cell A1 contains Mr. Fred Munster, the formula would return Fred Munster.

```
=IF(OR(LEFT(A1,2)="Mr",LEFT(A1,3)="Mrs",LEFT(A1,2)="Ms"),
    RIGHT(A1,LEN(A1) -FIND(" ",A1)),A1)
```

Creating an ordinal number

An *ordinal number* is an adjective form of a number. Examples include 1st, 2nd, 5th, 23rd, and so on.

The formula that follows displays the value in cell A1 as an ordinal number:

```
=A13&IF(OR(VALUE(RIGHT(A1,2))={11,12,13}),"th",
IF(OR(VALUE(RIGHT(A1))={1,2,3}),CHOOSE(RIGHT(A1),
"st","nd","rd"),"th"))
```

The formula is rather complex because it must determine whether the number will end in th, st, nd, or rd. This formula also uses literal arrays (enclosed in brackets), which are described in Chapter 17.

Counting the number of words in a cell

The following formula returns the number of words in cell A1:

```
=LEN(TRIM(A1))-LEN(SUBSTITUTE( (A1)," ",""))+1
```

The formula uses the TRIM function to remove excess spaces. It then uses the SUBSTITUTE function to create a new string (in memory) that has all the space characters removed. The length of this string is subtracted from the length of the original (trimmed) string to get the number of spaces. This value is then incremented by 1 to get the number of words.

Note that this formula will return 1 if the cell is empty. The following modification solves that problem:

```
=IF(LEN(A1)=0,0,LEN(TRIM(A1))-LEN(SUBSTITUTE(TRIM(A1)," ",""))+1)
```

Working with Dates and Times

IN THIS CHAPTER

An overview of using dates and times in Excel

Excel date-related functions

Excel time-related functions

Many worksheets contain dates and times in cells. For example, you might track information by date, or create a schedule based on time. Beginners often find that working with dates and times in Excel can be frustrating. To work with dates and times, you need a good understanding of how Excel handles time-based information. This chapter provides the information you need to create powerful formulas that manipulate dates and times.

Note
The dates in this chapter correspond to the U.S. English language date format: month/day/year. For example, the date 3/1/1952 refers to March 1, 1952, not January 3, 1952. I realize that this setup may seem illogical, but that's the way Americans have been trained. I trust that the non-American readers of this book can make the adjustment. ∎

How Excel Handles Dates and Times

This section presents a quick overview of how Excel deals with dates and times. It includes coverage of the Excel program's date and time serial number system, and it offers tips for entering and formatting dates and times.

Understanding date serial numbers

To Excel, a date is simply a number. More precisely, a date is a *serial number* that represents the number of days since the fictitious date of January 0, 1900.

A serial number of 1 corresponds to January 1, 1900; a serial number of 2 corresponds to January 2, 1900, and so on. This system makes it possible to deal with dates in formulas. For example, you can create a formula to calculate the number of days between two dates (just subtract one from the other).

Excel support dates from January 1, 1900, through December 31, 9999 (serial number = 2,958,465).

You may wonder about January 0, 1900. This *nondate* (which corresponds to date serial number 0) is actually used to represent times that aren't associated with a particular day. This concept becomes clear later in this chapter (see "Entering times").

To view a date serial number as a date, you must format the cell as a date. Choose Home ➪ Number ➪ Number Format. This drop-down control provides you with two date formats. To select from additional date formats, see "Formatting dates and times," later in this chapter.

Entering dates

You can enter a date directly as a serial number (if you know the serial number) and then format it as a date. More often, you enter a date by using any of several recognized date formats. Excel automatically converts your entry into the corresponding date serial number (which it uses for calculations), and it also applies the default date format to the cell so that it displays as an actual date rather than as a cryptic serial number.

Choose Your Date System: 1900 or 1904

Excel supports two date systems: the 1900 date system and the 1904 date system. Which system you use in a workbook determines what date serves as the basis for dates. The 1900 date system uses January 1, 1900 as the day assigned to date serial number 1. The 1904 date system uses January 1, 1904, as the base date. By default, Excel for Windows uses the 1900 date system, and Excel for Macintosh uses the 1904 date system. Excel for Windows supports the 1904 date system for compatibility with Macintosh files. You can choose the date system for the active workbook in the Advanced section of the Excel Options dialog box. (It's in the When Calculating This Workbook subsection.) You can't change the date system if you use Excel for Macintosh.

Generally, you should use the default 1900 date system. And you should exercise caution if you use two different date systems in workbooks that are linked. For example, assume that Book1 uses the 1904 date system and contains the date 1/15/1999 in cell A1. Assume that Book2 uses the 1900 date system and contains a link to cell A1 in Book1. Book2 displays the date as 1/14/1995. Both workbooks use the same date serial number (34713), but they're interpreted differently.

One advantage to using the 1904 date system is that it enables you to display negative time values. With the 1900 date system, a calculation that results in a negative time (for example, 4:00 PM–5:30 PM) cannot be displayed. When using the 1904 date system, the negative time displays as –1:30 (that is, a difference of 1 hour and 30 minutes).

For example, if you need to enter June 18, 2010 into a cell, you can enter the date by typing **June 18, 2010** (or any of several different date formats). Excel interprets your entry and stores the value 40347, the date serial number for that date. It also applies the default date format, so the cell contents may not appear exactly as you typed them.

Note

Depending on your regional settings, entering a date in a format such as June 18, 2010 may be interpreted as a text string. In such a case, you need to enter the date in a format that corresponds to your regional settings, such as 18 June, 2010. ■

When you activate a cell that contains a date, the Formula bar shows the cell contents formatted by using the default date format — which corresponds to your system's *short date format*. The Formula bar doesn't display the date's serial number. If you need to find out the serial number for a particular date, format the cell with a nondate number format.

Tip

To change the default date format, you need to change a system-wide setting. From the Windows Control Panel, select Regional and Language Options. The exact procedure varies, depending on the version of Windows you use. Look for the drop-down list that enables you to change the Short Date Format. The setting you choose determines the default date format that Excel uses to display dates in the Formula bar. ■

Table 12.1 shows a sampling of the date formats that Excel recognizes (using the U.S. settings). Results will vary if you use a different regional setting.

TABLE 12.1

Date Entry Formats Recognized by Excel

Entry	Excel Interpretation (U.S. Settings)
6-18-10	June 18, 2010
6-18-2010	June 18, 2010
6/18/10	June 18, 2010
6/18/2010	June 18, 2010
6-18/10	June 18, 2010
June 18, 2010	June 18, 2010
Jun 18	June 18 of the current year
June 18	June 18 of the current year
6/18	June 18 of the current year
6-18	June 18 of the current year
18-Jun-2010	June 18, 2010
2010/6/18	June 18, 2010

Searching for Dates

If your worksheet uses many dates, you may need to search for a particular date by using the Find and Replace dialog box (Home ➪ Editing ➪ Find & Select ➪ Find, or Ctrl+F). Excel is rather picky when it comes to finding dates. You must enter the date as it appears in the formula bar. For example, if a cell contains a date formatted to display as June 19, 2010, the date appears in the Formula bar using your system's short date format (for example, 6/19/2010). Therefore, if you search for the date as it appears in the cell, Excel won't find it. But it will find the cell if you search for date in the format that appears in the Formula bar.

As you can see in Table 12.1, Excel is rather flexible when it comes to recognizing dates entered into a cell. It's not perfect, however. For example, Excel does *not* recognize any of the following entries as dates:

- June 18 2010
- Jun-18 2010
- Jun-18/2010

Rather, it interprets these entries as text. If you plan to use dates in formulas, make sure that Excel can recognize the date you enter as a date; otherwise, the formulas that refer to these dates will produce incorrect results.

If you attempt to enter a date that lies outside of the supported date range, Excel interprets it as text. If you attempt to format a serial number that lies outside of the supported range as a date, the value displays as a series of hash marks (#########).

Understanding time serial numbers

When you need to work with time values, you extend the Excel date serial number system to include decimals. In other words, Excel works with times by using fractional days. For example, the date serial number for June 1, 2010 is 40330. Noon (halfway through the day) is represented internally as 40330.5.

The serial number equivalent of one minute is approximately 0.00069444. The formula that follows calculates this number by multiplying 24 hours by 60 minutes, and dividing the result into 1. The denominator consists of the number of minutes in a day (1,440).

```
=1/(24*60)
```

Similarly, the serial number equivalent of one second is approximately 0.00001157, obtained by the following formula:

1 / 24 hours × 60 minutes × 60 seconds

In this case, the denominator represents the number of seconds in a day (86,400).

```
=1/(24*60*60)
```

In Excel, the smallest unit of time is one one-thousandth of a second. The time serial number shown here represents 23:59:59.999 (one one-thousandth of a second before midnight):

```
0.99999999
```

Table 12.2 shows various times of day along with each associated time serial numbers.

TABLE 12.2

Times of Day and Their Corresponding Serial Numbers

Time of Day	Time Serial Number
12:00:00 AM (midnight)	0.00000000
1:30:00 AM	0.06250000
7:30:00 AM	0.31250000
10:30:00 AM	0.43750000
12:00:00 PM (noon)	0.50000000
1:30:00 PM	0.56250000
4:30:00 PM	0.68750000
6:00:00 PM	0.75000000
9:00:00 PM	0.87500000
10:30:00 PM	0.93750000

Entering times

As with entering dates, you normally don't have to worry about the actual time serial numbers. Just enter the time into a cell using a recognized format. Table 12.3 shows some examples of time formats that Excel recognizes.

TABLE 12.3

Time Entry Formats Recognized by Excel

Entry	Excel Interpretation
11:30:00 am	11:30 AM
11:30:00 AM	11:30 AM
11:30 pm	11:30 PM
11:30	11:30 AM
13:30	1:30 PM

Because the preceding samples don't have a specific day associated with them, Excel (by default) uses a date serial number of 0, which corresponds to the nonday January 0, 1900. Often, you'll want to combine a date and time. Do so by using a recognized date-entry format, followed by a space, and then a recognized time-entry format. For example, if you enter **6/18/2010 11:30** in a cell, Excel interprets it as 11:30 a.m. on June 18, 2010. Its date/time serial number is 40347.479166667.

When you enter a time that exceeds 24 hours, the associated date for the time increments accordingly. For example, if you enter **25:00:00** into a cell, it's interpreted as 1:00 a.m. on January 1, 1900. The day part of the entry increments because the time exceeds 24 hours. Keep in mind that a time value without a date uses January 0, 1900 as the date.

Similarly, if you enter a date *and* a time (and the time exceeds 24 hours), the date that you entered is adjusted. If you enter **9/18/2010 25:00:00**, for example, it's interpreted as 9/19/2010 1:00:00 a.m.

If you enter a time only (without an associated date) into an unformatted cell, the maximum time that you can enter into a cell is 9999:59:59 (just less than 10,000 hours). Excel adds the appropriate number of days. In this case, 9999:59:59 is interpreted as 3:59:59 p.m. on 02/19/1901. If you enter a time that exceeds 10,000 hours, the entry is interpreted as a text string rather than a time.

Formatting dates and times

You have a great deal of flexibility in formatting cells that contain dates and times. For example, you can format the cell to display the date part only, the time part only, or both the date and time parts.

You format dates and times by selecting the cells and then using the Number tab of the Format Cells dialog box, as shown in Figure 12.1. To display this dialog box, click the dialog box launcher icon in the Number group of the Home tab. Or, click Number Format and choose More Number Formats from the list that appears.

The Date category shows built-in date formats, and the Time category shows built-in time formats. Some formats include both date and time displays. Just select the desired format from the Type list and then click OK.

Tip

When you create a formula that refers to a cell containing a date or a time, Excel sometimes automatically formats the formula cell as a date or a time. Often, this automation is very helpful; other times, it's completely inappropriate and downright annoying. To return the number formatting to the default General format, choose Home ➪ Number ➪ Number Format and choose General from the drop-down list. Or, press Ctrl+Shift+~. ∎

If none of the built-in formats meets your needs, you can create a custom number format. Select the Custom category and then type the custom format codes into the Type box. (See Chapter 24 for information on creating custom number formats.)

Use the Number tab in the Format Cells dialog box to change the appearance of dates and times.

Problems with dates

Excel has some problems when it comes to dates. Many of these problems stem from the fact that Excel was designed many years ago. Excel designers basically emulated the Lotus 1-2-3 program's limited date and time features, which contain a nasty bug that was duplicated intentionally in Excel. (You can read why in a bit.) If Excel were being designed from scratch today, I'm sure it would be much more versatile in dealing with dates. Unfortunately, users are currently stuck with a product that leaves much to be desired in the area of dates.

Excel's leap year bug

A *leap year,* which occurs every four years, contains an additional day (February 29). Specifically, years that are evenly divisible by 100 are not leap years, unless they are also evenly divisible by 400. Although the year 1900 was not a leap year, Excel treats it as such. In other words, when you type **2/29/1900** into a cell, Excel interprets it as a valid date and assigns a serial number of 60.

If you type **2/29/1901**, however, Excel correctly interprets it as a mistake and doesn't convert it to a date. Rather, it simply makes the cell entry a text string.

How can a product used daily by millions of people contain such an obvious bug? The answer is historical. The original version of Lotus 1-2-3 contained a bug that caused it to treat 1900 as a leap year. When Excel was released some time later, the designers knew of this bug and chose to reproduce it in Excel to maintain compatibility with Lotus worksheet files.

Why does this bug still exist in later versions of Excel? Microsoft asserts that the disadvantages of correcting this bug outweigh the advantages. If the bug were eliminated, it would mess up millions of existing workbooks. In addition, correcting this problem would possibly affect compatibility between Excel and other programs that use dates. As it stands, this bug really causes very few problems because most users don't use dates prior to March 1, 1900.

Pre-1900 dates

The world, of course, didn't begin on January 1, 1900. People who use Excel to work with historical information often need to work with dates before January 1, 1900. Unfortunately, the only way to work with pre-1900 dates is to enter the date into a cell as text. For example, you can enter **July 4, 1776** into a cell, and Excel won't complain.

Tip

If you plan to sort information by old dates, you should enter your text dates with a four-digit year, followed by a two-digit month, and then a two-digit day: for example, 1776-07-04. This format will enable accurate sorting. ∎

Using text as dates works in some situation, but the main problem is that you can't perform any manipulation on a date that's entered as text. For example, you can't change its numeric formatting, you can't determine which day of the week this date occurred on, and you can't calculate the date that occurs seven days later.

On the CD

The companion CD-ROM contains a workbook named XDATE demo.xlsm. This workbook contains eight custom worksheet functions written in VBA. These functions enable you to work with any date in the years 0100 through 9999. Figure 12.2 shows a worksheet that uses these extended date functions in columns E though G to perform calculations that involve pre-1900 dates.

FIGURE 12.2

The author's Extended Date Functions add-in enables you to work with pre-1900 dates.

	A	B	C	D	E	F	G
1	President Birthdays						
2							
3	President	Year	Month	Day	XDATE	XDATEDOW	XDATEYEARDIF
4	George Washington	1732	2	22	2/22/1732	Friday	277
5	William Henry Harrison	1773	2	9	2/9/1773	Tuesday	236
6	Zachary Taylor	1784	11	24	11/24/1784	Wednesday	224
7	Abraham Lincoln	1809	2	12	2/12/1809	Sunday	200
8	James A. Garfield	1831	11	19	11/19/1831	Saturday	177
9	William McKinley	1843	1	29	1/29/1843	Sunday	166
10	Warren G. Harding	1865	11	2	11/2/1865	Thursday	143
11	Franklin D. Roosevelt	1882	1	30	1/30/1882	Monday	127
12	Harry S Truman	1884	5	8	5/8/1884	Thursday	125
13	Barack Obama	1961	8	4	8/4/1961	Friday	48
14							

Inconsistent date entries

You need to exercise caution when entering dates by using two digits for the year. When you do so, Excel has some rules that kick in to determine which century to use. And those rules vary, depending on the version of Excel that you use.

Two-digit years between 00 and 29 are interpreted as 21st century dates, and two-digit years between 30 and 99 are interpreted as 20th-century dates. For example, if you enter **12/15/28**, Excel interprets your entry as December 15, 2028. But if you enter **12/15/30**, Excel sees it as December 15, 1930 because Windows uses a default boundary year of 2029. You can keep the default as is or change it via the Windows Control Panel. From the Regional and Language Options dialog box, click the Customize button to display the Customize Regional Options dialog box. Select the Date tab and then specify a different year.

Figure 12.3 shows this dialog box in Windows Vista. This procedure may vary with different versions of Windows.

FIGURE 12.3

Use the Windows Control Panel to specify how Excel interprets two-digit years.

Tip

The best way to avoid any surprises is to simply enter all years using all four digits for the year. ■

Date-Related Worksheet Functions

Excel has quite a few functions that work with dates. These functions are accessible by choosing Formulas ➪ Function Library ➪ Date & Time.

Table 12.4 summarizes the date-related functions available in Excel.

TABLE 12.4

Date-Related Functions

Function	Description
DATE	Returns the serial number of a particular date
DATEVALUE	Converts a date in the form of text to a serial number
DAY	Converts a serial number to a day of the month
DAYS360	Calculates the number of days between two dates based on a 360-day year
EDATE*	Returns the serial number of the date that represents the indicated number of months before or after the start date
EOMONTH*	Returns the serial number of the last day of the month before or after a specified number of months
MONTH	Converts a serial number to a month
NETWORKDAYS*	Returns the number of whole work days between two dates
NETWORKDAYS.INTL**	An international version of the NETWORKDAYS function, which allows non-standard weekend days.
NOW	Returns the serial number of the current date and time
TODAY	Returns the serial number of today's date
WEEKDAY	Converts a serial number to a day of the week
WEEKNUM*	Returns the week number in the year
WORKDAY*	Returns the serial number of the date before or after a specified number of workdays
WORKDAY.INTL**	An international version of the WORKDAY function, which allows non-standard weekend days.
YEAR	Converts a serial number to a year
YEARFRAC*	Returns the year fraction representing the number of whole days between start_date and end_date

* In versions prior to Excel 2007, these functions are available only when the Analysis ToolPak add-in is installed.

** Indicates a function new to Excel 2010.

New Feature

Excel 2010 includes two new worksheet functions related to dates: NETWORKDAYS.INTL and WORKDAY.INTL. These functions include an additional argument in which you can specify non-standard weekend days. If you consider Saturday and Sunday to be non-working weekend days, the older versions of these functions will work fine. ∎

Displaying the current date

The following formula uses the TODAY function to display the current date in a cell:

```
=TODAY()
```

You can also display the date combined with text. The formula that follows, for example, displays text, such as Today is Friday, April 9, 2010:

```
="Today is "&TEXT(TODAY(),"dddd, mmmm d, yyyy")
```

It's important to understand that the TODAY function is not a date stamp. The function is updated whenever the worksheet is calculated. For example, if you enter either of the preceding formulas into a worksheet, the formulas display the current date. And when you open the workbook tomorrow, they will display the current date (*not* the date when you entered the formula).

Tip

To enter a date stamp into a cell, press Ctrl+; (semicolon). This action enters the date directly into the cell and does not use a formula. Therefore, the date will not change. ∎

Displaying any date

You can easily enter a date into a cell by simply typing it while using any of the date formats that Excel recognizes. You can also create a date by using the DATE function, which takes three arguments: the year, the month, and the day. The following formula, for example, returns a date comprising the year in cell A1, the month in cell B1, and the day in cell C1:

```
=DATE(A1,B1,C1)
```

Note

The DATE function accepts invalid arguments and adjusts the result accordingly. For example, the following formula uses 13 as the month argument and returns January 1, 2010. The month argument is automatically translated as month 1 of the following year.

```
=DATE(2009,13,1)
```

Often, you'll use the DATE function with other functions as arguments. For example, the formula that follows uses the YEAR and TODAY functions to return the date for the U.S. Independence Day (July 4) of the current year:

```
=DATE(YEAR(TODAY()),7,4)
```

The DATEVALUE function converts a text string that looks like a date into a date serial number. The following formula returns 40412, which is the date serial number for August 22, 2010:

```
=DATEVALUE("8/22/2010")
```

To view the result of this formula as a date, you need to apply a date number format to the cell.

Caution

Be careful when using the DATEVALUE function. A text string that looks like a date in your country may not look like a date in another country. The preceding example works fine if your system is set for U.S. date formats, but it returns an error for other regional date formats because Excel is looking for the eighth day of the 22nd month! ∎

Generating a series of dates

Often, you want to insert a series of dates into a worksheet. For example, in tracking weekly sales, you may want to enter a series of dates, each separated by seven days. These dates will serve to identify the sales figures.

In some cases you can use the Excel AutoFill feature to insert a series of dates. Enter the first date and drag the cell's fill handle while holding the right mouse button. Release the mouse button and select an option from the shortcut menu (see Figure 12.4) — Fill Days, Fill Weekdays, Fill Months, or Fill Years.

For more flexibility enter the first two dates in the series, and choose Fill Series from the shortcut menu. For example, to enter a series of dates separated by seven days, enter the first two dates of the series and select both cells. Drag the cell's fill handle while holding the right mouse button. In the shortcut menu, choose Fill Series. Excel completes the series by entering additional dates, separated by seven days.

The advantage of using formulas (instead of AutoFill) to create a series of dates is that when you change the first date, the others update automatically. You need to enter the starting date into a cell and then use formulas (copied down the column) to generate the additional dates.

The following examples assume that you enter the first date of the series into cell A1 and the formula into cell A2. You can then copy this formula down the column as many times as needed.

To generate a series of dates separated by seven days, use this formula:

```
=A1+7
```

FIGURE 12.4

Using AutoFill to create a series of dates.

To generate a series of dates separated by one month, you need to use a more complicated formula because months don't all have the same number of days. This formula creates a series of dates, separated by one month:

    =DATE(YEAR(A1),MONTH(A1)+1,DAY(A1))

To generate a series of dates separated by one year, use this formula:

    =DATE(YEAR(A1)+1,MONTH(A1),DAY(A1))

To generate a series of weekdays only (no Saturdays or Sundays), use the formula that follows. This formula assumes that the date in cell A1 is not a weekend day.

    =IF(WEEKDAY(A1)=6,A1+3,A1+1)

Converting a nondate string to a date

You may import data that contains dates coded as text strings. For example, the following text represents August 21, 2010 (a four-digit year followed by a two-digit month, followed by a two-digit day):

    20100821

To convert this string to an actual date, you can use a formula, such as the following. (It assumes that the coded data is in cell A1.)

    =DATE(LEFT(A1,4),MID(A1,5,2),RIGHT(A1,2))

This formula uses text functions (LEFT, MID, and RIGHT) to extract the digits, and then it uses these extracted digits as arguments for the DATE function.

Cross-Reference

See Chapter 11 for more information about using formulas to manipulate text. ∎

Calculating the number of days between two dates

A common type of date calculation determines the number of days between two dates. For example, say you have a financial worksheet that calculates interest earned on a deposit account. The interest earned depends on the number of days the account is open. If your sheet contains the open date and the close date for the account, you can calculate the number of days the account was open.

Because dates are stored as consecutive serial numbers, you can use simple subtraction to calculate the number of days between two dates. For example, if cells A1 and B1 both contain a date, the following formula returns the number of days between these dates:

```
=A1-B1
```

If cell B1 contains a more recent date than the date in cell A1, the result will be negative.

Note

If this formula does not display the correct value, make sure that A1 and B1 both contain actual dates — not text that looks like a date. ∎

Sometimes, calculating the difference between two days is more difficult. To demonstrate, consider the common *fence-post analogy*. If somebody asks you how many units make up a fence, you can respond with either of two answers: the number of fence posts or the number of gaps between the fence posts. The number of fence posts is always one more than the number of gaps between the posts.

To bring this analogy into the realm of dates, suppose that you start a sales promotion on February 1 and end the promotion on February 9. How many days was the promotion in effect? Subtracting February 1 from February 9 produces an answer of eight days. Actually, though, the promotion lasted nine days. In this case, the correct answer involves counting the fence posts, not the gaps. The formula to calculate the length of the promotion (assuming that you have appropriately named cells) appears like this:

```
=EndDay-StartDay+1
```

Calculating the number of work days between two dates

When calculating the difference between two dates, you may want to exclude weekends and holidays. For example, you may need to know how many business days fall in the month of November. This calculation should exclude Saturdays, Sundays, and holidays. The NETWORKDAYS function can help out.

Note

In versions prior to Excel 2007, the NETWORKDAYS **function was available only when the Analysis ToolPak add-in was installed. This function is now part of Excel and doesn't require an add-in. ■**

The NETWORKDAYS function calculates the difference between two dates, excluding weekend days (Saturdays and Sundays). As an option, you can specify a range of cells that contain the dates of holidays, which are also excluded. Excel has no way of determining which days are holidays, so you must provide this information in a range.

Figure 12.5 shows a worksheet that calculates the work days between two dates. The range A2:A11 contains a list of holiday dates. The two formulas in column C calculate the work days between the dates in column A and column B. For example, the formula in cell C15 is

```
=NETWORKDAYS(A15,B15,A2:A11)
```

FIGURE 12.5

Using the NETWORKDAYS function to calculate the number of working days between two dates.

This formula returns 4, which means that the seven-day period beginning with January 1 contains four work days. In other words, the calculation excludes one holiday, one Saturday, and one Sunday. The formula in cell C16 calculates the total number of work days in the year.

On the CD

This workbook is available on the companion CD-ROM. The file is named work days.xlsx.

New

Excel 2010 includes an updated version of the NETWORKDAYS function, named NETWORKDAYS.INTL. This new version is useful if you consider weekend days to be days other than Saturday and Sunday. ■

Offsetting a date using only work days

The WORKDAY function is the opposite of the NETWORKDAYS function. For example, if you start a project on January 4 and the project requires 10 working days to complete, the WORKDAY function can calculate the date you will finish the project.

Note

In versions prior to Excel 2007, the WORKDAY function was available only when the Analysis ToolPak add-in was installed. The function is now part of Excel and doesn't require an add-in. ■

The following formula uses the WORKDAY function to determine the date that is ten working days from January 4, 2010. A working day consists of a week day (Monday through Friday).

```
=WORKDAY("1/4/2010",10)
```

The formula returns a date serial number, which must be formatted as a date. The result is January 18, 2010 (four weekend dates fall between January 4 and January 18).

Caution

The preceding formula may return a different result, depending on your regional date setting. (The hard-coded date may be interpreted as April 1, 2010.) A better formula is

```
=WORKDAY(DATE(2010,1,4),10)
```

The second argument for the WORKDAY function can be negative. And, as with the NETWORKDAYS function, the WORKDAY function accepts an optional third argument (a reference to a range that contains a list of holiday dates).

New

Excel 2010 includes an updated version of the WORKDAY function, named WORKDAY.INTL. This new version is useful if you consider weekend days to be days other than Saturday and Sunday. ■

Calculating the number of years between two dates

The following formula calculates the number of years between two dates. This formula assumes that cells A1 and B1 both contain dates:

```
=YEAR(A1)-YEAR(B1)
```

This formula uses the YEAR function to extract the year from each date and then subtracts one year from the other. If cell B1 contains a more recent date than the date in cell A1, the result is negative.

Note that this function doesn't calculate *full* years. For example, if cell A1 contains 12/31/2010 and cell B1 contains 01/01/2011, the formula returns a difference of one year even though the dates differ by only one day. See the next section for another way to calculate the number of full years.

Calculating a person's age

A person's age indicates the number of full years that the person has been alive. The formula in the previous section (for calculating the number of years between two dates) won't calculate this value correctly. You can use two other formulas, however, to calculate a person's age.

The following formula returns the age of the person whose date of birth you enter into cell A1. This formula uses the YEARFRAC function.

```
=INT(YEARFRAC(TODAY(),A1,1))
```

Note

In versions prior to Excel 2007, the YEARFRAC function was available only when the Analysis ToolPak add-in was installed. The function is now part of Excel, and does not require an add-in. ■

The following formula uses the DATEDIF function to calculate an age. (See the sidebar, "Where's the DATEDIF Function?")

```
=DATEDIF(A1,TODAY(),"Y")
```

Where's the DATEDIF Function?

One of Excel's mysteries is the DATEDIF function. You may notice that this function does not appear in the drop-down function list for the Date & Time category, nor does it appear in the Insert Function dialog box. Therefore, when you use this function, you must always enter it manually.

The DATEDIF function has its origins in Lotus 1-2-3, and apparently Excel provides it for compatibility purposes. For some reason, Microsoft wants to keep this function a secret. The function has been available since Excel 5, but Excel 2000 is the only version that ever documented it in its Help system.

continued

continued

`DATEDIF` is a handy function that calculates the number of days, months, or years between two dates. The function takes three arguments: `start_date`, `end_date`, and a code that represents the time unit of interest. Here's an example of a formula that uses the `DATEDIF` function (it assumes cells A1 and A2 contain a date). The formula returns the number of complete years between those two dates.

`=DATEDIF(A1,A2,"y")`

The following table displays valid codes for the third argument. (You must enclose the codes in quotation marks.)

Unit Code	Returns
`"y"`	The number of complete years in the period.
`"m"`	The number of complete months in the period.
`"d"`	The number of days in the period.
`"md"`	The difference between the days in `start_date` and `end_date`. The months and years of the dates are ignored.
`"ym"`	The difference between the months in `start_date` and `end_date`. The days and years of the dates are ignored.
`"yd"`	The difference between the days of `start_date` and `end_date`. The years of the dates are ignored.

The `start_date` argument must be earlier than the `end_date` argument or else the function returns an error.

Determining the day of the year

January 1 is the first day of the year, and December 31 is the last day. But what about all those days in between? The following formula returns the day of the year for a date stored in cell A1:

`=A1-DATE(YEAR(A1),1,0)`

Here's a similar formula that returns the day of the year for the current date:

`=TODAY()-DATE(YEAR(TODAY()),1,0)`

The following formula returns the number of days remaining in the year after a particular date (assumed to be in cell A1):

`=DATE(YEAR(A1),12,31)-A1`

Here's the formula modified to use the current date:

```
=DATE(YEAR(TODAY()),12,31)-TODAY()
```

When you enter either formula, Excel applies date formatting to the cell. You need to apply a non-date number format to view the result as a number.

To convert a particular day of the year (for example, the 90th day of the year) to an actual date in a specified year, use the following formula, which assumes that the year is stored in cell A1 and that the day of the year is stored in cell B1:

```
=DATE(A1,1,B1)
```

Determining the day of the week

The WEEKDAY function accepts a date argument and returns an integer between 1 and 7 that corresponds to the day of the week. The following formula, for example, returns 7 because the first day of the year 2011 falls on a Saturday:

```
=WEEKDAY(DATE(2011,1,1))
```

The WEEKDAY function uses an optional second argument that specifies the day-numbering system for the result. If you specify 2 as the second argument, the function returns 1 for Monday, 2 for Tuesday, and so on. If you specify 3 as the second argument, the function returns 0 for Monday, 1 for Tuesday, and so on.

Tip

You can also determine the day of the week for a cell that contains a date by applying a custom number format. A cell that uses the following custom number format displays the day of the week, spelled out:

```
dddd
```

Determining the date of the most recent Sunday

You can use the following formula to return the date for the previous Sunday (or any other day of the week). If the current day is a Sunday, the formula returns the current date:

```
=TODAY()-MOD(TODAY()-1,7)
```

To modify this formula to find the date of a day other than Sunday, change the 1 to a different number between 2 (for Monday) and 7 (for Saturday).

Determining the first day of the week after a date

This next formula returns the specified day of the week that occurs after a particular date. For example, use this formula to determine the date of the first Monday after June 1, 2010. The formula assumes that cell A1 contains a date and cell A2 contains a number between 1 and 7 (1 for Sunday, 2 for Monday, and so on).

```
=A1+A2-WEEKDAY(A1)+(A2<WEEKDAY(A1))*7
```

If cell A1 contains June 1, 2010 (a Tuesday), and cell A2 contains 7 (for Saturday), the formula returns June 5, 2010. This is the first Saturday after June 1, 2010.

Determining the *n*th occurrence of a day of the week in a month

You may need a formula to determine the date for a particular occurrence of a week day. For example, suppose that your company payday falls on the second Friday of each month and you need to determine the paydays for each month of the year. The following formula makes this type of calculation:

```
=DATE(A1,A2,1)+A3-WEEKDAY(DATE(A1,A2,1))+
    (A4-(A3>=WEEKDAY(DATE(A1,A2,1))))*7
```

The formula in this section assumes that

- Cell A1 contains a year.
- Cell A2 contains a month.
- Cell A3 contains a day number (1 for Sunday, 2 for Monday, and so on).
- Cell A4 contains the occurrence number (for example, 2 to select the second occurrence of the weekday specified in cell A3).

If you use this formula to determine the date of the second Friday in November 2010, it returns November 12, 2010.

Note
If the value in cell A4 exceeds the number of the specified day in the month, the formula returns a date from a subsequent month. For example, if you attempt to determine the date of the fifth Friday in November 2010 (there is no such date), the formula returns the first Friday in December. ∎

Calculating dates of holidays

Determining the date for a particular holiday can be tricky. Some, such as New Year's Day and U.S. Independence Day are no-brainers because they always occur on the same date. For these kinds of holidays, you can simply use the DATE function. To enter New Year's Day (which always falls on January 1) for a specific year in cell A1, you can enter this function:

```
=DATE(A1,1,1)
```

Other holidays are defined in terms of a particular occurrence of a particular week day in a particular month. For example, Labor Day falls on the first Monday in September.

Figure 12.6 shows a workbook with formulas that calculate the date for 11 U.S. holidays. The formulas, which reference the year in cell A1, are listed in the sections that follow.

FIGURE 12.6

Using formulas to determine the date for various holidays.

On the CD

The workbook shown in Figure 12.5 also appears on the companion CD-ROM. The file is named holidays.xlsx.

New Year's Day

This holiday always falls on January 1:

```
=DATE(A1,1,1)
```

Martin Luther King, Jr. Day

This holiday occurs on the third Monday in January. This formula calculates Martin Luther King, Jr. Day for the year in cell A1:

```
=DATE(A1,1,1)+IF(2<WEEKDAY(DATE(A1,1,1)),7-WEEKDAY
    (DATE(A1,1,1))+2,2-WEEKDAY(DATE(A1,1,1)))+((3-1)*7)
```

Presidents' Day

Presidents' Day occurs on the third Monday in February. This formula calculates Presidents' Day for the year in cell A1:

```
=DATE(A1,2,1)+IF(2<WEEKDAY(DATE(A1,2,1)),7-WEEKDAY
    (DATE(A1,2,1))+2,2-WEEKDAY(DATE(A1,2,1)))+((3-1)*7)
```

Easter

Calculating the date for Easter is difficult because of the complicated manner in which Easter is determined. Easter Day is the first Sunday after the next full moon occurs after the vernal equinox. I found these formulas to calculate Easter on the Web. I have no idea how they work. And they don't work if your workbook uses the 1904 date system. (Read about the difference between the 1900 and the 1904 date system earlier in this chapter.)

```
=DOLLAR(("4/"&A1)/7+MOD(19*MOD(A1,19)-7,30)*14%,)*7-6
```

This one is slightly shorter, but equally obtuse:

```
=FLOOR("5/"&DAY(MINUTE(A1/38)/2+56)&"/"&A1,7)-34
```

Memorial Day

The last Monday in May is Memorial Day. This formula calculates Memorial Day for the year in cell A1:

```
=DATE(A1,6,1)+IF(2<WEEKDAY(DATE(A1,6,1)),7-WEEKDAY
    (DATE(A1,6,1))+2,2-WEEKDAY(DATE(A1,6,1)))+((1-1)*7)-7
```

Notice that this formula actually calculates the first Monday in June and then subtracts 7 from the result to return the last Monday in May.

Independence Day

This holiday always falls on July 4:

```
=DATE(A1,7,4)
```

Labor Day

Labor Day occurs on the first Monday in September. This formula calculates Labor Day for the year in cell A1:

```
=DATE(A1,9,1)+IF(2<WEEKDAY(DATE(A1,9,1)),7-WEEKDAY
    (DATE(A1,9,1))+2,2-WEEKDAY(DATE(A1,9,1)))+((1-1)*7)
```

Columbus Day

This holiday occurs on the second Monday in October. This formula calculates Columbus Day for the year in cell A1:

```
=DATE(A1,10,1)+IF(2<WEEKDAY(DATE(A1,10,1)),7-WEEKDAY
    (DATE(A1,10,1))+2,2-WEEKDAY(DATE(A1,10,1)))+((2-1)*7)
```

Veterans Day

This holiday always falls on November 11:

```
=DATE(A1,11,11)
```

Thanksgiving Day

Thanksgiving Day is celebrated on the fourth Thursday in November. This formula calculates Thanksgiving Day for the year in cell A1:

```
=DATE(A1,11,1)+IF(5<WEEKDAY(DATE(A1,11,1)),7-WEEKDAY
    (DATE(A1,11,1))+5,5-WEEKDAY(DATE(A1,11,1)))+((4-1)*7)
```

Christmas Day

This holiday always falls on December 25:

```
=DATE(A1,12,25)
```

Determining the last day of a month

To determine the date that corresponds to the last day of a month, you can use the DATE function. However, you need to increment the month by 1 and use a day value of 0. In other words, the "0th" day of the next month is the last day of the current month.

The following formula assumes that a date is stored in cell A1. The formula returns the date that corresponds to the last day of the month.

```
=DATE(YEAR(A1),MONTH(A1)+1,0)
```

You can use a variation of this formula to determine how many days are in a specified month. The formula that follows returns an integer that corresponds to the number of days in the month for the date in cell A1:

```
=DAY(DATE(YEAR(A1),MONTH(A1)+1,0))
```

Determining whether a year is a leap year

To determine whether a particular year is a leap year, you can write a formula that determines whether the 29th day of February occurs in February or March. You can take advantage of the fact that the Excel DATE function adjusts the result when you supply an invalid argument — for example, a day of 29 when February contains only 28 days.

The following formula returns TRUE if the year of the date in cell A1 is a leap year. Otherwise, it returns FALSE.

```
=IF(MONTH(DATE(YEAR(A1),2,29))=2,TRUE,FALSE)
```

Caution

This function returns the wrong result (TRUE) if the year is 1900. See "Excel's leap year bug," earlier in this chapter. ∎

Determining a date's quarter

For financial reports, you may find it useful to present information in terms of quarters. The following formula returns an integer between 1 and 4 that corresponds to the calendar quarter for the date in cell A1:

```
=ROUNDUP(MONTH(A1)/3,0)
```

This formula divides the month number by 3 and then rounds up the result.

Time-Related Functions

Excel also includes a number of functions that enable you to work with time values in your formulas. This section contains examples that demonstrate the use of these functions.

Table 12.5 summarizes the time-related functions available in Excel. These functions work with date serial numbers. When you use the Insert Function dialog box, these functions appear in the Date & Time function category.

TABLE 12.5

Time-Related Functions

Function	Description
HOUR	Returns the hour part of a serial number
MINUTE	Returns the minute part of a serial number
NOW	Returns the serial number of the current date and time
SECOND	Returns the second part of a serial number
TIME	Returns the serial number of a specified time
TIMEVALUE	Converts a time in the form of text to a serial number

Displaying the current time

This formula displays the current time as a time serial number (or as a serial number without an associated date):

```
=NOW()-TODAY()
```

You need to format the cell with a time format to view the result as a recognizable time. The quickest way is to choose Home ➪ Number ➪ Format Number and select Time from the drop-down list.

Note

This formula is updated only when the worksheet is calculated. ■

Tip

To enter a time stamp (that doesn't change) into a cell, press Ctrl+Shift+: (colon). ■

Displaying any time

One way to enter a time value into a cell is to just type it, making sure that you include at least one colon (:). You can also create a time by using the TIME function. For example, the following formula returns a time comprising of the hour in cell A1, the minute in cell B1, and the second in cell C1:

```
=TIME(A1,B1,C1)
```

Like the DATE function, the TIME function accepts invalid arguments and adjusts the result accordingly. For example, the following formula uses 80 as the minute argument and returns 10:20:15 AM. The 80 minutes are simply added to the hour, with 20 minutes remaining.

```
=TIME(9,80,15)
```

Caution

If you enter a value greater than 24 as the first argument for the TIME function, the result may not be what you expect. Logically, a formula such as the one that follows should produce a date/time serial number of 1.041667 (that is, one day and one hour).

```
=TIME(25,0,0)
```

In fact, this formula is equivalent to the following:

```
=TIME(1,0,0)
```

You can also use the DATE function along with the TIME function in a single cell. The formula that follows generates a date and time with a serial number of 39420.7708333333 — which represents 6:30 PM on December 4, 2010:

```
=DATE(2010,12,4)+TIME(18,30,0)
```

The TIMEVALUE function converts a text string that looks like a time into a time serial number. This formula returns 0.2395833333, the time serial number for 5:45 AM:

```
=TIMEVALUE("5:45 am")
```

To view the result of this formula as a time, you need to apply number formatting to the cell. The TIMEVALUE function doesn't recognize all common time formats. For example, the following formula returns an error because Excel doesn't like the periods in "a.m."

```
=TIMEVALUE("5:45 a.m.")
```

Calculating the difference between two times

Because times are represented as serial numbers, you can subtract the earlier time from the later time to get the difference. For example, if cell A2 contains 5:30:00 and cell B2 contains 14:00:00, the following formula returns 08:30:00 (a difference of 8 hours and 30 minutes):

```
=B2-A2
```

If the subtraction results in a negative value, however, it becomes an invalid time; Excel displays a series of hash marks (######) because a time without a date has a date serial number of 0. A negative time results in a negative serial number, which cannot be displayed — although you can still use the calculated value in other formulas.

If the direction of the time difference doesn't matter, you can use the ABS function to return the absolute value of the difference:

```
=ABS(B2-A2)
```

This "negative time" problem often occurs when calculating an elapsed time — for example, calculating the number of hours worked given a start time and an end time. This presents no problem if the two times fall in the same day. But if the work shift spans midnight, the result is an invalid negative time. For example, you may start work at 10:00 p.m. and end work at 6:00 a.m. the next day. Figure 12.7 shows a worksheet that calculates the hours worked. As you can see, the shift that spans midnight presents a problem (cell C3).

FIGURE 12.7

Calculating the number of hours worked returns an error if the shift spans midnight.

	A	B	C	D	E
1	Start Shift	End Shift	Hours Worked		
2	8:00 AM	5:30 PM	9:30		
3	10:00 PM	6:00 AM	##############		
4	9:00 AM	4:30 PM	7:30		
5	11:30 AM	7:45 PM	8:15		
6	6:15 AM	1:45 PM	7:30		
7					
8					

Using the ABS function (to calculate the absolute value) isn't an option in this case because it returns the wrong result (16 hours). The following formula, however, *does* work:

```
=IF(B2<A2,B2+1,B2)-A2
```

Tip

Negative times are permitted if the workbook uses the 1904 date system. To switch to the 1904 date system, use the Advanced section of the Excel Options dialog box. Select the Use 1904 Date System option. But beware! When changing the workbook's date system, if the workbook uses dates, the dates will be off by four years For more information about the 1904 date system, see the sidebar "Choose Your Date System: 1900 or 1904," earlier in this chapter. ■

Summing times that exceed 24 hours

Many people are surprised to discover that when you sum a series of times that exceed 24 hours, Excel doesn't display the correct total. Figure 12.8 shows an example. The range B2:B8 contains times that represent the hours and minutes worked each day. The formula in cell B9 is

```
=SUM(B2:B8)
```

As you can see, the formula returns a seemingly incorrect total (17 hours, 45 minutes). The total should read 41 hours, 45 minutes. The problem is that the formula is displaying the total as a date/time serial number of 1.7395833, but the cell formatting is not displaying the *date* part of the date/time. The answer is incorrect because cell B9 has the wrong number format.

FIGURE 12.8

Incorrect cell formatting makes the total appear incorrectly.

	A	B	C	D
1	Day	Hours Worked		
2	Sunday	0		
3	Monday	8:30		
4	Tuesday	8:00		
5	Wednesday	9:00		
6	Thursday	9:30		
7	Friday	4:15		
8	Saturday	2:30		
9	Total Hours	17:45		
10				
11				
12				
13				

To view a time that exceeds 24 hours, you need to apply a custom number format for the cell so that square brackets surround the *hour* part of the format string. Applying the number format here to cell B9 displays the sum correctly:

```
[h]:mm
```

Cross-Reference

For more information about custom number formats, see Chapter 24. ■

Figure 12.9 shows another example of a worksheet that manipulates times. This worksheet keeps track of hours worked during a week (regular hours and overtime hours).

On the CD

This workbook is available on the companion CD-ROM. The filename is `time sheet.xlsm`. The workbook contains a few macros to make it easier to use. ■

The week's starting date appears in cell D5, and the formulas in column B fill in the dates for the days of the week. Times appear in the range D8:G14, and formulas in column H calculate the number of hours worked each day. For example, the formula in cell H8 is

```
=IF(E8<D8,E8+1-D8,E8-D8)+IF(G8<F8,G8+1-G8,G8-F8)
```

An employee timesheet workbook.

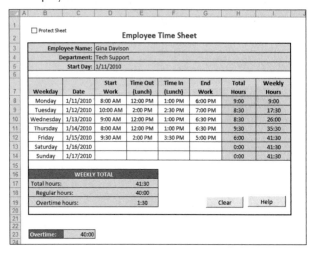

The first part of this formula subtracts the time in column D from the time in column E to get the total hours worked before lunch. The second part subtracts the time in column F from the time in column G to get the total hours worked after lunch. I use IF functions to accommodate graveyard shift cases that span midnight — for example, an employee may start work at 10:00 PM and begin lunch at 2:00 AM. Without the IF function, the formula returns a negative result.

The following formula in cell H17 calculates the weekly total by summing the daily totals in column H:

```
=SUM(H8:H14)
```

This worksheet assumes that hours in excess of 40 hours in a week are considered overtime hours. The worksheet contains a cell named *Overtime*, in cell C23. This cell contains a formula that returns 40:00. If your standard workweek consists of something other than 40 hours, you can change this cell.

The following formula (in cell H18) calculates regular (nonovertime) hours. This formula returns the smaller of two values: the total hours or the overtime hours.

```
=MIN(E17,Overtime)
```

The final formula, in cell H19, simply subtracts the regular hours from the total hours to yield the overtime hours.

```
=E17-E18
```

The times in H17:H19 may display time values that exceed 24 hours, so these cells use a custom number format:

```
[h]:mm
```

Converting from military time

Military time is expressed as a four-digit number from 0000 to 2359. For example, 1:00 a.m. is expressed as 0100 hours, and 3:30 p.m. is expressed as 1530 hours. The following formula converts such a number (assumed to be in cell A1) to a standard time:

```
=TIMEVALUE(LEFT(A1,2)&":"&RIGHT(A1,2))
```

The formula returns an incorrect result if the contents of cell A1 do not contain four digits. The following formula corrects the problem, and it returns a valid time for any military time value from 0 to 2359:

```
=TIMEVALUE(LEFT(TEXT(A1,"0000"),2)&":"&RIGHT(A1,2))
```

Following is a simpler formula that uses the TEXT function to return a formatted string, and then it uses the TIMEVALUE function to express the result in terms of a time.

```
=TIMEVALUE(TEXT(A1,"00\:00"))
```

Converting decimal hours, minutes, or seconds to a time

To convert decimal hours to a time, divide the decimal hours by 24. For example, if cell A1 contains 9.25 (representing hours), this formula returns 09:15:00 (nine hours, 15 minutes):

```
=A1/24
```

To convert decimal minutes to a time, divide the decimal hours by 1,440 (the number of minutes in a day). For example, if cell A1 contains 500 (representing minutes), the following formula returns 08:20:00 (eight hours, 20 minutes):

```
=A1/1440
```

To convert decimal seconds to a time, divide the decimal hours by 86,400 (the number of seconds in a day). For example, if cell A1 contains 65,000 (representing seconds), the following formula returns 18:03:20 (18 hours, three minutes, and 20 seconds):

```
=A1/86400
```

Adding hours, minutes, or seconds to a time

You can use the TIME function to add any number of hours, minutes, or seconds to a time. For example, assume that cell A1 contains a time. The following formula adds 2 hours and 30 minutes to that time and displays the result:

```
=A1+TIME(2,30,0)
```

You can use the TIME function to fill a range of cells with incremental times. Figure 12.10 shows a worksheet with a series of times in 10-minute increments. Cell A1 contains a time that was entered directly. Cell A2 contains the following formula, which copied down the column:

```
=A1+TIME(0,10,0)
```

FIGURE 12.10

Using a formula to create a series of incremental times.

	A	B	C	D
1	8:00 AM			
2	8:10 AM			
3	8:20 AM			
4	8:30 AM			
5	8:40 AM			
6	8:50 AM			
7	9:00 AM			
8	9:10 AM			
9	9:20 AM			
10	9:30 AM			
11	9:40 AM			
12	9:50 AM			
13				
14				

Rounding time values

You may need to create a formula that rounds a time to a particular value. For example, you may need to enter your company's time records rounded to the nearest 15 minutes. This section presents examples of various ways to round a time value.

The following formula rounds the time in cell A1 to the nearest minute:

```
=ROUND(A1*1440,0)/1440
```

The formula works by multiplying the time by 1440 (to get total minutes). This value is passed to the ROUND function, and the result is divided by 1440. For example, if cell A1 contains 11:52:34, the formula returns 11:53:00.

The following formula resembles this example, except that it rounds the time in cell A1 to the nearest hour:

```
=ROUND(A1*24,0)/24
```

If cell A1 contains 5:21:31, the formula returns 5:00:00.

The following formula rounds the time in cell A1 to the nearest 15 minutes (a quarter of an hour):

```
=ROUND(A1*24/0.25,0)*(0.25/24)
```

In this formula, 0.25 represents the fractional hour. To round a time to the nearest 30 minutes, change 0.25 to 0.5, as in the following formula:

```
=ROUND(A1*24/0.5,0)*(0.5/24)
```

Working with non–time-of-day values

Sometimes, you may want to work with time values that don't represent an actual time of day. For example, you may want to create a list of the finish times for a race or record the amount of time you spend in meetings each day. Such times don't represent a time of day. Rather, a value represents the time for an event (in hours, minutes, and seconds). The time to complete a test, for example, may be 35 minutes and 45 seconds. You can enter that value into a cell as:

```
00:35:45
```

Excel interprets such an entry as 12:35:45 a.m., which works fine. (Just make sure that you format the cell so that it appears as you like.) When you enter such times that do not have an hour component, you must include at least one zero for the hour. If you omit a leading zero for a missing hour, Excel interprets your entry as 35 hours and 45 minutes.

Figure 12.11 shows an example of a worksheet set up to keep track of a person's jogging activity. Column A contains simple dates. Column B contains the distance in miles. Column C contains the time it took to run the distance. Column D contains formulas to calculate the speed in miles per hour. For example, the formula in cell D2 is

```
=B2/(C2*24)
```

FIGURE 12.11

This worksheet uses times not associated with a time of day.

	A	B	C	D	E	F	G	H
1	Date	Distance	Time	Speed (mph)	Pace (min/mile)	YTD Distance	Cumulative Time	
2	1/1/2010	1.50	00:18:45	4.80	12.50	1.50	00:18:45	
3	1/2/2010	1.50	00:17:40	5.09	11.78	3.00	00:36:25	
4	1/3/2010	2.00	00:21:30	5.58	10.75	5.00	00:57:55	
5	1/4/2010	1.50	00:15:20	5.87	10.22	6.50	01:13:15	
6	1/5/2010	2.40	00:25:05	5.74	10.45	8.90	01:38:20	
7	1/6/2010	3.00	00:31:06	5.79	10.37	11.90	02:09:26	
8	1/7/2010	3.80	00:41:06	5.55	10.82	15.70	02:50:32	
9	1/8/2010	5.00	01:09:00	4.35	13.80	20.70	03:59:32	
10	1/9/2010	4.00	00:45:10	5.31	11.29	24.70	04:44:42	
11	1/10/2010	3.00	00:29:06	6.19	9.70	27.70	05:13:48	
12	1/11/2010	5.50	01:08:30	4.82	12.45	33.20	06:22:18	
13								
14								

Column E contains formulas to calculate the pace, in minutes per mile. For example, the formula in cell E2 is

```
=(C2*60*24)/B2
```

Columns F and G contain formulas that calculate the year-to-date distance (using column B) and the cumulative time (using column C). The cells in column G are formatted using the following number format (which permits time displays that exceed 24 hours):

```
[hh]:mm:ss
```

On the CD

You can also access the workbook shown in Figure 12.11 on the companion CD-ROM. The file is named jogging log.xlsx.

Creating Formulas That Count and Sum

IN THIS CHAPTER

Information on counting and summing cells

Basic counting formulas

Advanced counting formulas

Formulas for performing common summing tasks

Conditional summing formulas using a single criterion

Conditional summing formulas using multiple criteria

Many of the most common spreadsheet questions involve counting and summing values and other worksheet elements. It seems that people are always looking for formulas to count or to sum various items in a worksheet. If I've done my job, this chapter answers the vast majority of such questions. It contains many examples that you can easily adapt to your own situation.

Counting and Summing Worksheet Cells

Generally, a *counting formula* returns the number of cells in a specified range that meet certain criteria. A *summing formula* returns the sum of the values of the cells in a range that meet certain criteria. The range you want counted or summed may or may not consist of a worksheet database.

Table 13.1 lists the Excel worksheet functions that come into play when creating counting and summing formulas. Not all these functions are covered in this chapter. If none of the functions in Table 13.1 can solve your problem, it's likely that an array formula can come to the rescue.

Cross-Reference
See Chapters 16 and 17 for detailed information and examples of array formulas used for counting and summing. ■

Note

If your data is in the form of a table, you can use autofiltering to accomplish many counting and summing operations. Just set the autofilter criteria, and the table displays only the rows that match your criteria (the nonqualifying rows in the table are hidden). Then you can select formulas to display counts or sums in the table's total row. See Chapter 5 for more information on using tables. ∎

TABLE 13.1

Excel Counting and Summing Functions

Function	Description
COUNT	Returns the number of cells that contain a numeric value.
COUNTA	Returns the number of nonblank cells.
COUNTBLANK	Returns the number of blank cells.
COUNTIF	Returns the number of cells that meet a specified criterion.
COUNTIFS*	Returns the number of cells that meet multiple criteria.
DCOUNT	Counts the number of records that meet specified criteria; used with a worksheet database.
DCOUNTA	Counts the number of nonblank records that meet specified criteria; used with a worksheet database.
DEVSQ	Returns the sum of squares of deviations of data points from the sample mean; used primarily in statistical formulas.
DSUM	Returns the sum of a column of values that meet specified criteria; used with a worksheet database.
FREQUENCY	Calculates how often values occur within a range of values and returns a vertical array of numbers. Used only in a multicell array formula.
SUBTOTAL	When used with a first argument of 2, 3, 102, or 103, returns *a count* of cells that comprise a subtotal; when used with a first argument of 9 or 109, returns *the sum* of cells that comprise a subtotal.
SUM	Returns the sum of its arguments.
SUMIF	Returns the sum of cells that meet a specified criterion.
SUMIFS*	Returns the sum of cells that meet multiple criteria.
SUMPRODUCT	Multiplies corresponding cells in two or more ranges and returns the sum of those products.
SUMSQ	Returns the sum of the squares of its arguments; used primarily in statistical formulas.
SUMX2PY2	Returns the sum of the sum of squares of corresponding values in two ranges; used primarily in statistical formulas.
SUMXMY2	Returns the sum of squares of the differences of corresponding values in two ranges; used primarily in statistical formulas.
SUMX2MY2	Returns the sum of the differences of squares of corresponding values in two ranges; used primarily in statistical formulas.

* These functions were introduced in Excel 2007.

Getting a Quick Count or Sum

The Excel status bar can display useful information about the currently selected cells — no formulas required. Normally, the status bar displays the sum and count of the values in the selected range. You can, however, right-click to bring up a menu with other options. You can choose any or all the following: Average, Count, Numerical Count, Minimum, Maximum, and Sum.

	Paul	Jim	Hank	Joe
	101	115	107	114
	107	102	113	106
	105	107	120	114
	106	102	104	104
	117	119	120	100
	113	116	103	119
	113	111	103	104
	103	110	100	113
	106	117	112	114
	108	117	104	119
	120	109	107	100
	103	119	112	113
	110	105	115	111
	107	103	105	119

Count: 14   Sum: 1552   100%

Basic Counting Formulas

The basic counting formulas presented in this section are all straightforward and relatively simple. They demonstrate the capability of the Excel counting functions to count the number of cells in a range that meet specific criteria. Figure 13.1 shows a worksheet that uses formulas (in column E) to summarize the contents of range A1:B10 — a 20-cell range named *Data*. This range contains a variety of information, including values, text, logical values, errors, and empty cells.

On the CD

This workbook is available on the companion CD-ROM. The file is named `basic counting.xlsx`.

Counting the total number of cells

To get a count of the total number of cells in a range (empty and non-empty cells), use the following formula. This formula returns the number of cells in a range named *Data*. It simply multiplies the number of rows (returned by the ROWS function) by the number of columns (returned by the COLUMNS function).

```
=ROWS(Data)*COLUMNS(Data)
```

This formula will not work if the *Data* range consists of noncontiguous cells. In other words, *Data* must be a rectangular range of cells.

About This Chapter's Examples

Most of the examples in this chapter use named ranges for function arguments. When you adapt these formulas for your own use, you'll need to substitute either the actual range address or a range name defined in your workbook.

Also, some examples consist of array formulas. An *array formula* is a special type of formula that enables you to perform calculations that would not otherwise be possible. You can spot an array formula because it's enclosed in curly brackets when it's displayed in the Formula bar. In addition, I use this syntax for the array formula examples presented in this book. For example:

```
{=Data*2}
```

When you enter an array formula, press Ctrl+Shift+Enter (not just Enter) but *don't* type the curly brackets (Excel inserts the brackets for you.) If you need to edit an array formula, don't forget to use Ctrl+Shift+Enter when you finish editing (otherwise, the array formula will revert to a normal formula, and it will return an incorrect result). See Chapter 16 for an introduction to array formulas.

FIGURE 13.1

Formulas in column E display various counts of the data in A1:B10.

	A	B	C	D	E	F
1	Jan	Feb		Total cells:	20	
2	525	718		Blank cells:	6	
3				Nonblank cells:	14	
4	3			Numeric values:	7	
5	552	911		Non-text cells:	17	
6	250	98		Text cells:	3	
7				Logical values:	2	
8	TRUE	FALSE		Error values:	2	
9		#DIV/0!		#N/A errors:	0	
10	Total	#NAME?		#NULL! errors:	0	
11				#DIV/0! errors:	1	
12				#VALUE! errors:	0	
13				#REF! errors:	0	
14				#NAME? errors:	1	
15				#NUM! errors:	0	
16						

Counting blank cells

The following formula returns the number of blank (empty) cells in a range named *Data*:

```
=COUNTBLANK(Data)
```

The COUNTBLANK function also counts cells containing a formula that returns an empty string. For example, the formula that follows returns an empty string if the value in cell A1 is greater than 5. If the cell meets this condition, the COUNTBLANK function counts that cell.

```
=IF(A1>5,"",A1)
```

You can use the COUNTBLANK function with an argument that consists of entire rows or columns. For example, this next formula returns the number of blank cells in column A:

```
=COUNTBLANK(A:A)
```

The following formula returns the number of empty cells on the entire worksheet named Sheet1. You must enter this formula on a sheet other than Sheet1, or it will create a circular reference.

```
=COUNTBLANK(Sheet1!1:1048576)
```

Counting nonblank cells

To count nonblank cells, use the COUNTA function. The following formula uses the COUNTA function to return the number of nonblank cells in a range named *Data*:

```
=COUNTA(Data)
```

The COUNTA function counts cells that contain values, text, or logical values (TRUE or FALSE).

Note
If a cell contains a formula that returns an empty string, that cell is included in the count returned by COUNTA, even though the cell appears to be blank. ∎

Counting numeric cells

To count only the numeric cells in a range, use the following formula (which assumes the range is named *Data*):

```
=COUNT(Data)
```

Cells that contain a date or a time are considered to be numeric cells. Cells that contain a logical value (TRUE or FALSE) aren't considered to be numeric cells.

Counting text cells

To count the number of text cells in a range, you need to use an array formula. The array formula that follows returns the number of text cells in a range named *Data*:

```
{=SUM(IF(ISTEXT(Data),1))}
```

Counting nontext cells

The following array formula uses the Excel ISNONTEXT function, which returns TRUE if its argument refers to any nontext cell (including a blank cell). This formula returns the count of the number of cells not containing text (including blank cells):

```
{=SUM(IF(ISNONTEXT(Data),1))}
```

Counting logical values

The following array formula returns the number of logical values (TRUE or FALSE) in a range named *Data*:

```
{=SUM(IF(ISLOGICAL(Data),1))}
```

Counting error values in a range

Excel has three functions that help you determine whether a cell contains an error value:

- ISERROR: Returns TRUE if the cell contains any error value (#N/A, #VALUE!, #REF!, #DIV/0!, #NUM!, #NAME?, or #NULL!)
- ISERR: Returns TRUE if the cell contains any error value except #N/A
- ISNA: Returns TRUE if the cell contains the #N/A error value

You can use these functions in an array formula to count the number of error values in a range. The following array formula, for example, returns the total number of error values in a range named *Data*:

```
{=SUM(IF(ISERROR(data),1))}
```

Depending on your needs, you can use the ISERR or ISNA function in place of ISERROR.

If you would like to count specific types of errors, you can use the COUNTIF function. The following formula, for example, returns the number of #DIV/0! error values in the range named *Data*:

```
=COUNTIF(Data,"#DIV/0!")
```

Advanced Counting Formulas

Most of the basic examples I present earlier in this chapter use functions or formulas that perform conditional counting. The advanced counting formulas that I present here represent more complex examples for counting worksheet cells, based on various types of criteria.

Cross-Reference
Some of these examples are array formulas. See Chapters 16 and 17 for more information about array formulas. ∎

Counting cells by using the COUNTIF function

The COUNTIF function, which is useful for single-criterion counting formulas, takes two arguments:

- *range*: The range that contains the values that determine whether to include a particular cell in the count
- *criteria*: The logical criteria that determine whether to include a particular cell in the count

Table 13.2 lists several examples of formulas that use the COUNTIF function. These formulas all work with a range named *Data*. As you can see, the *criteria* argument proves quite flexible. You can use constants, expressions, functions, cell references, and even wildcard characters (* and ?).

TABLE 13.2

Examples of Formulas Using the COUNTIF Function

=COUNTIF(Data,12)	Returns the number of cells containing the value 12
=COUNTIF(Data,"<0")	Returns the number of cells containing a negative value
=COUNTIF(Data,"<>0")	Returns the number of cells not equal to 0
=COUNTIF(Data,">5")	Returns the number of cells greater than 5
=COUNTIF(Data,A1)	Returns the number of cells equal to the contents of cell A1
=COUNTIF(Data,">"&A1)	Returns the number of cells greater than the value in cell A1
=COUNTIF(Data,"*")	Returns the number of cells containing text
=COUNTIF(Data,"???")	Returns the number of text cells containing exactly three characters
=COUNTIF(Data,"budget")	Returns the number of cells containing the single word *budget* (not case sensitive)
=COUNTIF(Data,"*budget*")	Returns the number of cells containing the text *budget* anywhere within the text
=COUNTIF(Data,"A*")	Returns the number of cells containing text that begins with the letter *A* (not case sensitive)
=COUNTIF(Data,TODAY())	Returns the number of cells containing the current date
=COUNTIF(Data,">"&AVERAGE(Data))	Returns the number of cells with a value greater than the average
=COUNTIF(Data,">"&AVERAGE(Data)+STDEV(Data)*3)	Returns the number of values exceeding three standard deviations above the mean
=COUNTIF(Data,3)+COUNTIF(Data,-3)	Returns the number of cells containing the value 3 or −3
=COUNTIF(Data,TRUE)	Returns the number of cells containing logical TRUE
=COUNTIF(Data,TRUE)+COUNTIF(Data,FALSE)	Returns the number of cells containing a logical value (TRUE or FALSE)
=COUNTIF(Data,"#N/A")	Returns the number of cells containing the #N/A error value

Counting cells based on multiple criteria

In many cases, your counting formula will need to count cells only if two or more criteria are met. These criteria can be based on the cells that are being counted or based on a range of corresponding cells.

Figure 13.2 shows a simple worksheet that I use for the examples in this section. This sheet shows sales data categorized by Month, SalesRep, and Type. The worksheet contains named ranges that correspond to the labels in row 1.

On the CD

This workbook is available on the companion CD-ROM. The file is named `multiple criteria counting .xlsx`.

Note

Several of the examples in this section use the COUNTIFS function, which was introduced in Excel 2007. I also present alternative versions of the formulas, which should be used if you plan to share your workbook with others who use an earlier version of Excel. ∎

FIGURE 13.2

This worksheet demonstrates various counting techniques that use multiple criteria.

	A	B	C	D
1	Month	SalesRep	Type	Amount
2	January	Albert	New	85
3	January	Albert	New	675
4	January	Brooks	New	130
5	January	Cook	New	1350
6	January	Cook	Existing	685
7	January	Brooks	New	1350
8	January	Cook	New	475
9	January	Brooks	New	1205
10	February	Brooks	Existing	450
11	February	Albert	New	495
12	February	Cook	New	210
13	February	Cook	Existing	1050
14	February	Albert	New	140
15	February	Brooks	New	900
16	February	Brooks	New	900
17	February	Cook	New	95
18	February	Cook	New	780
19	March	Brooks	New	900
20	March	Albert	Existing	875
21	March	Brooks	New	50
22	March	Brooks	New	875
23	March	Cook	Existing	225
24	March	Cook	New	175
25	March	Brooks	Existing	400
26	March	Albert	New	840
27	March	Cook	New	132

Using And criteria

An And criterion counts cells if all specified conditions are met. A common example is a formula that counts the number of values that fall within a numerical range. For example, you may want to count cells that contain a value greater than 100 *and* less than or equal to 200. For this example, the COUNTIFS function will do the job:

```
=COUNTIFS(Amount,">100",Amount,"<=200")
```

Note

If the data is contained in a table, you can use table referencing in your formulas. For example, if the table is named Table1, you can rewrite the preceding formula as:

```
=COUNTIFS(Table1[Amount],">100",Table1[Amount],"<=200")
```

This method of writing formulas does not require named ranges. ■

The COUNTIFS function accepts any number of paired arguments. The first member of the pair is the range to be counted (in this case, the range named *Amount*); the second member of the pair is the criterion. The preceding example contains two sets of paired arguments and returns the number of cells in which *Amount* is greater than 100 and less than or equal to 200.

Prior to Excel 2007, you would need to use a formula like this:

```
=COUNTIF(Amount,">100")-COUNTIF(Amount,">200")
```

The formula counts the number of values that are greater than 100 and then subtracts the number of values that are greater than or equal to 200. The result is the number of cells that contain a value greater than 100 and less than or equal to 200. This formula can be confusing because the formula refers to a condition ">200" even though the goal is to count values that are less than or equal to 200. Yet another alternate technique is to use an array formula, like the one that follows. You may find it easier to create this type of formula:

```
{=SUM((Amount>100)*(Amount<=200))}
```

Note

When you enter an array formula, remember to use Ctrl+Shift+Enter but don't type the brackets. Excel includes the brackets for you. ■

Sometimes, the counting criteria will be based on cells other than the cells being counted. You may, for example, want to count the number of sales that meet the following criteria:

- Month is January, *and*
- SalesRep is Brooks, *and*
- Amount is greater than 1000

The following formula (for Excel 2007 and Excel 2010) returns the number of items that meets all three criteria. Note that the COUNTIFS function uses three sets of pairs of arguments.

```
=COUNTIFS(Month,"January",SalesRep,"Brooks",Amount,">1000")
```

An alternative formula, which works with all versions of Excel, uses the SUMPRODUCT function. The following formula returns the same result as the previous formula.

```
=SUMPRODUCT((Month="January")*(SalesRep="Brooks")*(Amount>1000))
```

Yet another way to perform this count is to use an array formula:

```
{=SUM((Month="January")*(SalesRep="Brooks")*(Amount>1000))}
```

Using Or criteria

To count cells by using an Or criterion, you can sometimes use multiple COUNTIF functions. The following formula, for example, counts the number of sales made in January or February:

```
=COUNTIF(Month,"January")+COUNTIF(Month,"February")
```

You can also use the COUNTIF function in an array formula. The following array formula, for example, returns the same result as the previous formula:

```
{=SUM(COUNTIF(Month,{"January","February"}))}
```

But if you base your Or criteria on cells other than the cells being counted, the COUNTIF function won't work. (Refer to Figure 13.2.) Suppose that you want to count the number of sales that meet the following criteria:

- Month is January, *or*
- SalesRep is Brooks, *or*
- Amount is greater than 1000

If you attempt to create a formula that uses COUNTIF, some double counting will occur. The solution is to use an array formula like this:

```
{=SUM(IF((Month="January")+(SalesRep="Brooks")+(Amount>1000),1))}
```

Combining And and Or criteria

In some cases, you may need to combine And and Or criteria when counting. For example, perhaps you want to count sales that meet the following criteria:

- Month is January, *and*
- SalesRep is Brooks, *or* SalesRep is Cook

This array formula returns the number of sales that meet the criteria:

```
{=SUM((Month="January")*IF((SalesRep="Brooks")+
    (SalesRep="Cook"),1))}
```

Counting the most frequently occurring entry

The MODE function returns the most frequently occurring value in a range. Figure 13.3 shows a worksheet with values in range A1:A10 (named *Data*). The formula that follows returns 10 because that value appears most frequently in the *Data* range:

```
=MODE(Data)
```

FIGURE 13.3

The MODE function returns the most frequently occurring value in a range.

	A	B	C	D	E	F
1	1		10	<- Mode		
2	4		5	<- Frequency of the mode		
3	4					
4	10					
5	10					
6	10					
7	10					
8	10					
9	12					
10	12					
11						

To count the number of times the most frequently occurring value appears in the range (in other words, the frequency of the mode), use the following formula:

```
=COUNTIF(Data,MODE(Data))
```

This formula returns 5 because the modal value (10) appears five times in the *Data* range.

The MODE function works only for numeric values. It simply ignores cells that contain text. To find the most frequently occurring text entry in a range, you need to use an array formula.

To count the number of times the most frequently occurring item (text or values) appears in a range named *Data*, use the following array formula:

```
{=MAX(COUNTIF(Data,Data))}
```

This next array formula operates like the MODE function except that it works with both text and values:

```
{=INDEX(Data,MATCH(MAX(COUNTIF(Data,Data)),COUNTIF(Data,Data),0))}
```

Counting the occurrences of specific text

The examples in this section demonstrate various ways to count the occurrences of a character or text string in a range of cells. Figure 13.4 shows a worksheet used for these examples. Various text strings appear in the range A1:A10 (named *Data*); cell B1 is named *Text*.

This worksheet demonstrates various ways to count character strings in a range.

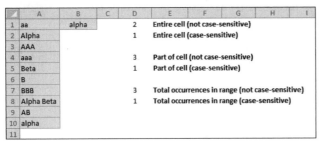

On the CD

The companion CD-ROM contains a workbook that demonstrates the formulas in this section. The file is named `counting text in a range.xlsx`.

Entire cell contents

To count the number of cells containing the contents of the *Text* cell (and nothing else), you can use the COUNTIF function as the following formula demonstrates.

```
=COUNTIF(Data,Text)
```

For example, if the *Text* cell contains the string `Alpha`, the formula returns 2 because two cells in the *Data* range contain this text. This formula is not case sensitive, so it counts both `Alpha` (cell A2) and `alpha` (cell A10). Note, however, that it does not count the cell that contains `Alpha Beta` (cell A8).

The following array formula is similar to the preceding formula, but this one is case sensitive:

```
{=SUM(IF(EXACT(Data,Text),1))}
```

Partial cell contents

To count the number of cells that contain a string that includes the contents of the *Text* cell, use this formula:

```
=COUNTIF(Data,"*"&Text&"*")
```

For example, if the *Text* cell contains the text Alpha, the formula returns 3 because three cells in the *Data* range contain the text alpha (cells A2, A8, and A10). Note that the comparison is not case sensitive.

If you need a case-sensitive count, you can use the following array formula:

```
{=SUM(IF(LEN(Data)-LEN(SUBSTITUTE(Data,Text,""))>0,1))}
```

If the *Text* cells contain the text Alpha, the preceding formula returns 2 because the string appears in two cells (A2 and A8).

Total occurrences in a range

To count the total number of occurrences of a string within a range of cells, use the following array formula:

```
{=(SUM(LEN(Data))-SUM(LEN(SUBSTITUTE(Data,Text,""))))
   /
   LEN(Text)}
```

If the *Text* cell contains the character B, the formula returns 7 because the range contains seven instances of the string. This formula is case sensitive.

The following array formula is a modified version that is not case sensitive:

```
{=(SUM(LEN(Data))-SUM(LEN(SUBSTITUTE(UPPER(Data),
   UPPER(Text),""))))/LEN(Text)}
```

Counting the number of unique values

The following array formula returns the number of unique values in a range named *Data*:

```
{=SUM(1/COUNTIF(Data,Data))}
```

Note
The preceding formula is one of those "classic" Excel formulas that gets passed around the Internet. I don't know who originated it. ■

Useful as it is, this formula does have a serious limitation: If the range contains any blank cells, it returns an error. The following array formula solves this problem:

```
{=SUM(IF(COUNTIF(Data,Data)=0,"",1/COUNTIF(Data,Data)))}
```

Cross-Reference
To find out how to create an array formula that returns a list of unique items in a range, see Chapter 17. ■

On the CD

The companion CD-ROM contains a workbook that demonstrates this technique. The file is named `count unique.xlsx`.

Creating a frequency distribution

A *frequency distribution* basically comprises a summary table that shows the frequency of each value in a range. For example, an instructor may create a frequency distribution of test scores. The table would show the count of A's, B's, C's, and so on. Excel provides a number of ways to create frequency distributions. You can

- Use the FREQUENCY function.
- Create your own formulas.
- Use the Analysis ToolPak add-in.
- Use a pivot table.

On the CD

A workbook that demonstrates these four techniques appears on the companion CD-ROM. The file is named `frequency distribution.xlsx`.

The FREQUENCY function

Using the FREQUENCY function to create a frequency distribution can be a bit tricky. This function always returns an array, so you must use it in an array formula that's entered into a multicell range.

Figure 13.5 shows some data in range A1:E25 (named *Data*). These values range from 1 to 500. The range G2:G11 contains the bins used for the frequency distribution. Each cell in this bin range contains the upper limit for the bin. In this case, the bins consist of <=50, 51–100, 101–150, and so on.

To create the frequency distribution, select a range of cells that corresponds to the number of cells in the bin range (in this example, select H2:H11 because the bins are in G2:G11). Then enter the following array formula into the selected range (press Ctrl+Shift+Enter it):

```
{=FREQUENCY(Data,G2:G11)}
```

The array formula returns the count of values in the *Data* range that fall into each bin. To create a frequency distribution that consists of percentages, use the following array formula:

```
{=FREQUENCY(Data,G2:G11)/COUNT(Data)}
```

Figure 13.6 shows two frequency distributions — one in terms of counts and one in terms of percentages. The figure also shows a chart (histogram) created from the frequency distribution.

FIGURE 13.5

Creating a frequency distribution for the data in A1:E25.

	A	B	C	D	E	F	G	H
1	55	316	223	185	124		**Bins**	
2	124	93	163	213	314		50	
3	211	41	231	241	212		100	
4	118	113	400	205	254		150	
5	262	1	201	12	101		200	
6	167	479	205	337	118		250	
7	489	15	89	362	148		300	
8	179	248	125	197	177		350	
9	456	153	269	49	127		400	
10	289	500	198	317	300		450	
11	126	114	303	314	270		500	
12	151	279	347	314	170			
13	250	175	93	209	61			
14	166	113	356	124	242			
15	152	384	157	233	99			
16	277	195	436	6	240			
17	147	80	173	211	244			
18	386	93	330	400	141			
19	332	173	129	323	188			
20	338	263	444	84	220			
21	221	402	498	98	2			
22	201	400	3	190	105			
23	35	225	12	265	329			
24	43	302	125	301	444			
25	56	9	135	500	398			

FIGURE 13.6

Frequency distributions created by using the FREQUENCY function.

Using formulas to create a frequency distribution

Figure 13.7 shows a worksheet that contains test scores for 50 students in column B (the range is named *Grades*). Formulas in columns G and H calculate a frequency distribution for letter grades. The minimum and maximum values for each letter grade appear in columns D and E. For example, a test score between 80 and 89 (inclusive) earns a B. In addition, a chart displays the distribution of the test scores.

The formula in cell G2 that follows counts the number of scores that qualify for an A:

    =COUNTIFS(Grades,">="&D2,Grades,"<="&E2)

You may recognize this formula from a previous section in this chapter (see "Counting cells by using multiple criteria"). This formula was copied to the four cells below G2.

Note

The preceding formula uses the COUNTIFS function, which first appeared in Excel 2007. For compatibility with previous Excel versions, use this array formula:

    {=SUM((Grades>=D2)*(Grades<=E2))}

FIGURE 13.7

Creating a frequency distribution of test scores.

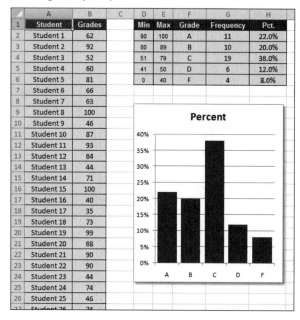

The formulas in column H calculate the percentage of scores for each letter grade. The formula in H2, which was copied to the four cells below H2, is

```
=G2/SUM($G$2:$G$6)
```

Using the Analysis ToolPak to create a frequency distribution

The Analysis ToolPak add-in, distributed with Excel, provides another way to calculate a frequency distribution.

1. **Enter your bin values in a range.**

2. **Choose Data ⇨ Analysis ⇨ Analysis to display the Data Analysis dialog box.** If this command is not available, see the sidebar, "Is the Analysis ToolPak Installed?".

3. **In the Data Analysis dialog box, select Histogram and then click OK.** You should see the Histogram dialog box shown in Figure 13.8.

4. **Specify the ranges for your data (Input Range), bins (Bin Range), and results (Output Range), and then select any options. Click OK.** Figure 13.9 shows a frequency distribution (and chart) created with the Histogram option.

Caution

Note that the frequency distribution consists of values, not formulas. Therefore, if you make any changes to your input data, you need to rerun the Histogram procedure to update the results. ■

FIGURE 13.8

The Analysis ToolPak's Histogram dialog box.

FIGURE 13.9

A frequency distribution and chart generated by the Analysis ToolPak's Histogram option.

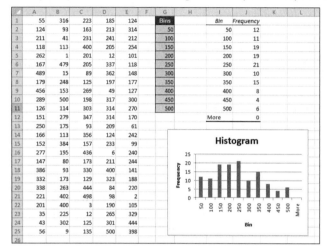

Using a pivot table to create a frequency distribution

If your data is in the form of a table, you may prefer to use a pivot table to create a histogram. Figure 13.10 shows the student grade data summarized in a pivot table in columns D and E. The data bars were added using conditional formatting.

Is the Analysis ToolPak Installed?

To make sure that the Analysis ToolPak add-in is installed, click the Data tab. If the Ribbon displays the Data Analysis command in the Analysis group, you're all set. If not, you'll need to install the add-in:

1. **Choose File ⇨ Options to display the Excel Options dialog box.**
2. **Click the Add-ins tab on the left.**
3. **Select Excel Add-Ins from the Manage drop-down list.**
4. **Click Go to display the Add-Ins dialog box.**
5. **Place a check mark next to Analysis ToolPak.**
6. **Click OK.**

If you've enabled the Developer tab, you can display the Add-Ins dialog box by choosing Developer ⇨ Add-Ins ⇨ Add-Ins.

Note: In the Add-Ins dialog box, you see an additional add-in, Analysis ToolPak - VBA. This add-in is for programmers, and you don't need to install it.

Cross-Reference

I cover pivot tables in detail in Chapters 34 and 35, and you can learn more about the conditional formatting data bars in Chapter 20. ■

FIGURE 13.10

Using data bars within a pivot table to display a histogram.

	A	B	C	D	E
1	Student	Grades		Row Labels ▾	Count of Grades
2	Student 1	62		30-39	3
3	Student 2	92		40-49	7
4	Student 3	52		50-59	6
5	Student 4	60		60-69	6
6	Student 5	81		70-79	7
7	Student 6	66		80-89	10
8	Student 7	63		90-100	11
9	Student 8	100		Grand Total	50
10	Student 9	46			
11	Student 10	87			
12	Student 11	93			
13	Student 12	84			
14	Student 13	44			
15	Student 14	71			
16	Student 15	100			
17	Student 16	40			
18	Student 17	35			
19	Student 18	73			
20	Student 19	99			
21	Student 20	88			
22	Student 21	90			

Summing Formulas

The examples in this section demonstrate how to perform common summing tasks by using formulas. The formulas range from very simple to relatively complex array formulas that compute sums by using multiple criteria.

Summing all cells in a range

It doesn't get much simpler than this. The following formula returns the sum of all values in a range named *Data*:

```
=SUM(Data)
```

The SUM function can take up to 255 arguments. The following formula, for example, returns the sum of the values in five noncontiguous ranges:

```
=SUM(A1:A9,C1:C9,E1:E9,G1:G9,I1:I9)
```

You can use complete rows or columns as an argument for the SUM function. The formula that follows, for example, returns the sum of all values in column A. If this formula appears in a cell in column A, it generates a circular reference error.

```
=SUM(A:A)
```

The following formula returns the sum of all values on Sheet1 by using a range reference that consists of all rows. To avoid a circular reference error, this formula must appear on a sheet other than Sheet1.

```
=SUM(Sheet1!1:1048576)
```

The SUM function is very versatile. The arguments can be numerical values, cells, ranges, text representations of numbers (which are interpreted as values), logical values, and even embedded functions. For example, consider the following formula:

```
=SUM(B1,5,"6",,SQRT(4),A1:A5,TRUE)
```

This odd formula, which is perfectly valid, contains all the following types of arguments, listed here in the order of their presentation:

- A single cell reference: B1
- A literal value: 5
- A string that looks like a value: "6"
- A missing argument: , ,
- An expression that uses another function: SQRT(4)
- A range reference: A1:A5
- A logical value: TRUE

Caution

The SUM function is versatile, but it's also inconsistent when you use logical values (TRUE or FALSE). Logical values stored in cells are always treated as 0. However, logical TRUE, when used as an argument in the SUM function, is treated as 1.

Computing a cumulative sum

You may want to display a cumulative sum of values in a range — sometimes known as a "running total." Figure 13.11 illustrates a cumulative sum. Column B shows the monthly amounts, and column C displays the cumulative (year-to-date) totals.

The formula in cell C2 is

```
=SUM(B$2:B2)
```

Notice that this formula uses a *mixed reference* — that is, the first cell in the range reference always refers to the same row (in this case, row 2). When this formula is copied down the column, the range argument adjusts such that the sum always starts with row 2 and ends with the current row. For example, after copying this formula down column C, the formula in cell C8 is

```
=SUM(B$2:B8)
```

FIGURE 13.11

Simple formulas in column C display a cumulative sum of the values in column B.

	A	B	C	D
1	Month	Amount	Year-to-Date	
2	January	850	850	
3	February	900	1,750	
4	March	750	2,500	
5	April	1,100	3,600	
6	May	600	4,200	
7	June	500	4,700	
8	July	1,200	5,900	
9	August		5,900	
10	September		5,900	
11	October		5,900	
12	November		5,900	
13	December		5,900	
14	TOTAL	5,900		
15				
16				

You can use an IF function to hide the cumulative sums for rows in which data hasn't been entered. The following formula, entered in cell C2 and copied down the column, is

```
=IF(B2<>"",SUM(B$2:B2),"")
```

Figure 13.12 shows this formula at work.

FIGURE 13.12

Using an IF function to hide cumulative sums for missing data.

	A	B	C	D
1	Month	Amount	Year-to-Date	
2	January	850	850	
3	February	900	1,750	
4	March	750	2,500	
5	April	1,100	3,600	
6	May	600	4,200	
7	June	500	4,700	
8	July	1,200	5,900	
9	August			
10	September			
11	October			
12	November			
13	December			
14	TOTAL	5,900		
15				
16				

On the CD

This workbook is available on the companion CD-ROM. The file is named `cumulative sum.xlsx`.

Summing the "top *n*" values

In some situations, you may need to sum the *n* largest values in a range — for example, the top ten values. If your data resides in a table, you can use autofiltering to hide all but the top *n* rows and then display the sum of the visible data in the table's total row.

Another approach is to sort the range in descending order and then use the SUM function with an argument consisting of the first *n* values in the sorted range.

A better solution — which doesn't require a table or sorting — uses an array formula like this one:

    {=SUM(LARGE(Data,{1,2,3,4,5,6,7,8,9,10}))}

This formula sums the ten largest values in a range named *Data*. To sum the ten smallest values, use the SMALL function instead of the LARGE function:

    {=SUM(SMALL(Data,{1,2,3,4,5,6,7,8,9,10}))}

These formulas use an array constant comprised of the arguments for the LARGE or SMALL function. If the value of *n* for your top-n calculation is large, you may prefer to use the following variation. This formula returns the sum of the top 30 values in the *Data* range. You can, of course, substitute a different value for 30.

    {=SUM(LARGE(Data,ROW(INDIRECT("1:30"))))}

Figure 13.13 shows this array formula in use.

FIGURE 13.13

Using an array formula to calculate the sum of the 30 largest values in a range.

Cross-Reference

See Chapter 16 for more information about using array constants. ■

Conditional Sums Using a Single Criterion

Often, you need to calculate a *conditional sum*. With a conditional sum, values in a range that meet one or more conditions are included in the sum. This section presents examples of conditional summing by using a single criterion.

The SUMIF function is very useful for single-criterion sum formulas. The SUMIF function takes three arguments:

- *range*: The range containing the values that determine whether to include a particular cell in the sum.

- *criteria*: An expression that determines whether to include a particular cell in the sum.

- *sum_range*: Optional. The range that contains the cells you want to sum. If you omit this argument, the function uses the range specified in the first argument.

The examples that follow demonstrate the use of the SUMIF function. These formulas are based on the worksheet shown in Figure 13.14, set up to track invoices. Column F contains a formula that subtracts the date in column E from the date in column D. A negative number in column F indicates a past-due payment. The worksheet uses named ranges that correspond to the labels in row 1.

On the CD

All the examples in this section also appear on the companion CD-ROM. The file is named conditional sum.xlsx.

FIGURE 13.14

A negative value in Column F indicates a past-due payment.

	A	B	C	D	E	F	G
1	InvoiceNum	Office	Amount	DateDue	Today	Difference	
2	AG-0145	Oregon	$5,000.00	4/1/2010	5/5/2010	-34	
3	AG-0189	California	$450.00	4/19/2010	5/5/2010	-16	
4	AG-0220	Washington	$3,211.56	4/28/2010	5/5/2010	-7	
5	AG-0310	Oregon	$250.00	4/30/2010	5/5/2010	-5	
6	AG-0355	Washington	$125.50	5/4/2010	5/5/2010	-1	
7	AG-0409	Washington	$3,000.00	5/10/2010	5/5/2010	5	
8	AG-0581	Oregon	$2,100.00	5/24/2010	5/5/2010	19	
9	AG-0600	Oregon	$335.39	5/24/2010	5/5/2010	19	
10	AG-0602	Washington	$65.00	5/28/2010	5/5/2010	23	
11	AG-0633	California	$250.00	5/31/2010	5/5/2010	26	
12	TOTAL		$14,787.45			29	
13							

Summing only negative values

The following formula returns the sum of the negative values in column F. In other words, it returns the total number of past-due days for all invoices. For this worksheet, the formula returns −63.

```
=SUMIF(Difference,"<0")
```

Because you omit the third argument, the second argument ("<0") applies to the values in the *Difference* range.

You don't need to hard-code the arguments for the SUMIF function into your formula. For example, you can create a formula, such as the following, which gets the criteria argument from the contents of cell G2:

```
=SUMIF(Difference,G2)
```

This formula returns a new result if you change the criteria in cell G2.

Summing values based on a different range

The following formula returns the sum of the past-due invoice amounts (in column C):

```
=SUMIF(Difference,"<0",Amount)
```

This formula uses the values in the *Difference* range to determine whether the corresponding values in the *Amount* range contribute to the sum.

Summing values based on a text comparison

The following formula returns the total invoice amounts for the Oregon office:

```
=SUMIF(Office,"=Oregon",Amount)
```

Using the equal sign in the argument is optional. The following formula has the same result:

```
=SUMIF(Office,"Oregon",Amount)
```

To sum the invoice amounts for all offices *except* Oregon, use this formula:

```
=SUMIF(Office,"<>Oregon",Amount)
```

Summing values based on a date comparison

The following formula returns the total invoice amounts that have a due date after May 1, 2010:

```
=SUMIF(DateDue,">="&DATE(2010,5,1),Amount)
```

Notice that the second argument for the SUMIF function is an expression. The *expression* uses the DATE function, which returns a date. Also, the comparison operator, enclosed in quotes, is concatenated (using the & operator) with the result of the DATE function.

The formula that follows returns the total invoice amounts that have a future due date (including today):

```
=SUMIF(DateDue,">="&TODAY(),Amount)
```

Conditional Sums Using Multiple Criteria

The examples in the preceding section all used a single comparison criterion. The examples in this section involve summing cells based on multiple criteria.

Figure 13.15 shows the sample worksheet again, for your reference. The worksheet also shows the result of several formulas that demonstrate summing by using multiple criteria.

Using And criteria

Suppose that you want to get a sum of the invoice amounts that are past due *and* associated with the Oregon office. In other words, the value in the *Amount* range will be summed only if both of the following criteria are met:

- The corresponding value in the *Difference* range is negative.
- The corresponding text in the Office range is Oregon.

If the worksheet won't be used by anyone running a version prior to Excel 2007, the following formula does the job:

```
=SUMIFS(Amount,Difference,"<0",Office,"Oregon")
```

The array formula that follows returns the same result and will work in all versions of Excel.

```
{=SUM((Difference<0)*(Office="Oregon")*Amount)}
```

FIGURE 13.15

This worksheet demonstrates summing based on multiple criteria.

	A	B	C	D	E	F
1	InvoiceNum	Office	Amount	DateDue	Today	Difference
2	AG-0145	Oregon	$5,000.00	4/1/2010	5/5/2010	-34
3	AG-0189	California	$450.00	4/19/2010	5/5/2010	-16
4	AG-0220	Washington	$3,211.56	4/28/2010	5/5/2010	-7
5	AG-0310	Oregon	$250.00	4/30/2010	5/5/2010	-5
6	AG-0355	Washington	$125.50	5/4/2010	5/5/2010	-1
7	AG-0409	Washington	$3,000.00	5/10/2010	5/5/2010	5
8	AG-0581	Oregon	$2,100.00	5/24/2010	5/5/2010	19
9	AG-0600	Oregon	$335.39	5/24/2010	5/5/2010	19
10	AG-0602	Washington	$65.00	5/28/2010	5/5/2010	23
11	AG-0633	California	$250.00	5/31/2010	5/5/2010	26
12	TOTAL		$14,787.45			29
13						
14						
15		-63	Total past due days			
16		-63	Total past due days (array formula)			
17						
18		$9,037.06	Total amount past due			
19		$9,037.06	Total amount past due (array formula)			
20						
21		$7,685.39	Total for Oregon only			
22						
23		$7,102.06	Total for all except Oregon			
24						
25		$14,787.45	Total amount with due date beyond May 1			
26						
27		$5,250.00	Total past due amount for Oregon (Excel 2007 or later only)			
28		$5,250.00	Total past due amount for Oregon (array formula)			
29						
30		$5,000.00	Total past due amounts OR amounts for Oregon (array formula)			
31						
32		$5,700.00	Total past due amounts for Oregon and California (array formula)			
33						

Using Or criteria

Suppose that you want to get a sum of past-due invoice amounts *or* ones associated with the Oregon office. In other words, the value in the *Amount* range will be summed if either of the following criteria is met:

- The corresponding value in the *Difference* range is negative.
- The corresponding text in the Office range is `Oregon`.

This example requires an array formula:

```
{=SUM(IF((Office="Oregon")+(Difference<0),1,0)*Amount)}
```

A plus sign (+) joins the conditions; you can include more than two conditions.

Using And and Or criteria

As you may expect, things get a bit tricky when your criteria consists of both And and Or operations. For example, you may want to sum the values in the *Amount* range when both of the following conditions are met:

- The corresponding value in the *Difference* range is negative.
- The corresponding text in the Office range is Oregon or California.

Notice that the second condition actually consists of two conditions joined with Or. The following array formula does the trick:

```
{=SUM((Difference<0)*IF((Office="Oregon")+
    (Office="California"),1)*Amount)}
```

Creating Formulas
That Look Up Values

This chapter discusses various techniques that you can use to look up a value in a range of data. Excel has three functions (LOOKUP, VLOOKUP, and HLOOKUP) designed for this task, but you may find that these functions don't quite cut it.

This chapter provides many lookup examples, including alternative techniques that go well beyond the Excel program's normal lookup capabilities.

Introducing Lookup Formulas

A *lookup formula* essentially returns a value from a table by looking up another related value. A common telephone directory provides a good analogy. If you want to find a person's telephone number, you first locate the name (look it up) and then retrieve the corresponding number.

Note
I use the term table to describe a rectangular range of data. The range does not necessarily need to be an "official" table, as created by choosing Insert ⇨ Tables ⇨ Table. ■

Figure 14.1 shows a worksheet that uses several lookup formulas. This worksheet contains a table of employee data, beginning in row 7. This range is named *EmpData*. When you enter a last name into cell C2, lookup formulas in D2:G2 retrieve the matching information from the table. If the last name does not appear in Column C, the formulas return #N/A.

IN THIS CHAPTER

An introduction to formulas that look up values in a table

An overview of the worksheet functions used to perform lookups

Basic lookup formulas

More sophisticated lookup formulas

About This Chapter's Examples

Most of the examples in this chapter use named ranges for function arguments. When you adapt these formulas for your own use, you need to substitute the actual range address or a range name defined in your workbook.

The following lookup formulas use the VLOOKUP function:

D2	=VLOOKUP(C2,EmpData,2,FALSE)
E2	=VLOOKUP(C2,EmpData,3,FALSE)
F2	=VLOOKUP(C2,EmpData,4,FALSE)
G2	=VLOOKUP(C2,EmpData,5,FALSE)

FIGURE 14.1

Lookup formulas in row 2 look up the information for the employee name in cell C2.

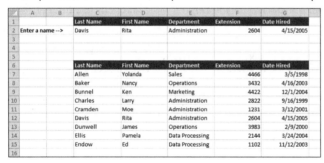

This particular example uses four formulas to return information from the *EmpData* range. In many cases, you want only a single value from the table, so use only one formula.

Functions Relevant to Lookups

Several Excel functions are useful when writing formulas to look up information in a table. Table 14.1 lists and describes these functions.

TABLE 14.1

Functions Used in Lookup Formulas

Function	Description
CHOOSE	Returns a specific value from a list of values supplied as arguments.
HLOOKUP	Horizontal lookup. Searches for a value in the top row of a table and returns a value in the same column from a row you specify in the table.
IF	Returns one value if a condition you specify is TRUE, and returns another value if the condition is FALSE.
IFERROR*	If the first argument returns an error, the second argument is evaluated and returned. If the first argument does not return an error, then it is evaluated and returned.
INDEX	Returns a value (or the reference to a value) from within a table or range.
LOOKUP	Returns a value either from a one-row or one-column range. Another form of the LOOKUP function works like VLOOKUP but is restricted to returning a value from the last column of a range.
MATCH	Returns the relative position of an item in a range that matches a specified value.
OFFSET	Returns a reference to a range that is a specified number of rows and columns from a cell or range of cells.
VLOOKUP	Vertical lookup. Searches for a value in the first column of a table and returns a value in the same row from a column you specify in the table.

* Introduced in Excel 2007.

The examples in this chapter use the functions listed in Table 14.1.

Using the IF Function for Simple Lookups

The IF function is very versatile and is often suitable for simple decision-making problems. The accompanying figure shows a worksheet with student grades in column B. Formulas in column C use the IF function to return text: either Pass (a score of 65 or higher) or Fail (a score below 65). For example, the formula in cell C2 is

```
=IF(B2>=65,"Pass","Fail")
```

	A	B	C	D
1	Student	Score	Grade	
2	Andy	82	Pass	
3	Barbara	57	Fail	
4	Chris	73	Pass	
5	Dennis	54	Fail	
6	Elsie	82	Pass	
7	Francine	72	Pass	
8				

continued

continued

You can "nest" IF functions to provide even more decision-making ability. This formula, for example, returns one of four strings: Excellent, Very Good, Fair, or Poor.

`=IF(B2>=90,"Excellent",IF(B2>=70,"Very Good",IF(B2>=50,"Fair","Poor")))`

This technique is fine for situations that involve only a few choices. However, using nested IF functions can quickly become complicated and unwieldy. The lookup techniques described in this chapter usually provide a much better solution.

Basic Lookup Formulas

You can use the Excel basic lookup functions to search a column or row for a lookup value to return another value as a result. Excel provides three basic lookup functions: HLOOKUP, VLOOKUP, and LOOKUP. In addition, the MATCH and INDEX functions are often used together to return a cell or relative cell reference for a lookup value.

The VLOOKUP function

The VLOOKUP function looks up the value in the first column of the lookup table and returns the corresponding value in a specified table column. The lookup table is arranged vertically (which explains the V in the function's name). The syntax for the VLOOKUP function is

VLOOKUP(lookup_value,table_array,col_index_num,range_lookup)

The VLOOKUP function's arguments are as follows:

- *lookup_value*: The value to be looked up in the first column of the lookup table.
- *table_array*: The range that contains the lookup table.
- *col_index_num*: The column number within the table from which the matching value is returned.
- *range_lookup*: Optional. If TRUE or omitted, an approximate match is returned. (If an exact match is not found, the next largest value that is less than *lookup_value* is returned.) If FALSE, VLOOKUP will search for an exact match. If VLOOKUP can't find an exact match, the function returns #N/A.

Caution

If the range_lookup argument is TRUE or omitted, the first column of the lookup table must be in ascending order. If lookup_value is smaller than the smallest value in the first column of table_array, VLOOKUP returns #N/A. If the range_lookup argument is FALSE, the first column of the lookup table need not be in ascending order. If an exact match is not found, the function returns #N/A.

Tip

If the lookup_value argument is text and the range_lookup argument is False, the lookup_value can include wildcard characters * and ?.

A very common use for a lookup formula involves an income tax rate schedule (see Figure 14.2). The tax rate schedule shows the income tax rates for various income levels. The following formula (in cell B3) returns the tax rate for the income in cell B2:

```
=VLOOKUP(B2,D2:F7,3)
```

On the CD

The examples in this section are available on the companion CD-ROM. They're contained in a file named basic lookup examples.xlsx.

FIGURE 14.2

Using VLOOKUP to look up a tax rate.

	A	B	C	D	E	F
1				Income is Greater Than or Equal To...	But Less Than or Equal To...	Tax Rate
2	Enter Income:	$45,500		$0	$2,650	15.00%
3	The Tax Rate is:	31.00%		$2,651	$27,300	28.00%
4				$27,301	$58,500	31.00%
5				$58,501	$131,800	36.00%
6				$131,801	$284,700	39.60%
7				$284,701		45.25%
8						

The lookup table resides in a range that consists of three columns (D2:F7). Because the last argument for the VLOOKUP function is 3, the formula returns the corresponding value in the third column of the lookup table.

Note that an exact match is not required. If an exact match is not found in the first column of the lookup table, the VLOOKUP function uses the next largest value that is less than the lookup value. In other words, the function uses the row in which the value you want to look up is greater than or equal to the row value but less than the value in the next row. In the case of a tax table, this is exactly what you want to happen.

The HLOOKUP function

The HLOOKUP function works just like the VLOOKUP function except that the lookup table is arranged horizontally instead of vertically. The HLOOKUP function looks up the value in the first row of the lookup table and returns the corresponding value in a specified table row.

The syntax for the HLOOKUP function is

```
HLOOKUP(lookup_value,table_array,row_index_num,range_lookup)
```

The HLOOKUP function's arguments are as follows

- *lookup_value*: The value to be looked up in the first row of the lookup table.
- *table_array*: The range that contains the lookup table.
- *row_index_num*: The row number within the table from which the matching value is returned.
- *range_lookup*: Optional. If TRUE or omitted, an approximate match is returned. (If an exact match is not found, the next largest value less than *lookup_value* is returned.) If FALSE, VLOOKUP will search for an exact match. If VLOOKUP can't find an exact match, the function returns #N/A.

Tip

If the lookup_value argument is text and the range_lookup argument is False, the lookup_value can include wildcard characters * and?.

Figure 14.3 shows the tax rate example with a horizontal lookup table (in the range E1:J3). The formula in cell B3 is

```
=HLOOKUP(B2,E1:J3,3)
```

FIGURE 14.3

Using HLOOKUP to look up a tax rate.

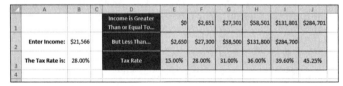

	A	B	C	D	E	F	G	H	I	J
1				Income is Greater Than or Equal To...	$0	$2,651	$27,301	$58,501	$131,801	$284,701
2	Enter Income:	$21,566		But Less Than...	$2,650	$27,300	$58,500	$131,800	$284,700	
3	The Tax Rate is:	28.00%		Tax Rate	15.00%	28.00%	31.00%	36.00%	39.60%	45.25%
4										

The LOOKUP function

The LOOKUP function looks in a one-row or one-column range (*lookup_vector*) for a value (*lookup_value*) and returns a value from the same position in a second one-row or one-column range (*result_vector*).

The LOOKUP function has the following syntax:

```
LOOKUP(lookup_value,lookup_vector,result_vector)
```

The function's arguments are as follows:

- *lookup_value*: The value to be looked up in the *lookup_vector*.
- *lookup_vector*: A single-column or single-row range that contains the values to be looked up. These values must be in ascending order.
- *result_vector*: The single-column or single-row range that contains the values to be returned. It must be the same size as the *lookup_vector*.

Caution

Values in the lookup_vector must be in ascending order. If lookup_value is smaller than the smallest value in lookup_vector, LOOKUP returns #N/A.

Figure 14.4 shows the tax table again. This time, the formula in cell B3 uses the LOOKUP function to return the corresponding tax rate. The formula in cell B3 is

```
=LOOKUP(B2,D2:D7,F2:F7)
```

Caution

If the values in the first column are not arranged in ascending order, the LOOKUP function may return an incorrect value. ■

Note that LOOKUP (as opposed to VLOOKUP) requires two range references (a range to be looked in, and a range that contains result values). VLOOKUP, on the other hand, uses a single range for the lookup table, and the third argument determines which column to use for the result. This argument, of course, can consist of a cell reference.

FIGURE 14.4

Using LOOKUP to look up a tax rate.

	A	B	C	D	E	F
1				Income is Greater Than or Equal To...	But Less Than...	Tax Rate
2	Enter Income:	$123,409		$0	$2,650	15.00%
3	The Tax Rate is:	36.00%		$2,651	$27,300	28.00%
4				$27,301	$58,500	31.00%
5				$58,501	$131,800	36.00%
6				$131,801	$284,700	39.60%
7				$284,701		45.25%
8						
9						

Combining the MATCH and INDEX functions

The MATCH and INDEX functions are often used together to perform lookups. The MATCH function returns the relative position of a cell in a range that matches a specified value. The syntax for MATCH is

```
MATCH(lookup_value,lookup_array,match_type)
```

The MATCH function's arguments are as follows:

- *lookup_value*: The value you want to match in *lookup_array*. If *match_type* is 0 and the *lookup_value* is text, this argument can include wildcard characters * and ?
- *lookup_array*: The range being searched.
- *match_type*: An integer (−1, 0, or 1) that specifies how the match is determined.

Note

If match_type is 1, MATCH finds the largest value less than or equal to lookup_value. (lookup_array must be in ascending order.) If match_type is 0, MATCH finds the first value exactly equal to lookup_value. If match_type is −1, MATCH finds the smallest value greater than or equal to lookup_value. (lookup_array must be in descending order.) If you omit the match_type argument, this argument is assumed to be 1.

The INDEX function returns a cell from a range. The syntax for the INDEX function is

```
INDEX(array,row_num,column_num)
```

The INDEX function's arguments are as follows:

- *array*: A range
- *row_num*: A row number within *array*
- *col_num*: A column number within *array*

Note

If array contains only one row or column, the corresponding row_num or column_num argument is optional. ■

Figure 14.5 shows a worksheet with dates, day names, and amounts in columns D, E, and F. When you enter a date in cell B1, the following formula (in cell B2) searches the dates in column D and returns the corresponding amount from column F. The formula in cell B2 is

```
=INDEX(F2:F21,MATCH(B1,D2:D21,0))
```

To understand how this formula works, start with the MATCH function. This function searches the range D2:D21 for the date in cell B1. It returns the relative row number where the date is found. This value is then used as the second argument for the INDEX function. The result is the corresponding value in F2:F21.

FIGURE 14.5

Using the INDEX and MATCH functions to perform a lookup.

	A	B	C	D	E	F
1	Date:	1/12/2010		Date	Weekday	Amount
2	Amount:	189		1/1/2010	Friday	23
3				1/2/2010	Saturday	179
4				1/3/2010	Sunday	149
5				1/4/2010	Monday	196
6				1/5/2010	Tuesday	131
7				1/6/2010	Wednesday	179
8				1/7/2010	Thursday	134
9				1/8/2010	Friday	179
10				1/9/2010	Saturday	193
11				1/10/2010	Sunday	191
12				1/11/2010	Monday	176
13				1/12/2010	Tuesday	189
14				1/13/2010	Wednesday	163
15				1/14/2010	Thursday	121
16				1/15/2010	Friday	100
17				1/16/2010	Saturday	109
18				1/17/2010	Sunday	151
19				1/18/2010	Monday	138
20				1/19/2010	Tuesday	114
21				1/20/2010	Wednesday	156
22						

When a Blank Is Not a Zero

The Excel lookup functions treat empty cells in the result range as zeros. The worksheet in the accompanying figure contains a two-column lookup table, and this formula looks up the name in cell B1 and returns the corresponding amount:

=VLOOKUP(B1,D2:E8,2)

Note that the Amount cell for Charlie is blank, but the formula returns a 0.

	A	B	C	D	E	F
1	Name:	Charlie		Name	Amount	
2	Amount:	0		Bob	45	
3				Charlie		
4				David	16	
5				Frank	32	
6				George	9	
7				Harry	0	
8				Mike	1	
9						

continued

continued

If you need to distinguish zeros from blank cells, you must modify the lookup formula by adding an IF function to check whether the length of the returned value is 0. When the looked up value is blank, the length of the return value is 0. In all other cases, the length of the returned value is non-zero. The following formula displays an empty string (a blank) whenever the length of the looked-up value is zero and the actual value whenever the length is anything but zero:

```
=IF(LEN(VLOOKUP(B1,D2:E8,2))=0,"",(VLOOKUP(B1,D2:E8,2)))
```

Alternatively, you can specifically check for an empty string, as in the following formula:

```
=IF(VLOOKUP(B1,D2:E8,2)="","",(VLOOKUP(B1,D2:E8,2)))
```

Specialized Lookup Formulas

You can use additional types of lookup formulas to perform more specialized lookups. For example, you can look up an exact value, search in another column besides the first in a lookup table, perform a case-sensitive lookup, return a value from among multiple lookup tables, and perform other specialized and complex lookups.

On the CD

The examples in this section are available on the companion CD-ROM. The file is named specialized lookup examples.xlsx.

Looking up an exact value

As demonstrated in the previous examples, VLOOKUP and HLOOKUP don't necessarily require an exact match between the value to be looked up and the values in the lookup table. An example is looking up a tax rate in a tax table. In some cases, you may require a perfect match. For example, when looking up an employee number, you would require a perfect match for the number.

To look up an exact value only, use the VLOOKUP (or HLOOKUP) function with the optional fourth argument set to FALSE.

Figure 14.6 shows a worksheet with a lookup table that contains employee numbers (column C) and employee names (column D). The lookup table is named *EmpList*. The formula in cell B2, which follows, looks up the employee number entered in cell B1 and returns the corresponding employee name:

```
=VLOOKUP(B1,EmpList,2,FALSE)
```

Because the last argument for the VLOOKUP function is FALSE, the function returns a value only if an exact match is found. If the value is not found, the formula returns #N/A. This result, of course, is exactly what you want to happen because returning an approximate match for an employee number makes no sense. Also, notice that the employee numbers in column C are not in ascending order. If the last argument for VLOOKUP is FALSE, the values need not be in ascending order.

Tip

If you prefer to see something other than #N/A when the employee number is not found, you can use the IFERROR function to test for the error result and substitute a different string. The following formula displays the text Not Found rather than #N/A:

```
=IFERROR(VLOOKUP(B1,EmpList,2,FALSE),"Not Found")
```

IFERROR works only with Excel 2007 and Excel 2010. For compatibility with previous versions, use the following formula:

```
=IF(ISNA(VLOOKUP(B1,EmpList,2,FALSE)),"Not Found",
   VLOOKUP(B1,EmpList,2,FALSE))
```

FIGURE 14.6

This lookup table requires an exact match.

	A	B	C	D
1	Employee No.:	1101	Employee Number	Employee Name
2	Employee Name:	Melinda Hindquest	873	Charles K. Barkley
3			1109	Francis Jenikins
4			1549	James Brackman
5			1334	Linda Harper
6			1643	Louise Victor
7			1101	Melinda Hindquest
8			1873	Michael Orenthal
9			983	Peter Yates
10			972	Sally Rice
11			1398	Walter Franklin
12				

Looking up a value to the left

The VLOOKUP function always looks up a value in the first column of the lookup range. But what if you want to look up a value in a column other than the first column? It would be helpful if you could supply a negative value for the third argument for VLOOKUP — but Excel doesn't allow it.

Figure 14.7 illustrates the problem. Suppose that you want to look up the batting average (column B, in a range named *Averages*) of a player in column C (in a range named *Players*). The player you want data for appears in a cell named *LookupValue*. The VLOOKUP function won't work because the data isn't arranged correctly. One option is to rearrange your data, but sometimes that's not possible.

One solution is to use the LOOKUP function, which requires two range arguments. The following formula (in cell F3) returns the batting average from column B of the player name contained in the cell named *LookupValue*:

```
=LOOKUP(LookupValue,Players,Averages)
```

Using the LOOKUP function requires that the lookup range (in this case, the *Players* range) is in ascending order. In addition to this limitation, the formula suffers from a slight problem: If you enter a nonexistent player (in other words, the *LookupValue* cell contains a value not found in the *Players* range), the formula returns an erroneous result.

A better solution uses the INDEX and MATCH functions. The formula that follows works just like the previous one except that it returns #N/A if the player is not found. Another advantage is that the player names need not be sorted.

    =INDEX(Averages,MATCH(LookupValue,Players,0))

FIGURE 14.7

The VLOOKUP function can't look up a value in column B, based on a value in column C.

Performing a case-sensitive lookup

The Excel lookup functions (LOOKUP, VLOOKUP, and HLOOKUP) are not case sensitive. For example, if you write a lookup formula to look up the text *budget*, the formula considers any of the following a match: *BUDGET*, *Budget*, or *BuDgEt*.

Figure 14.8 shows a simple example. Range D2:D7 is named *Range1*, and range E2:E7 is named *Range2*. The word to be looked up appears in cell B1 (named *Value*).

FIGURE 14.8

Using an array formula to perform a case-sensitive lookup.

The array formula that follows is in cell B2. This formula does a case-sensitive lookup in *Range1* and returns the corresponding value in *Range2*.

```
{=INDEX(Range2,MATCH(TRUE,EXACT(Value,Range1),0))}
```

The formula looks up the word *DOG* (uppercase) and returns 300. The following standard LOOKUP formula (which is not case sensitive) returns 400:

```
=LOOKUP(Value,Range1,Range2)
```

Note
When entering an array formula, remember to use Ctrl+Shift+Enter. ■

Looking up a value from multiple lookup tables

You can, of course, have any number of lookup tables in a worksheet. In some situations, your formula may need to decide which lookup table to use. Figure 14.9 shows an example.

This workbook calculates sales commission and contains two lookup tables: G3:H9 (named *CommTable1*) and J3:K8 (named *CommTable2*). The commission rate for a particular sales representative depends on two factors: the sales rep's years of service (column B) and the amount sold (column C). Column D contains formulas that look up the commission rate from the appropriate table. For example, the formula in cell D2 is

```
=VLOOKUP(C2,IF(B2<3,CommTable1,CommTable2),2)
```

FIGURE 14.9

This worksheet demonstrates the use of multiple lookup tables.

	A	B	C	D	E	F	G	H	I	J	K
1	Sales Rep	Years	Sales	Comm. Rate	Commission		<3 Years Tenure			3+ Years Tenure	
							Amt Sold	Rate		Amt Sold	Rate
2	Benson	2	120,000	7.00%	8,400		0	1.50%		0	2.00%
3	Davidson	1	210,921	7.00%	14,764		5,000	3.25%		50,000	6.25%
4	Ellison	1	100,000	7.00%	7,000		10,000	3.50%		100,000	7.25%
5	Gomez	2	87,401	6.00%	5,244		20,000	5.00%		200,000	8.25%
6	Hernandez	6	310,983	9.25%	28,766		50,000	6.00%		300,000	9.25%
7	Kelly	3	43,902	2.00%	878		100,000	7.00%		500,000	10.00%
8	Martin	2	121,021	7.00%	8,471		250,000	8.00%			
9	Oswald	3	908	2.00%	18						
10	Reginald	1	0	1.50%	0						
11	Veras	4	359,832	9.25%	33,284						
12	Wilmington	4	502,983	10.00%	50,298						
13											

The second argument for the VLOOKUP function consists of an IF formula that uses the value in column B to determine which lookup table to use.

The formula in column E simply multiplies the sales amount in column C by the commission rate in column D. The formula in cell E2, for example, is

```
=C2*D2
```

Determining letter grades for test scores

A common use of a lookup table is to assign letter grades for test scores. Figure 14.10 shows a worksheet with student test scores. The range E2:F6 (named *GradeList*) displays a lookup table used to assign a letter grade to a test score.

Column C contains formulas that use the VLOOKUP function and the lookup table to assign a grade based on the score in column B. The formula in cell C2, for example, is

```
=VLOOKUP(B2,GradeList,2)
```

When the lookup table is small (as in the example shown earlier in Figure 14.10), you can use a literal array in place of the lookup table. The formula that follows, for example, returns a letter grade without using a lookup table. Rather, the information in the lookup table is hard-coded into an array. See Chapter 17 for more information about arrays.

```
=VLOOKUP(B2,{0,"F";40,"D";70,"C";80,"B";90,"A"},2)
```

Another approach, which uses a more legible formula, is to use the LOOKUP function with two array arguments:

```
=LOOKUP(B2,{0,40,70,80,90},{"F","D","C","B","A"})
```

FIGURE 14.10

Looking up letter grades for test scores.

	A	B	C	D	E	F	G
1	Student	Score	Grade		Score	Grade	
2	Adams	36	F		0	F	
3	Baker	68	D		40	D	
4	Camden	50	D		70	C	
5	Dailey	77	C		80	B	
6	Gomez	92	A		90	A	
7	Hernandez	100	A				
8	Jackson	74	C				
9	Maplethorpe	45	D				
10	Paulson	60	D				
11	Ramirez	89	B				
12	Sosa	99	A				
13	Thompson	91	A				
14	Wilson	59	D				
15							

Calculating a grade-point average

A student's *grade-point average* (GPA) is a numerical measure of the average grade received for classes taken. This discussion assumes a letter grade system, in which each letter grade is assigned a numeric value (A=4, B=3, C=2, D=1, and F=0). The GPA comprises an average of the numeric grade values weighted by the credit hours of the course. A one-hour course, for example, receives less weight than a three-hour course. The GPA ranges from 0 (all Fs) to 4.00 (all As).

Figure 14.11 shows a worksheet with information for a student. This student took five courses, for a total of 13 credit hours. Range B2:B6 is named *CreditHours*. The grades for each course appear in column C. (Range C2:C6 is named *Grades*.) Column D uses a lookup formula to calculate the grade value for each course. The lookup formula in cell D2, for example, follows. This formula uses the lookup table in G2:H6 (named *GradeTable*).

```
=VLOOKUP(C2,GradeTable,2,FALSE)
```

FIGURE 14.11

Using multiple formulas to calculate a GPA.

	A	B	C	D	E	F	G	H
1	Course	Credit Hrs	Grade	Grade Val	Weighted Val		GradeTable	
2	Psych 101	3	A	4	12		A	4
3	PhysEd	2	C	2	4		B	3
4	PoliSci 101	4	B	3	12		C	2
5	IndepStudy	1	A	4	4		D	1
6	IntroMath	3	A	4	12		F	0
7								
8	GPA:	3.38	<-- Requires multiple formulas and lookup table					
9								

Formulas in column E calculate the weighted values. The formula in cell E2 is

```
=D2*B2
```

Cell B8 computes the GPA by using the following formula:

```
=SUM(E2:E6)/SUM(B2:B6)
```

The preceding formulas work fine, but you can streamline the GPA calculation quite a bit. In fact, you can use a single array formula to make this calculation and avoid using the lookup table and the formulas in columns D and E. This array formula does the job:

```
{=SUM((MATCH(Grades,{"F","D","C","B","A"},0)-1)*CreditHours)
    /SUM(CreditHours)}
```

Performing a two-way lookup

Figure 14.12 shows a worksheet with a table that displays product sales by month. To retrieve sales for a particular month and product, the user enters a month in cell B1 and a product name in cell B2.

FIGURE 14.12

This table demonstrates a two-way lookup.

	A	B	C	D	E	F	G	H
1	Month:	July			Widgets	Sprockets	Snapholytes	Combined
2	Product:	Sprockets		January	2,892	1,771	4,718	9,381
3				February	3,380	4,711	2,615	10,706
4	Month Offset:	8		March	3,744	3,223	5,312	12,279
5	Product Offset:	3		April	3,221	2,438	1,108	6,767
6	Sales:	3,337		May	4,839	1,999	1,994	8,832
7				June	3,767	5,140	3,830	12,737
8				July	5,467	3,337	3,232	12,036
9	Single-formula -->	3,337		August	3,154	4,895	1,607	9,656
10				September	1,718	2,040	1,563	5,321
11				October	1,548	1,061	2,590	5,199
12				November	5,083	3,558	3,960	12,601
13				December	5,753	2,839	3,013	11,605
14				Total	44,566	37,012	35,542	117,120
15								

To simplify things, the worksheet uses the following named ranges:

Month	B1
Product	B2
Table	D1:H14
MonthList	D1:D14
ProductList	D1:H1

The following formula (in cell B4) uses the MATCH function to return the position of the *Month* within the *MonthList* range. For example, if the month is January, the formula returns 2 because January is the second item in the *MonthList* range (the first item is a blank cell, D1).

```
=MATCH(Month,MonthList,0)
```

The formula in cell B5 works similarly but uses the *ProductList* range.

```
=MATCH(Product,ProductList,0)
```

The final formula, in cell B6, returns the corresponding sales amount. It uses the INDEX function with the results from cells B4 and B5.

```
=INDEX(Table,B4,B5)
```

You can, of course, combine these formulas into a single formula, as shown here:

```
=INDEX(Table,MATCH(Month,MonthList,0),MATCH(Product,ProductList,0))
```

Tip

Another way to accomplish a two-way lookup is to provide a name for each row and column of the table. A quick way to do so is to select the table and choose Formulas ⇨ Defined Names ⇨ Create from Selection. In the Create Names from Selection dialog box, select the Top Row and Left Column check boxes. After creating the names, you can use a simple formula, such as:

```
= Sprockets July
```

This formula, which uses the range intersection operator (a space), returns July sales for Sprockets. See Chapter 10 for details about the range intersection operator. ∎

Performing a two-column lookup

Some situations may require a lookup based on the values in two columns. Figure 14.13 shows an example.

FIGURE 14.13

This workbook performs a lookup by using information in two columns (D and E).

	A	B	C	D	E	F
1	Make:	Jeep		Make	Model	Code
2	Model:	Grand Cherokee		Chevy	Blazer	C-094
3	Code:	J-701		Chevy	Tahoe	C-823
4				Ford	Explorer	F-772
5				Ford	Expedition	F-229
6				Isuzu	Rodeo	I-897
7				Isuzu	Trooper	I-900
8				Jeep	Cherokee	J-983
9				Jeep	Grand Cherokee	J-701
10				Nissan	Pathfinder	N-231
11				Toyota	4Runner	T-871
12				Toyota	Land Cruiser	T-981
13						
14						

The lookup table contains automobile makes and models and a corresponding code for each. The worksheet uses named ranges, as shown here:

F2:F12	*Code*
B1	*Make*
B2	*Model*
D2:D12	*Makes*
E2:E12	*Models*

The following array formula displays the corresponding code for an automobile make and model:

```
{=INDEX(Code,MATCH(Make&Model,Makes&Models,0))}
```

This formula works by concatenating the contents of *Make* and *Model* and then searching for this text in an array consisting of the concatenated corresponding text in *Makes* and *Models*.

Determining the cell address of a value within a range

Most of the time, you want your lookup formula to return a value. You may, however, need to determine the cell address of a particular value within a range. For example, Figure 14.14 shows a worksheet with a range of numbers that occupies a single column (named *Data*). Cell B1, which contains the value to look up, is named *Target*.

The formula in cell B2 returns the address in the *Data* range for the value in cell B1.

	A	B	C	D
1	Target:	55	Data	
2	Address:	$C$10	74	
3			62	
4			60	
5			44	
6			50	
7			41	
8			77	
9			24	
10			55	
11			30	
12			12	
13			21	
14			7	
15			1	
16			22	
17			53	
18			36	
19			18	
20			68	
21				
22				

The formula in cell B2, which follows, returns the address of the cell in the *Data* range that contains the *Target* value:

```
=ADDRESS(ROW(Data)+MATCH(Target,Data,0)-1,COLUMN(Data))
```

If the *Data* range occupies a single row, use this formula to return the address of the *Target* value:

```
=ADDRESS(ROW(Data),COLUMN(Data)+MATCH(Target,Data,0)-1)
```

If the *Data* range contains more than one instance of the *Target* value, the address of the first occurrence is returned. If the *Target* value isn't found in the *Data* range, the formula returns #N/A.

Looking up a value by using the closest match

The VLOOKUP and HLOOKUP functions are useful in the following situations:

- You need to identify an exact match for a target value. Use FALSE as the function's fourth argument.

- You need to locate an approximate match. If the function's fourth argument is TRUE or omitted and an exact match is not found, the next largest value less than the lookup value is returned.

But what if you need to look up a value based on the *closest* match? Neither VLOOKUP nor HLOOKUP can do the job.

Figure 14.15 shows a worksheet with student names in column A and values in column B. Range B2:B20 is named *Data*. Cell E2, named *Target*, contains a value to search for in the *Data* range. Cell E3, named *ColOffset*, contains a value that represents the column offset from the *Data* range.

This workbook demonstrates how to perform a lookup by using the closest match.

	A	B	C	D	E
1	Student	Data			
2	Ann	9,101	Target Value -->		8025
3	Betsy	8,873	Column Offset -->		-1
4	Chuck	6,000			
5	David	9,820		Student:	Leslie
6	George	10,500			
7	Hilda	3,500			
8	James	12,873			
9	John	5,867			
10	Keith	8,989			
11	Leslie	8,000			
12	Michelle	1,124			
13	Nora	9,099			
14	Paul	6,800			
15	Peter	5,509			
16	Rasmusen	5,460			
17	Sally	8,400			
18	Theresa	7,777			
19	Violet	3,600			
20	Wendy	5,400			
21					

The array formula that follows identifies the closest match to the *Target* value in the *Data* range and returns the names of the corresponding student in column A (that is, the column with an offset of -1). The formula returns Leslie (with a matching value of 8,000, which is the one closest to the *Target* value of 8,025).

```
{=INDIRECT(ADDRESS(ROW(Data)+MATCH(MIN(ABS(Target-Data)),
    ABS(Target-Data),0)-1,COLUMN(Data)+ColOffset))}
```

If two values in the *Data* range are equidistant from the *Target* value, the formula uses the first one in the list.

The value in *ColOffset* can be negative (for a column to the left of *Data*), positive (for a column to the right of *Data*), or 0 (for the actual closest match value in the *Data* range).

To understand how this formula works, you need to understand the INDIRECT function. This function's first argument is a text string in the form of a cell reference (or a reference to a cell that contains a text string). In this example, the text string is created by the ADDRESS function, which accepts a row and column reference and returns a cell address.

CHAPTER 3

Creating Formulas for Financial Applications

I t's a safe bet that the most common use of Excel is to perform calculations involving money. Every day, people make hundreds of thousands
of financial decisions based on the numbers that are calculated in a
spreadsheet. These decisions range from simple (*Can I afford to buy a new
car?*) to complex (*Will purchasing XYZ Corporation result in a positive cash flow
in the next 18 months?*). This chapter discusses basic financial calculations that
you can perform with the assistance of Excel.

The Time Value of Money

The face value of money may not always be what it seems. A key consideration is the time value of money. This concept involves calculating the value
of money in the past, present, or future. It is based on the premise that
money increases in value over time because of interest earned by the money.
In other words, a dollar invested today will be worth more tomorrow.

For example, imagine that your rich uncle decided to give away some money
and asked you to choose one of the following options:

- Receive $8,000 today.
- Receive $9,500 in one year.
- Receive $12,000 in five years.
- Receive $150 per month for five years.

If your goal is to maximize the amount received, you need to take into
account not only the face value of the money but also the *time value* of the
money when it arrives in your hands.

IN THIS CHAPTER

**A brief overview of the Excel
functions that deal with the
time value of money**

**Formulas that perform various
types of loan calculations**

**Formulas that perform various
types of investment
calculations**

**An overview of Excel
depreciation functions**

The time value of money depends on your perspective. In other words, you're either a lender or a borrower. When you take out a loan to purchase an automobile, you're a borrower, and the institution that provides the funds to you is the lender. When you invest money in a bank savings account, you're a lender; you're lending your money to the bank, and the bank is borrowing it from you.

Several concepts contribute to the time value of money:

- **Present Value (PV):** This is the principal amount. If you deposit $5,000 in a bank savings account, this amount represents the *principal,* or present value, of the money you invested. If you borrow $15,000 to purchase a car, this amount represents the principal or present value of the loan. Present Value may be positive or negative.

- **Future Value (FV):** This is the principal plus interest. If you invest $5,000 for five years and earn 3 percent annual interest, your investment is worth $5,796.37 at the end of the five-year term. This amount is the future value of your $5,000 investment. If you take out a three-year auto loan for $15,000 and make monthly payments based on a 5.25 percent annual interest rate, you pay a total of $16,244.97. This amount represents the principal plus the interest you paid. Future Value may be positive or negative, depending on the perspective (lender or borrower).

- **Payment (PMT):** This is either principal or principal plus interest. If you deposit $100 per month into a savings account, $100 is the payment. If you have a monthly mortgage payment of $1,025, this amount is made up of principal and interest.

- **Interest Rate:** Interest is a percentage of the principal, usually expressed on an annual basis. For example, you may earn 2.5 percent annual interest on a bank CD (certificate of deposit). Or your mortgage loan may have a 6.75 percent interest rate.

- **Period:** This represents the point in time when interest is paid or earned (for example, a bank CD that pays interest quarterly, or an auto loan that requires monthly payments).

- **Term:** This is the amount of time of interest. A 12-month bank CD has a term of one year. A 30-year mortgage loan has a term of 360 months.

Loan Calculations

This section describes how to calculate various components of a loan. Think of a loan as consisting of the following components:

- The loan amount
- The interest rate
- The number of payment periods
- The periodic payment amount

If you know any three of these components, you can create a formula to calculate the unknown component.

Note
The loan calculations in this section all assume a fixed-rate loan with a fixed term. ■

Worksheet functions for calculating loan information

This section describes six commonly used financial functions: PMT, PPMT, IPMT, RATE, NPER, and PV. For information about the arguments used in these functions, see Table 15.1.

TABLE 15.1

Financial Function Arguments

Function Argument	Description
rate	The interest rate per period. If the rate is expressed as an annual interest rate, you must divide it by the number of periods.
nper	The total number of payment periods.
per	A particular period. The period must be less than or equal to nper.
pmt	The payment made each period (a constant value that does not change).
fv	The future value after the last payment is made. If you omit fv, it is assumed to be 0. (The future value of a loan, for example, is 0.)
type	Indicates when payments are due — either 0 (due at the end of the period) or 1 (due at the beginning of the period). If you omit type, it is assumed to be 0.

PMT

The PMT function returns the loan payment (principal plus interest) per period, assuming constant payment amounts and a fixed interest rate. The syntax for the PMT function is

```
PMT(rate,nper,pv,fv,type)
```

The following formula returns the monthly payment amount for a $5,000 loan with a 6 percent annual percentage rate. The loan has a term of four years (48 months).

```
=PMT(6%/12,48,-5000)
```

This formula returns $117.43, the monthly payment for the loan. The first argument, rate, is the annual rate divided by the number of months in a year. Also, notice that the third argument (pv, for present value) is negative and represents money owed.

PPMT

The PPMT function returns the principal part of a loan payment for a given period, assuming constant payment amounts and a fixed interest rate. The syntax for the PPMT function is

```
PPMT(rate,per,nper,pv,fv,type)
```

The following formula returns the amount paid to principal for the first month of a $5,000 loan with a 6 percent annual percentage rate. The loan has a term of four years (48 months).

```
=PPMT(6%/12,1,48,-5000)
```

The formula returns $92.43 for the principal, which is about 78.7 percent of the total loan payment. If I change the second argument to 48 (to calculate the principal amount for the last payment), the formula returns $116.84, or about 99.5 percent of the total loan payment.

Note

To calculate the cumulative principal paid between any two payment periods, use the CUMPRINC function. This function uses two additional arguments: start_period and end_period. In Excel versions prior to Excel 2007, CUMPRINC is available only when you install the Analysis ToolPak add-in. ■

IPMT

The IPMT function returns the interest part of a loan payment for a given period, assuming constant payment amounts and a fixed interest rate. The syntax for the IPMT function is

```
IPMT(rate,per,nper,pv,fv,type)
```

The following formula returns the amount paid to interest for the first month of a $5,000 loan with a 6 percent annual percentage rate. The loan has a term of four years (48 months).

```
=IPMT(6%/12,1,48,-5000)
```

This formula returns an interest amount of $25.00. By the last payment period for the loan, the interest payment is only $0.58.

Note

To calculate the cumulative interest paid between any two payment periods, use the CUMIPMT function. This function uses two additional arguments: start_period and end_period. In Excel versions prior to Excel 2007, CUMIPMT is available only when you install the Analysis ToolPak add-in. ■

RATE

The RATE function returns the periodic interest rate of a loan, given the number of payment periods, the periodic payment amount, and the loan amount. The syntax for the RATE function is

```
RATE(nper,pmt,pv,fv,type,guess)
```

The following formula calculates the annual interest rate for a 48-month loan for $5,000 that has a monthly payment amount of $117.43.

```
=RATE(48,117.43,-5000)*12
```

This formula returns 6.00 percent. Notice that the result of the function is multiplied by 12 to get the annual percentage rate.

NPER

The NPER function returns the number of payment periods for a loan, given the loan's amount, interest rate, and periodic payment amount. The syntax for the NPER function is

```
NPER(rate,pmt,pv,fv,type)
```

The following formula calculates the number of payment periods for a $5,000 loan that has a monthly payment amount of $117.43. The loan has a 6 percent annual interest rate.

```
=NPER(6%/12,117.43,-5000)
```

This formula returns 47.997 (that is, 48 months). The monthly payment was rounded to the nearest penny, causing the minor discrepancy.

PV

The PV function returns the present value (that is, the original loan amount) for a loan, given the interest rate, the number of periods, and the periodic payment amount. The syntax for the PV function is

```
PV(rate,nper,pmt,fv,type)
```

The following formula calculates the original loan amount for a 48-month loan that has a monthly payment amount of $117.43. The annual interest rate is 6 percent.

```
=PV(6%/12,48,-117.43)
```

This formula returns $5,000.21. The monthly payment was rounded to the nearest penny, causing the $0.21 discrepancy.

A loan calculation example

Figure 15.1 shows a worksheet set up to calculate the periodic payment amount for a loan.

On the CD

The workbook described in this section is available on the companion CD-ROM. The file is named loan payment.xlsx.

The loan amount is in cell B1, and the annual interest rate is in cell B2. Cell B3 contains the payment period expressed in months. For example, if cell B3 is 1, the payment is due monthly. If cell B3 is 3, the payment is due every three months, or quarterly. Cell B4 contains the number of periods of the loan. The example shown in this figure calculates the payment for a $25,000 loan at 6.25 percent annual interest with monthly payments for 36 months. The formula in cell B6 is

```
=PMT(B2*(B3/12),B4,-B1)
```

FIGURE 15.1

Using the PMT function to calculate a periodic loan payment amount.

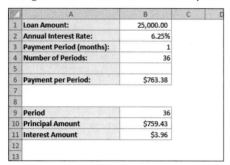

	A	B	C	D
1	Loan Amount:	25,000.00		
2	Annual Interest Rate:	6.25%		
3	Payment Period (months):	1		
4	Number of Periods:	36		
5				
6	Payment per Period:	$763.38		
7				
8				
9	Period	36		
10	Principal Amount	$759.43		
11	Interest Amount	$3.96		
12				
13				

Notice that the first argument is an expression that calculates the *periodic interest rate* by using the annual interest rate and the payment period. Therefore, if payments are made quarterly on a three-year loan, the payment period is 3, the number of periods is 12, and the periodic interest rate would be calculated as the annual interest rate multiplied by 3/12.

In the worksheet in Figure 15.1, range A9:B11 is set up to calculate the principal and interest amount for a particular payment period. Cell B9 contains the payment period used by the formulas in B10:B11. (The payment period must be less than or equal to the value in cell B4.)

The formula in cell B10, shown here, calculates the amount of the payment that goes toward principal for the payment period in cell B9:

```
=PPMT(B2*(B3/12),B9,B4,-B1)
```

The following formula, in cell B11, calculates the amount of the payment that goes toward interest for the payment period in cell B9:

```
=IPMT(B2*(B3/12),B9,B4,-B1)
```

You should note that the sum of B10 and B11 is equal to the total loan payment calculated in cell B6. However, the relative proportion of principal and interest amounts varies with the payment period. (An increasingly larger proportion of the payment is applied toward principal as the loan progresses.) Figure 15.2 shows the principal and interest portions graphically.

Credit card payments

Do you ever wonder how long it would take to pay off a credit card balance if you make the minimum payment amount each month? Figure 15.3 shows a worksheet set up to make this type of calculation.

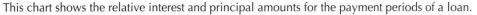

This chart shows the relative interest and principal amounts for the payment periods of a loan.

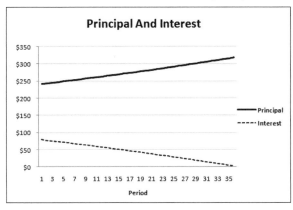

On the CD

The workbook shown in Figure 15.3 is available on the companion CD-ROM. The file is named `credit card payments.xlsx.`

Range B1:B5 stores input values. In this example, the credit card has a balance of $1,000, and the lender charges 21.25 percent annual percentage rate (APR). The minimum payment is 2.00 percent (typical of many credit card lenders). Therefore, the minimum payment amount for this example is $20. You can enter a different payment amount in cell B5, but it must be large enough to pay off the loan. For example, you may choose to pay $50 per month to pay off the balance more quickly. However, paying $10 per month isn't sufficient, and the formulas return an error.

Range B7:B9 holds formulas that perform various calculations. The formula in cell B7, which follows, calculates the number of months required to pay off the balance:

```
=NPER(B2/12,B5,-B1,0)
```

The formula in B8 calculates the total amount you will pay. This formula is

```
=B7*B5
```

The formula in cell B9 calculates the total interest paid:

```
=B8-B1
```

FIGURE 15.3

This worksheet calculates the number of payments required to pay off a credit card balance by paying the minimum payment amount each month.

	A	B
1	Credit Card Balance	$1,000.00
2	Annual Interest Rate:	21.25%
3	Minimum Payment Pct:	2.00%
4	Minimum Monthly Payment Amount:	$20.00
5	Your Actual Monthly Payment:	$20.00
6		
7	No. of Payments Required:	123.4
8	Total Amount Paid:	$2,468.42
9	Total Interest Paid:	$1,468.42
10		
11		

In this example, it would take about 123 months (more than ten years) to pay off the credit card balance if the borrower made only the minimum monthly payment. The total interest paid on the $1,000 loan would be $1,468.42. This calculation assumes, of course, that no additional charges are made on the account. This example may help explain why you receive so many credit card solicitations in the mail.

Figure 15.4 shows some additional calculations for the credit card example. For example, if you want to pay off the credit card in 12 months, you need to make monthly payments of $93.23. (This amount results in total payments of $1,118.81 with total interest of $118.81.) The formula in B13 is

```
=PMT($B$2/12,A13,-$B$1)
```

FIGURE 15.4

Column B shows the payment required to pay off the credit card balance for various payoff periods.

	A	B	C	D
11				
12	Other Payoff Periods (months)	Pmt Required	Total Pmts	Total Interest
13	2	$513.32	$1,026.64	$26.64
14	6	$177.15	$1,062.89	$62.89
15	12	$93.23	$1,118.81	$118.81
16	24	$51.51	$1,236.20	$236.20
17	36	$37.80	$1,360.93	$360.93
18	48	$31.10	$1,492.82	$492.82
19	60	$27.19	$1,631.65	$631.65
20	72	$24.68	$1,777.17	$777.17
21	84	$22.96	$1,929.06	$929.06
22	96	$21.74	$2,086.97	$1,086.97
23	108	$20.84	$2,250.54	$1,250.54
24	120	$20.16	$2,419.38	$1,419.38
25	132	$19.64	$2,593.09	$1,593.09
26				

Creating a loan amortization schedule

A *loan amortization schedule* is a table of values that shows various types of information for each payment period of a loan. Figure 15.5 shows a worksheet that uses formulas to calculate an amortization schedule.

FIGURE 15.5

A loan amortization schedule.

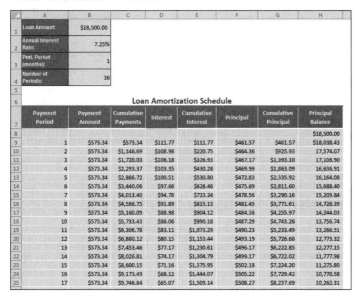

	A	B	C	D	E	F	G	H
1	Loan Amount:	$18,500.00						
2	Annual Interest Rate:	7.25%						
3	Pmt. Period (months):	1						
4	Number of Periods:	36						
5								
6				Loan Amortization Schedule				
7	Payment Period	Payment Amount	Cumulative Payments	Interest	Cumulative Interest	Principal	Cumulative Principal	Principal Balance
8								$18,500.00
9	1	$573.34	$573.34	$111.77	$111.77	$461.57	$461.57	$18,038.43
10	2	$573.34	$1,146.69	$108.98	$220.75	$464.36	$925.93	17,574.07
11	3	$573.34	$1,720.03	$106.18	$326.93	$467.17	$1,393.10	17,106.90
12	4	$573.34	$2,293.37	$103.35	$430.28	$469.99	$1,863.09	16,636.91
13	5	$573.34	$2,866.72	$100.51	$530.80	$472.83	$2,335.92	16,164.08
14	6	$573.34	$3,440.06	$97.66	$628.46	$475.69	$2,811.60	15,688.40
15	7	$573.34	$4,013.40	$94.78	$723.24	$478.56	$3,290.16	15,209.84
16	8	$573.34	$4,586.75	$91.89	$815.13	$481.45	$3,771.61	14,728.39
17	9	$573.34	$5,160.09	$88.98	$904.12	$484.36	$4,255.97	14,244.03
18	10	$573.34	$5,733.43	$86.06	$990.18	$487.29	$4,743.26	13,756.74
19	11	$573.34	$6,306.78	$83.11	$1,073.29	$490.23	$5,233.49	13,266.51
20	12	$573.34	$6,880.12	$80.15	$1,153.44	$493.19	$5,726.68	12,773.32
21	13	$573.34	$7,453.46	$77.17	$1,230.61	$496.17	$6,222.85	12,277.15
22	14	$573.34	$8,026.81	$74.17	$1,304.79	$499.17	$6,722.02	11,777.98
23	15	$573.34	$8,600.15	$71.16	$1,375.95	$502.18	$7,224.20	11,275.80
24	16	$573.34	$9,173.49	$68.12	$1,444.07	$505.22	$7,729.42	10,770.58
25	17	$573.34	$9,746.84	$65.07	$1,509.14	$508.27	$8,237.69	10,262.31

On the CD

This workbook available on the companion CD-ROM. The file is named `loan amortization schedule .xlsx`.

The loan parameters are entered into B1:B4, and the formulas beginning in row 9 use these values for the calculations. Table 15.2 shows the formulas in row 9 of the schedule. These formulas were copied down to row 488. Therefore, the worksheet can calculate amortization schedules for a loan with as many as 480 payment periods (40 years of monthly payments).

Note

Formulas in the rows that extend beyond the number of payments return an error value. The worksheet uses conditional formatting to hide the data in these rows. See Chapter 20 for more information about conditional formatting. ∎

TABLE 15.2

Formulas Used to Calculate an Amortization Schedule

Cell	Formula	Description
A9	=A8+1	Returns the payment number
B9	=PMT($B$2*($B$3/12),$B$4,-$B$1)	Calculates the periodic payment amount
C9	=C8+B9	Calculates the cumulative payment amounts
D9	=IPMT($B$2*($B$3/12),A9,$B$4,-$B$1)	Calculates the interest portion of the periodic payment
E9	=E8+D9	Calculates the cumulative interest paid
F9	=PPMT($B$2*($B$3/12),A9,$B$4,-$B$1)	Calculates the principal portion of the periodic payment
G9	=G8+F9	Calculates the cumulative amount applied toward principal
H9	=H8-F9	Returns the principal balance at the end of the period

Summarizing loan options by using a data table

The Excel Data Table feature is probably one of the most underutilized tools in Excel. Keep in mind that a data table is not the same as a table (created with Insert ⇨ Tables ⇨ Table). A data table is a handy way to summarize calculations that depend on one or two "changing" cells. In this example, I use a data table to summarize various loan options. This section describes how to create one-way and two-way data tables.

Cross-Reference

See Chapter 36 for more information about setting up data tables. ∎

On the CD

A workbook that demonstrates one- and two-way data tables is available on the companion CD-ROM. The file is named loan data tables.xlsx.

Creating a one-way data table

A *one-way data table* shows the results of any number of calculations for different values of a single input cell.

Figure 15.6 shows a one-way data table (in B10:I13) that displays three calculations (payment amount, total payments, and total interest) for a loan, using seven interest rates ranging from 7.00 percent to 8.50 percent. In this example, the input cell is cell B2.

FIGURE 15.6

Using a one-way data table to display three loan calculations for various interest rates.

To create this one-way data table, follow these steps:

1. **Enter the formulas that return the results for use in the data table.** In this example, the formulas are in B6:B8.

2. **Enter various values for a single input cell in successive columns.** In this example, the input value is interest rate, and the values for various interest rates appear in C10:I10.

3. **Create a reference to the formula cells in the column to the left of the input values.** In this example, the range B11:B13 contains simple formulas that reference other cells. For example, cell B11 contains the following formula:

   =B6

4. **Select the rectangular range that contains the entries from the previous steps.** In this example, select B10:I13.

5. **Choose Data ⇨ Data Tools ⇨ What-If Analysis ⇨ Data Table.** Excel displays the Data Table dialog box, shown in Figure 15.7.

FIGURE 15.7

The Data Table dialog box.

6. **For the Row input cell field, specify the cell reference that corresponds to the variable in your Data Table column header row.** In this example, the Row input cell is B2.

7. **Leave the Column input cell field empty.** The Column input field is used for two-way data tables, described in the next section.

8. **Click OK.** Excel inserts an array formula that uses the TABLE function with a single argument.

9. **(Optional) Format the data table.** For example, you may want to apply shading to the row and column headers.

Note that the array formula is not entered into the entire range that you selected in Step 4. The first column and first row of your selection are not changed.

Tip

When you create a data table, the leftmost column of the data table (the column that contains the references entered in Step 3) contains the calculated values for the input cell. In this example, those values are repeated in column D. You may want to hide the values in column B by making the font color the same color as the background. ■

Creating a two-way data table

A *two-way data table* shows the results of a single calculation for different values of two input cells. Figure 15.8 shows a two-way data table (in B10:I16) that displays a calculation (payment amount) for a loan, using seven interest rates and six loan amounts.

To create this two-way data table, follow these steps:

1. **Enter a formula that returns the results that will be used in the data table.** In this example, the formula is in cell B6. The formulas in B7:B8 are not used.

2. **Enter various values for the first input in successive columns.** In this example, the first input value is interest rate, and the values for various interest rates appear in C10:I10.

FIGURE 15.8

Using a two-way data table to display payment amounts for various loan amounts and interest rates.

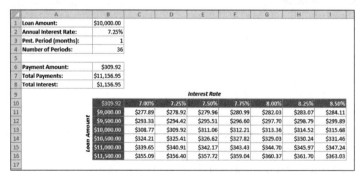

3. **Enter various values for the second input cell in successive rows, to the left and below the input values for the first input.** In this example, the second input value is the loan amount, and the values for various loan amounts are in B11:B16.

4. **Create a reference to the formula that will be calculated in the table.** This reference goes in the upper-left corner of the data table range. In this example, cell B10 contains the following formula:

   =B6

5. **Select the rectangular range that contains the entries from the previous steps.** In this example, select B10:I16.

6. **Choose Data ➪ Data Tools ➪ What-If Analysis ➪ Data Table.** Excel displays the Data Table dialog box. (Refer to Figure 15.7.)

7. **For the Row Input Cell field, specify the cell reference that corresponds to the first input cell.** In this example, the Row Input cell is B2.

8. **For the Column Input Cell field, specify the cell reference that corresponds to the second input cell.** In this example, the ColumnInput cell is B1.

9. **Click OK.** Excel inserts an array formula that uses the TABLE function with two arguments.

After you create the two-way data table, you can change the calculated cell by changing the cell reference in the upper-left cell of the data table. In this example, you can change the formula in cell B10 to =B8 so that the data table displays total interest rather than payment amounts.

Tip

If you create very large data tables, the calculation speed of your workbook may be slowed down. Excel has a special calculation mode for calculation-intensive data tables. To change the calculation mode, choose Formulas ➪ Calculation ➪ Calculation Options ➪ Automatic Except For Data Tables. ■

Calculating a loan with irregular payments

So far, the loan calculation examples in this chapter have involved loans with regular periodic payments. In some cases, loan payback is irregular. For example, you may loan some money to a friend without a formal agreement as to how he will pay the money back. You still collect interest on the loan, so you need a way to perform the calculations based on the actual payment dates.

Figure 15.9 shows a worksheet set up to keep track of such a loan. The annual interest rate for the loan is stored in cell B1 (named *APR*). The original loan amount and loan date are stored in row 5. Formulas, beginning in row 6, track the irregular loan payments and perform calculations.

FIGURE 15.9

This worksheet tracks loan payments that are made on an irregular basis.

	A	B	C	D	E	F	G	H
1	Interest Rate (APR):	6.50%						
2								
3								
4	Payment Number	Payment Amount	Payment Date	Amount to Interest	Amount to Principal	Cumulative Payments	Cumulative Interest	Loan Balance
5	Original Loan	($10,000.00)	06/08/08					$10,000.00
6	1	$200.00	07/25/08	$83.70	$116.30	$200.00	$83.70	$9,883.70
7	2	$200.00	08/09/08	$26.40	$173.60	$400.00	$110.10	$9,710.10
8	3	$200.00	09/24/08	$79.54	$120.46	$600.00	$189.64	$9,589.64
9	4	$100.00	12/09/08	$129.79	($29.79)	$700.00	$319.43	$9,619.43
10	5	$250.00	01/19/09	$70.24	$179.76	$950.00	$389.67	$9,439.67
11	Addition to Principal	($500.00)	02/01/09	$21.85	($521.85)	$450.00	$411.52	$9,961.52
12	6	$200.00	02/11/09	$17.74	$182.26	$650.00	$429.26	$9,779.26
13	7	$100.00	02/27/09	$27.86	$72.14	$750.00	$457.12	$9,707.12
14	8	$1,000.00	03/08/09	$15.56	$984.44	$1,750.00	$472.68	$8,722.68
15	9	$250.00	03/23/09	$23.30	$226.70	$2,000.00	$495.98	$8,495.98
16	10	$200.00	04/09/09	$25.72	$174.28	$2,200.00	$521.70	$8,321.70
17	11	$200.00	04/26/09	$25.19	$174.81	$2,400.00	$546.90	$8,146.90
18	12	$1,000.00	05/11/09	$21.76	$978.24	$3,400.00	$568.66	$7,168.66
19	13	$100.00	05/23/09	$15.32	$84.68	$3,500.00	$583.98	$7,083.98
20	14	$200.00	06/09/09	$21.45	$178.55	$3,700.00	$605.42	$6,905.42
21	15	$200.00	06/26/09	$20.91	$179.09	$3,900.00	$626.33	$6,726.33
22	16	$100.00	07/12/09	$19.17	$80.83	$4,000.00	$645.49	$6,645.49
23	17	$100.00	07/22/09	$11.83	$88.17	$4,100.00	$657.33	$6,557.33
24	Addition to Principal	($500.00)	09/08/09	$56.05	($556.05)	$3,600.00	$713.38	$7,113.38
25	18	$100.00	11/09/09	$78.54	$21.46	$3,700.00	$791.92	$7,091.92
26	19	$100.00	11/22/09	$16.42	$83.58	$3,800.00	$808.34	$7,008.34
27	20	$200.00	12/22/09	$37.44	$162.56	$4,000.00	$845.78	$6,845.78
28	21	$750.00	01/12/10	$25.60	$724.40	$4,750.00	$871.38	$6,121.38
29	22	$750.00	01/26/10	$15.26	$734.74	$5,500.00	$886.64	$5,386.64
30	23	$750.00	02/12/10	$16.31	$733.69	$6,250.00	$902.95	$4,652.95
31	24							

Column B stores the payment amount made on the date in column C. Notice that the payments are not made on a regular basis. Also, notice that in two cases (row 11 and row 24), the payment amount is negative. These entries represent additional borrowed money added to the loan balance. Formulas in columns D and E calculate the amount of the payment credited toward interest and principal. Columns F and G keep a running tally of the cumulative payments and interest amounts. Formulas in column H compute the new loan balance after each payment. Table 15.3 lists and describes the formulas in row 6. Note that each formula uses an IF function to determine whether the payment date in column C is missing. If so, the formula returns an empty string, so no data appears in the cell.

TABLE 15.3

Formulas to Calculate a Loan with Irregular Payments

Cell	Formula	Description
D6	=IF(C6<>"",(C6-C5)/365*H5*APR,"")	The formula calculates the interest, based on the payment date.
E6	=IF(C6<>"",B6-D6,"")	The formula subtracts the interest amount from the payment to calculate the amount credited to principal.

Cell	Formula	Description
F6	=IF(C6<>"",F5+B6,"")	The formula adds the payment amount to the running total.
G6	=IF(C6<>"",G5+D6,"")	The formula adds the interest to the running total.
H6	=IF(C6<>"",H5-E6,"")	The formula calculates the new loan balance by subtracting the principal amount from the previous loan balance.

On the CD

This workbook is available on the companion CD-ROM. The file name is `irregular payments.xlsx`.

Investment Calculations

Investment calculations involve calculating interest on fixed-rate investments, such as bank savings accounts, CDs, and annuities. You can make these interest calculations for investments that consist of a single deposit or multiple deposits.

On the CD

The companion CD-ROM contains a workbook with all the interest calculation examples in this section. The file is named `investment calculations.xlsx`.

Future value of a single deposit

Many investments consist of a single deposit that earns interest over the term of the investment. This section describes calculations for simple interest and compound interest.

Calculating simple interest

Simple interest refers to the fact that interest payments are not compounded. The basic formula for computing interest is

Interest = Principal * Rate * Term

For example, suppose that you deposit $1,000 into a bank CD that pays a 3 percent simple annual interest rate. After one year, the CD matures, and you withdraw your money. The bank adds $30, and you walk away with $1,030. In this case, the interest earned is calculated by multiplying the principal ($1,000) by the interest rate (.03) by the term (one year).

If the investment term is less than one year, the simple interest rate is adjusted accordingly, based on the term. For example, $1,000 invested in a six-month CD that pays 3 percent simple annual interest earns $15.00 when the CD matures. In this case, the annual interest rate multiplies by 6/12.

Figure 15.10 shows a worksheet set up to make simple interest calculations. The formula in cell B7, shown here, calculates the interest due at the end of the term:

```
=B3*B4*B5
```

The formula in B8 simply adds the interest to the original investment amount.

This worksheet calculates simple interest payments.

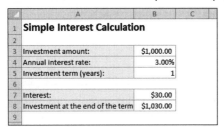

Calculating compound interest

Most fixed-term investments pay interest by using some type of compound interest calculation. *Compound interest* refers to interest credited to the investment balance, and the investment then earns interest on the interest.

For example, suppose that you deposit $1,000 into a bank CD that pays 3 percent annual interest rate, compounded monthly. Each month, the interest is calculated on the balance, and that amount is credited to your account. The next month's interest calculation will be based on a higher amount because it also includes the previous month's interest payment. One way to calculate the final investment amount involves a series of formulas (see Figure 15.11).

Column B contains formulas to calculate the interest for one month. For example, the formula in B10 is

```
=C9*($B$5*(1/12))
```

The formulas in column C simply add the monthly interest amount to the balance. For example, the formula in C10 is

```
=C9+B10
```

At the end of the 12-month term, the CD balance is $1,030.42. In other words, monthly compounding results in an additional $0.42 (compared with simple interest).

FIGURE 15.11

Using a series of formulas to calculate compound interest.

	A	B	C
1	**Compound Interest Calculation**		
2	*Monthly compounding*		
3			
4	Investment amount:	$1,000.00	
5	Annual interest rate:	3.00%	
6	Investment term (months):	12	
7			
8	Month	Interest Earned	Balance
9	Beginning Balance		$1,000.00
10	1	$2.50	$1,002.50
11	2	$2.51	$1,005.01
12	3	$2.51	$1,007.52
13	4	$2.52	$1,010.04
14	5	$2.53	$1,012.56
15	6	$2.53	$1,015.09
16	7	$2.54	$1,017.63
17	8	$2.54	$1,020.18
18	9	$2.55	$1,022.73
19	10	$2.56	$1,025.28
20	11	$2.56	$1,027.85
21	12	$2.57	$1,030.42
22			

You can use the FV (Future Value) function to calculate the final investment amount without using a series of formulas. Figure 15.12 shows a worksheet set up to calculate compound interest. Cell B6 is an input cell that holds the number of compounding periods per year. For monthly compounding, the value in B6 would be 12. For quarterly compounding, the value would be 4. For daily compounding, the value would be 365. Cell B7 holds the term of the investment expressed in years.

FIGURE 15.12

Using a single formula to calculate compound interest.

	A	B
1	**Compound Interest Calculation**	
2	*Single formula general solution*	
3		
4	Investment amount:	$5,000.00
5	Annual interest rate:	4.25%
6	Compounding periods/year	4
7	Term (years)	3
8		
9	Periodic interest rate:	1.06%
10	Investment value at end of term:	$5,676.11
11	Total interest earned:	$676.11
12		
13	Annual yield:	4.51%
14		
15		

Cell B9 contains the following formula that calculates the periodic interest rate. This value is the interest rate used for each compounding period.

```
=B5*(1/B6)
```

The formula in cell B10 uses the FV function to calculate the value of the investment at the end of the term. The formula is

```
=FV(B9,B6*B7,,-B4)
```

The first argument for the FV function is the periodic interest rate, which is calculated in cell B9. The second argument represents the total number of compounding periods. The third argument (pmt) is omitted, and the fourth argument is the original investment amount (expressed as a negative value).

The total interest is calculated with a simple formula in cell B11:

```
=B10-B4
```

Another formula, in cell B13, calculates the annual yield on the investment:

```
=(B11/B4)/B7
```

For example, suppose that you deposit $5,000 into a three-year CD with a 4.25 percent annual interest rate compounded quarterly. In this case, the investment has four compounding periods per year, so you enter **4** into cell B6. The term is three years, so you enter **3** into cell B7. The formula in B10 returns $5,676.11.

Perhaps you want to see how this rate stacks up against a competitor's account that offers daily compounding. Figure 15.13 shows a calculation with daily compounding, using a $5,000 investment (compare this with Figure 15.12). As you can see, the difference is very small ($679.88 versus $676.11). Over a period of three years, the account with daily compounding earns a total of $3.77 more interest. In terms of annual yield, quarterly compounding earns 4.51%, and daily compounding earns 4.53%.

Calculating interest with continuous compounding

The term *continuous compounding* refers to interest that is accumulated continuously. In other words, the investment has an infinite number of compounding periods per year. The following formula calculates the future value of a $5,000 investment at 4.25 percent compounded continuously for three years:

```
=5000*EXP(4.25%*3)
```

The formula returns $5,679.92, which is an additional $0.04 compared with daily compounding.

FIGURE 15.13

Calculating interest by using daily compounding.

	A	B
1	**Compound Interest Calculation**	
2	*Single formula general solution*	
3		
4	Investment amount:	$5,000.00
5	Annual interest rate:	4.25%
6	Compounding periods/year	365
7	Term (years)	3
8		
9	Periodic interest rate:	0.01%
10	Investment value at end of term:	$5,679.88
11	Total interest earned:	$679.88
12		
13	Annual yield:	4.53%
14		

Note

You can calculate compound interest without using the FV function. The general formula to calculate compound interest is

```
Principal * (1 + periodic rate) ^ number of periods
```

For example, consider a five-year, $5,000 investment that earns an annual interest rate of 4 percent, compounded monthly. The formula to calculate the future value of this investment is

```
=5000*(1+4%/12)^(12*5)
```

The Rule of 72

Need to make an investment decision, but don't have a computer handy? You can use the *Rule of 72* to determine the number of years required to double your money at a particular interest rate, using annual compounding. Just divide 72 by the interest rate. For example, consider a $10,000 investment at 4 percent interest. How many years will it take to turn that 10 grand into 20 grand? Take 72, divide it by 4, and you get 18 years. What if you can get a 5 percent interest rate? If so, you can double your money in a little over 14 years.

How accurate is the Rule of 72? The table that follows shows Rule of 72 estimated values versus the actual values for various interest rates. As you can see, this simple rule is remarkably accurate. However, for interest rates that exceed 30 percent, the accuracy drops off considerably.

continued

continued

Interest Rate	Rule of 72	Actual
1%	72.00	69.66
2%	36.00	35.00
3%	24.00	23.45
4%	18.00	17.67
5%	14.40	14.21
6%	12.00	11.90
7%	10.29	10.24
8%	9.00	9.01
9%	8.00	8.04
10%	7.20	7.27
15%	4.80	4.96
20%	3.60	3.80
25%	2.88	3.11
30%	2.40	2.64

The Rule of 72 also works in reverse. For example, if you want to double your money in six years, divide 6 into 72; you'll discover that you need to find an investment that pays an annual interest rate of about 12 percent. Good luck.

Future value of a series of deposits

Now, consider another type of investment, one in which you make a regular series of deposits into an account. This type of investment is known as an *annuity*.

The worksheet functions discussed in the "Loan Calculations" section earlier in this chapter also apply to annuities, but you need to use the perspective of a lender, not a borrower. A simple example of this type of investment is a holiday club savings program offered by some banking institutions. A fixed amount is deducted from each of your paychecks and deposited into an interest-earning account. At the end of the year, you withdraw the money (with accumulated interest) to use for holiday expenses.

Suppose that you deposit $200 at the beginning of each month (for 12 months) into an account that pays 2.5 percent annual interest compounded monthly. The following formula calculates the future value of your series of deposits:

```
=FV(2.5%/12,12,-200,,1)
```

This formula returns $2,432.75, which represents the total of your deposits ($2,400) plus the interest ($32.75). The last argument for the FV function is 1, which means that you make payments at the beginning of the month. Figure 15.14 shows a worksheet set up to calculate annuities. Table 15.4 describes the contents of this sheet.

FIGURE 15.14

This worksheet contains formulas to calculate annuities.

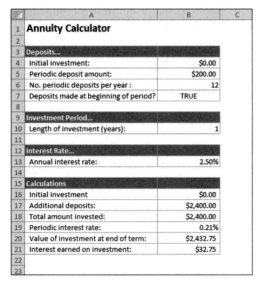

	A	B	C
1	**Annuity Calculator**		
2			
3	Deposits...		
4	Initial investment:	$0.00	
5	Periodic deposit amount:	$200.00	
6	No. periodic deposits per year :	12	
7	Deposits made at beginning of period?	TRUE	
8			
9	Investment Period...		
10	Length of investment (years):	1	
11			
12	Interest Rate...		
13	Annual interest rate:	2.50%	
14			
15	Calculations		
16	Initial investment	$0.00	
17	Additional deposits:	$2,400.00	
18	Total amount invested:	$2,400.00	
19	Periodic interest rate:	0.21%	
20	Value of investment at end of term:	$2,432.75	
21	Interest earned on investment:	$32.75	
22			
23			

On the CD

The workbook shown in Figure 15.14 is available on the companion CD-ROM. The file is named annuity calculator.xlsx.

TABLE 15.4

The Annuity Calculator Worksheet

Cell	Formula	Description
B4	None (input cell)	Initial investment (can be 0)
B5	None (input cell)	The amount deposited on a regular basis
B6	None (input cell)	The number of deposits made in 12 months
B7	None (input cell)	TRUE if you make deposits at the beginning of period; FALSE otherwise
B10	None (input cell)	The length of the investment, in years (can be fractional)

continued

TABLE 15.4	*(continued)*	
Cell	**Formula**	**Description**
B13	None (input cell)	The annual interest rate
B16	=B4	Displays the initial investment amount
B17	=B5*B6*B10	Calculates the total of all regular deposits
B18	=B16+B17	Adds the initial investment to the sum of the deposits
B19	=B13*(1/B6)	Calculates the periodic interest rate
B20	=FV(B19,B6*B10,-B5,-B4,IF(B7,1,0))	Calculates the future value of the investment
B21	=B20-B18	Calculates the interest earned from the investment

Depreciation Calculations

Excel offers five functions to calculate depreciation of an asset over time. Depreciating an asset places a value on the asset at a point in time, based on the original value and its useful life. The function that you choose depends on the type of *depreciation method* that you use.

Table 15.5 summarizes the Excel depreciation functions and the arguments used by each. For complete details, consult the Excel online Help system.

TABLE 15.5		

Excel Depreciation Functions

Function	Depreciation Method	Arguments*
SLN	Straight-line. The asset depreciates by the same amount each year of its life.	Cost, Salvage, Life
DB	Declining balance. Computes depreciation at a fixed rate.	Cost, Salvage, Life, Period, [Month]
DDB	Double-declining balance. Computes depreciation at an accelerated rate. Depreciation is highest in the first period and decreases in successive periods.	Cost, Salvage, Life, Period, [Factor

Function	Depreciation Method	Arguments*
SYD	Sum of the year's digits. Allocates a large depreciation in the earlier years of an asset's life.	Cost, Salvage, Life, Period
VDB	Variable-declining balance. Computes the depreciation of an asset for any period (including partial periods) using the double-declining balance method or some other method you specify.	Cost, Salvage, Life, Start _Period, End_Period, [Factor], [No Switch]

* Arguments in brackets are optional.

Here are the arguments for the depreciation functions:

- Cost: Original cost of the asset.
- Salvage: Salvage cost of the asset after it has fully depreciated.
- Life: Number of periods over which the asset will depreciate.
- Period: Period in the life for which the calculation is being made.
- Month: Number of months in the first year; if omitted, Excel uses 12.
- Start_Period:Starting period for the depreciation calculation.
- End_Period: Ending period for the depreciation calculation.
- Factor: Rate at which the balance declines; if omitted, it is assumed to be 2 (that is, double-declining).
- No Switch: TRUE or FALSE. Specifies whether to switch to straight-line depreciation when depreciation is greater than the declining balance calculation.

Figure 15.15 shows depreciation calculations using the SLN, DB, DDB, and SYD functions. The asset's original cost, $10,000, is assumed to have a useful life of 10 years, with a salvage value of $1,000. The range labeled *Depreciation Amount* shows the annual depreciation of the asset. The range labeled *Value of Asset* shows the asset's depreciated value over its life.

On the CD

This workbook is available on the companion CD-ROM. The file is named depreciation calculations .xlsx.

Figure 15.16 shows a chart that graphs the asset's value. As you can see, the SLN function produces a straight line; the other functions produce a curved line because the depreciation is greater in the earlier years of the asset's life.

FIGURE 15.15

A comparison of four depreciation functions.

	A	B	C	D	E
1	Asset:	Office Furniture			
2	Original Cost:	$10,000			
3	Life (years):	10			
4	Salvage Value:	$1,000			
5					
6	*Depreciation Amount*				
7	Year	SLN	DB	DDB	SYD
8	1	$900.00	$2,060.00	$2,000.00	$1,636.36
9	2	$900.00	$1,635.64	$1,600.00	$1,472.73
10	3	$900.00	$1,298.70	$1,280.00	$1,309.09
11	4	$900.00	$1,031.17	$1,024.00	$1,145.45
12	5	$900.00	$818.75	$819.20	$981.82
13	6	$900.00	$650.08	$655.36	$818.18
14	7	$900.00	$516.17	$524.29	$654.55
15	8	$900.00	$409.84	$419.43	$490.91
16	9	$900.00	$325.41	$335.54	$327.27
17	10	$900.00	$258.38	$268.44	$163.64
18					
19					
20	*Value of Asset*				
21	Year	SLN	DB	DDB	SYD
22	0	$10,000.00	$10,000.00	$10,000.00	$10,000.00
23	1	$9,100.00	$7,940.00	$8,000.00	$8,363.64
24	2	$8,200.00	$6,304.36	$6,400.00	$6,890.91
25	3	$7,300.00	$5,005.66	$5,120.00	$5,581.82
26	4	$6,400.00	$3,974.50	$4,096.00	$4,436.36
27	5	$5,500.00	$3,155.75	$3,276.80	$3,454.55
28	6	$4,600.00	$2,505.67	$2,621.44	$2,636.36
29	7	$3,700.00	$1,989.50	$2,097.15	$1,981.82
30	8	$2,800.00	$1,579.66	$1,677.72	$1,490.91
31	9	$1,900.00	$1,254.25	$1,342.18	$1,163.64
32	10	$1,000.00	$995.88	$1,073.74	$1,000.00
33					

FIGURE 15.16

This chart shows an asset's value over time, using four depreciation functions.

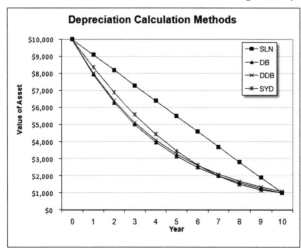

The VBD function is useful if you need to calculate depreciation for multiple periods (for example, years 2 and 3). Figure 15.17 shows a worksheet set up to calculate depreciation using the VBD function. The formula in cell B11 is

```
=VDB(B2,B4,B3,B6,B7,B8,B9)
```

FIGURE 15.17

Using the VBD function to calculate depreciation for multiple periods.

	A	B	C
1	Asset:	Office Furniture	
2	Original Cost:	$10,000	
3	Life (years):	10	
4	Salvage Value:	$1,000	
5			
6	Starting Period:	0	
7	Ending Period:	3	
8	Factor:	2	
9	No-Switch:	TRUE	
10			
11	Depreciation:	$4,880.00	
12			

The formula displays the depreciation for the first three years of an asset (starting period of 0 and ending period of 3).

Introducing Array Formulas

O ne of Excel's most interesting (and most powerful) features is its
ability to work with arrays in formulas. When you understand this
concept, you'll be able to create elegant formulas that appear to perform spreadsheet magic.

This chapter introduces the concept of arrays and is required reading for
anyone who wants to become a master of Excel formulas. Chapter 17 continues with lots of useful examples.

On the CD
Most of the examples in this chapter are available on the companion CD-ROM.
The filename is `array examples.xlsx`.

Understanding Array Formulas

If you do any computer programming, you've probably been exposed to the
concept of an array. An *array* is simply a collection of items operated on collectively or individually. In Excel, an array can be one dimensional or two
dimensional. These dimensions correspond to rows and columns. For example, a *one-dimensional array* can be stored in a range that consists of one row
(a horizontal array) or one column (a vertical array). A *two-dimensional array*
can be stored in a rectangular range of cells. Excel doesn't support three-
dimensional arrays (but its VBA programming language does).

As you'll see, arrays need not be stored in cells. You can also work with
arrays that exist only in Excel's memory. You can then use an *array formula*
to manipulate this information and return a result. An array formula can
occupy multiple cells or reside in a single cell.

IN THIS CHAPTER

The definition of an array and
an array formula

One-dimensional versus two-
dimensional arrays

How to work with array
constants

Techniques for working with
array formulas

Examples of multicell array
formulas

Examples of array formulas that
occupy a single cell

This section presents two array formula examples: an array formula that occupies multiple cells and another array formula that occupies only one cell.

A multicell array formula

Figure 16.1 shows a simple worksheet set up to calculate product sales. Normally, you'd calculate the value in column D (total sales per product) with a formula such as the one that follows, and then you'd copy this formula down the column.

```
=B2*C2
```

After copying the formula, the worksheet contains six formulas in column D.

Column D contains formulas to calculate the total for each product.

	A	B	C	D	E
1	Product	Units Sold	Unit Price	Total	
2	AR-998	3	$50	$150	
3	BZ-011	10	$100	$1,000	
4	MR-919	5	$20	$100	
5	TR-811	9	$10	$90	
6	TS-333	3	$60	$180	
7	ZL-001	1	$200	$200	
8					

An alternative method uses a *single* formula (an array formula) to calculate all six values in D2:D7. This single formula occupies six cells and returns an array of six values.

To create a single array formula to perform the calculations, follow these steps:

1. **Select a range to hold the results.** In this case, the range is D2:D7. Because you can't display more than one value in a single cell, six cells are required to display the resulting array — so you select six cells to make this array work.

2. **Type the following formula:**
   ```
   =B2:B7*C2:C7
   ```

3. **Press Ctrl+Shift+Enter to enter the formula.** Normally, you press Enter to enter a formula. Because this is an array formula, however, press Ctrl+Shift+Enter.

Caution
You can't insert a multicell array formula into a range that has been designated a table (using Insert ➪ Tables ➪ Table). In addition, you can't convert a range that contains a multicell array formula to a table. ■

The formula is entered into all six selected cells. If you examine the Formula bar, you see the following:

```
{=B2:B7*C2:C7}
```

Excel places curly brackets around the formula to indicate that it's an array formula.

This formula performs its calculations and returns a six-item array. The array formula actually works with two other arrays, both of which happen to be stored in ranges. The values for the first array are stored in B2:B7, and the values for the second array are stored in C2:C7.

This array formula returns exactly the same values as these six normal formulas entered into individual cells in D2:D7:

```
=B2*C2
=B3*C3
=B4*C4
=B5*C5
=B6*C6
=B7*C7
```

Using a single array formula rather than individual formulas does offer a few advantages:

- It's a good way to ensure that all formulas in a range are identical.
- Using a multicell array formula makes it less likely that you'll overwrite a formula accidentally. You can't change one cell in a multicell array formula. Excel displays an error message if you attempt to do so.
- Using a multicell array formula will almost certainly prevent novices from tampering with your formulas.

Using a multicell array formula as described in the preceding list also has some potential disadvantages:

- It's impossible to insert a new row into the range. But in some cases, the inability to insert a row is a positive feature. For example, you might not want users to add rows because it would affect other parts of the worksheet.
- If you add new data to the bottom of the range, you need to modify the array formula to accommodate the new data.

A single-cell array formula

Now it's time to take a look at a single-cell array formula. Check out Figure 16.2, which is similar to Figure 16.1. Notice, however, that the formulas in column D have been deleted. The goal is to calculate the sum of the total product sales without using the individual calculations that were in column D.

FIGURE 16.2

The array formula in cell C9 calculates the total sales without using intermediate formulas.

	A	B	C	D
1	Product	Units Sold	Unit Price	
2	AR-998	3	$50	
3	BZ-011	10	$100	
4	MR-919	5	$20	
5	TR-811	9	$10	
6	TS-333	3	$60	
7	ZL-001	1	$200	
8				
9		Total Sales:	$1,720	
10				

The following array formula is in cell C9:

```
{=SUM(B2:B7*C2:C7)}
```

When you enter this formula, make sure that you use Ctrl+Shift+Enter (and don't type the curly brackets because Excel automatically adds them for you).

This formula works with two arrays, both of which are stored in cells. The first array is stored in B2:B7, and the second array is stored in C2:C7. The formula multiplies the corresponding values in these two arrays and creates a new array (which exists only in memory). The SUM function then operates on this new array and returns the sum of its values.

Note

In this case, you can use the SUMPRODUCT function to obtain the same result without using an array formula:

```
=SUMPRODUCT(B2:B7,C2:C7)
```

As you see, however, array formulas allow many other types of calculations that are otherwise not possible.

Creating an array constant

The examples in the preceding section used arrays stored in worksheet ranges. The examples in this section demonstrate an important concept: An array need not be stored in a range of cells. This type of array, which is stored in memory, is referred to as an *array constant*.

To create an array constant, list its items and surround them with brackets. Here's an example of a five-item horizontal array constant:

```
{1,0,1,0,1}
```

The following formula uses the SUM function, with the preceding array constant as its argument. The formula returns the sum of the values in the array (which is 3):

```
=SUM({1,0,1,0,1})
```

Notice that this formula uses an array, but the formula itself isn't an array formula. Therefore, you don't use Ctrl+Shift+Enter to enter the formula — although entering it as an array formula will still produce the same result.

Note

When you specify an array directly (as shown previously), you must provide the curly brackets around the array elements. When you enter an array formula, on the other hand, you do not supply the brackets. ∎

At this point, you probably don't see any advantage to using an array constant. The following formula, for example, returns the same result as the previous formula. The advantages, however, will become apparent.

```
=SUM(1,0,1,0,1)
```

This formula uses two array constants:

```
=SUM({1,2,3,4}*{5,6,7,8})
```

This formula creates a new array (in memory) that consists of the product of the corresponding elements in the two arrays. The new array is

```
{5,12,21,32}
```

This new array is then used as an argument for the SUM function, which returns the result (70). The formula is equivalent to the following formula, which doesn't use arrays:

```
=SUM(1*5,2*6,3*7,4*8)
```

Alternatively, you can use the SUMPRODUCT function. The formula that follows is not an array formula, but it uses two array constants as its arguments.

```
=SUMPRODUCT({1,2,3,4},{5,6,7,8})
```

A formula can work with both an array constant and an array stored in a range. The following formula, for example, returns the sum of the values in A1:D1, each multiplied by the corresponding element in the array constant:

```
=SUM((A1:D1*{1,2,3,4}))
```

This formula is equivalent to

```
=SUM(A1*1,B1*2,C1*3,D1*4)
```

Array constant elements

An array constant can contain numbers, text, logical values (TRUE or FALSE), and even error values, such as #N/A. Numbers can be in integer, decimal, or scientific format. You must enclose text in double quotation marks. You can use different types of values in the same array constant, as in this example:

```
{1,2,3,TRUE,FALSE,TRUE,"Moe","Larry","Curly"}
```

An array constant can't contain formulas, functions, or other arrays. Numeric values can't contain dollar signs, commas, parentheses, or percent signs. For example, the following is an invalid array constant:

```
{SQRT(32),$56.32,12.5%}
```

Understanding the Dimensions of an Array

As stated previously, an array can be one dimensional or two dimensional. A one-dimensional array's orientation can be horizontal (corresponding to a single row) or vertical (corresponding to a single column).

One-dimensional horizontal arrays

The elements in a one-dimensional horizontal array are separated by commas, and the array can be displayed in a row of cells. The following example is a one-dimensional horizontal array constant:

```
{1,2,3,4,5}
```

Displaying this array in a range requires five consecutive cells in a row. To enter this array into a range, select a range of cells that consists of one row and five columns. Then enter ={1,2,3,4,5} and press Ctrl+Shift+Enter.

Note

If you enter this array into a horizontal range that consists of more than five cells, the extra cells will contain #N/A (which denotes unavailable values). If you enter this array into a vertical range of cells, only the first item (1) will appear in each cell. ∎

The following example is another horizontal array; it has seven elements and is made up of text strings:

```
{"Sun","Mon","Tue","Wed","Thu","Fri","Sat"}
```

To enter this array, select seven cells in a row and type the following (followed by Ctrl+Shift+Enter):

```
={"Sun","Mon","Tue","Wed","Thu","Fri","Sat"}
```

One-dimensional vertical arrays

The elements in a one-dimensional vertical array are separated by semicolons, and the array can be displayed in a column of cells. The following is a six-element vertical array constant:

```
{10;20;30;40;50;60}
```

Displaying this array in a range requires six cells in a column. To enter this array into a range, select a range of cells that consists of six rows and one column. Then enter the following formula, followed by Ctrl+Shift+Enter:

```
={10;20;30;40;50;60}
```

The following is another example of a vertical array; this one has four elements:

```
{"Widgets";"Sprockets";"Doodads";"Thingamajigs"}
```

Two-dimensional arrays

A two-dimensional array uses commas to separate its horizontal elements and semicolons to separate its vertical elements. The following example shows a 3 × 4 array constant:

```
{1,2,3,4;5,6,7,8;9,10,11,12}
```

Displaying this array in a range requires 12 cells. To enter this array into a range, select a range of cells that consists of three rows and four columns. Then type the following formula, followed by Ctrl+Shift+Enter:

```
={1,2,3,4;5,6,7,8;9,10,11,12}
```

Figure 16.3 shows how this array appears when entered into a range (in this case, B3:E5).

If you enter an array into a range that has more cells than array elements, Excel displays #N/A in the extra cells. Figure 16.4 shows a 3 × 4 array entered into a 10 × 5 cell range.

Each row of a two-dimensional array must contain the same number of items. The array that follows, for example, isn't valid, because the third row contains only three items:

```
{1,2,3,4;5,6,7,8;9,10,11}
```

Excel doesn't allow you to enter a formula that contains an invalid array.

A 3 × 4 array entered into a range of cells.

A 3 × 4 array entered into a 10 × 5 cell range.

Naming Array Constants

You can create an array constant, give it a name, and then use this named array in a formula. Technically, a named array is a named formula.

Cross-Reference

Chapter 3 covers the topic of names and named formulas. ∎

Figure 16.5 shows a named array being created from the New Name dialog box. (Access this dialog box by choosing Formulas ➪ Defined Names ➪ Define Name.) The name of the array is *DayNames*, and it refers to the following array constant:

```
{"Sun","Mon","Tue","Wed","Thu","Fri","Sat"}
```

Notice that, in the New Name dialog box, the array is defined (in the Refers To field) using a leading equal sign (=). Without this equal sign, the array is interpreted as a text string rather than an array. Also, you must type the curly brackets when defining a named array constant; Excel does not enter them for you.

After creating this named array, you can use it in a formula. Figure 16.6 shows a worksheet that contains a single array formula entered into the range A1:G1. The formula is

    {=DayNames}

FIGURE 16.5

Creating a named array constant.

FIGURE 16.6

Using a named array in an array formula.

Because commas separate the array elements, the array has a horizontal orientation. Use semicolons to create a vertical array. Or you can use the Excel TRANSPOSE function to insert a horizontal array into a vertical range of cells (see "Transposing an array," later in this chapter). The following array formula, which is entered into a seven-cell vertical range, uses the TRANSPOSE function:

    {=TRANSPOSE(DayNames)}

You also can access individual elements from the array by using the Excel INDEX function. The following formula, for example, returns Wed, the fourth item in the DayNames array:

    =INDEX(DayNames,4)

Working with Array Formulas

This section deals with the mechanics of selecting cells that contain arrays and entering and editing array formulas. These procedures differ a bit from working with ordinary ranges and formulas.

Entering an array formula

When you enter an array formula into a cell or range, you must follow a special procedure so that Excel knows that you want an array formula rather than a normal formula. You enter a normal formula into a cell by pressing Enter. You enter an array formula into one or more cells by pressing Ctrl+Shift+Enter.

Don't enter the curly brackets when you create an array formula; Excel inserts them for you. If the result of an array formula consists of more than one value, you must select all the cells in the results range *before* you enter the formula. If you fail to do so, only the first element of the result is returned.

Selecting an array formula range

You can select the cells that contain a multicell array formula manually by using the normal cell selection procedures. Or you can use either of the following methods:

- Activate any cell in the array formula range. Display the Go To dialog box (choose Home ⇨ Editing ⇨ Find & Select ⇨ Go To, or just press F5). In the Go To dialog box, click the Special button and then choose the Current Array option. Click OK to close the dialog box.

- Activate any cell in the array formula range and press Ctrl+/ to select the entire array.

Editing an array formula

If an array formula occupies multiple cells, you must edit the entire range as though it were a single cell. The key point to remember is that you can't change just one element of a multicell array formula. If you attempt to do so, Excel displays the message shown in Figure 16.7.

FIGURE 16.7

Excel's warning message reminds you that you can't edit just one cell of a multicell array formula.

The following rules apply to multicell array formulas. If you try to do any of these things, Excel lets you know about it:

- You can't change the contents of any individual cell that makes up an array formula.
- You can't move cells that make up part of an array formula (but you can move an entire array formula).
- You can't delete cells that form part of an array formula (but you can delete an entire array).
- You can't insert new cells into an array range. This rule includes inserting rows or columns that would add new cells to an array range.
- You can't use multicell array formulas inside of a table that was created by choosing Insert ⇨ Tables ⇨ Table. Similarly, you can't convert a range to a table if the range contains a multicell array formula.

To edit an array formula, select all the cells in the array range and activate the Formula bar as usual (click it or press F2). Excel removes the brackets from the formula while you edit it. Edit the formula and then press Ctrl+Shift+Enter to enter the changes. All the cells in the array now reflect your editing changes.

Caution

If you accidentally press Ctrl+Enter (instead of Ctrl+Shift+Enter) after editing an array formula, the formula will be entered into each selected cell, but it will no longer be an array formula. And it will probably return an incorrect result. Just reselect the cells, press F2, and then press Ctrl+Shift+Enter. ■

Although you can't change any individual cell that makes up a multicell array formula, you can apply formatting to the entire array or to only parts of it.

Expanding or contracting a multicell array formula

Often, you may need to expand a multicell array formula (to include more cells) or contract it (to include fewer cells). Doing so requires a few steps:

1. **Select the entire range that contains the array formula.**
2. **Press F2 to enter Edit mode.**
3. **Press Ctrl+Enter.** This step enters an identical (non-array) formula into each selected cell.
4. **Change your range selection to include additional or fewer cells, but make sure the active cell is in a cell that's part of the original array.**
5. **Press F2 to re-enter Edit mode.**
6. **Press Ctrl+Shift+Enter.**

Array Formulas: The Downside

If you've followed along in this chapter, you probably understand some of the advantages of using array formulas. The main advantage, of course, is that an array formula enables you to perform otherwise impossible calculations. As you gain more experience with arrays, however, you undoubtedly will also discover some disadvantages.

Array formulas are one of the least understood features of Excel. Consequently, if you plan to share a workbook with someone who may need to make modifications, you should probably avoid using array formulas. Encountering an array formula when you don't know what it is can be very confusing.

You might also discover that you can easily forget to enter an array formula by pressing Ctrl+Shift+Enter. (And don't forget: If you edit an existing array, you must remember to use this key combination to complete the edits.) Except for logical errors, this is probably the most common problem that users have with array formulas. If you press Enter by mistake after editing an array formula, just press F2 to get back into Edit mode and then press Ctrl+Shift+Enter.

Another potential problem with array formulas is that they can slow your worksheet's recalculations, especially if you use very large arrays. On a faster system, this delay in speed may not be a problem. But, conversely, using an array formula is almost always faster than using a custom VBA function. See Chapter 40 for more information about creating custom VBA functions.

Using Multicell Array Formulas

This section contains examples that demonstrate additional features of *multicell array formulas* (array formulas that are entered into a range of cells). These features include creating arrays from values, performing operations, using functions, transposing arrays, and generating consecutive integers.

Creating an array from values in a range

The following array formula creates an array from a range of cells. Figure 16.8 shows a workbook with some data entered into A1:C4. The range D8:F11 contains a single array formula:

```
{=A1:C4}
```

The array in D8:F11 is linked to the range A1:C4. Change any value in A1:C4, and the corresponding cell in D8:F11 reflects that change. It's a one-way link, of course. You can't change a value in D8:F11.

FIGURE 16.8

Creating an array from a range.

	A	B	C	D	E	F	G
				D8	▼	f_x {=A1:C4}	
1	1	dog	3				
2	4	5	cat				
3	7	FALSE	9				
4	monkey	8	12				
5							
6							
7							
8				1	dog	3	
9				4	5	cat	
10				7	FALSE	9	
11				monkey	8	12	
12							

Creating an array constant from values in a range

In the preceding example, the array formula in D8:F11 essentially created a link to the cells in A1:C4. It's possible to sever this link and create an array constant made up of the values in A1:C4:

1. **Select the cells that contain the array formula (the range D8:F11, in this example).**
2. **Press F2 to edit the array formula.**
3. **Press F9 to convert the cell references to values.**
4. **Press Ctrl+Shift+Enter to re-enter the array formula (which now uses an array constant).**

The array constant is

```
{1,"dog",3;4,5,"cat";7,False,9;"monkey",8,12}
```

Figure 16.9 shows how this looks in the Formula bar.

FIGURE 16.9

After you press F9, the Formula bar displays the array constant.

	C	D	E	F	G	H	I	J
		D8	▼	f_x {={1,"dog",3;4,5,"cat";7,FALSE,9;"monkey",8,12}}			
6								
7								
8		1	dog	3				
9		4	5	cat				
10		7	FALSE	9				
11		monkey	8	12				
12								

Performing operations on an array

So far, most of the examples in this chapter simply entered arrays into ranges. The following array formula creates a rectangular array and multiplies each array element by 2:

```
{={1,2,3,4;5,6,7,8;9,10,11,12}*2}
```

Figure 16.10 shows the result when you enter this formula into a range:

FIGURE 16.10

Performing a mathematical operation on an array.

The following array formula multiplies each array element by itself:

```
{={1,2,3,4;5,6,7,8;9,10,11,12}*{1,2,3,4;5,6,7,8;9,10,11,12}}
```

The following array formula is a simpler way of obtaining the same result. Figure 16.11 shows the result when you enter this formula into a range:

```
{={1,2,3,4;5,6,7,8;9,10,11,12}^2}
```

If the array is stored in a range (such asB8:E10), the array formula returns the square of each value in the range, as follows:

```
{=B8:E10^2}
```

FIGURE 16.11

Multiplying each array element by itself.

Using functions with an array

As you may expect, you also can use worksheet functions with an array. The following array formula, which you can enter into a 10-cell vertical range, calculates the square root of each array element in the array constant:

```
{=SQRT({1;2;3;4;5;6;7;8;9;10})}
```

If the array is stored in a range, a multicell array formula such as the one that follows returns the square root of each value in the range:

```
{=SQRT(A1:A10)}
```

Transposing an array

When you transpose an array, you essentially convert rows to columns and columns to rows. In other words, you can convert a horizontal array to a vertical array (and vice versa). Use the TRANSPOSE function to transpose an array.

Consider the following one-dimensional horizontal array constant:

```
{1,2,3,4,5}
```

You can enter this array into a vertical range of cells by using the TRANSPOSE function. To do so, select a range of five cells that occupy five rows and one column. Then enter the following formula and press Ctrl+Shift+Enter:

```
=TRANSPOSE({1,2,3,4,5})
```

The horizontal array is transposed, and the array elements appear in the vertical range.

Transposing a two-dimensional array works in a similar manner. Figure 16.12 shows a two-dimensional array entered into a range normally and entered into a range by using the TRANSPOSE function. The formula in A1:D3 is

```
{={1,2,3,4;5,6,7,8;9,10,11,12}}
```

The formula in A6:C9 is

```
{=TRANSPOSE({1,2,3,4;5,6,7,8;9,10,11,12})}
```

You can, of course, use the TRANSPOSE function to transpose an array stored in a range. The following formula, for example, uses an array stored in A1:C4 (four rows, three columns). You can enter this array formula into a range that consists of three rows and four columns.

```
{=TRANSPOSE(A1:C4)}
```

FIGURE 16.12

Using the TRANSPOSE function to transpose a rectangular array.

Generating an array of consecutive integers

As you see in Chapter 17, generating an array of consecutive integers for use in an array formula is often useful. The ROW function, which returns a row number, is ideal for this. Consider the array formula shown here, entered into a vertical range of 12 cells:

```
{=ROW(1:12)}
```

This formula generates a 12-element array that contains integers from 1 to 12. To demonstrate, select a range that consists of 12 rows and one column and enter the array formula into the range. You'll find that the range is filled with 12 consecutive integers (as shown in Figure 16.13).

FIGURE 16.13

Using an array formula to generate consecutive integers.

Worksheet Functions That Return an Array

Several of the Excel worksheet functions use arrays; you must enter a formula that uses one of these functions into multiple cells as an array formula. These functions are FORECAST, FREQUENCY, GROWTH, LINEST, LOGEST, MINVERSE, MMULT, and TREND. Consult the Excel Help system for more information.

If you want to generate an array of consecutive integers, a formula like the one shown previously is good — but not perfect. To see the problem, insert a new row above the range that contains the array formula. Excel adjusts the row references so that the array formula now reads

    {=ROW(2:13)}

The formula that originally generated integers from 1 to 12 now generates integers from 2 to 13.

For a better solution, use this formula:

    {=ROW(INDIRECT("1:12"))}

This formula uses the INDIRECT function, which takes a text string as its argument. Excel does not adjust the references contained in the argument for the INDIRECT function. Therefore, this array formula *always* returns integers from 1 to 12.

Cross-Reference

Chapter 17 contains several examples that use the technique for generating consecutive integers. ∎

Using Single-Cell Array Formulas

The examples in the preceding section all used a multicell array formula — a single array formula that's entered into a range of cells. The real power of using arrays becomes apparent when you use single-cell array formulas. This section contains examples of array formulas that occupy a single cell.

Counting characters in a range

Suppose that you have a range of cells that contains text entries (see Figure 16.14). If you need to get a count of the total number of characters in that range, the "traditional" method involves creating a formula like the one that follows and copying it down the column:

    =LEN(A1)

Then you use a SUM formula to calculate the sum of the values returned by these intermediate formulas.

The following array formula does the job without using any intermediate formulas:

```
{=SUM(LEN(A1:A14))}
```

The goal is to count the number of characters in a range of text.

	A	B	C	D
1	aboriginal			
2	aborigine	Total characters:	112	
3	aborting			
4	abort			
5	abound			
6	about			
7	above			
8	aboveboard			
9	aboveground			
10	abovementioned			
11	abrade			
12	abrasion			
13	abrasive			
14	abreact			
15				

The array formula uses the LEN function to create a new array (in memory) that consists of the number of characters in each cell of the range. In this case, the new array is

```
{10,9,8,5,6,5,5,10,11,14,6,8,8,7}
```

The array formula is then reduced to

```
=SUM({10,9,8,5,6,5,5,10,11,14,6,8,8,7})
```

The formula returns the sum of the array elements, 112.

Summing the three smallest values in a range

If you have values in a range named *Data*, you can determine the smallest value by using the SMALL function:

```
=SMALL(Data,1)
```

You can determine the second smallest and third smallest values by using these formulas:

```
=SMALL(Data,2)
=SMALL(Data,3)
```

To add the three smallest values, you could use a formula like this:

```
=SUM(SMALL(Data,1), SMALL(Data,2), SMALL(Data,3)
```

This formula works fine, but using an array formula is more efficient. The following array formula returns the sum of the three smallest values in a range named *Data*:

```
{=SUM(SMALL(Data,{1,2,3}))}
```

The formula uses an array constant as the second argument for the SMALL function. This generates a new array, which consists of the three smallest values in the range. This array is then passed to the SUM function, which returns the sum of the values in the new array.

Figure 16.15 shows an example in which the range A1:A10 is named *Data*. The SMALL function is evaluated three times, each time with a different second argument. The first time, the SMALL function has a second argument of 1, and it returns −5. The second time, the second argument for the SMALL function is 2, and it returns 0 (the second smallest value in the range). The third time, the SMALL function has a second argument of 3 and returns the third smallest value of 2.

FIGURE 16.15

An array formula returns the sum of the three smallest values in A1:A10.

	A	B	C	D	E
1	12				
2	-5		Sum of three smallest:	-3	
3	3				
4	2				
5	0				
6	6				
7	13				
8	7				
9	4				
10	8				
11					
12					

Therefore, the array that's passed to the SUM function is

```
{-5,0,2}
```

The formula returns the sum of the array (−3).

Counting text cells in a range

Suppose that you need to count the number of text cells in a range. The COUNTIF function seems like it might be useful for this task — but it's not. COUNTIF is useful only if you need to count values in a range that meet some criterion (for example, values greater than 12).

To count the number of text cells in a range, you need an array formula. The following array formula uses the IF function to examine each cell in a range. It then creates a new array (of the same size and dimensions as the original range) that consists of 1s and 0s, depending on whether the cell contains text. This new array is then passed to the SUM function, which returns the sum of the items in the array. The result is a count of the number of text cells in the range:

```
{=SUM(IF(ISTEXT(A1:D5),1,0))}
```

Cross-Reference

This general array formula type (that is, an IF function nested in a SUM function) is very useful for counting. See Chapter 13 for additional examples of IF and SUM functions. ∎

Figure 16.16 shows an example of the preceding formula in cell C7. The array created by the IF function is

```
{0,1,1,1;1,0,0,0;1,0,0,0;1,0,0,0;1,0,0,0}
```

Notice that this array contains four rows of three elements (the same dimensions as the range).

Here is a slightly more efficient variation on this formula:

```
{=SUM(ISTEXT(A1:D5)*1)}
```

This formula eliminates the need for the IF function and takes advantage of the fact that

```
TRUE * 1 = 1
```

and

```
FALSE * 1 = 0
```

FIGURE 16.16

An array formula returns the number of text cells in the range.

	A	B	C	D	E
1		Jan	Feb	Mar	
2	Region 1	7	4	9	
3	Region 2	8	2	8	
4	Region 3	12	1	9	
5	Region 4	14	6	10	
6					
7	No. of text cells:		7		
8					

Eliminating intermediate formulas

One key benefit of using an array formula is that you can often eliminate intermediate formulas in your worksheet, which makes your worksheet more compact and eliminates the need to display irrelevant calculations. Figure 16.17 shows a worksheet that contains pre-test and post-test scores for students. Column D contains formulas that calculate the changes between the pre-test and the post-test scores. Cell D17 contains a formula, shown here, that calculates the average of the values in column D:

=AVERAGE(D2:D15)

With an array formula, you can eliminate column D. The following array formula calculates the average of the changes but does not require the formulas in column D:

{=AVERAGE(C2:C15-B2:B15)}

How does it work? The formula uses two arrays, the values of which are stored in two ranges (B2:B15 and C2:C15). The formula creates a *new* array that consists of the differences between each corresponding element in the other arrays. This new array is stored in Excel's memory, not in a range. The AVERAGE function then uses this new array as its argument and returns the result.

The new array consists of the following elements:

{11,15,-6,1,19,2,0,7,15,1,8,23,21,-11}

The formula, therefore, is equivalent to

=AVERAGE({11,15,-6,1,19,2,0,7,15,1,8,23,21,-11})

Excel evaluates the function and displays the results, 7.57.

You can use additional array formulas to calculate other measures for the data in this example. For example, the following array formula returns the largest change (that is, the greatest improvement). This formula returns 23, which represents Linda's test scores.

{=MAX(C2:C15-B2:B15)}

FIGURE 16.17

Without an array formula, calculating the average change requires intermediate formulas in column D.

	A	B	C	D	E
1	Student	Pre-Test	Post-Test	Change	
2	Andy	56	67	11	
3	Beth	59	74	15	
4	Cindy	98	92	-6	
5	Duane	78	79	1	
6	Eddy	81	100	19	
7	Francis	92	94	2	
8	Georgia	100	100	0	
9	Hilda	92	99	7	
10	Isabel	54	69	15	
11	Jack	91	92	1	
12	Kent	80	88	8	
13	Linda	45	68	23	
14	Michelle	71	92	21	
15	Nancy	94	83	-11	
16					
17		Average Change:		7.57	
18					

The following array formula returns the smallest value in the Change column. This formula returns –11, which represents Nancy's test scores.

```
{=MIN(C2:C15-B2:B15)}
```

Using an array in lieu of a range reference

If your formula uses a function that requires a range reference, you may be able to replace that range reference with an array constant. This is useful in situations in which the values in the referenced range do not change.

Note

A notable exception to using an array constant in place of a range reference in a function is with the database functions that use a reference to a criteria range (for example, DSUM). Unfortunately, using an array constant instead of a reference to a criteria range does not work. ■

Cross-Reference

For information about lookup formulas, see Chapter 14. ■

Figure 16.18 shows a worksheet that uses a lookup table to display a word that corresponds to an integer. For example, looking up a value of 9 returns Nine from the lookup table in D1:E10. The formula in cell C1 is

```
=VLOOKUP(B1,D1:E10,2,FALSE)
```

FIGURE 16.18

You can replace the lookup table in D1:E10 with an array constant.

	A	B	C	D	E	F
1	Number->	9	Nine	1	One	
2				2	Two	
3				3	Three	
4				4	Four	
5				5	Five	
6				6	Six	
7				7	Seven	
8				8	Eight	
9				9	Nine	
10				10	Ten	
11						
12						

You can use a two-dimensional array in place of the lookup range. The following formula returns the same result as the previous formula, but it does not require the lookup range in D1:E1:

```
=VLOOKUP(B1,{1,"One";2,"Two";3,"Three";4,"Four";5,"Five";
    6,"Six";7,"Seven";8,"Eight";9,"Nine";10,"Ten"},2,FALSE)
```

This chapter introduced arrays. Chapter 17 explores the topic further and provides some additional examples.

Performing Magic with Array Formulas

The preceding chapter provides an introduction to arrays and array formulas and presented some basic examples to whet your appetite. This chapter continues the saga and provides many useful examples that further demonstrate the power of this feature.

I selected the examples in this chapter to provide a good assortment of the various uses for array formulas. You can use most of them as-is. You will, of course, need to adjust the range names or references used. Also, you can modify many of the examples easily to work in a slightly different manner.

Working with Single-Cell Array Formulas

As I describe in the preceding chapter, you enter single-cell array formulas into a single cell (not into a range of cells). These array formulas work with arrays contained in a range or that exist in memory. This section provides some additional examples of such array formulas.

On the CD

The examples in this section are available on the companion CD-ROM. The file is named single-cell array formulas.xlsx.

Summing a range that contains errors

You may have discovered that the SUM function doesn't work if you attempt to sum a range that contains one or more error values (such as #DIV/0! or

#N/A). Figure 17.1 shows an example. The formula in cell C11 returns an error value because the range that it sums (C4:C10) contains errors.

The following array formula, in cell C13, overcomes this problem and returns the sum of the values, even if the range contains error values:

```
{=SUM(IFERROR(C4:C10,""))}
```

This formula works by creating a new array that contains the original values but without the errors. The IFERROR function effectively filters out error values by replacing them with an empty string. The SUM function then works on this "filtered" array. This technique also works with other functions, such as AVERAGE, MIN, and MAX.

Note

The IFERROR function was introduced in Excel 2007. Following is a modified version of the formula that's compatible with older versions of Excel:

```
{=SUM(IF(ISERROR(C4:C10),"",C4:C10))}
```

New Feature

The new AGGREGATE function, which works only in Excel 2010, provides another way to sum a range that contains one or more error values. Here's an example:

```
=AGGREGATE(9,2,C4:C10)
```

The first argument, 9, is the code for SUM. The second argument, 2, is the code for "ignore error values." ■

FIGURE 17.1

An array formula can sum a range of values, even if the range contains errors.

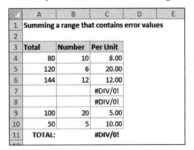

Counting the number of error values in a range

The following array formula is similar to the previous example, but it returns a count of the number of error values in a range named *Data*:

```
{=SUM(IF(ISERROR(Data),1,0))}
```

This formula creates an array that consists of 1s (if the corresponding cell contains an error) and 0s (if the corresponding cell does not contain an error value).

You can simplify the formula a bit by removing the third argument for the IF function. If this argument isn't specified, the IF function returns FALSE if the condition is not satisfied (that is, the cell does not contain an error value). In this context, Excel treats FALSE as a 0 value. The array formula shown here performs exactly like the previous formula, but it doesn't use the third argument for the IF function:

```
{=SUM(IF(ISERROR(Data),1))}
```

Actually, you can simplify the formula even more:

```
{=SUM(ISERROR(Data)*1)}
```

This version of the formula relies on the fact that

```
TRUE * 1 = 1
```

and

```
FALSE * 1 = 0
```

Summing the *n* largest values in a range

The following array formula returns the sum of the 10 largest values in a range named *Data*:

```
{=SUM(LARGE(Data,ROW(INDIRECT("1:10"))))}
```

The LARGE function is evaluated 10 times, each time with a different second argument (1, 2, 3, and so on up to 10). The results of these calculations are stored in a new array, and that array is used as the argument for the SUM function.

To sum a different number of values, replace the 10 in the argument for the INDIRECT function with another value.

If the number of cells to sum is contained in cell C17, use the following array formula, which uses the concatenation operator (&) to create the range address for the INDIRECT function:

```
{=SUM(LARGE(Data,ROW(INDIRECT("1:"&C17))))}
```

To sum the *n smallest* values in a range, use the SMALL function instead of the LARGE function.

Computing an average that excludes zeros

Figure 17.2 shows a simple worksheet that calculates average sales. The formula in cell B13 is

```
=AVERAGE(B4:B11)
```

FIGURE 17.2

The calculated average includes cells that contain a 0.

Two of the sales staff had the week off, however, so including their 0 sales in the calculated average doesn't accurately describe the average sales per representative.

Note

The AVERAGE function ignores blank cells, but it does not ignore cells that contain 0.

The following array formula returns the average of the range but excludes the cells containing 0:

```
{=AVERAGE(IF(B5:B12<>0,B5:B12))}
```

This formula creates a new array that consists only of the nonzero values in the range. The AVERAGE function then uses this new array as its argument.

You also can get the same result with a regular (non-array) formula:

```
=SUM(B5:B12)/COUNTIF(B5:B12,"<>0")
```

This formula uses the COUNTIF function to count the number of nonzero values in the range. This value is divided into the sum of the values.

Note

The only reason to use an array formula to calculate an average that excludes zero values is for compatibility with versions prior to Excel 2007. A simple approach is to use the AVERAGEIF function in a non-array formula:

```
=AVERAGEIF(B5:B12,"<>0",B5:B12)
```

Determining whether a particular value appears in a range

To determine whether a particular value appears in a range of cells, you can choose Home ⇨ Editing ⇨ Find & Select ⇨ Find and do a search of the worksheet. But you also can make this determination by using an array formula.

Figure 17.3 shows a worksheet with a list of names in A5:E24 (named *NameList*). An array formula in cell D3 checks the name entered into cell C3 (named *TheName*). If the name exists in the list of names, the formula displays the text Found. Otherwise, it displays Not Found.

FIGURE 17.3

Using an array formula to determine whether a range contains a particular value.

	A	B	C	D	E
1	Is a value contained in a range?				
2					
3	Enter a Name -->		Merle	Found	
4					
5	Al	Daniel	Harold	Lyle	Richard
6	Allen	Dave	Ian	Maggie	Rick
7	Andrew	David	Jack	Margaret	Robert
8	Anthony	Dennis	James	Marilyn	Rod
9	Arthur	Don	Jan	Mark	Roger
10	Barbara	Donald	Jeff	Marvin	Ronald
11	Bernard	Doug	Jeffrey	Mary	Russ
12	Beth	Douglas	Jerry	Matt	Sandra
13	Bill	Ed	Jim	Mel	Scott
14	Bob	Edward	Joe	Merle	Simon
15	Brian	Eric	John	Michael	Stacy
16	Bruce	Fran	Joseph	Michelle	Stephen
17	Cark	Frank	Kathy	Mike	Steven
18	Carl	Fred	Kathy	Norman	Stuart
19	Charles	Gary	Keith	Patrick	Susan
20	Chris	George	Kenneth	Paul	Terry
21	Chuck	Glenn	Kevin	Peter	Thomas
22	Clark	Gordon	Larry	Phillip	Timothy
23	Curt	Greg	Leonard	Ray	Vincent
24	Dan	Gregory	Louise	Rebecca	Wendy
25					

The array formula in cell D3 is

```
{=IF(OR(TheName=NameList),"Found","Not Found")}
```

This formula compares *TheName* to each cell in the *NameList* range. It builds a new array that consists of logical TRUE or FALSE values. The OR function returns TRUE if any one of the values in the new array is TRUE. The IF function uses this result to determine which message to display.

A simpler form of this formula follows. This formula displays TRUE if the name is found and returns FALSE otherwise.

```
{=OR(TheName=NameList)}
```

Yet another approach uses the COUNTIF function in a non-array formula:

```
=IF(COUNTIF(NameList,TheName)>0,"Found","Not Found")
```

Counting the number of differences in two ranges

The following array formula compares the corresponding values in two ranges (named *MyData* and *YourData*) and returns the number of differences in the two ranges. If the contents of the two ranges are identical, the formula returns 0.

```
{=SUM(IF(MyData=YourData,0,1))}
```

Note

The two ranges must be the same size and of the same dimensions. ■

This formula works by creating a new array of the same size as the ranges being compared. The IF function fills this new array with 0s and 1s: 1 if a difference is found, and 0 if the corresponding cells are the same. The SUM function then returns the sum of the values in the array.

The following array formula, which is simpler, is another way of calculating the same result:

```
{=SUM(1*(MyData<>YourData))}
```

This version of the formula relies on the fact that

```
TRUE * 1 = 1
```

and

```
FALSE * 1 = 0
```

Returning the location of the maximum value in a range

The following array formula returns the row number of the maximum value in a single-column range named *Data*:

```
{=MIN(IF(Data=MAX(Data),ROW(Data), ""))}
```

The IF function creates a new array that corresponds to the *Data* range. If the corresponding cell contains the maximum value in *Data*, the array contains the row number; otherwise, it contains an empty string. The MIN function uses this new array as its second argument, and it returns the smallest value, which corresponds to the row number of the maximum value in *Data*.

I use the MIN function to handle ties. If the *Data* range contains more than one cell that has the maximum value, the row of the *first* occurrence of the maximum cell is returned. If you change MIN to MAX, then the formula returns the last occurrence of the maximum cell.

The following array formula is similar to the previous one, but it returns the actual cell address of the maximum value in the *Data* range. It uses the ADDRESS function, which takes two arguments: a row number and a column number.

```
{=ADDRESS(MIN(IF(Data=MAX(Data),ROW(Data), "")),COLUMN(Data))}
```

The previous formulas work only with a single-column range. The following variation works with any sized range and returns the address of the smallest value in the range named *Data*:

```
{=ADDRESS(MIN(IF(Data=MAX(Data),ROW(Data), "")),
    MIN(IF(Data=MAX(Data),COLUMN(Data), "")))}
```

Note that this formula may not work correctly if the range contains two or more cells that are tied for the maximum valve.

Finding the row of a value's *n*th occurrence in a range

The following array formula returns the row number within a single-column range named *Data* that contains the *n*th occurrence of the value in a cell named *Value*:

```
{=SMALL(IF(Data=Value,ROW(Data), ""),n)}
```

The IF function creates a new array that consists of the row number of values from the *Data* range that are equal to *Value*. Values from the *Data* range that aren't equal to *Value* are replaced with an empty string. The SMALL function works on this new array and returns the *n*th smallest row number.

The formula returns #NUM! if the *Value* is not found or if *n* exceeds the number of occurences of *Value* in the range.

Returning the longest text in a range

The following array formula displays the text string in a range (named *Data*) that has the most characters. If multiple cells contain the longest text string, the first cell is returned.

```
{=INDEX(Data,MATCH(MAX(LEN(Data)),LEN(Data),FALSE),1)}
```

This formula works with two arrays, both of which contain the length of each item in the *Data* range. The MAX function determines the largest value, which corresponds to the longest text item. The MATCH function calculates the offset of the cell that contains the maximum length. The INDEX function returns the contents of the cell containing the most characters. This function works only if the *Data* range consists of a single column.

Determining whether a range contains valid values

You may have a list of items that you need to check against another list. For example, you may import a list of part numbers into a range named *MyList*, and you want to ensure that all the part numbers are valid. You can do so by comparing the items in the imported list to the items in a master list of part numbers (named *Master*).

The following array formula returns TRUE if every item in the range named *MyList* is found in the range named *Master*. Both ranges must consist of a single column, but they don't need to contain the same number of rows.

```
{=ISNA(MATCH(TRUE,ISNA(MATCH(MyList,Master,0)),0))}
```

The array formula that follows returns the number of invalid items. In other words, it returns the number of items in *MyList* that do not appear in *Master*.

```
{=SUM(1*ISNA(MATCH(MyList,Master,0)))}
```

To return the first invalid item in *MyList*, use the following array formula:

```
{=INDEX(MyList,MATCH(TRUE,ISNA(MATCH(MyList,Master,0)),0))}
```

Summing the digits of an integer

I can't think of any practical application for the example in this section, but it's a good demonstration of the power of an array formula. The following array formula calculates the sum of the digits in a positive integer, which is stored in cell A1. For example, if cell A1 contains the value 409, the formula returns 13 (the sum of 4, 0, and 9).

```
{=SUM(MID(A1,ROW(INDIRECT("1:"&LEN(A1))),1)*1)}
```

To understand how this formula works, start with the ROW function, as shown here:

```
{=ROW(INDIRECT("1:"&LEN(A1)))}
```

This function returns an array of consecutive integers beginning with 1 and ending with the number of digits in the value in cell A1. For example, if cell A1 contains the value 409, the LEN function returns 3, and the array generated by the ROW functions is

```
{1,2,3}
```

Cross-Reference

For more information about using the INDIRECT function to return this array, see Chapter 16. ∎

This array is then used as the second argument for the MID function. The MID part of the formula, simplified a bit and expressed as values, is the following:

```
{=MID(409,{1,2,3},1)*1}
```

This function generates an array with three elements:

{4,0,9}

By simplifying again and adding the SUM function, the formula looks like this:

{=SUM({4,0,9})}

This formula produces the result of 13.

Note

The values in the array created by the MID function are multiplied by 1 because the MID function returns a string. Multiplying by 1 forces a numeric value result. Alternatively, you can use the VALUE function to force a numeric string to become a numeric value. ∎

Notice that the formula doesn't work with a negative value because the negative sign is not a numeric value. Also, the formula fails if the cell contains non-numeric values (such as 123A6). The following formula solves this problem by checking for errors in the array and replacing them with zero.

{=SUM(IFERROR(MID(A1,ROW(INDIRECT("1:"&LEN(A1))),1)*1,0))}

Note

This formula uses the IFERROR function, which was introduced in Excel 2007.

Figure 17.4 shows a worksheet that uses both versions of this formula.

FIGURE 17.4

Two versions of an array formula calculate the sum of the digits in an integer.

	A	B	C
1	Sum of the digits of a value		
2			
3	Number	Sum of Digits	Improved Version
4	132	6	6
5	9	9	9
6	111111	6	6
7	980991	36	36
8	-980991	#VALUE!	36
9	409	13	13
10	123A6	#VALUE!	12
11	12	3	3
12	98,763,023	38	38
13	111,111,111	9	9
14			

Summing rounded values

Figure 17.5 shows a simple worksheet that demonstrates a common spreadsheet problem: rounding errors. As you can see, the grand total in cell E7 appears to display an incorrect amount. (That is, it's off by a penny.) The values in column E use a number format that displays two decimal places. The actual values, however, consist of additional decimal places that do not display due to rounding (as a result of the number format). The net effect of these rounding errors is a seemingly incorrect total. The total, which is actually $168.320997, displays as $168.32.

FIGURE 17.5

Using an array formula to correct rounding errors.

The following array formula creates a new array that consists of values in column E, rounded to two decimal places:

```
{=SUM(ROUND(E4:E6,2))}
```

This formula returns $168.31.

You also can eliminate these types of rounding errors by using the ROUND function in the formula that calculates each row total in column E (which does not require an array formula).

Summing every *n*th value in a range

Suppose that you have a range of values and you want to compute the sum of every third value in the list — the first, the fourth, the seventh, and so on. One solution is to hard-code the cell addresses in a formula. A better solution, though, is to use an array formula.

Note

In Figure 17.6, the values are stored in a range named Data, and the value of n is in cell D2 (named n). ■

FIGURE 17.6

An array formula returns the sum of every *n*th value in the range.

The following array formula returns the sum of every *n*th value in the range:

```
{=SUM(IF(MOD(ROW(INDIRECT("1:"&COUNT(Data)))-1,n)=0,Data,""))}
```

This formula returns 70, which is the sum of every third value in the range.

This formula generates an array of consecutive integers, and the MOD function uses this array as its first argument. The second argument for the MOD function is the value of *n*. The MOD function creates another array that consists of the remainders when each row number is divided by *n*. When the array item is 0 (that is, the row is evenly divisible by *n*), the corresponding item in the *Data* range will be included in the sum.

You find that this formula fails when *n* is 0: that is, when it sums no items. The modified array formula that follows uses an IF function to handle this case:

```
{=IF(n=0,0,SUM(IF(MOD(ROW(INDIRECT("1:"&COUNT(Data)))-
    1,n)=0,Data,"")))}
```

This formula works only when the *Data* range consists of a single column of values. It does not work for a multicolumn range or for a single row of values.

Using the Excel Formula Evaluator

If you would like to better understand how some of these complex array formulas work, consider using a handy tool: the Formula Evaluator. Select the cell that contains the formula and then choose Formulas ➪ Formula Auditing ➪ Evaluate Formula. The Evaluate Formula dialog box is shown in the figure here.

Click the Evaluate button repeatedly to see the intermediate results as the formula is being calculated. It's like watching a formula calculate in slow motion.

To make the formula work with a horizontal range, you need to transpose the array of integers generated by the ROW function. The TRANSPOSE function is just the ticket. The modified array formula that follows works only with a horizontal *Data* range:

```
{=IF(n=0,0,SUM(IF(MOD(TRANSPOSE(ROW(INDIRECT
    ("1:"&COUNT(Data))))-1,n)=0,Data,"")))}
```

Removing non-numeric characters from a string

The following array formula extracts a number from a string that contains text. For example, consider the string *ABC145Z*. The formula returns the numeric part, 145.

```
{=MID(A1,MATCH(0,(ISERROR(MID(A1,ROW(INDIRECT
    ("1:"&LEN(A1))),1)*1)*1),0),LEN(A1)-SUM((ISERROR
    (MID(A1,ROW(INDIRECT("1:"&LEN(A1))),1)*1)*1)))}
```

This formula works only with a single embedded number. For example, it fails with a string like *X45Z99* because the string contains two embedded numbers.

Determining the closest value in a range

The formula in this section performs an operation that none of Excel's lookup functions can do. The array formula that follows returns the value in a range named *Data* that is closest to another value (named *Target*):

```
{=INDEX(Data,MATCH(SMALL(ABS(Target-Data),1),ABS(Target-Data),0))}
```

If two values in the *Data* range are equidistant from the *Target* value, the formula returns the first one in the list. Figure 17.7 shows an example of this formula. In this case, the *Target* value is 45. The array formula in cell D4 returns 48 — the value closest to 45.

FIGURE 17.7

An array formula returns the closest match.

Returning the last value in a column

Suppose that you have a worksheet that you update frequently by adding new data to columns. You may need a way to reference the last value in column A (the value most recently entered). If column A contains no empty cells, the solution is relatively simple and doesn't require an array formula:

```
=OFFSET(A1,COUNTA(A:A)-1,0)
```

This formula uses the COUNTA function to count the number of nonempty cells in column A. This value (minus 1) is used as the second argument for the OFFSET function. For example, if the last value is in row 100, COUNTA returns 100. The OFFSET function returns the value in the cell 99 rows down from cell A1 in the same column.

If column A has one or more empty cells interspersed, which is frequently the case, the preceding formula won't work because the COUNTA function doesn't count the empty cells.

The following array formula returns the contents of the last nonempty cell in the first 500 rows of column A:

```
{=INDEX(A1:A500,MAX(ROW(A1:A500)*(A1:A500<>"")))}
```

You can, of course, modify the formula to work with a column other than column A. To use a different column, change the four column references from A to whatever column you need. If the last nonempty cell occurs in a row beyond row 500, you need to change the two instances of 500 to a larger number. The fewer rows referenced in the formula, the faster the calculation speed.

Caution
You can't use this formula, as written, in the same column with which it's working. Attempting to do so generates a circular reference. You can, however, modify it. For example, to use the function in cell A1, change the references so that they begin with row 2 instead of row 1. ■

Returning the last value in a row

The following array formula is similar to the previous formula, but it returns the last nonempty cell in a row (in this case, row 1):

```
{=INDEX(1:1,MAX(COLUMN(1:1)*(1:1<>"")))}
```

To use this formula for a different row, change the 1:1 reference to correspond to the row.

Ranking data with an array formula

Often, computing the rank orders for the values in a range of data is helpful. If you have a worksheet containing the annual sales figures for 20 salespeople, for example, you may want to know how each person ranks, from highest to lowest.

If you've used the Excel RANK function, you may have noticed that the ranks produced by this function don't handle ties the way that you may like. For example, if two values are tied for third place, RANK gives both of them a rank of 3. You may prefer a commonly used approach that assigns each an average (or midpoint) of the ranks — in other words, a rank of 3.5 for both values tied for third place.

Figure 17.8 shows a worksheet that uses two methods to rank a column of values (named *Sales*). The first method (column C) uses the RANK function. Column D uses array formulas to compute the ranks.

The following is the array formula in cell D4:

```
{=SUM(1*(B4<=Sales))-(SUM(1*(B4=Sales))-1)/2}
```

This formula is copied to the cells below it.

Note

Each ranking is computed with a separate array formula, not with an array formula entered into multiple cells. ■

Each array function works by computing the number of higher values and subtracting one half of the number of equal values minus 1.

New Feature

Excel 2010 includes a new worksheet function, RANK.AVG, that eliminates the need for an array formula. The formula that follows returns the same rankings as shown in Column D in Figure 17.8. This formula is in cell D4, and copied to the cells below.

```
=RANK.AVG(B4,Sales)
```

FIGURE 17.8

Ranking data with the Excel's RANK function and with array formulas.

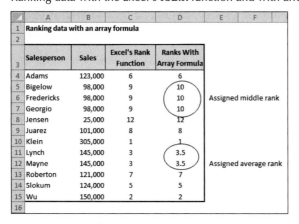

Working with Multicell Array Formulas

The preceding chapter introduced array formulas entered into multicell ranges. In this section, I present a few more array multicell formulas. Most of these formulas return some or all the values in a range, but rearranged in some way.

On the CD

The examples in this section are available on the companion CD-ROM. The file is named `multi-cell array formulas.xlsx`**.**

Returning only positive values from a range

The following array formula works with a single-column vertical range (named *Data*). The array formula is entered into a range that's the same size as *Data* and returns only the positive values in the *Data* range. (Zeroes and negative numbers are ignored.)

```
{=INDEX(Data,SMALL(IF(Data>0,ROW(INDIRECT("1:"&ROWS(Data)))),
    ROW(INDIRECT("1:"&ROWS(Data)))))}
```

As you can see in Figure 17.9, this formula works, but not perfectly. The *Data* range is A4:A22, and the array formula is entered into C4:C23. However, the array formula displays #NUM! error values for cells that don't contain a value.

This modified array formula, entered into range E4:E23, uses the IFERROR function to avoid the error value display:

```
{=IFERROR(INDEX(Data,SMALL(IF(Data>0,ROW
    (INDIRECT("1:"&ROWS(Data)))),ROW
    (INDIRECT("1:"&ROWS(Data))))),"")}
```

The IFERROR function was introduced in Excel 2007. For compatibility with older versions, use this formula:

```
{=IF(ISERR(SMALL(IF(Data>0,ROW(INDIRECT("1:"&ROWS(Data)))),ROW
    (INDIRECT("1:"&ROWS(Data))))),"",INDEX(Data,SMALL(IF
    (Data>0,ROW(INDIRECT("1:"&ROWS(Data)))),ROW(INDIRECT
    ("1:"&ROWS(Data))))))}
```

Returning nonblank cells from a range

The following formula is a variation on the formula in the preceding section. This array formula works with a single-column vertical range named *Data*. The array formula is entered into a range of the same size as *Data* and returns only the nonblank cells in the *Data* range.

```
{=IFERROR(INDEX(Data,SMALL(IF(Data<>"",ROW(INDIRECT
    ("1:"&ROWS(Data)))),ROW(INDIRECT("1:"&ROWS(Data)))))),"")}
```

For compatibility with versions prior to Excel 2007, use this formula:

```
{=IF(ISERR(SMALL(IF(Data<>"",ROW(INDIRECT("1:"&ROWS(Data))))),
    ROW(INDIRECT("1:"&ROWS(Data))))),"",INDEX(Data,SMALL(IF
    (Data<>"",ROW(INDIRECT("1:"&ROWS(Data)))),ROW(INDIRECT
    ("1:"&ROWS(Data)))))))}
```

FIGURE 17.9

Using an array formula to return only the positive values in a range.

	A	B	C	D	E	F	G
1	Return only positive values from a range						
2							
3	Data		Positive Vals		Positive Vals		Positive Vals
4	33		33		33		33
5	-33		44		44		44
6	44		4		4		4
7	4		43		43		43
8	-5		99		99		99
9	0		5		5		5
10	43		6		6		6
11	-1		8		8		8
12	-2		9		9		9
13	-3		10		10		10
14	-33		11		11		11
15	99		12		12		12
16	5		#NUM!				
17	6		#NUM!				
18	-14		#NUM!				
19	8		#NUM!				
20	9		#NUM!				
21	10		#NUM!				
22	11		#NUM!				
23	12		#NUM!				
24							

Reversing the order of cells in a range

In Figure 17.10, cells C4:C13 contain a multicell array formula that reverses the order of the values in the range A4:A13 (which is named *Data*).

The array formula is

```
{=IF(INDEX(Data,ROWS(Data)-ROW(INDIRECT
    ("1:"&ROWS(Data)))+1)="","",INDEX(Data,ROWS(Data)-ROW(INDIRECT("1
    :"&ROWS(Data)))+1))}
```

FIGURE 17.10

A multicell array formula displays the entries in A4:A13 in reverse order.

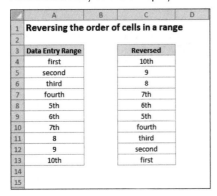

Sorting a range of values dynamically

Figure 17.11 shows a data entry range in column A (named *Data*). As the user enters values into that range, the values are displayed sorted from largest to smallest in column C. The array formula in column C is rather simple:

```
{=LARGE(Data,ROW(INDIRECT("1:"&ROWS(Data))))}
```

If you prefer to avoid the #NUM! error display, the formula gets a bit more complex:

```
{=IF(ISERR(LARGE(Data,ROW(INDIRECT("1:"&ROWS(Data))))),
    "",LARGE(Data,ROW(INDIRECT("1:"&ROWS(Data)))))}
```

Note that this formula works only with values. The companion CD-ROM has a similar array formula example that works only with text.

Returning a list of unique items in a range

If you have a single-column range named *Data*, the following array formula returns a list of the unique items in the range (the list with no duplicated items):

```
{=INDEX(Data,SMALL(IF(MATCH(Data,Data,0)=ROW(INDIRECT
    ("1:"&ROWS(Data))),MATCH(Data,Data,0),""),ROW(INDIRECT
    ("1:"&ROWS(Data)))))}
```

This formula doesn't work if the *Data* range contains any blank cells. The unfilled cells of the array formula display #NUM!.

The following modified version eliminates the #NUM! display by using the Excel 2007 IFERROR function.

```
{=IFERROR(INDEX(Data,SMALL(IF(MATCH(Data,Data,0)=ROW(INDIRECT
("1:"&ROWS(data))),MATCH(Data,Data,0),""),ROW(INDIRECT
("1:"&ROWS(Data)))))),"")}
```

FIGURE 17.11

A multicell array formula displays the values in column A, sorted.

	A	B	C	D	E
1	**Sorting a range of values dynamically**				
2					
3	**Data Entry Range**		**SORTED (with #NUM!)**		**SORTED (no #NUM!)**
4	44		233		233
5	25		105		105
6	89		89		89
7	43		55		55
8	31		44		44
9	105		43		43
10			31		31
11	55		25		25
12			#NUM!		
13	233		#NUM!		
14			#NUM!		
15			#NUM!		
16			#NUM!		
17			#NUM!		
18			#NUM!		
19			#NUM!		
20			#NUM!		
21			#NUM!		
22			#NUM!		
23			#NUM!		
24			#NUM!		
25			#NUM!		
26			#NUM!		
27			#NUM!		
28			#NUM!		
29			#NUM!		
30			#NUM!		
31			#NUM!		
32			#NUM!		
33			#NUM!		
34			#NUM!		
35					

Figure 17.12 shows an example. Range A4:A22 is named *Data*, and the array formula is entered into range C4:C22. Range E4:E22 contains the array formula that uses the IFERROR function.

FIGURE 17.12

Using an array formula to return unique items from a list.

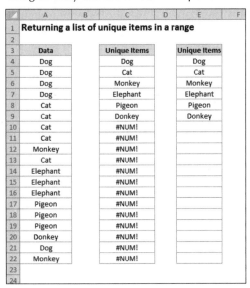

Displaying a calendar in a range

Figure 17.13 shows the results of one of my favorite multicell array formulas, a "live" calendar displayed in a range of cells. If you change the date at the top, the calendar recalculates to display the dates for the month and year.

On the CD

This workbook is available on the companion CD-ROM. The file is named `array formula calendar.xlsx`. In addition, you'll find a workbook (`yearly calendar.xlsx`) that uses this technique to display a calendar for a complete year. ■

After you create this calendar, you can easily copy it to other worksheets or workbooks.

To create this calendar in the range B2:H9, follow these steps:

1. **Select B2:H2 and merge the cells by choosing Home ➪ Alignment ➪ Merge & Center.**

2. **Enter a date into the merged range.** The day of the month isn't important.

3. **Enter the abbreviated day names in the range B3:H3.**

4. **Select B4:H9 and enter this array formula.** Remember: To enter an array formula, press Ctrl+Shift+Enter (not just Enter).

```
{=IF(MONTH(DATE(YEAR(B2),MONTH(B2),1))<>MONTH(DATE(YEAR(B2),
    MONTH(B2),1)-(WEEKDAY(DATE(YEAR(B2),MONTH(B2),1))-1)+
    {0;1;2;3;4;5}*7+{1,2,3,4,5,6,7}-1),"",
    DATE(YEAR(B2),MONTH(B2),1)-(WEEKDAY(DATE(YEAR(B2),MONT
    H(B2),1))-1)+
    {0;1;2;3;4;5}*7+{1,2,3,4,5,6,7}-1)}
```

5. **Format the range B4:H9 to use this custom number format: d.** This step formats the dates to show only the day. Use the Custom category in the Number tab of the Format Cells dialog box to specify this custom number format.

6. **Adjust the column widths and format the cells as you like.**

7. **Change the month and year in cell B2.** The calendar updates automatically.

After creating this calendar, you can copy the range to any other worksheet or workbook.

FIGURE 17.13

Displaying a calendar by using a single array formula.

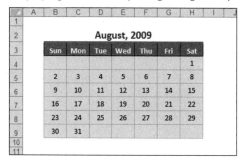

The array formula actually returns date values, but the cells are formatted to display only the day portion of the date. Also, notice that the array formula uses array constants.

Cross-Reference

See Chapter 16 for more information about array constants. ■

Part III

Creating Charts and Graphics

The five chapters in this section deal with charts and graphics — including the new Sparkline graphics. You'll discover how to use Excel's graphics capabilities to display your data in a chart. In addition, you'll learn to use Excel's other drawing tools to enhance your worksheets.

IN THIS PART

Chapter 18
Getting Started Making Charts

Chapter 19
Learning Advanced Charting

Chapter 20
Visualizing Data Using Conditional Formatting

Chapter 21
Creating Sparkline Graphics

Chapter 22
Enhancing Your Work with Pictures and SmartArt

18

Getting Started Making Charts

IN THIS CHAPTER

Charting overview

How Excel handles charts

Embedded charts versus chart sheets

The parts of a chart

Examples of each chart type

When most people think of Excel, they think of crunching rows and columns of numbers. But as you probably know already, Excel is no slouch when it comes to presenting data visually in the form of a chart. In fact, Excel is probably the most commonly used software for creating charts.

This chapter presents an introductory overview of the Excel program's charting ability.

New Feature

One of the new features in Excel 2010 is Sparklines. A *Sparkline* is a mini-chart that's displayed in a single cell. Because this feature is significantly different from standard charts, I devote Chapter 21 to Sparklines. ■

What Is a Chart?

A *chart* is a visual representation of numeric values. Charts (also known as *graphs*) have been an integral part of spreadsheets since the early days of Lotus 1-2-3. Charts generated by early spreadsheet products were quite crude, but they have improved significantly over the years. Excel provides you with the tools to create a wide variety of highly customizable charts.

Displaying data in a well-conceived chart can make your numbers more understandable. Because a chart presents a picture, charts are particularly useful for summarizing a series of numbers and their interrelationships. Making a chart can often help you spot trends and patterns that may otherwise go unnoticed. If you're unfamiliar with the elements of a chart, see the sidebar later in this chapter, "The Parts of a Chart."

Figure 18.1 shows a worksheet that contains a simple column chart that depicts a company's sales volume by month. Viewing the chart makes it very apparent that sales were down in the summer months (June through August), but they increased steadily during the final four months of the year. You could, of course, arrive at this same conclusion simply by studying the numbers. But viewing the chart makes the point much more quickly.

FIGURE 18.1

A simple column chart depicts the monthly sales volume.

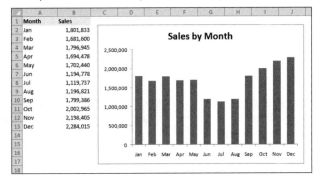

A column chart is just one of many different types of charts that you can create with Excel. I discuss all chart types so you can make the right choice for your data later in this chapter.

Understanding How Excel Handles Charts

Before you can create a chart, you must have some numbers — sometimes known as *data*. The data, of course, is stored in the cells in a worksheet. Normally, the data that a chart uses resides in a single worksheet, but that's not a strict requirement. A chart can use data that's stored in a different worksheet or even in a different workbook.

A chart is essentially an object that Excel creates upon request. This object consists of one or more data series, displayed graphically. The appearance of the data series depends on the selected chart type. For example, if you create a line chart that uses two data series, the chart contains two lines, each representing one data series. The data for each series is stored in a separate row or column. Each point on the line is determined by the value in a single cell and is represented by a marker. You can distinguish each of the lines by its thickness, line style, color, or data markers (squares, circles, and so on).

Figure 18.2 shows a line chart that plots two data series across an 11-month period. I used different data markers (squares versus circles) to identify the two series, as shown in the legend at the bottom of the chart. The chart clearly shows the sales in the Eastern Region are declining steadily, while Western Region sales are relatively constant.

A key point to keep in mind is that charts are *dynamic*. In other words, a chart series is linked to the data in your worksheet. If the data changes, the chart is updated automatically to reflect those changes.

After you create a chart, you can always change its type, change the formatting, add new data series to it, or change an existing data series so that it uses data in a different range.

This line chart displays two data series.

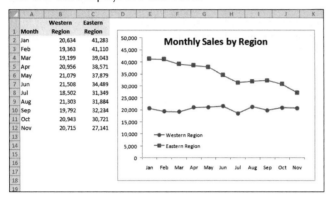

A chart is either embedded in a worksheet, or displayed on a separate chart sheet. It's very easy to move an embedded chart to a chart sheet (and vice versa).

Embedded charts

An *embedded chart* basically floats on top of a worksheet, on the worksheet's drawing layer. The charts shown previously in this chapter are both embedded charts.

As with other drawing objects (such as Shapes or SmartArt), you can move an embedded chart, resize it, change its proportions, adjust its borders, and perform other operations. Using embedded charts enables you to print the chart next to the data that it uses.

To make any changes to the actual chart in an embedded chart object, you must click it to *activate* the chart. When a chart is activated, Excel displays the Chart Tools context tab. The Ribbon provides many tools for working with charts.

With one exception, every chart starts out as an embedded chart. The exception is when you create a default chart by selecting the data and pressing F11. In that case, the chart is created on a chart sheet.

Chart sheets

When a chart is on a chart sheet, you view it by clicking its sheet tab. Chart sheets and worksheets can be interspersed in a workbook.

To move an embedded chart to a chart sheet, click the chart to select it and then choose Chart Tools ⇨ Design ⇨ Location ⇨ Move Chart. Excel displays the Move Chart dialog box, shown in Figure 18.3. Select the New Sheet option and provide a name for the chart sheet (or accept Excel's default name). Click OK, and the chart is moved, and the new chart sheet is activated.

Tip

This operation also works in the opposite direction: You can select a chart on a chart sheet and relocate it to a worksheet as an embedded chart. In the Move Chart dialog box, choose Object In, and then select the worksheet from the drop-down list. ■

FIGURE 18.3

The Move Chart dialog box lets you move a chart to a chart sheet.

When you place a chart on a chart sheet, the chart occupies the entire sheet. If you plan to print a chart on a page by itself, using a chart sheet is often your better choice. If you have many charts, you may want to put each one on a separate chart sheet to avoid cluttering your worksheet. This technique also makes locating a particular chart easier because you can change the names of the chart sheets' tabs to provide a description of the chart that it contains.

The Excel Ribbon changes when a chart sheet is active, similar to the way it changes when you select an embedded chart.

Excel displays a chart in a chart sheet in WYSIWYG (What You See Is What You Get) mode: The printed chart looks just like the image on the chart sheet. If the chart doesn't fit in the window, you can use the scroll bars to scroll it or adjust the zoom factor. You also can change its orientation (tall or wide) by choosing Page Layout ⇨ Page Setup ⇨ Orientation.

Parts of a Chart

Refer to the accompanying chart as you read the following description of the chart's elements.

The particular chart is a *combination chart* that displays two *data series:* Calls and Sales. Calls are plotted as vertical columns, and the Sales are plotted as a line with square markers. Each column (or marker on the line) represents a single *data point* (the value in a cell). The chart data is stored in the range A1:C7.

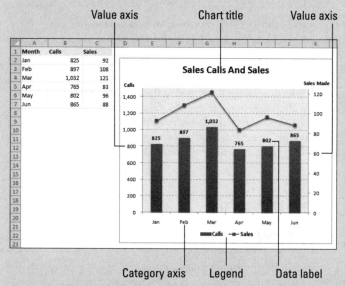

It has a horizontal axis, known as the *category axis.* This axis represents the category for each data point (January, February, and so on).

It has two vertical axes, known as value axes, and each one has a different scale. The axis on the left is for the columns (Calls), and the axis on the right is for the line (Sales).

The value axes also display scale values. The axis on the left displays scale values from 0 to 1,400, in major unit increments of 200. The value axis on the right uses a different scale: 0 to 120, in increments of 20.

Note

A chart with two value axes is appropriate because the two data series vary dramatically in scale. If the Sales data were plotted using the left axis, the line would barely be visible. ∎

Most charts provide some method of identifying the data series or data points. A legend, for example, is often used to identify the various series in a chart. In this example, the legend appears on the bottom of the chart. Some charts also display data labels to identify specific data points. This chart displays data labels for the Calls series, but not for the Sales series. In addition, most charts (including the example chart) contain a chart title and additional labels to identify the axes or categories.

Creating a Chart

Creating a chart is fairly simple:

1. **Make sure that your data is appropriate for a chart.**

2. **Select the range that contains your data.**

3. **Choose Insert ➪ Charts and select a chart type.** These icons display drop-down lists that display subtypes. Excel creates the chart and places it in the center of the window.

4. **(Optional) Use the commands in the Chart Tools contextual menu to change the look or layout of the chart or add or delete chart elements.**

Tip

You can create a chart with a single keystroke. Select the range to be used in the chart and then press Alt+F1 (for an embedded chart) or F11 (for a chart on a chart sheet). Excel displays the chart of the selected data, using the default chart type. The default chart type is a column chart, but you can change it. Start by creating a chart of the type that you want to be the default type. Select the chart and choose Chart Tools ➪ Design ➪ Change Chart Type. In the Change Chart Type dialog box, click Set As Default Chart. ∎

Hands On: Creating and Customizing a Chart

This section contains a step-by-step example of creating a chart and applying some customizations. If you've never created a chart, this is a good opportunity to get a feel for how it works.

Figure 18.4 shows a worksheet with a range of data. This data is customer survey results by month, broken down by customers in three age groups. In this case, the data resides in a table (created by choosing Insert ➪ Tables ➪ Table), but that's not a requirement to create a chart.

On the CD

This workbook, named hands-on example.xlsx, **is available on the companion CD-ROM. ∎**

Selecting the data

The first step is to select the data for the chart. Your selection should include such items as labels and series identifiers (row and column headings). For this example, select the range A4:D10. This range includes the category labels but not the title (which is in A1).

FIGURE 18.4

The source data for the hands-on chart example.

	A	B	C	D	E
1	**Customer Satisfaction by Age Group**				
2	*Percent 'Very Satisfied' by customer age*				
3					
4	**Month**	**< 30**	**30-49**	**50+**	
5	Jan	42%	46%	75%	
6	Feb	39%	51%	76%	
7	Mar	29%	38%	73%	
8	Apr	33%	39%	75%	
9	May	48%	53%	70%	
10	Jun	51%	57%	78%	
11					
12					

Tip

If your chart data is in a table (or is in a rectangular range separated from other data), you can select just a single cell. Excel will almost always guess the range for the chart accurately. ■

Note

The data that you use in a chart need not be in contiguous cells. You can press Ctrl and make a multiple selection. The initial data, however, must be on a single worksheet. If you need to plot data that exists on more than one worksheet, you can add more series after the chart is created. In all cases, however, data for a single chart series must reside on one sheet. ■

Choosing a chart type

After you select the data, select a chart type from the Insert ➪ Charts group. Each control in this group is a drop-down list, which lets you further refine your choice by selecting a subtype.

For this example, choose Insert ➪ Charts ➪ Column ➪ Clustered Column. In other words, you're creating a column chart, using the clustered column subtype. Excel displays the chart shown in Figure 18.5.

You can move the chart by dragging any of its borders. You can also resize it by clicking and dragging in one of its corners.

Experimenting with different layouts

The chart looks pretty good, but it's just one of several predefined layouts for a clustered column chart.

To see some other configurations for the chart, select the chart and apply a few other layouts in the Chart Tools ➪ Design ➪ Chart Layouts group.

A clustered columns chart.

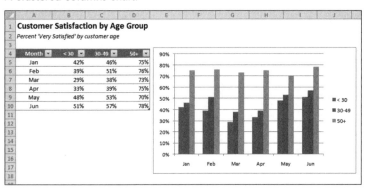

Note

Every chart type has a set of layouts that you can choose from. A layout contains additional chart elements, such as a title, data labels, axes, and so on. You can add your own elements to your chart, but often, using a predefined layout saves time. Even if the layout isn't exactly what you want, it may be close enough that you need to make only a few adjustments. ■

Figure 18.6 shows the chart after selecting a layout that adds a chart title and moves the legend to the bottom. The chart title is a text element that you can select and edit (the figure shows the generic title). For this example, *Customer Satisfaction by Age Group* is a good title.

The chart, after selecting a different layout.

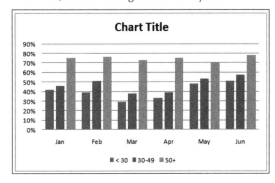

Tip

You can link the chart title to a cell so the title always displays the contents of a particular cell. To create a link to a cell, click the chart title, type an equal sign (=), click the cell, and press Enter. Excel displays the link in the Formula bar. In the example, the contents of cell A1 is perfect for the chart title. ■

Experiment with the Chart Tools ⇨ Layout tab to make other changes to the chart. For example, you can remove the grid lines, add axis titles, relocate the legend, and so on. Making these changes is easy and fairly intuitive.

Trying another view of the data

The chart, at this point, shows six clusters (months) of three data points in each (age groups). Would the data be easier to understand if you plotted the information in the opposite way?

Try it. Select the chart and then choose Chart Tools ⇨ Design ⇨ Data ⇨ Switch Row/Column. Figure 18.7 shows the result of this change. I also selected a different layout, which provides more separation between the three clusters.

Note

The orientation of the data has a drastic effect on the look of your chart. Excel has its own rules that it uses to determine the initial data orientation when you create a chart. If Excel's orientation doesn't match your expectation, it's easy enough to change. ■

The chart, with this new orientation, reveals information that wasn't so apparent in the original version. The <30 and 30–49 age groups both show a decline in satisfaction for March and April. The 50+ age group didn't have this problem, however.

FIGURE 18.7

The chart, after changing the row and column orientation, and choosing a different layout.

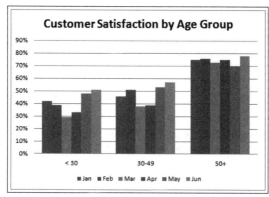

Trying other chart types

Although a clustered column chart seems to work well for this data, there's no harm in checking out some other chart types. Choose Design ➪ Type ➪ Change Chart Type to experiment with other chart types. This command displays the Change Chart Type dialog box, shown in Figure 18.8. The main categories are listed on the left, and the subtypes are shown as icons. Select an icon and click OK, and Excel displays the chart using the new chart type. If you don't like the result, select Undo.

Tip
You can also change the chart type by selecting the chart and using the controls in the Insert ➪ Charts group. ■

FIGURE 18.8

Use this dialog box to change the chart type.

Trying other chart styles

If you'd like to try some of the prebuilt chart styles, select the chart and choose Chart Tools ➪ Design ➪ Chart Styles gallery. You'll find an amazing selection of different colors and effects, all available with a single mouse click.

Tip
The styles displayed in the gallery depend on the workbook's theme. When you choose Page Layout ➪ Themes ➪ Themes to apply a different theme, you'll have a new selection of chart styles designed for the selected theme. ■

Figure 18.9 shows a few different chart type options using the customer satisfaction data.

FIGURE 18.9

The customer satisfaction chart, using four different chart types.

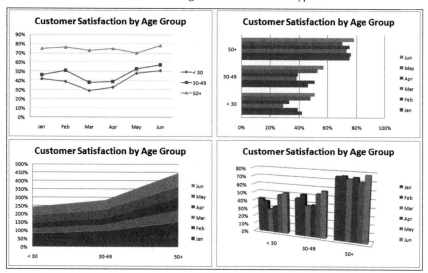

Working with Charts

This section covers some common chart modifications:

- Resizing and moving charts
- Copying a chart
- Deleting a chart
- Adding chart elements
- Moving and deleting chart elements
- Formatting chart elements
- Printing charts

Note
Before you can modify a chart, the chart must be activated. To activate an embedded chart, click it. Doing so activates the chart and also selects the element that you click. To activate a chart on a chart sheet, just click its sheet tab. ■

Resizing a chart

If your chart is an embedded chart, you can freely resize it with you mouse. Click the chart's border. Handles (gray dots) appear on the chart's corners and edges. When the mouse pointer turns into a double arrow, click and drag to resize the chart.

When a chart is selected, choose Chart Tools ➪ Format ➪ Size to adjust the height and width of the chart. Use the spinners, or type the dimensions directly into the Height and Width controls.

Moving a chart

To move a chart to a different location on a worksheet, click the chart and drag one of its borders. You can use standard cut and paste techniques to move an embedded chart. In fact, this is the only way to move a chart from one worksheet to another. Select the chart and choose Home ➪ Clipboard ➪ Cut (or press Ctrl+X). Then activate a cell near the desired location and choose Home ➪ Clipboard ➪ Paste (or press Ctrl+V). The new location can be in a different worksheet or even in a different workbook. If you paste the chart to a different workbook, it will be linked to the data in the original workbook.

To move an embedded chart to a chart sheet (or vice versa), select the chart and choose Chart Tools ➪ Design ➪ Location ➪ Move Chart to display the Move Chart dialog box. Choose New Sheet and provide a name for the chart sheet (or use the Excel proposed name).

Copying a chart

To make an exact copy of an embedded chart on the same worksheet, activate the chart, press and hold the Ctrl key, and drag. Release the mouse button, and a new copy of the chart is created.

To make a copy of a chart sheet, use the same procedure, but drag the chart sheet's tab.

You also can use standard copy and paste techniques to copy a chart. Select the chart (an embedded chart or a chart sheet) and choose Home ➪ Clipboard ➪ Copy (or press Ctrl+C). Then activate a cell near the desired location and choose Home ➪ Clipboard ➪ Paste (or press Ctrl+V). The new location can be in a different worksheet or even in a different workbook. If you paste the chart to a different workbook, it will be linked to the data in the original workbook.

Deleting a chart

To delete an embedded chart, press Ctrl and click the chart (to select the chart as an object). Then press Delete. When the Ctrl key is pressed, you can select multiple charts, and then delete them all with a single press of the Delete key.

To delete a chart sheet, right-click its sheet tab and choose Delete from the shortcut menu. To delete multiple chart sheets, select them by pressing Ctrl while you click the sheet tabs.

Adding chart elements

To add new elements to a chart (such as a title, legend, data labels, or gridlines), use the controls on the Chart Tools ⇨ Layout tab. These controls are arranged into logical groups, and they all display a drop-down list of options.

Moving and deleting chart elements

Some elements within a chart can be moved: titles, legend, and data labels. To move a chart element, simply click it to select it. Then drag its border.

The easiest way to delete a chart element is to select it and then press Delete. You can also use the controls on the Chart Tools ⇨ Layout tab to turn off the display of a particular chart element. For example, to delete data labels, choose Chart Tools ⇨ Layout ⇨ Labels ⇨ Data Labels ⇨ None.

Note

A few chart elements consist of multiple objects. For example, the data labels element consists of one label for each data point. To move or delete one data label, click once to select the entire element and then click a second time to select the specific data label. You can then move or delete the single data label. ■

Formatting chart elements

Many users are content to stick with the predefined chart layouts and chart styles. For more precise customizations, Excel allows you to work with individual chart elements and apply additional formatting. You can use the Ribbon commands for some modifications, but the easiest way to format chart elements is to right-click the element and choose Format from the shortcut menu. The exact command depends on the element you select. For example, if you right-click the chart's title, the shortcut menu command is Format Chart Title.

The Format command displays a stay-on-top tabbed dialog box with options for the selected element. Changes that you make are displayed immediately, but in some cases you need to deactivate the control by pressing tab to move to the next control. You can keep this dialog box displayed while you work on the chart. When you select a new chart element, the dialog box changes to display the properties for the newly selected element.

New Feature

In Excel 2007, the designers removed the ability to double-click a chart element to display the corresponding Format dialog box. In response to user complaints, double-clicking a chart element has been reinstated in Excel 2010. ■

Figure 18.10 shows the Format Axis dialog box, which is displayed by right-clicking the vertical axis and selecting Format Axis from the shortcut menu — or by simply double-clicking the vertical axis.

Tip

If you apply formatting to a chart element and decide that it wasn't such a good idea, you can revert to the original formatting for the particular chart style. Right-click the chart element and choose Reset to Match Style from the shortcut menu. To reset the entire chart, select the chart area when you issue the command. ■

FIGURE 18.10

Each chart element has a formatting dialog box. This one is used to format a chart axis.

Cross-Reference

See Chapter 19 for more information about customizing and formatting charts. ■

Printing charts

Printing embedded charts is nothing special; you print them the same way that you print a worksheet. As long as you include the embedded chart in the range that you want to print, Excel prints the chart as it appears onscreen. When printing a sheet that contains embedded charts, it's a good idea to preview first (or use Page Layout view) to ensure that your charts do not span multiple pages. If you created the chart on a chart sheet, Excel always prints the chart on a page by itself.

Tip

If you select an embedded chart and choose File ➪ Print, Excel prints the chart on a page by itself and does not print the worksheet. ■

If you don't want a particular embedded chart to appear on your printout, use the Properties tab of the Format Chart Area dialog box. To display this dialog box, double-click the background area of the chart. In the Properties tab of the Format Chart Area dialog box, clear the Print Object check box.

Understanding Chart Types

People who create charts usually do so to make a point or to communicate a specific message. Often, the message is explicitly stated in the chart's title or in a text box within the chart. The chart itself provides visual support.

Choosing the correct chart type is often a key factor in the effectiveness of the message. Therefore, it's often well worth your time to experiment with various chart types to determine which one conveys your message best.

In almost every case, the underlying message in a chart is some type of *comparison*. Examples of some general types of comparisons include

- **Compare item to other items.** A chart may compare sales in each of a company's sales regions.

- **Compare data over time.** A chart may display sales by month and indicate trends over time.

- **Make relative comparisons.** A common pie chart can depict relative proportions in terms of pie "slices."

- **Compare data relationships.** An XY chart is ideal for this comparison. For example, you might show the relationship between marketing expenditures and sales.

- **Frequency comparison.** You can use a common histogram, for example, to display the number (or percentage) of students who scored within a particular grade range.

- **Identify "outliers" or unusual situations.** If you have thousands of data points, creating a chart may help identify data that is not representative.

Choosing a chart type

A common question among Excel users is "How do I know which chart type to use for my data?" Unfortunately, this question has no cut-and-dried answer. Perhaps the best answer is a vague one: Use the chart type that gets your message across in the simplest way.

Figure 18.11 shows the same set of data plotted by using six different chart types. Although all six charts represent the same information (monthly Web site visitors), they look quite different from one another.

FIGURE 18.11

The same data, plotted by using six chart types.

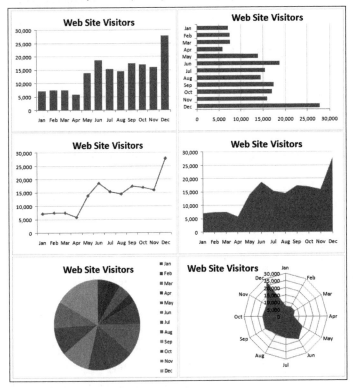

On the CD

This workbook is available on the companion CD-ROM. The file is named six chart types.xlsx.

The column chart (upper left) is probably the best choice for this particular set of data because it clearly shows the information for each month in discrete units. The bar chart (upper right) is similar to a column chart, but the axes are swapped. Most people are more accustomed to seeing time-based information extend from left to right rather than from top to bottom.

The line chart (middle left) may not be the best choice because it seems to imply that the data is continuous — that points exist in between the 12 actual data points. This same argument may be made against using an area chart (middle right).

The pie chart (lower left) is simply too confusing and does nothing to convey the time-based nature of the data. Pie charts are most appropriate for a data series in which you want to emphasize proportions among a relatively small number of data points. If you have too many data points, a pie chart can be impossible to interpret.

The radar chart (lower right) is clearly inappropriate for this data. People aren't accustomed to viewing time-based information in a circular direction!

Fortunately, changing a chart's type is easy, so you can experiment with various chart types until you find the one that represents your data accurately, clearly, and as simply as possible.

The remainder of this chapter contains more information about the various Excel chart types. The examples and discussion may give you a better handle on determining the most appropriate chart type for your data.

Column

Probably the most common chart type is column charts. A *column chart* displays each data point as a vertical column, the height of which corresponds to the value. The value scale is displayed on the vertical axis, which is usually on the left side of the chart. You can specify any number of data series, and the corresponding data points from each series can be stacked on top of each other. Typically, each data series is depicted in a different color or pattern.

Column charts are often used to compare discrete items, and they can depict the differences between items in a series or items across multiple series. Excel offers seven column-chart subtypes.

On the CD

A workbook that contains the charts in this section is available on the companion CD-ROM. The file is named `column charts.xlsx.`

Figure 18.12 shows an example of a clustered column chart that depicts monthly sales for two products. From this chart, it is clear that Sprocket sales have always exceeded Widget sales. In addition, Widget sales have been declining over the five-month period, whereas Sprocket sales are increasing.

FIGURE 18.12

This clustered column chart compares monthly sales for two products.

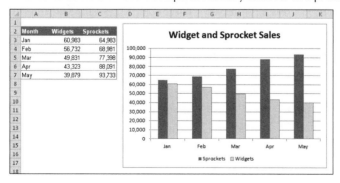

The same data, in the form of a stacked column chart, is shown in Figure 18.13. This chart has the added advantage of depicting the combined sales over time. It shows that total sales have remained fairly steady each month, but the relative proportions of the two products have changed.

Figure 18.14 shows the same sales data plotted as a 100% stacked column chart. This chart type shows the relative contribution of each product by month. Notice that the vertical axis displays percentage values, not sales amounts. This chart provides no information about the actual sales volumes. This type of chart is often a good alternative to using several pie charts. Instead of using a pie to show the relative sales volume in each year, the chart uses a column for each year.

FIGURE 18.13

This stacked column chart displays sales by product and depicts the total sales.

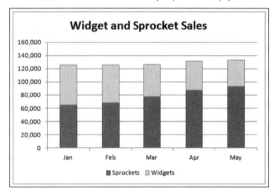

FIGURE 18.14

This 100% stacked column chart display monthly sales as a percentage.

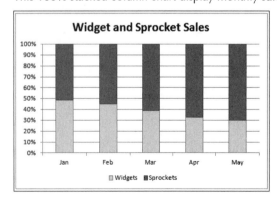

The data is plotted with a 3-D clustered column chart in Figure 18.15. The name is a bit deceptive, because the chart uses only two dimensions, not three. Many people use this type of chart because it has more visual pizzazz. Compare this chart with a "true" 3-D column chart, shown in Figure 18.16. This type of chart may be appealing visually, but precise comparisons are difficult because of the distorted perspective view.

You can also choose from column variations known as cylinder, cone, and pyramid charts. The only difference among these chart types and a standard column chart is the shape of the columns.

FIGURE 18.15

A 3-D column chart.

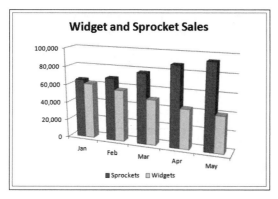

FIGURE 18.16

A true 3-D column chart.

Bar

A *bar chart* is essentially a column chart that has been rotated 90 degrees clockwise. One distinct advantage to using a bar chart is that the category labels may be easier to read. Figure 18.17 shows a bar chart that displays a value for each of ten survey items. The category labels are lengthy, and displaying them legibly with a column chart would be difficult. Excel offers six bar chart subtypes.

On the CD

A workbook that contains the chart in this section is available on the companion CD-ROM. The file is named bar charts.xlsx.

Note

Unlike a column chart, no subtype displays multiple series along a third axis. (That is, Excel does not provide a 3-D Bar Chart subtype.) You can add a 3-D look to a column chart, but it will be limited to two axes. ∎

You can include any number of data series in a bar chart. In addition, the bars can be "stacked" from left to right.

FIGURE 18.17

If you have lengthy category labels, a bar chart may be a good choice.

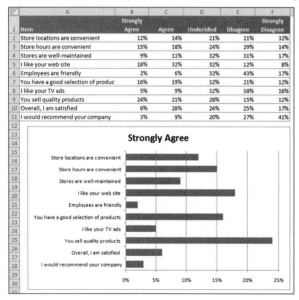

Line

Line charts are often used to plot continuous data and are useful for identifying trends. For example, plotting daily sales as a line chart may enable you to identify sales fluctuations over time. Normally, the category axis for a line chart displays equal intervals. Excel supports seven line chart subtypes.

See Figure 18.18 for an example of a line chart that depicts daily sales (200 data points). Although the data varies quite a bit on a daily basis, the chart clearly depicts an upward trend.

On the CD

A workbook that contains the charts in this section is available on the companion CD-ROM. The file is named line charts.xlsx.

The final line chart example, shown in Figure 18.20, is a *3-D line chart*. Although it has a nice visual appeal, it's certainly not the clearest way to present the data. In fact, it's fairly worthless.

A line chart can use any number of data series, and you distinguish the lines by using different colors, line styles, or markers. Figure 18.19 shows a line chart that has three series. The series are distinguished by markers (circles, squares, and diamonds) and different line colors.

FIGURE 18.18

A line chart often can help you spot trends in your data.

FIGURE 18.19

This line chart displays three series.

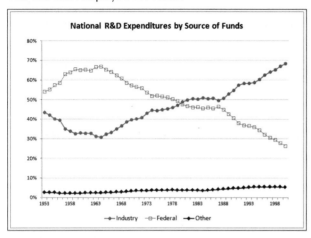

FIGURE 18.20

This 3-D line chart does not present the data very well.

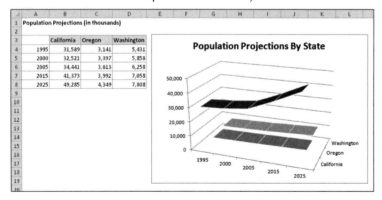

Pie

A *pie chart* is useful when you want to show relative proportions or contributions to a whole. A pie chart uses only one data series. Pie charts are most effective with a small number of data points. Generally, a pie chart should use no more than five or six data points (or slices). A pie chart with too many data points can be very difficult to interpret.

Caution

The values used in a pie chart must all be positive numbers. If you create a pie chart that uses one or more negative values, the negative values will be converted to positive values — which is probably not what you intended! ■

You can "explode" one or more slices of a pie chart for emphasis (see Figure 18.21). Activate the chart and click any pie slice to select the entire pie. Then click the slice that you want to explode and drag it away from the center.

On the CD

A workbook that contains the charts in this section is available on the companion CD-ROM. The file is named pie charts.xlsx.

FIGURE 18.21

A pie chart with one slice exploded.

The pie of pie and bar of pie chart types enables you to display a secondary chart that provides more detail for one of the pie slices. Figure 18.22 shows an example of a bar of pie chart. The pie chart shows the breakdown of four expense categories Rent, Supplies, Miscellaneous, and Salary. The secondary bar chart provides an additional regional breakdown of the Salary category.

The data used in the chart resides in A2:B8. When the chart was created, Excel made a guess at which categories belong to the secondary chart. In this case, the guess was to use the last three data points for the secondary chart — and the guess was incorrect.

To correct the chart, right-click any of the pie slices and choose Format Data Series. In the dialog box that appears, select the Series Options tab and make the changes. In this example, I chose Split Series by Position and specified that the Second Plot Contains the Last 4 Values in The Series.

FIGURE 18.22

A bar of pie chart that shows detail for one of the pie slices.

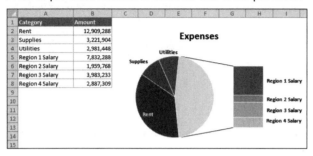

XY (scatter)

Another common chart type is an *XY chart* (also known as scattergrams or scatter plots). An XY chart differs from most other chart types in that both axes display values. (An XY chart has no category axis.)

This type of chart often is used to show the relationship between two variables. Figure 18.23 shows an example of an XY chart that plots the relationship between sales calls made (horizontal axis) and sales (vertical axis). Each point in the chart represents one month. The chart shows that these two variables are positively related: Months in which more calls were made typically had higher sales volumes.

FIGURE 18.23

An XY chart shows the relationship between two variables.

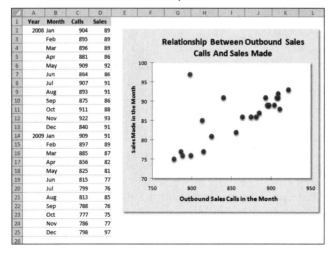

On the CD

A workbook that contains the charts in this section is available on the companion CD-ROM. The file is named `xy charts.xlsx`.

Note

Although these data points correspond to time, the chart doesn't convey any time-related information. In other words, the data points are plotted based only on their two values. ■

Figure 18.24 shows another XY chart, this one with lines that connect the XY points. This chart plots a hypocycloid curve with 200 data points. It's set up with three parameters. Change any of the parameters, and you'll get a completely different curve. This is a very minimalist chart. I deleted all the chart elements except the data series itself.

If this type of design looks familiar, it's because a hypocycloid curve is the basis for a popular children's drawing toy.

FIGURE 18.24

A hypocycloid curve, plotted as an XY chart.

Area

Think of an *area chart* as a line chart in which the area below the line has been colored in. Figure 18.25 shows an example of a stacked area chart. Stacking the data series enables you to see clearly the total, plus the contribution by each series.

FIGURE 18.25

A stacked area chart.

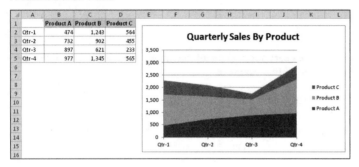

On the CD

A workbook that contains the charts in this section is available on the companion CD-ROM. The file is named `area charts.xlsx`.

Figure 18.26 shows the same data, plotted as a 3-D area chart. As you can see, it's not an example of an effective chart. The data for products B and C are obscured. In some cases, the problem can be resolved by rotating the chart or using transparency. But usually the best way to salvage a chart like this is to select a new chart type.

FIGURE 18.26

This 3-D area chart is not a good choice.

Doughnut

A *doughnut chart* is similar to a pie chart, with two differences: It has a hole in the middle, and it can display more than one series of data. Doughnut charts are listed in the Other Charts category.

Figure 18.27 shows an example of a doughnut chart with two series (1st Half Sales and 2nd Half Sales). The legend identifies the data points. Because a doughnut chart doesn't provide a direct way to identify the series, I added arrows and series descriptions manually.

On the CD

A workbook that contains the charts in this section is available on the companion CD-ROM. The file is named `doughnut charts.xlsx`.

FIGURE 18.27

A doughnut chart with two data series.

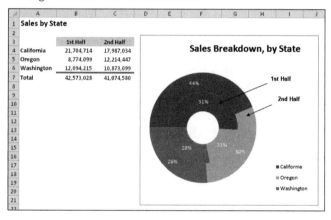

Notice that Excel displays the data series as concentric rings. As you can see, a doughnut chart with more than one series can be very difficult to interpret. For example, the relatively larger sizes of the slices toward the outer part of the doughnut can be deceiving. Consequently, you should use doughnut charts sparingly. Perhaps the best use for a doughnut chart is to plot a single series as a visual alternative to a pie chart.

In many cases, a stacked column chart for such comparisons expresses your meaning better than does a doughnut chart (see Figure 18.28).

FIGURE 18.28

Using a stacked column chart is a better choice.

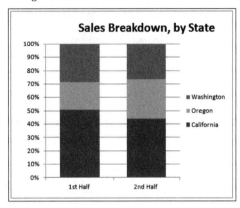

Radar

Radar charts are listed in the Other Charts category. You may not be familiar with this type of chart. A *radar chart* is a specialized chart that has a separate axis for each category, and the axes extend outward from the center of the chart. The value of each data point is plotted on the corresponding axis.

Figure 18.29 shows an example of a radar chart. This chart plots two data series across 12 categories (months) and shows the seasonal demand for snow skis versus water skis. Note that the water-ski series partially obscures the snow-ski series.

On the CD

A workbook that contains the charts in this section is available on the companion CD-ROM. The file is named `radar charts.xlsx`.

Using a radar chart to show seasonal sales may be an interesting approach, but it's not the best. As you can see in Figure 18.30, a stacked bar chart shows the information much more clearly.

A more appropriate use for radar charts is shown in Figure 18.31. These four charts each plot a color. More precisely, each chart shows the RGB components (the contributions of red, green, and blue) that make up a color. Each chart has one series, and three categories. The categories extend from 0 to 255.

FIGURE 18.29

Plotting ski sales using a radar chart with 12 categories and 2 series.

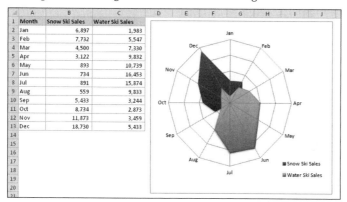

FIGURE 18.30

A stacked bar chart is a better choice for the ski sales data.

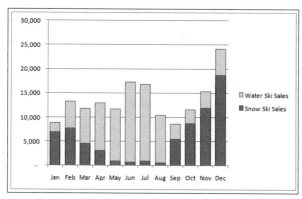

Note

If you view the charts in color, you'll see that they actually depict the color that they describe. The data series colors were applied manually. ■

FIGURE 18.31

These radar charts depict the red, green, and blue contributions for each of four colors.

Surface

Surface charts display two or more data series on a surface. Surface charts are listed in the Other Charts category.

As Figure 18.32 shows, these charts can be quite interesting. Unlike other charts, Excel uses color to distinguish values, not to distinguish the data series. The number of colors used is determined by the major unit scale setting for the value axis. Each color corresponds to one major unit.

On the CD

A workbook that contains the charts in this section is available on the companion CD-ROM. The file is named surface charts.xlsx.

Note

A surface chart does not plot 3-D data points. The series axis for a surface chart, like with all other 3-D charts, is a category axis — not a value axis. In other words, if you have data that is represented by x, y, and z coordinates, it can't be plotted accurately on a surface chart unless the x and y values are equally spaced. ■

FIGURE 18.32

A surface chart.

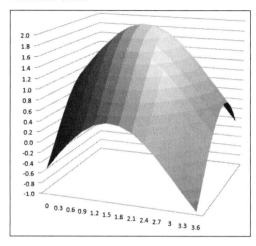

Bubble

Think of a *bubble chart* as an XY chart that can display an additional data series, which is represented by the size of the bubbles. As with an XY chart, both axes are value axes (there is no category axis). Bubble charts are listed in the Other Charts category.

Figure 18.33 shows an example of a bubble chart that depicts the results of a weight-loss program. The horizontal value axis represents the original weight, the vertical value axis shows the number of weeks in the program, and the size of the bubbles represents the amount of weight lost.

On the CD

A workbook that contains the charts in this section is available on the companion CD-ROM. The file is named bubble charts.xlsx.

Figure 18.34 shows another bubble chart, made up of nine series that represent mouse face parts. The size and position of each bubble required some experimentation.

Stock

Stock charts are most useful for displaying stock-market information. These charts require three to five data series, depending on the subtype. This chart type is listed in the Other Charts category.

FIGURE 18.33

A bubble chart.

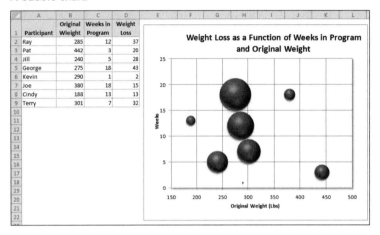

FIGURE 18.34

This bubble chart depicts a mouse.

Figure 18.35 shows an example of each of the four stock chart types. The two charts on the bottom display the trade volume and use two value axes. The daily volume, represented by columns, uses the axis on the left. The *up-bars,* sometimes referred to as *candlesticks,* are the vertical lines that

depict the difference between the opening and closing price. A black up-bar indicates that the closing price was lower than the opening price.

On the CD

A workbook that contains the charts in this section is available on the companion CD-ROM. The file is named `stock charts.xlsx`.

Stock charts aren't just for stock price data. Figure 18.36 shows a chart that depicts the high, low, and average temperatures for each day in May. This is a high-low-close chart.

The four stock chart subtypes.

FIGURE 18.36

Plotting temperature data with a stock chart.

Learning More

This chapter introduced Excel charts, including examples of the types of charts that you can create. For many uses, the information in this chapter is sufficient to create a wide variety of charts.

Those who require control over every aspect of their charts can find the information they need in the next chapter. It picks up where this one left off and covers the details involved in creating the perfect chart.

19

Learning Advanced Charting

E xcel makes creating a basic chart very easy. Select your data, choose a chart type, and you're finished. You may take a few extra seconds and select one of the prebuilt Chart Layouts, and maybe even select one of the Chart Styles. But if your goal is to create the most effective chart possible, you probably want to take advantage of the additional customization techniques available in Excel.

Customizing a chart involves changing its appearance as well as possibly adding new elements to it. These changes can be purely cosmetic (such as changing colors modifying line widths, or adding a shadow) or quite substantial (say, changing the axis scales or adding a second Value Axis). Chart elements that you might add include such features as a data table, a trend line, or error bars.

The preceding chapter introduced charting in Excel and described how to create basic charts. This chapter takes the topic to the next level. You learn how to customize your charts to the maximum so that they look exactly as you want. You also pick up some slick charting tricks that will make your charts even more impressive.

IN THIS CHAPTER

Understanding chart customization

Changing basic chart elements

Working with data series

Discovering some chart-making tricks

Selecting Chart Elements

Modifying a chart is similar to everything else you do in Excel: First you make a selection (in this case, select a chart element), and then you issue a command to do something with the selection.

You can select only one chart element (or one group of chart elements) at a time. For example, if you want to change the font for two axis labels, you must work on each set of axis labels separately.

Excel provides three ways, described in the following sections, to select a particular chart element:

- Mouse
- Keyboard
- Chart Elements control

Selecting with the mouse

To select a chart element with your mouse, just click the element. The chart element appears with small circles at the corners.

Tip

Some chart elements are a bit tricky to select. To ensure that you select the chart element that you intended to select, view the Chart Element control, located in the Chart Tools ⇨ Format ⇨ Current Selection group of the Ribbon (see Figure 19.1). ■

FIGURE 19.1

The Chart Element control displays the name of the selected chart element. In this example, the Legend is selected.

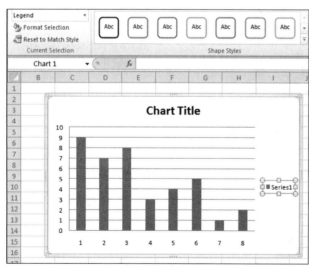

When you move the mouse over a chart, a small *chart tip* displays the name of the chart element under the mouse pointer. When the mouse pointer is over a data point, the chart tip also displays the value of the data point.

Tip

If you find these chart tips annoying, you can turn them off. Choose File ➪ Options and click the Advanced tab in the Excel Options dialog box. Locate the Chart section and clear either or both the Show Chart Element Names on Hover or the Show Data Point Values on Hover check boxes. ∎

Some chart elements (such as a series, a legend, and data labels) consist of multiple items. For example, a chart series element is made up of individual data points. To select a particular data point, click twice: First click the series to select it and then click the specific element within the series (for example, a column or a line chart marker). Selecting the element enables you to apply formatting to only a particular data point in a series.

You may find that some chart elements are difficult to select with the mouse. If you rely on the mouse for selecting a chart element, you may have to click it several times before the desired element is actually selected. Fortunately, Excel provides other ways to select a chart element, and it's worth your while to be familiar with them. Keep reading to see how.

Selecting with the keyboard

When a chart is active, you can use the up-arrow and down-arrow navigation keys on your keyboard to cycle among the chart's elements. Again, keep your eye on the Chart Elements control to ensure that the selected chart element is what you think it is.

- **When a chart series is selected:** Use the left-arrow and right-arrow keys to select an individual item within the series.
- **When a set of data labels is selected:** You can select a specific data label by using the left-arrow or right-arrow key.
- **When a legend is selected:** Select individual elements within the legend by using the left-arrow or right-arrow keys.

Selecting with the Chart Element control

The Chart Element control is located in the Chart Tools ➪ Format ➪ Current Selection group and also in the Chart Tools ➪ Layout ➪ Current Selection group. This control displays the name of the currently selected chart element. It's a drop-down control, and you can also use it to select a particular element in the active chart (see Figure 19.2).

The Chart Element control also appears in the Mini toolbar, which is displayed when you right-click a chart element.

The Chart Element control enables you to select only the top-level elements in the chart. To select an individual data point within a series, for example, you need to select the series and then use the navigation keys (or your mouse) to select the desired data point.

FIGURE 19.2

Using the Chart Element drop-down control to select a chart element.

Note

When a single data point is selected, the Chart Element control will display the name of the selected element even though it's not actually available for selection from the drop-down list. ∎

Tip

If you do a lot of work with charts, you may want to add the Chart Element control to your Quick Access toolbar. That way, it will always be visible regardless of which Ribbon tab is showing. To add the control to your Quick Access toolbar, right-click the down arrow in the control and choose Add to Quick Access Toolbar. ∎

User Interface Choices for Modifying Chart Elements

You have three main ways of working with chart elements: the Format dialog box, the Ribbon, and the Mini toolbar.

Using the Format dialog box

When a chart element is selected, use the element's Format dialog box to format or set options for the element. Each chart element has a unique Format dialog box that contains controls specific to the element (although many Format dialog boxes have controls in common). To access the Format dialog box, use any of these methods:

- Double-click the chart element.
- Right-click the chart element and then choose Format *xxxx* from the shortcut menu (where *xxxx* is the name of the element).
- Select a chart element and then choose Chart Tools ➪ Format ➪ Current Selection ➪ Format Selection.
- Select a chart element and press Ctrl+1.

Any of these actions displays a tabbed Format dialog box from which you can make many changes to the selected chart element. For example, Figure 19.3 shows the dialog box that appears when a chart's legend is selected.

Tip

The Format dialog box is a modeless dialog box, so you can leave it open while you're working on a chart. If you select a different chart element, the Format dialog box changes to display the options appropriate for the new element. ∎

FIGURE 19.3

Use the Format dialog box to set the properties of a selected chart element — in this case, the chart's legend.

Using the Ribbon

When a chart element is selected, you can also use the commands on the Ribbon to change some aspects of its formatting. For example, to change the color of the bars in a column chart, use the commands from the Chart Tools ➪ Format ➪ Shape Styles group. For some types of chart element formatting, you need to leave the Chart Tools tab. For example, to adjust font-related properties, use the commands from the Home ➪ Font Group.

The Ribbon controls do *not* comprise a comprehensive set of tools for chart elements. The Format dialog box usually presents options that aren't available on the Ribbon.

Using the Mini toolbar

When you right-click an element in a chart, Excel displays a shortcut menu and the Mini toolbar. The Mini toolbar contains commonly used formatting commands, plus a copy of the Chart Elements control (which you can use to select another chart element).

Commands that are inappropriate for the selected chart element are disabled in the Mini toolbar. For example, if you select an element that doesn't contain text, the text-related tools are disabled.

Modifying the Chart Area

The *Chart Area* is an object that contains all other elements in the chart. You can think of it as a chart's master background or container.

The only modifications that you can make to the Chart Area are cosmetic. You can change its fill color; outline; or effects, such as shadow and soft edges.

Note that if you set the Chart Area of an embedded chart to use No Fill, the underlying cells are visible. Figure 19.4 shows a chart that uses No Fill and No Outline in its Chart Area. The Plot Area, Legend, and Chart Title *do* use a fill color. Adding a shadow to these other elements make them appear to be floating on the worksheet.

The Chart Area element also controls all the fonts used in the chart. For example, if you want to change every font in the chart, you don't need to format each text element separately. Just select the Chart Area and then make the change from options of the Home ➪ Font group or by using the Mini toolbar.

The Chart Area element uses No Fill, so the underlying cells are visible.

Resetting Chart Element Formatting

If you go overboard formatting a chart element, you can always reset it to its original state. Just select the element and choose Chart Tools ➪ Format ➪ Current Selection ➪ Reset to Match Style. Or, right-click the chart element and choose Reset to Match Style from the shortcut menu.

To reset all formatting changes in the entire chart, select the Chart Area before you issue the Reset to Match Style command.

Modifying the Plot Area

The *Plot Area* is the part of the chart that contains the actual chart. More specifically, the Plot Area is a container for the chart series.

Tip

If you set the Shape Fill property to No Fill, the Plot Area will be transparent. Therefore, the fill color applied to the Chart Area will show through. ■

You can move and resize the Plot Area. Select the Plot Area and then drag a border to move it. To change the size of the Plot Area, drag one of the corner handles.

Different chart types vary in how they respond to changes in the Plot Area dimensions. For example, you can't change the relative dimensions of the Plot Area of a pie chart or a radar chart. The Plot Area of these charts is always square. With other chart types, though, you can change the aspect ratio of the Plot Area by changing either the height or the width.

Figure 19.5 shows a chart in which the Plot Area was resized to make room for a Shape that contains text.

FIGURE 19.5

Reducing the size of the Plot Area makes room for the Shape.

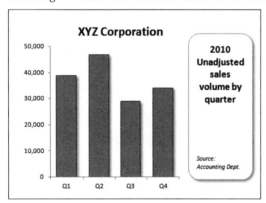

In some cases, the size of the Plot Area changes automatically when you adjust other elements of your chart. For example, if you add a legend to a chart, the size of the Plot Area may be reduced to accommodate the legend.

Tip

Changing the size and position of the Plot Area can have a dramatic effect on the overall look of your chart. When you're fine-tuning a chart, you'll probably want to experiment with various sizes and positions for the Plot Area. ∎

Working with Chart Titles

A chart can have several different types of titles:

- Chart title
- Category (X) axis title
- Value (Y) axis title
- Second category (X) axis title
- Second value (Y) axis title
- Depth axis title (for true 3-D charts)

The number of titles that you can use depends on the chart type. For example, a pie chart supports only a chart title because it has no axes.

To add a chart title, activate the chart and choose Chart Tools ➪ Layout ➪ Labels ➪ Chart Title. To add a title to one or more of the axes, choose Chart Tools ➪ Layout ➪ Labels ➪ Axis Titles. These controls are drop-down lists, and each has several options.

After you add a title, you can replace the default text and drag the titles to a different position. However, you can't change the size of a title by dragging. The only way to change the size of a title is to change the font size.

Adding Free-Floating Text to a Chart

Text in a chart is not limited to titles. In fact, you can add free-floating text anywhere you want. To do so, activate the chart and choose Chart Tools ➪ Layout ➪ Insert ➪ Text Box. Click in the chart to create the text box and enter the text. You can resize the text box, move it, change its formatting, and so on. You can also add a Shape to the chart and then add text to the Shape (if the Shape is one that accepts text).

Many people prefer to use a text box in place of a chart's "official" title elements. Resizing a title is not possible (except by changing its font size). If you use a text box, though, you can resize it by dragging its corners, change the text alignment, and even rotate it.

The chart title or any of the axis titles can also use a cell reference. For example, you can create a link so the chart always displays the text contained in cell A1 as its title. To create a link, select the title, type an equal sign (=), point to the cell, and press Enter. After you create the link, the Formula bar displays the cell reference when you select the title.

Working with a Legend

A chart's *legend* consists of text and keys that identify the data series in the chart. A *key* is a small graphic that corresponds to the chart's series (one key for each series).

To add a legend to your chart, choose Chart Tools ➪ Layout ➪ Labels ➪ Legend. This drop-down control contains several options for the legend placement. After you add a legend, you can drag it to move it anywhere you like.

Tip

If you move a legend from its default position, you may want to change the size of the Plot Area to fill in the gap left by the legend. Just select the Plot Area and drag a border to make it the desired size. ■

The quickest way to remove a legend is to select the legend and then press Delete.

You can select individual items within a legend and format them separately. For example, you may want to make the text bold to draw attention to a particular data series. To select an element in the legend, first select the legend and then click the desired element.

If you didn't include legend text when you originally selected the cells to create the chart, Excel displays Series 1, Series 2, and so on in the legend. To add series names, choose Chart Tools ➪ Design ➪ Data ➪ Select Data to display the Select Data Source dialog box (see Figure 19.6). Select the series name and click the Edit button. In the Edit Series dialog box, type the series name or enter a cell reference that contains the series name. Repeat for each series that needs naming.

FIGURE 19.6

Use the Select Data Source dialog box to change the name of a data series.

In some cases, you may prefer to omit the legend and use callouts to identify the data series. Figure 19.7 shows a chart with no legend. Instead, it uses Shapes to identify each series. These Shapes are from the Callouts section of the Chart Tools ⇨ Layout ⇨ Insert ⇨ Shapes Gallery.

FIGURE 19.7

Using Shapes as callouts in lieu of a legend.

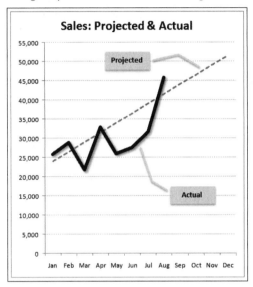

Copying Chart Formatting

You created a killer chart and spent hours customizing it. Now you need to create another one just like it, but with a different set of data. What are your options? You have several choices:

- **Copy the formatting.** Create your new chart with the default formatting. Then select your original chart and choose Home ⇨ Clipboard ⇨ Copy (or press Ctrl+C). Click your new chart and choose Home ⇨ Clipboard ⇨ Paste ⇨ Paste Special. In the Paste Special dialog box, select the Formats option.

- **Copy the chart; change the data sources.** Press Ctrl while you click the original chart and drag. This creates an exact copy of your chart. Then choose Chart Tools ⇨ Design ⇨ Data ⇨ Select Data. In the Select Data Source dialog box, specify the data for the new chart.

- **Create a chart template.** Select your chart and then choose Chart Tools ⇨ Design ⇨ Type ⇨ Save as Template. Excel prompts you for a name. When you create your next chart, use this template as the chart type.

Cross-Reference

For more information about using chart templates, see "Creating Chart Templates," later in this chapter. ■

Working with Gridlines

Gridlines can help the viewer determine what the chart series represents numerically. Gridlines simply extend the tick marks on an axis. Some charts look better with gridlines; others appear more cluttered. Sometimes, horizontal gridlines alone are enough although XY charts often benefit from both horizontal and vertical gridlines.

To add or remove gridlines, choose Chart Tools ⇨ Layout ⇨ Axes ⇨ Gridlines. This drop-down control contains options for all possible gridlines in the active chart.

Note

Each axis has two sets of gridlines: major and minor. Major units display a label. Minor units are located between the labels. ■

To modify the color or thickness of a set of gridlines, click one of the gridlines and use the commands from the Chart Tools ⇨ Format ⇨ Shape Styles group.

If gridlines seem too overpowering, consider changing them to a lighter color or use one of the dashed options.

Modifying the Axes

Charts vary in the number of axes that they use. Pie and doughnut charts have no axes. All 2-D charts have two axes (three, if you use a secondary-value axis; four, if you use a secondary-category axis in an XY chart). True 3-D charts have three axes.

Excel gives you a great deal of control over these axes, via the Format Axis dialog box. The content of this dialog box varies depending on the type of axis selected.

Value axis

To change a value axis, right-click it and choose Format Axis. Figure 19.8 shows the Axis Options tab of the Format Axis dialog box. The other tabs in the dialog box deal with cosmetic formatting.

On the Axis Options tab, the four sets of option buttons at the top determine the scale of the axis (its minimum, maximum, and intervals). By default, Excel determines these values based on the numerical range of the data, and the settings are set to Auto. You can override Excel's choice and set any or all of them to Fixed and then enter your own values.

FIGURE 19.8

These options are available for a Value Axis.

Adjusting the scale of a value axis can dramatically affect the chart's appearance. Manipulating the scale, in some cases, can present a false picture of the data. Figure 19.9 shows two line charts that depict the same data. The chart on the left uses Excel's default (Auto) axis scale values, which extend from 7,400 to 9,400. In the chart on the right, the Minimum scale value was set to 0, and the Maximum scale value was set to 10,000. The first chart makes the differences in the data seem more prominent. The second chart gives the impression that there is not much change over time.

FIGURE 19.9

These two charts show the same data, but use a different Value Axis scales.

The actual scale that you use depends on the situation. There are no hard-and-fast rules regarding setting scale values except that you shouldn't misrepresent data by manipulating the chart to prove a point that doesn't exist.

Tip

If you're preparing several charts that use similarly scaled data, keeping the scales the same is a good idea so that the charts can be compared more easily. ■

Another option in the Format Axis dialog box is Values in Reverse Order. The left chart in Figure 19.10 uses default axis settings. The right chart uses the Values in Reverse Order option, which reverses the scale's direction. Notice that the Category Axis is at the top. If you would prefer that it remain at the bottom of the chart, select the Maximum Axis Value option for the Horizontal Axis Crosses setting.

FIGURE 19.10

The right chart uses the Values in Reverse Order option.

If the values to be plotted cover a very large numerical range, you may want to use a logarithmic scale for the value axis. A log scale is most often used for scientific applications. Figure 19.11 shows two charts. The left chart uses a standard scale, and the right chart uses a logarithmic scale.

Note

The Base setting is 10, so each scale value in the chart is 10 times greater than the one below it. Increasing the major unit to 100 results in a scale in which each tick mark value is 100 times greater than the one below. You can specify a base value between 2 and 1,000. ■

On the CD

This workbook, `log scale.xlsx`, is available on the companion CD-ROM. ■

FIGURE 19.11

These charts display the same data, but the right chart uses a logarithmic scale.

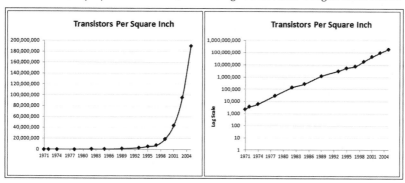

If your chart uses very large numbers, you may want to change the Display Units settings. Figure 19.12 shows a chart that uses very large numbers. The chart on the right uses the Display Units as Millions settings, with the option to Show Display Units Labels on Chart.

FIGURE 19.12

The chart on the right uses display units of millions.

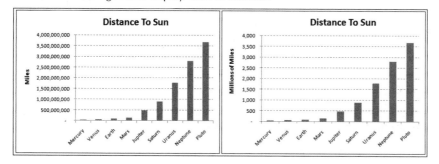

The Major and Minor Tick Mark options control how the tick marks are displayed. *Major tick marks* are the axis tick marks that normally have labels next to them. *Minor tick marks* fall between the major tick marks.

Excel lets you position the axis labels at three different locations: Next to Axis, High, and Low. Each axis extends from −10 to +10. When you combine these settings with the Axis Crosses At option, you have a great deal of flexibility, as shown in Figure 19.13.

FIGURE 19.13

Various ways to display axis labels and crossing points.

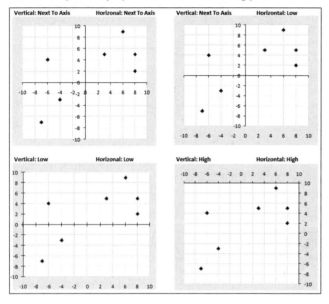

Category axis

Figure 19.14 shows the Axis Options tab of the Format Axis dialog box when a category axis is selected. Some options are the same as those for a value axis.

Excel chooses how to display category labels, but you can override its choice. Figure 19.15 shows a column chart with month labels. Because of the lengthy category labels, Excel displays the text at an angle. If you make the chart wider, the labels will then appear horizontally. You can also adjust the labels from the Alignment tab of the Format Axis dialog box.

In some cases, you really don't need every category label. You can adjust the Interval between Labels settings to skip some labels (and cause the text to display horizontally). Figure 19.16 shows such a chart; the Interval between Labels setting is 3.

FIGURE 19.14

These options are available for a category axis.

FIGURE 19.15

Excel determines how to display category axis labels.

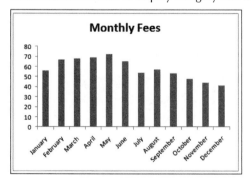

FIGURE 19.16

Changing the Interval between Labels setting makes labels display horizontally.

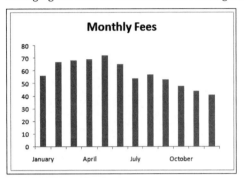

When you create a chart, Excel recognizes whether your category axis contains date or time values. If so, it uses a time-based category axis. Figure 19.17 shows a simple example. Column A contains dates, and column B contains the values plotted in the column chart. The data consists of values for only 10 dates, yet Excel created the chart with 30 intervals on the category axis. It recognized that the category axis values were dates and created an equal-interval scale.

FIGURE 19.17

Excel recognizes dates and creates a time-based category axis.

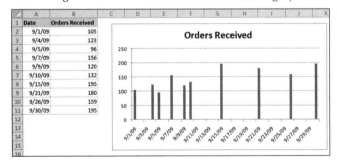

You can override Excel's decision to use a time-based category axis by choosing the Text Axis option for Axis Type. Figure 19.18 shows the chart after making this change. In this case, using a time-based category axis presents a truer picture of the data.

Don't Be Afraid to Experiment (But on a Copy)

I'll let you in on a secret: The key to mastering charts in Excel is experimentation, otherwise known as trial and error. Excel's charting options can be overwhelming, even to experienced users. This book doesn't even pretend to cover all the charting features and options. Your job, as a potential charting guru, is to dig deep and try out the various options in your charts. With a bit of creativity, you can create original-looking charts.

After you create a basic chart, make a copy of the chart for your experimentation. That way, if you mess it up, you can always revert to the original and start again. To make a copy of an embedded chart, click the chart and press Ctrl+C. Then activate a cell and press Ctrl+V. To make a copy of a chart sheet, press Ctrl while you click the sheet tab and then drag it to a new location among the other tabs.

FIGURE 19.18

Overriding the Excel time-based category axis.

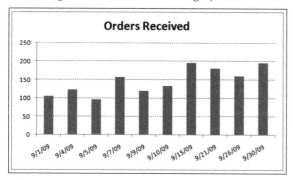

Working with Data Series

Every chart consists of one or more data series. This data translates into chart columns, bars, lines, pie slices, and so on. This section discusses some common operations that involve a chart's data series.

When you select a data series in a chart, Excel does the following:

- Displays the series name in the Chart Elements control (located in the Chart Tools ➪ Layout ➪ Current Selection group and also in the Chart Tools ➪ Format ➪ Current Selection group)
- Displays the `Series` formula in the Formula bar
- Highlights the cells used for the selected series by outlining them in color

You can make changes to a data series by using options on the Ribbon or from the Format Data Series dialog box. This dialog box varies, depending on the type of data series you're working on (column, line, pie, and so on).

Caution

The easiest way to display the Format Data Series dialog box is to double-click the chart series. Be careful, however: If a data series is already selected, double-clicking brings up the Format Data Point dialog box. Changes that you make affect only one point in the data series. To edit the entire series, make sure that a chart element other than the data series is selected before you double-click the data series. ∎

Deleting a data series

To delete a data series in a chart, select the data series and press Delete. The data series disappears from the chart. The data in the worksheet, of course, remains intact.

Note

You can delete all data series from a chart. If you do so, the chart appears empty. It retains its settings, however. Therefore, you can add a data series to an empty chart, and it again looks like a chart. ∎

Adding a new data series to a chart

If you want to add another data series to an existing chart, re-create the chart and include the new data series. However, adding the data to the existing chart is usually easier, and your chart retains any customization that you've made.

Figure 19.19 shows a column chart that has two data series (Jan and Feb). The March figures just became available and were entered into the worksheet in row 4. Now the chart needs to be updated to include the new data series.

Excel provides two ways to add a new data series to a chart:

- Activate the chart and choose Chart Tools ⇨ Design ⇨ Data ⇨ Select Data. In the Select Data Source dialog box, click the Add button, and Excel displays the Edit Series dialog box. Specify the Series Name (as a cell reference or text) and the range that contains the Series Values.
- Select the range to add and press Ctrl+C to copy it to the Clipboard. Then activate the chart and press Ctrl+V to paste the data into the chart.

Note

In previous versions of Excel, you could add a new data series by selecting a range of data and "dragging" it into an embedded chart. That feature was removed, beginning with Excel 2007. ∎

FIGURE 19.19

This chart needs a new data series.

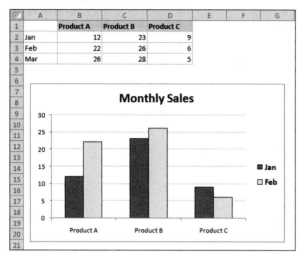

Tip

If the chart was originally made from data in a table (created via Insert ⇨ Tables ⇨ Table), the chart is updated automatically when you add new data to the table. If you have a chart that is updated frequently with new data, you can save time and effort by creating the chart from data in a table. ■

Changing data used by a series

You may find that you need to modify the range that defines a data series. For example, say you need to add new data points or remove old ones from the data set. The following sections describe several ways to change the range used by a data series.

Changing the data range by dragging the range outline

If you have an embedded chart, the easiest way to change the data range for a data series is to drag the range outline. When you select a series in a chart, Excel outlines the data range used by that series (see Figure 19.20). You can drag the small dot in the lower-right corner of the range outline to extend or contract the data series.

You can also click and drag one of the sides of the outline to move the outline to a different range of cells.

In some cases, you'll also need to adjust the range that contains the category labels as well. The labels are also outlined, and you can drag the outline to expand or contract the range of labels used in the chart.

If your chart is on a chart sheet, you need to use one of the two methods described next.

Changing a chart's data series by dragging the range outline.

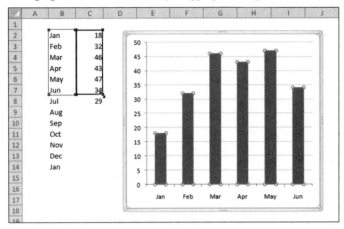

Using the Edit Series dialog box

Another way to update the chart to reflect a different data range is to use the Edit Series dialog box. A quick way to display this dialog box is to right-click the series in the chart and then choose Select Data from the shortcut menu. Excel displays the Select Source Data dialog box. Select the data series in the list, and click Edit to display the Edit Series dialog box, shown in Figure 19.21.

You can change the entire data range used by the chart by adjusting the range references in the Chart Data Range field. Or, select a Series from the list and click Edit to modify the selected series.

The Edit Series dialog box.

Editing the Series formula

Every data series in a chart has an associated Series formula, which appears in the Formula bar when you select a data series in a chart. If you understand how a Series formula is constructed, you can edit the range references in the Series formula directly to change the data used by the chart.

Note

The Series formula is not a real formula: In other words, you can't use it in a cell, and you can't use worksheet functions within the Series formula. You can, however, edit the arguments in the Series formula. ∎

A Series formula has the following syntax:

```
=SERIES(series_name, category_labels, values, order, sizes)
```

The arguments that you can use in the Series formula include

- series_name: (Optional). A reference to the cell that contains the series name used in the legend. If the chart has only one series, the name argument is used as the title. This argument can also consist of text in quotation marks. If omitted, Excel creates a default series name (for example, Series 1).

- category_labels: (Optional). A reference to the range that contains the labels for the category axis. If omitted, Excel uses consecutive integers beginning with 1. For XY charts, this argument specifies the X values. A noncontiguous range reference is also valid. The ranges' addresses are separated by commas and enclosed in parentheses. The argument could also consist of an array of comma-separated values (or text in quotation marks) enclosed in curly brackets.

- values: (Required). A reference to the range that contains the values for the series. For XY charts, this argument specifies the Y values. A noncontiguous range reference is also valid. The ranges addresses are separated by a comma and enclosed in parentheses. The argument could also consist of an array of comma-separated values enclosed in curly brackets.

- order: (Required). An integer that specifies the plotting order of the series. This argument is relevant only if the chart has more than one series. Using a reference to a cell is not allowed.

- sizes: (Only for bubble charts). A reference to the range that contains the values for the size of the bubbles in a bubble chart. A noncontiguous range reference is also valid. The ranges addresses are separated by commas and enclosed in parentheses. The argument can also consist of an array of values enclosed in curly brackets.

Range references in a Series formula are always absolute (contain two dollar signs), and they always include the sheet name. For example

```
=SERIES(Sheet1!$B$1,,Sheet1!$B$2:$B$7,1)
```

Tip

You can substitute range names for the range references. If you do so, Excel changes the reference in the `Series` **formula to include the workbook name. For example if you use a range named MyData (in a workbook named budget.xlsx), the** `Series` **formula looks like this:**

```
=SERIES(Sheet1!$B$1,,budget.xlsx!MyData,1)
```

Displaying data labels in a chart

Sometimes, you may want your chart to display the actual numerical values for each data point. You specify data labels by choosing Chart Tools ➪ Layout ➪ Labels ➪ Data Labels. This drop-down control contains several data label positioning options.

Figure 19.22 shows three minimalist charts with data labels.

These charts use data labels.

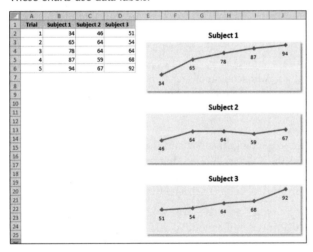

To change the type of information that appears in data labels, select the data labels in the chart and press Ctrl+F1. Then use the Label Options tab of the Format Data Labels dialog box to customize the data labels. For example, you can include the series name and the category name along with the value.

The data labels are linked to the worksheet, so if your data changes, the labels also change. If you want to override the data label with other text, select the label and enter the new text.

Tip

Often, the data labels aren't positioned properly — for example, a label may be obscured by another data point. If you select an individual data label, you can drag the label to a better location. To select an individual data label, click once to select them all and then click the single data label. ■

As you work with data labels, you discover that the Excel data labels feature leaves a bit to be desired. For example, it would be nice to be able to specify an arbitrary range of text to be used for the data labels. This capability would be particularly useful in XY charts in which you want to identify each data point with a particular text item. Despite what must amount to thousands of requests, Microsoft still hasn't added this feature to Excel. You need to add data labels and then manually edit each label.

Handling missing data

Sometimes, data that you're charting may be missing one or more data points. As shown in Figure 19.23, Excel offers three ways to handle the missing data:

- **Gaps:** Missing data is simply ignored, and the data series will have a gap. This is the default.

- **Zero:** Missing data is treated as zero.

- **Connect Data Points with Line:** Missing data is interpolated, calculated by using data on either side of the missing point(s). This option is available for line charts, area charts, and XY charts only.

To specify how to deal with missing data for a chart, choose Chart Tools ➪ Design ➪ Data ➪ Select Data. In the Select Data Source dialog box, click the Hidden and Empty Cells button. Excel displays its Hidden and Empty Cell Settings dialog box. Make your choice in the dialog box. The option that you choose applies to the entire chart, and you can't set a different option for different series in the same chart.

Tip

Normally, a chart doesn't display data that's in a hidden row or column. You can use the Hidden and Empty Cell Settings dialog box to force a chart to use hidden data, though. ■

Adding error bars

Some chart types support error bars. *Error bars* often are used to indicate "plus or minus" information that reflects uncertainty in the data. Error bars are appropriate for area, bar, column, line, and XY charts only.

FIGURE 19.23

Three options for dealing with missing data.

To add error bars, select a data series and then choose Chart Tools ➪ Layout ➪ Analysis ➪ Error Bars. This drop-down control has several options. You can then fine-tune the error bar settings from the Format Error Bars dialog box. The types of error bars are

- **Fixed value:** The error bars are fixed by an amount that you specify.
- **Percentage:** The error bars are a percentage of each value.
- **Standard Deviation(s):** The error bars are in the number of standard deviation units that you specify. (Excel calculates the standard deviation of the data series.)
- **Standard Error:** The error bars are one standard error unit. (Excel calculates the standard error of the data series.)
- **Custom:** You set the error bar units for the upper or lower error bars. You can enter either a value or a range reference that holds the error values that you want to plot as error bars.

The chart shown in Figure 19.24 displays error bars based on percentage.

Tip
A data series in an XY chart can have error bars for both the X values and Y values. ∎

FIGURE 19.24

This line chart series displays error bars based on percentage.

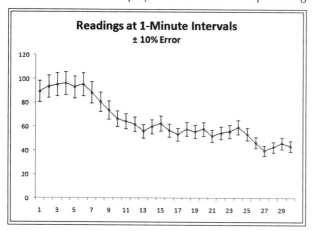

Adding a trendline

When you're plotting data over time, you may want to plot a trendline that describes the data. A *trendline* points out general trends in your data. In some cases, you can forecast future data with trendlines. A single series can have more than one trendline.

To add a trendline, select the data series and choose Chart Tools ➪ Layout ➪ Analysis ➪ Trendline. This drop-down control contains options for the type of trendline. The type of trendline that you choose depends on your data. Linear trends are most common, but some data can be described more effectively with another type.

Figure 19.25 shows an XY chart with a linear trendline and the (optional) equation for the trendline. The trendline describes the "best fit" of the height and weight data.

For more control over a trendline, right-click it and choose Format Trendline to open the Format Trendline dialog box. One option, Moving Average, is useful for smoothing out data that has a lot of variation (that is, "noisy" data).

The Moving Average option enables you to specify the number of data points to include in each average. For example, if you select 5, Excel averages every five data points. Figure 19.26 shows a chart that uses a moving average trendline.

FIGURE 19.25

An XY chart with a linear trendline.

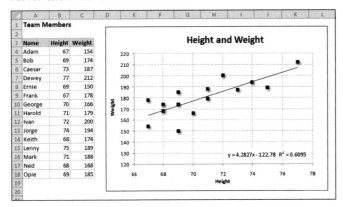

FIGURE 19.26

The dashed line displays a seven-interval moving average.

Modifying 3-D charts

3-D charts have a few additional elements that you can customize. For example, most 3-D charts have a floor and walls, and true 3-D charts also have an additional axis. You can select these chart elements and format them to your liking using the Format dialog box.

One area in which Excel 3-D charts differ from 2-D charts is in the perspective — or *viewpoint* — from which you see the chart. In some cases, the data may be viewed better if you change the order of the series.

Figure 19.27 shows two versions of 3-D column chart with two data series. The left chart is the original, and the right chart shows the effect of changing the series order. To change the series order, choose Chart Tools ➪ Design ➪ Data ➪ Select Data. In the Select Data Source dialog box, select a series and use the arrow buttons to change its order.

FIGURE 19.27

A 3-D column chart, before and after changing the series order.

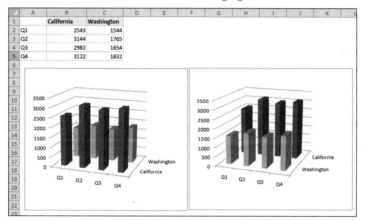

Fortunately, Excel allows you to change the viewing angle of 3-D charts. Doing so may reveal portions of the chart that are otherwise hidden. To rotate a 3-D chart, choose Chart Tools ➪ Layout ➪ Background ➪ 3-D Rotation, which displays the 3-D Rotation tab of the Format Chart Area dialog box. You can make your rotations and perspective changes by clicking the appropriate controls.

Figure 19.28 shows four different views of the same chart. As you can see, you can accidentally distort the chart to make it virtually worthless in terms of visualizing information. If accuracy of presentation is important, a 3-D chart is hardly ever the best choice.

Creating combination charts

A *combination chart* is a single chart that consists of series that use different chart types. A combination chart may also include a second value axis. For example, you may have a chart that shows both columns and lines, with two value axes. The value axis for the columns is on the left, and the value axis for the line is on the right. A combination chart requires at least two data series.

Creating a combination chart involves changing one or more of the data series to a different chart type. Select the data series to change and then choose Chart Tools ➪ Design ➪ Type ➪ Change Chart Type. In the Change Chart Type dialog box, select the chart type that you want to apply to the selected series. Using a second Value Axis is optional.

FIGURE 19.28

Changing the viewing angle to show different views of the same 3-D column chart.

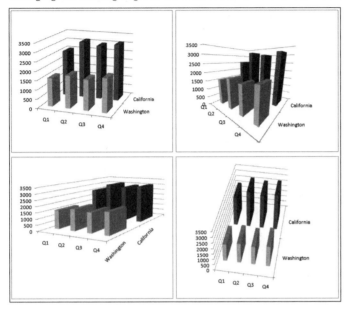

Note

If anything other than a series is selected when you choose Chart Tools ➪ Design ➪ Type ➪ Change Chart Type, all the series in the chart change. ∎

Figure 19.29 shows a column chart with two data series. The values for the Precipitation series are very low — so low that they're barely visible on the Value Axis scale. This is a good candidate for a combination chart.

The following steps describe how to convert this chart into a combination chart (column and line) that uses a second Value Axis.

1. **Double-click the Precipitation data series to display the Format Data Series dialog box.**

2. **Click the Series Options tab and select the Secondary Axis option.**

3. **With the Precipitation data series still selected, choose Chart Tools ➪ Design ➪ Type ➪ Change Chart Type.**

4. **In the Change Chart Type dialog box, select the Line type and click OK.**

Figure 19.30 shows the modified chart. The Precipitation data appears as a line, and it uses the Value Axis on the right.

FIGURE 19.29

The Precipitation series is barely visible.

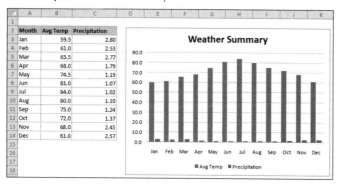

FIGURE 19.30

The Precipitation series is now visible.

On the CD

This workbook is available on the companion CD-ROM. The filename is `weather combination chart.xlsx`.

Note

In some cases, you can't combine chart types. For example, you can't create a combination chart that involves a bubble chart or a 3-D chart. If you choose an incompatible chart type for the series, Excel lets you know. ∎

Figure 19.31 demonstrates just how far you can go with a combination chart. This chart combines five different chart types: Pie, Area, Column, Line, and XY. I can't think of any situation that would warrant such a chart, but it's an interesting demo.

A five-way combination chart.

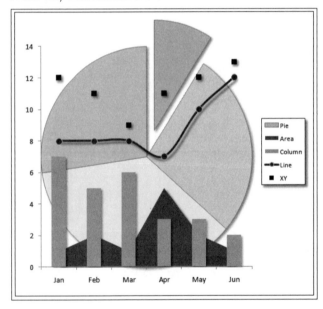

Displaying a data table

In some cases, you may want to display a *data table*, which displays the chart's data in tabular form, directly in the chart.

To add a data table to a chart, choose Chart Tools ➪ Layout ➪ Labels ➪ Data Table. This control is a drop-down list with a few options to choose from. For more options, use the Format Data Table dialog box. Figure 19.32 shows a combination chart that includes a data table.

FIGURE 19.32

This combination chart includes a data table that displays the values of the data points.

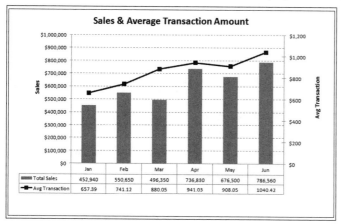

	Jan	Feb	Mar	Apr	May	Jun
Total Sales	452,940	550,650	496,350	736,830	676,500	786,560
Avg Transaction	657.39	741.12	880.05	941.03	908.05	1040.42

Tip

Using a data table is probably best suited for charts on chart sheets. If you need to show the data used in an embedded chart, you can do so using data in cells, which provide you with a lot more flexibility in terms of formatting. ■

Creating Chart Templates

This section describes how to create custom chart templates. A template includes customized chart formatting and settings. When you create a new chart, you can choose to use your template rather than a built-in chart type.

If you find that you are continually customizing your charts in the same way, you can probably save some time by creating a template. Or, if you create lots of combination charts, you can create a combination chart template and avoid making the manual adjustments required for a combination chart.

To create a chart template

1. **Create a chart to serve as the basis for your template.** The data you use for this chart is not critical, but for best results, it should be typical of the data that you'll eventually be plotting with your custom chart type.

2. **Apply any formatting and customizations that you like.** This step determines how the appearance of the charts created from the template.

3. **Activate the chart and choose Chart Tools ➪ Design ➪ Type ➪ Save as Template.** Excel displays its Save Chart Template dialog box.

4. **Provide a name for the template and click Save.**

To create a chart based on a template

1. **Select the data to be used in the chart.**

2. **Choose Insert ➪ Charts ➪ Other Charts ➪ All Chart Types.** Excel displays its Insert Chart dialog box.

3. **From the left side of the Insert Chart dialog box, select Templates.** Excel displays an icon for each custom template that has been created.

4. **Click the icon that represents the template you want to use and then click OK.** Excel creates the chart based on the template you selected.

Note
You can also apply a template to an existing chart. Select the chart and choose Chart Tools ➪ Design ➪ Change Chart Type. ∎

Learning Some Chart-Making Tricks

This section describes some interesting (and perhaps useful) chart-making tricks. Some of these tricks use little-known features, and several tricks enable you to make charts that you may have considered impossible to create.

Creating picture charts

Excel makes it easy to incorporate a pattern, texture, or graphics file for elements in your chart. Figure 19.33 shows a chart that uses a photo as the background for a chart's Chart Area element.

To display an image in a chart element, use the Fill tab in the element's Format dialog box. Select the Picture or Texture Fill option and then click the button that corresponds to the image source (File, Clipboard, or ClipArt). If you use the Clipboard button, make sure that you copied your image first. The other two options prompt you for the image.

Figure 19.34 shows two more examples: a pie chart that uses Office clipart as its fill; and a column chart that uses a Shape, which was inserted on a worksheet and then copied to the Clipboard.

On the CD
The examples in this section are available on the companion CD-ROM. The filename is `picture charts. xlsx`.

FIGURE 19.33

The Chart Area contains a photo.

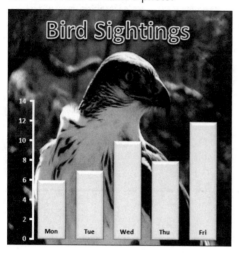

Using images in a chart offers unlimited potential for creativity. The key, of course, is to resist the temptation to go overboard. A chart's primary goal is to convey information, not to impress the viewer with your artistic skills.

Caution

Using images, especially photos, in charts can dramatically increase the size of your workbooks. ■

FIGURE 19.34

The left chart uses clip art, and the right chart uses a Shape that was copied to the Clipboard.

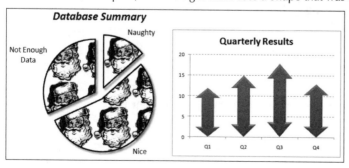

Creating a thermometer chart

You're probably familiar with a "thermometer" type display that shows the percentage of a task that has been completed. Creating such a display in Excel is very easy. The trick involves creating a chart that uses a single cell (which holds a percentage value) as a data series.

Figure 19.35 shows a worksheet set up to track daily progress toward a goal: 1,000 new customers in a 15-day period. Cell B18 contains the goal value, and cell B19 contains a simple formula that calculates the sum. Cell B21 contains a formula that calculates the percent of goal:

    =B19/B18

As you enter new data in column B, the formulas display the current results.

FIGURE 19.35

This single-point chart displays progress toward a goal.

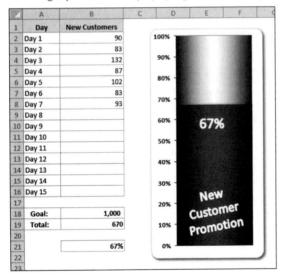

On the CD

A workbook with this example is available on the companion CD-ROM. The filename is thermometer chart.xlsx.

To make the thermometer chart, select cell B21 and create a column chart from that single cell. Notice the blank cell above cell B21. Without this blank cell, Excel uses the entire data block for the chart, not just the single cell. Because B21 is isolated from the other data, only the single cell is used.

Other changes required are to

- Select the horizontal category axis and press Delete to remove the category axis from the chart.

- Remove the legend.

- Add a text box, linked to cell B21 to display the percent accomplished.

- In the Format Data Series dialog box (Series Options tab), set the Gap width to 0, which makes the column occupy the entire width of the plot area.

- Select the Value Axis and display the Format Value Axis dialog box. In the Axis Options tab, set the Minimum to 0 and the Maximum to 1.

Make any other cosmetic adjustments to get the look you desire.

Creating a gauge chart

Figure 19.36 shows another chart based on a single cell. It's a pie chart set up to resemble a gauge. Although this chart displays only one value (entered in cell B1), it actually uses three data points (in A4:A6).

On the CD

A workbook with this example is available on the companion CD-ROM. The filename is `gauge chart.`
`xlsx.`

One slice of the pie — the slice at the bottom — always consists of 50 percent. I rotated the pie so that the 50 percent slice was at the bottom. Then I hid that slice by specifying No Fill and No Border for the data point.

FIGURE 19.36

This chart resembles a speedometer gauge and displays a value between 0 and 100 percent.

The other two slices are apportioned based on the value in cell B1. The formula in cell A4 is

```
=MIN(B1,100%)/2
```

This formula uses the MIN function to display the smaller of two values: either the value in cell B1 or 100 percent. It then divides this value by 2 because only the top half of the pie is relevant. Using the MIN function prevents the chart from displaying more than 100 percent.

The formula in cell A5 simply calculates the remaining part of the pie — the part to the right of the gauge's "needle":

```
=50%-A4
```

The chart's title was moved below the half-pie. The chart also contains a text box, linked to cell B1, that displays the percent completed.

Displaying conditional colors in a column chart

You may have noticed the Vary Colors by Point option on the Fill tab of the Format Data Series dialog box. This option simply uses more colors for the data series. Unfortunately, the colors aren't related to the values of the data series.

This section describes how to create a column chart in which the color of each column depends on the value that it's displaying. Figure 19.37 shows such a chart (more impressive when you see it in color). The data used to create the chart is in range A1:F14.

FIGURE 19.37

The color of the column depends varies with the value.

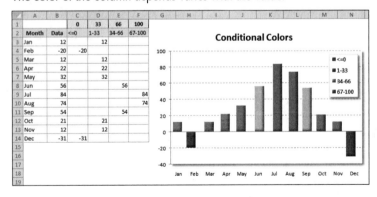

On the CD

A workbook with this example is available on the companion CD-ROM. The filename is `conditional colors.xlsx`.

This chart displays four data series, but some data is missing for each series. The data for the chart is entered in column B. Formulas in columns C:F determine which series the number belongs to by referencing the bins in Row 1. For example, the formula in cell C3 is

```
=IF(B3<=$C$1,B3,"")
```

If the value in column B is less than the value in cell C1, the value goes in this column. The formulas are set up such that a value in column B goes into only one column in the row.

The formula in cell D3 is a bit more complex because it must determine whether cell C3 is greater than the value in cell C1 and less than or equal to the value in cell D1:

```
=IF(AND($B3>C$1,$B3<=D$1),$B3,"")
```

The four data series are overlaid on top of each other in the chart. The trick involves setting the Series Overlap value to a large number. This setting determines the spacing between the series. Use the Series Options tab of the Format Data Series dialog box to adjust this setting.

Note

Series Overlap is a single setting for the chart. If you change the setting for one series, the other series change to the same value. ∎

Creating a comparative histogram

With a bit of creativity, you can create charts that you may have considered impossible. For example, Figure 19.38 shows a chart sometimes referred to as a *comparative histogram chart*. Such charts often display population data.

On the CD

A workbook with this example is available on the companion CD-ROM. The filename is `comparative histogram.xlsx`.

Here's how to create the chart:

1. **Enter the data in A1:C8, as shown in Figure 19.38.** Notice that the values for females are entered as negative values, which is very important.
2. **Select A1:C8 and create a bar chart.** Use the subtype labeled Clustered Bar.
3. **Select the horizontal axis and display the Format Axis dialog box.**
4. **Click the Number tab and specify the 0%;0%;0% custom number format.** This custom format eliminates the negative signs in the percentages.

5. Select the vertical axis and display the Format Axis dialog box.

6. **On the Axis Options tab, set all tick marks to None and set the Axis Labels option to Low.** This setting keeps the vertical axis in the center of the chart but displays the axis labels at the left side.

7. Select either data series and display the Format Data Series dialog box.

8. **On the Series Options tab, set the Series Overlap to 100% and the Gap Width to 0%.**

9. Delete the legend and add two text boxes to the chart (Females and Males) to substitute for the legend.

10. Apply other formatting and labels as desired.

FIGURE 19.38

A comparative histogram.

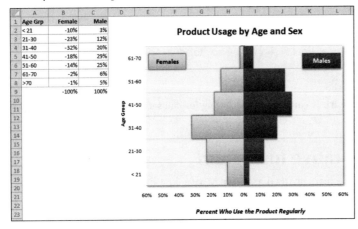

Creating a Gantt chart

A *Gantt chart* is a horizontal bar chart often used in project management applications. Although Excel doesn't support Gantt charts per se, creating a simple Gantt chart is possible. The key is getting your data set up properly.

Figure 19.39 shows a Gantt chart that depicts the schedule for a project, which is in the range A2:C13. The horizontal axis represents the total time span of the project, and each bar represents a project task. The viewer can quickly see the duration for each task and identify overlapping tasks.

On the CD

A workbook with this example is available on the companion CD-ROM. The filename is `gantt chart.xlsx`.

FIGURE 19.39

You can create a simple Gantt chart from a bar chart.

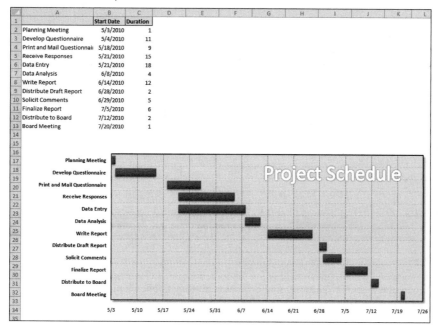

Column A contains the task name, column B contains the corresponding start date, and column C contains the duration of the task, in days.

Follow these steps to create this chart:

1. Select the range A2:C13, and create a stacked bar chart.

2. Delete the legend.

3. Select the category (vertical) axis and display the Format Axis dialog box.

4. From the Format Axis dialog box, specify Categories in Reverse Order to display the tasks in order, starting at the top. Choose Horizontal Axis Crosses at Maximum Category to display the dates at the bottom.

5. Select the Start Date data series and display the Format Data Series dialog box.

6. Still in the Format Data Series dialog box, click the Series Options tab and set the Series Overlap to 100%. From the Fill tab, specify No Fill. From the Border Color tab, specify No Line. These steps effectively hide the data series.

7. Select the value (horizontal) axis and display the Format Axis dialog box.

8. In the Format Axis dialog box, adjust the Minimum and Maximum settings to accommodate the dates that you want to display on the axis. Unfortunately, you must enter these values as date serial numbers, not actual dates. In this example, the Minimum

is 40301 (May 3, 2010) and the Maximum is 40385 (July 26, 2010). Specify 7 for the Major Unit, to display one-week intervals. Use the number tab to specify a date format for the axis labels.

9. **Apply other formatting as desired.**

Plotting mathematical functions with one variable

An XY chart is useful for plotting various mathematical and trigonometric functions. For example, Figure 19.40 shows a plot of the SIN function. The charts plots *y* for values of *x* (expressed in radians) from –5 to +5 in increments of 0.5. Each pair of *x* and *y* values appears as a data point in the chart, and the points connect with a line.

The function is expressed as

```
y = SIN(x)
```

The corresponding formula in cell B2 (which is copied to the cells below) is

```
=SIN(A2)
```

On the CD

The companion CD-ROM contains a general-purpose, single-variable plotting application. The file is named function plot 2D.xlsx.

FIGURE 19.40

This chart plots the SIN(x).

Plotting mathematical functions with two variables

The preceding section describes how to plot functions that use a single variable (x). You also can plot functions that use two variables. For example, the following function calculates a value of z for various values of two variables (x and y):

```
z = SIN(x)*COS(y)
```

Figure 19.41 shows a surface chart that plots the value of z for 21 x values ranging from 1 to 5, and for 21 y values ranging from 1 to 5. Both x and y use an increment of 0.2.

The formula in cell B2, copied across and down, is

```
=SIN($A2*COS(B$1))
```

On the CD

The companion CD-ROM contains a general–purpose, two-variable plotting application. The file is named `function plot 3D.xlsm`. **This workbook contains a few simple VBA macros to allow you to change the chart's rotation and elevation.** ■

FIGURE 19.41

Using a surface chart to plot a function with two variables.

Visualizing Data Using Conditional Formatting

T his chapter explores conditional formatting, one of Excel's most versatile features. You can apply conditional formatting to a cell so that
the cell looks different, depending on its contents.

Microsoft made significant enhancements to conditional formatting in Excel
2007, and it's now a useful tool for visualizing numeric data. You'll find a
few more conditional formatting improvements in Excel 2010.

About Conditional Formatting

Conditional formatting enables you to apply cell formatting selectively and
automatically, based on the contents of the cells. For example, you can set
things up so that all negative values in a range have a light-yellow background color. When you enter or change a value in the range, Excel examines the value and checks the conditional formatting rules for the cell. If the
value is negative, the background is shaded. If not, no formatting is applied.

Conditional formatting is a useful way to quickly identify erroneous cell
entries or cells of a particular type. You can use a format (such as bright-red
cell shading) to make particular cells easy to identify.

Figure 20.1 shows a worksheet with nine ranges, each with a different type
of conditional formatting rule applied. Here's a brief explanation of each:

- **Greater than 10:** Values greater than 10 are highlighted with a different background color. This rule is just one of many numeric
  value related rules that you can apply.

- **Above average:** Values that are higher than the average value are
  highlighted.

- **Duplicate values:** Values that appear more than one time are highlighted.

- **Words that contain X:** If the cell contains X (upper- or lowercase), the cell is highlighted.

- **Data bars:** Each cell displays a horizontal bar, proportional to its value.

- **Color Scale:** The background color varies, depending on the value of the cells. You can choose from several different color scales or create your own.

- **Icon Set:** One of several icon sets. It displays a small graphic in the cell. The graphic varies, depending on the cell value.

- **Icon Set:** Another icon set, with all but one icon hidden.

- **Custom rule:** The rule for this checkerboard pattern is based on a formula:

  `=MOD(ROW(),2)=MOD(COLUMN(),2)`

On the CD

This workbook, named `conditional formatting examples.xlsx`, is available on the companion CD-ROM. ∎

FIGURE 20.1

This worksheet demonstrates a few conditional formatting rules.

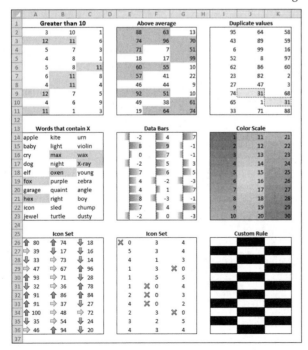

Specifying Conditional Formatting

To apply a conditional formatting rule to a cell or range, select the cells and then use one of the commands from the Home ⇨ Styles ⇨ Conditional Formatting drop-down list to specify a rule. The choices are

- **Highlight Cell Rules:** Examples rules include highlighting cells that are greater than a particular value, between two values, contain specific text string, a date, or are duplicated.

- **Top Bottom Rules:** Examples include highlighting the top 10 items, the items in the bottom 20 percent, and items that are above average.

- **Data Bars:** Applies graphic bars directly in the cells, proportional to the cell's value.

- **Color Scales:** Applies background color, proportional to the cell's value.

- **Icon Sets:** Displays icons directly in the cells. The icons depend on the cell's value.

- **New Rule:** Enables you to specify other conditional formatting rules, including rules based on a logical formula.

- **Clear Rules:** Deletes all the conditional formatting rules from the selected cells.

- **Manage Rules:** Displays the Conditional Formatting Rules Manager dialog box, in which you create new conditional formatting rules, edit rules, or delete rules.

Formatting types you can apply

When you select a conditional formatting rule, Excel displays a dialog box specific to that rule. These dialog boxes have one thing in a common: a drop-down list with common formatting suggestions.

Figure 20.2 shows the dialog box that appears when you choose Home ⇨ Styles ⇨ Conditional Formatting ⇨ Highlight Cells Rules ⇨ Between. This particular rule applies the formatting if the value in the cell falls between two specified values. In this case, you enter the two values (or specify cell references), and then use choices from the drop-down list to set the type of formatting to display if the condition is met.

FIGURE 20.2

One of several different conditional formatting dialog boxes.

Excel 2010 Improvements

If you've used conditional formatting in Excel 2007, you'll find several improvements in Excel 2010:

- Data bars display proportionally.
- Data bars can display in a solid color with a border. Previously, data bars always displayed with a gradient.
- Data bars handle negative values much better.
- You can specify minimum and maximum values for data bars.
- You can create customized Icon sets.
- Hiding one or more icons in an icon set is easy.

The formatting suggestions in the drop-down list are just a few of thousands of different formatting combinations. If none of Excel's suggestions are what you want, choose the Custom Format option to display the Format Cells dialog box. You can specify the format in any or all of the four tabs: Number, Font, Border, and Fill.

Note
The Format Cells dialog box used for conditional formatting is a modified version of the standard Format Cells dialog box. It doesn't have the Alignment and Protection tabs, and some of the Font formatting options are disabled. The dialog box also includes a Clear button that clears any formatting already selected. ■

Making your own rules

For do-it-yourself types, Excel provides the New Formatting Rule dialog box, shown in Figure 20.3. Access this dialog box by choosing Home ➪ Styles ➪ Conditional Formatting ➪ New Rules.

Use the New Formatting Rule dialog box to re-create all the conditional format rules available via the Ribbon, as well as new rules. First, select a general rule type from the list at the top of the dialog box. The bottom part of the dialog box varies, depending on your selection at the top. After you specify the rule, click the Format button to specify the type of formatting to apply if the condition is met. An exception is the first rule type, which doesn't have a Format button (it uses graphics rather than cell formatting).

Here is a summary of the rule types:

- **Format all cells based on their values:** Use this rule type to create rules that display data bars, color scales, or icon sets.
- **Format only cells that contain:** Use this rule type to create rules that format cells based on mathematical comparisons (greater than, less than, greater than or equal to, less than or equal to, equal to, not equal to, between, not between). You can also create rules based

on text, dates, blanks, nonblanks, and errors. This rule type is very similar to how conditional formatting was set up in previous versions of Excel.

- **Format only top or bottom ranked values:** Use this rule type to create rules that involve identifying cells in the top *n*, top *n* percent, bottom *n*, and bottom *n* percent.

- **Format only values that are above or below average:** Use this rule type to create rules that identify cells that are above average, below average, or within a specified standard deviation from the average.

- **Format only unique or duplicate values**: Use this rule type to create rules that format unique or duplicate values in a range.

- **Use a formula to determine which cells to format:** Use this rule type to create rules based on a logical formula. See "Formula-Based Conditions," later in this chapter.

FIGURE 20.3

Use the New Formatting Rule dialog box to create your own conditional formatting rules.

Conditional Formats That Use Graphics

This section describes the three conditional formatting options that display graphics: data bars, color scales, and icons sets. These types of conditional formatting can be useful for visualizing the values in a range.

Using data bars

The *data bars conditional format* displays horizontal bars directly in the cell. The length of the bar is based on the value of the cell, relative to the other values in the range.

New Feature

The data bars feature is improved significantly in Excel 2010. Data bars now display proportionally (just like a bar chart), and there is now an option to display data bars in a solid color (no more forced color gradient) and with a border. In addition, negative values can now display in a different color, and to the left of an axis. ■

A simple data bar

Figure 20.4 shows an example of data bars. It's a list of tracks on Bob Dylan albums, with the length of each track in column D. I applied data bar conditional formatting to the values in column D. You can tell at a glance which tracks are longer.

On the CD

The examples in the section are available on the companion CD-ROM. The workbook is named `data bars examples.xlsx`.

FIGURE 20.4

The length of the data bars is proportional to the track length in the cell in column D.

	A	B	C	D
11	Bob Dylan	Another Side of Bob Dylan	Spanish Harlem Incident	0:02:24
12	Bob Dylan	Another Side of Bob Dylan	To Ramona	0:03:52
13	Bob Dylan	Blonde On Blonde	4th Time Around	0:04:36
14	Bob Dylan	Blonde On Blonde	Absolutely Sweet Marie	0:04:57
15	Bob Dylan	Blonde On Blonde	I Want You	0:03:08
16	Bob Dylan	Blonde On Blonde	Just Like A Woman	0:04:54
17	Bob Dylan	Blonde On Blonde	Leopard-Skin Pill-Box Hat	0:04:00
18	Bob Dylan	Blonde On Blonde	Most Likely You Go Your Way (And I'll Go Mine)	0:03:29
19	Bob Dylan	Blonde On Blonde	Obviously 5 Believers	0:03:36
20	Bob Dylan	Blonde On Blonde	One Of Us Must Know (Sooner Or Later)	0:04:56
21	Bob Dylan	Blonde On Blonde	Pledging My Time	0:03:49
22	Bob Dylan	Blonde On Blonde	Rainy Day Women #12 And #35	0:04:38
23	Bob Dylan	Blonde On Blonde	Sad Eyed Lady Of the Lowlands	0:11:20
24	Bob Dylan	Blonde On Blonde	Stuck Inside Of Mobile With the Memphis Blues Again	0:07:05
25	Bob Dylan	Blonde On Blonde	Temporary Like Achilles	0:05:06
26	Bob Dylan	Blonde On Blonde	Visions Of Johanna	0:07:34
27	Bob Dylan	Blood On The Tracks	Buckets Of Rain	0:03:22
28	Bob Dylan	Blood On The Tracks	Idiot Wind	0:07:49
29	Bob Dylan	Blood On The Tracks	If You See Her, Say Hello	0:04:49
30	Bob Dylan	Blood On The Tracks	Lily Rosemary And The Jack Of Hearts	0:08:53
31	Bob Dylan	Blood On The Tracks	Meet Me In The Morning	0:04:22
32	Bob Dylan	Blood On The Tracks	Shelter From The Storm	0:05:02
33	Bob Dylan	Blood On The Tracks	Simple Twist Of Fate	0:04:19
34	Bob Dylan	Blood On The Tracks	Tangled Up In Blue	0:05:42
35	Bob Dylan	Blood On The Tracks	You're A Big Girl Now	0:04:36
36	Bob Dylan	Blood On The Tracks	You're Gonna Make Me Lonesome When You Go	0:02:55
37	Bob Dylan	Bringing it All Back Home	Bob Dylan's 115th Dream	0:06:33
38	Bob Dylan	Bringing it All Back Home	Gates of Eden	0:05:44

Tip

When you adjust the column width, the bar lengths adjust accordingly. The differences among the bar lengths are more prominent when the column is wider. ■

Excel provides quick access to 12 data bar styles via Home ⇨ Styles ⇨ Conditional Formatting ⇨ Data Bars. For additional choices, click the More Rules option, which displays the New Formatting Rule dialog box. Use this dialog box to

- Show the bar only (hide the numbers).
- Specify Minimum and Maximum values for the scaling.
- Change the appearance of the bars.
- Specify how negative values and the axis is handled.
- Specify the direction of the bars.

Note
Oddly, the colors used for data bars are not theme colors. If you apply a new document theme, the data bar colors do not change. ■

Using data bars in lieu of a chart

Using the data bars conditional formatting can sometimes serve as a quick alternative to creating a chart. Figure 20.5 shows a three-column table of data (created by using Insert ➪ Tables ➪ Table), with data bars conditional formatting applied in the third column. The third column of the table contains references to the values in the second column. The conditional formatting in the third column uses the Show Bars Only option, so the values are not displayed.

FIGURE 20.5

This table uses data bars conditional formatting.

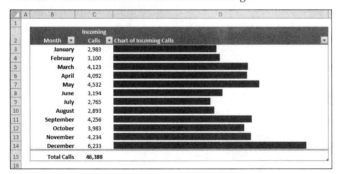

Figure 20.6 shows an actual bar chart created from the same data. The bar chart takes about the same amount of time to create and is a lot more flexible. But for a quick-and-dirty chart, data bars are a good option — especially when you need to create several such charts.

Using color scales

The *color scale conditional formatting option* varies the background color of a cell based on the cell's value, relative to other cells in the range.

FIGURE 20.6

A real Excel bar chart (not conditional formatting data bars).

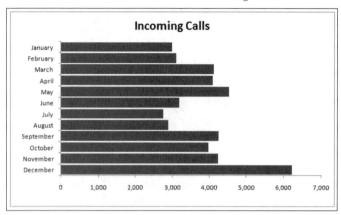

A color scale example

Figure 20.7 shows a range of cells that use color scale conditional formatting. It depicts the number of employees on each day of the year. This is a 3-color scale that uses red for the lowest value, yellow for the midpoint, and green for the highest value. Values in between are displayed using a color within the gradient.

FIGURE 20.7

A range that uses color scale conditional formatting.

On the CD

This workbook, named `color scale example.xlsx`, is available on the companion CD-ROM. ∎

Excel provides four 2-color scale presets and four 3-color scales presets, which you can apply to the selected range by choosing Home ⇨ Styles ⇨ Conditional Formatting ⇨ Color Scales.

To customize the colors and other options, choose Home ⇨ Styles ⇨ Conditional Formatting ⇨ Color Scales ⇨ More Rules. This command displays the New Formatting Rule dialog box, shown in Figure 20.8. Adjust the settings, and watch the Preview box to see the effects of your changes.

FIGURE 20.8

Use the New Formatting Rule dialog box to customize a color scale.

An extreme color scale example

It's important to understand that color scale conditional formatting uses a gradient. For example, if you format a range using a 2-color scale, you will get a lot more than two colors. You'll get colors with the gradient between the two specified colors.

Figure 20.9 shows an extreme example that uses color scale conditional formatting on a range of 10,000 cells (100 rows x 100 columns). The worksheet is zoomed down to 20% to display a very smooth three-color gradient. The range contains formulas like this one, in cell C5:

```
=SIN($A2)+COS(B$1)
```

Values in column A and row 1 range from 0 to 4.0, in increments of 0.04.

When viewed onscreen, the result is stunning; it loses a lot when converted to grayscale.

On the CD

This workbook, named extreme color scale.xlsx, is available on the companion CD-ROM. ∎

FIGURE 20.9

This worksheet, which uses color scale conditional formatting, displays an impressive color gradient.

Note

You can't hide the cell contents when using a color scale rule, so I formatted the cells using this custom number format (which effectively hides the cell content):

```
;;;
```

Using icon sets

Yet another conditional formatting option is to display an icon in the cell. The icon displayed depends on the value of the cell.

To assign an icon set to a range, select the cells and choose Home ➪ Styles ➪ Conditional Formatting ➪ Icon Sets. Excel provides 20 icon sets to choose from. The number of icons in the sets ranges from three to five. You cannot supply your own icons.

An icon set example

Figure 20.10 shows an example that uses an icon set. The symbols graphically depict the status of each project, based on the value in column C.

On the CD

All the icon set examples in this section are available on the companion CD-ROM. The workbook is named `icon set examples.xlsx.`

Using an icon set to indicate the status of projects.

By default, the symbols are assigned using percentiles. For a 3-symbol set, the items are grouped into three percentiles. For a 4-symbol set, they're grouped into four percentiles. And for a 5-symbol set, the items are grouped into five percentiles.

If you would like more control over how the icons are assigned, choose Home ➪ Styles ➪ Conditional Formatting ➪ Icon Sets ➪ More Rules to display the New Formatting Rule dialog box. To modify an existing rule, choose Home ➪ Styles ➪ Conditional Formatting ➪ Manage Rules. Then select the rule to modify and click the Edit Rule button.

Figure 20.11 shows how to modify the icon set rules such that only projects that are 100% completed get the check mark icons. Projects that are 0% completed get the X icon. All other projects get no icon.

Figure 20.12 shows project status list after making this change.

FIGURE 20.11

Changing the icon assignment rule.

FIGURE 20.12

Using a modified rule and eliminating an icon makes the table more readable.

Another icon set example

Figure 20.13 shows a table that contains two test scores for each student. The Change column contains a formula that calculates the difference between the two tests. The Trend column uses an icon set to display the trend graphically.

This example uses the icon set named 3 Arrows, and I customized the rule:

- **Up Arrow:** When value is >= 5

- **Level Arrow:** When value < 5 and > −5

- **Down Arrow:** When value is <= −5

In other words, a difference of no more than five points in either direction is considered an even trend. An improvement of at least five points is considered a positive trend, and a decline of five points or more is considered a negative trend.

Note

The Trend column contains a formula that references the Change column. I used the Show Icon Only option in the Trend column, which also centers the icon in the column. ■

FIGURE 20.13

The arrows depict the trend from Test 1 to Test 2.

	A	B	C	D	E
1					
2	Student	Test 1	Test 2	Change	Trend
3	Amy	59	65	6	⬆
4	Bob	82	78	-4	⇨
5	Calvind	98	92	-6	⬇
6	Doug	56	60	4	⇨
7	Ephraim	98	89	-9	⬇
8	Frank	67	75	8	⬆
9	Gretta	78	81	3	⇨
10	Harold	87	92	5	⬆
11	Inez	56	85	29	⬆
12	June	87	72	-15	⬇
13	Kenny	87	88	1	⇨
14	Lance	92	92	0	⇨
15	Marvin	82	73	-9	⬇
16	Noel	98	100	2	⇨
17	Opie	84	73	-11	⬇
18	Paul	94	93	-1	⇨
19	Quinton	68	92	24	⬆
20	Rasmus	91	90	-1	⇨
21	Sam	85	86	1	⇨
22	Ted	72	92	20	⬆
23	Ursie	80	82	2	⇨
24	Valerie	77	78	1	⇨
25	Wally	64	45	-19	⬇
26	Xerxes	59	63	4	⇨
27	Yolanda	89	99	10	⬆
28	Zippy	85	82	-3	⇨
29					

In some cases, using icon sets can cause your worksheet to look very cluttered. Displaying an icon for every cell in a range might result in visual overload.

Figure 20.14 shows the test results table after hiding the level arrow by choosing No Cell Icon in the Edit Formatting Rule dialog box.

FIGURE 20.14

Hiding one of the icons makes the table less cluttered.

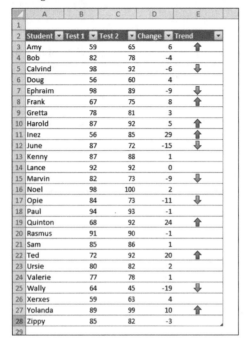

	Student	Test 1	Test 2	Change	Trend
3	Amy	59	65	6	⬆
4	Bob	82	78	-4	
5	Calvind	98	92	-6	⬇
6	Doug	56	60	4	
7	Ephraim	98	89	-9	⬇
8	Frank	67	75	8	⬆
9	Gretta	78	81	3	
10	Harold	87	92	5	⬆
11	Inez	56	85	29	⬆
12	June	87	72	-15	⬇
13	Kenny	87	88	1	
14	Lance	92	92	0	
15	Marvin	82	73	-9	⬇
16	Noel	98	100	2	
17	Opie	84	73	-11	⬇
18	Paul	94	93	-1	
19	Quinton	68	92	24	⬆
20	Rasmus	91	90	-1	
21	Sam	85	86	1	
22	Ted	72	92	20	⬆
23	Ursie	80	82	2	
24	Valerie	77	78	1	
25	Wally	64	45	-19	⬇
26	Xerxes	59	63	4	
27	Yolanda	89	99	10	⬆
28	Zippy	85	82	-3	

Creating Formula-Based Rules

Excel's conditional formatting feature is versatile, but sometimes it's just not quite versatile enough. Fortunately, you can extend its versatility by writing conditional formatting formulas.

The examples later in this section describe how to create conditional formatting formulas for the following:

- To identify text entries
- To identify dates that fall on a weekend
- To format cells that are in odd-numbered rows or columns (for dynamic alternate row or columns shading)
- To format groups of rows (for example, shade every two groups of rows)
- To display a sum only when all precedent cells contain values

Some of these formulas may be useful to you. If not, they may inspire you to create other conditional formatting formulas.

On the CD

The companion CD-ROM contains all the examples in this section. The file is named `conditional formatting formulas.xlsx.`

To specify conditional formatting based on a formula, select the cells and then choose Home ➪ Styles ➪ Conditional Formatting ➪ New Rule. This command displays the New Formatting Rule dialog box. Click the rule type Use a Formula to Determine Which Cells to Format, and you can specify the formula.

You can type the formula directly into the box, or you can enter a reference to a cell that contains a logical formula. As with normal Excel formulas, the formula you enter here must begin with an equal sign (=).

Note

The formula must be a logical formula that returns either TRUE or FALSE. If the formula evaluates to TRUE, the condition is satisfied, and the conditional formatting is applied. If the formula evaluates to FALSE, the conditional formatting is not applied. ■

Understanding relative and absolute references

If the formula that you enter into the Conditional Formatting dialog box contains a cell reference, that reference is considered a *relative reference,* based on the upper-left cell in the selected range.

For example, suppose that you want to set up a conditional formatting condition that applies shading to cells in range A1:B10 only if the cell contains text. None of Excel's conditional formatting options can do this task, so you need to create a formula that will return TRUE if the cell contains text and FALSE otherwise. Follow these steps:

1. **Select the range A1:B10 and ensure that cell A1 is the active cell.**
2. **Choose Home ➪ Styles ➪ Conditional Formatting ➪ New Rule to display the New Formatting Rule dialog box.**
3. **Click the Use a Formula to Determine Which Cells to Format rule type.**
4. **Enter the following formula in the Formula box:**
   `=ISTEXT(A1)`
5. **Click the Format button to display the Format Cells dialog box.**
6. **From the Fill tab, specify the cell shading that will be applied if the formula returns** TRUE.
7. **Click OK to return to the New Formatting Rule dialog box (see Figure 20.15).**
8. **In the New Formatting Rule dialog box, click the Preview button.** Make sure that the formula is working correctly and to see a preview of your selected formatting.
9. **If the preview looks correct, click OK to close the New Formatting Rule dialog box.**

Notice that the formula entered in Step 4 contains a relative reference to the upper-left cell in the selected range.

FIGURE 20.15

Creating a conditional formatting rule based on a formula.

Generally, when entering a conditional formatting formula for a range of cells, you'll use a reference to the active cell, which is typically the upper-left cell in the selected range. One exception is when you need to refer to a specific cell. For example, suppose that you select range A1:B10, and you want to apply formatting to all cells in the range that exceed the value in cell C1. Enter this conditional formatting formula:

    =A1>$C$1

In this case, the reference to cell C1 is an *absolute reference;* it will not be adjusted for the cells in the selected range. In other words, the conditional formatting formula for cell A2 looks like this:

    =A2>$C$1

The relative cell reference is adjusted, but the absolute cell reference is not.

Conditional formatting formula examples

Each of these examples uses a formula entered directly into the New Formatting Rule dialog box, after selecting the Use a Formula to Determine Which Cells to Format rule type. You decide the type of formatting that you apply conditionally.

Identifying weekend days

Excel provides a number of conditional formatting rules that deal with dates, but it doesn't let you identify dates that fall on a weekend. Use this formula to identify weekend dates:

    =OR(WEEKDAY(A1)=7,WEEKDAY(A1)=1)

This formula assumes that a range is selected and that cell A1 is the active cell.

Displaying alternate-row shading

The conditional formatting formula that follows was applied to the range A1:D18, as shown in Figure 20.16, to apply shading to alternate rows.

```
=MOD(ROW(),2)=0
```

Alternate row shading can make your spreadsheets easier to read. If you add or delete rows within the conditional formatting area, the shading is updated automatically.

This formula uses the ROW function (which returns the row number) and the MOD function (which returns the remainder of its first argument divided by its second argument). For cells in even-numbered rows, the MOD function returns 0, and cells in that row are formatted.

For alternate shading of columns, use the COLUMN function instead of the ROW function.

FIGURE 20.16

Using conditional formatting to apply formatting to alternate rows.

	A	B	C	D	E
1	430	470	843	319	
2	283	788	119	658	
3	821	426	265	269	
4	921	809	382	186	
5	282	287	289	712	
6	727	885	0	126	
7	395	83	836	351	
8	121	922	541	798	
9	885	426	109	234	
10	455	66	177	919	
11	562	794	743	145	
12	109	847	116	310	
13	748	65	740	259	
14	524	293	537	541	
15	475	71	831	370	
16	472	522	823	414	
17	467	608	963	278	
18	484	667	758	426	
19					

Creating checkerboard shading

The following formula is a variation on the example in the preceding section. It applies formatting to alternate rows and columns, creating a checkerboard effect.

```
=MOD(ROW(),2)=MOD(COLUMN(),2)
```

Shading groups of rows

Here's another rows shading variation. The following formula shades alternate groups of rows. It produces four rows of shaded rows, followed by four rows of unshaded rows, followed by four more shaded rows, and so on.

```
=MOD(INT((ROW()-1)/4)+1,2)
```

Figure 20.17 shows an example.

For different sized groups, change the 4 to some other value. For example, use this formula to shade alternate groups of two rows:

```
=MOD(INT((ROW()-1)/2)+1,2)
```

Conditional formatting produces these groups of alternate shaded rows.

	A	B	C	D	E
1	250	589	585	878	
2	660	865	956	473	
3	229	322	298	669	
4	200	69	282	248	
5	387	584	924	119	
6	304	604	445	486	
7	122	887	534	809	
8	797	846	482	148	
9	846	99	384	234	
10	339	499	736	228	
11	78	574	216	33	
12	481	177	127	566	
13	881	772	437	408	
14	697	459	342	786	
15	474	541	216	634	
16	71	719	764	96	
17	15	805	966	180	
18	415	76	568	752	
19	573	492	165	483	
20	355	795	811	667	
21	623	942	122	23	
22	589	195	966	588	
23					

Displaying a total only when all values are entered

Figure 20.18 shows a range with a formula that uses the SUM function in cell C6. Conditional formatting is used to hide the sum if any of the four cells above is blank. The conditional formatting formula for cell C6 (and cell C5, which contains a label) is

```
=COUNT($C$2:$C$5)=4
```

This formula returns TRUE only if C2:C5 contains no empty cells.

Figure 20.19 shows the worksheet when one of the values is missing.

The sum is displayed only when all four values have been entered.

A missing value causes the sum to be hidden.

Working with Conditional Formats

This section describes some additional information about conditional formatting that you may find useful.

Managing rules

The Conditional Formatting Rules Manager dialog box is useful for checking, editing, deleting, and adding conditional formats. First select any cell in the range that contains conditional formatting. Then choose Home ⇨ Styles ⇨ Conditional Formatting ⇨ Manage Rules.

You can specify as many rules as you like by clicking the New Rule button. As you can see in Figure 20.20, cells can even use data bars, color scales, and icon sets all at the same time — although I can't think of a good reason to do so.

FIGURE 20.20

This range uses data bars, color scales, and icon sets.

Copying cells that contain conditional formatting

Conditional formatting information is stored with a cell much like standard formatting information is stored with a cell. As a result, when you copy a cell that contains conditional formatting, you also copy the conditional formatting.

Tip

To copy only the formatting (including conditional formatting), use the Paste Special dialog box and select the Formats option. Or, use Home ➪ Clipboard ➪ Paste ➪ Formatting (R). ■

If you insert rows or columns within a range that contains conditional formatting, the new cells have the same conditional formatting.

Deleting conditional formatting

When you press Delete to delete the contents of a cell, you do not delete the conditional formatting for the cell (if any). To remove all conditional formats (as well as all other cell formatting), select the cell. Then choose Home ➪ Editing ➪ Clear ➪ Clear Formats. Or, choose Home ➪ Editing ➪ Clear ➪ Clear All to delete the cell contents and the conditional formatting.

To remove only conditional formatting (and leave the other formatting intact), use Home ➪ Styles ➪ Conditional Formatting ➪ Clear Rules.

Locating cells that contain conditional formatting

You can't tell, just by looking at a cell, whether it contains conditional formatting. You can, however, use the Go To dialog box to select such cells.

1. Choose Home ⇨ Editing ⇨ Find & Select ⇨ Go To Special.

2. In the Go To Special dialog box, select the Conditional Formats option.

3. To select all cells on the worksheet containing conditional formatting, select the All option; to select only the cells that contain the same conditional formatting as the active cell, select the Same option.

4. Click OK. Excel selects the cells for you.

Note

The Excel Find and Replace dialog box includes a feature that allows you to search your worksheet to locate cells that contain specific formatting. This feature does not locate cells that contain formatting resulting from conditional formatting. ∎

Creating Sparkline Graphics

O ne of the new features in Excel 2010 is Sparklines graphics. A *Sparkline* is a small chart displayed in a single cell. A Sparkline allows you to quickly spot time-based trends or variations in data. Because they are so compact, Sparklines are often used in a group.

Although Sparklines look like miniature charts (and can sometimes take the place of a chart), this feature is completely separate from the charting feature. For example, charts are placed on a worksheet's draw layer, and a single chart can display several series of data. A Sparkline is displayed inside a cell and displays only one series of data. See Chapters 18 and 19 for information about *real* charts.

This chapter introduces Sparklines, and presents examples that demonstrate how they can be used in your worksheets.

New Feature

Sparklines are new to Excel 2010. If you create a workbook that uses Sparklines, and that workbook is opened using a previous version of Excel, the Sparkline cells will be empty. ■

On the CD

All examples in this chapter are available on the companion CD-ROM. The filename is `sparkline examples.xlsx`.

IN THIS CHAPTER

An introduction to the new Sparkline graphics feature

How to add Sparklines to a worksheet

How to customize Sparklines

How make a Sparkline display only the most recent data

Sparkline Types

Excel 2010 supports three types of Sparklines. Figure 21.1 shows examples of the three types of Sparkline graphics, displayed in column H. Each Sparkline depicts the six data points to the left.

- **Line:** Similar to a line chart. As an option, the line can display with a marker for each data point. The first group in Figure 21.1 shows line Sparklines, with markers. A quick glance reveals that with the exception of Fund Number W-91, the funds have been losing value over the six-month period.

- **Column:** Similar to a column chart. The second group in Figure 21.1 shows the same data displayed with column Sparklines.

- **Win/Loss:** A "binary" type chart that displays each data point as a high block or a low block. The third group shows win/loss Sparklines. Notice that the data is different. Each cell displays the *change* from the previous month. In the Sparkline, each data point is depicted as a high block (win) or a low block (loss). In this example, a positive change from the previous month is a win, and a negative change from the previous month is a loss.

FIGURE 21.1

Three groups of Sparklines.

	A	B	C	D	E	F	G	H
1	Line Sparklines							
2								
3	Fund Number	Jan	Feb	Mar	Apr	May	Jun	Sparklines
4	A-13	103.98	98.92	88.12	86.34	75.58	71.2	
5	C-09	212.74	218.7	202.18	198.56	190.12	181.74	
6	K-88	75.74	73.68	69.86	60.34	64.92	59.46	
7	W-91	91.78	95.44	98.1	99.46	98.68	105.86	
8	M-03	324.48	309.14	313.1	287.82	276.24	260.9	
9								
10	Column Sparklines							
11								
12	Fund Number	Jan	Feb	Mar	Apr	May	Jun	Sparklines
13	A-13	103.98	98.92	88.12	86.34	75.58	71.2	
14	C-09	212.74	218.7	202.18	198.56	190.12	181.74	
15	K-88	75.74	73.68	69.86	60.34	64.92	59.46	
16	W-91	91.78	95.44	98.1	99.46	98.68	105.86	
17	M-03	324.48	309.14	313.1	287.82	276.24	260.9	
18								
19	Win/Loss Sparklines							
20								
21	Fund Number	Jan	Feb	Mar	Apr	May	Jun	Sparklines
22	A-13	#N/A	-5.06	-10.8	-1.78	-10.76	-4.38	
23	C-09	#N/A	5.96	-16.52	-3.62	-8.44	-8.38	
24	K-88	#N/A	-2.06	-3.82	-9.52	4.58	-5.46	
25	W-91	#N/A	3.66	2.66	1.36	-0.78	7.18	
26	M-03	#N/A	-15.34	3.96	-25.28	-11.58	-15.34	

Why Sparklines?

If the term *Sparkline* seems odd, don't blame Microsoft. Edward Tufte coined the term *sparkline*, and in his book, *Beautiful Evidence* (Graphics Press, 2006), he described it as

> Sparklines: Intense, simple, word-sized graphics

In the case of Excel, Sparklines are cell-sized graphics. As you see in this chapter, Sparklines aren't limited to lines.

Creating Sparklines

Figure 21.2 shows some data to be summarized with Sparklines. To create Sparkline graphics, follow these steps:

1. **Select the data that will be depicted. If you are creating multiple Sparklines, select all the data.** In this example, start by selecting B4:M12.

FIGURE 21.2

Data to be summarized with Sparklines.

2. **With the data selected, choose Insert ➪ Sparklines, and click one of the three Sparkline types: Line, Column, or Win/Loss.** Excel displays the Create Sparklines dialog box, as shown in Figure 21.3.

3. **Specify the location for the Sparklines.** Typically, you'll put the Sparklines next to the data, but that's not a requirement. Most of the time, you'll use an empty range to hold the Sparklines. However, Excel does not prevent your from inserting Sparklines into cells that already contain data. The Sparkline location that you specify must match the source data in terms of number of rows or number of columns. For this example, specify N4:N12 as the Location Range.

4. **Click OK.** Excel creates the Sparklines graphics of the type you specified.

The Sparklines are linked to the data, so if you change any of the values in the data range, the Sparkline graphic will update.

FIGURE 21.3

Use the Create Sparklines dialog box to specify the data range and the location for the Sparkline graphics.

Tip

Most of the time, you'll create Sparklines on the same sheet that contains the data. If you want to create Sparklines on a different sheet, start by activating the sheet where the Sparklines will be displayed. Then, in the Create Sparklines dialog box, specify the source data either by pointing or by typing the complete sheet reference (for example, Sheet1A1:C12). The Create Sparklines dialog box lets you specify a different sheet for the Data Range, but not for the Location Range. ■

Understanding Sparkline Groups

Most of the time, you'll probably create a group of Sparklines — one for each row or column of data. A worksheet can hold any number of Sparkline groups. Excel remembers each group, and you can work with the group as a single unit. For example, you can select one Sparkline in a group, and then modify the formatting of all Sparklines in the group. When you select one Sparkline cell, Excel displays an outline of all the other Sparklines in the group.

You can, however, perform some operations on an individual Sparkline in a group:

- **Change the Sparkline's data source.** Select the Sparkline cell and choose Sparkline Tools ➪ Design ➪ Sparkline ➪ Edit Data ➪ Edit Single Sparkline's Data. Excel displays a dialog box that lets you change the data source for the selected Sparkline.

- **Delete the Sparkline.** Select the Sparkline cell and choose Sparkline Tools ➪ Design ➪ Group ➪ Clear ➪ Clear Selected Sparklines.

Both operations are available from the shortcut menu that appears when you right-click a Sparkline cell.

You can also ungroup a set of Sparklines by selecting any Sparkline in the group and choosing Sparkline Tools ➪ Design ➪ Group ➪ Ungroup. After you ungroup a set of Sparklines, you can work with each Sparkline individually.

Figure 21.4 shows column Sparklines for the precipitation data.

Column Sparklines summarize the precipitation data for nine cities.

	Jan	Feb	Mar	Apr	May	Jun	Jul	Aug	Sep	Oct	Nov	Dec	
Average Monthly Precipitation (Inches)													
ASHEVILLE, NC	4.06	3.83	4.59	3.5	4.41	4.38	3.87	4.3	3.72	3.17	3.82	3.39	
BAKERSFIELD, CA	1.18	1.21	1.41	0.45	0.24	0.12	0	0.08	0.15	0.3	0.59	0.76	
BATON ROUGE, LA	6.19	5.1	5.07	5.56	5.34	5.33	5.96	5.86	4.84	3.81	4.76	5.26	
BILLINGS, MT	0.81	0.57	1.12	1.74	2.48	1.89	1.28	0.85	1.34	1.26	0.75	0.67	
DAYTONA BEACH, FL	3.13	2.74	3.84	2.54	3.26	5.69	5.17	6.09	6.61	4.48	3.03	2.71	
EUGENE, OR	7.65	6.35	5.8	3.66	2.66	1.53	0.64	0.99	1.54	3.35	8.44	8.29	
HONOLULU,HI	2.73	2.35	1.89	1.11	0.78	0.43	0.5	0.46	0.74	2.18	2.26	2.85	
ST. LOUIS, MO	2.14	2.28	3.6	3.69	4.11	3.76	3.9	2.98	2.96	2.76	3.71	2.86	
TUCSON, AZ	0.99	0.88	0.81	0.28	0.24	0.24	2.07	2.3	1.45	1.21	0.67	1.03	

Customizing Sparklines

When you activate a cell that contains a Sparkline, Excel displays an outline around all the Sparklines in its group. You can then use the commands on the Sparkline Tools ⇨ Design tab to customize the group of Sparklines.

Sizing Sparkline cells

When you change the width or height of a cell that contains a Sparkline, the Sparkline adjusts accordingly. In addition, you can insert a Sparkline into merged cells.

Figure 21.5 shows the same Sparkline, displayed at four sizes resulting from column width, row height, and merged cells.

A Sparkline at various sizes.

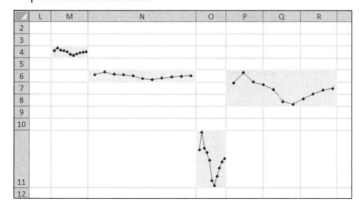

Handling hidden or missing data

By default, if you hide rows or columns that are used in a Sparkline graphic, the hidden data does not appear in the Sparkline. Also, missing data is displayed as a gap in the graphic.

To change these settings, choose Sparkline Tools ➪ Design ➪ Sparkline ➪ Edit Data ➪ Hidden and Empty Cells. In the Hidden and Empty Cell Settings dialog box that appears (see Figure 21.6), specify how to handle hidden data and empty cells.

The Hidden and Empty Cell Settings dialog box.

Changing the Sparkline type

As I mentioned earlier, Excel supports three Sparkline types: Line, Column, and Win/Loss. After you create a Sparkline or group of Sparklines, you can easily change the type by selecting the Sparkline and clicking one of the three icons in the Sparkline Tools ➪ Design ➪ Type group. If the selected Sparkline is part of a group, all Sparklines in the group are changed to the new type.

Tip

If you've customized the appearance, Excel remembers your customization settings for each type if you switch among Sparkline types. ■

Changing Sparkline colors and line width

After you've created a Sparkline, changing the color is easy. Use the controls in the Sparkline Tools ➪ Design ➪ Style group.

Note

Colors used in Sparkline graphics are tied to the document theme. Thus, if you change the theme (by choosing Page Layout ➪ Themes ➪ Themes), the Sparkline colors will change to the new theme colors. See Chapter 6 for more information about document themes. ■

For Line Sparklines, you can also specify the line width. Choose Sparkline Tools ➪ Design ➪ Style ➪ Sparkline Color ➪ Weight.

Highlighting certain data points

Use the commands in the Sparkline Tools ➪ Design ➪ Show group to customize the Sparklines to highlight certain aspects of the data. The options are

- **High Point:** Apply a different color to the highest data point in the Sparkline.
- **Low Point:** Apply a different color to the lowest data point in the Sparkline.
- **Negative Points:** Apply a different color to negative values in the Sparkline.
- **First Point:** Apply a different color to the first data point in the Sparkline.
- **Last Point:** Apply a different color to the last data point in the Sparkline.
- **Markers:** Show data markers in the Sparkline. This option is available only for Line Sparklines.

You control the color of the highlighting by using the Marker Color control in the Sparkline Tools ➪ Design ➪ Style group. Unfortunately, you cannot change the size of the markers in Line Sparklines.

Figure 21.7 shows some Line Sparklines with various types of highlighting applied.

FIGURE 21.7

Highlighting options for Line Sparklines.

	A	B	C	D	E	F	G	H	I	J	K
1											
2											
3		12	9	-6	-12	2	8	16	14		Default
4		12	9	-6	-12	2	8	16	14		Markers
5		12	9	-6	-12	2	8	16	14		High Point, Low Point
6		12	9	-6	-12	2	8	16	14		First Point, Last Point
7		12	9	-6	-12	2	8	16	14		Negative Points
8											

Adjusting Sparkline axis scaling

When you create one or more Sparklines, they all use (by default) automatic axis scaling. In other words, the minimum and maximum vertical axis values are determined automatically for each Sparkline in the group, based on the numeric range of the data used by the Sparkline.

The Sparkline Tools ➪ Design ➪ Group ➪ Axis command lets you override this automatic behavior and control the minimum and maximum value for each Sparkline, or for a group of Sparklines. For even more control, you can use the Custom Value option and specify the minimum and maximum for the Sparkline group.

Figure 21.8 shows two groups of Sparklines. The group at the top uses the default axis settings (Automatic for Each Sparkline). Each Sparkline shows the six-month trend for the product, but there is no indication of the magnitude of the values.

The bottom group of Sparklines shows the effect of using the same axis minimum and maximum values for all Sparklines in a group.

For the Sparkline group at the bottom (which uses the same data), I changed the vertical axis minimum and maximum to use the Same for All Sparklines setting. With these settings in effect, the magnitude of the values *across* the products is apparent — but the trend across the months within a product is not apparent.

The axis scaling option you choose depends upon what aspect of the data you want to emphasize.

Faking a reference line

One useful feature that's missing in the Excel 2010 implementation of Sparklines is a reference line. For example, it might be useful to show performance relative to a goal. If the goal is displayed as a reference line in a Sparkline, the viewer can quickly see whether the performance for a period exceeded the goal.

You can, however, to transform the data and then use a Sparkline axis as a fake reference line. Figure 21.9 shows an example. Students have a monthly reading goal of 500 pages. The range of data shows the actual pages read, with Sparklines in column H. The Sparklines show the six-month page data, but it's impossible to tell who exceeded the goal, and when they did it.

Figure 21.10 shows another approach: Transforming the data such that meeting the goal is expressed as a 1, and failing to meet the goal is expressed as a −1. I used the following formula (in cell B18) to transform the original data:

```
=IF(B6>$C$2,1,-1)
```

FIGURE 21.9

Sparklines display the number of pages read per month.

	A	B	C	D	E	F	G	H
1	**Pages Read**							
2	Monthly Goal:		500					
3								
4					Pages Read			
5		Jan	Feb	Mar	Apr	May	Jun	
6	Ann	450	412	632	663	702	512	
7	Bob	309	215	194	189	678	256	
8	Chuck	608	783	765	832	483	763	
9	Dave	409	415	522	598	421	433	
10	Ellen	790	893	577	802	874	763	
11	Frank	211	59	0	0	185	230	
12	Giselle	785	764	701	784	214	185	
13	Henry	350	367	560	583	784	663	

FIGURE 21.10

Using Win/Loss Sparklines to display goal achievement.

	A	B	C	D	E	F	G	H
15								
16			Pages Read (Did or Did Not Meet Goal)					
17		Jan	Feb	Mar	Apr	May	Jun	
18	Ann	-1	-1	1	1	1	1	
19	Bob	-1	-1	-1	-1	1	-1	
20	Chuck	1	1	1	1	-1	1	
21	Dave	-1	-1	1	1	-1	-1	
22	Ellen	1	1	1	1	1	1	
23	Frank	-1	-1	-1	-1	-1	-1	
24	Giselle	1	1	1	1	-1	-1	
25	Henry	-1	-1	1	1	1	1	
26								

I copied this formula to the other cells in B18:G25 range.

Using the transformed data, I created Win/Loss Sparklines to visualize the results. This approach is better than the original, but it doesn't convey any magnitude differences. For example, you cannot tell whether the student missed the goal by 1 page or by 500 pages.

Figure 21.11 shows a better approach. Here, I transformed the original data by subtracting the goal from the pages read. The formula in cell B31 is

```
=B6-$C$2
```

I copied this formula to the other cells in the B31:G38 range, and created a group of Line Sparklines, with the axis turned on. I also enabled the Negative Points option so that negative values (failure to meet the goal) clearly stand out.

The axis in the Sparklines represents the goal.

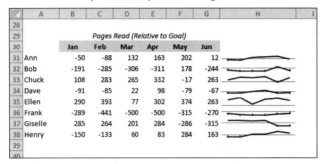

	Jan	Feb	Mar	Apr	May	Jun	
		Pages Read (Relative to Goal)					
Ann	-50	-88	132	163	202	12	
Bob	-191	-285	-306	-311	178	-244	
Chuck	108	283	265	332	-17	263	
Dave	-91	-85	22	98	-79	-67	
Ellen	290	393	77	302	374	263	
Frank	-289	-441	-500	-500	-315	-270	
Giselle	285	264	201	284	-286	-315	
Henry	-150	-133	60	83	284	163	

Specifying a Date Axis

Normally, data displayed in a Sparkline is assumed to be at equal intervals. For example, a Sparkline might display a daily account balance, sales by month, or profits by year. But what if the data aren't at equal intervals?

Figure 21.12 shows data, by date, along with a Sparklines graphic created from Column B. Notice that some dates are missing, but the Sparkline shows the columns as if the values were spaced at equal intervals.

The Sparkline displays the values as if they are at equal time intervals.

	Date	Amount
1	Date	Amount
2	1/1/2010	154
3	1/2/2010	201
4	1/3/2010	245
5	1/4/2010	176
6	1/11/2010	267
7	1/12/2010	289
8	1/13/2010	331
9	1/14/2010	365
10	1/18/2010	298
11	1/19/2010	424

To better depict the data, the solution is to specify a date axis. Select the Sparkline and choose Sparkline Tools ➪ Design ➪ Group ➪ Axis ➪ Date Axis Type. Excel displays a dialog box, asking for the range that contains the dates. In this example, specify range A2:A11. Click OK, and the Sparkline displays gaps for the missing dates (see Figure 21.13).

FIGURE 21.13

After specifying a date axis, the Sparkline shows the values accurately.

Auto-Updating Sparklines

If a Sparkline uses data in a normal range of cells, adding new data to the beginning or end of the range does *not* force the Sparkline to use the new data. You need to use the Edit Sparklines dialog box to update the data range (choose Sparkline Tools ➪ Design ➪ Sparkline ➪ Edit Data). But, if the Sparkline data is in a column within a table (created by using Insert ➪ Tables ➪ Table), then the Sparkline will use new data that's added to the end of the table.

Figure 21.14 shows an example. The Sparkline was created using the data in the Rate column of the table. When you add the new rate for September, the Sparkline will automatically update its Data Range.

FIGURE 21.14

Creating a Sparkline from data in a table.

Displaying a Sparkline for a Dynamic Range

The example in this section describes how to create a Sparkline that display only the most recent data points in a range. Figure 21.15 shows a worksheet that tracks daily sales. The Sparkline, in cell F4, displays only the seven most recent data points in column B.

Using a dynamic range name to display only the last seven data points in a Sparkline.

Need More about Sparklines?

This chapter describes pretty much everything there is to know about Excel 2010 Sparklines. You may be left asking, *Is that all there is?* Unfortunately, it is.

The Sparklines feature in Excel 2010 certainly leaves much to be desired. For example, you're limited to three types (Line, Column, and Win/Loss). It would be useful to have access to other Sparkline types, such as a column chart with no gaps, an area chart, and a stacked bar chart. Although Excel provides some basic formatting options, many users would prefer to have more control over the appearance of their Sparklines.

If you like the idea of Sparklines — and you're disappointed by the implementation in Excel 2010 — check out some add-ins that provide Sparklines in Excel. These products provide many additional Sparkline types, and most provide many additional customization options. Search the Web for *sparklines excel*, and you'll find several add-ins to choose from.

I started by creating a dynamic range name. Here's how:

1. **Choose Formulas ⇨ Defined Names ⇨ Define Name, specify Last7 as the Name, and enter the following formula in the Refers To field:**

   `=OFFSET($B$2,COUNTA($B:$B)-7-1,0,7,1)`

   This formula calculates a range by using the OFFSET function. The first argument is the first cell in the range (B2). The second argument is the number of cells in the column (minus the number to be returned and minus 1 to accommodate the label in B1).

   This name always refers to the last seven non-empty cells in column B. To display a different number of data points, change both instances of 7 to a different value.

2. **Chose Insert ⇨ Sparklines ⇨ Line.**

3. **In the Data Range field, type** Last7 **(the dynamic range name). Specify cell E4 as the Location Range**. The Sparkline shows the data in range B11:B17.

4. **Add new data to column B.** The Sparkline adjusts to display only the last seven data points.

Enhancing Your Work with Pictures and Drawings

W hen it comes to visual presentation, Excel has a lot more up its sleeve than charts. As you may know, you can insert a wide variety of graphics into your worksheet to add pizzazz to an otherwise boring report.

This chapter describes the non–chart-related graphic tools available in Excel. These tools consist of Shapes, SmartArt, WordArt, and imported or pasted images. In addition to enhancing your worksheets, you'll find that working with these objects can be a nice diversion. When you need a break from crunching numbers, you might enjoy creating an artistic masterpiece using Excel's graphic tools.

On the CD
Most of the examples in this chapter are available on the companion CD-ROM. ■

Using Shapes

Microsoft Office, including Excel, provides access to a variety of customizable graphic images known as *Shapes*. You might want to insert shapes to create diagrams, store text, or just add some visual appeal to a worksheet.

IN THIS CHAPTER

Inserting and customizing Shapes

An overview of SmartArt and WordArt

Working with other types of graphics

Inserting a Shape

You can add a Shape to a worksheet's draw layer by choosing Insert ➪ Illustrations ➪ Shapes, which opens the Shapes gallery, shown in Figure 22.1. Shapes are organized into categories, and the category at the top displays the Shapes that you've used recently. To insert a Shape on a worksheet, you can do one of the following:

- **Click the Shape in the Shapes gallery and then click in the worksheet.** A default-sized shape is added to your worksheet.

- **Click the Shape and then drag in the worksheet** to create a larger or smaller Shape, or a Shape with different proportions than the default

When you release the mouse button, the object is selected, and its name appears in the Name field (as shown in Figure 22.2).

FIGURE 22.1

The Shapes gallery.

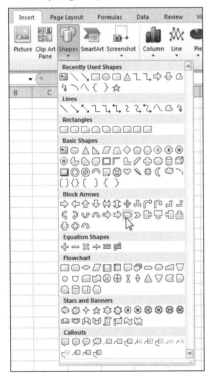

FIGURE 22.2

This Shape was drawn on the worksheet. Its name (Quad Arrow 1) appears in the Name field.

Tip

You can also insert a Shape into a chart. Just select the chart before you choose the Shape from the gallery and then click inside the chart to insert the Shape. When a chart is selected, the Chart Tools contextual tab also displays an icon to access the Shapes gallery: Chart Tools ⇨ Layout ⇨ Insert ⇨ Shapes. ■

A few Shapes require a slightly different approach. For example, when adding a FreeForm Shape (from the Lines category), you can click repeatedly to create lines. Or click and drag to create a nonlinear shape. Double-click to finish drawing and create the Shape. The Curve and Scribble Shapes (in the Lines category) also require several clicks while drawing.

Here are a few tips to keep in mind when creating Shapes:

- Every Shape has a name. Some have generic names like *Shape 1* and *Shape 2,* but others are given more descriptive names (for example, *Rectangle 1*). To change the name of a Shape, select it, type a new name in the Name field, and press Enter.

- To select a specific shape, type its name in the Name field and press Enter.

- When you create a Shape by dragging, hold down the Shift key to maintain the object's default proportions.

- You can control how objects appear onscreen in the Advanced tab of the Excel Options dialog box (File ⇨ Excel). This setting appears in the Display Options for This Workbook section. Normally, the All option is selected under For Objects Show. You can hide all objects by choosing Nothing (Hide Objects). Hiding objects may speed things up if your worksheet contains complex objects that take a long time to redraw.

About the Drawing Layer

Every worksheet and chart sheet has a *drawing layer*. This invisible surface can hold Shapes, SmartArt, WordArt, graphic images, embedded charts, inserted objects, and so on.

You can move, resize, copy, and delete objects placed on the drawing layer, with no effect on any other elements in the worksheet. Objects on the drawing layer have properties that relate to how they're moved and sized when underlying cells are moved and sized. When you right-click a graphic object and choose Size and Properties from the shortcut menu that appears, you get a tabbed dialog box. Click the Properties tab to adjust how the object moves or resizes with its underlying cells. Your choices are as follows:

- **Move and Size with Cells:** If this option is selected, the object appears to be attached to the cells beneath it. For example, if you insert rows above the object, the object moves down. If you increase the column width, the object gets wider.

- **Move But Don't Size with Cells:** If this option is selected, the object moves whenever rows or columns are inserted, but it never changes its size when you change row heights or column widths.

- **Don't Move or Size with Cells:** This option makes the object completely independent of the underlying cells.

The preceding options control how an object is moved or sized with respect to the underlying cells.

Excel also lets you *attach* an object to a cell. To do so, open the Excel Options dialog box, click the Advanced tab, and select the Cut, Copy, and Sort Inserted Objects With Their Parent Cells check box. After you do so, graphic objects on the drawing layer are attached to the underlying cells. If you copy a range of cells that includes an object, the object is also copied. Note that this is a general option that affects all objects and, by default, this option is enabled.

Adding text to a Shape

Many Shape objects can display text. To add text to such a Shape, select the Shape and start typing the text.

To change the formatting for all text in a Shape, Ctrl-click the Shape object. You can then use the formatting commands on the Home tab of the Ribbon. To change the formatting of specific characters within the text, select only those characters, and use the Ribbon buttons. Or, right-click and use the Mini toolbar to format the text.

In addition, you can dramatically change the look of the text by using the tools in the Drawing Tools ➪ Format ➪ WordArt Styles group. You can read more about WordArt later in the chapter.

Formatting Shapes

When you select a Shape, the Drawing Tools ➪ Format contextual tab is available, with the following groups of commands:

- **Insert Shapes:** Insert new Shapes; change a Shape to a different Shape.
- **Shape Styles:** Change the overall style of a Shape; modify the Shape's fill, outline, or effects.
- **WordArt Styles:** Modify the appearance of the text within a Shape.
- **Arrange:** Adjust the "stack order" of Shapes, align Shapes, group multiple Shapes, and rotate Shapes.
- **Size:** Change the size of a Shape.

Additional commands are available from the Shape's shortcut menu (which you access by right-clicking the Shape). In addition, you can use your mouse to perform some operations directly: for example, resize or rotate a Shape.

Selecting and Hiding Objects

An easy way to select an object is to use the Selection and Visibility task pane. Just select any Shape and then choose Drawing Tools ⇨ Format ⇨ Arrange ⇨ Selection Pane. Or, choose Home ⇨ Editing ⇨ Find & Select ⇨ Selection Pane.

Like with all task panes, you can undock this pane from the side of the window and make it free-floating. The accompanying figure shows the Selection and Visibility task pane as a floating window.

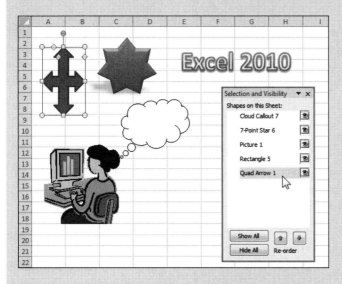

Each object on the active worksheet is listed in the Selection and Visibility pane. Just click the object's name to select it. To select multiple objects, press Ctrl while you click the names.

To hide an object, click the "eye" icon to the right of its name. Use the buttons at the bottom of the task pane to quickly hide (or show) all items.

Figure 22.3 shows a worksheet with some Shapes that use various types of formatting.

As an alternative to the Ribbon, you can use the Format Shape dialog box. Right-click the Shape and choose Format Shape from the shortcut menu. You'll get a stay-on-top tabbed dialog box that contains some additional formatting options that aren't on the Ribbon. Changes appear immediately, and you can keep the Format Shape dialog box open while you work.

I could probably write 20 pages about formatting Shapes, but it would be a waste of paper and certainly not a very efficient way of learning about Shape formatting. The best way, by far, to learn about formatting Shapes is to experiment. Create some shapes, click some commands, and see what happens. The commands are fairly intuitive, and you can always use Undo if a command doesn't do what you expected it to do.

FIGURE 22.3

A variety of Shapes.

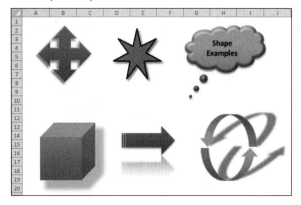

Grouping objects

Excel lets you combine (or *group*) two or more Shape objects into a single object. For example, if you create a design that uses four separate Shapes, you can combine them into a group. Then, you can manipulate this group as a single object (move it, resize it, apply formatting, and so on).

To group objects, press Ctrl while you click the objects to be included in the group. Then right-click and choose Group ➪ Group from the shortcut menu.

When objects are grouped, you can still work with an individual object in the group. Click once to select the group; then click again to select the object.

To ungroup a group, right-click the group object and choose Group ➪ Ungroup from the shortcut menu. This command breaks the object into its original components.

Aligning and spacing objects

When you have several objects on a worksheet, you may want to align and evenly space these objects. You can, of course, drag the objects with your mouse (which isn't very precise). Or, you can use the navigation arrow keys to move a selected object one pixel at a time. The fastest way to align and space objects is to let Excel do it for you.

To align multiple objects, start by selecting them (press Ctrl and click the objects). Then use the tools in the Drawing Tools ➪ Format ➪ Arrange ➪ Align drop-down list.

Note

Unfortunately, you can't specify which object is used as the basis for the alignment. When you're aligning objects to the left (or right), they're always aligned with the leftmost (or rightmost) object that's selected. When you're aligning objects to the top (or bottom), they're always aligned with the topmost (or bottommost) object. Aligning the centers (or middles) of objects will align them along an axis halfway between the left and right (or top and bottom) extremes of the selected shapes. ■

You can instruct Excel to distribute three or more objects so that they're equally spaced horizontally or vertically. Choose Drawing Tools ➪ Format ➪ Arrange ➪ Align and then select either Distribute Horizontally or Distribute Vertically.

Reshaping Shapes

Excel has many Shapes to choose from, but sometimes the Shape you need isn't in the gallery. In such a case, you may be able to modify one of the existing shapes using one of these techniques:

- **Rotate the Shape.** When you select a Shape, it displays a small green dot. Click and drag this dot to rotate the Shape.

- **Group multiple Shapes.** You may be able to create the Shape you need by combining two or more Shapes and then grouping them. (See "Grouping objects," earlier in this chapter.)

- **Reconfigure the Shape.** Many Shapes display one or more small yellow diamonds when the Shape is selected. You can click and drag this diamond to change the Shape's outline. The exact behavior varies with the Shape, so you should experiment and see what happens. Figure 22.4 shows six variations of an up-down arrow. This particular shape, when selected, has two yellow diamonds, which allows lots of variations.

- **Create a Freeform Shape.** Select the Freeform Shape (in the Lines category of the Shapes gallery) to create a custom Shape. Figure 22.5 shows a Freeform Shape, with eyes and a mouth added. The shadow effect completes the masterpiece.

- **Editing a Shape's Points.** Another way to create a unique Shape is to edit its points. Select the Shape and choose Drawing Tools ➪ Format ➪ Insert Shapes ➪ Edit Shape ➪ Edit Points. You can then drag the points to reconfigure the Shape. Figure 22.6 shows an example of a Shape that has been edited beyond all recognition.

FIGURE 22.4

Six variations on a Shape.

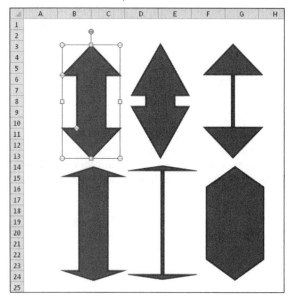

FIGURE 22.5

When none of the existing Shapes will do, create your own Freeform Shape.

Printing objects

By default, objects are printed along with the worksheet. To avoid printing a Shape, right-click the Shape and choose Size and Properties. In the Format Shape dialog box, click the Properties tab and then clear the Print Object check box.

Exporting Graphic Objects

If you create a graphic in Excel using Shapes, SmartArt, or WordArt, you may want to save the graphic as a separate file for use in another program. Unfortunately, Excel doesn't provide a direct way to export a graphic, but here's a trick you can use. Make sure that your graphic appears the way you want it and then follow these steps:

1. **Save your workbook.**

2. **Choose File ⇨ Save As to save your workbook as a Web Page.** In the Save As dialog box, select Web Page (*.htm; *.html) from the Save as Type drop-down list.

3. **Close the workbook.**

4. **Use Windows Explorer to locate the HTML file you saved in Step 2.** You'll notice that Excel also created a companion directory for the HTML file. If you save the file as `myart.htm`, the directory will be named `myart_files`.

5. **Open the directory, and you'll find `*.png` graphic files — one for each graphic object in your workbook.** The `*.png` files have a transparent background.

FIGURE 22.6

A Shape, before and after editing its points.

Using SmartArt

Excel's Shapes are certainly impressive, but the SmartArt feature is downright amazing. Using SmartArt, you can insert a wide variety of highly customizable diagrams into a worksheet, and you can change the overall look of the diagram with a few mouse clicks. This feature was introduced in Office 2007, and is probably more useful for PowerPoint users. But many Excel users will be able to make good use of SmartArt.

Inserting SmartArt

To insert SmartArt into a worksheet, choose Insert ⇨ SmartArt. Excel displays the dialog box shown in Figure 22.7. The diagrams are arranged in categories along the left. When you find one that looks appropriate, click it for a larger view in the panel on the right, which also provides some usage tips. Then click OK to insert the graphic.

Note

Don't be concerned about the number of elements contained in the SmartArt graphics. You can customize the SmartArt to display the number of elements you need. ■

FIGURE 22.7

Inserting a SmartArt graphic.

Figure 22.8 shows a SmartArt diagram after I customized it and added text. When you insert or select a SmartArt diagram, Excel displays its SmartArt Tools contextual tab, which provides many customization options.

FIGURE 22.8

This SmartArt shows a simple organizational chart.

Customizing SmartArt

Figure 22.9 shows a SmartArt graphic (named Vertical Equation, from the Process category) immediately after I inserted it into a worksheet. The Type Your Text Here window makes it very easy to enter text into the elements of the image. If you prefer, you can click one of the [Text] areas in the image and type the text directly.

FIGURE 22.9

This SmartArt needs to be customized.

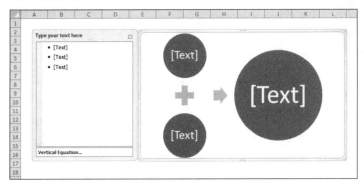

Figure 22.10 shows the SmartArt after I added some text.

This particular diagram depicts two items combining into a third item. Suppose that your boss sees this graphic and tells you that you need a third item: Advanced Technology. To add an element to the SmartArt graphic, just select an item and choose SmartArt Tools ➪ Design ➪ Create Graphic ➪ Add Shape. Or you can just select an item and press Enter. Figure 22.11 shows the modified SmartArt.

FIGURE 22.10

The SmartArt now has text.

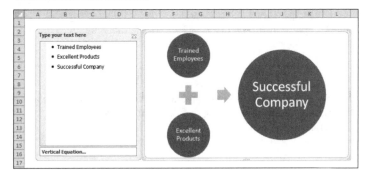

FIGURE 22.11

The SmartArt, after adding a new element.

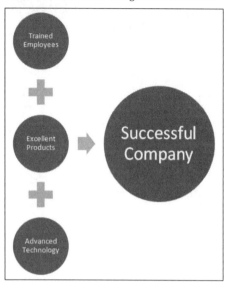

When working with SmartArt, keep in mind that you can move, resize, or format individually any element within the graphic. Select the element and then use the tools on the SmartArt Tools ➪ Format tab.

Changing the layout

You can easily change the layout of a SmartArt diagram. Select the object and then choose SmartArt Tools ➪ Design ➪ Layouts. Any text that you've entered remains intact. Figure 22.12 shows a few alternate layouts for the previous example.

Changing the style

After you decide on a layout, you may want to consider other styles or colors available in the SmartArt Tools ➪ Design ➪ SmartArt Styles group. Figure 22.13 shows the diagram after I chose a different style and changed the colors.

Tip

SmartArt styles available vary depending upon the document theme assigned to the workbook. To change a workbook's theme, choose Page Layout ➪ Themes ➪ Themes. Switching to a different theme can have a dramatic impact on the appearance of SmartArt diagrams. ■

FIGURE 22.12

A few different layouts for the SmartArt.

FIGURE 22.13

A few mouse clicks changed the style of this diagram.

Learning more about SmartArt

This section provided a basic introduction to SmartArt. The topic is complex enough to warrant an entire book, but I recommend simply experimenting with the commands.

Using WordArt

WordArt is available in previous versions of Excel, but this feature got a well-needed facelift in Excel 2007. You can use WordArt to create graphical effects in text. Figure 22.14 shows a few examples of WordArt.

To insert a WordArt graphic on a worksheet, choose Insert ➪ WordArt and then select a style from the gallery. Excel inserts an object with the placeholder text Your text here. Replace that text with your own, resize it, and apply other formatting if you like.

When you select a WordArt image, Excel displays its Drawing Tools contextual menu. Use the controls to vary the look of your WordArt.

Note

The controls in the Drawing Tools ➪ Format ➪ Shape Styles group operate on the Shape that contains the text — not the text. To apply text formatting, use the controls in the Drawing Tools ➪ Format ➪ WordArt Styles group. You can also use some of the standard formatting controls on the Home tab or the Mini toolbar. In addition, right-click the WordArt and choose Format Text Effects for more formatting options. ∎

FIGURE 22.14

WordArt examples.

Working with Other Graphic Types

Excel can import a wide variety of graphics into a worksheet. You have several choices:

- Use the Clip Art task pane to locate and insert an image.
- Import a graphic file directly.
- Copy and paste an image using the Windows Clipboard.

About graphics files

Graphics files come in two main categories: *bitmap* and *vector* (picture).

- **Bitmap images** are made up of discrete dots. They usually look pretty good at their original size, but often lose clarity if you increase the size. Examples of common bitmap file formats include BMP, PNG, JPEG, TIFF, and GIF.
- **Vector-based images**, on the other hand, are comprised of points and paths that are represented by mathematical equations, so they retain their crispness regardless of their size. Examples of common vector file formats include CGM, WMF, and EPS.

You can find hundreds of thousands of graphics files free for the taking on the Internet. Be aware, however, that some graphic files have copyright restrictions.

Caution
Using bitmap graphics in a worksheet can dramatically increase the size of your workbook, resulting in more memory usage and longer load and save times. ∎

Using the Clip Art task pane

Clip art refers to pre-made images (as opposed to custom image) that are used to illustrate just about any medium. The term originated back in the days when images were actually clipped from books and reused in new print projects. Nowadays, clip art is almost always in electronic form.

Want a Great Graphics File Viewer?

Many users are content to use the graphics file-viewing capabilities built into Windows. If you do a lot of work with graphics files, though, you owe it to yourself to get a *real* file-viewing program.

Many graphics viewers are available, but one of the best products in its class is IrfanView. It enables you to view just about any graphics file you can find, and it has features and options that will satisfy even hard-core graphics mavens. Best of all, it's free. To download a copy, visit www.irfanview.com.

Microsoft Office includes lots of clip art images, and you access them via the Clip Art task pane. This task pane provides an easy way to locate and insert images into a worksheet.

Note

The Clip Art task pane also allows you to insert sound and video files, and gives you direct access to the Microsoft Design Gallery Live on the Web. ■

Display the Clip Art task pane by choosing Insert ➪ Clip Art. You can search for clip art by using the controls at the top of the task pane. Figure 22.15 shows the task pane, along with the thumbnail images resulting from a search for "people". To insert an image into the active worksheet, just double-click the thumbnail. For additional options, right-click the thumbnail image.

FIGURE 22.15

Use the Clip Art task pane to search for clip art and other multimedia files.

If you can't find a suitable image, go online and browse through the extensive clip art at the Microsoft Clip Gallery Live Web site. Click the Find More at Office.com link (at the bottom of the task pane), and your Web browser will be activated, at which point you can view the images (or listen to the sounds) and add those you want to your Clip Organizer.

Inserting graphics files

If the graphic image that you want to insert is available in a file, you can easily import the file into your worksheet. Choose Insert ➪ Picture. Excel displays its Insert Picture dialog box, from which you can browse for the file.

When you insert a picture on a worksheet, you can modify the picture in a number of ways from the Picture Tools ⇨ Format contextual tab, which becomes available when you select a picture object. For example, you can adjust the color, contrast, and brightness. In addition, you can add borders, shadows, reflections, and so on — similar to the operations available for Shapes.

And don't overlook the Picture Tools ⇨ Format ⇨ Picture Styles group. These commands can transform your image in some very interesting ways. Figure 22.16 shows various styles for a picture.

FIGURE 22.16

Displaying a picture in a number of different styles.

New Feature

A new feature in Office 2010 is Artistic Effects. This command can apply a number of Photoshop-like effects to an image. To access this feature, right-click and image and choose Format Picture. Then, in the Format Picture dialog box, choose Artistic Effects. Each effect is somewhat customizable, so if you're not happy with the default effect, try adjusting some options.

You might be surprised by some of the image enhancements that are available. The best way to learn this feature is to dig in and experiment. Even if you have no need for image enhancement, you might find that it's a fun diversion when you need a break from working with numbers. ■

Inserting screenshots

A new feature in Excel 2010 allows you to insert an image of any program currently running on your computer. To use the new screenshot feature

1. **Make sure that the window you want to use displays the content that you want.**

2. **Choose Insert ⇨ Illustrations ⇨ Shapes.** You'll see a gallery that contains thumbnails of all windows open on your computer.

3. **Click the image you want.** Excel inserts it into your worksheet.

When the image is selected, you can use any of the normal picture tools.

Taking Pictures of Ranges

One of Excel's best-kept secrets is its ability to copy and paste "live" pictures of cells and charts. You can copy a cell or range and then paste a picture (as an object) of the cell or range on any worksheet or chart. If you change the contents of a cell that's in a picture, the picture changes. The accompanying image shows a picture of a range after applying some picture effects.

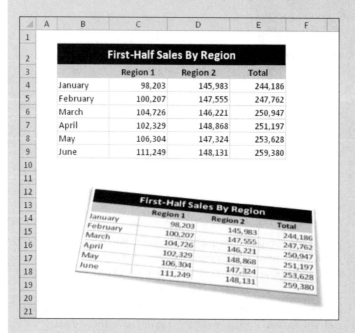

To "take a picture" of a range

1. **Select the range.**

2. **Press Ctrl+C to copy the range.**

3. **Activate another cell.**

4. **Choose Home ⇨ Clipboard ⇨ Paste ⇨ Linked Picture (I).**

The result is a live picture of the range you selected in Step 1.

If you use this feature frequently, you can save some time by adding the Excel Camera tool to your Quick access toolbar:

1. **Right-click the Quick Access toolbar and choose Customize Quick Access Toolbar from the shortcut menu that appears.**
2. **On the Customization tab of the Excel Options dialog box, select Command Not in the Ribbon from the drop-down list on the left.**
3. **Select Camera from the list and click Add.**
4. **Click OK to close the Excel Options dialog box.**

After you add the Camera tool to your Quick Access toolbar, you can select a range of cells and click the Camera tool to take a "picture" of the range. Then click in the worksheet, and Excel places a live picture of the selected range on the worksheet's draw layer. If you make changes to the original ranges, the changes are shown in the picture of the range.

Note

Keep in mind that the image is static. If the program from which it was taken updates its window, the image in your worksheet will not change. ■

In many cases, you don't want the entire window — just a portion of it. The solution is to crop the inserted screenshot by choosing Picture Tools ➪ Format ➪ Size ➪ Crop. This command adds cropping marks to the corners of the image. Just drag the cropping marks to crop the image.

Displaying a worksheet background image

If you want to use a graphics image for a worksheet's background (similar to wallpaper on the Windows desktop), choose Page Layout ➪ Page Setup ➪ Background and select a graphics file. The selected graphics file is tiled on the worksheet. Unfortunately, worksheet background images are for onscreen display only. These images do not appear when the worksheet is printed.

Using the Equation Editor

New Feature

The final topic in this chapter deals with the new Equation Editor. Use this feature to insert a nicely formatted mathematical equation as a graphic object. ■

Figure 22.17 shows an example of an equation in a worksheet. Keep in mind that these equations do not perform calculations: They are for display purposes only.

FIGURE 22.17

An equation created by the new Equation Editor.

$$x = \frac{-b \pm \sqrt{b^2 - 4ac}}{2a}$$

The best way to become familiar with the Equation Editor is to insert one of the pre-made equations. Choose Insert ➪ Symbols ➪ Equation, and choose one of equations from the gallery. The equation is inserted in your worksheet.

When you select an Equation object, you have access to two contextual tabs:

- **Drawing Tools:** Used to format the container object
- **Equation Tools:** Used to edit the equation

The Equation Tools ➪ Design tab contains three groups of controls:

- **Tools:** Used to insert a new equation, or control how the equation is displayed. Click the dialog box launcher in the bottom-right corner of the Tools group to display the Equation Options dialog box, where you can specify how the equation is copied and also define keyboard shortcuts (click Math AutoCorrect).
- **Symbols:** Contains common mathematical symbols and operators that you can use in your equations.
- **Structures:** Contains templates for various structures that are used in equations.

Describing how to use the Equation tools is more difficult than actually using them. Generally, you add a structure, and then edit the various parts by adding text or symbols. You can put structures inside of structures, and there is no limit to the complexity of the equations. It might be a bit tricky at first, but it doesn't take long before you understand how it works.

Figure 22.18 shows two equations that illustrate an old calculus joke.

FIGURE 22.18

Two Equation objects on a worksheet.

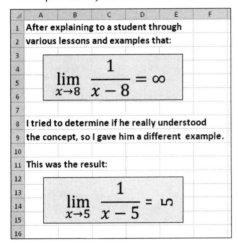

Part IV

Using Advanced Excel Features

A number of Excel features can probably be fairly called "advanced" features if for no better reason than the ways in which they expand the definitions of what a spreadsheet program can do. The chapters in this part cover some useful features that you may not have used in the past but may find very valuable.

IN THIS PART

Chapter 23
Customizing the Excel User Interface

Chapter 24
Using Custom Number Formats

Chapter 25
Using Data Validation

Chapter 26
Creating and Using Worksheet Outlines

Chapter 27
Linking and Consolidating Worksheets

Chapter 28
Excel and the Internet

Chapter 29
Sharing Data with Other Office Applications

Chapter 30
Using Excel in a Workgroup

Chapter 31
Protecting Your Work

Chapter 32
Making Your Worksheets Error-Free

Customizing the Excel User Interface

A software program's *user interface* consists of all the ways that the user interacts with the software. In Excel, the user interface consists of

- The Ribbon
- The Quick Access toolbar
- Right-click shortcut menus
- Keyboard shortcuts

This chapter describes how to make changes to two Excel user interface components: the Ribbon and the Quick Access toolbar. You might want to customize these elements to make Excel more suited to the way you use it.

Customizing the Quick Access Toolbar

The Quick Access toolbar is always visible, regardless of which Ribbon tab is selected. After you customize the Quick Access toolbar, your frequently used commands will always be one click away.

Note
The only situation in which the Quick Access toolbar is not visible is in Full Screen mode, which is enabled by choosing View ⇨ Workbook Views ⇨ Full Screen. To cancel Full Screen mode, right-click any cell and choose Close Full Screen, or just press Esc(ape). ■

About the Quick Access toolbar

By default, the Quick Access toolbar is located on the left side of Excel title bar, above the Ribbon (see Figure 23.1). It includes three tools:

- **Save:** Saves the active workbook
- **Undo:** Reverses the effect of the last action
- **Redo:** Reverses the effect of the last undo

If you prefer, you can move the Quick Access toolbar below the Ribbon. To do so, right-click the Quick Access toolbar and choose Show Quick Access Toolbar below the Ribbon. Moving the Quick Access toolbar below the Ribbon uses additional vertical space on your screen. In other words, you'll be able to see one less row of your worksheet if you move the Quick Access Toolbar from its default location. Unlike traditional toolbars, the Quick Access Toolbar cannot be made free-floating so you can move it to a convenient location. It always appears either above or below the Ribbon.

FIGURE 23.1

The default location for the Quick Access toolbar is on the left side of the Excel title bar.

Commands on the Quick Access toolbar always appear as a small icon, with no text. When you hover your mouse pointer over an icon, you see the name of the command and a brief description.

Customizing the Quick Access toolbar consists of adding new commands to it. If you find that you use some Excel commands frequently, you can make these commands easily accessible by adding them to your Quick Access toolbar. You can also rearrange the order of the icons.

As far as I can tell, there is no limit to the number of commands that you can add. The Quick Access toolbar always displays only a single line of icons. If the number of icons exceeds the Excel window width, it displays an additional icon at the end: More Controls. Click the More Controls icon, and the hidden Quick Access toolbar icons appear in a pop-up window.

Adding new commands to the Quick Access toolbar

You can add a new command to the Quick Access toolbar in three ways:

- Click the Quick Access toolbar drop-down control, which is located on the right side of the Quick Access toolbar (see Figure 23.2). The list contains a few commonly used commands. Select a command from the list, and Excel adds it to your Quick Access toolbar.

- Right-click any control on the Ribbon and choose Add to Quick Access Toolbar. The control is added to your Quick Access toolbar, after the last control.

- Use the Quick Access Toolbar tab in the Excel Options dialog box. A quick way to access this dialog box is to right-click any Ribbon control and choose Customize Quick Access Toolbar.

FIGURE 23.2

This drop-down list is one way to add a new command to the Quick Access toolbar.

The remainder of this section discusses the Quick Access Toolbar tab of the Excel Options dialog box, shown in Figure 23.3.

The left side of the dialog box displays a list of Excel commands, and the right side shows the commands currently on your Quick Access toolbar. Above the command list on the left is the Choose Commands From drop-down list from which you can filter the list. Select an item from the drop-down list, and the list displays only the commands for that item. In Figure 23.3, the list shows commands in the Popular Commands category.

FIGURE 23.3

Use the Quick Access Toolbar tab in the Excel Options dialog box to customize the Quick Access toolbar.

Some of the items in the drop-down list are

- **Popular Commands:** Displays commands that Excel users commonly use
- **Commands Not in the Ribbon:** Displays a list of commands that you cannot access from the Ribbon
- **All Commands:** Displays a complete list of Excel commands
- **Macros:** Displays a list of all available macros
- **File Tab:** Displays the commands available in the Backoffice menu
- **Home Tab:** Displays all commands available when the Home tab is active

In addition, the Choose Commands From drop-down list contains an item for every other tab. To add an item to your Quick Access toolbar, select it from the list on the left and then click Add. The command appears in the list on the right.

Tip

You can create a Quick Access toolbar configuration that's specific to a particular workbook. In other words, the commands on the Quick Access toolbar appear only when a particular workbook is active. Start by activating the workbook, and then display the Customize Quick Access Toolbar tab of the Excel Options dialog box. When you add a command to the Quick Access toolbar, use the drop-down list in the upper right to specify the workbook (only the active workbook is available as a choice). By default, customizations are For All Documents option. ∎

Sometimes, you need to do some guessing to find a particular command. For example, the command that displays the recent file list is named Open Recent File, not Recent Files.

Note

Some commands simply aren't available. For example, I would like the Quick Access toolbar to display the command to toggle page break display on a worksheet. As far as I can tell, the only way to issue that command is to display the Advanced tab of the Excel Options dialog box, and then scroll down until you find the Show Page Breaks check box. ■

When you select Macros from the Choose Commands From drop-down, Excel lists all available macros. You can attach a macro to a Quick Access Toolbar icon so that when you click the icon, the macro is executed. If you add a macro to your Quick Access toolbar, you can click the Modify button to change the text and choose a different icon for the macro.

When you finish making your Quick Access Toolbar customizations, click OK to close the Excel Options dialog box. The new icon will appear on the Quick Access toolbar.

Tip

The only times you ever need to use the Quick Access Toolbar tab in the Excel Options dialog box is when you want to add a command that's not on the Ribbon, add a command that executes a macro, or rearrange the order of the icons. In all other situations, it's much easier to locate the command in the Ribbon, right-click the command, and choose Add to Quick Access Toolbar. ■

Other Quick Access toolbar actions

Other Quick Access toolbar actions include the following:

- **Rearranging the Quick Access toolbar icons:** If you want to change the order of your Quick Access toolbar icons, you can do so from the Quick Access Toolbar tab of the Excel Options dialog box. Select the command and then use the Up and Down arrow buttons on the right to move the icon.

- **Removing Quick Access toolbar icons:** The easiest way to remove an icon from your Quick Access toolbar is to right-click the icon and choose Remove from Quick Access Toolbar. You can also use the Quick Access Toolbar tab of the Excel Options dialog box. Just select the command in the list on the right and click Remove.

- **Resetting the Quick Access toolbar:** If you want to return the Quick Access toolbar to its default state, display the Quick Access Toolbar tab of the Excel Options dialog box and click the Reset button. Then choose Rest Only Quick Access Toolbar. All your customizations disappear, and the Quick Access toolbar then displays its three default commands.

Caution

You can't undo resetting the Quick Access toolbar. Also, restoring defaults also resets any Ribbon customizations that you made. ■

Sharing User Interface Customizations

In the Excel Options dialog box, the Quick Access Toolbar tab and the Customize Ribbon tab both have an Import/Export button. You can use this button to save and open files that contain user interface customizations. For example, you might create a new Ribbon tab and want to share it with your office mates.

Click the Import/Export button, and you get two options:

- **Import Customization File:** You are prompted to locate the file. Before you load a file, you are asked whether you want to replace all existing Ribbon and Quick Access toolbar customizations.

- **Export All Customization:** You are prompted to provide a filename and location for the file.

The information is stored in a file that has a `*.exportedUI` extension. Unfortunately, importing and exporting is not implemented very well. Excel does not allow you to save or load only the Quick Access toolbar customization or only the Ribbon customizations. Both types of customizations are exported and imported. Therefore, you cannot share your Quick Access toolbar customization without also sharing your Ribbon customizations.

Customizing the Ribbon

The Ribbon is Excel's primary user interface. It consists of tabs along the top. When you click a tab, it displays a set of commands, and the commands are arranged in groups.

New Feature

The Ribbon was introduced in Excel 2007, but it could not be customized. Excel 2010, however, makes it fairly easy to modify the Ribbon in a number of ways. ■

Why customize the Ribbon?

Most users will have no need to customize the Ribbon. If you find that you tend to use the same command over and over, though — and you are constantly clicking tabs to access these commands — then you might benefit for customizing the Ribbon in such a way that the commands you need are on the same tab.

What can be customized

You can customize the Ribbon in these ways:

- Tabs
  - Add a new custom tab.
  - Delete custom tabs.

- Add a new group to tab.
- Change the order of the tabs.
- Change the name of a tab.
- Hide built-in tabs.

- **Groups**
  - Add new custom groups.
  - Add commands to a custom group.
  - Remove commands from custom groups.
  - Remove groups from a tab.
  - Move a group to a different tab.
  - Change the order of the groups within a tab.
  - Change the name of a group.

Note

To restore all or part of the Ribbon to its default state, use the Reset button on the Customize Ribbon tab of the Excel Options dialog box. Click this button to display two options: Reset Only Selected Ribbon Tab, and Rest All Customizations. If you choose the latter, you will also lose any Quick Access toolbar customizations that you made. ∎

That's a fairly comprehensive list of customization options, but there are some actions that you *cannot* do:

- Remove built-in tabs — but you *can* hide them.
- Remove commands from built-in groups.
- Change the order of commands in a built-in group.

Note

Unfortunately, you cannot customize the Ribbon (or Quick Access toolbar) by using VBA macros. However, developers can write RibbonX code and store it in workbook files. When the file is open, the Ribbon is modified to display new commands. Writing RibbonX is relatively complicated, and beyond the scope of this book. ∎

How to customize the Ribbon

Customizing the Ribbon is done via the Customize Ribbon panel of the Excel Options dialog box (see Figure 23.4). The quickest way to display this dialog box is to right-click anywhere on the Ribbon, and choose Customize The Ribbon.

FIGURE 23.4

The Customize Ribbon tab of the Excel Options dialog box.

Customizing the Ribbon is very similar to customizing the Quick Access toolbar, which I describe earlier in this chapter. The only difference is that you need to decide where to put the command within the Ribbon. The general procedure is

1. **Use the Choose Command From drop-down list on the left to display various groups of commands.**

2. **Locate the command in the list box on the left, and select it.**

3. **Use the Customize the Ribbon drop-down list on the right to choose a group of tabs.** *Main Tabs* refer to the tabs that are always visible; *Tool Tabs* refer to the contextual tabs that appear when a particular object is selected.

4. **In the list box on the right, select the tab and the group where you would like to put the command.** You'll need to click the plus-sign control to expand the tab name so that it displays its group names.

5. **Click the Add button to add the selected command from the left to the selected group on the right.**

Use the New Tab button to create a new tab, and the New Group button to create a new group within a tab. New tabs and groups are given generic names, so you'll probably want to give them more meaningful names. Use the Rename button to rename the selected tab or group. You can also rename built-in tabs and groups.

To rearrange the order of tabs, groups, or commands, select the item and use the Move Up and Move Down buttons on the right. Note that you can move a group into a different tab.

Note

Although you cannot remove a built-in tab, you can hide the tab by clearing the check box next to its name. ■

Figure 23.5 shows a part of a customized Ribbon. In this case, I added two groups to the View tab (to the right of the Zoom group): Extra Commands (with four new commands), and Text to Speech (with two new commands).

FIGURE 23.5

The View tab, with two new groups added.

Using Custom Number Formats

IN THIS CHAPTER

An overview of custom number formatting

How to create a custom number format

A list of all custom number format codes

Examples of custom number formats

When you enter a number into a cell, you can display that number in a variety of different formats. Excel has quite a few built-in number formats, but you may find that none of them suit your needs.

This chapter describes how to create custom number formats and provides many examples that you can use as-is, or adapt to your needs.

About Number Formatting

By default, all cells use the General number format. This format is basically "what you type is what you get." But if the cell isn't wide enough to show the entire number, the General format rounds numbers with decimals and uses scientific notation for large numbers. In many cases, the General number format works just fine, but most people prefer to specify a different number format for consistency.

The key thing to remember about number formatting is that it affects only how a value is *displayed*. The actual number remains intact, and any formulas that use a formatted number use the actual number.

Note
An exception to this rule occurs if you specify the Set Precision as Displayed option on the Advanced tab in the Excel Options dialog box. If that option is in effect, formulas use the values that are actually displayed in the cells. In general, using this option is not a good idea because it changes the underlying values in your worksheet. ■

One more thing to keep in mind: If you use the Find and Replace dialog box (Home ➪ Editing ➪ Find & Select ➪ Find), characters that are displayed as a result of number formatting (for example, a currency symbol) are not searchable by default. To be able to locate information based on formatting, use the Search In Value option in the Find and Replace dialog box.

Automatic number formatting

Excel is smart enough to perform some formatting for you automatically. For example, if you enter **12.3%** into a cell, Excel assumes that you want to use a percentage format and applies it automatically. If you use commas to separate thousands (such as 123,456), Excel applies comma formatting for you. And if you precede your value with a currency symbol, Excel formats the cell for currency.

Note
You have an option when it comes to entering values into cells formatted as percentages. Access the Excel Options and click the Advanced tab. If the Enable Automatic Percent Entry check box is selected (the default setting), you can simply enter a normal value into a cell that has been formatted to display as a percent (for example, enter 12.5 for 12.5%). If this check box isn't selected, you must enter the value as a decimal (for example, .125 for 12.5%). ■

Excel automatically applies a built-in number format to a cell based on the following criteria:

- If a number contains a slash (/), it may be converted to a date format or a fraction format.
- If a number contains a hyphen (-), it may be converted to a date format.
- If a number contains a colon (:) or is followed by a space and the letter *A* or *P*, it may be converted to a time format.
- If a number contains the letter *E* (uppercase or lowercase), it may be converted to scientific notation or exponential format.

Tip
To avoid automatic number formatting when you enter a value, preformat the cell with the desired number format or precede your entry with an apostrophe. (The apostrophe makes the entry text, so number formatting is not applied to the cell.) ■

Formatting numbers by using the Ribbon

The Number group on the Home tab of the Ribbon contains several controls for applying common number formats quickly. The Number Format drop-down control gives you quick access to 11 common number formats. In addition, the Number group contains some buttons. When you click one of these buttons, the selected cells take on the specified number format. Table 24.1 summarizes the formats that these buttons perform in the U.S. English version of Excel.

Note

Some of these buttons actually apply predefined styles to the selected cells. Access Excel's styles by using the Style gallery, in the Styles group on the Home tab. ■

TABLE 24.1

Number-Formatting Buttons on the Ribbon

Button Name	Formatting Applied
Accounting Number Format	Adds a dollar sign to the left, separates thousands with a comma, and displays the value with two digits to the right of the decimal point. This is a drop-down control, so you can select other common currency symbols.
Percent Style	Displays the value as a percentage, with no decimal places.
Comma Style	Separates thousands with a comma and displays the value with two digits to the right of the decimal place. It's like the Accounting number format, but without the currency symbol.
Increase Decimal	Increases the number of digits to the right of the decimal point by one.
Decrease Decimal	Decreases the number of digits to the right of the decimal point by one.

Using shortcut keys to format numbers

Another way to apply number formatting is to use shortcut keys. Table 24.2 summarizes the shortcut key combinations that you can use to apply common number formatting to the selected cells or range. Notice that these are the shifted versions of the number keys along the top of a typical keyboard.

TABLE 24.2

Number-Formatting Keyboard Shortcuts

Key Combination	Formatting Applied
Ctrl+Shift+~	General number format (that is, unformatted values).
Ctrl+Shift+!	Two decimal places, thousands separator, and a hyphen for negative values.
Ctrl+Shift+@	Time format with the hour, minute, and AM or PM.
Ctrl+Shift+#	Date format with the day, month, and year.
Ctrl+Shift+$	Currency format with two decimal places. (Negative numbers appear in parentheses.)
Ctrl+Shift+%	Percentage format with no decimal places.
Ctrl+Shift+^	Scientific notation number format with two decimal places.

Using the Format Cells dialog box to format numbers

For maximum control of number formatting, use the Number tab in the Format Cells dialog box. You can access this dialog box in any of several ways:

- Click the dialog box launcher at the bottom right of the Home ➪ Number group.
- Choose Home ➪ Number ➪ Number Format ➪ More Number Formats.
- Press Ctrl+1.

The Number tab in the Format Cells dialog box contains 12 categories of number formats from which to choose. When you select a category from the list box, the right side of the dialog box changes to display appropriate options.

Here are the number-format categories, along with some general comments:

- **General:** The default format; it displays numbers as integers, decimals, or in scientific notation if the value is too wide to fit into the cell.

- **Number:** Specify the number of decimal places, whether to use your system thousands separator (for example, a comma) to separate thousands, and how to display negative numbers.

- **Currency:** Specify the number of decimal places, choose a currency symbol, and display negative numbers. This format always uses the system thousands separator symbol (for example, a comma) to separate thousands.

- **Accounting:** Differs from the Currency format in that the currency symbols always line up vertically, regardless of the number of digits displayed in the value.

- **Date:** Choose from a variety of date formats and select the locale for your date formats.

- **Time:** Choose from a number of time formats and select the locale for your time formats.

- **Percentage:** Choose the number of decimal places; always displays a percent sign.

- **Fraction:** Choose from among nine fraction formats.

- **Scientific:** Displays numbers in exponential notation (with an E): `2.00E+05` = `200,000`. You can choose the number of decimal places to display to the left of E.

- **Text:** When applied to a value, causes Excel to treat the value as text (even if it looks like a value). This feature is useful for such items as numerical part numbers and credit card numbers.

- **Special:** Contains additional number formats. The list varies, depending on the Locale you choose. For the English (United States) locale, the formatting options are Zip Code, Zip Code +4, Phone Number, and Social Security Number.

- **Custom:** Define custom number formats not included in any of the other categories.

Note

If the cell displays a series of hash marks after you apply a number format (such as ##########), it usually means that the column isn't wide enough to display the value by using the number format that you selected. Either make the column wider (by dragging the right border of the column header) or change the number format. A series of hash marks also can mean that the cell contains an invalid date or time. ■

Creating a Custom Number Format

When you create a custom number format, it can be used to format any cells in the workbook. You can create about 200 custom number formats in each workbook.

Figure 24.1 shows the Custom category in the Number tab of the Format Cells dialog box. Here, you can create number formats not included in any of the other categories. Excel gives you a great deal of flexibility in creating custom number formats.

The Custom category of the Number tab in the Format Cells dialog box.

Tip

Custom number formats are stored with the workbook in which they are defined. To make the custom format available in a different workbook, you can just copy a cell that uses the custom format to the other workbook. ■

You construct a number format by specifying a series of codes as a *number format string*. You enter this code sequence in the Type field after you select the Custom category on the Number tab of the Format Cells dialog box. Here's an example of a simple number format code:

```
0.000
```

This code consists of placeholders and a decimal point; it tells Excel to display the value with three digits to the right of the decimal place. Here's another example:

```
00000
```

This custom number format has five placeholders and displays the value with five digits (no decimal point). This format is good to use when the cell holds a five-digit zip code. (In fact, this is the code actually used by the Zip Code format in the Special category.) When you format the cell with this number format and then enter a Zip Code, such as 06604 (Bridgeport, CT), the value is displayed with the leading zero. If you enter this number into a cell with the General number format, it displays 6604 (no leading zero).

Scroll through the list of number formats in the Custom category in the Format Cells dialog box to see many more examples. In many cases, you can use one of these codes as a starting point, and you'll need to customize it only slightly.

On the CD

The companion CD-ROM contains a workbook with many custom number format examples (see Figure 24.2). The file is named `number formats.xlsx`.

Changing the Default Number Format for a Workbook

As I mention earlier, the default number format is General. If you prefer a different default number format, you have two choices: Preformat the cells with the number format of your choice, or change the number format for the Normal style.

You can preformat specific cells, entire rows or columns, or even the entire worksheet.

Rather than preformat an entire worksheet, however, a better solution is to change the number format for the Normal style. Unless you specify otherwise, all cells use the Normal style. Therefore, by changing the number format for the Normal style you are essentially creating a new default number format for the workbook.

Change the Normal style by displaying the Style gallery. Right-click the Normal style icon (in the Home ➪ Styles group) and choose Modify to display the Style dialog box. In the Style dialog box, click the Format button and then choose the new number format that you want to use for the Normal style.

FIGURE 24.2

Examples of custom number formatting.

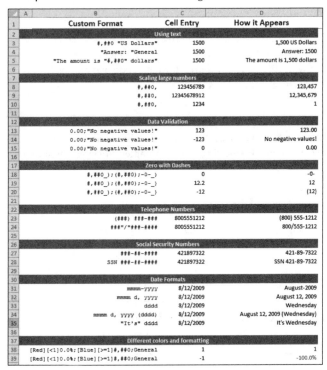

	Custom Format	Cell Entry	How it Appears
	Using text		
	#,##0 "US Dollars"	1500	1,500 US Dollars
	"Answer: "General	1500	Answer: 1500
	"The amount is "#,##0" dollars"	1500	The amount is 1,500 dollars
	Scaling large numbers		
	#,##0,	123456789	123,457
	#,##0,	12345678912	12,345,679
	#,##0,	1234	1
	Data Validation		
	0.00;"No negative values!"	123	123.00
	0.00;"No negative values!"	-123	No negative values!
	0.00;"No negative values!"	0	0.00
	Zero with Dashes		
	#,##0_);(#,##0);-0-_)	0	-0-
	#,##0_);(#,##0);-0-_)	12.2	12
	#,##0_);(#,##0);-0-_)	-12	(12)
	Telephone Numbers		
	(###) ###-####	8005551212	(800) 555-1212
	###"/"###-####	8005551212	800/555-1212
	Social Security Numbers		
	###-##-####	421897322	421-89-7322
	SSN ###-##-####	421897322	SSN 421-89-7322
	Date Formats		
	mmmm-yyyy	8/12/2009	August-2009
	mmmm d, yyyy	8/12/2009	August 12, 2009
	dddd	8/12/2009	Wednesday
	mmmm d, yyyy (dddd)	8/12/2009	August 12, 2009 (Wednesday)
	"It's" dddd	8/12/2009	It's Wednesday
	Different colors and formatting		
	[Red][<1]0.0%;[Blue][>=1]#,##0;General	1	1
	[Red][<1]0.0%;[Blue][>=1]#,##0;General	-1	-100.0%

Parts of a number format string

A custom format string can have up to four sections, which enables you to specify different format codes for positive numbers, negative numbers, zero values, and text. You do so by separating the codes with a semicolon. The codes are arranged in the following order:

```
Positive format; Negative format; Zero format; Text format
```

If you don't use all four sections of a format string, Excel interprets the format string as follows:

- **If you use only one section:** The format string applies to all types of entries.
- **If you use two sections:** The first section applies to positive values and zeros, and the second section applies to negative values.
- **If you use three sections:** The first section applies to positive values, the second section applies to negative values, and the third section applies to zeros.
- **If you use all four sections:** The last section applies to text stored in the cell.

The following is an example of a custom number format that specifies a different format for each of these types:

```
[Green]General;[Red]General;[Black]General;[Blue]General
```

This custom number format example takes advantage of the fact that colors have special codes. A cell formatted with this custom number format displays its contents in a different color, depending on the value. When a cell is formatted with this custom number format, a positive number is green, a negative number is red, a zero is black, and text is blue.

Cross-Reference

If you want to apply cell formatting automatically (such as text or background color) based on the cell's contents, a much better solution is to use the Excel Conditional Formatting feature. Chapter 20 covers conditional formatting. ■

Custom number format codes

Table 24.3 lists the formatting codes available for custom formats, along with brief descriptions. I use most of these codes in examples later in this chapter.

TABLE 24.3

Codes Used to Create Custom Number Formats

Code	Comments
General	Displays the number in General format.
#	Digit placeholder. Displays only significant digits, and does not display insignificant zeros.
0 (zero)	Digit placeholder. Displays insignificant zeros if a number has fewer digits than there are zeros in the format.
?	Digit placeholder. Adds spaces for insignificant zeros on either side of the decimal point so that decimal points align when formatted with a fixed-width font. You can also use ? for fractions that have varying numbers of digits.
.	Decimal point.
%	Percentage.
,	Thousands separator.
E- E+ e- e+	Scientific notation.
$ - + / ( ) : space	Displays this character.
\	Displays the next character in the format.
*	Repeats the next character, to fill the column width.
_ (underscore)	Leaves a space equal to the width of the next character.

Code	Comments
"text"	Displays the text inside the double quotation marks.
@	Text placeholder.
[color]	Displays the characters in the color specified. Can be any of the following text strings (not case sensitive): Black, Blue, Cyan, Green, Magenta, Red, White, or Yellow.
[Color n]	Displays the corresponding color in the color palette, where n is a number from 0 to 56.
[condition value]	Set your own criterion for each section of a number format.

Table 24.4 lists the codes used to create custom formats for dates and times.

TABLE 24.4

Codes Used in Creating Custom Formats for Dates and Times

Code	Comments
m	Displays the month as a number without leading zeros (1–12).
mm	Displays the month as a number with leading zeros (01–12).
mmm	Displays the month as an abbreviation (Jan–Dec).
mmmm	Displays the month as a full name (January–December).
mmmmm	Displays the first letter of the month (J–D).
d	Displays the day as a number without leading zeros (1–31).
dd	Displays the day as a number with leading zeros (01–31).
ddd	Displays the day as an abbreviation (Sun–Sat).
dddd	Displays the day as a full name (Sunday–Saturday).
yy or yyyy	Displays the year as a two-digit number (00–99) or as a four-digit number (1900–9999).
h or hh	Displays the hour as a number without leading zeros (0–23) or as a number with leading zeros (00–23).
m or mm	Displays the minute as a number without leading zeros (0–59) or as a number with leading zeros (00–59).
s or ss	Displays the second as a number without leading zeros (0–59) or as a number with leading zeros (00–59).
[ ]	Displays hours greater than 24 or minutes or seconds greater than 60.
AM/PM	Displays the hour using a 12-hour clock; if no AM/PM indicator is used, the hour uses a 24 hour clock.

Where Did Those Number Formats Come From?

Excel may create custom number formats without you realizing it. When you use the Increase Decimal or Decrease Decimal button on the Home ➪ Number group of the Ribbon (or on the Mini toolbar), Excel creates new custom number formats, which appear on the Number tab in the Format Cells dialog box. For example, if you click the Increase Decimal button five times, the following custom number formats are created:

```
0.0
0.000
0.0000
0.000000
```

A format string for two decimal places is not created because that format string is built-in.

Custom Number Format Examples

The remainder of this chapter consists of useful examples of custom number formats. You can use most of these format codes as-is. Others may require slight modification to meet your needs.

Scaling values

You can use a custom number format to scale a number. For example, if you work with very large numbers, you may want to display the numbers in thousands (that is, display 1,200,000 as 1,200). The actual number, of course, will be used in calculations that involve that cell. The formatting affects only how it is displayed.

Displaying values in thousands

The following format string displays values without the last three digits to the left of the decimal place and no decimal places. In other words, the value appears as if it's divided by 1,000 and rounded to no decimal places.

```
#,###,
```

A variation of this format string follows. A value with this number format appears as if it's divided by 1,000 and rounded to two decimal places.

```
#,###.00,
```

Table 24.5 shows examples of these number formats:

TABLE 24.5

Examples of Displaying Values in Thousands

Value	Number Format	Display
123456	#,###,	123
1234565	#,###,	1,235
−323434	#,###,	−323
123123.123	#,###,	123
499	#,###,	(blank)
500	#,###,	1
123456	#,###.00,	123.46
1234565	#,###.00,	1,234.57
−323434	#,###.00,	−323.43
123123.123	#,###.00,	123.12
499	#,###.00,	.50
500	#,###.00,	.50

Displaying values in hundreds

The following format string displays values in hundreds, with two decimal places. A value with this number format appears as if it's divided by 100 and rounded to two decimal places.

```
0"."00
```

Table 24.6 shows examples of these number formats:

TABLE 24.6

Examples of Displaying Values in Hundreds

Value	Number Format	Display
546	0"."00	5.46
100	0"."00	1.00
9890	0"."00	98.90
500	0"."00	5.00
−500	0"."00	−5.00
0	0"."00	0.00

Displaying values in millions

The following format string displays values in millions with no decimal places. A value with this number appears as if it's divided by 1,000,000 and rounded to no decimal places.

```
#,###,,
```

A variation of this format string follows. A value with this number appears as if it's divided by 1,000,000 and rounded to two decimal places.

```
#,###.00,,
```

Another variation follows. This adds the letter M to the end of the value.

```
#,###,,M
```

The following format string is a bit more complex. It adds the letter M to the end of the value — and also displays negative values in parentheses as well as displaying zeros.

```
#,###.0,,"M"_);(#,###.0,,"M)";0.0"M"_)
```

Table 24.7 shows examples of these format strings.

TABLE 24.7

Examples of Displaying Values in Millions

Value	Number Format	Display
123456789	#,###,,	123
1.23457E+11	#,###,,	123,457
1000000	#,###,,	1
5000000	#,###,,	5
–5000000	#,###,,	–5
0	#,###,,	(blank)
123456789	#,###.00,,	123.46
1.23457E+11	#,###.00,,	123,457.00
1000000	#,###.00,,	1.00
5000000	#,###.00,,	5.00
–5000000	#,###.00,,	–5.00
0	#,###.00,,	.00
123456789	#,###,,"M"	123M
1.23457E+11	#,###,,"M"	123,457M
1000000	#,###,,"M"	1M

Value	Number Format	Display
5000000	#,###,,"M"	5M
−5000000	#,###,,"M"	−5M
0	#,###,,"M"	M
123456789	#,###.0,,"M"_);(#,###.0,,"M)";0.0"M"_)	123.5M
1.23457E+11	#,###.0,,"M"_);(#,###.0,,"M)";0.0"M"_)	123,456.8M
1000000	#,###.0,,"M"_);(#,###.0,,"M)";0.0"M"_)	1.0M
5000000	#,###.0,,"M"_);(#,###.0,,"M)";0.0"M"_)	5.0M
−5000000	#,###.0,,"M"_);(#,###.0,,"M)";0.0"M"_)	(5.0M)
0	#,###.0,,"M"_);(#,###.0,,"M)";0.0"M"_)	0.0M

Adding zeros to a value

The following format string displays a value with three additional zeros and no decimal places. A value with this number format appears as if it's rounded to no decimal places and then multiplied by 1,000.

    #",000"

Examples of this format string, plus a variation that adds six zeros, are shown in Table 24.8.

TABLE 24.8

Examples of Displaying a Value with Extra Zeros

Value	Number Format	Display
1	#",000"	1,000
1.5	#",000"	2,000
43	#",000"	43,000
−54	#",000"	−54,000
5.5	#",000"	6,000
0.5	#",000,000"	1,000,000
0	#",000,000"	,000,000
1	#",000,000"	1,000,000
1.5	#",000,000"	2,000,000
43	#",000,000"	43,000,000
−54	#",000,000"	−54,000,000
5.5	#",000,000"	6,000,000
0.5	#",000,000"	1,000,000

Displaying leading zeros

To display leading zeros, create a custom number format that uses the 0 character. For example, if you want all numbers to display with ten digits, use the number format string that follows. Values with fewer than ten digits will display with leading zeros.

```
0000000000
```

You also can force all numbers to display with a fixed number of leading zeros. The format string that follows, for example, appends three zeros to the beginning of each number:

```
"000"#
```

In the following example, the format string uses the repeat character code (an asterisk) to apply enough leading zeros to fill the entire width of the cell:

```
*00
```

Displaying fractions

Excel supports quite a few built-in fraction number formats (select the Fraction category on the Number tab in the Format Cells dialog box). For example, to display the value .125 as a fraction with 8 as the denominator, select As Eighths (4/8) from the Type list (see Figure 24.3).

FIGURE 24.3

Selecting a number format to display a value as a fraction.

Testing Custom Number Formats

When you create a custom number format, don't overlook the Sample box on the Number tab in the Format Cells dialog box. This box displays the value in the active cell using the format string in the Type box.

It's a good idea to test your custom number formats by using the following data: a positive value, a negative value, a zero value, and text. Often, creating a custom number format takes several attempts. Each time you edit a format string, it is added to the list. When you finally get the correct format string, access the Format Cells dialog box one more time and delete your previous attempts.

You can use a custom format string to create other fractional formats. For example, the following format string displays a value in 50ths:

```
# ??/50
```

To display the fraction reduced to its lowest terms, use a question mark after the slash symbol. For example, the value 0.125 can be expressed as 2/16, and 2/16 can be reduced to 1/8. Here's an example of a number format that displays the value as a fraction reduced to its simplest terms:

```
# ?/?
```

If you omit the leading hash symbol, the value is displayed without a leading value. For example, the value 2.5 would display as 5/2 using this number format code:

```
?/?
```

The following format string displays a value in terms of fractional dollars. For example, the value 154.87 is displayed as 154 and 87/100 Dollars.

```
0 "and "??/100 "Dollars"
```

The following example displays the value in sixteenths, with a quotation mark appended to the right. This format string is useful when you deal with fractions of inches (for example, 2/16").

```
# ??/16\"
```

Displaying a negative sign on the right

The following format string displays negative values with the negative sign to the right of the number. Positive values have an additional space on the right, so both positive and negative numbers align properly on the right.

```
0.00_-;0.00-
```

To make the negative numbers more prominent, you can add a color code to the negative part of the number format string:

```
0.00_-;[Red]0.00-
```

Formatting dates and times

When you enter a date into a cell, Excel formats the date using the system short date format. You can change this format by using the Windows Control Panel (Regional and Language Options).

Excel provides many useful, built-in dates and time formats. Table 24.9 shows some other date and time formats that you may find useful. The first column of the table shows the date/time serial number.

Useful Built-In Date and Time Formats

Value	Number Format	Display
40360	mmmm d, yyyy (dddd)	July 1, 2007 (Thursday)
40360	"It's" dddd!	It's Thursday!
40360	dddd, mm/dd/yyyy	Thursday, 07/01/2010
40360	"Month: "mmm	Month: July
40360	General (m/d/yyyy)	40360 (7/1/2010)
0.345	h "Hours"	8 Hours
0.345	h:mm o'clock	8:16 o'clock
0.345	h:mm a/p"m"	8:16 am
0.78	h:mm a/p".m."	6:43 p.m.

Cross-Reference

See Chapter 13 for more information about the Excel date and time serial number system.

Displaying text with numbers

The ability to display text with a value is one of the most useful benefits of using a custom number format. To add text, just create the number format string as usual (or use a built-in number format as a starting point) and put the text within quotation marks. The following number format string, for example, displays a value with the text (US Dollars) added to the end:

```
#,##0.00 "(US Dollars)"
```

Using the TEXT Function to Format Numbers

The TEXT function accepts a number format string as its second argument. For example, the following formula displays the contents of cell A1 using a custom number format that displays a fraction:

```
=TEXT(A1,"# ??/50")
```

However, not all formatting codes work when used in this manner. For example, colors and repeating characters are ignored. The following formula does not display the contents of cell A1 in red:

```
=TEXT(A1,"[Red]General")
```

Here's another example that displays text before the number:

```
"Average: "0.00
```

If you use the preceding number format, you'll find that the negative sign appears before the text for negative values. To display number signs properly, use this variation:

```
"Average: "0.00;"Average: "-0.00
```

The following format string displays a value with the words Dollars and Cents. For example, the number 123.45 displays as 123 Dollars and .45 Cents.

```
0 "Dollars and" .00 "Cents"
```

Suppressing certain types of entries

You can use number formatting to hide certain types of entries. For example, the following format string displays text but not values:

```
;;
```

This format string displays values but not text or zeros:

```
0.0;-0.0;;
```

This format string displays everything except zeros:

```
0.0;-0.0;;@
```

You can use the following format string to completely hide the contents of a cell:

```
;;;
```

Note that when the cell is activated, however, the cell's contents are visible on the Formula bar.

Filling a cell with a repeating character

The asterisk (*) symbol specifies a repeating character in a number format string. The repeating character completely fills the cell and adjusts if the column width changes. The following format string, for example, displays the contents of a cell padded on the right with dashes:

```
General*-;-General*-;General*-;General*-
```

Using Data Validation

This chapter explores a very useful Excel feature: data validation. Data validation enables you to add dynamic elements to your worksheet without using any macro programming.

IN THIS CHAPTER

An overview of Excel's data validation feature

Practical examples of using data validation formulas

About Data Validation

The Excel *data validation* feature allows you to set up certain rules that dictate what can be entered into a cell. For example, you may want to limit data entry in a particular cell to whole numbers between 1 and 12. If the user makes an invalid entry, you can display a custom message, such as the one shown in Figure 25.1.

FIGURE 25.1

Displaying a message when the user makes an invalid entry.

Excel makes it easy to specify the validation criteria, and you can also use a formula for more complex criteria.

Caution

The Excel data validation feature suffers from a potentially serious problem: If the user copies a cell that does not use data validation and pastes it to a cell that does use data validation, the data validation rules are deleted. In other words, the cell then accepts any type of data. ■

Specifying Validation Criteria

To specify the type of data allowable in a cell or range, follow the steps below while you refer to Figure 25.2, which shows all three tabs of the Data Validation dialog box.

1. **Select the cell or range.**

2. **Choose Data ⇨ Data Tools ⇨ Data Validation.** Excel displays its Data Validation dialog box.

3. **Click the Settings tab.**

4. **Choose an option from the Allow drop-down list.** The contents of the Data Validation dialog box will change, displaying controls based on your choice. To specify a formula, select Custom.

FIGURE 25.2

The three tabs of the Data Validation dialog box.

5. **Specify the conditions by using the displayed controls.** Your selection in Step 4 determines what other controls you can access.

6. **(Optional) Click the Input Message tab and specify which message to display when a user selects the cell.** You can use this optional step to tell the user what type of data is expected. If this step is omitted, no message will appear when the user selects the cell.

7. **(Optional) Click the Error Alert tab and specify which error message to display when a user makes an invalid entry.** The selection for Style determines what choices users have when they make invalid entries. To prevent an invalid entry, choose Stop. If this step is omitted, a standard message will appear if the user makes an invalid entry.

8. **Click OK.** The cell or range contains the validation criteria you specified.

Caution

Even with data validation in effect, a user can enter invalid data. If the Style setting on the Error Alert tab of the Data Validation dialog box is set to anything except Stop, invalid data *can* **be entered. Also, remember that data validation does not apply to the calculated results of formulas. In other words, if the cell contains a formula, applying conditional formatting to that cell will have no effect. ∎**

Types of Validation Criteria You Can Apply

From the Settings tab of the Data Validation dialog box, you can specify a wide variety of data validation criteria. The following options are available from the Allow drop-down list. Keep in mind that the other controls on the Settings tab vary, depending on your choice from the Allow drop-down list.

- **Any Value:** Selecting this option removes any existing data validation. Note, however, that the input message, if any, still displays if the check box is checked on the Input Message tab.

- **Whole Number:** The user must enter a whole number. You specify a valid range of whole numbers by using the Data drop-down list. For example, you can specify that the entry must be a whole number greater than or equal to 100.

- **Decimal:** The user must enter a number. You specify a valid range of numbers by refining the criteria from choices in the Data drop-down list. For example, you can specify that the entry must be greater than or equal to 0 and less than or equal to 1.

- **List:** The user must choose from a list of entries you provide. This option is very useful, and I discuss it in detail later in this chapter. (See "Creating a drop-down list.").

- **Date:** The user must enter a date. You specify a valid date range from choices in the Data drop-down list. For example, you can specify that the entered data must be greater than or equal to January 1, 2010, and less than or equal to December 31, 2010.

- **Time:** The user must enter a time. You specify a valid time range from choices in the Data drop-down list. For example, you can specify that the entered data must be later than 12:00 p.m.

- **Text Length:** The length of the data (number of characters) is limited. You specify a valid length by using the Data drop-down list. For example, you can specify that the length of the entered data be 1 (a single alphanumeric character).

- **Custom:** To use this option, you must supply a logical formula that determines the validity of the user's entry (a logical formula returns either TRUE or FALSE). You can enter the formula directly into the Formula control (which appears when you select the Custom option), or you can specify a cell reference that contains a formula. This chapter contains examples of useful formulas.

The Settings tab of the Data Validation dialog box contains two other check boxes:

- **Ignore Blank:** If selected, blank entries are allowed.

- **Apply These Changes to All Other Cells with the Same Setting:** If selected, the changes you make apply to all other cells that contain the original data validation criteria.

Tip

The Data ➪ Data Tools ➪ Data Validation drop-down list contains an item named Circle Invalid Data. When you select this item, circles appear around cells that contain incorrect entries. If you correct an invalid entry, the circle disappears. To get rid of the circles, choose Data ➪ Data Tools ➪ Data Validation ➪ Clear Validation Circles. In Figure 25.3, invalid entries are defined as values that are greater than 100. ■

FIGURE 25.3

Excel can draw circles around invalid entries (in this case, cells that contain values greater than 100).

	A	B	C	D	E	F	G
1	11	26	67	26	67	24	93
2	52	63	72	17	38	104	105
3	105	11	25	51	98	90	83
4	89	97	33	95	14	18	101
5	65	102	36	94	13	87	94
6	42	95	67	94	26	85	99
7	84	14	48	4	23	97	48
8	18	17	1	64	49	47	15
9	97	49	61	35	57	99	9
10	56	37	96	6	81	92	8
11	82	18	26	54	8	73	50
12	10	77	68	67	13	59	60
13	31	65	19	24	82	14	4
14	29	58	24	3	68	86	50
15	68	46	74	24	38	80	104
16	102	43	26	78	78	36	94
17	15	20	45	49	40	12	89
18	16	88	49	87	74	63	72
19	28	58	31	5	65	104	45
20	7	80	76	78	25	19	7
21	67	86	46	32	15	35	102
22	84	55	30	44	9	44	89
23	82	48	90	43	82	22	19

Creating a Drop-Down List

Perhaps one of the most common uses of data validation is to create a drop-down list in a cell. Figure 25.4 shows an example that uses the month names in A1:A12 as the list source.

This drop-down list (with an Input Message) was created using data validation.

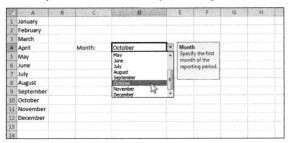

To create a drop-down list in a cell

1. **Enter the list items into a single-row or single-column range.** These items will appear in the drop-down list.

2. **Select the cell that will contain the drop-down list and then access the Data Validation dialog box (choose Data ➪ Data Tools ➪ Data Validation).**

3. **From the Settings tab, select the List option (from the Allow drop-down list) and specify the range that contains the list, using the Source control.**

4. **Make sure that the In-Cell Dropdown check box is selected.**

5. **Set any other Data Validation options as desired.**

6. **Click OK.** The cell displays an input message (if specified) and a drop-down arrow when it's activated. Click the arrow and choose an item from the list that appears.

Tip

If you have a short list, you can enter the items directly into the Source control of the Settings tab of the Data Validation dialog box. (This control appears when you choose the List option in the Allow drop-down list.) Just separate each item with list separators specified in your regional settings (a comma if you use the U.S. regional settings). ■

New

In previous versions of Excel the range that contains the list must be on the same worksheet as the cell that contains the data validation. That restriction was removed in Excel 2010. The list range can be on any worksheet in the workbook. ■

Using Formulas for Data Validation Rules

For simple data validation, the data validation feature is quite straightforward and easy to use. The real power of this feature, though, becomes apparent when you use data validation formulas.

Note

The formula that you specify must be a logical formula that returns either TRUE or FALSE. If the formula evaluates to TRUE, the data is considered valid and remains in the cell. If the formula evaluates to FALSE, a message box appears that displays the message that you specify on the Error Alert tab of the Data Validation dialog box. Specify a formula in the Data Validation dialog box by selecting the Custom option from the Allow drop-down list of the Settings tab. Enter the formula directly into the Formula control, or enter a reference to a cell that contains a formula. The Formula control appears on the Setting tab of the Data Validation dialog box when the Custom option is selected. ∎

I have several examples of formulas used for data validation in the upcoming section "Data Validation Examples."

Understanding Cell References

If the formula that you enter into the Data Validation dialog box contains a cell reference, that reference is considered a *relative reference,* based on the upper-left cell in the selected range.

The following example clarifies this concept. Suppose that you want to allow only an odd number to be entered into the range B2:B10. None of the Excel data validation rules can limit entry to odd numbers, so a formula is required.

Follow these steps:

1. **Select the range (B2:B10 for this example) and ensure that cell B2 is the active cell.**
2. **Choose Data ➪ Data Tools ➪ Data Validation.** The Data Validation dialog box appears.
3. **Click the Settings tab and select Custom from the Allow drop-down list.**
4. **Enter the following formula in the Formula field, as shown in Figure 25.5:**

   `=ISODD(B2)`

   This formula uses the ISODD function, which returns TRUE if its numeric argument is an odd number. Notice that the formula refers to the active cell, which is cell B2.
5. **On the Error Alert tab, choose Stop for the Style and then type An odd number is required here as the Error Message.**
6. **Click OK to close the Data Validation dialog box.**

Notice that the formula entered contains a reference to the upper-left cell in the selected range. This data validation formula was applied to a range of cells, so you might expect that each cell would contain the same data validation formula. Because you entered a relative cell reference as the argument for the ISODD function, Excel adjusts the formula for the other cells in the B2:B10 range. To demonstrate that the reference is relative, select cell B5 and examine its formula displayed in the Data Validation dialog box . You'll see that the formula for this cell is

```
=ISODD(B5)
```

FIGURE 25.5

Entering a data validation formula.

Generally, when entering a data validation formula for a range of cells, you use a reference to the active cell, which is normally the upper-left cell in the selected range. An exception is when you need to refer to a specific cell. For example, suppose that you select range A1:B10, and you want your data validation to allow only values that are greater than C1. You would use this formula:

```
=A1>$C$1
```

In this case, the reference to cell C1 is an *absolute reference;* it will not be adjusted for the cells in the selected range — which is just what you want. The data validation formula for cell A2 looks like this:

```
=A2>$C$1
```

The relative cell reference is adjusted, but the absolute cell reference is not.

Data Validation Formula Examples

The following sections contain a few data validation examples that use a formula entered directly into the Formula control on the Settings tab of the Data Validation dialog box. These examples help you understand how to create your own Data Validation formulas.

On the CD

All the examples in this section are available on the companion CD-ROM. The file is named `data validation examples.xlsx.`

Accepting text only

Excel has a data validation option to limit the length of text entered into a cell, but it doesn't have an option to force text (rather than a number) into a cell. To force a cell or range to accept only text (no values), use the following data validation formula:

```
=ISTEXT(A1)
```

This formula assumes that the active cell in the selected range is cell A1.

Accepting a larger value than the previous cell

The following data validation formula enables the user to enter a value only if it's greater than the value in the cell directly above it:

```
=A2>A1
```

This formula assumes that A2 is the active cell in the selected range. Note that you can't use this formula for a cell in row 1.

Accepting nonduplicate entries only

The following data validation formula does not permit the user to make a duplicate entry in the range A1:C20:

```
=COUNTIF($A$1:$C$20,A1)=1
```

This is a logical formula that returns TRUE if the value in the cell occurs only one time in the A1:C20 range. Otherwise, it returns FALSE, and the Duplicate Entry dialog box is displayed.

This formula assumes that A1 is the active cell in the selected range. Note that the first argument for COUNTIF is an absolute reference. The second argument is a relative reference, and it adjusts for each cell in the validation range. Figure 25.6 shows this validation criterion in effect, using a custom error alert message. The user is attempting to enter 16 into cell B5.

FIGURE 25.6

Using data validation to prevent duplicate entries in a range.

Accepting text that begins with a specific character

The following data validation formula demonstrates how to check for a specific character. In this case, the formula ensures that the user's entry is a text string that begins with the letter *A* (uppercase or lowercase).

```
=LEFT(A1)="a"
```

This is a logical formula that returns TRUE if the first character in the cell is the letter *A*. Otherwise, it returns FALSE. This formula assumes that the active cell in the selected range is cell A1.

The following formula is a variation of this validation formula. It uses wildcard characters in the second argument of the COUNTIF function. In this case, the formula ensures that the entry begins with the letter *A* and contains exactly five characters:

```
=COUNTIF(A1,"A????")=1
```

Accepting dates by the day of the week

The following data validation formula ensures that the cell entry is a date, and that the date is a Monday:

```
=WEEKDAY(A1)=2
```

This formula assumes that the active cell in the selected range is cell A1. It uses the WEEKDAY function, which returns 1 for Sunday, 2 for Monday, and so on.

Accepting only values that don't exceed a total

Figure 25.7 shows a simple budget worksheet, with the budget item amounts in the range B1:B6. The planned budget is in cell E5, and the user is attempting to enter a value in cell B4 that would cause the total (cell E6) to exceed the budget. The following data validation formula ensures that the sum of the budget items does not exceed the budget:

```
=SUM($B$1:$B$6)<=$E$5
```

FIGURE 25.7

Using data validation to ensure that the sum of a range does not exceed a certain value.

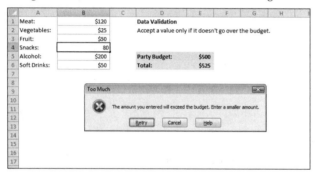

Creating a dependent list

As I describe previously, you can use data validation to create a drop-down list in a cell (see "Creating a Drop-Down List"). This section explains how to use a drop-down list to control the entries that appear in a second drop-down list. In other words, the second drop-down list is dependent upon the value selected in the first drop-down list.

Figure 25.8 shows a simple example of a dependent list created by using data validation. Cell E2 contains data validation that displays a three-item list from the range A1:C1 (Vegetables, Fruits, and Meats). When the user chooses an item from the list, the second list (in cell F2) displays the appropriate items.

This worksheet uses three named ranges:

- Vegetables: A2:A15
- Fruits: B2:B9
- Meats: C2:C5

Cell F2 contains data validation that uses this formula:

```
=INDIRECT($E$2)
```

Therefore, the drop-down list displayed in F2 depends on the value displayed in cell E2.

FIGURE 25.8

The items displayed in the list in cell F2 depend on the list item selected in cell E2.

Creating and Using Worksheet Outlines

I f you use a word processor, you may be familiar with the concept of an outline. Most word processors (including Microsoft Word) have an outline mode that lets you view only the headings and subheadings in your document. You can easily expand a heading to show the text below it. Using an outline makes visualizing the structure of your document easy.

Excel also is capable of using outlines, and understanding this feature can make working with certain types of worksheets much easier for you.

IN THIS CHAPTER

Introducing worksheet outlines

Creating an outline

Using outlines

Introducing Worksheet Outlines

You'll find that some worksheets are more suitable for outlines than others. You can use outlines to create summary reports in which you don't want to show all the details. If your worksheet uses hierarchical data with subtotals, it's probably a good candidate for an outline.

The best way to understand how worksheet outlining works is to look at an example. Figure 26.1 shows a simple sales summary sheet without an outline. Formulas are used to calculate subtotals by region and by quarter.

Figure 26.2 shows the same worksheet after I created the outline. Notice that Excel adds a new section to the left of the screen. This section contains outline controls that enable you to determine which level to view. This particular outline has three levels: States, Regions (each region consists of states grouped into categories such as West, East, and Central), and Grand Total (the sum of each region's subtotal).

FIGURE 26.1

A simple sales summary with subtotals.

State	Jan	Feb	Mar	Qtr-1	Apr	May	Jun	Qtr-2	Total
California	1,118	1,960	1,252	4,330	1,271	1,557	1,679	4,507	8,837
Washington	1,247	1,238	1,028	3,513	1,345	1,784	1,574	4,703	8,216
Oregon	1,460	1,954	1,726	5,140	1,461	1,764	1,144	4,369	9,509
Arizona	1,345	1,375	1,075	3,795	1,736	1,555	1,372	4,663	8,458
West Total	5,170	6,527	5,081	16,778	5,813	6,660	5,769	18,242	35,020
New York	1,429	1,316	1,993	4,738	1,832	1,740	1,191	4,763	9,501
New Jersey	1,735	1,406	1,224	4,365	1,706	1,320	1,290	4,316	8,681
Massachusetts	1,099	1,233	1,110	3,442	1,637	1,512	1,006	4,155	7,597
Florida	1,705	1,792	1,225	4,722	1,946	1,327	1,357	4,630	9,352
East Total	5,968	5,747	5,552	17,267	7,121	5,899	4,844	17,864	35,131
Kentucky	1,109	1,078	1,155	3,342	1,993	1,082	1,551	4,626	7,968
Oklahoma	1,309	1,045	1,641	3,995	1,924	1,499	1,941	5,364	9,359
Missouri	1,511	1,744	1,414	4,669	1,243	1,493	1,820	4,556	9,225
Illinois	1,539	1,493	1,211	4,243	1,165	1,013	1,445	3,623	7,866
Kansas	1,973	1,560	1,243	4,776	1,495	1,125	1,387	4,007	8,783
Central Total	7,441	6,920	6,664	21,025	7,820	6,212	8,144	22,176	43,201
Grand Total	18,579	19,194	17,297	55,070	20,754	18,771	18,757	58,282	113,352

FIGURE 26.2

The worksheet after creating an outline.

State	Jan	Feb	Mar	Qtr-1	Apr	May	Jun	Qtr-2	Total
California	1,118	1,960	1,252	4,330	1,271	1,557	1,679	4,507	8,837
Washington	1,247	1,238	1,028	3,513	1,345	1,784	1,574	4,703	8,216
Oregon	1,460	1,954	1,726	5,140	1,461	1,764	1,144	4,369	9,509
Arizona	1,345	1,375	1,075	3,795	1,736	1,555	1,372	4,663	8,458
West Total	5,170	6,527	5,081	16,778	5,813	6,660	5,769	18,242	35,020
New York	1,429	1,316	1,993	4,738	1,832	1,740	1,191	4,763	9,501
New Jersey	1,735	1,406	1,224	4,365	1,706	1,320	1,290	4,316	8,681
Massachusetts	1,099	1,233	1,110	3,442	1,637	1,512	1,006	4,155	7,597
Florida	1,705	1,792	1,225	4,722	1,946	1,327	1,357	4,630	9,352
East Total	5,968	5,747	5,552	17,267	7,121	5,899	4,844	17,864	35,131
Kentucky	1,109	1,078	1,155	3,342	1,993	1,082	1,551	4,626	7,968
Oklahoma	1,309	1,045	1,641	3,995	1,924	1,499	1,941	5,364	9,359
Missouri	1,511	1,744	1,414	4,669	1,243	1,493	1,820	4,556	9,225
Illinois	1,539	1,493	1,211	4,243	1,165	1,013	1,445	3,623	7,866
Kansas	1,973	1,560	1,243	4,776	1,495	1,125	1,387	4,007	8,783
Central Total	7,441	6,920	6,664	21,025	7,820	6,212	8,144	22,176	43,201
Grand Total	18,579	19,194	17,297	55,070	20,754	18,771	18,757	58,282	113,352

Figure 26.3 depicts the outline after clicking the 2 button, which displays the second level of details. Now, the outline shows only the totals for the regions (the detail rows are hidden). You can partially expand the outline to show the detail for a particular region by clicking one of the + buttons. Collapsing the outline to level 1 shows only the headers and the Grand Total row.

Excel can create outlines in both directions. In the preceding examples, the outline is a row (vertical) outline. Figure 26.4 shows the same model after a column (horizontal) outline was added. Now, Excel also displays outline controls at the top.

FIGURE 26.3

The worksheet after collapsing the outline to the second level.

		A	B	C	D	E	F	G	H	I	J
	1	State	Jan	Feb	Mar	Qtr-1	Apr	May	Jun	Qtr-2	Total
	6	West Total	5,170	6,527	5,081	16,778	5,813	6,660	5,769	18,242	35,020
	11	East Total	5,968	5,747	5,552	17,267	7,121	5,899	4,844	17,864	35,131
	17	Central Total	7,441	6,920	6,664	21,025	7,820	6,212	8,144	22,176	43,201
	18	Grand Total	18,579	19,194	17,297	55,070	20,754	18,771	18,757	58,282	113,352
	19										

FIGURE 26.4

The worksheet after adding a column outline.

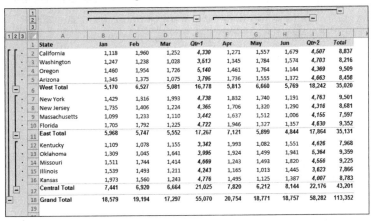

	A	B	C	D	E	F	G	H	I	Total
1	State	Jan	Feb	Mar	Qtr-1	Apr	May	Jun	Qtr-2	Total
2	California	1,118	1,960	1,252	4,330	1,271	1,557	1,679	4,507	8,837
3	Washington	1,247	1,238	1,028	3,513	1,345	1,784	1,574	4,703	8,216
4	Oregon	1,460	1,954	1,726	5,140	1,461	1,764	1,144	4,369	9,509
5	Arizona	1,345	1,375	1,075	3,795	1,736	1,555	1,372	4,663	8,458
6	West Total	5,170	6,527	5,081	16,778	5,813	6,660	5,769	18,242	35,020
7	New York	1,429	1,316	1,993	4,738	1,832	1,740	1,191	4,763	9,501
8	New Jersey	1,735	1,406	1,224	4,365	1,706	1,320	1,290	4,316	8,681
9	Massachusetts	1,099	1,233	1,110	3,442	1,637	1,512	1,006	4,155	7,597
10	Florida	1,705	1,792	1,225	4,722	1,946	1,327	1,357	4,630	9,352
11	East Total	5,968	5,747	5,552	17,267	7,121	5,899	4,844	17,864	35,131
12	Kentucky	1,109	1,078	1,155	3,342	1,993	1,082	1,551	4,626	7,968
13	Oklahoma	1,309	1,045	1,641	3,995	1,924	1,499	1,941	5,364	9,359
14	Missouri	1,511	1,744	1,414	4,669	1,243	1,493	1,820	4,556	9,225
15	Illinois	1,539	1,493	1,211	4,243	1,165	1,013	1,445	3,623	7,866
16	Kansas	1,973	1,560	1,243	4,776	1,495	1,125	1,387	4,007	8,783
17	Central Total	7,441	6,920	6,664	21,025	7,820	6,212	8,144	22,176	43,201
18	Grand Total	18,579	19,194	17,297	55,070	20,754	18,771	18,757	58,282	113,352
19										

If you create both a row and a column outline in a worksheet, you can work with each outline independent of the other. For example, you can show the row outline at the second level and the column outline at the first level. Figure 26.5 shows the model with both outlines collapsed at the second level. The result is a nice high-level summary table that gives regional totals by quarter.

FIGURE 26.5

The worksheet with both outlines collapsed at the second level.

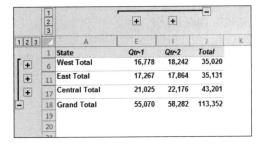

	A	E	I	J	K
1	State	Qtr-1	Qtr-2	Total	
6	West Total	16,778	18,242	35,020	
11	East Total	17,267	17,864	35,131	
17	Central Total	21,025	22,176	43,201	
18	Grand Total	55,070	58,282	113,352	
19					
20					

On the CD

You can find the workbook used in the preceding examples on this book's CD-ROM. The file is named `outline example.xlsx`.

Keep in mind the following points about worksheet outlines:

- A worksheet can have only one outline. If you need to create more than one outline, move the data to a new worksheet.

- You can either create an outline manually or have Excel do it for you automatically. If you choose the latter option, you may need to do some preparation to get the worksheet in the proper format. You can read later in this chapter how to use both methods.

- You can create an outline for either all data on a worksheet or just a selected data range.

- You can remove an outline with a single command. (Read how in the upcoming section, "Removing an outline.") However, the data remains.

- You can hide the outline symbols (to free screen space) but retain the outline. I show you how in this chapter.

- An outline can have up to eight nested levels.

Worksheet outlines can be quite useful. If your main objective is to summarize a large amount of data, though, you may be better off using a pivot table. A pivot table is much more flexible and doesn't require that you create the subtotal formulas; it does the summarizing for you automatically. The ultimate solution depends upon your data source. If you're entering data from scratch, the most flexible approach is to enter it in a normalized table format, and create a pivot table.

Cross-Reference

I discuss pivot tables (and normalized data) in Chapters 34 and 35. ∎

Creating an Outline

This section describes the two ways to create an outline: automatically and manually. Before you create an outline, you need to ensure that data is appropriate for an outline and that the formulas are set up properly.

Preparing the data

What type of data is appropriate for an outline? Generally, the data should be arranged in a hierarchy, such as a budget that consists of an arrangement similar to the following:

> Company
> > Division
> > > Department
> > > > Budget Category
> > > > > Budget Item

In this case, each budget item (for example, airfare and hotel expenses) is part of a budget category (for example, travel expenses). Each department has its own budget, and the departments are rolled up into divisions. The divisions make up the company. This type of arrangement is well suited for a row outline.

Cross-Reference

The data arrangement suitable for an outline is essentially a summary table of your data. In some situations, your data will be "normalized" data — one data point per row. You can easily create a pivot table to summarize such data, and a pivot table is much more flexible than dealing with an outline. See Chapters 34 and 35 for more information on pivot tables. ■

After you create such an outline, you can view the information at any level of detail that you want by clicking the outline controls. When you need to create reports for different levels of management, consider using an outline. For example, upper management may want to see only the division totals. Division managers may want to see totals by department, and each department manager needs to see the full details for his or her department.

Keep in mind that using an outline isn't a security feature. The data that's hidden when an outline is collapsed can easily be revealed when the outline is expanded.

You can include time-based information that is rolled up into larger units (such as months and quarters) in a column outline. Column outlines work just like row outlines, however, and the levels need not be time based.

Before you create an outline, you need to make sure that all the summary formulas are entered correctly and consistently. In this context, *consistently* means that the formulas are in the same relative location. Generally, formulas that compute summary formulas (such as subtotals) are entered below the data to which they refer. In some cases, however, the summary formulas are entered above the referenced cells. Excel can handle either method, but you must be consistent throughout the range that you outline. If the summary formulas aren't consistent, automatic outlining won't produce the results that you want.

Note

If your summary formulas aren't consistent (that is, some are above and some are below the data), you still can create an outline, but you must do it manually. ■

Creating an outline automatically

Excel can create an outline for you automatically in a few seconds, whereas it may take you 10 minutes or more to do the same thing manually.

Note

If you have created a table for your data (Insert ➪ Tables ➪ Table), Excel can't create an outline automatically. You can create an outline from a table, but you must do so manually. ■

To have Excel create an outline, move the cell pointer anywhere within the range of data that you're outlining. Then, choose Data ➪ Outline ➪ Group ➪ Auto Outline. Excel analyzes the formulas in the range and creates the outline. Depending on the formulas that you have, Excel creates a row outline, a column outline, or both.

If the worksheet already has an outline, Excel asks whether you want to modify the existing outline. Click Yes to force Excel to remove the old outline and create a new one.

Note

Excel automatically creates an outline when you choose Data ➪ Outline ➪ Subtotal, which inserts subtotal formulas automatically. ■

Creating an outline manually

Usually, letting Excel create the outline is the best approach. It's much faster and less error prone. If the outline that Excel creates isn't what you have in mind, however, you can create an outline manually.

When Excel creates a row outline, the summary rows must all be below the data or all above the data: They can't be mixed. Similarly, for a column outline, the summary columns must all be to the right of the data or to the left of the data. If your worksheet doesn't meet these requirements, you have two choices:

- Rearrange the worksheet so that it does meet the requirements.
- Create the outline manually.

You also need to create an outline manually if the range doesn't contain any formulas. You may have imported a file and want to use an outline to display it better. Because Excel uses the positioning of the formulas to determine how to create the outline, it cannot make an outline without formulas.

Creating an outline manually consists of creating groups of rows (for row outlines) or groups of columns (for column outlines). To create a group of rows

1. **Click the row numbers for all the rows that you want to include in the group.**

Caution

Do not select the row that has the summary formulas. You don't want these rows to be included in the group. ■

2. **Choose Data ➪ Outline ➪ Group ➪ Group.** Excel displays outline symbols for the group.

3. **Repeat this process for each group that you want to create.** When you collapse the outline, Excel hides rows in the group, but the summary row, which isn't in the group, remains in view.

Note

If you select a range of cells (rather than entire rows or columns) before you create a group, Excel displays a dialog box asking what you want to group. It then groups entire rows or columns based on the range that you select. ∎

You can also select groups of groups to create multilevel outlines. When you create multilevel outlines, always start with the innermost groupings and then work your way out. If you realize that you grouped the wrong rows, you can ungroup the group by selecting the rows and choosing Data ➪ Outline ➪ Ungroup ➪ Ungroup.

Here are keyboard shortcuts you can use that speed up grouping and ungrouping:

- **Alt+Shift+right arrow:** Groups selected rows or columns
- **Alt+Shift+left arrow:** Ungroups selected rows or columns

Creating outlines manually can be confusing at first, but if you stick with it, you'll become a pro in no time.

Working with Outlines

This section discusses the basic operations that you can perform with a worksheet outline.

Displaying levels

To display various outline levels, click the appropriate outline symbol. These symbols consist of buttons with numbers on them (1, 2, and so on) or a plus sign (+) or a minus sign (−). Refer to Figure 26.5, which shows these symbols for a row and column outline.

Clicking the 1 button collapses the outline so that it displays no detail (just the highest summary level of information), clicking the 2 button expands the outline to show one level, and so on. The number of numbered buttons depends on the number of outline levels. Choosing a level number displays the detail for that level, plus any lower levels. To display all levels (the most detail), click the highest-level number.

You can expand a particular section by clicking its + button, or you can collapse a particular section by clicking its − button. In short, you have complete control over the details that Excel exposes or hides in an outline.

If you prefer, you can use the Hide Detail and Show Detail commands on the Data ➪ Outline group to hide and show details, respectively.

Tip

If you constantly adjust the outline to show different reports, consider using the Custom Views feature to save a particular view and give it a name. Then you can quickly switch among the named views. Choose View ➪ Workbook Views ➪ Custom Views. ∎

Adding data to an outline

You may need to add additional rows or columns to an outline. In some cases, you may be able to insert new rows or columns without disturbing the outline, and the new rows or columns become part of the outline. In other cases, you'll find that the new row or column is not part of the outline. If you create the outline automatically, choose Data ➪ Outline ➪ Group ➪ Auto Outline. Excel makes you verify that you want to modify the existing outline. If you create the outline manually, you need to make the adjustments manually, as well.

Removing an outline

After you no longer need an outline, you can remove it by choosing Data ➪ Outline ➪ Ungroup ➪ Clear Outline. Excel fully expands the outline by displaying all hidden rows and columns, and the outline symbols disappear. Be careful before you remove an outline, however. You can't make it reappear by using the Undo button. You must re-create the outline from scratch.

Hiding the outline symbols

The outline symbols Excel displays when an outline is present take up quite a bit of space. (The exact amount depends on the number levels.) If you want to see as much as possible onscreen, you can temporarily hide these symbols without removing the outline. Use Ctrl+8 to toggle the outline symbols on and off. When the outline symbols are hidden, you cannot expand or collapse the outline.

Note
When you hide the outline symbols, the outline still is in effect, and the worksheet displays the data at the current outline level. That is, some rows or columns may be hidden. ■

The Custom Views feature, which saves named views of your outline, also saves the status of the outline symbols as part of the view, enabling you to name some views with the outline symbols and other views without them.

CHAPTER 2

Linking and Consolidating Worksheets

I n this chapter, I discuss two procedures that you might find helpful: linking and consolidation. *Linking* is the process of using references to cells in external workbooks to get data into your worksheet. *Consolidation* combines or summarizes information from two or more worksheets (which can be in multiple workbooks).

Linking Workbooks

As you may know, Excel allows you to create formulas that contain references to other workbook files. In such a case, the workbooks are linked in such a way that one depends upon the other. The workbook that contains the external reference formulas is the *dependent* workbook (because it contains formulas that depend upon another workbook). The workbook that contains the information used in the external reference formula is the *source* workbook (because it's the source of the information).

When you consider linking workbooks, you may ask yourself the following question: If Workbook A needs to access data in another workbook (Workbook B), why not just enter the data into Workbook A in the first place? In some cases, you can. But the real value of linking becomes apparent when the source workbook is being continually updated by another person or group. Creating a link in Workbook A to Workbook B means that in Workbook A, you always have access to the most recent information in Workbook B because Workbook A is updated whenever Workbook B changes.

Linking workbooks also can be helpful if you need to consolidate different files. For example, each regional sales manager may store data in a separate workbook. You can create a summary workbook that first uses link formulas to retrieve specific data from each manager's workbook and then calculates totals across all regions.

Linking also is useful as a way to break up a large workbook into smaller files. You can create smaller workbooks that are linked with a few key external references.

Linking has its downside, however. External reference formulas are somewhat fragile, and accidentally severing the links that you create is relatively easy. You can prevent this mistake if you understand how linking works. Later in the chapter, I discuss some problems that may arise as well as how to avoid them. (See "Avoiding Potential Problems with External Reference Formulas.")

On the CD

The companion CD-ROM contains two linked files that you can use to get a feel for how linking works. The files are named `source.xlsx` and `dependent.xlsx`. As long as these files remain in the same folder, the links will be maintained. ∎

Creating External Reference Formulas

You can create an external reference formula by using several different techniques:

- **Type the cell references manually.** These references may be lengthy because they include workbook and sheet names (and, possibly, even drive and path information). The advantage of manually typing the cell references is that the source workbook doesn't have to be open. The disadvantage is that it's very error prone. Mistyping a single character makes the formula return an error (or possibly return a wrong value from the file).

- **Point to the cell references.** If the source workbook is open, you can use the standard pointing techniques to create formulas that use external references.

- **Paste the links.** Copy your data to the Clipboard. Then, with the source workbook open, choose Home ➪ Clipboard ➪ Paste ➪ Paste Link (N). Excel pastes the copied data as external reference formulas.

- **Choose Data ➪ Data Tools ➪ Consolidate.** For more on this method, see the section "Consolidating worksheets by using the Consolidate command," later in this chapter.

Understanding link formula syntax

The general syntax for an external reference formula is as follows:

```
=[WorkbookName]SheetName!CellAddress
```

Precede the cell address with the workbook name (in brackets), followed by the worksheet name and an exclamation point. Here's an example of a formula that uses cell A1 in the Sheet1 worksheet of a workbook named Budget:

```
=[Budget.xlsx]Sheet1!A1
```

If the workbook name or the sheet name in the reference includes one or more spaces, you must enclose the text in single quotation marks. For example, here's a formula that refers to cell A1 on Sheet1 in a workbook named Annual Budget.xlsx:

```
='[Annual Budget.xlsx]Sheet1'!A1
```

When a formula links to a different workbook, you don't need to open the other workbook. However, if the workbook is closed and not in the current folder, you must add the complete path to the reference. For example

```
='C:\Data\Excel\Budget\[Annual Budget.xlsx]Sheet1'!A1
```

Creating a link formula by pointing

Entering external reference formulas manually is usually not the best approach because you can easily make an error. Instead, have Excel build the formula for you, as follows:

1. **Open the source workbook.**
2. **Select the cell in the dependent workbook that will hold the formula.**
3. **Enter the formula.** When you get to the part that requires the external reference, activate the source workbook and select the cell or range and press Enter. If you're simply creating a link to a cell, just enter an equal sign (=) and then select the cell and press Enter.
4. **After you press Enter, return to the dependent workbook, where you can finish the formula.**

When you point to the cell or range, Excel automatically takes care of the details and creates a syntactically correct external reference. When using this method, the cell reference is always an absolute reference (such as $A$1). If you plan to copy the formula to create additional link formulas, you need to change the absolute reference to a relative reference by removing the dollar signs for the cell address.

As long as the source workbook remains open, the external reference doesn't include the path to the workbook. If you close the source workbook, however, the external reference formulas change to include the full path.

Pasting links

Pasting links provides another way to create external reference formulas. This method is applicable when you want to create formulas that simply reference other cells. Follow these steps:

1. **Open the source workbook.**
2. **Select the cell or range that you want to link and then copy it to the Clipboard.**
3. **Activate the dependent workbook and select the cell in which you want the link formula to appear.** If you're pasting a copied range, just select the upper-left cell.
4. **Choose Home ➪ Clipboard ➪ Paste ➪ Paste Link (N).**

Working with External Reference Formulas

This section discusses some key points that you need to know about when working with links. Understanding these details can help prevent some common errors.

Creating links to unsaved workbooks

Excel enables you to create link formulas to unsaved workbooks (and even to nonexistent workbooks). Assume that you have two workbooks open (Book1 and Book2), and you haven't saved either of them. If you create a link formula to Book1 in Book2 and then save Book2, Excel displays the confirmation dialog box shown in Figure 27.1.

Typically, you don't want to save a workbook that has links to an unsaved document. To avoid this prompt, save the source workbook first.

FIGURE 27.1

This confirmation message indicates that the workbook you're saving contains references to a workbook that you haven't yet saved.

You also can create links to documents that don't exist. You may want to do so if you'll be using a source workbook from a colleague, but the file hasn't yet arrived. When you enter an external reference formula that refers to a nonexistent workbook, Excel displays its Update Values dialog box, which resembles the Open dialog box. If you click Cancel, the formula retains the workbook name that you entered, but it returns a #REF! error.

When the source workbook becomes available, you can choose File ➪ Info ➪ Related Documents ➪ Edit Links to Files to update the link; see "Updating links," later in this chapter) After doing so, the error goes away, and the formula displays its proper value.

Opening a workbook with external reference formulas

When you open a workbook that contains links, Excel displays a dialog box (shown in Figure 27.2) that asks you what to do.

- **Update:** The links are updated with the current information in the source file(s).
- **Don't Update:** The links are not updated, and the workbook displays the previous values returned by the link formulas.
- **Help:** The Excel Help screen displays so you can read about links.

Security Warning for Links

Excel 2010 features a new security feature. The first time you open a workbook that contains links to other files, you see a security warning below the Ribbon. The links will not be updated unless you click the Enable Content button.

However, Excel remembers that you've deemed the workbook safe, so you won't see that Security Warning again. If you would like to disable these Security Warnings, use the External Content tab of the Trust Center dialog box and change the option for Security Settings for Workbook Links. To display this dialog box, choose File ➪ Options. Then click the Trust Center tab, and click the Trust Center Settings button.

What if you choose to update the links, but the source workbook is no longer available? If Excel can't locate a source workbook that's referred to in a link formula, it displays its Edit Links dialog box, shown in Figure 27.3. Click the Change Source button to specify a different workbook, or click the Break Link to destroy the link.

Note

You can also access the Edit Links dialog box by choosing File ➪ Info ➪ Related Documents ➪ Edit Links to Files. The dialog box that appears lists all source workbooks, plus other types of links to other documents. ■

FIGURE 27.2

Excel displays this dialog box when you open a workbook that contains links to other files.

FIGURE 27.3

The Edit Links dialog box.

Changing the startup prompt

When you open a workbook that contains one or more external reference formulas, Excel, by default, displays the dialog box (shown in Figure 27.2) that asks how you want to handle the links. You can eliminate this prompt by changing a setting in the Startup Prompt dialog box (see Figure 27.4).

To display the Startup Prompt dialog box, choose File ➪ Info ➪ Related Documents ➪ Edit Links to Files, which displays the Edit Links dialog box (refer to Figure 27.3). There, click the Startup Prompt button and then select the option that describes how you want to handle the links.

FIGURE 27.4

Use the Startup Prompt dialog box to specify how Excel handles links when the workbook is opened.

Updating links

If you want to ensure that your link formulas have the latest values from their source workbooks, you can force an update. For example, say that you just discovered that someone made changes to the source workbook and saved the latest version to your network server. In such a case, you may want to update the links to display the current data.

To update linked formulas with their current value, open the Edit Links dialog box (choose File ➪ Info ➪ Related Documents ➪ Edit Links to Files), choose the appropriate source workbook in the list, and then click the Update Values button. Excel updates the link formulas with the latest version of the source workbook.

Note

Excel always sets worksheet links to the Automatic Update option in the Edit Links dialog box, and you can't change them to Manual, which means that Excel updates the links only when you open the workbook. Excel doesn't automatically update links when the source file changes (unless the source workbook is open). ∎

Changing the link source

In some cases, you may need to change the source workbook for your external references. For example, say you have a worksheet that has links to a file named Preliminary Budget, but you later receive a finalized version named Final Budget.

You can change the link source using the Edit Links dialog box (choose File ➪ Info ➪ Related Documents ➪ Edit Links to Files). Select the source workbook that you want to change and click the Change Source button. Excel displays its Change Source dialog box, from which you can select a new source file. After you select the file, all external reference formulas that referred to the old file are updated.

Severing links

If you have external references in a workbook and then decide that you no longer need the links, you can convert the external reference formulas to values, thereby severing the links. To do so, access the Edit Links dialog box (choose File ➪ Info ➪ Related Documents ➪ Edit Links to Files), select the linked file in the list, and then click Break Link.

Caution

Excel prompts you to verify your intentions because you can't undo this operation. ∎

Avoiding Potential Problems with External Reference Formulas

Using external reference formulas can be quite useful, but the links may be unintentionally severed. As long as the source file hasn't been deleted, you can almost always re-establish lost links. If you open the workbook and Excel can't locate the file, you see a dialog box that enables you to specify the workbook and re-create the links. You also can change the source file by using the Change Source button in the Edit Links dialog box. The following sections discuss some pointers that you must remember when you use external reference formulas.

Renaming or moving a source workbook

If you rename the source document or move it to a different folder, Excel won't be able to update the links. You need to use the Edit Links dialog box and specify the new source document. See "Changing the link source," earlier in this chapter.

Note

If the source and dependent folder reside in the same folder, you can move both of the files to a different folder. In such a case, the links remain intact. ■

Using the Save As command

If both the source workbook and the dependent workbook are open, Excel doesn't display the full path to the source file in the external reference formulas. If you use the File ➪ Save As command to give the source workbook a new name, Excel modifies the external references to use the new workbook name. In some cases, this change may be what you want. But in other cases, it may not.

Here's an example of how using File ➪ Save As can cause a problem: You finished working on a source workbook and save the file. Then you decide to be safe and make a backup copy on a different drive, using File ➪ Save As. The formulas in the dependent workbook now refer to the backup copy, not the original source file. This is *not* what you want.

Bottom line? Be careful when you choose File ➪ Save As with a workbook that is the source of a link in another open workbook.

Modifying a source workbook

If you open a workbook that is a source workbook for another workbook, be extremely careful if the dependent workbook isn't open. For example, if you add a new row to the source workbook, the cells all move down one row. When you open the dependent workbook, it continues to use the old cell references — which is probably not what you want.

Note

It's easy to determine the source workbooks for a particular dependent workbook: Just examine the files listed in the Edit Links dialog box (choose File ➪ Info ➪ Related Documents ➪ Edit Links to Files). However, it's not possible to determine whether a particular workbook is used as the source for another workbook. ■

You can avoid this problem in the following ways:

- **Always open the dependent workbook(s) when you modify the source workbook.** If you do so, Excel adjusts the external references in the dependent workbook when you make changes to the source workbook.
- **Use names rather than cell references in your link formula.** This approach is the safest.

The following link formula refers to cell C21 on Sheet1 in the `budget.xlsx` workbook:

```
=[budget.xlsx]Sheet1!$C$21
```

If cell C21 is named *Total*, you can write the formula using that name:

```
=budget.xlsx!total
```

Using a name ensures that the link retrieves the correct value, even if you add or delete rows or columns from the source workbook.

Cross-Reference

See Chapter 4 for more information about creating names for cells and ranges. ■

Intermediary links

Excel doesn't place many limitations on the complexity of your network of external references. For example, Workbook A can contain external references that refer to Workbook B, which can contain an external reference that refers to Workbook C. In this case, a value in Workbook A can ultimately depend on a value in Workbook C. Workbook B is an *intermediary link.*

I don't recommend using intermediary links, but if you must use them, be aware that Excel doesn't update external reference formulas if the dependent workbook isn't open. In the preceding example, assume that Workbooks A and C are open. If you change a value in Workbook C, Workbook A won't reflect the change because you didn't open Workbook B (the intermediary link).

Consolidating Worksheets

The term *consolidation,* in the context of worksheets, refers to several operations that involve multiple worksheets or multiple workbook files. In some cases, consolidation involves creating link formulas. Here are two common examples of consolidation:

- The budget for each department in your company is stored in a single workbook, with a separate worksheet for each department. You need to consolidate the data and create a company-wide budget on a single sheet.
- Each department head submits a budget to you in a separate workbook file. Your job is to consolidate these files into a company-wide budget.

These types of tasks can be very difficult or quite easy. The task is easy if the information is laid out *exactly* the same in each worksheet. If the worksheets aren't laid out identically, they may be similar enough. In the second example, some budget files submitted to you may be missing categories that aren't used by a particular department. In this case, you can use a handy feature in Excel that matches data by using row and column titles. I discuss this feature in "Consolidating worksheets by using the Consolidate command," later in this chapter.

If the worksheets bear little or no resemblance to each other, your best bet may be to edit the sheets so that they correspond to one another. Better yet, return the files to the department heads and ask that they submit them using a standardized format.

You can use any of the following techniques to consolidate information from multiple workbooks:

- Use external reference formulas.
- Copy the data and choose Home ➪ Clipboard ➪ Paste ➪ Paste Link (N).
- Use the Consolidate dialog box, displayed by choosing Data ➪ Data Tools ➪ Consolidate.

Consolidating worksheets by using formulas

Consolidating with formulas simply involves creating formulas that use references to other worksheets or other workbooks. The primary advantages to using this method of consolidation are

- **Dynamic updating:** If the values in the source worksheets change, the formulas are updated automatically.
- **Open versus closed:** The source workbooks don't need to be open when you create the consolidation formulas.

If you're consolidating the worksheets in the same workbook and all the worksheets are laid out identically, the consolidation task is simple. You can just use standard formulas to create the consolidations. For example, to compute the total for cell A1 in worksheets named Sheet2 through Sheet10, enter the following formula:

```
=SUM(Sheet2:Sheet10!A1)
```

You can enter this formula manually or use the multisheet selection technique discussed in Chapter 4. You can then copy this formula to create summary formulas for other cells.

If the consolidation involves other workbooks, you can use external reference formulas to perform your consolidation. For example, if you want to add the values in cell A1 from Sheet1 in two workbooks (named Region1 and Region2), you can use the following formula:

```
=[Region1.xlsx]Sheet1!B2+[Region2.xlsx]Sheet1!B2
```

You can include any number of external references in this formula, up to the 8,000-character limit for a formula. However, if you use many external references, such a formula can be quite lengthy and confusing if you need to edit it.

If the worksheets that you're consolidating aren't laid out the same, you can still use formulas, but you need to ensure that each formula refers to the correct cell.

Consolidating worksheets by using Paste Special

Another method of consolidating information is to use the Paste Special dialog box. This technique takes advantage of the fact that the Paste Special dialog box can perform a mathematical operation when it pastes data from the Clipboard. For example, you can use the Add option to add the copied data to the selected range. Figure 27.5 shows the Paste Special dialog box.

This method is applicable only when all the worksheets that you're consolidating are open. The disadvantage is that the consolidation isn't dynamic. In other words, it doesn't generate formulas. So, if any data that was consolidated changes, the consolidation is no longer accurate.

FIGURE 27.5

Choosing the Add operation in the Paste Special dialog box.

Here's how to use this method:

1. **Copy the data from the first source range.**

2. **Activate the dependent workbook and select a location for the consolidated data.** A single cell is sufficient.

3. **Display the Paste Special dialog box (choose Home ⇨ Clipboard ⇨ Paste ⇨ Paste Special).**

4. **Choose the Values option and the Add operation, and then click OK.**

Repeat these steps for each source range that you want to consolidate. Make sure that the consolidation location in Step 2 is the same for each paste operation.

Caution

This method is probably the worst way of consolidating data. It can be rather error prone, and the lack of formulas means that you have no way to verify the accuracy of the data. ■

Consolidating worksheets by using the Consolidate command

For the ultimate in data consolidation, use the Consolidate dialog box. This method is very flexible, and in some cases, it even works if the source worksheets aren't laid out identically. This technique can create consolidations that are *static* (no link formulas) or *dynamic* (with link formulas). The Data Consolidate feature supports the following methods of consolidation:

- **By position:** This method is accurate only if the worksheets are laid out identically.

- **By category:** Excel uses row and column labels to match data in the source worksheets. Use this option if the data is laid out differently in the source worksheets or if some source worksheets are missing rows or columns.

Figure 27.6 shows the Consolidate dialog box, which appears when you choose Data ⇨ Data Tools ⇨ Consolidate. Following is a description of the controls in this dialog box:

FIGURE 27.6

The Consolidate dialog box enables you to specify ranges to consolidate.

- **Function drop-down list:** Specify the type of consolidation. Sum is the most commonly used consolidation function, but you also can select from ten other options.

- **Reference text box:** Specify a range from a source file that you want to consolidate. You can enter the range reference manually or use any standard pointing technique (if the workbook is open). Named ranges are also acceptable. After you enter the range in this box, click Add to add it to the All References list. If you consolidate by position, don't include labels in the range. If you consolidate by category, *do* include labels in the range.

- **All References list box:** Contains the list of references that you have added with the Add button.

- **Use Labels In check boxes:** Use to instruct Excel to perform the consolidation by examining the labels in the top row, the left column, or both positions. Use these options when you consolidate by category.

- **Create Links to Source Data check box:** When you select this option, Excel adds summary formulas for each label and creates an outline. If you don't select this option, the consolidation doesn't use formulas, and an outline isn't created.

- **Browse button:** Click to display a dialog box that enables you to select a workbook to open. It inserts the filename in the Reference box, but you have to supply the range reference. You'll find that your job is much easier if all the workbooks to be consolidated are open.

- **Add button:** Click to add the reference in the Reference box to the All References list. Make sure that you click this button after you specify each range.

- **Delete button:** Click to delete the selected reference from the All References list.

A workbook consolidation example

The simple example in this section demonstrates the power of the Data Consolidate feature. Figure 27.7 shows three single-sheet workbooks that will be consolidated. These worksheets report product sales for three months. Notice, however, that they don't all report on the same products. In addition, the products aren't even listed in the same order. In other words, these worksheets aren't laid out identically. Creating consolidation formulas manually would be a very tedious task.

FIGURE 27.7

Three worksheets to be consolidated.

On the CD

These workbooks are available on the companion CD-ROM. The files are named `region1.xlsx`, `region2.xlsx`, and `region3.xlsx`.

To consolidate this information, start with a new workbook. You don't need to open the source workbooks, but consolidation is easier if they are open. Follow these steps to consolidate the workbooks:

1. **Choose Data ⇨ Data Tools ⇨ Consolidate.** Excel displays its Consolidate dialog box.

2. **Use the Function drop-down list to select the type of consolidation summary that you want to use.** Use Sum for this example.

3. **Enter the reference for the first worksheet to consolidate.** If the workbook is open, you can point to the reference. If it's not open, click the Browse button to locate the file on disk. The reference must include a range. You can use a range that includes complete columns, such as A:K. This range is larger than the actual range to consolidate, but using this range ensures that the consolidation will still work if new rows and columns are added to the source file. When the reference in the Reference box is correct, click Add to add it to the All References list.

4. **Enter the reference for the second worksheet.** You can point to the range in the Region2 workbook, or you can simply edit the existing reference by changing Region1 to Region2 and then clicking Add. This reference is added to the All References list.

5. **Enter the reference for the third worksheet.** Again, you can edit the existing reference by changing Region2 to Region3 and then clicking Add. This final reference is added to the All References list.

6. **Because the worksheets aren't laid out the same, select the Left Column and the Top Row check boxes to force Excel to match the data by using the labels.**

7. **Select the Create Links to Source Data check box to make Excel create an outline with external references.**

8. **Click OK to begin the consolidation.**

Excel creates the consolidation, beginning at the active cell. Notice that Excel created an outline, which is collapsed to show only the subtotals for each product. If you expand the outline (by clicking the number 2 or the + symbols in the outline), you can see the details. Examine it further, and you discover that each detail cell is an external reference formula that uses the appropriate cell in the source file. Therefore, the consolidated results are updated automatically values are changed in any of the source workbooks.

Figure 27.8 shows the result of the consolidation, and Figure 27.9 shows the summary information (with the outline collapsed to hide the details).

Cross-Reference

For more information about Excel outlines, see Chapter 26. ∎

FIGURE 27.8

The result of consolidating the information in three workbooks.

	A	B	C	D	E	F
1			Jan	Feb	Mar	
2		Region2	5,344	5,211	5,526	
3	A-402		5,344	5,211	5,526	
4		Region3	3,453	3,478	3,301	
5	A-407		3,453	3,478	3,301	
6		Region1	1,000	1,094	1,202	
7		Region2	5,000	5,600	5,451	
8		Region3	3,000	3,246	3,224	
9	A-401		9,000	9,940	9,877	
10		Region1	1,188	1,324	1,236	
11	A-403		1,188	1,324	1,236	
12		Region1	1,212	1,002	1,018	
13		Region2	5,436	5,350	5,210	
14	A-404		6,648	6,352	6,228	
15		Region1	1,173	1,116	1,110	
16	A-409		1,173	1,116	1,110	
17		Region1	1,298	1,218	1,467	
18	A-412		1,298	1,218	1,467	
19		Region2	5,336	5,358	5,653	
20	A-408		5,336	5,358	5,653	
21		Region2	5,278	5,676	5,257	
22	A-490		5,278	5,676	5,257	
23		Region1	1,217	1,346	1,006	
24		Region2	5,497	5,266	5,611	
25	A-415		6,714	6,612	6,617	
26		Region1	1,285	1,054	1,298	
27	A-503		1,285	1,054	1,298	
28		Region1	1,192	1,408	1,010	

FIGURE 27.9

Collapsing the outline to show only the totals.

	A	B	C	D	E	F
1			Jan	Feb	Mar	
3	A-402		5,344	5,211	5,526	
5	A-407		3,453	3,478	3,301	
9	A-401		9,000	9,940	9,877	
11	A-403		1,188	1,324	1,236	
14	A-404		6,648	6,352	6,228	
16	A-409		1,173	1,116	1,110	
18	A-412		1,298	1,218	1,467	
20	A-408		5,336	5,358	5,653	
22	A-490		5,278	5,676	5,257	
25	A-415		6,714	6,612	6,617	
27	A-503		1,285	1,054	1,298	
29	A-511		1,192	1,408	1,010	
31	A-536		1,202	1,544	1,732	
33	A-502		5,626	5,517	5,564	
35	A-505		5,497	5,239	5,348	
37	A-515		5,374	5,337	5,443	
39	A-405		3,039	3,221	3,299	
41	A-406		3,282	3,255	3,263	
43	A-512		3,218	3,217	3,023	
45	A-514		3,177	3,024	3,011	
47	A-523		3,348	3,482	3,209	
49	A-533		3,327	3,252	3,447	
51	A-535		3,426	3,026	3,074	
52						

Refreshing a consolidation

When you choose the option to create formulas, the external references in the consolidation workbook are created only for data that exists at the time of the consolidation. Therefore, if new rows are added to any of the original workbooks, the consolidation must be re-done. Fortunately, the consolidation parameters are stored with the workbook, so it's a simple matter to re-run the consolidation if necessary. That's why specifying complete columns and including extra columns (in Step 3 in the preceding section) is a good idea.

Excel remembers the references that you entered in the Consolidate dialog box and saves them with the workbook. That way, if you want to refresh a consolidation, you won't have to re-enter the references. Just display the Consolidate dialog box, verify that the ranges are correct, and then click OK.

More about consolidation

Excel is very flexible regarding the sources that you can consolidate. You can consolidate data from the following:

- **Open workbooks**
- **Closed workbooks.** You need to enter the reference manually, but you can use the Browse button to get the filename part of the reference.
- **The same workbook in which you're creating the consolidation**

And, of course, you can mix and match any of the preceding choices in a single consolidation.

If you perform the consolidation by matching labels, be aware that the matches must be exact. For example, *Jan* doesn't match *January*. The matching is not case sensitive, however, so *April* does match *APRIL*. In addition, the labels can be in any order, and they don't need to be in the same order in all the source ranges.

If you don't select the Create Links to Source Data check box, Excel generates a static consolidation. (It doesn't create formulas.) Therefore, if the data on any of the source worksheets changes, the consolidation won't update automatically. To update the summary information, you need to choose Data ➪ Data Tools ➪ Consolidate again.

If you do select the Create Links to Source Data check box, Excel creates a standard worksheet outline that you can manipulate by using the techniques described in Chapter 26.

Excel and the Internet

M ost people who use a computer are connected to the Internet. The Web has become an important way to share and gather informa- tion from myriad sources. To help you with these tasks, Excel has the capability to create files that you can use on the Internet and also to gather and process data from the Web. This chapter covers topics related to Excel and the Internet.

Note
Four of the Office 2010 applications are available in online versions: Excel, Word, PowerPoint, and OneNote. You can run these applications from within your Web browser. The online version of Excel is not the topic of this chapter, and is not covered in this book. Rather, the chapter deals with Internet-related features for the standard version of Excel. ■

IN THIS CHAPTER

Saving Excel files in HTML format

Creating hyperlinks

Importing data from a Web page

Understanding How Excel Uses HTML

HTML (HyperText Markup Language) is the language of the World Wide Web. When you browse the Web, most documents that your browser retrieves and displays are in HTML format. An HTML file consists of text information plus special tags that describe how the text is to be formatted. The browser interprets the tags, applies the formatting, and displays the information.

Understanding the Different Web Formats

You can save an Excel workbook so that it's viewable in a Web browser. When you save an Excel workbook for viewing on the Web, you have two options:

- **An HTML file:** Produces a static Web page, plus a folder that contains support files. You can create the HTML file from the entire workbook or from a specific sheet.

- **A single file Web page:** Produces a MIME HTML file (*.mht; *.mhtml). Not all browsers can open these files.

These options are described in the following sections. Both examples use a simple two-sheet workbook file. Each sheet has a table and a chart. Figure 28.1 shows one of these worksheets.

Keep in mind that these files are intended to be only displayed by a Web browser. They are *not* interactive files. In other words, the user cannot make any changes while viewing the file.

FIGURE 28.1

This workbook will be saved in Excel Web formats.

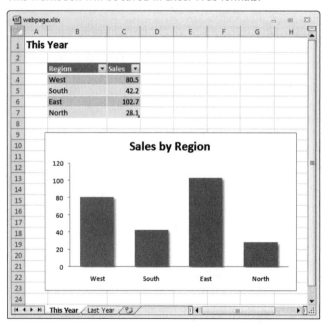

On the CD

This workbook, named webpage.xlsx, is available on the companion CD-ROM. ■

Creating an HTML file

To save a workbook as an HTML file:

1. **(Optional but recommended) Save the workbook as a normal Excel file.**
2. **Choose File ⇨ Save As to display the Save As dialog box.**
3. **Select Web Page (*.htm; *.html) from the Save as Type drop-down list.**
4. **Specify what to save (either Entire Workbook or the active sheet).**
5. **Specify a filename and then choose a location for the file.**
6. **Click Save to create the HTML file.** Excel may display a message warning you that some features in the workbook are not compatible with the Web page format. You can just ignore this message.

Caution

Although Excel can open the HTML files that it creates, essential information is lost. For example, formulas are lost, and charts appear as static graphic images. Therefore, if you might need to make changes later on, make sure you keep a copy of your work in a standard Excel file format. ■

Figure 28.2 shows how Sheet1 of the example file looks in a browser: Firefox, in this case. Notice that the workbook's sheet tabs appear along the bottom, and you can switch sheets just like you do in Excel.

In addition to the `webpage1.htm` file, Excel also created a folder named `webpage1_files`. This folder contains additional files that must be kept with the main HTML file. Therefore, if you post such a file on a Web server, don't forget to also post the accompanying directory.

Creating a single file Web page

In the previous section, I discuss how creating an HTML file with Excel also creates a folder of additional files. The procedure for creating a Web page that uses a single file is exactly the same, except for Step 3. In Step 3, select Single File Web Page (*.mht; *.mhtml) from the Save as Type drop-down list.

Figure 28.3 shows the example file displayed in Internet Explorer.

Caution

As I mention previously, not all browsers can open single-file MHTM files. Two that can are Microsoft Internet Explorer (IE) and Opera. Other browsers (such as Firefox and Google Chrome) may require an add-on to display these files. ■

FIGURE 28.2

Viewing the HTML file in a browser.

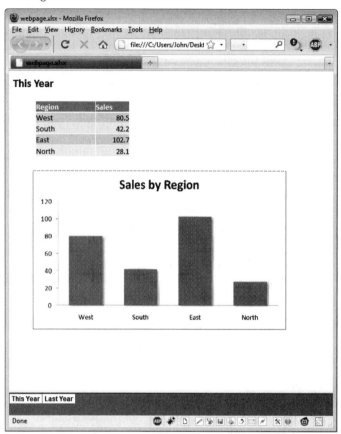

Web Options

If you save your work in HTML format, you should be aware of some additional options. In the Save As dialog box, click Tools and then choose Web Options to display the Web Options dialog box. From this dialog box you can control some aspects of the HTML file, such as target browser version (Internet Explorer only), target monitor resolution, and fonts. Most of the time, the default settings work just fine. However, if you plan to save Excel files in HTML format, familiarizing yourself with the options available is worthwhile. These options are described in the Help system.

FIGURE 28.3

Viewing the single file Web page in Internet Explorer.

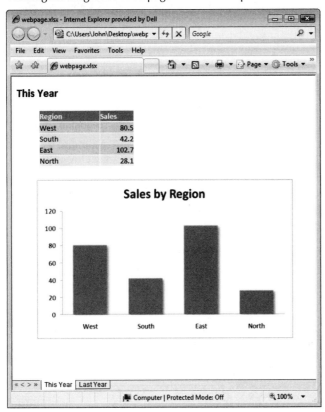

Opening an HTML File

Excel can open most HTML files, which can be stored on your local drive or on a Web server. Choose File ➪ Open and locate the HTML file. If the file is on a Web server, you'll need to copy the URL and paste it into the File Name field in the Open dialog box.

How the HTML code renders in Excel varies considerably. Sometimes, the HTML file may look exactly as it does in a browser. Other times, it may bear little resemblance, especially if the HTML file uses Cascading Style Sheets (CSS) for layout.

After opening an HTML file, you can work with the information using the normal Excel tools.

Another way to open an HTML file from a Web server is to use a Web query, which is discussed later in this chapter (see "Using Web Queries").

Working with Hyperlinks

A *hyperlink* is clickable text that provides a quick way to jump to other workbooks and files. You can set up hyperlinks to display files on your own computer, your network, and the Web. For example, you can create a series of hyperlinks to serve as a table of contents for a workbook. Or, you can insert a hyperlink that displays a Web page in the default Web browser.

Inserting a hyperlink

You can create hyperlinks from cell text or graphic objects, such as shapes and pictures. To create a text hyperlink in a cell, select the cell and choose Insert ➪ Links ➪ Hyperlink (or press Ctrl+K). Excel responds with the Insert Hyperlink dialog box, as shown in Figure 28.4.

FIGURE 28.4

Use the Insert Hyperlink dialog box to add hyperlinks to your Excel worksheets.

Select an icon in the Link To column that represents the type of hyperlink you want to create. You can create hyperlinks to a file on your hard drive, a Web page on the Internet, a new document, or a location in your current workbook. In addition, you can create a hyperlink that consists of an e-mail address. Then, specify the location of the file that you want to link to. The dialog box changes, depending upon the icon selected. If you like, click the ScreenTip button to provide some additional text that appears as a mouse-hover–activated ToolTip. Click OK, and Excel creates the hyperlink in the active cell.

Figure 28.5 shows a worksheet with hyperlinks that function as a table of contents for a workbook. Clicking a link activates a worksheet in the workbook. The example also shows an e-mail address that when clicked, activates the default e-mail program.

The appearance of hyperlinks in cells is controlled by two styles in the Style Gallery. The Hyperlink style controls the appearance of hyperlinks that haven't been clicked, and the Followed Hyperlink style controls the appearance of "visited" hyperlinks. To change the appearance of your hyperlinks, modify either or both of those styles. See Chapter 6 for information about using and modifying document styles.

To add a hyperlink to a Shape, select the Shape and then choose Insert ➪ Links ➪ Hyperlink (or, press Ctrl+K). Specify the required information in the Insert Hyperlink dialog box, as outlined earlier in this section. (Read more about Shapes in Chapter 22.)

FIGURE 28.5

Hyperlinks in a workbook.

	A	B	C
1			
2		**Workbook Contents**	
3		Click a hyperlink to activate a regional worksheet	
4			
5		Region 1	
6		Region 2	
7		Region 3	
8		Region 4	
9		Region 5	
10			
11		*Created by Mark J. Smith*	
12		mjsmith@xyzcorp.com	
13			

Using hyperlinks

When you hover your mouse pointer over a cell that contains a hyperlink, the mouse pointer turns into a hand. Click the hyperlink, and you're taken to the hyperlinked document.

Tip
To select a cell that has a hyperlink with your mouse (without following the hyperlink), position your mouse over the cell, click, and hold for a second or two before you release the mouse button. Or just activate a nearby cell and use the navigation keys to select the cell that contains the hyperlink. ∎

When you hover your pointer over a Shape that contains a hyperlink, the mouse pointer turns into a hand. To follow a hyperlink from a Shape, just point to the Shape and click.

If the hyperlink contains an e-mail address, your default e-mail program launches so that you can send an e-mail to the address specified when you created the hyperlink.

Using Web Queries

Excel enables you to pull in data contained in an HTML file by performing a Web query. The data is transferred to a worksheet, where you can manipulate it any way you like. Web queries are especially useful for data that is frequently updated, such as stock market quotes.

The term "Web Query" is a bit misleading. You can perform a Web Query on a local HTML file, a file stored on a network server, or a file stored on a Web server on the Internet. To retrieve information from a Web server, you must be connected to the Internet. After the information is retrieved, an Internet connection is not required to work with the information (unless you need to refresh the query).

Note
Performing a Web query doesn't actually open the HTML file in Excel. Rather, it copies the information from the HTML file. ∎

The best part about a Web query is that Excel remembers where the data came from. Therefore, after you create a Web query, you can *refresh* the query to pull in the most recent data.

To create a Web query

1. **Choose Data ⇨ Get External Data ⇨ From Web.** Excel displays the New Web Query dialog box, shown in Figure 28.6. This dialog box is actually a resizable dialog box that functions as a Web browser.

2. **Click links to navigate, or just type the URL of the HTML file in the Address field.** The HTML file can be on the Internet, on a corporate intranet, or on a local or network drive. Each table in the document is indicated by an arrow in a yellow box.

3. **Click an arrow to select the table or tables you want to import.**

4. **You can also control how the imported data is formatted. In the New Web Query dialog box, click Options (upper right) to display the Web Query Options dialog box. Select the desired formatting and then click OK to return to the New Web Query dialog box.**

5. **When you're ready to retrieve the information, click Import.**

6. **In the Import Data dialog box that opens, choose where you want to place the data.** The information on the Web page is retrieved and placed on your worksheet.

After you create your Web query, you have some options. Right-click any cell in the data range and choose Data Range Properties from the shortcut menu. Excel displays the External Data Range Properties dialog box, shown in Figure 28.7. These settings control when the data is refreshed, how it is formatted, and what happens if the amount of data changes when the query is refreshed.

To force a refresh at any time, right-click any cell in the data range and choose Refresh. The data in your worksheet is replaced by the latest of content of the Web page.

FIGURE 28.6

Use the New Web Query dialog box to specify the source of the data.

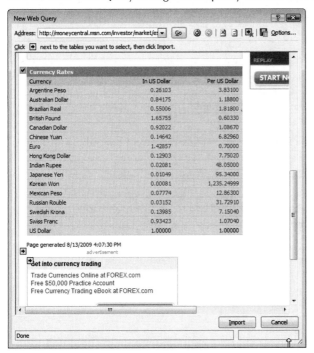

FIGURE 28.7

Use the External Data Range Properties dialog box to specify how Excel handles the imported data.

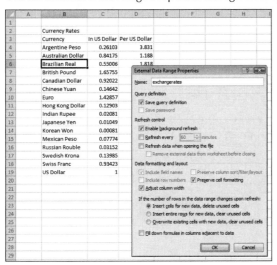

Other Internet-Related Features

Excel offers a few other Internet-related features, which I briefly describe here. Access these features from the Share tab of Backstage View (choose File ➪ Share). Figure 28.8 shows the Share options:

- **Send Using E-Mail:** Enables you to send the active workbook to one or more recipients via e-mail. The file can be the actual workbook, a PDF file, or an XPS file. If the workbook is saved to a shared location, you can send a link to the file (rather than the actual file). An additional option lets you fax the workbook (assuming that your system has a fax service provider).

- **Save to SkyDrive:** If you have a SkyDrive account, you can save the workbook to a folder on the Internet, where it can be accessed by others. *SkyDrive* is a free service offered by Microsoft (part of Windows Live). Go to www.windowslive.com for details.

- **Save to SharePoint:** Publish the workbook to your SharePoint server. A *SharePoint server* is a central location where files can be shared and worked on in collaborative manner. Check with your system administrator to see whether you have access to a SharePoint server.

- **Publish to Excel Services:** Excel Services also requires a SharePoint server.

FIGURE 28.8

The Share tab of Backstage View.

Sharing Data with Other Office Applications

T he applications in Microsoft Office are designed to work together. These programs have a common look and feel, and sharing data among these applications is usually quite easy.

Excel can import and export a variety of different file types. Besides sharing data using files, you can also transfer data to and from other open Windows applications in several other ways:

- Copy and paste, using either the Windows Clipboard or the Office Clipboard. Copying and pasting information creates a static copy of the data.

- Create a link so that subsequent changes in the source data will be reflected in the destination document.

- Embed an entire object from one application into another application's document.

This chapter explores some ways in which you can make use of other applications while working with Excel, as well as some ways in which you can use Excel while working with other applications.

IN THIS CHAPTER

Understanding data sharing

Pasting and linking data

Embedding objects in a worksheet

Embedding a workbook in a Word document

Copying and Pasting

Copying information from one Windows application to another is quite easy. The application that contains the information that you're copying is the *source application,* and the application to which you're copying the information is the *destination application.*

Here are the general steps that are required to copy from one application to another:

1. **Activate the source document window that contains the information that you want to copy.**

2. **Select the information, using the mouse or the keyboard.**

3. **If the source application is a Microsoft Office 2010 application, choose Home ➪ Clipboard ➪ Copy.** Most other applications have an Edit ➪ Copy menu command. In most cases, pressing Ctrl+C works as well. The selection is copied to the Clipboard.

Tip

You also can choose Home ➪ Clipboard ➪ Cut (or Edit ➪ Cut) from the source application menu. This step deletes your selection from the source application after placing the selection on the Clipboard. ■

4. **Activate the destination application.** If the program isn't running, you can usually start it without affecting the contents of the Clipboard.

5. **Move to the appropriate position in the destination application (where you want to paste the copied material).**

6. **If the destination application is a Microsoft Office 2010 application, choose Home ➪ Clipboard ➪ Paste.** Most other applications have an Edit ➪ Paste command, and you can usually use Ctrl+V to paste. If the Clipboard contents aren't appropriate for pasting, the Paste command is disabled. You can sometimes select other paste options by choosing Home ➪ Clipboard ➪ Paste (or Edit ➪ Paste Special).

Note

If you repeat Step 3 in any Office application, the Office Clipboard task pane appears automatically. If it doesn't appear, click the dialog launcher in the Home ➪ Clipboard group. Use the Options button at the bottom of the Office Clipboard to control when this task pane appears. ■

Two Clipboards

If you copy or cut information while working in a Microsoft Office application, the application places the copied information on both the Windows Clipboard *and* the Office Clipboard. After you copy information to the Windows Clipboard, it remains on the Windows Clipboard even after you paste it so that you can use it multiple times.

Because the Windows Clipboard can hold only one item at a time, when you copy or cut something else, the information previously stored on the Windows Clipboard is replaced. The Office Clipboard, unlike the Windows Clipboard, can hold up to 24 separate selections. The Office Clipboard operates in all Office applications; for example, you can copy two selections from Word and three from Excel and paste any or all of them in PowerPoint.

Cross-Reference

See Chapter 4 for more information about the Office Clipboard. ■

Copying from Excel to Word

One of the most frequently used software combinations is a spreadsheet and a word processor. This section describes some of the ways to copy information from an Excel worksheet to a Word document. Although I talk about Word here, most of the information in this section also applies to PowerPoint.

Generally speaking, you can copy something from Excel and paste it into Word in one of two ways:

- **As static information:** If the Excel data changes, the changes aren't reflected in the Word document.
- **As a link:** If the Excel data changes, the changes are shown in the Word document.

You can find all the various paste options for Word in the Paste drop-down list of Word's Home Clipboard group. In addition, various paste options are available from the Paste Special dialog box, which appears when you choose Home ➪ Clipboard ➪ Paste ➪ Paste Special.

Note

If you use Word's standard paste command (Home ➪ Clipboard ➪ Paste, or Ctrl+V), you'll find that the paste method varies, depending on what is pasted. An Excel range copied and pasted to Word is pasted as a static table. An Excel chart, on the other hand, is pasted as a link. ■

Pasting static information

Often, you don't need a link when you copy data from Excel to Word. For example, if you're preparing a report in your word processor and you simply want to include a range of data from an Excel worksheet, you probably don't need to create a link (unless the data in the Excel worksheet may be changed).

After you've copied an Excel range, activate Word and choose Home ➪ Clipboard ➪ Paste, or press Ctrl+V. The range appears as a Word table and is not linked to the Excel workbook.

New Feature

When you paste information from Excel into a Word document, Word 2010 displays a Paste Options Smart Tag, shown in Figure 29.1. This lets you choose a formatting option for the pasted information. ■

A Paste Options Smart Tag appears when you paste Excel 2010 data into a Word 2010 document.

For more control over pasting, use Home ➪ Clipboard ➪ Paste ➪ Paste Special, which displays the Paste Special dialog box (see Figure 29.2).

The Paste Special dialog box in Word.

Notice the two option buttons: Paste and Paste Link. If you select one of the choices in the Paste Special dialog box with the Paste option selected, the data is pasted without creating a link.

The paste options in Word's Paste Special dialog box when a range is copied include

- **Microsoft Excel Worksheet Object:** You can edit this object with Excel. Double-click, and the Word Ribbon is replaced with the Excel Ribbon. See "Embedding an Excel range in a Word document," later in this chapter.

- **Formatted Text (RTF):** The range is pasted as a table, with some formatting retained.

- **Unformatted Text:** Only the raw information is pasted, with no formatting. Cells are separated with a Tab character.

- **Picture (Windows Metafile):** The range is pasted as a picture.

- **Bitmap:** The range is pasted as a picture.

- **Picture (Enhanced Metafile):** The range is pasted as a picture.

- **HTML Format:** The range is pasted as a table, with all formatting retained. This format is pasted when you choose Home ➪ Clipboard ➪ Paste.

- **Unformatted Unicode Text:** Only the raw information is pasted, with no formatting. Cells are separated with a Tab character.

If you've copied an Excel chart to the Clipboard, Word's Paste Special dialog box displays different options. Figure 29.3 shows the Paste Special dialog box when an Excel chart is copied. The options are

- **Microsoft Excel Chart Object:** You can edit this object with Excel. Double-click, and the Word Ribbon is replaced with the Excel Ribbon.

- **Picture (Windows Metafile):** The chart is pasted as a picture.

- **Bitmap:** The chart is pasted as bitmap image.

- **Picture (Enhanced Metafile):** The chart is pasted as a picture.

- **Picture (GIF):** The chart is pasted as a GIF image.

- **Picture (PNG):** The chart is pasted as a PNG (Portable Network Graphics) image.

- **Picture (JPEG):** The chart is pasted as a JPEG image, which usually results in a fuzzy image.

- **Microsoft Office Graphic Object:** The image is linked to the Excel range, and you can also edit it in Word. This format is pasted when you choose Home ➪ Clipboard ➪ Paste.

FIGURE 29.3

Word paste options when an Excel chart is on the Clipboard.

Pasting a link

If the Excel data that you're copying will change, you may want to paste a link. Use the Paste Link option in the Paste Special dialog box.

When would you want to use this technique? If you generate proposals using Word, for example, you may need to refer to pricing information that you store in an Excel worksheet. If you set up a link between your Word document and the Excel worksheet, you can be sure that your proposals always quote the latest prices.

The link is a one-way link. You cannot make changes to the linked Excel worksheet in Word.

If you paste the data by using the Paste Link option in the Paste Special dialog box, you can make changes to the source document, and those changes appear in the destination application. You can test these changes by displaying both applications onscreen, making changes to the source document, and watching for them to appear in the destination document.

Caution
You can break links rather easily. For example, if you move the source document to another directory or save it under a different name, the destination document's application can't update the link. In such a case, you need to re-establish the link manually (described later in this section). ■

Figure 29.4 shows the Word Paste Special dialog box when an Excel range has been copied and the Paste Link option is specified. Note that, with one exception, these options are the same ones available when you select the Paste option. The only format that isn't available for pasting a link is Picture (Enhanced Metafile).

FIGURE 29.4

The Word paste link options for an Excel range.

When an Excel chart is on the Clipboard, you can also choose the Paste Link option from Word's Paste Special dialog box.

Note

When you paste an Excel chart to Word using the Microsoft Office Graphic Object option, only the chart's data is linked. All other modifications (such as formatting or changing the chart type) aren't reflected in the copy pasted in the Word document. When you activate the chart in Word, you can use the Chart Tools contextual menu to make changes to the chart. ■

To edit (or break) a link, activate Word and choose File ➪ Info ➪ Edit Links To Files, which displays the Links dialog box shown in Figure 29.5. Select the file from the Source File list and then click the Break Link button. After breaking a link, the data remains in the destination document, but it's no longer linked to the source document.

If the link has been broken (for example, the source file was moved or renamed), use the Change Source button to specify the source file and re-establish the link.

If the link isn't showing updated information from the source file, you can force an update by using the Update Now button.

Use Word's Links dialog box to modify or break links.

Embedding Objects in a Worksheet

Using *Object Linking and Embedding* (OLE), you can also embed an object to share information between Windows applications. This technique enables you to insert an object from another program and use that program's editing tools to manipulate it. The OLE objects can be such items as

- Text documents from other products, such as word processors
- Drawings or pictures from other products
- Information from special OLE server applications, such as Microsoft Equation
- Sound files
- Video or animation files

Many (but certainly not all) Windows applications support OLE. Embedding is often used for a document that you will distribute to others. It can eliminate the need to send multiple document files and help avoid broken link problems.

To embed an object into an Excel workbook, choose Insert ➪ Text ➪ Object, which displays the Object dialog box. This dialog box has two tabs: one for creating a new object and one for creating an object from an existing file.

Embedding Word documents

To embed an empty Word document into an Excel worksheet, choose Insert ➪ Text ➪ Object in Excel. In the Object dialog box, click the Create New tab and then select Microsoft Office Word Document from the Object type list.

The result is a blank Word document, activated and ready for you to enter text. Notice that Word's Ribbon replaces Excel's Ribbon, giving you access to all of Word's features.

To embed a copy of an existing Word file, click the Create from File tab in the Object dialog box and then locate the file on your hard drive. The Word document is inserted into your Excel worksheet. Double-click the document to display the Word Ribbon.

Embedding other types of documents

You can embed many other types of objects, including audio clips, video clips, MIDI sequences, and even an entire Microsoft PowerPoint presentation.

Figure 29.6 shows an MP3 audio file embedded in a worksheet. Clicking the object plays the song on the default MP3 player.

FIGURE 29.6

An MP3 file embedded in a worksheet.

Tip

Some of the object types listed in the Object dialog box can result in quite useful and interesting items when inserted into an Excel worksheet. If you're not sure what an object type is, try adding the object to a blank Excel workbook to see what is available. Keep in mind that not all the objects listed in this dialog box actually work with Excel. Attempting to use some of them may even crash Excel. ■

Embedding an Excel Workbook in a Word Document

You can embed an Excel workbook in a Word document in three ways:

- Copy a range and use Word's Paste Special dialog box.
- Open an existing Excel file using Word's Object dialog box.
- Create a new Excel workbook using Word's Object dialog box.

The following sections cover these methods.

Embedding a workbook in Word by copying

The example in this section describes how to embed an Excel workbook (shown in Figure 29.7) in a Word document.

FIGURE 29.7

This workbook will be embedded in a Word document.

	A	B	C	D
1				
2				
3	Region	Manager	ID	
4	Region 1	Logan Tipton	L12172	
5	Region 2	David D. Hill	D13168	
6	Region 3	Rene Martin	R1139	
7	Region 4	Janet Crane	J1169	
8	Region 5	Albert Thomas	A13124	
9	Region 6	Angel K. Bluhm	A1424	
10	Region 7	Carol P. Barger	C15118	
11	Region 8	Cassie Jones	C1287	
12	Region 9	Lori V. Moore	L1315	
13	Region 10	Jeffrey P. Moore	J1688	
14	Region 11	Beverly Glenn	B1360	
15	Region 12	Henry Baker	H1117	
16				
17				

To start, select A3:C15 and copy the range to the Clipboard. Then activate (or start) Word, open the document in which you want to embed the range, and move the insertion point to the location in the document where you want the table to appear. Choose Word's Home ➪ Clipboard ➪ Paste ➪ Paste Special command. Select the Paste option (not the Paste Link option) and then choose the Microsoft Excel Worksheet Object format. Click OK, and the range appears in the Word document. Although it appears that only the range is embedded, the entire Excel workbook is actually embedded.

If you double-click the embedded object, you notice that Word's Ribbon is replaced by the Excel Ribbon. In addition, the embedded object appears with Excel's familiar row and column borders. In other words, you can edit this object *in place* by using Excel's commands. Figure 29.8 shows the Word document after double-clicking the embedded Excel workbook. To return to Word, just click anywhere in the Word document.

FIGURE 29.8

Double-clicking the embedded Excel object enables you to edit it in place. Note that Word now displays Excel's Ribbon.

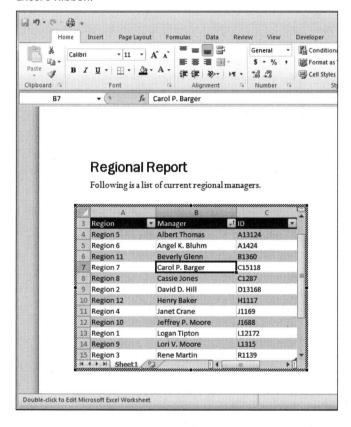

Caution

Remember that no link is involved here. If you make changes to the embedded object in Word, these changes don't appear in the original Excel worksheet. Because the embedded object is a copy of the original workbook, it is completely independent from the original source. ∎

You may have noticed that Microsoft Excel Worksheet Object also appears in the Paste Special dialog box when you select the Paste Link option. If you paste the range using this option, the workbook isn't embedded in the Word document. When you double-click the object, Excel is activated so that you can edit the workbook.

Embedding a saved workbook in Word

Another way to embed an Excel workbook in a Word document is to choose Insert ➪ Text ➪ Object in Word, which displays the Object dialog box. Select the Create from File tab, click Browse and locate the Excel document. When you click OK, a copy of the workbook is embedded in the document. No link is created.

Note

If you select the Link to File check box in the Object dialog box, you create a link to the workbook. In such a case, double-clicking the object in Word activates Excel so that you can edit the workbook. ■

Creating a new Excel object in Word

The preceding examples embed an existing workbook into a Word document. This section demonstrates how to create a new (empty) Excel object in Word, which is useful if you're creating a report and need to insert a table of values. If those values aren't available in an existing Excel workbook, you can embed a new Excel object and type them.

Tip

You could insert a normal Word table, but you can take advantage of Excel's formulas and functions in an embedded Excel worksheet. ■

To create a new Excel object in a Word document, choose Insert ➪ Text ➪ Object in Word. Word responds with the Object dialog box. Click the Create New tab, and you see a list of the types of objects that you can create. Select Microsoft Office Excel Worksheet from the list and then click OK.

Word inserts an empty Excel worksheet object into the document and activates it for you. Again, you have full access to the Excel Ribbon, so you can enter whatever you want into the worksheet object. After you finish, click anywhere in the Word document. You can double-click this object at any time to make changes or additions.

You can change the size of the object while it's activated by dragging any of the sizing handles (the little black squares and rectangles) that appear on the borders of the object.

Using Excel in a Workgroup

Most people who use a computer in an office connect to others via a network. In fact, networks are also common in homes. By enabling users to easily share data (and peripheral devices), networks make it much easier for you to work together with several people on projects. Excel has a number of features that facilitate this type of cooperation, and those features are the subject of this chapter.

Note

If you're working on a corporate network, you may need to consult with your network administrator before using any of the features described in this chapter. ■

IN THIS CHAPTER

Using Excel on a network

Understanding file reservations

Using shared workbooks

Tracking changes in a workbook

Using Excel on a Network

A computer *network* consists of two or more PCs that are linked electronically. You can perform these tasks on a network:

- Access files on other systems.
- Share files with other users.
- Share resources, such as printers, scanners, and fax modems.
- Communicate with each other electronically.

Excel has tools that enable you to work cooperatively with other Excel users on a project.

Understanding File Reservations

Networks provide you with the ability to share information stored on other computer systems. Sharing files on a network has two major advantages:

- It eliminates the need to have multiple copies of a file stored locally on user PCs.

- It ensures that the file is always up to date. For example, a group of users can work on a single document, as opposed to everyone working on his or her own document and then merging them.

Note

Some networks — generally known as client-server networks — designate specific computers as file servers. On these types of networks, the shared data files are typically stored on the file server. Excel doesn't care whether you're working on a client-server or a peer-to-peer network (where all the PCs have essentially equal functions). ■

Some software applications are *multiuser applications*. Most database software applications, for example, enable multiple users to work simultaneously on the same database files. One user may be updating customer records in the database, while another is extracting information for a report. But what if two users attempt to change a particular customer record at the same time? Multiuser database software contains record-locking safeguards that ensure that only one user at a time can modify a particular record.

Excel, however, is *not* a multiuser application. When you open an Excel file, the entire file is loaded into memory. If the file is accessible to other users, you wouldn't want someone else to change the stored copy of a file that you've opened. If Excel allowed you to open and change a file that someone else on a network had already opened, the following scenario could happen.

Assume that your company keeps its sales information in an Excel file that is stored on a network server. Esther wants to add this week's data to the file, so she loads it from the server and begins adding new information. A few minutes later, Jim loads the file to correct some errors that he noticed last week. Esther finishes her work and saves the file. Later, Jim finishes his corrections and saves the file. Jim's file overwrites the copy that Esther saved, and her additions are gone.

This scenario *can't happen* because Excel uses a concept known as *file reservation*. When Esther opens the sales workbook, she has the reservation for the file. When Jim tries to open the file, Excel informs him that Esther is using the file. If he insists on opening it, Excel opens the file as *read-only*. In other words, Jim can open the file, but he can't save it with the same name.

Figure 30.1 shows the message that appears if you try to open a file that is in use by someone else.

FIGURE 30.1

The File in Use dialog box appears if you try to open a file that someone else is using.

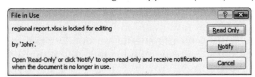

The File in Use dialog box has three choices:

- **Click Cancel, wait a while, and try again.** You may call the person who has the file reservation and ask when the file will be available.

- **Click Read Only.** Open the file to read it, but you cannot save changes to the same filename.

- **Click Notify.** This opens the file as read-only. Excel later pops up a message that notifies you when the person who has the file reservation is finished using the file.

Figure 30.2 shows the message that appears when the file is available. If you open the file as Read-Write, you receive another message if you makes any changes to this read-only version. You will have an opportunity to discard your changes or to save his file with a new name.

FIGURE 30.2

The File Now Available dialog box pops up with a new message when the file is available for editing.

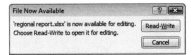

Sharing Workbooks

Although Excel isn't a true multiuser application, it does support a feature known as *shared workbooks,* which enables multiple users to work on the same workbook simultaneously. Excel keeps track of the changes and provides appropriate prompts to handle conflicts.

Caution

Although the ability to share workbooks sounds great in theory, it can be confusing if more than a few users are sharing a single workbook. Also, be warned that this feature has been known to cause problems, and it's certainly not 100-percent reliable. Therefore, use caution and make frequent backup copies of your workbooks. ∎

Understanding shared workbooks

You can share any Excel workbook with any number of users. Here are a few examples of workbooks that work well as shared workbooks:

- **Project tracking:** You may have a workbook that contains status information for projects. If multiple people are involved in the project, they can make changes and updates to the parts that are relevant to them.

- **Customer lists:** With a customer list, records are often added, deleted, and modified by multiple users.

- **Consolidations:** You may create a budget workbook in which each department manager is responsible for his or her department's budget. Usually, each department's budget appears on a separate worksheet, with one sheet serving as the consolidation sheet.

If you plan to designate a workbook as shared, be aware that Excel imposes quite a few restrictions on the workbook. For example, a shared workbook cannot contain tables (created with Insert ⇨ Tables ⇨ Table).

In addition, you can't perform any of the following actions while sharing the workbook. You can tell that these actions are not allowed because the relevant commands are disabled on the Ribbon.

- Delete worksheets or chart sheets.

- Insert or delete a blocks of cells. However, you can insert or delete entire rows and columns.

- Merge cells.

- Define or apply conditional formats.

- Change or delete array formulas.

- Set up or change data validation restrictions and messages.

- Insert or change charts, pictures, drawings, objects, or hyperlinks.

- Assign or modify a password to protect individual worksheets or the entire workbook.

- Create or modify pivot tables, scenarios, outlines, or data tables.

- Insert automatic subtotals.

- Write, change, view, record, or assign macros. However, you can record a macro while a shared workbook is active as long as you store the macro in another unshared workbook (such as your Personal Macro Workbook).

Tip

You may want to choose Review ⇨ Protect Sheet to further control what users can do while working in a shared workbook. ∎

Caution

If you save an Excel 2010 shared workbook to an earlier version file format (such as *.xls), sharing is turned off, and the revision history (if any) is lost. ∎

Designating a workbook as a shared workbook

To designate a workbook as a shared workbook, choose Review ➪ Changes ➪ Share Workbook. Excel displays the Share Workbook dialog box, shown in Figure 30.3. This dialog box has two tabs: Editing and Advanced. On the Editing tab, select the Allow Changes check box to allow changes by multiple users and then click OK. Excel then prompts you to save the workbook.

When you open a shared workbook, the workbook window's title bar displays [Shared]. If you no longer want other users to be able to use the workbook, remove the check mark from the Editing tab of the Share Workbook dialog box and save the workbook.

Tip

Whenever you're working with a shared workbook, you can find out whether any other users are working on the workbook. Choose Review ➪ Changes ➪ Share Workbook, and the Editing tab of the Share Workbook dialog box lists the names of the other users who have the file open, as well as the time that each user opened the workbook. ∎

FIGURE 30.3

Use the Share Workbook dialog box to control the sharing of your workbooks.

Sharing a Workbook with Yourself

If you plan to use shared workbooks, spend time experimenting with the various settings to ensure that you understand how sharing works. You don't need to enlist a colleague to help you — you can share a workbook with yourself. Just launch a second instance of Excel and then open a shared workbook in both instances. Make changes, save the file, adjust the settings, and so on. Before long, you'll have a good understanding of Excel's shared workbooks.

Controlling the advanced sharing settings

Excel enables you to set options for shared workbooks. Choose Review ➪ Changes ➪ Share Workbook and click the Advanced tab of the Share Workbook dialog box to access these options (see Figure 30.4).

FIGURE 30.4

Use the Advanced tab of the Share Workbook dialog box to set the advanced sharing options for your workbook.

Tracking changes

Excel can keep track of the workbook's changes: its *change history*. When you designate a work-book as a shared workbook, Excel automatically turns on the Change History option, enabling you to view information about previous (and perhaps conflicting) changes to the workbook. You can turn off change history by selecting the Don't Keep Change History button. You can also specify the number of days for which Excel tracks change history.

Updating changes

While you're working on a shared workbook, you can choose File ➪ Save to update the workbook with your changes. The Update Changes settings determine what happens when you save a shared workbook:

- **When File Is Saved:** You receive updates from other users when you save your copy of the shared workbook.

- **Automatically Every:** Lets you specify a time period for receiving updates from other users of the workbook. You can also specify whether Excel should save your changes automatically, too, or just show you the changes made by other users.

Resolving conflicting changes between users

As you may expect, multiple users working on the same file can result in some conflicts. For example, assume that you're working on a shared customer information workbook, and another user also has the workbook open. If you and the other user both make a change to the same cell, a conflict occurs. You can specify the manner in which Excel resolves the conflicts by selecting one of two options from the Advanced tab of the Share Workbook dialog box:

- **Ask Me Which Changes Win:** If you select this option, Excel displays a dialog box to let you determine how to settle the conflict.

- **The Changes Being Saved Win:** If you select this option, the most recently saved version always takes precedence.

Caution
The second option, The Changes Being Saved Win, has slightly deceptive wording. Even if the other user saves his changes, any changes you make will automatically override his changes when you save the workbook. This option may result in a loss of data because you won't have any warning that you've overwritten another user's changes. ■

Controlling the Include in Personal View settings

The final section of the Advanced tab of the Share Workbook dialog box enables you to specify settings that are specific to your view of the shared workbook. You can choose to use your own print settings and your own data-filtering settings. If you don't enable these check boxes, you can't save your own print and filter settings.

Tracking Workbook Changes

Excel has a feature that enables you to track changes made to a workbook. You may want to use this feature if you send a workbook to someone for reviewing. When the file is returned, you can see what changes were made and then accept or reject them accordingly.

Turning Track Changes on and off

To enable change tracking, choose Review ➪ Changes ➪ Track Changes ➪ Highlight Changes, which displays the Highlight Changes dialog box, shown in Figure 30.5. Then select the Track Changes While Editing check box.

FIGURE 30.5

Use the Highlight Changes dialog box to track changes made to a workbook.

You can also specify the period to track (When), which users to track (Who), and specify a range of cells to track (Where). If you enable the Highlight Changes on Screen option, each changed cell displays a small triangle in its upper-left corner. And when a changed cell is selected, you see a cell comment that describes what change was made (see Figure 30.6).

After you select the option(s) that you want, click OK to close the Highlight Changes dialog box and enable tracking. To stop tracking changes, choose Review ➪ Changes ➪ Track Changes ➪ Highlight Changes again, and then clear the Track Changes While Editing check box.

Caution

When tracking changes is enabled, the workbook always becomes a shared workbook, which severely limits the types of changes you can make. Shared workbooks are discussed earlier in this chapter (see "Sharing Workbooks"). ■

FIGURE 30.6

Excel displays a descriptive note when you select a cell that has changed.

	A	B	C	D	E	F	G
1		January					
2	Region 1	32,874					
3	Region 2	87,109					
4	Region 3	109,344	, 8/16/2009 9:40 AM: Changed cell B4 from '109,433.00' to '109,344.00'.				
5							
6							
7							
8							
9							
10							
11							
12							
13							
14							
15							

Keep in mind the following when using the Track Changes feature:

- Changes made to cell contents are tracked, but other changes (such as formatting changes) aren't tracked.

- The change history is kept only for a set interval. When you turn on Track Changes, changes are kept for 30 days. You can increase or decrease the number of days of history to keep in from Highlight Changes dialog box (use the When setting).

- If you would like to generate a list of the changes made, choose Review ➪ Changes ➪ Track Changes ➪ Highlight Changes and then enable the List Changes on a New Sheet check box. Click OK, and Excel inserts a new worksheet named History. This sheet shows detailed information about each change made.

- Only one level of changes is maintained. Thus, if you change the value of a cell several times, only the most recent change is remembered.

Reviewing the changes

To review the changes made while using the Track Changes features, choose Review ➪ Changes ➪ Track Changes ➪ Accept/Reject Changes. The Select Changes to Accept or Reject dialog box appears, enabling you to select the types of changes that you want to review. This dialog box is similar to the Highlight Changes dialog box. You can specify When, Who, and Where.

Click OK, and Excel displays each change in a new dialog box, as shown in Figure 30.7. You then click Accept to accept the change or click Reject to reject the change. You can also click Accept All (to accept all changes) or Reject All (to reject all changes).

FIGURE 30.7

The Accept or Reject Changes dialog box displays information about each cell that was changed.

Protecting Your Work

IN THIS CHAPTER

Protecting worksheets

Protecting workbooks

Protecting Visual Basic Projects

Other related topics

T he concept of "protection" gets a lot of attention in the Excel news-groups and forums. It seems that many users want to learn how to protect their workbooks from being copied or modified. Excel has several protection-related features, and those features are covered in this chapter.

Types of Protection

Excel's protection-related features fall into three categories:

- **Worksheet protection:** Protecting a worksheet from being modi-fied, or restricting the modifications to certain users

- **Workbook protection:** Protecting a workbook from having sheets inserted or deleted, and also requiring the use of password to open the workbook

- **Visual Basic (VB) protection:** Using a password to prevent others from viewing or modifying your VBA code

Caution

Before I discuss these features, you should understand the notion of security. Using a password to protect some aspect of your work doesn't guarantee that it's secure. Password-cracking utilities (and some simple tricks) have been around for a long time. Using passwords work in the vast majority of cases, but if someone is truly intent on getting to your data, he or she can usually find a way. If absolute security is critical, perhaps Excel isn't the proper tool. ∎

About Information Rights Management

Excel supports an Information Rights Management (IRM) feature, which allows you to specify access permissions for workbooks. Using IRM may help prevent sensitive information from being printed, e-mailed, or copied by unauthorized people. When IRM is applied to a workbook, the permission information is stored in the document file itself.

To use IRM, you must install the Microsoft Windows Rights Management Services (RMS) — an extra-cost product that isn't included with Microsoft Office. You can access the IRM settings by choosing File ➪ Info ➪ Protect Workbooks ➪ Restrict Permission By People.

IRM is not covered in this book. If your company uses RMS, consult your system administrator for more information about how this feature is used within your organization.

Protecting a Worksheet

You may want to protect a worksheet for a variety of reasons. One reason is to prevent yourself or others from accidentally deleting formulas or other critical data. A common scenario is to protect a worksheet so that the data can be changed, but the formulas can't be changed.

To protect a worksheet, activate the worksheet and choose Review ➪ Changes ➪ Protect Sheet. Excel displays the Protect Sheet dialog box shown in Figure 31.1. Note that providing a password is optional. If you enter a password, that password will be required to unprotect the worksheet. If you accept the default options in the Protect Sheet dialog box (and if you haven't unlocked any cells), none of the cells on the worksheet can be modified.

To unprotect a protected sheet, choose Review ➪ Changes ➪ Unprotect Sheet. If the sheet was protected with a password, you're prompted to enter that password.

FIGURE 31.1

Use the Protect Sheet dialog box to protect a worksheet.

Unlocking cells

In many cases, you will want to allow *some* cells to be changed when the worksheet is protected. For example, your worksheet may have some input cells that are used by formula cells. In such a case, you would want the user to be able to change the input cells, but not the formula cells. Every cell has a Locked attribute, and that attribute determines whether the cell can be changed when the sheet is protected.

By default, all cells are locked. To change the locked attribute, select the cell or range, right-click, and choose Format Cells from the shortcut menu (or press Ctrl+1). The Protection tab of the Format Cells dialog box opens (see Figure 31.2); clear the Locked check box and then click OK.

FIGURE 31.2

Use the Protection tab in the Format Cells dialog box to change the Locked attribute of a cell or range.

Note

The Protection tab of the Format Cells dialog box has another attribute: Hidden. If this check box is selected, the contents of the cell don't appear in the Formula bar when the sheet is protected. The cell isn't hidden in the worksheet. You may want to set the Hidden attribute for formula cells to prevent users from seeing the formula when the cell is selected. ■

After you unlock the desired cells, choose Review ➪ Changes ➪ Protect Sheet to protect the sheet. After doing so, you can change the unlocked cells, but if you attempt to change a locked cell, Excel displays the warning alert shown in Figure 31.3.

FIGURE 31.3

Excel warns you if you attempt to change a locked cell.

Sheet protection options

The Protect Sheet dialog box has several options, which determine what the user can do when the worksheet is protected.

- **Select Locked Cells:** If checked, the user can select locked cells using the mouse or the keyboard. This setting is enabled by default.
- **Select Unlocked Cells:** If checked, the user can select unlocked cells using the mouse or the keyboard. This setting is enabled by default.
- **Format Cells:** If checked, the user can apply formatting to locked cells.
- **Format Columns:** If checked, the user can hide or change the width of columns.
- **Format Rows:** If checked, the user can hide or change the height of rows.
- **Insert Columns:** If checked, the user can insert new columns.
- **Insert Rows:** If checked, the user can insert new rows.
- **Insert Hyperlinks:** If checked, the user can insert hyperlinks (even in locked cells).
- **Delete Columns:** If checked, the user can delete columns.
- **Delete Rows:** If checked, the user can delete rows.
- **Sort:** If checked, the user can sort data in a range as long as the range doesn't contain any locked cells.
- **Use AutoFilter:** If checked, the user can use existing autofiltering.
- **Use PivotTable Reports:** If checked, the user can change the layout of pivot tables or create new pivot tables.
- **Edit Objects:** If checked, the user can make changes to objects (such as Shapes) and charts, as well as insert or delete comments.
- **Edit Scenarios:** If checked, the user can use scenarios (see Chapter 36).

Tip

When the worksheet is protected and the Select Unlocked Cells option is set, pressing Tab moves to the next unlocked cell, making data entry much easier. ■

Assigning user permissions

Excel also offers the ability to assign user-level permissions to different areas on a protected worksheet. You can specify which users can edit a particular range while the worksheet is protected. As an option, you can require a password to make changes.

This feature is rarely used, and the setup procedure is rather complicated. But if you need this level of protection, setting it up might be worth the effort.

1. **Unprotect the worksheet if it's protected.**
2. **Choose Review ⇨ Changes ⇨ Allow Users to Edit Ranges.** The dialog box shown in Figure 31.4 opens.
3. **Follow the prompts in the series of dialog boxes that follow.**
4. **Protect the sheet.**

FIGURE 31.4

The Allow Users to Edit Ranges dialog box.

Protecting a Workbook

Excel provides three ways to protect a workbook:

- Require a password to open the workbook.
- Prevent users from adding sheets, deleting sheets, hiding sheets, and unhiding sheets.
- Prevent users from changing the size or position of windows.

I discuss each of these methods in the sections that follow.

Requiring a password to open a workbook

Excel lets you save a workbook with a password. After doing so, whoever tries to open the workbook must enter the password.

To add a password to a workbook, follow these steps:

1. **Choose File ⇨ Info ⇨ Protect Workbook ⇨ Encrypt With Password.** Excel displays the Encrypt Document dialog box shown in Figure 31.5.

2. **Type a password and click OK.**

3. **Type the password again and click OK.**

4. **Save the workbook.**

FIGURE 31.5

Specify a workbook password in the Encrypt Document dialog box.

Note

You need to perform these steps only one time. You don't need to specify the password every time you resave the workbook. ■

To remove a password from a workbook, repeat the same procedure. In Step 2, however, delete the existing password symbols from the Encrypt Document dialog box, click OK, and save your workbook.

Figure 31.6 shows the Password dialog box that appears when you try to open a file saved with a password.

FIGURE 31.6

Opening this workbook requires a password.

Excel provides another way to add a password to a document:

1. **Choose File ⇨ Save As.**

2. **In the Save As dialog box, click the Tools button and choose General Options.** Excel displays the General Options dialog box.

3. **In the General Options dialog box, enter a password in the Password to Open field.**

4. **Click OK.** You're asked to re-enter the password before you return to the Save As dialog box.

5. **In the Save As dialog box, make sure that the filename, location, and type are correct; then click Save.**

Note

The General Options dialog box has another password field: Password to Modify. If you specify a password for this field, the file opens in read-only mode (it can't be saved under the same name) unless the user knows the password. If you use the Read-Only Recommended check box without a password, Excel suggests that the file be opened in read-only mode, but the user can override this suggestion. ■

Protecting a workbook's structure

To prevent others (or yourself) from performing certain actions in a workbook, you can protect the workbook's structure. When a workbook's structure is protected, the user may not

- Add a sheet.
- Delete a sheet.
- Hide a sheet.
- Unhide a sheet.
- Rename a sheet.
- Move a sheet.

To protect a worksheet's structure

1. **Choose Review ⇨ Changes ⇨ Protect Workbook to display the Protect Workbook dialog box (see Figure 31.7).**

2. **In the Protect Workbook dialog box, select the Structure check box.**

3. **(Optional) Enter a password.**

4. **Click OK.**

To unprotect the workbook's structure, choose Review ⇨ Changes ⇨ Unprotect Workbook. If the workbook's structure was protected with a password, you are prompted to enter the password.

FIGURE 31.7

The Protect Workbook dialog box.

Protecting a workbook's windows

To prevent others (or yourself) from changing the size or position of a workbook's windows, you can protect the workbook's windows:

1. **Choose Review ⇨ Changes ⇨ Protect Workbook.**
2. **In the Protect Workbook dialog box, select the Windows check box.**
3. **(Optional) Enter a password.**
4. **Click OK.**

When a workbook's windows are protected, the user can't change anything related to the window size or position. For example, if the workbook window is maximized when the windows are protected, the user cannot unmaximize the window. The windows can, however, be zoomed.

To unprotect the workbook's windows, choose Review ⇨ Changes ⇨ Unprotect Workbook. If the workbook's windows were protected with a password, you are prompted to enter the password.

VB Project Protection

If your workbook contains any VBA macros, you may want to protect the VB Project to prevent others from viewing or modifying your macros. Another reason to protect a VB Project is to prevent its components from being expanded in the VB Editor Project window (which can avoid clutter while you're working on other VB project). To protect a VB Project

1. **Press Alt+F11 to activate the VB Editor.**
2. **Select your project in the Projects window.**
3. **Choose Tools - xxxx Properties (where xxxx corresponds to your Project name).** Excel displays the Project Properties dialog box.
4. **In the Project Properties dialog box, click the Protection tab (see Figure 31.8).**
5. **Select the Lock Project for Viewing check box.**

6. **Enter a password (twice).**

7. **Click OK and then save your file.** When the file is closed and then re-opened, a password will be required to view or modify the VBA code.

Protecting a VB Project with a password.

Cross-Reference
Part VI discusses VBA macros. ■

Related Topics

This section covers additional topics related to protecting and distributing your work.

Saving a worksheet as a PDF file

The PDF (Portable Document Format) file format is widely used as a way to present information in a read-only manner, with precise control over the layout. Software to display PDF files is available from a number of sources. Excel can create PDF files, but it cannot open them.

XPS is another "electronic paper" format, developed by Microsoft as an alternative to the PDF format. At this time, there is very little third-party support for the XPS format.

Save a worksheet in PDF or XPS format by choosing File ➪ Save and Send ➪ Create PDF/XPS Document ➪ Create a PDF/XPS. Excel displays its Publish as PDF Or XPS dialog box, in which you can specify a filename and location and set some other options.

Note

Only the active sheet is saved. If your workbook has multiple sheets, you must save each sheet to a separate PDF or XPS file. ■

Marking a workbook final

Excel lets you mark a document as "final." This action makes two changes to the workbook:

- It makes the workbook read-only so that the file can't be saved using the same name.
- It makes the workbook view-only so that nothing may be changed. When you open a finalized document, you see a message below the Ribbon. You can override its "final" status by clicking the Edit Anyway button.

To finalize a workbook, choose File ➪ Info ➪ Protect Workbook ➪ Mark as Final. Excel displays a dialog box in which you can confirm your choice.

Caution

Marking a document as final is not a security measure. Anyone who opens the workbook can cancel the mark as final designation. Therefore, this method doesn't guarantee that others will not change the workbook. ■

Inspecting a workbook

If you plan to distribute a workbook to others, you may want to have Excel check the file for hidden data and personal information. This tool can locate hidden information about you, your organization, or about the workbook. In some situations, you may not want to share this information with others.

To inspect a workbook, choose File ➪ Info ➪ Check for Issues ➪ Inspect Document. The Document Inspector dialog box opens, as shown in Figure 31.9. Click Inspect, and Excel displays the results of the inspection and gives you the opportunity to remove the items it finds.

Caution

If Excel identifies items in the Document Inspector, it doesn't necessarily mean that they should be removed. In other words, you should not blindly use the Remove All buttons to remove the items that Excel locates. For example, you may have a hidden sheet that serves a critical purpose. Excel will identify that hidden sheet and make it very easy for you to delete it. To be on the safe side, always make a backup copy of your workbook before running the Document Inspector. ■

Using a digital signature

Excel lets you add a *digital signature* to a workbook. Using a digital signature is somewhat analogous to signing a paper document. A digital signature helps to assure the authenticity of the workbook and also ensures that the content hasn't been modified since it was signed.

The Document Inspector dialog box identifies hidden and personal information in a workbook.

After you sign a workbook, the signature is valid until you make changes and resave the file.

Getting a digital ID

To digitally sign a workbook, you must obtain a certificate from a certified authority who is able to verify the authenticity of your signature. Prices vary, depending on the certificate granting company.

Another option is to create your own digital ID, but others will not be able to verify the authenticity. Creating your own digital ID is useful if you want to ensure that no one tampers with one of your signed workbooks.

Signing a workbook

Excel supports two types of digital signatures: a visible signature and an invisible signature.

To add a visible digital signature, choose Insert ➪ Text ➪ Signature Line ➪ Microsoft Office Signature Line. Excel displays its Signature Setup dialog box, and you're prompted for the information for the signature. After you add the signature box, double-click it to display the Sign dialog box, where you actually sign the document either by typing your name or uploading a scanned image of your signature.

Figure 31.10 shows a document with a visible digital signature.

FIGURE 31.10

This document has a digital signature.

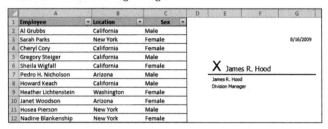

To add an invisible digital signature, choose File ⇨ Info ⇨ Protect ⇨ Add a Digital Signature. If the signed workbook is changed in any way, the digital signature is invalidated.

Making Your Worksheets Error-Free

I t goes without saying that you want your Excel worksheets to produce accurate results. Unfortunately, it's not always easy to be certain that the results are correct — especially if you deal with large, complex worksheets. This chapter introduces the tools and techniques available to help identify, correct, and prevent errors.

Finding and Correcting Formula Errors

Making a change in a worksheet — even a relatively minor change — may produce a ripple effect that introduces errors in other cells. For example, accidentally entering a value into a cell that previously held a formula is all too easy to do. This simple error can have a major impact on other formulas, and you may not discover the problem until long after you make the change — or you may never discover the problem.

Formula errors tend to fall into one of the following general categories:

- **Syntax errors:** You have a problem with the syntax of a formula. For example, a formula may have mismatched parentheses, or a function may not have the correct number of arguments.

- **Logical errors:** A formula doesn't return an error, but it contains a logical flaw that causes it to return an incorrect result.

- **Incorrect reference errors:** The logic of the formula is correct, but the formula uses an incorrect cell reference. As a simple example, the range reference in a Sum formula may not include all the data that you want to sum.

IN THIS CHAPTER

How to identify and correct common formula errors

Using Excel auditing tools

Using formula AutoCorrect

Tracing cell relationships

Checking spelling and related features

- **Semantic errors:** An example is a function name that is spelled incorrectly. Excel will attempt to interpret it as a name and will display the #NAME? error.

- **Circular references:** A circular reference occurs when a formula refers to its own cell, either directly or indirectly. Circular references are useful in a few cases, but most of the time, a circular reference indicates a problem.

- **Array formula entry error:** When entering (or editing) an Array formula, you must press Ctrl+Shift+Enter to enter the formula. If you fail to do so, Excel doesn't recognize the formula as an Array formula, and you may get an error or incorrect results.

- **Incomplete calculation errors:** The formulas simply aren't calculated fully. Microsoft has acknowledged some problems with Excel's calculation engine in some versions of Excel. To ensure that your formulas are fully calculated, press Ctrl+Alt+Shift+F9.

Syntax errors are usually the easiest to identify and correct. In most cases, you'll know when your formula contains a syntax error. For example, Excel won't permit you to enter a formula with mismatched parentheses. Other syntax errors also usually result in an error display in the cell.

The following sections describe common formula problems and offers advice on identifying and correcting them.

Mismatched parentheses

In a formula, every left parenthesis must have a corresponding right parenthesis. If your formula has mismatched parentheses, Excel usually won't permit you to enter it. An exception to this rule involves a simple formula that uses a function. For example, if you enter the following formula (which is missing a closing parenthesis), Excel accepts the formula and provides the missing parenthesis.

```
=SUM(A1:A500
```

A formula may have an equal number of left and right parentheses, but the parentheses may not match properly. For example, consider the following formula, which converts a text string such that the first character is uppercase and the remaining characters are lowercase. This formula has five pairs of parentheses, and they match properly.

```
=UPPER(LEFT(A1))&RIGHT(LOWER(A1),LEN(A1)-1)
```

The following formula also has five pairs of parentheses, but they are mismatched. The result displays a syntactically correct formula that simply returns the wrong result.

```
=UPPER(LEFT(A1)&RIGHT(LOWER(A1),LEN(A1)-1))
```

Often, parentheses that are in the wrong location will result in a *syntax error,* which is usually a message that tells you that you entered too many or too few arguments for a function.

Using Formula AutoCorrect

When you enter a formula that has a syntax error, Excel attempts to determine the problem and offers a suggested correction. The accompanying figure shows an example of a proposed correction.

Be careful when accepting corrections for your formulas from Excel because it doesn't always guess correctly. For example, I entered the following formula (which has mismatched parentheses):

=AVERAGE(SUM(A1:A12,SUM(B1:B12))

Excel then proposed the following correction to the formula:

=AVERAGE(SUM(A1:A12,SUM(B1:B12)))

You may be tempted to accept the suggestion without even thinking. In this case, the proposed formula is syntactically correct — but not what I intended. The correct formula is

=AVERAGE(SUM(A1:A12),SUM(B1:B12))

Tip

Excel can help you out with mismatched parentheses. When you're editing a formula and you move the cursor over a parenthesis, Excel displays it (and its matching parenthesis) in bold for about one-half second. In addition, Excel color codes pairs of nested parentheses while you are editing a formula. ∎

Cells are filled with hash marks

A cell is filled with a series of hash marks (#) for one of two reasons:

- The column is not wide enough to accommodate the formatted numeric value. To correct it, you can make the column wider or use a different number format (see Chapter 24).

- The cell contains a formula that returns an invalid date or time. For example, Excel doesn't support dates prior to 1900 or the use of negative time values. A formula that returns either of these values results in a cell filled with hash marks. Widening the column won't fix it.

Blank cells are not blank

Some Excel users have discovered that by pressing the spacebar, the contents of a cell seem to erase. Actually, pressing the spacebar inserts an invisible space character, which isn't the same as erasing the cell.

For example, the following formula returns the number of nonempty cells in range A1:A10. If you "erase" any of these cells by using the spacebar, these cells are included in the count, and the formula returns an incorrect result.

```
=COUNTA(A1:A10)
```

If your formula doesn't ignore blank cells the way that it should, check to make sure that the blank cells are really blank cells. Here's how to search for cells that contain only blank characters:

1. **Press Ctrl+F to display the Find and Replace dialog box.**
2. **Click the Options button to expand the dialog box so it displays additional options.**
3. **In the Find What box, enter * *.** That's an asterisk, followed by a space, and followed by another asterisk.
4. **Make sure the Match Entire Cell Contents check box is selected.**
5. **Click Find All.** If any cells that contain only space characters are found, Excel will list the cell address at the bottom of the Find and Replace dialog box.

Extra space characters

If you have formulas or use procedures that rely on comparing text, be careful that your text doesn't contain additional space characters. Adding an extra space character is particularly common when data has been imported from another source.

Excel automatically removes trailing spaces from values that you enter, but trailing spaces in text entries are not deleted. It's impossible to tell just by looking at a cell whether it contains one or more trailing space characters.

The TRIM function removes leading spaces, trailing spaces, and multiple spaces within a text string. Figure 32.1 shows some text in column A. The formula in B1, which was copied down the column is

```
=TRIM(A1)=A1
```

This formula returns FALSE if the text in column A contains leading spaces, trailing spaces, or multiple spaces. In this case, the word *Dog* in cell A3 contains a trailing space.

FIGURE 32.1

Using a formula to identify cells that contain extra space characters.

	A	B	C	D
1	Monkey	TRUE		
2	Rat	TRUE		
3	Dog	FALSE		
4	Elephant	TRUE		
5	Zebra	TRUE		
6				
7				

Tracing Error Values

Often, an error in one cell is the result of an error in a precedent cell. For help in identifying the cell causing an error value to appear, activate the cell that contains the error and then choose Formulas ⇨ Formula Auditing ⇨ Error Checking ⇨ Trace Error. Excel draws arrows to indicate which cell is the source of the error. After you identify the error, choose Formulas ⇨ Formula Auditing ⇨ Remove Arrows to get rid of the arrow display.

Formulas returning an error

A formula may return any of the following error values:

- #DIV/0!
- #N/A
- #NAME?
- #NULL!
- #NUM!
- #REF!
- #VALUE!

The following sections summarize possible problems that may cause these errors.

Tip

Excel allows you to choose how error values are printed. To access this feature, display the Page Setup dialog box and click the Sheet tab. You can choose to print error values as displayed (the default), or as blank cells, dashes, or #N/A. To display the Page Setup dialog box, click the dialog box launcher of the Page Layout ⇨ Page Setup group. ■

#DIV/0! errors

Division by zero is not a valid operation. If you create a formula that attempts to divide by zero, Excel displays its familiar #DIV/0! error value.

Because Excel considers a blank cell to be zero, you also get this error if your formula divides by a missing value. This problem is common when you create formulas for data that you haven't entered yet, as shown in Figure 32.2. The formula in cell D2, which was copied to the cells below it, is

```
=(C2-B2)/C2
```

FIGURE 32.2

#DIV/0! errors occur when the data in column C is missing.

	A	B	C	D	E	F
1	Month	Last Year	This Year	Change		
2	January	87,093	74,023	-17.7%		
3	February	86,166	72,997	-18.0%		
4	March	86,426	73,522	-17.6%		
5	April	86,062	76,597	-12.4%		
6	May	87,427	77,753	-12.4%		
7	June	88,152		#DIV/0!		
8	July	87,920		#DIV/0!		
9	August	85,078		#DIV/0!		
10	September	82,994		#DIV/0!		
11	October	84,679		#DIV/0!		
12	November	85,626		#DIV/0!		
13	December	83,304		#DIV/0!		
14						

This formula calculates the percent change between the values in columns B and C. Data isn't available for months beyond May, so the formula returns a #DIV/0! error.

To avoid the error display, you can use an IF function to check for a blank cell in column C:

```
= IF(C2=0,"",(C2-B2)/C2)
```

This formula displays an empty string if cell C2 is blank or contains 0; otherwise, it displays the calculated value.

Another approach is to use an IFERROR function to check for *any* error condition. The following formula, for example, displays an empty string if the formula results in any type of error:

```
=IFERROR((C2-B2)/C2,"")
```

Note

The IFERROR function was introduced in Excel 2007. For compatibility with previous versions, use this formula:

```
=IF(ISERROR((C2-B2)/C2),"",(C2-B2)/C2)
```

#N/A errors

The #N/A error occurs if any cell referenced by a formula displays #N/A.

Note

Some users like to use =NA() or #N/A explicitly for missing data. This method makes it perfectly clear that the data is not available and hasn't been deleted accidentally. ■

The #N/A error also occurs when a LOOKUP function (HLOOKUP, LOOKUP, MATCH, or VLOOKUP) can't find a match.

#NAME? errors

The #NAME? error occurs under these conditions:

- The formula contains an undefined range or cell name.

- The formula contains text that Excel *interprets* as an undefined name. A misspelled function name, for example, generates a #NAME? error.

- The formula uses a worksheet function that's defined in an add-in, and the add-in is not installed.

Caution

Excel has a bit of a problem with range names. If you delete a name for a cell or range and the name is used in a formula, the formula continues to use the name, even though it's no longer defined. As a result, the formula displays #NAME?. You may expect Excel to automatically convert the names to their corresponding cell references, but this doesn't happen. ■

#NULL! errors

A #NULL! error occurs when a formula attempts to use an intersection of two ranges that don't actually intersect. Excel's intersection operator is a space. The following formula, for example, returns #NULL! because the two ranges don't intersect:

```
=SUM(B5:B14 A16:F16)
```

The following formula doesn't return #NULL! but displays the contents of cell B9, which represents the intersection of the two ranges:

```
=SUM(B5:B14 A9:F9)
```

#NUM! errors

A formula returns a #NUM! error if any of the following occurs:

- You pass a non-numeric argument to a function when a numeric argument is expected.

- You pass an invalid argument to a function. For example, this formula returns #NUM!:
  ```
  =SQRT(-12).
  ```

- A function that uses iteration can't calculate a result. Examples of functions that use iteration are IRR and RATE.

- A formula returns a value that is too large or too small. Excel supports values between $-1E-307$ and $1E+307$.

#REF! errors

A #REF! error occurs when a formula uses an invalid cell reference. This error can occur in the following situations:

- You delete the row column of a cell that is referenced by the formula. For example, the following formula displays a #REF! error if row 1, column A, or column B is deleted:

  =A1/B1

- You delete the worksheet of a cell that is reference by the formula. For example, the following formula displays a #REF! error if Sheet2 is deleted:

  =Sheet2!A1

- You copy a formula to a location that invalidates the relative cell references. For example, if you copy the following formula from cell A2 to cell A1, the formula returns #REF! because it attempts to refer to a nonexistent cell.

  =A1-1

- You cut a cell (choose Home ➪ Clipboard ➪ Cut) and then paste it to a cell that's referenced by a formula. The formula will display #REF!.

#VALUE! errors

A #VALUE! error is very common and can occur under the following conditions:

- An argument for a function is of an incorrect data type, or the formula attempts to perform an operation using incorrect data. For example, a formula that adds a value to a text string returns the #VALUE! error.

- A function's argument is a range when it should be a single value.

- A custom worksheet function is not calculated. You can press Ctrl+Alt+F9 to force a recalculation.

- A custom worksheet function attempts to perform an operation that is not valid. For example, custom functions can't modify the Excel environment or make changes to other cells.

- You forget to press Ctrl+Shift+Enter when entering an Array formula.

Pay Attention to the Colors

When you edit a cell that contains a formula, Excel color-codes the cell and range references in the formula. Excel also outlines the cells and ranges used in the formula by using corresponding colors. Therefore, you can see at a glance the cells that are used in the formula.

You also can manipulate the colored outline to change the cell or range reference. To change the references used in a formula, drag the outline's border or fill handle (at the lower right of the outline). This technique is often easier than editing the formula.

Absolute/relative reference problems

As I describe in Chapter 10, a cell reference can be relative (for example, A1), absolute (for example, $A$1), or mixed (for example, $A1 or A$1). The type of cell reference that you use in a formula is relevant only if the formula will be copied to other cells.

A common problem is using a relative reference when you should use an absolute reference. As shown in Figure 32.3, cell C1 contains a tax rate, which is used in the formulas in column C. The formula in cell C4 is

```
=B4+(B4*$C$1)
```

Formulas in the range C4:C7 use an absolute reference to cell C1.

	A	B	C	D	E
1		Tax Rate:	7.35%		
2					
3	Item	Price	Price + Tax		
4	Z-93w	149.95	160.97		
5	K-092	59.95	64.36		
6	M-119	32.29	34.66		
7	A-091	11.49	12.33		
8					
9					

Notice that the reference to cell C1 is an absolute reference. When the formula is copied to other cells in column C, the formula continues to refer to cell C1. If the reference to cell C1 were a relative reference, the copied formulas would return an incorrect result.

Operator precedence problems

As I describe in Chapter 10, Excel has some straightforward rules about the order in which mathematical operations are performed. When in doubt (or when you simply need to clarify your intentions), you should use parentheses to ensure that operations are performed in the correct order. For example, the following formula multiplies A1 by A2 and then adds 1 to the result. The multiplication is performed first because it has a higher order of precedence.

```
=1+A1*A2
```

The following is a clearer version of this formula. The parentheses aren't necessary, but in this case, the order of operations is perfectly obvious.

```
=1+(A1*A2)
```

Notice that the negation operator symbol is exactly the same as the subtraction operator symbol. This, as you may expect, can cause some confusion. Consider these two formulas:

```
=-3^2
=0-3^2
```

The first formula, as expected, returns 9. The second formula, however, returns −9. Squaring a number always produces a positive result, so how is it that Excel can return the −9 result?

In the first formula, the minus sign is a *negation* operator and has the highest precedence. However, in the second formula, the minus sign is a *subtraction* operator, which has a lower precedence than the exponentiation operator. Therefore, the value 3 is squared, and then the result is subtracted from 0 (zero), which produces a negative result.

Using parentheses, as shown in the following formula, causes Excel to interpret the operator as a minus sign rather than a negation operator. This formula returns −9.

```
=-(3^2)
```

Formulas are not calculated

If you use custom worksheet functions written in VBA, you may find that formulas that use these functions fail to get recalculated and may display incorrect results. To force a single formula to be recalculated, select the cell, press F2, and then press Enter. To force a recalculation of all formulas, press Ctrl+Alt+F9.

Actual versus displayed values

You may encounter a situation in which values in a range don't appear to add up properly. For example, Figure 32.4 shows a worksheet with the following formula entered into each cell in the range B2:B4:

```
=1/3
```

FIGURE 32.4

A simple demonstration of numbers that appear to add up incorrectly.

⊿	A	B	C	D	E
1					
2		0.333			
3		0.333			
4		0.333			
5		1.000			
6					
7					

Cell B5 contains the following formula:

```
=SUM(B2:B4)
```

All the cells are formatted to display with three decimal places. As you can see, the formula in cell B5 appears to display an incorrect result. (You may expect it to display 0.999.) The formula, of course, *does* return the correct result. The formula uses the *actual* values in the range B2:B4 not the *displayed* values.

You can instruct Excel to use the displayed values by selecting the Set Precision as Displayed check box of the Advanced section of the Excel Options dialog box. (Choose File ➪ Excel Options to display this dialog box.)

Caution
Be very careful with the Set Precision as Displayed option. This option also affects normal values (nonformulas) that have been entered into cells. For example, if a cell contains the value 4.68 and is displayed with no decimal places (that is, 5), selecting the Precision as Displayed check box converts 4.68 to 5.00. This change is permanent, and you can't restore the original value if you later clear the Set Precision as Displayed check box. A better approach is to use the ROUND function to round off the values to the desired number of decimal places. ■

Floating point number errors

Computers, by their very nature, don't have infinite precision. Excel stores numbers in binary format by using eight bytes, which can handle numbers with 15-digit accuracy. Some numbers can't be expressed precisely by using eight bytes, so the number stores as an approximation.

To demonstrate how this lack of precision may cause problems, enter the following formula into cell A1:

```
=(5.1-5.2)+1
```

The result should be 0.9. However, if you format the cell to display 15 decimal places, you discover that Excel calculates the formula with a result of 0.899999999999999. This result occurs because the operation in parentheses is performed first, and this intermediate result stores in binary format by using an approximation. The formula then adds 1 to this value, and the approximation error is propagated to the final result.

In many cases, this type of error doesn't present a problem. However, if you need to test the result of that formula by using a logical operator, it *may* present a problem. For example, the following formula (which assumes that the previous formula is in cell A1) returns FALSE:

```
=A1=.9
```

One solution to this type of error is to use the ROUND function. The following formula, for example, returns TRUE because the comparison is made by using the value in A1 rounded to one decimal place.

```
=ROUND(A1,1)=0.9
```

Here's another example of a "precision" problem. Try entering the following formula:

```
=(1.333-1.233)-(1.334-1.234)
```

This formula should return 0, but it actually returns -2.220446E-16 (a number very close to zero).

If that formula is in cell A1, the following formula returns Not Zero.

```
=IF(A1=0,"Zero","Not Zero")
```

One way to handle these "very close to zero" rounding errors is to use a formula like this:

```
=IF(ABS(A1)<1E-6,"Zero","Not Zero")
```

This formula uses the less-than (<) operator to compare the absolute value of the number with a very small number. This formula returns Zero.

"Phantom link" errors

You may open a workbook and see a message like the one shown in Figure 32.5. This message sometimes appears even when a workbook contains no linked formulas. Often, these phantom links are created when you copy a worksheet that contains names.

FIGURE 32.5

Excel's way of asking whether you want to update links in a workbook.

First, try choosing File ➪ Info ➪ Edit Links to Files to display the Edit Links dialog box. Then select each link and click Break Link. If that doesn't solve the problem, this phantom link may be caused by an erroneous name. Choose Formulas ➪ Defined Names ➪ Name Manager and scroll through the list of names. If you see a name that refers to #REF!, delete the name. The Name Manager dialog box has a Filter button that lets you filter the names. For example, you can filter the lists to display only the names with errors.

Using Excel Auditing Tools

Excel includes a number of tools that can help you track down formula errors. This section describes the auditing tools built in to Excel.

Identifying cells of a particular type

The Go to Special dialog box (as shown in Figure 32.6) is a handy tool that enables you to locate cells of a particular type. To display this dialog box, choose Home ⇨ Editing ⇨ Find & Select ⇨ Go to Special.

Note

If you select a multicell range before displaying the Go to Special dialog box, the command operates only within the selected cells. If a single cell is selected, the command operates on the entire worksheet. ∎

FIGURE 32.6

The Go to Special dialog box.

You can use the Go to Special dialog box to select cells of a certain type, which can often help you identify errors. For example, if you choose the Formulas option, Excel selects all the cells that contain a formula. If you zoom the worksheet out to a small size, you can get a good idea of the worksheet's organization (see Figure 32.7). To zoom a worksheet, use the zoom controls on the right side of the status bar. Or, press Ctrl while you move the scroll wheel on your mouse.

FIGURE 32.7

Zooming out and selecting all formula cells can give you a good overview of how the worksheet is designed.

Tip

Selecting the formula cells may also help you spot a common error: namely, a formula that has been replaced accidentally with a value. If you find a cell that's not selected amid a group of selected formula cells, chances are good that the cell previously contained a formula that has been replaced by a value. ∎

Viewing formulas

You can become familiar with an unfamiliar workbook by displaying the formulas rather than the results of the formulas. To toggle the display of formulas, choose Formulas ➪ Formula Auditing ➪ Show Formulas. You may want to create a second window for the workbook before issuing this command. This way, you can see the formulas in one window and the results of the formula in the other window. Choose View ➪ Window ➪ New Window to open a new window.

Tip

You can also press Ctrl+` (the accent grave key, typically located above the Tab key) to toggle between Formula view and Normal view. ∎

Figure 32.8 shows an example of a worksheet displayed in two windows. The window on the top shows Normal view (formula results), and the window on the bottom displays the formulas. Choosing View ➪ Window ➪ View Side by Side, which allows synchronized scrolling, is also useful for viewing two windows. (See Chapter 4 for more information about this command.)

FIGURE 32.8

Displaying formulas (bottom window) and their results (top window).

Tracing cell relationships

To understand how to trace cell relationships, you need to familiarize yourself with the following two concepts:

- **Cell precedents:** Applicable only to cells that contain a formula, a formula cell's precedents are all the cells that contribute to the formula's result. A *direct precedent* is a cell that you use directly in the formula. An *indirect precedent* is a cell that isn't used directly in the formula but is used by a cell that you refer to in the formula.

- **Cell dependents:** These formula cells depend upon a particular cell. A cell's dependents consist of all formula cells that use the cell. Again, the formula cell can be a *direct dependent* or an *indirect dependent*.

For example, consider this simple formula entered into cell A4:

```
=SUM(A1:A3)
```

Cell A4 has three precedent cells (A1, A2, and A3), which are all direct precedents. Cells A1, A2, and A3 each have a dependent cell (cell A4), and they're all direct dependents.

Identifying cell precedents for a formula cell often sheds light on why the formula isn't working correctly. Conversely, knowing which formula cells depend on a particular cell is also helpful. For example, if you're about to delete a formula, you may want to check whether it has any dependents.

Identifying precedents

You can identify cells used by a formula in the active cell in a number of ways:

- **Press F2.** The cells that are used directly by the formula are outlined in color, and the color corresponds to the cell reference in the formula. This technique is limited to identifying cells on the same sheet as the formula.

- **Display the Go to Special dialog box.** (Choose Home ➪ Editing ➪ Find & Select ➪ Go to Special.) Select the Precedents option and then select either Direct Only (for direct precedents only) or All Levels (for direct and indirect precedents). Click OK, and Excel selects the precedent cells for the formula. This technique is limited to identifying cells on the same sheet as the formula.

- **Press Ctrl+[.** This selects all direct precedent cells on the active sheet.

- **Press Ctrl+Shift+{.** This selects all precedent cells (direct and indirect) on the active sheet.

- **Choose Formulas ➪ Formula Auditing ➪ Trace Precedents.** Excel will draw arrows to indicate the cell's precedents. Click this button multiple times to see additional levels of precedents. Choose Formulas ➪ Formula Auditing ➪ Remove Arrows to hide the arrows. Figure 32.9 shows a worksheet with precedent arrows drawn to indicate the precedents for the formula in cell C13.

FIGURE 32.9

This worksheet displays arrows that indicate cell precedents for the formula in cell C13.

Identifying dependents

You can identify formula cells that use a particular cell in a number of ways:

- **Display the Go to Special dialog box.** Select the Dependents option and then select either Direct Only (for direct dependents only) or All Levels (for direct and indirect dependents). Click OK. Excel selects the cells that depend upon the active cell. This technique is limited to identifying cells on the active sheet only.

- **Press Ctrl+].** This selects all direct dependent cells on the active sheet.

- **Press Ctrl+Shift+}.** This selects all dependent cells (direct and indirect) on the active sheet.

- **Choose Formulas ⇨ Formula Auditing ⇨ Trace Dependents.** Excel will draw arrows to indicate the cell's dependents. Click this button multiple times to see additional levels of dependents. Choose Formulas ⇨ Formula Auditing ⇨ Remove Arrows to hide the arrows.

Tracing error values

If a formula displays an error value, Excel can help you identify the cell that is causing that error value. An error in one cell is often the result of an error in a precedent cell. Activate a cell that contains an error value and then choose Formulas ⇨ Formula Auditing ⇨ Error Checking ⇨ Trace Error. Excel draws arrows to indicate the error source.

Fixing circular reference errors

If you accidentally create a circular reference formula, Excel displays a warning message — `Circular Reference` — with the cell address, in the status bar, and also draws arrows on the worksheet to help you identify the problem. If you can't figure out the source of the problem, choose Formulas ⇨ Formula Auditing ⇨ Error Checking ⇨ Circular References. This command displays a list of all cells that are involved in the circular references. Start by selecting the first cell listed and then work your way down the list until you figure out the problem.

Using background error-checking feature

Some people may find it helpful to take advantage of the Excel automatic error-checking feature. This feature is enabled or disabled via the Enable Background Error Checking check box, found on the Formulas tab of the Excel Options dialog box, shown in Figure 32.10. In addition, you can use the check boxes in the Error Checking Rules section to specify which types of errors to check.

When error checking is turned on, Excel continually evaluates the formulas in your worksheet. If a potential error is identified, Excel places a small triangle in the upper-left corner of the cell. When the cell is activated, a Smart Tag appears. Clicking this Smart Tag provides you with options. Figure 32.11 shows the options that appear when you click the Smart Tag in a cell that contains a `#DIV/0!` error. The options vary, depending on the type of error.

FIGURE 32.10

Excel can check your formulas for potential errors.

FIGURE 32.11

After you click an error, Smart Tag gives you a list of options.

In many cases, you will choose to ignore an error by selecting the Ignore Error option. Selecting this option eliminates the cell from subsequent error checks. However, all previously ignored errors can be reset so that they appear again. (Use the Reset Ignored Errors button in the Formulas tab of the Excel Options dialog box.)

You can choose Formulas ⇨ Formula Auditing ⇨ Error Checking to display a dialog box that describes each potential error cell in sequence, much like using a spell-checking command. This command is available even if you disable background error checking. Figure 32.12 shows the Error Checking dialog box. This dialog box is *modeless:* that is, you can still access your worksheet when the Error Checking dialog box is displayed.

Caution

The error-checking feature isn't perfect. In fact, it's not even close to perfect. In other words, you can't assume that you have an error-free worksheet simply because Excel doesn't identify any potential errors! Also, be aware that this error-checking feature won't catch a very common type of error: namely, overwriting a formula cell with a value. ■

FIGURE 32.12

Use the Error Checking dialog box to cycle through potential errors identified by Excel.

Using the Excel Formula Evaluator

Formula Evaluator lets you see the various parts of a nested formula evaluated in the order that the formula is calculated. To use Formula Evaluator, select the cell that contains the formula and then choose Formula ⇨ Formula Auditing ⇨ Evaluate Formula to display the Evaluate Formula dialog box (see Figure 32.13).

FIGURE 32.13

The Evaluate Formula dialog box shows a formula being calculated one step at a time.

Click the Evaluate button to show the result of calculating the expressions within the formula. Each click of the button performs another calculation. This feature may seem a bit complicated at first, but if you spend some time working with it, you'll understand how it works and see the value.

Excel provides another way to evaluate a part of a formula:

1. **Select the cell that contains the formula.**

2. **Press F2 to get into Cell Edit mode.**

3. **Use your mouse to highlight the portion of the formula you want to evaluate.** Or, press Shift and use the navigation keys.

4. **Press F9.**

The highlighted portion of the formula displays the calculated result. You can evaluate other parts of the formula or press Esc(ape) to cancel and return your formula to its previous state.

Caution

Be careful when using this technique because if you press Enter (rather than Esc), the formula will be modified to use the calculated values. ■

Searching and Replacing

Excel has a powerful search-and-replace feature that makes it easy to locate information in a worksheet or across multiple worksheets in a workbook. As an option, you can also search for text and replace it with other text.

To access the Find and Replace dialog box, start by selecting the range that you want to search. If you select any single cell, Excel searches the entire sheet. Choose Home ➪ Editing ➪ Find & Select ➪ Find (or, click Ctrl+F). You'll see the Find and Replace dialog box shown in Figure 32.14. If you're simply looking for information in the worksheet, click the Find tab. If you want to replace existing text with new text, use the Replace tab. Also note that you can use the Options button to display (or hide) additional options. The dialog box shown in the figure displays these additional options.

FIGURE 32.14

Use the Find and Replace dialog box to locate information in a worksheet or workbook.

Searching for information

Enter the information to search for in the Find What text box and then specify any of the following options.

- **Within drop-down list:** Specify where to search (the current sheet or the entire workbook).
- **Search drop-down list:** Specify the direction (by rows or by columns).
- **Look In drop-down list:** Specify what cell parts to search (formulas, values, or comments).
- **Match Case check box:** Specify whether the search should be case sensitive.
- **Match Entire Cell Contents check box:** Specify whether the entire cell contents must be matched.
- **Format button:** Click to search for cells that have a particular formatting (see the upcoming "Searching for formatting" section).

Click Find Next to locate the matching cells one at a time or click Find All to locate all matches. If you use the Find All button, the Find and Replace dialog box expands to display the addresses of all matching cells in a list (see Figure 32.15). When you select an entry in this list, Excel scrolls the worksheet so that you can view it in context.

Tip

After using Find All, press Ctrl+A to select all the found cells. ■

FIGURE 32.15

Displaying the result of a search in the Find and Replace dialog box.

Note

Because the Find and Replace dialog box is modeless, you can access the worksheet and make changes without the need to dismiss the dialog box. ∎

Replacing information

To replace text with other text, use the Replace tab in the Find and Replace dialog box. Enter the text to be replaced in the Find What field and then enter the new text in the Replace With field. Specify other options as described in the previous section.

Click Find Next to locate the first matching item and then click Replace to do the replacement. When you click the Replace button, Excel then locates the next matching item. To override the replacement, click Find Next. To replace all items without verification, click Replace All. If the replacement didn't occur as you planned, you can use the Undo button on the Quick Access toolbar (or press Ctrl+Z).

Tip

To delete information, enter the text to be deleted in the Find What field but leave the Replace With field empty. ∎

Searching for formatting

From the Find and Replace dialog box, you can also locate cells that contain a particular type of formatting. As an option, you can replace that formatting with another type of formatting. For example, assume that you want to locate all cells that are formatted as bold and then change that formatting to bold and italic. Follow these steps:

1. Choose Home ➪ Editing ➪ Find & Select ➪ Replace to display the Find and Replace dialog box (or, press Ctrl+H).

2. Make sure that the Replace tab is displayed.

3. If the Find What and Replace With fields are not empty, delete their contents.

4. Click the top Format button to display the Find Format dialog box. This dialog box resembles the standard Format Cells dialog box.

5. In the Find Format dialog box, click the Font tab.

6. Select Bold in the Font Style list and then click OK.

7. Click the bottom Format button to display the Replace Format dialog box.

8. In the Replace Format dialog box, click the Font tab.

9. Select Bold Italic from the Font Style list and then click OK. At this point, the Find and Replace dialog box resembles Figure 32.16. Notice that it displays previews of the formatting that will be found and replaced.

10. **In the Find and Replace dialog box, click Replace All.** Excel locates all cells that have bold formatting and changes the formatting to bold italic.

You can also find formatting based on a particular cell. In the Find Format dialog box, click the Choose Format from Cell button and then click the cell that contains the formatting you're looking for.

FIGURE 32.16

Use the Find and Replace dialog box to change formatting.

Caution
The Find and Replace dialog box cannot find background color formatting in tables that was applied using table styles, or formatting that is applied based on conditional formatting. ∎

Spell Checking Your Worksheets

If you use a word processing program, you probably take advantage of its spell checker feature. Spelling mistakes can be just as embarrassing when they appear in a spreadsheet. Fortunately, Microsoft includes a spell checker with Excel.

To access the spell checker, choose Review ➪ Proofing ➪ Spelling, or press F7. To check the spelling in just a particular range, select the range before you activate the spell checker.

If the spell checker finds any words it does not recognize as correct, it displays the Spelling dialog box, shown in Figure 32.17.

Note
The spell checker checks cell contents, text in graphic objects and charts, and page headers and footers. Even the contents of hidden rows and columns are checked. ∎

FIGURE 32.17

Use the Spelling dialog box to locate and correct spelling errors in your worksheets.

The Spelling dialog box works similarly to other spell checkers with which you may be familiar. If Excel encounters a word that isn't in the current dictionary or that is misspelled, it offers a list of suggestions. You can respond by clicking one of these buttons:

- **Ignore Once:** Ignore the word and continues the spell check.
- **Ignore All:** Ignore the word and all subsequent occurrences of it.
- **Add to Dictionary:** Add the word to the dictionary.
- **Change:** Change the word to the selected word in the Suggestions list.
- **Change All:** Change the word to the selected word in the Suggestions list and change all subsequent occurrences of it without asking.
- **AutoCorrect:** Add the misspelled word and its correct spelling (which you select from the list) to the AutoCorrect list.

Using AutoCorrect

AutoCorrect is a handy feature that automatically corrects common typing mistakes. You can also add words to the list that Excel corrects automatically. The AutoCorrect dialog box appears in Figure 32.18. To access this feature, choose File ➪ Options. In the Excel Options dialog box, click the Proofing tab and then click the AutoCorrect Options button.

This dialog box has several options:

- **Correct TWo INitial CApitals:** Automatically corrects words with two initial uppercase letters. For example, BUdget is converted to Budget. This mistake is common among fast typists. You can click the Exceptions button to specify a list of exceptions to this rule.
- **Capitalize First Letter of Sentences:** Capitalizes the first letter in a sentence. All other letters are unchanged.

- **Capitalize Names of Days:** Capitalizes the days of the week. If you enter *monday*, Excel converts it to *Monday*.

- **Correct Accidental Use of cAPS LOCK key:** Corrects errors caused if you accidentally pressed the CapsLock key while typing.

- **Replace Text as You Type:** AutoCorrect automatically changes incorrect words as you type them.

FIGURE 32.18

Use the AutoCorrect dialog box to control the spelling corrections Excel makes automatically.

Excel includes a long list of AutoCorrect entries for commonly misspelled words. In addition, it has AutoCorrect entries for some symbols. For example, (c) is replaced with ©, and (r) is replaced with ®. You can also add your own AutoCorrect entries. For example, if you find that you frequently misspell the word *January* as *Janruary,* you can create an AutoCorrect entry so that it's changed automatically. To create a new AutoCorrect entry, enter the misspelled word in the Replace box and the correctly spelled word in the With field. You can also delete entries that you no longer need.

Tip

You also can use the AutoCorrect feature to create shortcuts for commonly used words or phrases. For example, if you work for a company named Consolidated Data Processing Corporation, you can create an AutoCorrect entry for an abbreviation, such as cdp. Then, whenever you type cdp, Excel automatically changes it to Consolidated Data Processing Corporation. Just make sure that you don't use a combination of characters that might normally appear in your text. ∎

Note

In some cases, you may want to override the AutoCorrect feature. For example, you may need to literally enter (c) rather than a copyright symbol. Just click the Undo button on the Quick Access toolbar or press Ctrl+Z. ■

You can use the AutoFormat as You Type tab of the AutoCorrect dialog box to control a few other automatic settings in Excel.

Use the Smart Tags tab to make Excel show Smart Tags — similar to hyperlinks — for certain types of data in your worksheets. The types of Smart Tags Excel recognizes vary depending on the types of software that are installed on your system.

The Math AutoCorrect tab contains shortcuts used to enter symbols when working in the Equation Editor (see Chapter 22).

Part V

Analyzing Data with Excel

Excel is a superb data analysis tool — if you know how to extract the information you really need. In this part, you'll learn how to obtain and analyze data in Excel. As you'll see, many of the data-analysis capabilities in Excel are both surprisingly powerful and easy to use.

IN THIS PART

Chapter 33
Getting Data from External Database Files

Chapter 34
Understanding Pivot Tables

Chapter 35
Analyzing Data with Pivot Tables

Chapter 36
Performing Spreadsheet What-If Analysis

Chapter 37
Analyzing Data Using Goal Seeking and Solver

Chapter 38
Analyzing Data with the Analysis ToolPak

Getting Data from External Database Files

Excel has some great analysis and presentation tools, but these tools require data. In many cases, the data that you need is available in an external database. For example, your company may have a database that contains customer information, sales data, and so on. This chapter is an introduction to retrieving data from external database files for use in Excel.

Understanding External Database Files

When you work with an Excel workbook, the entire workbook must be loaded into memory before you can begin working. Although loading all the data provides you with immediate access to the entire file and all the data it contains, it also means that you can't work with extremely large amounts of data. Although Excel 2010 supports more than a million rows, actually using that many rows can slow your system to a crawl — even if your system has plenty of memory.

Note
Using the 64-bit version of Excel allows you to work with much larger workbooks. But for extremely large data sets, it's usually more efficient to work with a subset of the data. ■

When you access an external database file using Excel, you can perform a query to load just a subset of the data into your workbook.

Accessing external database files from Excel is useful in the following situations:

- You need to work with a subset of a very large database.

- The subset of data changes over time. It's very easy to refresh a query and replace the old data with updated information.

- The database is in a format that Excel can't import, or the database may be too large to import.

- The database contains multiple tables with relationships between those tables.

If you need to work with data in an external database, you may prefer to use Excel rather than the tools available in database programs. The advantage? After you bring the data into Excel, you can manipulate and format it by using familiar tools such as formulas, charts, and pivot tables. Of course, real database programs, such as Access, have advantages, too. For example, creating a complex database report in Access may be easier than creating it in Excel.

Understanding Some Database Terminology

People who spend their days working with databases seem to have their own special language. The following terms can help you hold your own among a group of database experts:

- **External database:** A collection of data stored in one or more files (not Excel files). A database contains one or more tables, and tables are composed of records and fields.

- **Field**: A component of a database table, it corresponds to a column in Excel.

- **ODBC**: Open DataBase Connectivity is a standard developed by Microsoft that uses drivers to access database files in different formats. Microsoft Query comes with drivers for Access, dBASE, FoxPro, Paradox, SQL Server, Excel workbooks, and ASCII text files. ODBC drivers for other databases are available from Microsoft and from third-party providers.

- **OLAP Cube:** A multidimensional aggregate data source, often created from various other sources. OLAP is an acronym for OnLine Analytical Processing.

- **Query**: Search a database for records that meet specific criteria. This term is also used as a noun; you can write a query, for example.

- **Record**: In a database table, a single element that corresponds to a row.

- **Refresh**: Rerun a query to get the latest data. It's applicable when the database contains information that is subject to change, as in a multiuser environment.

- **Relational database**: A database stored in more than one table or file. At least one common field (sometimes called the *key field*) connects the tables.

- **Result set**: The data returned by a query, usually a subset of the original database. Query returns the result set to your Excel workbook or to a pivot table. (I discuss pivot tables in Chapter 34.)

- **SQL**: An acronym for Structured Query Language (pronounced *see*-quel). Microsoft Query (discussed in this chapter) uses SQL to search data stored in ODBC databases.

- **Table**: A record- and field-oriented collection of data. A database consists of one or more tables.

Importing Access Tables

Microsoft Access is included with some versions of Office 2010. An Access database contains one or more tables of data, and you can import an Access table directly into a worksheet by choosing Data ⇨ Get External Data ⇨ From Access. When you choose this command, Excel displays the Select Data Source dialog box, which you use to locate the Access file.

After you locate the Access database file, Excel displays the Select Table dialog box, from which you select the table (or view) to import. Figure 33.1 shows the tables and views available for the Microsoft Northwind Traders database, which is a sample Access database that you can download from the Microsoft Web site. Select the table that contains the data you need, click OK, and Excel displays its Import Data dialog box, shown in Figure 33.2. Use this dialog box to specify the location and whether you want a normal table or a pivot table. See Chapter 34 for information about pivot tables.

FIGURE 33.1

Selecting an Access table to import.

Note

Importing an Access table in this manner is all or none. You're not given an opportunity to query the database for specific records. ■

Figure 33.3 shows part of the Customers table from the Northwind Traders database. Excel converts the data to a table. You can use all of Excel's tools to work with the data. Note, however, that you cannot make changes and send the changed data back to the Access database.

FIGURE 33.2

Use this dialog box to specify the location of the imported table.

FIGURE 33.3

An Access table, imported into Excel.

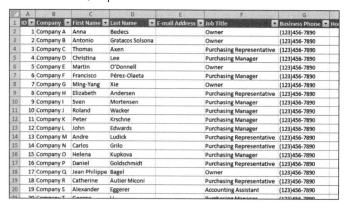

Retrieving Data with Query: An Example

This section discusses *Microsoft Query*, an application that ships with Excel. Use Query to import a subset of a database.

Note

To perform queries using external databases, Microsoft Query must be installed on your system. If Query isn't installed, you're prompted to install it when you first choose Data ➪ Get External Data ➪ From Other Sources ➪ From Microsoft Query. ∎

The best way to become familiar with Microsoft Query is to walk through an example. In the following sections, you learn how to use Query to open a database file and import a specified set of records.

On the CD

The database file used in this example is available on the companion CD-ROM. It's an Access 2010 file named `budget data.accdb`.

The database file

The database file used in this example is a single-table Access file that consists of 31,680 records. This table contains the following fields:

- **Sort:** A numeric field that holds record sequence numbers.
- **Division:** A text field that specifies the company division (Asia, Europe, N. America, Pacific Rim, or S. America).
- **Department:** A text field that specifies the department within the division. Each division is organized into the following departments: Accounting, Advertising, Data Processing, Human Resources, Operations, Public Relations, R&D, Sales, Security, Shipping, and Training.
- **Category:** A text field that specifies the budget category. The four categories are Compensation, Equipment, Facility, and Supplies & Services.
- **Item:** A text field that specifies the budget item. Each budget category has different budget items. For example, the Compensation category includes the following items: Benefits, Bonuses, Commissions, Conferences, Entertainment, Payroll Taxes, Salaries, and Training.
- **Month:** A text field that specifies the month (abbreviated as Jan, Feb, and so on).
- **Year:** A numeric field that stores the year (either 2008 or 2009).
- **Budget:** A numeric field that stores the budgeted amount.
- **Actual:** A numeric field that stores the actual amount spent.
- **Variance:** A numeric field that stores the difference between the Budget and Actual.

The task

The objective of this exercise is to create a report that shows the first quarter 2009 (January through March) Compensation expenditures of the Training Department in the North American Division. In other words, the query will extract records that meet all the following criteria:

- **Division:** N. America
- **Department:** Training
- **Category:** Compensation
- **Month:** Jan, Feb, or Mar
- **Year:** 2009

One approach to this task is to import the entire Access file into a worksheet using the method described earlier in this chapter (see "Importing Access Tables"). When the table is imported, you can filter it to display only the rows that meet the specified criteria. This approach works because this particular table isn't very large. However, in some cases, the number of records in the table may exceed the number of rows in a worksheet.

The advantage of using Query is that it imports only the data that's required. And, after you import the data, you can refresh the query at any time to bring in updated data.

Selecting a data source

Begin with an empty worksheet. Choose Data ➪ Get External Data ➪ From Other Sources ➪ From Microsoft Query, which displays the Choose Data Source dialog box, as shown in Figure 33.4. This dialog box contains three tabs:

- **Databases:** Lists the data sources that are known to Query. This tab may be empty, depending on which data sources are defined on your system.
- **Queries:** Contains a list of stored queries. Again, this tab may or may not be empty.
- **OLAP Cubes:** Lists OLAP databases available for query.

FIGURE 33.4

The Choose Data Source dialog box.

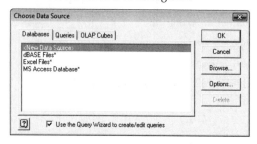

Your system may have some data sources already defined. If so, they appear in the list on the Databases tab. To set up a new data source, use the New Data Source option. For this example, choose New Data Source and click OK. The Create New Data Source dialog box, which has four parts, appears:

1. **Enter a descriptive name for the data source.** For this example, use the name Budget Database.

2. **Select a driver for the data source by selecting from the list of installed drivers.** For this example, choose Microsoft Access Driver (*.mdb, *.accdb).

3. **Click the Connect button to display another dialog box that asks for information specific to the driver that you selected in Step 2.** In this example, you need to click the Select button and then locate the `budget data.accdb` file. Click OK to return to the previous dialog box and click OK again to return to the Create New Data Source dialog box.

4. **Select the default data table that you want to use.** For this example, the database file contains a single table named `budget`. If the database requires a password, you can also specify that the password be saved with the data source definition. Figure 33.5 shows the Create New Data Source dialog box at this point.

5. **After you supply all the information in the Create New Data Source dialog box, click OK.** You're returned to the Choose Data Source dialog box, which now displays the name of the data source that you created.

FIGURE 33.5

The Create New Data Source dialog box.

Note

You have to go through these steps only once for each data source. The next time that you need to access this data source, the Budget Database (and any other database sources that you've defined) appears in the Choose Data Source dialog box. ■

Note

The preceding steps are general steps that work with all supported database types. In some situations, you may prefer to open the database file directly and not create a named data source that will appear in the Choose Data Source dialog box. For example, if you won't be using the database again, you can open the file directly and not have to bother creating a new named data source. If you're using an Access file, you can select MS Access Database from the Databases tab in the Choose Data Source dialog box. Then, you can specify the file, and you're taken directly to Microsoft Query. ■

Using Query with Excel Files

You may have noticed that one of the options in the Choose Data Source dialog box is Excel Files. If you choose this option, you can use Query to bring in data stored in Excel workbooks. You can put any number of data tables in a workbook, but each one must have a range name because that's how Query identifies the tables.

Using the Query Wizard

The Choose Data Source dialog box has a check box at the bottom that lets you specify whether to use the Query Wizard to create your query. (Refer to Figure 33.4.) The Query Wizard walks you through the steps used to create your query; if you use the Query Wizard, you don't have to deal directly with Query. I highly recommend using the Query Wizard, and the examples in this chapter use this tool.

In the Choose Data Source dialog box, do the following:

1. **Select your data source (Budget Database, for this example).**
2. **Make sure that the Query Wizard check box is selected.**
3. **Click OK to start the Query Wizard.**

Query Wizard: Choosing the columns

In the first step of the Query Wizard, select the database columns that you want to appear in your query. Select one or more columns and click the > button to add them (see Figure 33.6). To select all fields, click the table name (budget) and then click the > button.

FIGURE 33.6

In the first step of Query Wizard, you select the columns to use in your query.

If you want to see the data for a particular column, select the column and click the Preview Now button. If you accidentally add a column that you don't need, select it in the right panel and click the < button to remove it.

For this example, add all the fields and then click the Next button.

Query Wizard: Filtering data

In the second step of the Query Wizard , specify your record selection criteria — how you want to filter the data. This step is optional. If you want to retrieve all the data, just click the Next button to proceed.

Figure 33.7 shows the Filter Data dialog box of the Query Wizard.

FIGURE 33.7

In the second step of the Query Wizard, you specify how you want to filter the data.

For the example, not all records are needed. Recall that you're interested only in the records in which all the following applies:

- The Division is N. America.
- The Department is Training.
- The Category is Compensation.
- The Year is 2009.
- The Month is Jan, Feb, or Mar.

The criteria are entered by column. In this case, you have five criteria (one for each of five columns):

- From the Column to Filter list, select Division. In the right panel, select *equals* from the first drop-down list and then select N. America from the second drop-down list.
- From the Column to Filter list, select Department. In the right panel, select *equals* from the first drop-down list and then select Training from the second drop-down list.

- From the Column to Filter list, select Category. In the right panel, select *equals* from the first drop-down list and then select Compensation from the second drop-down list.

- From the Column to Filter list, select Year. In the right panel, select *equals* from the first drop-down list and then select 2009 from the second drop-down list.

- From the Column to Filter list, select Month. In the right panel, select *equals* from the first drop-down list and then select Jan from the second drop-down list. And because this column is filtered by multiple values, select the Or option button and then select *equals* and *Feb* from the drop-down lists in the second row. Finally, select *equals* and *Mar* from the drop-down lists in the third row.

To review the criteria that you entered, select the column from the Column to Filter list. The Query Wizard displays the criteria that you entered for the selected column. Notice that columns that are used in the query display in bold.

After you enter all the criteria, click Next.

Query Wizard: Sort order

The third step of the query lets you specify how you want the records to be sorted (see Figure 33.8). This step is optional, and you can click Next to move to the next step if you don't want the data sorted or if you prefer to sort it after it's returned to your worksheet.

For this example, sort by Category in ascending order. You can specify as many sort fields as you like. Click Next to move on to the next step.

Query Wizard: Finish

The final step of the Query Wizard, shown in Figure 33.9, lets you save the query so that you can reuse it. To save the query, click Save Query and then enter a filename.

Select an option that corresponds to what you want to do with the returned data. Normally, you want to return the data to Excel. If you know how to use the Microsoft Query application, you can return the data to Query and examine it or even modify the selection criteria.

FIGURE 33.8

In the third step of the Query Wizard, you specify the sort order.

For this example, select the Return Data to Microsoft Excel option button and then click Finish.

FIGURE 33.9

The final step of the Query Wizard.

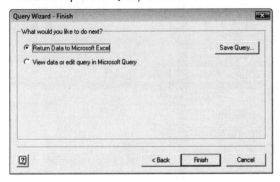

Specifying a location for the data

Figure 33.10 shows the Import Data dialog box, which appears after you click the Finish button in the Query Wizard.

For this example, select the Table option button and place the data beginning in cell A1 of the existing worksheet. Click OK to import the data.

Note

If you choose PivotTable Report, or PivotChart and PivotTable Report, you can specify the layout for a pivot table (see Chapters 34 and 35). In such a case, the database is used as the source for the pivot table, and the original data table does not appear in your workbook. ■

FIGURE 33.10

Specifying what to do with the data.

Figure 33.11 shows the data that is returned to a worksheet.

The results of the query.

	A	B	C	D	E	F	G	H	I	J	K
1	ID	SORT	DIVISION	DEPARTMENT	CATEGORY	ITEM	YEAR	MONTH	BUDGET	ACTUAL	VARIANCE
2	15913	15913	N. America	Training	Compensation	Salaries	2009	Jan	3184	4063	879
3	15914	15914	N. America	Training	Compensation	Benefits	2009	Jan	4179	2883	-1296
4	15915	15915	N. America	Training	Compensation	Bonuses	2009	Jan	4257	3435	-822
5	15916	15916	N. America	Training	Compensation	Commissions	2009	Jan	3182	2976	-206
6	15917	15917	N. America	Training	Compensation	Payroll Taxes	2009	Jan	3523	3618	95
7	15918	15918	N. America	Training	Compensation	Training	2009	Jan	4784	3690	-1094
8	15919	15919	N. America	Training	Compensation	Conferences	2009	Jan	2690	3718	1028
9	15920	15920	N. America	Training	Compensation	Entertainment	2009	Jan	3265	3454	189
10	17233	17233	N. America	Training	Compensation	Salaries	2009	Feb	2678	3985	1307
11	17234	17234	N. America	Training	Compensation	Benefits	2009	Feb	2517	4075	1558
12	17235	17235	N. America	Training	Compensation	Bonuses	2009	Feb	3830	2309	-1521
13	17236	17236	N. America	Training	Compensation	Commissions	2009	Feb	2209	2815	606
14	17237	17237	N. America	Training	Compensation	Payroll Taxes	2009	Feb	2917	2972	55
15	17238	17238	N. America	Training	Compensation	Training	2009	Feb	3180	3726	546
16	17239	17239	N. America	Training	Compensation	Conferences	2009	Feb	3897	4042	145
17	17240	17240	N. America	Training	Compensation	Entertainment	2009	Feb	3017	3029	12
18	18553	18553	N. America	Training	Compensation	Salaries	2009	Mar	3095	4090	995
19	18554	18554	N. America	Training	Compensation	Benefits	2009	Mar	2955	4348	1393
20	18555	18555	N. America	Training	Compensation	Bonuses	2009	Mar	2820	3178	358
21	18556	18556	N. America	Training	Compensation	Commissions	2009	Mar	4851	3643	-1208
22	18557	18557	N. America	Training	Compensation	Payroll Taxes	2009	Mar	2750	3298	548
23	18558	18558	N. America	Training	Compensation	Training	2009	Mar	2792	3979	1187
24	18559	18559	N. America	Training	Compensation	Conferences	2009	Mar	4229	3799	-430
25	18560	18560	N. America	Training	Compensation	Entertainment	2009	Mar	3769	3265	-504
26											

Working with Data Returned by Query

Excel stores the data that Query returns in either a worksheet or a pivot table cache. When Excel stores data in a worksheet, it stores the data in a table that's a specially named range known as an *external data range;* Excel creates the name for this range automatically. In this example, the external data range is named `Table_Query_from_Budget_Database`.

You can manipulate data returned from a query just like any other worksheet range. For example, you can sort the data, format it, or create formulas that use the data.

The following sections describe what you can do with the data that Excel receives from Query and stores in a worksheet.

Adjusting the external data range properties

You can adjust various properties of the external data range by using the External Data Properties dialog box (see Figure 33.12).

To display this dialog box, the cell pointer must be within the external data range. Open this dialog box by using either of these methods:

- Right-click and choose Table ➪ External Data Properties from the shortcut menu.
- Choose Data ➪ Connections ➪ Properties.

For more settings (applicable for advanced users), click the Properties icon, which is directly to the right of the Name field in the External Data Properties dialog box. Excel displays the Connection Properties dialog box.

The External Data Properties dialog box enables you to specify various options for an external data range.

Refreshing a query

After performing a query, you can save the workbook file and then retrieve it later. The file contains the data that you originally retrieved from the external database. The external database may have changed, however, in the interim.

Fortunately, Excel saves the query definition with the workbook. Simply move the cell pointer anywhere within the external data table in the worksheet and then use one of the following methods to refresh the query:

- Right-click and choose Refresh from the shortcut menu.
- Choose Data ➪ Connections ➪ Refresh All.
- Click Refresh in the Workbook Connections dialog box (displayed by choosing Data ➪ Connections ➪ Connections).

Excel uses your original query to bring in the current data from the external database.

Tip
If you find that refreshing the query causes undesirable results, use the Undo button to "unrefresh" the data. ∎

Note
A single workbook can hold as many external data ranges as you need. Excel gives each query a unique name, and you can work with each query independently. Excel automatically keeps track of the query that produces each external data range. ∎

Caution

After performing a query, you may want to copy or move the external data range, which you can do by using the normal copy, cut, and paste techniques. However, make sure that you copy or cut the entire external data range: Otherwise, the underlying query is not copied, and the copied data can't be refreshed. ■

Deleting a query

If you decide that you no longer need the data returned by a query, you can delete it by selecting the entire external data range and pressing Delete. Excel displays a warning and asks you to verify your intentions. Your data source definition remains intact, so you can always re-specify your original query.

Changing your query

If you bring the query results into your worksheet and discover that you don't have what you want, you can modify the query. Move the cell pointer anywhere within the external data table in the worksheet. Right-click and choose Table ⇨ Edit Query from the shortcut menu. You need to edit the query using Microsoft Query. See the next section to learn how to work with Query directly.

Using Query without the Wizard

When you choose Data ⇨ Get External Data ⇨ From Other Sources ⇨ From Microsoft Query, the Choose Data Source dialog box gives you the option of whether to use Query Wizard to create your query. If you choose not to use Query Wizard, Microsoft Query is launched in a new window. You also work directly with Query if you choose to edit a query that was created with Query Wizard.

Note

Microsoft Query is a relatively old application, and its user interface hasn't been updated to match the other Office programs. It works fine. It just looks old-fashioned. ■

Creating a query manually

Before you can create a query, you must display the Criteria pane. In Query, open the View menu and place a check next to the Criteria menu item. The Criteria pane appears in the middle of the window. Figure 33.13 shows Microsoft Query, after selecting the Budget Database from the Choose Data Source dialog box.

FIGURE 33.13

Display the Criteria pane as shown here so that you'll be able to create your query.

Tables pane

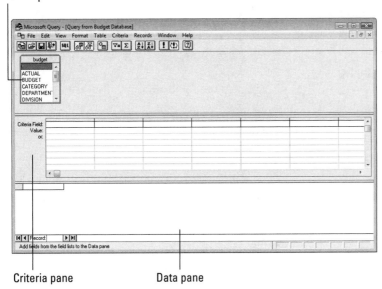

Criteria pane   Data pane

The Query window has three panes, which are split horizontally:

- **Tables pane:** The top pane, which holds the selected data tables for the database. Each data table window has a list of the fields in the table.

- **Criteria pane:** The middle pane, which holds the criteria that determine the rows that the query returns.

- **Data pane:** The bottom pane, which holds the data that passes the criteria.

Creating a query consists of the following steps:

1. **Drag fields from the Tables pane to the Data pane.** You can drag as many fields as you want. These fields are the columns that the query will return. You can also double-click a field instead of dragging it.

2. **Enter criteria in the Criteria pane.** When you activate this pane, the first row (labeled Criteria Field) displays a drop-down list that contains all the field names. Select a field and enter the criteria below it. Query updates the Data pane automatically, treating each row like an OR operator.

3. **Choose File ➪ Return Data to Microsoft Excel to execute the query and place the data in a worksheet or pivot table.**

Figure 33.14 shows how the query for the example presented earlier in this chapter appears in Query. Recall that the goal is to retrieve records in which all of the following applies:

- The Division is N. America.
- The Department is Training.
- The Category is Compensation.
- The Year is 2009.
- The Month is Jan, Feb, or Mar.

FIGURE 33.14

Add the fields and criteria to complete your query.

Tip

Double-clicking a criteria box to display the Edit Criteria dialog box enables you to select an operator and value. ∎

Using multiple database tables

The example in this chapter uses only one database table. Some databases, however, use multiple tables. These databases are *relational databases* because a common field links the tables. Query lets you use any number of tables in your queries.

Note

When you add tables to a query, the Tables pane in Query connects the linked fields with a line between the tables. If no links exist, you can create a link yourself by dragging a field from one table to the corresponding field in the other table. ■

Adding and editing records in external database tables

To add, delete, and edit data when you're using Query, make sure that a check mark appears next to the Records ➪ Allow Editing menu item. Of course, you'll need the proper permissions, and you can't edit a database file that's set up as read-only.

Caution

Be careful with this feature because your changes are saved to disk as soon as you move the cell pointer out of the record that you're editing. You do not need to choose File ➪ Save. ■

Formatting data

If you don't like the data's appearance in the Data pane, you can change the font used by choosing Format ➪ Font. Be aware that selective formatting isn't allowed (unlike in Excel); changing the font affects all the data in the Data pane.

Tip

If you need to view the data in the Data pane in a different order, choose Records ➪ Sort (or click the Sort Ascending or Sort Descending toolbar icon). ■

Learning More about Query

This chapter isn't intended to cover every aspect of Microsoft Query; rather, it discusses the basic features that are used most often. In fact, if you use the Query Wizard, you may never need to interact with Query itself. But if you do need to use Query, you can experiment and consult the online Help to learn more. As with anything related to Excel, the best way to master Query is to use it — preferably with data that's meaningful to you.

Introducing Pivot Tables

The Pivot Table feature is perhaps the most technologically sophisticated component in Excel. With only a few mouse clicks, you can slice and dice a data table in dozens of different ways and produce just about any type of summary you can think of.

If you haven't yet discovered the power of pivot tables, this chapter provides an introduction, and Chapter 35 continues with many examples that demonstrate how easy it is to create powerful data summaries using pivot tables.

About Pivot Tables

A *pivot table* is essentially a dynamic summary report generated from a database. The database can reside in a worksheet (in the form of a table) or in an external data file. A pivot table can help transform endless rows and columns of numbers into a meaningful presentation of the data.

For example, a pivot table can create frequency distributions and cross-tabulations of several different data dimensions. In addition, you can display subtotals and any level of detail that you want. Perhaps the most innovative aspect of a pivot table is its interactivity. After you create a pivot table, you can rearrange the information in almost any way imaginable and even insert special formulas that perform new calculations. You even can create post hoc groupings of summary items (for example, combine Northern Region totals with Western Region totals). And the icing on the cake: With a few mouse clicks, you can apply formatting to a pivot table to convert it into an attractive report.

IN THIS CHAPTER

An introduction to pivot tables

Types of data appropriate for a pivot table

Pivot table terminology

How to create pivot tables

Pivot table examples that answer specific questions about data

One minor drawback to using a pivot table is that unlike a formula-based summary report, a pivot table does not update automatically when you change information in the source data. This drawback doesn't pose a serious problem, however, because a single click of the Refresh button forces a pivot table to update itself with the latest data.

Pivot tables were introduced in Excel 97. Unfortunately, many users overlook this feature because they think it's too complicated. The pivot table feature was improved significantly in Excel 2007, and you'll find a few new twists in Excel 2010. Creating and working with pivot tables is easier than ever.

A pivot table example

The best way to understand the concept of a pivot table is to see one. Start with Figure 34.1, which shows a portion of the data used in creating the pivot table in this chapter.

FIGURE 34.1

This table is used to create a pivot table.

	A	B	C	D	E	F	G
1	Date	Weekday	Amount	AcctType	OpenedBy	Branch	Customer
2	Sep-01	Friday	5,000	IRA	New Accts	Central	Existing
3	Sep-01	Friday	14,571	CD	Teller	Central	New
4	Sep-01	Friday	500	Checking	New Accts	Central	Existing
5	Sep-01	Friday	15,000	CD	New Accts	Central	Existing
6	Sep-01	Friday	4,623	Savings	New Accts	North County	Existing
7	Sep-01	Friday	8,721	Savings	New Accts	Westside	New
8	Sep-01	Friday	15,276	Savings	New Accts	North County	Existing
9	Sep-01	Friday	5,000	Savings	New Accts	Westside	Existing
10	Sep-01	Friday	15,759	CD	Teller	Westside	Existing
11	Sep-01	Friday	12,000	CD	New Accts	Westside	Existing
12	Sep-01	Friday	7,177	Savings	Teller	North County	Existing
13	Sep-01	Friday	6,837	Savings	New Accts	Westside	Existing
14	Sep-01	Friday	3,171	Checking	New Accts	Westside	Existing
15	Sep-01	Friday	50,000	Savings	New Accts	Central	Existing
16	Sep-01	Friday	4,690	Checking	New Accts	North County	New
17	Sep-01	Friday	12,438	Checking	New Accts	Central	Existing
18	Sep-01	Friday	5,000	Checking	New Accts	North County	Existing
19	Sep-01	Friday	7,000	Savings	New Accts	North County	New
20	Sep-01	Friday	11,957	Checking	New Accts	Central	Existing
21	Sep-01	Friday	13,636	CD	New Accts	North County	Existing
22	Sep-01	Friday	16,000	CD	New Accts	Central	New
23	Sep-01	Friday	5,879	Savings	New Accts	Central	Existing
24	Sep-01	Friday	4,000	Savings	New Accts	Central	Existing
25	Sep-01	Friday	10,000	CD	Teller	North County	Existing
26	Sep-01	Friday	7,427	Checking	New Accts	North County	Existing
27	Sep-01	Friday	4,500	Checking	New Accts	North County	New
28	Sep-01	Friday	12,962	Checking	Teller	Central	Existing
29	Sep-01	Friday	500	Checking	New Accts	Central	New
30	Sep-01	Friday	5,364	Checking	Teller	Central	New
31	Sep-01	Friday	45,000	CD	Teller	North County	Existing
32	Sep-01	Friday	14,867	Checking	Teller	North County	Existing
33	Sep-01	Friday	13,061	Checking	Teller	Central	New
34	Sep-01	Friday	11,779	CD	Teller	Central	New
35	Sep-02	Saturday	4,995	Checking	New Accts	Central	New
36	Sep-02	Saturday	10,096	Savings	New Accts	Central	New

This table consists of a month's worth of new account information for a three-branch bank. The table contains 712 rows, and each row represents a new account. The table has the following columns:

- The date the account was opened
- The day of the week the account was opened
- The opening amount
- The account type (CD, checking, savings, or IRA)
- Who opened the account (a teller or a new-account representative)
- The branch at which it was opened (Central, Westside, or North County)
- The type of customer (an existing customer or a new customer)

On the CD

This workbook, named `bank accounts.xlsx`, **is available on the companion CD-ROM.** ∎

The bank accounts database contains quite a bit of information. In its current form, though, the data doesn't reveal much. To make the data more useful, you need to summarize it. Summarizing a database is essentially the process of answering questions about the data. Following are a few questions that may be of interest to the bank's management:

- What is the daily total new deposit amount for each branch?
- Which day of the week accounts for the most deposits?
- How many accounts were opened at each branch, broken down by account type?
- What's the dollar distribution of the different account types?
- What types of accounts do tellers open most often?
- How does the Central branch compare with the other two branches?
- In which branch do tellers open the most checking accounts for new customers?

You can, of course, spend time sorting the data and creating formulas to answer these questions. But almost always, a pivot table is a better choice. Creating a pivot table takes only a few seconds, doesn't require a single formula, and produces a nice-looking report. In addition, pivot tables are much less prone to error than creating formulas. (Later in this chapter, you'll see several pivot tables that answer the preceding questions.)

Figure 34.2 shows a pivot table created from the bank data. This pivot table shows the amount of new deposits, broken down by branch and account type. This particular summary represents one of dozens of summaries that you can produce from this data.

Figure 34.3 shows another pivot table generated from the bank data. This pivot table uses a drop-down Report Filter for the Customer item (in row 1). In the figure, the pivot table displays the data only for Existing customers. (The user can also select New or All from the drop-down control.) Notice the change in the orientation of the table? For this pivot table, branches appear as column labels, and account types appear as row labels. This change, which took about five seconds to make, is another example of the flexibility of a pivot table.

FIGURE 34.2

A simple pivot table.

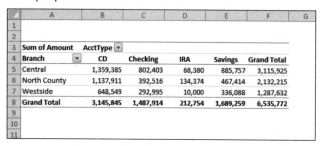

FIGURE 34.3

A pivot table that uses a report filter.

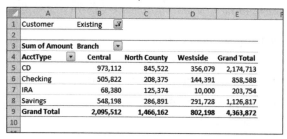

Data appropriate for a pivot table

A pivot table requires that your data is in the form of a rectangular database. You can store the database in either a worksheet range (which can be a table or just a normal range) or an external database file. And although Excel can generate a pivot table from any database, not all databases benefit.

Generally speaking, fields in a database table consist of two types:

- **Data:** Contains a value or data to be summarized. For the bank account example, the Amount field is a data field.

- **Category:** Describes the data. For the bank account data, the Date, AcctType, OpenedBy, Branch, and Customer fields are category fields because they describe the data in the Amount field.

Note

A database table that's appropriate for a pivot table is said to be "normalized." In other words, each record (or row) contains information that describes the data. ■

Why "Pivot?"

Are you curious about the term "pivot?"

Pivot, as a verb, means to rotate or revolve. If you think of your data as a physical object, a pivot table lets you rotate the data summary and look at it from different angles or perspectives. A pivot table allows you to move fields around easily, nest fields within each other, and even create ad hoc groups of items.

If you were handed a strange object and asked to identify it, you'd probably look at it from several different angles in an attempt to figure it out. Working with a pivot table is similar to investigating a strange object. In this case, the object happens to be your data. A pivot table invites experimentation, so feel free to rotate and manipulate the pivot table until you're satisfied. You may be surprised at what you discover.

A single database table can have any number of data fields and category fields. When you create a pivot table, you usually want to summarize one or more of the data fields. Conversely, the values in the category fields appear in the pivot table as rows, columns, or filters.

Exceptions exist, however, and you may find the Excel Pivot Table feature useful even for databases that don't contain actual numerical data fields. Chapter 35 has an example of a pivot table created from non-numeric data.

Figure 34.4 shows an example of an Excel range that is *not* appropriate for a pivot table. You might recognize this data from the outline example in Chapter 26. Although the range contains descriptive information about each value, it does *not* consist of normalized data. In fact, this range actually resembles a pivot table summary, but it is much less flexible.

FIGURE 34.4

This range is not appropriate for a pivot table.

	A	B	C	D	E	F	G	H	I	J
1	State	Jan	Feb	Mar	Qtr-1	Apr	May	Jun	Qtr-2	Total
2	California	1,118	1,960	1,252	4,330	1,271	1,557	1,679	4,507	8,837
3	Washington	1,247	1,238	1,028	3,513	1,345	1,784	1,574	4,703	8,216
4	Oregon	1,460	1,954	1,726	5,140	1,461	1,764	1,144	4,369	9,509
5	Arizona	1,345	1,375	1,075	3,795	1,736	1,555	1,372	4,663	8,458
6	West Total	5,170	6,527	5,081	16,778	5,813	6,660	5,769	18,242	35,020
7	New York	1,429	1,316	1,993	4,738	1,832	1,740	1,191	4,763	9,501
8	New Jersey	1,735	1,406	1,224	4,365	1,706	1,320	1,290	4,316	8,681
9	Massachusetts	1,099	1,233	1,110	3,442	1,637	1,512	1,006	4,155	7,597
10	Florida	1,705	1,792	1,225	4,722	1,946	1,327	1,357	4,630	9,352
11	East Total	5,968	5,747	5,552	17,267	7,121	5,899	4,844	17,864	35,131
12	Kentucky	1,109	1,078	1,155	3,342	1,993	1,082	1,551	4,626	7,968
13	Oklahoma	1,309	1,045	1,641	3,995	1,924	1,499	1,941	5,364	9,359
14	Missouri	1,511	1,744	1,414	4,669	1,243	1,493	1,820	4,556	9,225
15	Illinois	1,539	1,493	1,211	4,243	1,165	1,013	1,445	3,623	7,866
16	Kansas	1,973	1,560	1,243	4,776	1,495	1,125	1,387	4,007	8,783
17	Central Total	7,441	6,920	6,664	21,025	7,820	6,212	8,144	22,176	43,201
18	Grand Total	18,579	19,194	17,297	55,070	20,754	18,771	18,757	58,282	113,352
19										

Figure 34.5 shows the same data, but normalized. This range contains 78 rows of data — one for each of the six monthly sales values for the 13 states. Notice that each row contains category information for the sales value. This table is an ideal candidate for a pivot table, and contains all information necessary to summarize the information by region or quarter.

This range contains normalized data and is appropriate for a pivot table.

	A	B	C	D	E
1	State	Region	Month	Qtr	Sales
2	California	West	Jan	Qtr-1	1,118
3	California	West	Feb	Qtr-1	1,960
4	California	West	Mar	Qtr-1	1,252
5	California	West	Apr	Qtr-2	1,271
6	California	West	May	Qtr-2	1,557
7	California	West	Jun	Qtr-2	1,679
8	Washington	West	Jan	Qtr-1	1,247
9	Washington	West	Feb	Qtr-1	1,238
10	Washington	West	Mar	Qtr-1	1,028
11	Washington	West	Apr	Qtr-2	1,345
12	Washington	West	May	Qtr-2	1,784
13	Washington	West	Jun	Qtr-2	1,574
14	Oregon	West	Jan	Qtr-1	1,460
15	Oregon	West	Feb	Qtr-1	1,954
16	Oregon	West	Mar	Qtr-1	1,726
17	Oregon	West	Apr	Qtr-2	1,461
18	Oregon	West	May	Qtr-2	1,764
19	Oregon	West	Jun	Qtr-2	1,144
20	Arizona	West	Jan	Qtr-1	1,345
21	Arizona	West	Feb	Qtr-1	1,375
22	Arizona	West	Mar	Qtr-1	1,075
23	Arizona	West	Apr	Qtr-2	1,736
24	Arizona	West	May	Qtr-2	1,555

Figure 34.6 shows a pivot table created from the normalized data. As you can see, it's virtually identical to the non-normalized data shown in Figure 34.4.

On the CD

This workbook, named `normalized data.xlsx`, is available on the companion CD-ROM. ■

A pivot table created from normalized data.

Sum of Sales	Column									
	Qtr-1			Qtr-1 Total	Qtr-2			Qtr-2 Total	Grand Total
Row Labels	Jan	Feb	Mar		Apr	May	Jun		
West	5,170	6,527	5,081	16,778	5,813	6,660	5,769	18,242	35,020
Arizona	1,345	1,375	1,075	3,795	1,736	1,555	1,372	4,663	8,458
California	1,118	1,960	1,252	4,330	1,271	1,557	1,679	4,507	8,837
Oregon	1,460	1,954	1,726	5,140	1,461	1,764	1,144	4,369	9,509
Washington	1,247	1,238	1,028	3,513	1,345	1,784	1,574	4,703	8,216
East	5,968	5,747	5,552	17,267	7,121	5,899	4,844	17,864	35,131
Florida	1,705	1,792	1,225	4,722	1,946	1,327	1,357	4,630	9,352
Massachusetts	1,099	1,233	1,110	3,442	1,637	1,512	1,006	4,155	7,597
New Jersey	1,735	1,406	1,224	4,365	1,706	1,320	1,290	4,316	8,681
New York	1,429	1,316	1,993	4,738	1,832	1,740	1,191	4,763	9,501
Central	7,441	6,920	6,664	21,025	7,820	6,212	8,144	22,176	43,201
Illinois	1,539	1,493	1,211	4,243	1,165	1,013	1,445	3,623	7,866
Kansas	1,973	1,560	1,243	4,776	1,495	1,125	1,387	4,007	8,783
Kentucky	1,109	1,078	1,155	3,342	1,993	1,082	1,551	4,626	7,968
Missouri	1,511	1,744	1,414	4,669	1,243	1,493	1,820	4,556	9,225
Oklahoma	1,309	1,045	1,641	3,995	1,924	1,499	1,941	5,364	9,359
Grand Total	18,579	19,194	17,297	55,070	20,754	18,771	18,757	58,282	113,352

Creating a Pivot Table

In this section, I describe the basic steps required to create a pivot table, using the bank account data described earlier in this chapter. Creating a pivot table is an interactive process. It's not at all uncommon to experiment with various layouts until you find one that you're satisfied with. If you're unfamiliar with the elements of a pivot table, see the upcoming sidebar, "Pivot Table Terminology."

Specifying the data

If your data is in a worksheet range, select any cell in that range and then choose Insert ⇨ Tables ⇨ PivotTable, which displays the dialog box shown in Figure 34.7.

Excel attempts to guess the range, based on the location of the active cell. If you're creating a pivot table from an external data source, you need to select that option and then click Choose Connection to specify the data source.

Tip

If you're creating a pivot table from data in a worksheet, it's a good idea to first create a table for the range (choose Insert ⇨ Tables ⇨ Table). Then, if you expand the table by adding new rows of data, Excel will refresh the pivot table without the need to manually indicate the new data range. ■

FIGURE 34.7

In the Create PivotTable dialog box, you tell Excel where the data is and where you want the pivot table.

Specifying the location for the pivot table

Use the bottom section of the Create PivotTable dialog box to indicate the location for your pivot table. The default location is on a new worksheet, but you can specify any range on any worksheet, including the worksheet that contains the data.

Click OK, and Excel creates an empty pivot table and displays its PivotTable Field List task pane, as shown in Figure 34.8.

FIGURE 34.8

Use the PivotTable Field List to build the pivot table.

Tip

The PivotTable Field List is typically docked on the right side of the Excel window. Drag its title bar to move it anywhere you like. Also, if you click a cell outside the pivot table, the PivotTable Field List is hidden. ∎

Laying out the pivot table

Next, set up the actual layout of the pivot table. You can do so by using either of any techniques:

- Drag the field names (at the top) to one of the four boxes at the bottom of the PivotTable Field List.

- Place a check mark next to the item at the top of the PivotTable Field List. Excel will place the field into one of the four boxes at the bottom.

- Right-click a field name at the top of the PivotTable Field List and choose its location from the shortcut menu.

Note

In versions prior to Excel 2007, you could drag items from the field list directly into the appropriate area of the pivot table. This feature is still available, but it's turned off by default. To enable this feature, choose PivotTable Tools ⇨ Options ⇨ PivotTable Options ⇨ Options to display the PivotTable Options dialog box. Click the Display tab and then select the Classic PivotTable Layout check box. ∎

The following steps create the pivot table presented earlier in this chapter (see "A pivot table example"). For this example, I drag the items from the top of the PivotTable Field List to the areas in the bottom of the PivotTable Field List.

1. **Drag the Amount field into the Values area.** At this point, the pivot table displays the total of all the values in the Amount column.

2. **Drag the AcctType field into the Row Labels area.** Now the pivot table shows the total amount for each of the account types.

3. **Drag the Branch field into the Column Labels area.** The pivot table shows the amount for each account type, cross-tabulated by branch (see Figure 34.9). The pivot table updates itself automatically with every change you make in the PivotTable Field List.

FIGURE 34.9

After a few simple steps, the pivot table shows a summary of the data.

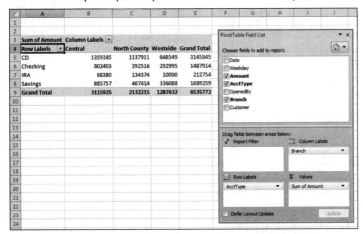

Formatting the pivot table

Notice that the pivot table uses General number formatting. To change the number format for all data, right-click any value and choose Number Format from the shortcut menu. Then use the Format Cells dialog box to change the number format for the displayed data.

You can apply any of several built-in styles to a pivot table. Select any cell in the pivot table and then choose PivotTable Tools ➪ Design ➪ PivotTable Styles to select a style.

You also can use the controls from the PivotTable ➪ Design ➪ Layout group to control various elements in the pivot table. For example, you can choose to hide the grand totals if you prefer.

The PivotTable Tools ➪ Options ➪ Show group contains additional options that affect the appearance of your pivot table. For example, you use the Show Field Headers button to toggle the display of the field headings.

Still more pivot table options are available from the PivotTable Options dialog box, shown in Figure 34.10. To display this dialog box, choose PivotTable Tools ➪ Options ➪ PivotTable ➪ Options. Or, right-click any cell in the pivot table and choose Table Options from the shortcut menu.

Pivot Table Terminology

Understanding the terminology associated with pivot tables is the first step in mastering this feature. Refer to the accompanying figure to get your bearings.

- **Column labels:** A field that has a column orientation in the pivot table. Each item in the field occupies a column. In the figure, Customer represents a column field that contains two items (Existing and New). You can have nested column fields.

- **Grand totals:** A row or column that displays totals for all cells in a row or column in a pivot table. You can specify that grand totals be calculated for rows, columns, or both (or neither). The pivot table in the figure shows grand totals for both rows and columns.

- **Group:** A collection of items treated as a single item. You can group items manually or automatically (group dates into months, for example). The pivot table in the figure does not have any defined groups.

- **Item:** An element in a field that appears as a row or column header in a pivot table. In the figure, Existing and New are items for the Customer field. The Branch field has three items: Central, North County, and Westside. AcctType has four items: CD, Checking, IRA, and Savings.

- **Refresh:** Recalculates the pivot table after making changes to the source data.

- **Row labels:** A field that has a row orientation in the pivot table. Each item in the field occupies a row. You can have nested row fields. In the figure, Branch and AcctType both represent row fields.

- **Source data:** The data used to create a pivot table. It can reside in a worksheet or an external database.

- **Subtotals:** A row or column that displays subtotals for detail cells in a row or column in a pivot table. The pivot table in the figure displays subtotals for each branch.

- **Table Filter:** A field that has a page orientation in the pivot table — similar to a slice of a three-dimensional cube. You can display only one item (or all items) in a page field at one time. In the figure, OpenedBy represents a page field that displays All (that is, not filtered). In previous version of Excel, a table filter was known as a Page field.

- **Values area:** The cells in a pivot table that contain the summary data. Excel offers several ways to summarize the data (sum, average, count, and so on).

FIGURE 34.10

The PivotTable Options dialog box.

Modifying the pivot table

After you create a pivot table, changing it is easy. For example, you can add further summary information by using the PivotTable Field List. Figure 34.11 shows the pivot table after I dragged a second field (OpenedBy) to the Row Labels section in the PivotTable Field List.

FIGURE 34.11

Two fields are used for row labels.

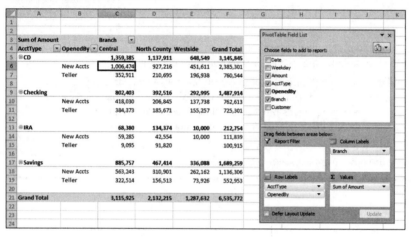

The following are some tips on other pivot table modifications you can make:

- To remove a field from the pivot table, select it in the bottom part of the PivotTable Field List and then drag it away.

- If an area has more than one field, you can change the order in which the fields are listed by dragging the field names. Doing so affects the appearance of the pivot table.

- To temporarily remove a field from the pivot table, remove the check mark from the field name in the top part of the PivotTable Field List. The pivot table is redisplayed without that field. Place the check mark back on the field name, and it appears in its previous section.

- If you add a field to the Report Filter section, the field items appear in a drop-down list, which allows you to filter the displayed data by one or more items. Figure 34.12 shows an example. I dragged the Date field to the Report Filter area. The report is now showing the data only for a single day (which I selected from the drop-down list in cell B1).

Pivot Table Calculations

Pivot table data is most frequently summarized using a sum. However, you can display your data using a number of different summary techniques. Select any cell in the Values area of your pivot table and then choose PivotTable Tools ➪ Options ➪ Active Field ➪ Field Settings to display the Value Field Settings dialog box. This dialog box has two tabs: Summarize Values By and Show Values As.

Use the Summarize Values By tab to select a different summary function. Your choices are Sum, Count, Average, Max, Min, Product, Count Numbers, StdDev, StdDevp, Var, and Varp.

To display your values in a different form, use the drop-down control on the Show Values As tab. You have many options to choose from, including as a percentage of the total or subtotal.

FIGURE 34.12

The pivot table is filtered by date.

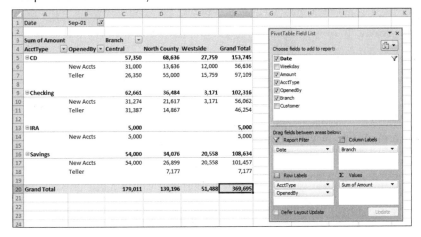

Copying a Pivot Table

A pivot table is very flexible, but it does have some limitations. For example, you can't add new rows or columns, change any of the calculated values, or enter formulas within the pivot table. If you want to manipulate a pivot table in ways not normally permitted, make a copy of it.

To copy a pivot table, select the entire table and choose Home ➪ Clipboard ➪ Copy (or, press Ctrl+C). Then select a new worksheet and choose Home Clipboard ➪ Paste ➪ Paste Values. The pivot table formatting is not copied — even if you repeat the operation and use the Formats option in the Paste Special dialog box.

To copy the pivot table and its formatting, use the Office Clipboard to paste. If the Office Clipboard is not displayed, click the dialog box launcher in the bottom right of the Home ➪ Clipboard group.

The contents of the pivot table are copied to the new location so that you can do whatever you like to them.

Note that the copied information is not a pivot table, and it is no longer linked to the source data. If the source data changes, your copied pivot table will not reflect these changes.

More Pivot Table Examples

To demonstrate the flexibility of this feature, I created some additional pivot tables. The examples use the bank account data and answer the questions posed earlier in this chapter (see "A pivot table example").

Question 1

What is the daily total new deposit amount for each branch?

Figure 34.13 shows the pivot table that answers this question.

- The Branch field is in the Column Labels section.
- The Date field is in the Row Labels section.
- The Amount field is in the Values section and is summarized by Sum.

Note that the pivot table can also be sorted by any column. For example, you can sort the Grand Total column in descending order to find out which day of the month had the largest amount of new funds. To sort, just right-click any cell in the column to sort and choose Sort from the short-cut menu.

FIGURE 34.13

This pivot table shows daily totals for each branch.

Date	Central	North County	Westside	Grand Total
Sep-01	135,345	57,402	51,488	244,235
Sep-02	79,642	81,794		161,436
Sep-03	59,119	65,530	20,117	144,766
Sep-04	123,451	126,580	109,899	359,930
Sep-05	101,480	50,294	97,415	249,189
Sep-06	188,018	91,724	52,738	332,480
Sep-07	271,227	196,188	53,525	520,940
Sep-08	67,999	24,123	47,329	139,451
Sep-09	14,475	41,248	36,172	91,895
Sep-10	91,367	24,238	8,512	124,117
Sep-11	104,166	32,018	89,258	225,442
Sep-12	70,300	43,621	39,797	153,718
Sep-13	143,921	176,698	29,075	349,694
Sep-14	117,800	114,418	36,064	268,282
Sep-15	88,566	41,635	78,481	208,682
Sep-16	79,579	21,152	6,534	107,265
Sep-17	56,187	29,380	7,037	92,604
Sep-18	46,673	42,882	41,300	130,855
Sep-19	208,916	213,728	53,721	476,365
Sep-20	125,276	140,739	56,444	322,459
Sep-21	79,355	35,753	3,419	118,527
Sep-22	132,403	149,447	97,210	379,060
Sep-23	56,106	15,823		71,929
Sep-24	75,606	23,285	28,457	127,348
Sep-25	143,283	113,740	57,371	314,394
Sep-26	150,139	29,040	94,310	273,489
Sep-27	56,379	72,948	43,472	172,799
Sep-28	62,192	43,217	12,128	117,537
Sep-29	186,955	33,570	36,359	256,884
Grand Total	**3,115,925**	**2,132,215**	**1,287,632**	**6,535,772**

Question 2

Which day of the week accounts for the most deposits?

Figure 34.14 shows the pivot table that answers this question.

- The Weekday field is in the Row Labels section.
- The Amount field is in the Values section and is summarized by Sum.

I added conditional formatting data bars to make it easier to see how the days compare.

Cross-Reference

See Chapter 20 for more information about conditional formatting. ∎

FIGURE 34.14

This pivot table shows totals by day of the week.

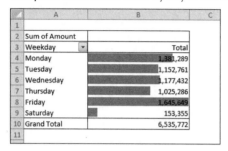

	A	B	C
1			
2	Sum of Amount		
3	Weekday	Total	
4	Monday	1,381,289	
5	Tuesday	1,152,761	
6	Wednesday	1,177,432	
7	Thursday	1,025,286	
8	Friday	1,645,649	
9	Saturday	153,355	
10	Grand Total	6,535,772	
11			

Question 3

How many accounts were opened at each branch, broken down by account type?

Figure 34.15 shows a pivot table that answers this question.

- The AcctType field is in the Column Labels section.
- The Branch field is in the Row Labels section.
- The Amount field is in the Values section and is summarized by Count.

The most common summary function used in pivot tables is Sum. In this case, I changed the summary function to Count. To change the summary function to Count, right-click any cell in the Value area and choose Summarize Data By ➪ Count from the shortcut menu.

FIGURE 34.15

This pivot table uses the Count function to summarize the data.

	A	B	C	D	E	F
1						
2	Count of Amount	AcctType				
3	Branch	CD	Checking	IRA	Savings	Grand Total
4	Central	97	158	8	99	362
5	North County	60	61	15	61	197
6	Westside	54	59	5	35	153
7	Grand Total	211	278	28	195	712
8						
9						

Question 4

What's the dollar distribution of the different account types?

Figure 34.16 shows a pivot table that answers this question. For example, 253 of the new accounts were for an amount of $5,000 or less.

FIGURE 34.16

This pivot table counts the number of accounts that fall into each value range.

This pivot table is unusual because it uses only one field: Amount.

- The Amount field is in the Row Labels section (grouped).
- The Amount field is also in the Values section and is summarized by Count.
- A third instance of the Amount field is the Values section, summarized by Percent of Total.

When I initially added the Amount field to the Row Labels section, the pivot table showed a row for each unique dollar amount. I right-clicked one of the Row Labels and chose Group from the shortcut menu. Then I used the Grouping dialog box to set up bins of $5,000 increments.

The second instance of the Amount field (in the Values section) is summarized by Count. I right-clicked a value and chose Summarize Data By ➪ Count from the shortcut menu.

I added another instance of Amount to the Values section, and I set it up to display the percentage. I right-clicked a value in column C and chose Show Values As ➪ % of Grand Total. This option is also available in the Show Values As tab of the Value Field Settings dialog box.

Question 5

What types of accounts do tellers open most often?

Figure 34.17 shows that the most common account opened by tellers is a Checking account.

- The AcctType field is in the Row Labels section.
- The OpenedBy field is in the Report Filters section.

- The Amount field is in the Values section (summarized by Count).

- A second instance of the Amount field is in the Values section (summarized by % of Total).

This pivot table uses the OpenedBy field as a Report Filter and is showing the data only for Tellers. I sorted the data so that the largest value is at the top, and I also used conditional formatting to display data bars for the percentages.

Cross-Reference

See Chapter 20 for more information about conditional formatting. ∎

FIGURE 34.17

This pivot table uses a Report Filter to show only the Teller data.

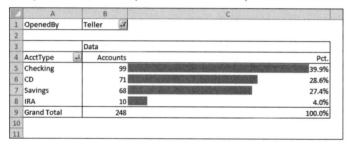

Question 6

How does the Central branch compare with the other two branches?

Figure 34.18 shows a pivot table that sheds some light on this rather vague question. It simply shows how the Central branch compares with the other two branches combined.

- The AcctType field is in the Row Labels section.

- The Branch field is in the Column Labels section.

- The Amount field is in the Values section.

I grouped the North County and Westside branches together and named the group Other. The pivot table shows the amount, by account type. I also created a pivot chart for good measure. See Chapter 35 for more information about pivot charts.

FIGURE 34.18

This pivot table (and pivot chart) compares the Central branch with the other two branches combined.

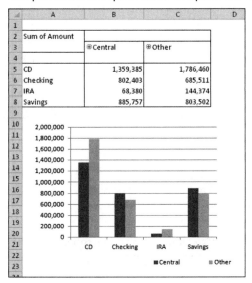

	⊞ Central	⊞ Other	
Sum of Amount			
CD	1,359,385	1,786,460	
Checking	802,403	685,511	
IRA	68,380	144,374	
Savings	885,757	803,502	

Question 7

In which branch do tellers open the most checking accounts for new customers?

Figure 34.19 shows a pivot table that answers this question. At the Central branch, tellers opened 23 checking accounts for new customers.

- The Customer field is in the Report Filters section.
- The OpenedBy field is in the Report Filters section.
- The AcctType field is in the Report Filters section.
- The Branch field is in the Row Labels section.
- The Amount field is in the Values section, summarized by Count.

This pivot table uses three Report Filters. The Customer field is filtered to show only New, the OpenedBy field is filtered to show only Teller, and the AcctType field is filtered to show only Checking.

FIGURE 34.19

This pivot table uses three Report Filters.

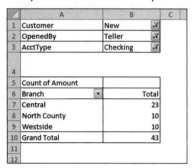

Learning More

The examples in this chapter should give you an appreciation for the power and flexibility of Excel pivot tables. The next chapter digs a bit deeper and covers some advanced features — with lots of examples.

Analyzing Data with Pivot Tables

IN THIS CHAPTER

How to create a pivot table from non-numeric data

How to group items in a pivot table

How to create a calculated field or a calculated item in a pivot table

How to create an attractive report using a pivot table

The previous chapter introduces pivot tables. There, I present several examples to demonstrate the types of pivot table summaries that you can generate from a set of data.

This chapter continues the discussion and explores the details of creating effective pivot tables. Creating a basic pivot table is very easy, and the examples in this chapter demonstrate additional pivot table features that you may find helpful. I urge you to try these techniques with your own data. If you don't have suitable data, use the files on the companion CD-ROM.

Working with Non-Numeric Data

Most pivot tables are created from numeric data, but pivot tables are also useful with some types of non-numeric data. Because you can't sum non-numbers, this technique involves counting.

Figure 35.1 shows a table and a pivot table generated from the table. The table is a list of 400 employees, along with their location and gender. As you can see, the table has no numeric values, but you can create a useful pivot table that counts the items rather than sums them. The pivot table cross-tabulates the Location field by the Sex field for the 400 employees and shows the count for each combination of location and gender.

On the CD

A workbook that demonstrates the pivot table created from non-numeric data is available on the companion CD-ROM. The file is named employee list. xlsx.

Here are the settings I used for this pivot table:

- The Sex field is used for the Column Labels.
- The Location field is used for the Row Labels.
- Location is used for the Values and is summarized by Count.
- The pivot table has the field headers turned off (by choosing PivotTable Tools ➪ Options ➪ Show ➪ Show Field headers).

This table doesn't have any numeric fields, but you can use it to generate a pivot table, shown next to the table.

Note

The Employee field is not used. This example uses the Location field for the Values section, but you can actually use any of the three fields because the pivot table is displaying a count. ■

Figure 35.2 shows the pivot table after making some additional changes:

- I added a second instance of the Location field to the Values section. To display percentages, I right-clicked a value in that column, and chose Show Values As ➪ Percent of Column Total.
- I changed the field names in the pivot table to Count and Pct.
- I selected a Pivot Table Style that makes it easier to distinguish the columns.

FIGURE 35.2

The pivot table, after making a few changes.

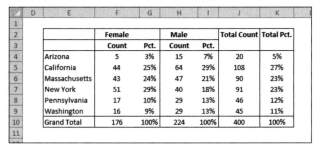

	Female		Male		Total Count	Total Pct.
	Count	Pct.	Count	Pct.		
Arizona	5	3%	15	7%	20	5%
California	44	25%	64	29%	108	27%
Massachusetts	43	24%	47	21%	90	23%
New York	51	29%	40	18%	91	23%
Pennsylvania	17	10%	29	13%	46	12%
Washington	16	9%	29	13%	45	11%
Grand Total	176	100%	224	100%	400	100%

Grouping Pivot Table Items

One of the most useful features of a pivot table is the ability to combine items into groups. You can group items that appear as Row Labels or Column Labels. Excel offers two ways to group items:

- **Manually:** After creating the pivot table, select the items to be grouped and then choose PivotTable Tools ➪ Options ➪ Group ➪ Group Selection. Or, you can right-click and choose Group from the shortcut menu.

- **Automatically:** If the items are numeric (or dates), use the Grouping dialog box to specify how you would like to group the items. Select any item in the Row Labels or Column Labels and then choose PivotTable Tools ➪ Options ➪ Group ➪ Group Selection. Or, you can right-click and choose Group from the shortcut menu. In either case, Excel displays its Grouping dialog box.

A manual grouping example

Figure 35.3 shows the pivot table example from the previous sections, with two groups created from the Row Labels. To create the first group, I held the Ctrl key while I selected Arizona, California, and Washington. Then I right-clicked and chose Group from the shortcut menu. Excel created a second group automatically. Then I replaced the default group names (Group 1 and Group 2) with more meaningful names (Western Region and Eastern Region).

You can create any number of groups, and even create groups of groups.

Excel provides a number of options for displaying a pivot table, and you may want to experiment with these options when you use groups. These commands are on the PivotTable Tools ➪ Design tab of the Ribbon. There are no rules for choosing a particular option. The key is to try a few and see which makes your pivot table look the best. In addition, try various PivotTable Styles, with options for banded rows or banded columns. Often, the style that you choose can greatly enhance readability.

FIGURE 35.3

A pivot table with two groups.

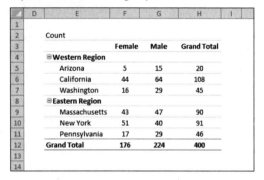

	Female	Male	Grand Total
Count			
Western Region			
Arizona	5	15	20
California	44	64	108
Washington	16	29	45
Eastern Region			
Massachusetts	43	47	90
New York	51	40	91
Pennsylvania	17	29	46
Grand Total	176	224	400

Figure 35.4 shows pivot tables using various options for displaying subtotals, grand totals, and styles.

FIGURE 35.4

Pivot tables with options for subtotals and grand totals.

Automatic grouping examples

When a field contains numbers, dates, or times, Excel can create groups automatically. The two examples in this section demonstrate automatic grouping.

Grouping by date

Figure 35.5 shows a portion of a simple table with two fields: Date and Sales. This table has 730 rows and covers the dates between January 1, 2008 and December 31, 2009. The goal is to summarize the sales information by month.

FIGURE 35.5

You can use a pivot table to summarize the sales data by month.

	A	B	C	D
1	Date	Sales		
2	1/1/2008	3,830		
3	1/2/2008	3,763		
4	1/3/2008	4,362		
5	1/4/2008	3,669		
6	1/5/2008	3,942		
7	1/6/2008	4,488		
8	1/7/2008	4,416		
9	1/8/2008	3,371		
10	1/9/2008	3,628		
11	1/10/2008	4,548		
12	1/11/2008	5,493		
13	1/12/2008	5,706		
14	1/13/2008	6,579		
15	1/14/2008	6,333		
16	1/15/2008	6,101		
17	1/16/2008	5,289		
18	1/17/2008	5,349		
19	1/18/2008	5,814		
20	1/19/2008	6,501		

On the CD

A workbook demonstrating how to group pivot table items by date is available on the companion CD-ROM. The file is named sales by date.xlsx.

Figure 35.6 shows part of a pivot table created from the data. The Date field is in the Row Labels section, and the Sales field is in the Values section. Not surprisingly, the pivot table looks exactly like the input data because the dates have not been grouped.

To group the items by month, select any date and choose PivotTable Tools ➪ Options ➪ Group ➪ Group Field (or, right-click and choose Group from the shortcut menu). You see the Grouping dialog box, shown in Figure 35.7. Excel supplies values for the Starting At and Ending At fields. The values cover the entire range of data, and you can change them if you like.

FIGURE 35.6

The pivot table, before grouping by month.

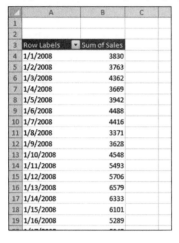

FIGURE 35.7

Use the Grouping dialog box to group pivot table items by dates.

In the By list box, select Months and Years and verify that the starting and ending dates are correct for your data. Click OK. The Date items in the pivot table are grouped by years and by months, as shown in Figure 35.8.

Note

If you select only Months in the By list box in the Grouping dialog box, months in different years combine together. For example, the January item would display sales for both 2008 and 2009. ■

FIGURE 35.8

The pivot table, after grouping by month and year.

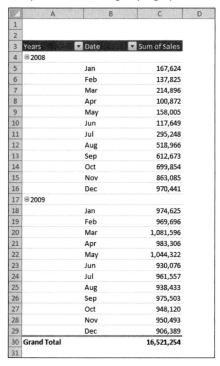

Years	Date	Sum of Sales
2008		
	Jan	167,624
	Feb	137,825
	Mar	214,896
	Apr	100,872
	May	158,005
	Jun	117,649
	Jul	295,248
	Aug	518,966
	Sep	612,673
	Oct	699,854
	Nov	863,085
	Dec	970,441
2009		
	Jan	974,625
	Feb	969,696
	Mar	1,081,596
	Apr	983,306
	May	1,044,322
	Jun	930,076
	Jul	961,557
	Aug	938,433
	Sep	975,503
	Oct	948,120
	Nov	950,493
	Dec	906,389
Grand Total		16,521,254

Figure 35.9 shows another view of the data, grouped by quarter and by year.

FIGURE 35.9

This pivot table shows sales by quarter and by year.

Years	Date	Sum of Sales
2008		
	Qtr1	520,345
	Qtr2	376,526
	Qtr3	1,426,887
	Qtr4	2,533,380
2009		
	Qtr1	3,025,917
	Qtr2	2,957,704
	Qtr3	2,875,493
	Qtr4	2,805,002
Grand Total		16,521,254

Grouping by time

Figure 35.10 shows a set of data in columns A:B. Each row is a reading from a measurement instrument, taken at one-minute intervals throughout an entire day. The table has 1,440 rows, each representing one minute. The pivot table summarizes the data by hour.

On the CD

This workbook, named `hourly readings.xlsx`, is available on the companion CD-ROM. ∎

Here are the settings I used for this pivot table:

- The Values area has three instances of the Reading field and each instance displays a different summary method (Average, Minimum, and Maximum). To change the summary method for a column, right-click any cell in the column and choose the Summarize Values By and then appropriate option.

- The Time field is in the Row Labels section, and I used the Grouping dialog box to group by Hours.

FIGURE 35.10

This pivot table is grouped by Hours.

	A	B	C	D	E	F	G	H
1	Time	Reading			Average	Minimum	Maximum	
2	6/15/2009 0:00	105.32		12 AM	110.50	104.37	116.21	
3	6/15/2009 0:01	105.35		1 AM	118.57	112.72	127.14	
4	6/15/2009 0:02	104.37		2 AM	124.39	115.75	130.36	
5	6/15/2009 0:03	106.40		3 AM	122.74	112.85	132.90	
6	6/15/2009 0:04	106.42		4 AM	129.29	123.99	133.52	
7	6/15/2009 0:05	105.45		5 AM	132.91	125.88	141.04	
8	6/15/2009 0:06	107.46		6 AM	139.67	132.69	146.06	
9	6/15/2009 0:07	109.49		7 AM	128.18	117.53	139.65	
10	6/15/2009 0:08	110.54		8 AM	119.24	112.10	129.38	
11	6/15/2009 0:09	110.54		9 AM	134.36	129.11	142.79	
12	6/15/2009 0:10	110.55		10 AM	136.16	130.91	142.89	
13	6/15/2009 0:11	109.56		11 AM	122.79	108.63	138.10	
14	6/15/2009 0:12	107.60		12 PM	111.76	106.43	116.71	
15	6/15/2009 0:13	107.68		1 PM	104.91	98.48	111.86	
16	6/15/2009 0:14	109.69		2 PM	119.71	110.37	130.55	
17	6/15/2009 0:15	107.76		3 PM	131.83	121.92	139.65	
18	6/15/2009 0:16	107.81		4 PM	131.05	123.36	137.94	
19	6/15/2009 0:17	108.83		5 PM	138.90	133.05	145.06	
20	6/15/2009 0:18	109.85		6 PM	134.71	129.29	139.89	
21	6/15/2009 0:19	111.94		7 PM	123.09	113.97	135.23	
22	6/15/2009 0:20	114.04		8 PM	118.13	112.64	125.65	
23	6/15/2009 0:21	112.12		9 PM	112.64	108.09	117.72	
24	6/15/2009 0:22	112.21		10 PM	103.19	96.13	110.49	
25	6/15/2009 0:23	112.25		11 PM	106.01	100.03	111.76	
26	6/15/2009 0:24	113.34		Grand Total	123.11	96.13	146.06	
27	6/15/2009 0:25	112.41						
28	6/15/2009 0:26	112.42						

Creating a Frequency Distribution

Excel provides a number of ways to create a frequency distribution (see Chapter 13), but none of these methods is easier than using a pivot table.

Figure 35.11 shows part of a table of 221 students and the test score for each. The goal is to determine how many students are in each 10-point range (1–10, 11–20, and so on).

FIGURE 35.11

Creating a frequency distribution for these test scores is simple.

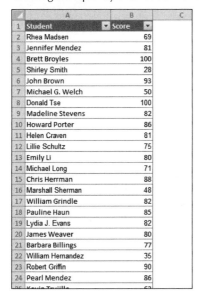

	A	B	C
1	Student	Score	
2	Rhea Madsen	69	
3	Jennifer Mendez	81	
4	Brett Broyles	100	
5	Shirley Smith	28	
6	John Brown	93	
7	Michael G. Welch	50	
8	Donald Tse	100	
9	Madeline Stevens	82	
10	Howard Porter	86	
11	Helen Craven	81	
12	Lillie Schultz	75	
13	Emily Li	80	
14	Michael Long	71	
15	Chris Herrman	88	
16	Marshall Sherman	48	
17	William Grindle	82	
18	Pauline Haun	85	
19	Lydia J. Evans	82	
20	James Weaver	80	
21	Barbara Billings	77	
22	William Hernandez	35	
23	Robert Griffin	90	
24	Pearl Mendez	86	

On the CD

This workbook, named `test scores.xlsx`, **is available on the companion CD-ROM.** ∎

The pivot table is simple:

- The Score field is in the Row Labels section (grouped).
- Another instance of the Score field is in the Values section (summarized by Count).

The Grouping dialog box that generated the bins specified that the groups start at 1, end at 100, and are incremented by 10.

Note

By default, Excel does not display items with a count of zero. In this example, no test scores are less than 21, so the 1–10 and 11–20 items are hidden. To force the display of empty bins, choose PivotTable Tools ⇨ Options ⇨ Field Settings to display the Field Settings dialog box. Click the Layout & Print tab, and select Show Items with No Data. ∎

Figure 35.12 show the frequency distribution of the test scores, along with a pivot chart. (See "Creating Pivot Charts," later in this chapter).

FIGURE 35.12

The pivot table and pivot chart show the frequency distribution for the test scores.

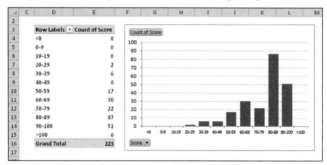

Note

This example uses the Excel Grouping dialog box to create the groups automatically. If you don't want to group in equal-sized bins, you can create your own groups. For example, you may want to assign letter grades based on the test score. Select the rows for the first group, right-click, and then choose Group from the shortcut menu. Repeat these steps for each additional group. Then replace the default group names with more meaningful names. ■

Creating a Calculated Field or Calculated Item

Perhaps the most confusing aspect of pivot tables is calculated fields versus calculated items. Many pivot table users simply avoid dealing with calculated fields and items. However, these features can be useful, and they really aren't that complicated once you understand how they work.

First, some basic definitions:

- **A calculated field:** A new field created from other fields in the pivot table. If your pivot table source is a worksheet table, an alternative to using a calculated field is to add a new column to the table, and create a formula to perform the desired calculation. A calculated field must reside in the Values area of the pivot table. You can't use a calculated field in the Column Labels, in the Row Labels, or in a Report Filter.

- **A calculated item:** Uses the contents of other items within a field of the pivot table. If your pivot table source is a worksheet table, an alternative to using a calculated item is to insert one or more rows and write formulas that use values in other rows. A calculated item must reside in the Column Labels, Row Labels, or Report Filter area of a pivot table. You can't use a calculated item in the Values area.

The formulas used to create calculated fields and calculated items aren't standard Excel formulas. In other words, you don't enter the formulas into cells. Rather, you enter these formulas in a dialog box, and they're stored along with the pivot table data.

The examples in this section use the worksheet table shown in Figure 35.13. The table consists of five columns and 48 rows. Each row describes monthly sales information for a particular sales representative. For example, Amy is a sales rep for the North region, and she sold 239 units in January for total sales of $23,040.

FIGURE 35.13

This data demonstrates calculated fields and calculated items.

	SalesRep	Region	Month	Sales	Units Sold	F
1	SalesRep	Region	Month	Sales	Units Sold	
2	Amy	North	Jan	$23,040	239	
3	Amy	North	Feb	$24,131	79	
4	Amy	North	Mar	$24,646	71	
5	Amy	North	Apr	$22,047	71	
6	Amy	North	May	$24,971	157	
7	Amy	North	Jun	$24,218	92	
8	Amy	North	Jul	$25,735	175	
9	Amy	North	Aug	$23,638	87	
10	Amy	North	Sep	$25,749	557	
11	Amy	North	Oct	$24,437	95	
12	Amy	North	Nov	$25,355	706	
13	Amy	North	Dec	$25,899	180	
14	Bob	North	Jan	$20,024	103	
15	Bob	North	Feb	$23,822	267	
16	Bob	North	Mar	$24,854	96	
17	Bob	North	Apr	$22,838	74	
18	Bob	North	May	$25,320	231	
19	Bob	North	Jun	$24,733	164	
20	Bob	North	Jul	$21,184	68	
21	Bob	North	Aug	$23,174	114	
22	Bob	North	Sep	$25,999	84	
23	Bob	North	Oct	$22,639	260	
24	Bob	North	Nov	$23,949	109	
25	Bob	North	Dec	$23,179	465	
26	Chuck	South	Jan	$19,886	95	
27	Chuck	South	Feb	$23,494	148	

On the CD

A workbook demonstrating calculated fields and items is available on the companion CD-ROM. The file is named `calculated fields and items.xlsx`.

Figure 35.14 shows a pivot table created from the data. This pivot table shows Sales (Values area), cross-tabulated by Month (Row Labels) and by SalesRep (Column Labels).

The examples that follow create

- A calculated field, to compute average sales per unit
- Four calculated items, to compute the quarterly sales commission

This pivot table was created from the sales data.

	Sum of Sales	Column Labels			
	Row Labels	Amy	Bob	Chuck	Doug
Jan		23,040	20,024	19,886	26,264
Feb		24,131	23,822	23,494	29,953
Mar		24,646	24,854	21,824	25,041
Apr		22,047	22,838	22,058	29,338
May		24,971	25,320	20,280	25,150
Jun		24,218	24,733	23,965	27,371
Jul		25,735	21,184	23,032	25,044
Aug		23,638	23,174	21,273	29,506
Sep		25,749	25,999	21,584	29,061
Oct		24,437	22,639	19,625	27,113
Nov		25,355	23,949	19,832	25,953
Dec		25,899	23,179	20,583	28,670
Grand Total		293,866	281,715	257,436	328,464

Creating a calculated field

Because a pivot table is a special type of range, you can't insert new rows or columns within the pivot table, which means that you can't insert formulas to perform calculations with the data in a pivot table. However, you can create calculated fields for a pivot table. A *calculated field* consists of a calculation that can involve other fields.

A calculated field is basically a way to display new information (derived from other fields) in a pivot table. It essentially presents an alternative to creating a new column field in your source data. In many cases, you may find it easier to insert a new column in the source range with a formula that performs the desired calculation. A calculated field is most useful when the data comes from a source that you can't easily manipulate — such as an external database.

In the sales example, for example, suppose that you want to calculate the average sales amount per unit. You can compute this value by dividing the Sales field by the Units Sold field. The result shows a new field (a calculated field) for the pivot table.

Use the following procedure to create a calculated field that consists of the Sales field divided by the Units Sold field:

1. **Select any cell within the pivot table.**
2. **Choose PivotTable Tools ⇨ Options ⇨ Calculations ⇨ Fields, Items & Sets ⇨ Calculated Field.** Excel displays the Insert Calculated Field dialog box.
3. **Enter a descriptive name in the Name box and specify the formula in the Formula box (see Figure 35.15).** The formula can use worksheet functions and other fields from

the data source. For this example, the calculated field name is Average Unit Price, and the formula is

```
=Sales/'Units Sold'
```

4. **Click Add to add this new field.**

5. **Click OK to close the Insert Calculated Field dialog box.**

The Insert Calculated Field dialog box.

Note

You can create the formula manually by typing it or by double-clicking items in the Fields list box. Double-clicking an item transfers it to the Formula field. Because the Units Sold field contains a space, Excel adds single quotes around the field name. ■

After you create the calculated field, Excel adds it to the Values area of the pivot table (and it also appears in the PivotTable Field List). You can treat it just like any other field, with one exception: You can't move it to the Row Labels, Column Labels, or Report Filter areas. It must remain in the Values area.

Figure 35.16 shows the pivot table after adding the calculated field. The new field displayed Sum of Average Unit Price, but I shortened this label to Avg Price. I also changed the style to display banded columns.

Tip

The formulas that you develop can also use worksheet functions, but the functions can't refer to cells or named ranges. ■

FIGURE 35.16

This pivot table uses a calculated field.

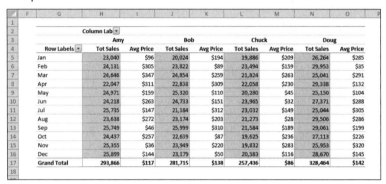

Row Labels	Amy		Bob		Chuck		Doug	
	Tot Sales	Avg Price	Tot Sales	Avg Price	Tot Sales	Avg Price	Tot Sales	Avg Price
Jan	23,040	$96	20,024	$194	19,886	$209	26,264	$285
Feb	24,131	$305	23,822	$89	23,494	$159	29,953	$35
Mar	24,646	$347	24,854	$259	21,824	$263	25,041	$291
Apr	22,047	$311	22,838	$309	22,058	$230	29,338	$132
May	24,971	$159	25,320	$110	20,280	$45	25,150	$104
Jun	24,218	$263	24,733	$151	23,965	$32	27,371	$288
Jul	25,735	$147	21,184	$312	23,032	$149	25,044	$305
Aug	23,638	$272	23,174	$203	21,273	$28	29,506	$286
Sep	25,749	$46	25,999	$310	21,584	$189	29,061	$199
Oct	24,437	$257	22,639	$87	19,625	$236	27,113	$226
Nov	25,355	$36	23,949	$220	19,832	$283	25,953	$320
Dec	25,899	$144	23,179	$50	20,583	$116	28,670	$145
Grand Total	293,866	$117	281,715	$138	257,436	$86	328,464	$142

Inserting a calculated item

The preceding section describes how to create a calculated field. Excel also enables you to create a *calculated item* for a pivot table field. Keep in mind that a calculated field can be an alternative to adding a new field to your data source. A calculated item, on the other hand, is an alternative to adding a new row to the data source — a row that contains a formula that refers to other rows.

In this example, you create four calculated items. Each item represents the commission earned on the quarter's sales, according to the following schedule:

- **Quarter 1:** 10% of January, February, and March sales
- **Quarter 2:** 11% of April, May, and June sales
- **Quarter 3:** 12% of July, August, and September sales
- **Quarter 4:** 12.5% of October, November, and December sales

Note
Modifying the source data to obtain this information would require inserting 16 new rows, each with formulas. So, for this example, creating four calculated items may be an easier task. ∎

To create a calculated item to compute the commission for January, February, and March, follow these steps:

1. **Move the cell pointer to the Row Labels or Column Labels area of the pivot table and choose PivotTable Tools ➪ Options ➪ Calculations ➪ Fields, Items & Sets ➪ Calculated Item.** Excel displays the Insert Calculated Item dialog box.

2. **Enter a name for the new item in the Name field and specify the formula in the Formula field (see Figure 35.17).** The formula can use items in other fields, but it can't use worksheet functions. For this example, the new item is named Qtr1 Commission, and the formula appears as follows:

```
=10%*(Jan+Feb+Mar)
```

3. **Click Add.**

4. **Repeat Steps 2 and 3 to create three additional calculated items:**

   Qtr2 Commission: = 11%*(Apr+May+Jun)

   Qtr3 Commission: = 12%*(Jul+Aug+Sep)

   Qtr4 Commission: = 12.5%*(Oct+Nov+Dec)

5. **Click OK to close the dialog box.**

FIGURE 35.17

The Insert Calculated Item dialog box.

Note

A calculated item, unlike a calculated field, does not appear in the PivotTable Field List. Only fields appear in the field list. ■

Caution

If you use a calculated item in your pivot table, you may need to turn off the Grand Total display for columns to avoid double counting. In this example, the Grand Total includes the calculated items, so the commission amounts are included with the sales amounts. To turn off Grand Totals, choose PivotTable Tools ➪ Design ➪ Layout ➪ Grand Totals. ■

After you create the calculated items, they appear in the pivot table. Figure 35.18 shows the pivot table after adding the four calculated items. Notice that the calculated items are added to the end of the Month items. You can rearrange the items by selecting the cell and dragging its border. Another option is to create two groups: One for the sales numbers, and one for the commission calculations. Figure 35.19 shows the pivot table after creating the two groups and adding subtotals.

FIGURE 35.18

This pivot table uses calculated items for quarterly totals.

Row Labels	Amy	Bob	Chuck	Doug	Grand Total
Jan	23,040	20,024	19,886	26,264	89,214
Feb	24,131	23,822	23,494	29,953	101,400
Mar	24,646	24,854	21,824	25,041	96,365
Apr	22,047	22,838	22,058	29,338	96,281
May	24,971	25,320	20,280	25,150	95,721
Jun	24,218	24,733	23,965	27,371	100,287
Jul	25,735	21,184	23,032	25,044	94,995
Aug	23,638	23,174	21,273	29,506	97,591
Sep	25,749	25,999	21,584	29,061	102,393
Oct	24,437	22,639	19,625	27,113	93,814
Nov	25,355	23,949	19,832	25,953	95,089
Dec	25,899	23,179	20,583	28,670	98,331
Qtr1 Commission	7,182	6,870	6,520	8,126	28,698
Qtr2 Commission	7,836	8,018	7,293	9,004	32,152
Qtr3 Commission	9,015	8,443	7,907	10,033	35,397
Qtr4 Commission	9,461	8,721	7,505	10,217	35,904

FIGURE 35.19

The pivot table, after creating two groups and adding subtotals.

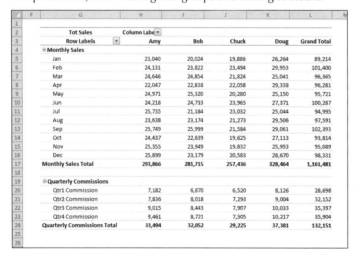

Row Labels	Amy	Bob	Chuck	Doug	Grand Total
Monthly Sales					
Jan	23,040	20,024	19,886	26,264	89,214
Feb	24,131	23,822	23,494	29,953	101,400
Mar	24,646	24,854	21,824	25,041	96,365
Apr	22,047	22,838	22,058	29,338	96,281
May	24,971	25,320	20,280	25,150	95,721
Jun	24,218	24,733	23,965	27,371	100,287
Jul	25,735	21,184	23,032	25,044	94,995
Aug	23,638	23,174	21,273	29,506	97,591
Sep	25,749	25,999	21,584	29,061	102,393
Oct	24,437	22,639	19,625	27,113	93,814
Nov	25,355	23,949	19,832	25,953	95,089
Dec	25,899	23,179	20,583	28,670	98,331
Monthly Sales Total	**293,866**	**281,715**	**257,436**	**328,464**	**1,161,481**
Quarterly Commissions					
Qtr1 Commission	7,182	6,870	6,520	8,126	28,698
Qtr2 Commission	7,836	8,018	7,293	9,004	32,152
Qtr3 Commission	9,015	8,443	7,907	10,033	35,397
Qtr4 Commission	9,461	8,721	7,505	10,217	35,904
Quarterly Commissions Total	**33,494**	**32,052**	**29,225**	**37,381**	**132,151**

A Reverse Pivot Table

The Excel Pivot Table feature creates a summary table from a list. But what if you want to perform the opposite operation? Often, you may have a two-way summary table, and it would be convenient if the data were in the form of a list.

In the figure here, range A1:E13 contains a summary table with 48 data points. Notice that this summary table is similar to a pivot table. Column G:I shows part of a 48-row table that was derived from the summary table. In other words, every value in the original summary table gets converted to a row, which also contains the region name and month. This type of table is useful because it can be sorted and manipulated in other ways. And, you can create a pivot table from this transformed table.

	A	B	C	D	E	F	G	H	I	J
1		North	South	East	West		Month	Region	Sales	
2	Jan	132	233	314	441		Jan	North	132	
3	Feb	143	251	314	447		Jan	South	233	
4	Mar	172	252	345	450		Jan	East	314	
5	Apr	184	290	365	452		Jan	West	441	
6	May	212	299	401	453		Feb	North	143	
7	Jun	239	317	413	457		Feb	South	251	
8	Jul	249	350	427	460		Feb	East	314	
9	Aug	263	354	448	468		Feb	West	447	
10	Sep	291	373	367	472		Mar	North	172	
11	Oct	294	401	392	479		Mar	South	252	
12	Nov	302	437	495	484		Mar	East	345	
13	Dec	305	466	504	490		Mar	West	450	
14							Apr	North	184	
15							Apr	South	290	
16							Apr	East	365	
17							Apr	West	452	
18							May	North	212	
19							May	South	299	
20							May	East	401	
21							May	West	453	
22							Jun	North	239	
23							Jun	South	317	
24							Jun	East	413	
25							Jun	West	457	
26							Jul	North	249	

The companion CD-ROM contains a workbook, `reverse pivot.xlsm`, which has a macro that will convert any two-way summary table into a three-column normalized table.

Filtering Pivot Tables with Slicers

A *Slicer* is an interactive control that makes it easy to filter data in a pivot table. Figure 35.20 shows a pivot table with three Slicers. Each Slicer represents a particular field. In this case, the pivot table is displaying data for New customers, opened by tellers at the Westside branch.

New Feature

Slicers are new to Excel 2010. ■

The same type of filtering can be accomplished by using the field labels in the pivot table, but Slicers are intended for those who might not understand how to filter data in a pivot table. Slicers can also be used to create an attractive and easy-to-use interactive "dashboard."

FIGURE 35.20

Using Slicers to filter the data displayed in a pivot table.

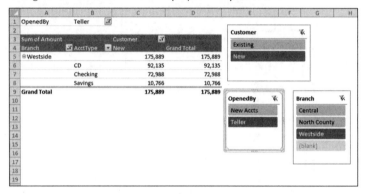

To add one or more Slicers to a worksheet, start by selecting any cell in a pivot table. Then choose Insert ➪ Filter ➪ Slicer. The Insert Slicers dialog box appears, with a list of all fields in the pivot table. Place a check mark next to the Slicers you want, and then click OK.

Slicers can be moved and resized, and you can change the look. To remove the effects of filtering by a particular Slicer, click the icon in the Slicer's upper-right corner.

To use a Slicer to filter data in a pivot table, just click a button. To display multiple values, press Ctrl while you click the buttons in a Slicer.

Figure 35.21 shows a pivot table and a pivot chart. Two Slicers are used to filter the data (by state and by month). In this case, the pivot table (and pivot chart) shows only the data for Missouri for the months of January through March. Slicers provide quick and easy way to create an interactive chart.

On the CD

This workbook, named `pivot chart slicer.xlsx`, **is available on the companion CD-ROM.** ■

FIGURE 35.21

Using Slicers to filter a pivot table by state and by month.

Referencing Cells within a Pivot Table

After you create a pivot table, you may want to create a formula that references one or more cells within a pivot table. Figure 35.22 shows a simple pivot table that displays income and expense information for three years. In this pivot table, the Month field is hidden, so the pivot table shows the year totals.

On the CD

This workbook, named income and expenses.xlsx, is available on the companion CD-ROM. ■

FIGURE 35.22

The formulas in column F reference cells in the pivot table.

Year	Month	Sum of Income	Sum of Expenses		Ratio
⊞2007		1,256,274	525,288		41.8%
⊞2008		1,357,068	533,893		39.3%
⊞2009		1,583,717	646,181		40.8%
Grand Total		4,197,059	1,705,362		40.6%

Column F contains formulas, and this column is not part of the pivot table. These formulas calculate the expense-to-income ratio for each year. I created these formulas by pointing to the cells. You may expect to see this formula in cell F5:

```
=D5/C5
```

In fact, the formula in cell F5 is

```
=GETPIVOTDATA("Sum of Expenses",$A$3,"Year",2007)/GETPIVOTDATA
    ("Sum of Income",$A$3,"Year",2007)
```

When you use the pointing technique to create a formula that references a cell in a pivot table, Excel replaces those simple cell references with a much more complicated GETPIVOTDATA function. If you type the cell references manually (rather than pointing to them), Excel does not use the GETPIVOTDATA function.

The reason? Using the GETPIVOTDATA function helps ensure that the formula will continue to reference the intended cells if the pivot table layout is changed. Figure 35.23 shows the pivot table after expanding the years to show the month detail. As you can see, the formulas in column F still show the correct result even though the referenced cells are in a different location. Had I used simple cell references, the formula would return incorrect results after expanding the years.

Caution

Using the GETPIVOTDATA function has one caveat: The data that it retrieves must be visible. If you modify the pivot table so that the value returned by GETPIVOTDATA is no longer visible, the formula returns an error. ■

Tip

If, for some reason, you want to prevent Excel from using the GETPIVOTDATA function when you point to pivot table cells when creating a formula, choose PivotTable Tools ➪ Options ➪ PivotTable ➪ Options ➪ Generate GetPivot Data. (This command is a toggle.) ■

FIGURE 35.23

After expanding the pivot table, formulas that use the GETPIVOTDATA function continue to display the correct result.

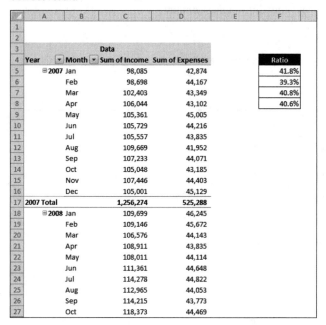

	Year	Month	Sum of Income	Sum of Expenses		Ratio
	2007	Jan	98,085	42,874		41.8%
		Feb	98,698	44,167		39.3%
		Mar	102,403	43,349		40.8%
		Apr	106,044	43,102		40.6%
		May	105,361	45,005		
		Jun	105,729	44,216		
		Jul	105,557	43,835		
		Aug	109,669	41,952		
		Sep	107,233	44,071		
		Oct	105,048	43,185		
		Nov	107,446	44,403		
		Dec	105,001	45,129		
	2007 Total		1,256,274	525,288		
	2008	Jan	109,699	46,245		
		Feb	109,146	45,672		
		Mar	106,576	44,143		
		Apr	108,911	43,835		
		May	108,011	44,114		
		Jun	111,361	44,648		
		Jul	114,278	44,822		
		Aug	112,965	44,053		
		Sep	114,215	43,773		
		Oct	118,373	44,469		

Creating Pivot Charts

A *pivot chart* is a graphical representation of a data summary displayed in a pivot table. A pivot chart is always based on a pivot table. Although Excel lets you create a pivot table and a pivot chart at the same time, you can't create a pivot chart without a pivot table.

If you're familiar with creating charts in Excel, you'll have no problem creating and customizing pivot charts. All Excel charting features are available in a pivot chart.

Cross-Reference
I cover charting in Chapters 18 and 19. ∎

Excel provides two ways to create a pivot chart:

- Select any cell in an existing pivot table and then choose PivotTable Tools ⇨ Options ⇨ Tools ⇨ PivotChart.
- Choose Insert ⇨ Tables ⇨ Pivot Table ⇨ Pivot Chart. Excel creates a pivot table and a pivot chart.

A pivot chart example

Figure 35.24 shows part of a table that tracks daily sales by region. The Date field contains dates for the entire year (excluding weekends), the Region field contains the region name (Eastern, Southern, or Western), and the Sales field contains the sales amount.

On the CD

This workbook, named `sales by region pivot chart.xlsx`, is available on the companion CD-ROM. ■

FIGURE 35.24

This data will be used to create a pivot chart.

	A	B	C	D
1	Date	Region	Sales	
2	1/2/2009	Eastern	10,909	
3	1/3/2009	Eastern	11,126	
4	1/4/2009	Eastern	11,224	
5	1/5/2009	Eastern	11,299	
6	1/6/2009	Eastern	11,265	
7	1/9/2009	Eastern	11,328	
8	1/10/2009	Eastern	11,494	
9	1/11/2009	Eastern	11,328	
10	1/12/2009	Eastern	11,598	
11	1/13/2009	Eastern	11,868	
12	1/16/2009	Eastern	11,702	
13	1/17/2009	Eastern	11,846	
14	1/18/2009	Eastern	11,898	
15	1/19/2009	Eastern	11,871	
16	1/20/2009	Eastern	12,053	
17	1/23/2009	Eastern	12,073	
18	1/24/2009	Eastern	12,153	
19	1/25/2009	Eastern	12,226	
20	1/26/2009	Eastern	12,413	
21	1/27/2009	Eastern	12,663	
22	1/30/2009	Eastern	12,571	
23	1/31/2009	Eastern	12,508	
24	2/1/2009	Eastern	12,390	
25	2/2/2009	Eastern	12,649	

The first step is to create a pivot table to summarize the data. Figure 35.25 shows the pivot table. The Date field is in the Row Labels area, and the daily dates have been grouped into months. The Region field is in the Column Labels area. The Sales field is in the Values area.

The pivot table is certainly easier to interpret than the raw data, but the trends would be easier to spot in a chart.

To create a pivot chart, select any cell in the pivot table and choose PivotTable Tools ➪ Options ➪ Tools ➪ PivotChart. Excel displays its Create Chart dialog box, from which you can choose a chart type. For this example, select a standard line chart and then click OK. Excel creates the pivot chart shown in Figure 35.26.

The chart makes it easy to see an upward sales trend for the Western division, a downward trend for the Southern division, and relatively flat sales for the Eastern division.

A pivot chart includes field buttons that let you filter the chart's data. To remove the field buttons, right-click a button and choose the Hide command from the shortcut menu.

When you select a pivot chart, the Ribbon displays a new contextual tab: PivotChart Tools. The commands are virtually identical to those for a standard Excel chart, so you can manipulate the pivot chart any way you like.

FIGURE 35.25

This pivot table summarizes sales by region and by month.

	A	B	C	D	E
1					
2					
3	Sum of Sales				
4		Eastern	Southern	Western	Grand Total
5	Jan	259,416	171,897	99,833	531,146
6	Feb	255,487	135,497	100,333	491,317
7	Mar	296,958	147,425	107,884	552,267
8	Apr	248,956	131,401	110,628	490,985
9	May	293,192	132,165	144,889	570,246
10	Jun	281,641	122,156	133,153	536,950
11	Jul	263,899	110,844	147,484	522,227
12	Aug	283,917	107,935	176,325	568,177
13	Sep	252,049	101,233	181,518	534,800
14	Oct	273,592	104,542	212,932	591,066
15	Nov	292,585	98,041	232,032	622,658
16	Dec	288,378	95,986	239,514	623,878
17	Grand Total	3,290,070	1,459,122	1,886,525	6,635,717
18					

FIGURE 35.26

The pivot chart uses the data displayed in the pivot table.

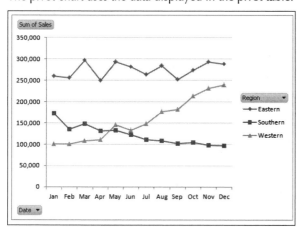

If you modify the underlying pivot table, the chart adjusts automatically to display the new summary data. Figure 35.27 shows the pivot chart after I changed the Date group to quarters.

FIGURE 35.27

If you modify the pivot table, the pivot chart is also changed.

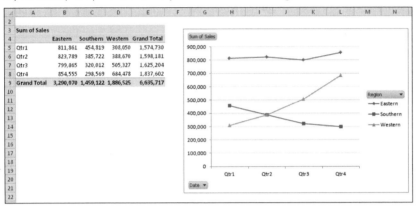

More about pivot charts

Keep in mind these points when using pivot charts:

- **A pivot table and a pivot chart are joined in a two-way link.** If you make structural or filtering changes to one, the other is also changed.

- **The field buttons in a pivot chart contain the same controls as the pivot chart's field headers.** These controls allow you to filter the data that's displayed in the pivot table (and pivot chart). If you make changes to the chart using these buttons, those changes are also reflected in the pivot table.

- **If you have a pivot chart and you delete the underlying pivot table, the pivot chart remains.** The chart's Series formulas contain the original data, stored in arrays.

- **By default, pivot charts are embedded in the sheet that contains the pivot table.** To move the pivot chart to a different worksheet (or to a Chart sheet), choose PivotChart Tools ➪ Tools ➪ Design ➪ Location ➪ Move Chart.

- **You can create multiple pivot charts from a pivot table, and you can manipulate and format the charts separately.** However, all the charts display the same data.

- **Slicers also work with pivot charts.** See the example in the earlier previous section, "Filtering Pivot Tables with Slicers."

- **Don't forget about themes.** You can choose Page Layout ➪ Themes ➪ Themes to change the workbook theme, and your pivot table and pivot chart will both reflect the new theme.

Another Pivot Table Example

The pivot table example in this section demonstrates some useful ways to work with pivot tables.

Figure 35.28 shows part of a table with 3,144 data rows, one for each county in the United States. The fields are

- **County:** The name of the county
- **State Name:** The state of the county
- **Region:** The region (Roman number ranging from I to XII)
- **Census 2000:** The population of the county, according to the 2000 Census
- **Census 1990:** The population of the county, according to the 1990 Census
- **LandArea:** The area, in square miles (excluding water-covered area)
- **WaterArea:** The area, in square miles, covered by water

On the CD
This workbook, named `county data.xlsx`, **is available on the companion CD-ROM.** ∎

FIGURE 35.28

This table contains data for each county in the United States.

County	State Name	Region	Census 2000	Census 1990	Land Area	WaterArea
Los Angeles	California	Region IX	9,519,338	8,863,164	4,060.87	691.45
Cook	Illinois	Region V	5,376,741	5,105,067	945.68	689.36
Harris	Texas	Region VI	3,400,578	2,818,199	1,728.83	48.87
San Diego	California	Region IX	2,813,833	2,498,016	4,199.89	325.62
Orange	California	Region IX	2,846,289	2,410,556	789.40	158.57
Kings	New York	Region II	2,465,326	2,300,664	70.61	26.29
Maricopa	Arizona	Region IX	3,072,149	2,122,101	9,203.14	21.13
Wayne	Michigan	Region V	2,061,162	2,111,687	614.15	58.05
Queens	New York	Region II	2,229,379	1,951,598	109.24	69.04
Dade	Florida	Region IV	2,253,362	1,937,094	1,946.21	77.85
Dallas	Texas	Region VI	2,218,899	1,852,810	879.60	28.96
Philadelphia	Pennsylvania	Region III	1,517,550	1,585,577	135.09	7.55
King	Washington	Region X	1,737,034	1,507,319	2,126.04	180.48
Santa Clara	California	Region IX	1,682,585	1,497,577	1,290.69	13.32
New York	New York	Region II	1,537,195	1,487,536	22.96	10.81
San Bernardino	California	Region IX	1,709,434	1,418,380	20,052.50	52.82
Cuyahoga	Ohio	Region V	1,393,978	1,412,140	458.49	787.07
Middlesex	Massachusetts	Region I	1,465,396	1,398,468	823.46	24.08
Allegheny	Pennsylvania	Region III	1,281,666	1,336,449	730.17	14.54
Suffolk	New York	Region II	1,419,369	1,321,864	912.20	1,460.87
Nassau	New York	Region II	1,334,544	1,287,348	286.69	166.39
Alameda	California	Region IX	1,443,741	1,279,182	737.57	83.57
Broward	Florida	Region IV	1,623,018	1,255,488	1,205.40	114.24
Bronx	New York	Region II	1,332,650	1,203,789	42.03	15.40
Bexar	Texas	Region VI	1,392,931	1,185,394	1,246.82	9.84
Riverside	California	Region IX	1,545,387	1,170,413	7,207.37	95.76

Figure 35.29 shows a pivot table created from the county data. The pivot table uses the Region and State Name fields for the Row Labels, and uses Census 2000 and Census 1990 as the Column Labels.

FIGURE 35.29

This pivot table was created from the county data.

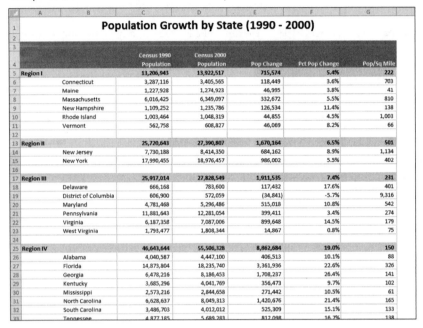

		Census 1990 Population	Census 2000 Population	Pop Change	Pct Pop Change	Pop/Sq Mile
Region I		**13,206,943**	**13,922,517**	**715,574**	**5.4%**	**222**
	Connecticut	3,287,116	3,405,565	118,449	3.6%	703
	Maine	1,227,928	1,274,923	46,995	3.8%	41
	Massachusetts	6,016,425	6,349,097	332,672	5.5%	810
	New Hampshire	1,109,252	1,235,786	126,534	11.4%	138
	Rhode Island	1,003,464	1,048,319	44,855	4.5%	1,003
	Vermont	562,758	608,827	46,069	8.2%	66
Region II		**25,720,643**	**27,390,807**	**1,670,164**	**6.5%**	**501**
	New Jersey	7,730,188	8,414,350	684,162	8.9%	1,134
	New York	17,990,455	18,976,457	986,002	5.5%	402
Region III		**25,917,014**	**27,828,549**	**1,911,535**	**7.4%**	**231**
	Delaware	666,168	783,600	117,432	17.6%	401
	District of Columbia	606,900	572,059	(34,841)	-5.7%	9,316
	Maryland	4,781,468	5,296,486	515,018	10.8%	542
	Pennsylvania	11,881,643	12,281,054	399,411	3.4%	274
	Virginia	6,187,358	7,087,006	899,648	14.5%	179
	West Virginia	1,793,477	1,808,344	14,867	0.8%	75
Region IV		**46,643,644**	**55,506,328**	**8,862,684**	**19.0%**	**150**
	Alabama	4,040,587	4,447,100	406,513	10.1%	88
	Florida	14,873,804	18,235,740	3,361,936	22.6%	326
	Georgia	6,478,216	8,186,453	1,708,237	26.4%	141
	Kentucky	3,685,296	4,041,769	356,473	9.7%	102
	Mississippi	2,573,216	2,844,658	271,442	10.5%	61
	North Carolina	6,628,637	8,049,313	1,420,676	21.4%	165
	South Carolina	3,486,703	4,012,012	525,309	15.1%	133
	Tennessee	4,877,185	5,689,283	812,098	16.7%	138

I created three calculated fields to display additional information:

- Change (displayed as **Pop Change**): The difference between Census 2000 and Census 1990

- Pct Change (displayed as **Pct Pop Change**): The population change expressed as a percentage of the 1990 population

- Density (displayed as **Pop/Sq Mile**): The population per square mile of land

Tip

To view (or document) calculated fields and calculated items in a pivot table, choose PivotTable Tools ➪ Options ➪ Calculations ➪ Fields, Items & Sets ➪ List Formulas. Excel inserts a new worksheet with information about your calculated fields and items. Figure 35.30 shows an example. ■

FIGURE 35.30

This worksheet lists calculated fields and items for the pivot table.

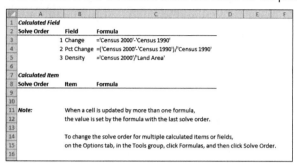

This pivot table is sorted on two columns. The main sort is by Region, and states within each region are sorted alphabetically. To sort, just select a cell that contains a data point to be included in the sort. Right-click and choose from the shortcut menu.

Sorting by Region requires some additional effort because Roman numerals are not in alphabetical order. Therefore, I had to create a custom list. To create a custom sort list, access the Excel Options dialog box, click the Advanced tab, and click Edit Custom Lists. Click New List, type your list entries, and click Add. Figure 35.31 shows the custom list I created for the region names.

FIGURE 35.31

This custom list ensures that the Region names are sorted correctly.

Producing a Report with a Pivot Table

By using a pivot table, you can convert a huge table of data into an attractive printed report. Figure 35.32 shows a small portion of a pivot table that I created from a table that has more than 40,000 rows of data. This data happens to be my digital music collection, and each row contains information about a single music file: the genre, the artist name, the album, the filename, the file size, and the duration.

FIGURE 35.32

A 132-page pivot table report.

Heartland An Appalachian Anthology	16	105 Mb	1:06:08
The Great Dobro Sessions	21	117 Mb	1:13:33
The Rebel Records Sampler	10	42 Mb	0:32:19
Wayne Henderson	**27**	**130 Mb**	**1:21:24**
Les Pick	13	71 Mb	0:44:36
Rugby Guitar	14	60 Mb	0:36:48
Blues Acoustic	**884**	**4,829 Mb**	**54:11:09**
Alberta Hunter	**10**	**61 Mb**	**0:39:26**
Amtrak Blues	10	61 Mb	0:39:26
Beth Scalet	**1**	**4 Mb**	**0:03:48**
Blues In Paradise	1	4 Mb	0:03:48
Big Joe Duskin	**7**	**29 Mb**	**0:18:15**
Big Joe Jumps Again!	7	29 Mb	0:18:15
Black Ace	**23**	**84 Mb**	**1:09:41**
I'm The Boss Card In Your Hand	23	84 Mb	1:09:41
Bluff City Backsliders	**12**	**71 Mb**	**0:45:47**
Bluff City Backsliders	12	71 Mb	0:45:47
Bo Ramsey	**2**	**7 Mb**	**0:10:06**
Downloads	2	7 Mb	0:10:06
Buddy Guy & Junior Wells	**15**	**93 Mb**	**0:59:30**
Alone & Acoustic	15	93 Mb	0:59:30
Chris Whitley	**20**	**97 Mb**	**1:06:06**
Dirt Floor	9	37 Mb	0:27:06
Perfect Day	11	60 Mb	0:39:00
Doug MacLeod	**35**	**230 Mb**	**2:40:53**
A Little Sin	10	59 Mb	0:45:55
Dubb	12	80 Mb	0:55:25
Unmarked Road	12	86 Mb	0:54:29
Where I Been	1	6 Mb	0:05:04
Etta Baker	**3**	**13 Mb**	**0:07:53**
Downloads	3	13 Mb	0:07:53

Page 8 of 132

Music List			
Geoff Muldaur	**10**	**72 Mb**	**0:46:01**
The Secret Handshake	10	72 Mb	0:46:01
Guitar Gabriel	**8**	**36 Mb**	**0:38:22**
Unknown	8	36 Mb	0:38:22

The pivot table report created from this data is 132 pages long, and it took about five minutes to set up (and a little longer to fine-tune it).

On the CD

This workbook, named `music list.xlsx`**, is available on the companion CD-ROM.** ∎

Here's a quick summary of how I created this report:

1. I selected a cell in the table and chose Insert ⇨ Tables ⇨ PivotTable.

2. In the Create PivotTable dialog box, I clicked OK to accept the default settings.

3. In the new worksheet, I used the PivotTable Field List and dragged the following fields to the Row Labels area: Genre, Artist, and Album.

4. I dragged these fields to the Values area: Track, Size, and Duration.

5. I used the Data Field Settings dialog box to summarize Track as Count, Size as Sum, and Duration as Sum.

6. I wanted the information in the Size column to display in megabytes, so I formatted the column using this custom number format:

   `###,###, "Mb";;`

7. I wanted the information in the Duration column to display as hours, minutes, and seconds, so I formatted the column using this custom number format:

   `[h]:mm:ss;;`

8. I edited the column headings. For example, I replaced *Count of Track* with *Tracks*.

9. I changed the layout to outline format by choosing PivotTable Tools ⇨ Design ⇨ Layout ⇨ Report Layout ⇨ Show In Outline Form.

10. I turned off the field headers by choosing PivotTable Tools ⇨ Options ⇨ Show ⇨ Show Field Headers.

11. I turned off the buttons by choosing PivotTable Tools ⇨ Options ⇨ Show ⇨ +/- Buttons.

12. I displayed a blank row after each artist's section by choosing PivotTable Tools ⇨ Design ⇨ Layout ⇨ Blank Rows ⇨ Insert Blank Line after Each Item.

13. I applied a built-in style by choosing PivotTable Tools ⇨ Design ⇨ PivotTable Styles.

14. I increased the font size for the Genre.

15. I went into Page Layout view and adjusted the column widths so that the report would fit horizontally on the page.

Note

Step 14 was actually kind of tricky. I wanted to increase the size of the genre names, but leave the subtotals in the same font size. Therefore, I couldn't modify the style for the PivotTable Style I chose. I selected the entire column A and pressed Ctrl+G to bring up the Go To dialog box. I clicked Special to display the Go To Special dialog box. Then I selected the Constants option and clicked OK, which selected only the nonempty cells in column A. I then adjusted the font size for the selected cells. ∎

Performing Spreadsheet What-If Analysis

O ne of the most appealing aspects of Excel is its ability to create dynamic models. A *dynamic model* uses formulas that instantly recalculate when you change values in cells that are used by the formulas. When you change values in cells in a systematic manner and observe the effects on specific formula cells, you're performing a type of *what-if* analysis.

What-if analysis is the process of asking such questions as "What if the interest rate on the loan changes to 7.5 percent rather than 7.0 percent?" or "What if we raise our product prices by 5 percent?"

If you set up your worksheet properly, answering such questions is simply a matter of plugging in new values and observing the results of the recalculation. Excel provides useful tools to assist you in your what-if endeavors.

IN THIS CHAPTER

A what-if example

Types of what-if analyses

Manual what-if analyses

Creating one-input and two-input data tables

Using Scenario Manager

A What-If Example

Figure 36.1 shows a simple worksheet model that calculates information pertaining to a mortgage loan. The worksheet is divided into two sections: the input cells and the result cells (which contain formulas).

On the CD

This workbook is available on the companion CD-ROM. The filename is
`mortgage loan.xlsx`.

With this worksheet, you can easily answer the following what-if questions:

- What if I can negotiate a lower purchase price on the property?
- What if the lender requires a 20-percent down payment?
- What if I can get a 40-year mortgage?
- What if the interest rate increases to 7.0 percent?

FIGURE 36.1

This simple worksheet model uses four input cells to produce the results.

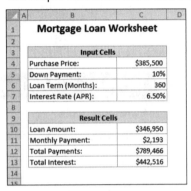

You can answer these questions by simply changing the values in the cells in range C4:C7 and observing the effects in the dependent cells (C10:C13). You can, of course, vary any number of input cells simultaneously.

Avoid Hard-Coding Values in a Formula

The mortgage calculation example, simple as it is, demonstrates an important point about spreadsheet design: You should always set up your worksheet so that you have maximum flexibility to make changes. Perhaps the most fundamental rule of spreadsheet design is the following:

> *Do not hard-code values in a formula. Rather, store the values in separate cells and use cell references in the formula.*

The term *hard-code* refers to the use of actual values, or *constants*, in a formula. In the mortgage loan example, all the formulas use references to cells, not actual values.

You *could* use the value 360, for example, for the loan term argument of the pmt function in cell C11 of Figure 36.1. Using a cell reference has two advantages. First, you have no doubt about the values that the formula uses (they aren't buried in the formula). Second, you can easily change the value — which is easier than editing the formula.

Using values in formulas may not seem like much of an issue when only one formula is involved, but just imagine what would happen if this value were hard-coded into several hundred formulas that were scattered throughout a worksheet.

Types of What-If Analyses

Not surprisingly, Excel can handle much more sophisticated models than the preceding example. To perform a what-if analysis using Excel, you have three basic options:

- **Manual what-if analysis:** Plug in new values and observe the effects on formula cells.
- **Data tables:** Create a special type of table that displays the results of selected formula cells as you systematically change one or two input cells.
- **Scenario Manager:** Create named scenarios and generate reports that use outlines or pivot tables.

I discuss each of these types of what-if analysis in the rest of this chapter.

Manual What-If Analysis

A manual what-if analysis doesn't require too much explanation. In fact, the example that opens this chapter demonstrates how it's done. Manual what-if analysis is based on the idea that you have one or more input cells that affect one or more key formula cells. You change the value in the input cells and see what happens to the formula cells. You may want to print the results or save each scenario to a new workbook. The term *scenario* refers to a specific set of values in one or more input cells.

Manual what-if analysis is very common, and people often use this technique without even realizing that they're doing a type of what-if analysis. This method of performing what-if analysis certainly has nothing wrong with it, but you should be aware of some other techniques.

Tip

If your input cells are not located near the formula cells, consider using a Watch Window to monitor the formula results in a movable window. I discuss this feature in Chapter 3. ∎

Creating Data Tables

This section describes one of Excel's most underutilized features: data tables. A *data table* is a dynamic range that summarizes formula cells for varying input cells. You can create a data table fairly easily, but data tables have some limitations. In particular, a data table can deal with only one or two input cells at a time. This limitation becomes clear as you view the examples.

Note
Scenario Manager, discussed later in this chapter (see "Using Scenario Manager"), can produce a report that summarizes any number of input cells and result cells. ■

Don't confuse a data table with a standard table (created by choosing Insert ➪ Tables ➪ Table). These two features are completely independent.

Creating a one-input data table

A *one-input data table* displays the results of one or more formulas for various values of a single input cell. Figure 36.2 shows the general layout for a one-input data table. You need to set up the table yourself, manually. This is not something that Excel will do for you.

How a one-input data table is set up.

You can place the data table anywhere in a worksheet. The left column contains various values for the single input cell. The top row contains references to formulas located elsewhere in the worksheet. You can use a single formula reference or any number of formula references. The upper-left cell of the table remains empty. Excel calculates the values that result from each value of the input cell and places them under each formula reference.

This example uses the mortgage loan worksheet from earlier in the chapter (see "A What-If Example"). The goal of this exercise is to create a data table that shows the values of the four formula cells (loan amount, monthly payment, total payments, and total interest) for various interest rates ranging from 6 to 8 percent, in 0.25-percent increments.

On the CD

This workbook is available on the companion CD-ROM. The file is named `mortgage loan data table.xlsx`.

Figure 36.3 shows the setup for the data table area. Row 3 consists of references to the formulas in the worksheet. For example, cell F3 contains the formula =C10, and cell G3 contains the formula =C11. Row 2 contains optional descriptive labels, and these are not actually part of the data table. Column E contains the values of the single input cell (interest rate) that Excel will use in the table.

To create the table, select the data table range (in this case, E3:I12) and then choose Data ➪ Data Tools ➪ What-If Analysis ➪ Data Table. Excel displays the Data Table dialog box, shown in Figure 36.4.

FIGURE 36.3

Preparing to create a one-input data table.

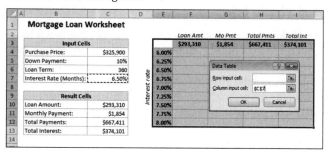

FIGURE 36.4

The Data Table dialog box.

You must specify the worksheet cell that contains the input value. Because variables for the input cell appear in the left column in the data table, you place this cell reference in the Column Input Cell field. Enter **C7** or point to the cell in the worksheet. Leave the Row Input Cell field blank. Click OK, and Excel fills in the table with the calculated results (see Figure 36.5).

FIGURE 36.5

The result of the one-input data table.

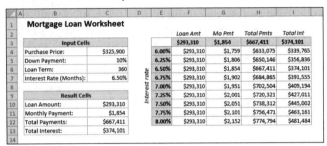

Using this table, you can now see the calculated loan values for varying interest rates. If you examine the contents of the cells that Excel entered as a result of this command, you'll see that the data is generated with a multicell array formula:

```
{=TABLE(,C7)}
```

As I discuss in Chapter 16, an *array formula* is a single formula that can produce results in multiple cells. Because the table uses formulas, Excel updates the table that you produce if you change the cell references in the first row or plug in different interest rates in the first column.

Note

You can arrange a one-input table vertically (as in this example) or horizontally. If you place the values of the input cell in a row, you enter the input cell reference in the Row Input Cell field of the Data Table dialog box. ■

Creating a two-input data table

As the name implies, a *two-input data table* lets you vary *two* input cells. You can see the setup for this type of table in Figure 36.6. Although it looks similar to a one-input table, the two-input table has one critical difference: It can show the results of only one formula at a time. With a one-input table, you can place any number of formulas, or references to formulas, across the top row of the table. In a two-input table, this top row holds the values for the second input cell. The upper-left cell of the table contains a reference to the single result formula.

Using the mortgage loan worksheet, you could create a two-input data table that shows the results of a formula (say, monthly payment) for various combinations of two input cells (such as interest rate and down-payment percent). To see the effects on other formulas, you simply create multiple data tables — one for each formula cell that you want to summarize.

The example in this section uses the worksheet shown in Figure 36.7 to demonstrate a two-input data table. In this example, a company wants to conduct a direct-mail promotion to sell its product. The worksheet calculates the net profit from the promotion.

FIGURE 36.6

The setup for a two-input data table.

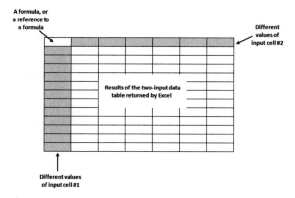

A formula, or a reference to a formula

Different values of input cell #2

Results of the two-input data table returned by Excel

Different values of input cell #1

FIGURE 36.7

This worksheet calculates the net profit from a direct-mail promotion.

	A	B	C
1	**Direct Mail Profit Model**		
2			
3	**Input Cells**		
4	Number mailed:	275,000	
5	Response rate:	2.50%	
6			
7	**Parameters**		
8	Printing costs per unit:	$0.15	
9	Mailing costs per unit:	$0.28	
10	Responses:	6,875	
11	Profit per response:	$18.50	
12	Gross profit:	$127,188	
13	Printing + mailing costs:	$118,250	
14	Net Profit	$8,937	
15			

On the CD

This workbook, named `direct mail.xlsx`, **is available on the companion CD-ROM.** ∎

This model uses two input cells: the number of promotional pieces mailed and the anticipated response rate. The following items appear in the Parameters area:

- **Printing costs per unit:** The cost to print a single mailer. The unit cost varies with the quantity: $0.20 each for quantities less than 200,000; $0.15 each for quantities of 200,001 through 300,000; and $0.10 each for quantities of more than 300,000. The following formula is used:

  `=IF(B4<200000,0.2,IF(B4<300000,0.15,0.1))`

- **Mailing costs per unit:** A fixed cost, $0.28 per unit mailed.

- **Responses:** The number of responses, calculated from the response rate and the number mailed. The formula in this cell is the following:

  `=B4*B5`

- **Profit per response:** A fixed value. The company knows that it will realize an average profit of $18.50 per order.

- **Gross profit:** This is a simple formula that multiplies the profit-per-response by the number of responses:

  `=B10*B11`

- **Print + mailing costs:** This formula calculates the total cost of the promotion:

  `=B4*(B8+B9)`

- **Net Profit:** This formula calculates the bottom line — the gross profit minus the printing and mailing costs.

If you enter values for the two input cells, you see that the net profit varies quite a bit, often going negative to produce a net loss.

Figure 36.8 shows the setup of a two-input data table that summarizes the net profit at various combinations of quantity and response rate; the table appears in the range E4:M14. Cell E4 contains a formula that references the Net Profit cell:

`=B14`

FIGURE 36.8

Preparing to create a two-input data table.

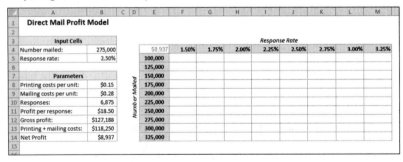

To create the data table

1. **Enter the response rate values in F4:M4.**

2. **Enter the number mailed values in E5:E14.**

3. **Select the range E4:M14 and choose Data ⇨ Data Tools ⇨ What-If Analysis ⇨ Data Table.**

4. **In the Data Table dialog box, specify B5 as the Row input cell (the response rate) and cell B4 as the Column input (the number mailed).**

5. **Click OK.** Excel fills in the data table.

Figure 36.9 shows the result. As you see, quite a few of the combinations of response rate and quantity mailed result in a loss rather than a profit.

As with the one-input data table, this data table is dynamic. You can change the formula in cell E4 to refer to another cell (such a gross profit). Or, you can enter some different values for Response Rate and Number Mailed.

The result of the two-input data table.

Using Scenario Manager

Data tables are useful, but they have a few limitations:

- You can vary only one or two input cells at a time.

- Setting up a data table is not very intuitive.

- A two-input table shows the results of only one formula cell although you can create additional tables for more formulas.

- In many situations, you're interested in a few select combinations, not an entire table that shows all possible combinations of two input cells.

The Scenario Manager feature makes automating your what-if models easy. You can store different sets of input values (called *changing cells* in the terminology of Scenario Manager) for any number of variables and give a name to each set. You can then select a set of values by name, and Excel displays the worksheet by using those values. You can also generate a summary report that shows the effect of various combinations of values on any number of result cells. These summary reports can be an outline or a pivot table.

For example, your annual sales forecast may depend upon several factors. Consequently, you can define three scenarios: best case, worst case, and most likely case. You then can switch to any of these scenarios by selecting the named scenario from a list. Excel substitutes the appropriate input values in your worksheet and recalculates the formulas.

Defining scenarios

To introduce you to Scenario Manager, this section starts with an example that uses a simplified production model, as shown in Figure 36.10.

On the CD
This workbook, named `production model.xlsx`, is available on the companion CD-ROM. ∎

This worksheet contains two input cells: the hourly labor cost (cell B2) and the unit cost for materials (cell B3). The company produces three products, and each product requires a different number of hours and a different amount of materials to produce.

FIGURE 36.10

A simple production model to demonstrate Scenario Manager.

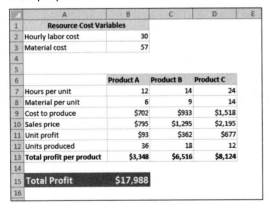

	A	B	C	D	E
1	Resource Cost Variables				
2	Hourly labor cost	30			
3	Material cost	57			
4					
5					
6		Product A	Product B	Product C	
7	Hours per unit	12	14	24	
8	Material per unit	6	9	14	
9	Cost to produce	$702	$933	$1,518	
10	Sales price	$795	$1,295	$2,195	
11	Unit profit	$93	$362	$677	
12	Units produced	36	18	12	
13	Total profit per product	$3,348	$6,516	$8,124	
14					
15	Total Profit	$17,988			
16					

Formulas calculate the total profit per product (row 13) and the total combined profit (cell B15). Management — trying to predict the total profit, but uncertain what the hourly labor cost and material costs will be — has identified three scenarios, listed in Table 36.1.

TABLE 36.1

Three Scenarios for the Production Model

Scenario	Hourly Cost	Materials Cost
Best Case	30	57
Worst Case	38	62
Most Likely	34	59

The Best Case scenario has the lowest hourly cost and lowest materials cost. The Worst Case scenario has high values for both the hourly cost and the materials cost. The third scenario, Most Likely Case, has intermediate values for both of these input cells. The managers need to be prepared for the worst case, however, and they're interested in what would happen under the Best Case scenario.

Choose Data ➪ Data Tools ➪ What-If Analysis ➪ Scenario Manger to display the Scenario Manager dialog box. When you first open this dialog box, it tells you that no scenarios are defined — which is not too surprising because you're just starting. As you add named scenarios, they appear in the Scenarios list in this dialog box.

Tip

I strongly suggest that you create names for the changing cells and all the result cells that you want to examine. Excel uses these names in the dialog boxes and in the reports that it generates. If you use names, keeping track of what's going on is much easier; names also make your reports more readable. ■

To add a scenario, click the Add button in the Scenario Manager dialog box. Excel displays its Add Scenario dialog box, shown in Figure 36.11.

FIGURE 36.11

Use the Add Scenario dialog box to create a named scenario.

This dialog box consists of four parts:

- **Scenario Name:** You can give the scenario any name that you like — preferably something meaningful.

- **Changing Cells:** The input cells for the scenario. You can enter the cell addresses directly or point to them. If you've created a name for the cells, type the name. Nonadjacent cells are allowed; if pointing to multiple cells, press Ctrl while you click the cells. Each named scenario can use the same set of changing cells or different changing cells. The number of changing cells for a scenario is limited to 32.

- **Comment:** By default, Excel displays the name of the person who created the scenario and the date when it was created. You can change this text, add new text to it, or delete it.

- **Protection:** The two Protection options (preventing changes and hiding a scenario) are in effect only when you protect the worksheet and choose the Scenario option in the Protect Sheet dialog box. Protecting a scenario prevents anyone from modifying it; a hidden scenario doesn't appear in the Scenario Manager dialog box.

In this example, define the three scenarios that are listed in Table 36.1. The changing cells are Hourly_Cost (B2) and Materials_Cost (B3).

After you enter the information in the Add Scenario dialog box, click OK. Excel then displays the Scenario Values dialog box, shown in Figure 36.12. This dialog box displays one field for each changing cell that you specified in the previous dialog box. Enter the values for each cell in the scenario. If you click OK, you return to the Scenario Manager dialog box, which then displays your named scenario in its list. If you have more scenarios to create, click the Add button to return to the Add Scenario dialog box.

You enter the values for the scenario in the Scenario Values dialog box.

Displaying scenarios

After you define all the scenarios and return to the Scenario Manager dialog box, the dialog box displays the names of your defined scenarios. Select one of the scenarios and then click the Show button. Excel inserts the corresponding values into the changing cells and calculates the worksheet to show the results for that scenario. Figure 36.13 shows an example of selecting a scenario.

Selecting a scenario to display.

Using the Scenarios Drop-Down List

The Scenarios drop-down list shows all the defined scenarios and enables you to quickly display a scenario. Oddly, this useful tool doesn't appear on the Ribbon. But, if you use Scenario Manager, you can add the Scenarios control to your Quick Access toolbar. Here's how:

1. **Right-click the Quick Access toolbar and choose Customize Quick Access Toolbar from the shortcut menu.** Excel displays the Quick Access Toolbar tab of the Excel Options dialog box.

2. **From the Choose Commands From drop-down list, select Commands Not in the Ribbon.**

3. **Scroll down the list and select Scenario.**

4. **Click the Add button.**

5. **Click OK to close the Excel Options dialog box.**

Alternatively, you can add the Scenarios control to the Ribbon. See Chapter 23 for additional details on customizing the Quick Access toolbar and the Ribbon.

Modifying scenarios

After you've created scenarios, you may need to change them. Click the Edit button in the Scenario Manager dialog box to change one or more of the values for the changing cells of a scenario. From the Scenarios list, select the scenario that you want to change and then click the Edit button. In the Edit Scenario dialog box that appears, click OK to access the Scenario Values dialog box. Make your changes and then click OK to return to the Scenario Manager dialog box. Notice that Excel automatically updates the Comments box with new text that indicates when the scenario was modified.

Merging scenarios

In workgroup situations, you may have several people working on a spreadsheet model, and several people may have defined various scenarios. The marketing department, for example, may have its opinion of what the input cells should be, the finance department may have another opinion, and your CEO may have yet another opinion.

Excel makes it easy to merge these various scenarios into a single workbook. Before you merge scenarios, make sure that the workbook from which you're merging is open:

1. **Click the Merge button in the Scenario Manager dialog box.**

2. **From the Merge Scenarios dialog box that appears, choose the workbook that contains the scenarios you're merging in the Book drop-down list.**

3. **Choose the sheet that contains the scenarios you want to merge from the Sheet list box.** Notice that the dialog box displays the number of scenarios in each sheet as you scroll through the Sheet list box.

4. **Click OK.** You return to the previous dialog box, which now displays the scenario names that you merged from the other workbook.

Generating a scenario report

If you've created multiple scenarios, you may want to document your work by creating a scenario summary report. When you click the Summary button in the Scenario Manager dialog box, Excel displays the Scenario Summary dialog box.

You have a choice of report types:

- **Scenario Summary:** The summary report appears in the form of a worksheet outline.
- **Scenario PivotTable:** The summary report appears in the form of a pivot table.

Cross-Reference
See Chapter 26 for more information about outlines, and Chapter 34 for more information about pivot tables. ∎

For simple cases of scenario management, a standard Scenario Summary report is usually suffi-cient. If you have many scenarios defined with multiple result cells, however, you may find that a Scenario Pivot Table provides more flexibility.

The Scenario Summary dialog box also asks you to specify the *result cells* (the cells that contain the formulas in which you're interested). For this example, select B13:D13 and B15 (a multiple selec-tion) to make the report show the profit for each product, plus the total profit.

Note

As you work with Scenario Manager, you may discover its main limitation: namely, that a scenario can use no more than 32 changing cells. If you attempt to use more cells, you get an error message. ■

Excel creates a new worksheet to store the summary table. Figure 36.14 shows the Scenario Summary form of the report. If you gave names to the changing cells and result cells, the table uses these names. Otherwise, it lists the cell references.

FIGURE 36.14

A Scenario Summary report produced by Scenario Manager.

759

Analyzing Data Using Goal Seeking and Solver

The preceding chapter discusses *what-if analysis* — the process of changing input cells to observe the results on other dependent cells. This chapter looks at that process from the opposite perspective: finding the value of one or more input cells that produces a desired result in a formula cell.

This chapter covers two tools: Goal Seeking and the Solver add-in.

IN THIS CHAPTER

What-if analysis — in reverse

Single-cell goal seeking

Introducing Solver

Solver examples

What-If Analysis, in Reverse

Consider the following what-if question: "What is the total profit if sales increase by 20 percent?" If you set up your worksheet model properly, you can change the value in one cell to see what happens to the profit cell. The examples in this chapter take the opposite approach. If you know what a formula result *should* be, Excel can tell you the values that you need to enter in one or more input cells to produce that result. In other words, you can ask a question such as "How much do sales need to increase to produce a profit of $1.2 million?" Excel provides two tools that are relevant:

- **Goal Seek:** Determines the value that you need to enter in a single input cell to produce a result that you want in a dependent (formula) cell.

- **Solver:** Determines the values that you need to enter in multiple input cells to produce a result that you want. Moreover, because you can specify certain constraints to the problem, you gain significant problem-solving ability.

Single-Cell Goal Seeking

Single-cell goal seeking is a rather simple concept. Excel determines what value in an input cell produces a desired result in a formula cell. The following example shows you how single-cell goal seeking works.

A goal-seeking example

Figure 37.1 shows the mortgage loan worksheet used in the preceding chapter. This worksheet has four input cells (C4:C7) and four formula cells (C10:C13). Originally, this worksheet was used for a what-if analysis example. This example demonstrates the opposite approach. Rather than supply different input cell values to look at the calculated formulas, this example lets Excel determine one of the input values that will produce the desired result.

On the CD

This workbook is available on the companion CD-ROM. The file is named `mortgage loan.xlsx`.

FIGURE 37.1

This worksheet is a good demonstration of goal seeking.

Assume that you're in the market for a new home and you know that you can afford an $1,800 monthly mortgage payment. You also know that a lender can issue a 30-year fixed-rate mortgage loan for 6.50%, based on an 80% loan-to-value (that is, a 20% down payment). The question is "What is the maximum purchase price I can handle?" In other words, what value in cell C4 causes the formula in cell C11 to result in $1,800? In this simple example, you could plug values into cell C4 until C11 displays $1,800. With more complex models, Excel can usually determine the answer much more efficiently.

To answer the question posed in the preceding paragraph, first set up the input cells to match what you already know. Specifically:

- Enter **20%** in cell C5 (the down payment percent)
- Enter **360** in cell C6 (the loan term, in months)
- Enter **6.5%** in cell C7 (the annual interest rate)

Next, choose Data ➪ Data Tools ➪ What-If Analysis ➪ Goal Seek. Excel displays the Goal Seek dialog box, shown in Figure 37.2. Completing this dialog box is similar to forming a sentence. You want to set cell C11 to 1800 by changing cell C4. Enter this information in the dialog box either by typing the cell references or by pointing with the mouse. Click OK to begin the goal-seeking process.

FIGURE 37.2

The Goal Seek dialog box.

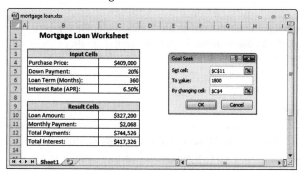

In less than a second, Excel displays the Goal Seek Status box, which shows the target value and the value that Excel calculated. In this case, Excel found an exact value. The worksheet now displays the found value in cell C4 ($355,974). As a result of this value, the monthly payment amount is $1,800. At this point, you have two options:

- Click OK to replace the original value with the found value.
- Click Cancel to restore your worksheet to the form that it had before you chose Goal Seek.

More about goal seeking

Excel can't always find a value that produces the result that you're seeking. Sometimes, a solution simply doesn't exist. In such a case, the Goal Seek Status box informs you of that fact.

Other times, however, Excel may report that it can't find a solution, but you're pretty sure that one exists. If that's the case, you can try the following options:

- Change the current value of the By Changing Cell field in the Goal Seek dialog box (refer to Figure 37.2) to a value that is closer to the solution and then reissue the command.

- Adjust the Maximum iterations setting on the Formulas tab of the Excel Options dialog box (choose File ➪ Excel Options). Increasing the number of iterations (or calculations) makes Excel try more possible solutions.

- Double-check your logic and make sure that the formula cell does, indeed, depend upon the specified changing cell.

Note

Like all computer programs, Excel has limited precision. To demonstrate this limitation, enter =A1^2 into cell A2. Then, use the Goal Seek dialog box to find the value in cell A1 (which is empty) that makes the formula return 16. Excel comes up with a value of 4.00002269, which is close to the square root of 16, but certainly not exact. You can adjust the precision on the Formulas tab of the Excel Options dialog box (make the Maximum Change value smaller). ■

Note

In some cases, multiple values of the input cell produce the same desired result. For example, the formula =A1^2 returns 16 if cell A1 contains either –4 or +4. If you use goal seeking when multiple solutions are possible, Excel gives you the solution that is closest to the current value. ■

Introducing Solver

The Excel Goal Seek feature is a useful tool, but it clearly has limitations. It can solve for only one adjustable cell, and it returns only a single solution. Excel's powerful Solver tool extends this concept by enabling you to do the following:

- Specify multiple adjustable cells.

- Specify constraints on the values that the adjustable cells can have.

- Generate a solution that maximizes or minimizes a particular worksheet cell.

- Generate multiple solutions to a problem.

Although goal seeking is a relatively simple operation, using Solver can be much more complicated. In fact, Solver is probably one of the most difficult (and potentially frustrating) features in Excel. I'm the first to admit that Solver isn't for everyone. In fact, most Excel users have no use for this feature. However, many users find that having this much power is worth spending the extra time to learn about it.

New Feature

In Excel 2010, the Solver add-in received a much-needed facelift. In addition to the cosmetic improvements, the product also performs better. ■

No Solver Command?

You access Solver by choosing Data ➪ Analysis ➪ Solver. If this command isn't available, you need to install the Solver add-in. It's a simple process:

1. **Choose File ➪ Options.**

2. **In the Excel Options dialog box, click the Add-Ins tab.**

3. **At the bottom of the dialog box, select Excel Add-Ins from the Manage drop-down list and then click Go.** Excel displays its Add-Ins dialog box.

4. **In the Add-Ins dialog box, place a check mark next to Solver Add-In and then click OK.**

After performing these steps, the Solver add-in loads whenever you start Excel.

Appropriate problems for Solver

Problems that are appropriate for Solver fall into a relatively narrow range. They typically involve situations that meet the following criteria:

- A target cell depends upon other cells and formulas. Typically, you want to maximize or minimize this target cell or set it equal to some value.

- The target cell depends on a group of cells (called *changing cells*) that Solver can adjust to affect the target cell.

- The solution must adhere to certain limitations, or *constraints*.

After you set up your worksheet appropriately, you can use Solver to adjust the changing cells and produce the result that you want in your target cell — and simultaneously meet all the constraints that you defined.

A simple Solver example

I start with a simple example to introduce Solver and then present some increasingly complex examples to demonstrate what this feature can do.

Figure 37.3 shows a worksheet that is set up to calculate the profit for three products. Column B shows the number of units of each product, Column C shows the profit per unit for each product, and Column D contains formulas that calculate the total profit for each product by multiplying the units by the profit per unit.

On the CD

This workbook, named `three products.xlsx`, is available on this book's CD-ROM. ∎

FIGURE 37.3

Use Solver to determine the number of units to maximize the total profit.

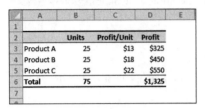

	A	B	C	D	E
1					
2		Units	Profit/Unit	Profit	
3	Product A	25	$13	$325	
4	Product B	25	$18	$450	
5	Product C	25	$22	$550	
6	Total	75		$1,325	
7					

You don't need an MBA degree to realize that the greatest profit comes from Product C. Therefore, to maximize total profit, the logical solution is to produce only Product C. If things were really this simple, you wouldn't need tools such as Solver. As in most situations, this company has some constraints that must be met:

- The combined production capacity is 300 total units per day.
- The company needs 50 units of Product A to fill an existing order.
- The company needs 40 units of Product B to fill an anticipated order.
- Because the market for Product C is relatively limited, the company doesn't want to produce more than 40 units of this product.

These four constraints make the problem more realistic and a bit more challenging. In fact, it's a perfect problem for Solver.

I go into more detail in a moment, but here is the basic procedure for using Solver:

1. **Set up the worksheet with values and formulas.** Make sure that you format cells logically; for example, if you can't produce partial units of your products, format those cells to contain numbers with no decimal values.
2. **Choose Data ⇨ Analysis ⇨ Solver to bring up the Solver Parameters dialog box.**
3. **Specify the target cell.**
4. **Specify the range that contains the changing cells.**
5. **Specify the constraints.**
6. **Change the Solver options, if necessary.**
7. **Let Solver solve the problem.**

To start Solver to tackle this example, choose Data ⇨ Analysis ⇨ Solver. Excel displays its Solver Parameters dialog box, shown in Figure 37.4.

FIGURE 37.4

The Solver Parameters dialog box.

In this example, the target cell is D6 — the cell that calculates the total profit for three products.

1. **Enter D6 in the Set Objective field of the Solver Parameters dialog box.**

2. **Because the objective is to maximize this cell, select the Max option button.**

3. **Specify the changing cells (which are in the range B3:B5) in the By Changing Variable Cells field.** The next step is to specify the constraints on the problem. The constraints are added one at a time and appear in the Subject to the Constraints list.

4. **To add a constraint, click the Add button.** Excel displays the Add Constraint dialog box, shown in Figure 37.5. This dialog box has three parts: a Cell Reference, an operator, and a Constraint value.

FIGURE 37.5

The Add Constraint dialog box.

5. To set the first constraint (that the total production capacity is 300 units), enter B6 as the Cell Reference, choose equal (=) from the drop-down list of operators, and enter 300 as the Constraint value.

6. Click Add, and enter the remaining constraints. Table 37.1 summarizes the constraints for this problem.

TABLE 37.1

Constraints Summary

Constraint	Expressed As
Capacity is 300 units	B6=300
At least 50 units of Product A	B3>=50
At least 40 units of Product B	B4>=40
No more than 40 units of Product C	B5<=40

7. After you enter the last constraint, click OK to return to the Solver Parameters dialog box, which now lists the four constraints.

8. For the Solving Method, use the default, GRG Nonlinear.

9. Click the Solve button to start the solution process. You can watch the progress onscreen, and Excel soon announces that it has found a solution. The Solver Results dialog box is shown in Figure 37.6.

FIGURE 37.6

Solver displays this dialog box when it finds a solution to the problem.

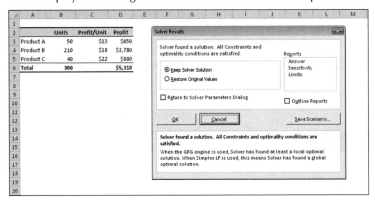

At this point, you have the following options:

- Keep the solution that Solver found.
- Restore the original changing cell values.
- Create any or all three reports that describe what Solver did.
- Click the Save Scenario button to save the solution as a scenario so that Scenario Manager can use it (see Chapter 36).

The Reports section of the Solver Results dialog box lets you select any or all of three optional reports. If you specify any report options, Excel creates each report on a new worksheet, with an appropriate name. Figure 37.7 shows an Answer Report, in the form of a collapsible outline (I chose the Outline Reports check box in the Solver Results dialog box). In the Constraints section of the report, three of the four constraints are *binding,* which means that these constraints were satisfied at their limit with no more room to change.

This simple example illustrates how Solver works. The fact is, you could probably solve this particular problem manually just as quickly. That, of course, isn't always the case.

FIGURE 37.7

One of three reports that Solver can produce.

Caution

When you close the Solver Results dialog box (by clicking either OK or Cancel) the Undo stack is cleared. In other words, you cannot undo any changes that Solver makes to your workbook. ■

More about Solver

Before presenting more complex examples, this section discusses the Solver Options dialog box. From this dialog box, you control many aspects of the solution process, as well as load and save model specifications in a worksheet range.

Usually, you want to save a model only when you're using more than one set of Solver parameters with your worksheet. This is because Excel saves the first Solver model automatically with your worksheet (using hidden names). If you save additional models, Excel stores the information in the form of formulas that correspond to the specifications. (The last cell in the saved range is an array formula that holds the options settings.)

It's not unusual for Solver to report that it can't find a solution, even when you know that one should exist. Often, you can change one or more of the Solver options and try again. When you click the Options button in the Solver Parameters dialog box, Excel displays the Solver Options dialog box, shown in Figure 37.8.

FIGURE 37.8

You can control many aspects of how Solver solves a problem.

This list describes Solver's options:

- **Constraint Precision:** Specify how close the Cell Reference and Constraint formulas must be to satisfy a constraint. Excel may solve the problem more quickly if you specify less precision.

- **Use Automatic Scaling:** Use when the problem involves large differences in magnitude — when you attempt to maximize a percentage, for example, by varying cells that are very large.

- **Show Iteration Results:** Instruct Solver to pause and display the results after each iteration by selecting this check box.

- **Ignore Integer Constraints:** When this check box is selected, Solver ignores constraints that specify that a particular cell must be an integer. Using this option may allow Solver to find a solution that cannot be found otherwise.

- **Max Time:** Specify the maximum amount of time (in seconds) that you want Solver to spend on a problem. If Solver reports that it exceeded the time limit, you can increase the amount of time that it spends searching for a solution.

- **Iterations:** Enter the maximum number of trial solutions that you want Solver to perform.

- **Max Subproblems:** For complex problems. Specify the maximum number of subproblems that may be explored by the Evolutionary algorithm.

- **Max Feasible Solutions:** For complex problems. Specify the maximum number of feasible solutions that may be explored by the Evolutionary algorithm.

Note

The other two tabs in the Options dialog box contain additional options used by the GRG Nonlinear and Evolutionary algorithms. ■

Solver Examples

The remainder of this chapter consists of examples of using Solver for various types of problems.

Solving simultaneous linear equations

This example describes how to solve a set of three linear equations with three variables. Here's an example of a set of linear equations:

```
4x + y -2z =0
2x - 3y +3z =9
-6x -2y +z = 0
```

The question that Solver will answer is *What values of x, y, and z satisfy all three equations?*

Figure 37.9 shows a workbook set up to solve this problem. This workbook has three named cells, which makes the formulas more readable:

- x: C11
- y: C12
- z: C13

The three named cells are all initialized to 1 (which certainly doesn't solve the equations).

FIGURE 37.9

Solver will attempt to solve this series of linear equations.

	A	B	C	D
1	4x + y −2z =0			
2	2x − 3y +3z =9			
3	−6x −2y +z = 0			
4				
5		Formula	Desired Value	
6	Equation 1:	3	0	
7	Equation 2:	2	9	
8	Equation 3:	-7	0	
9				
10		Variable	Value	
11		x:	1.00	
12		y:	1.00	
13		z:	1.00	
14				

On the CD

This workbook, named `linear equations.xlsx`, **is available on the companion CD-ROM.** ■

The three equations are represented by formulas in the range B6:B8:

- B6: = (4*x) + (y) − (2*z)
- B7: = (2*x) − (3*y) + (3*z)
- B8: =− (6*x) − (2*y) + (z)

These formulas use the values in the x, y, and z named cells. The range C6:C8 contains the "desired" result for these three formulas.

Solver will adjust the values in x, y, and z — that is, the changing cells in C11:C13 — subject to these constraints:

- B6=C6
- B7=C7
- B8=C8

Note

This problem doesn't have a target cell because it's not trying to maximize or minimize anything. However, the Solver Parameters dialog box insists that you specify a formula for the Set Target Cell field. Therefore, just enter a reference to any cell that has a formula. ■

Figure 37.10 shows the solution. The x (0.75), y (−2.0), and z (0.5) values satisfy all three equations.

FIGURE 37.10

Solver solved the simultaneous equations.

▲	A	B	C	D
1	4x + y −2z =0			
2	2x − 3y +3z =9			
3	−6x −2y +z = 0			
4				
5		Formula	Desired Value	
6	Equation 1:	0	0	
7	Equation 2:	9	9	
8	Equation 3:	0	0	
9				
10		Variable	Value	
11		x:	0.75	
12		y:	-2.00	
13		z:	0.50	
14				

Note

A set of linear equations may have one solution, no solution, or an infinite number of solutions. ■

Minimizing shipping costs

This example involves finding alternative options for shipping materials, while keeping total shipping costs at a minimum (see Figure 37.11). A company has warehouses in Los Angeles, St. Louis, and Boston. Retail outlets throughout the United States place orders, which the company then ships from one of the warehouses. The company wants to meet the product needs of all six retail outlets from available inventory and keep total shipping charges as low as possible.

On the CD

This workbook, named shipping costs.xlsx, is available on the companion CD-ROM. ■

FIGURE 37.11

This worksheet determines the least expensive way to ship products from warehouses to retail outlets.

This workbook is rather complicated, so each part is explained individually:

- **Shipping Costs Table:** This table, in range B2:E8, is a matrix that contains per-unit shipping costs from each warehouse to each retail outlet. The cost to ship a unit from Los Angeles to Denver, for example, is $58.

- **Product needs of each retail store:** This information appears in C12:C17. For example, Denver needs 150 units, Houston needs 225, and so on. C18 contains a formula that calculates the total needed.

- **Number to ship from:** Range D12:F17 holds the adjustable cells that Solver varies. These cells are all initialized with a value of 25 to give Solver a starting value. Column G contains formulas that sum the number of units the company needs to ship to each retail outlet.

- **Warehouse inventory:** Row 21 contains the amount of inventory at each warehouse, and row 22 contains formulas that subtract the amount shipped (row 18) from the inventory.

- **Calculated shipping costs:** Row 24 contains formulas that calculate the shipping costs. Cell D24 contains the following formula, which is copied to the two cells to the right of Cell D24:

  `=SUMPRODUCT(C3:C8,D12:D17)`

Cell G24 is the bottom line, the total shipping costs for all orders.

Solver fills in values in the range D12:F17 in such a way that minimizes shipping costs while still supplying each retail outlet with the desired number of units. In other words, the solution minimizes the value in cell G24 by adjusting the cells in D12:F17, subject to the following constraints:

- The number of units needed by each retail outlet must equal the number shipped. (In other words, all the orders are filled.) These constraints are represented by the following specifications:

    C12=G12   C14=G14   C16=G16
    C13=G13   C15=G15   C17=G17

- The adjustable cells can't be negative because shipping a negative number of units makes no sense. These constraints are represented by the following specifications:

    D12>=0   E12>=0   F12>=0
    D13>=0   E13>=0   F13>=0
    D14>=0   E14>=0   F14>=0
    D15>=0   E15>=0   F15>=0
    D16>=0   E16>=0   F16>=0
    D17>=0   E17>=0   F17>=0

- The number of units remaining in each warehouse's inventory must not be negative (that is, they can't ship more than what's available). This is represented by the following constraint specifications:

    D22>=0   E22>=0   F22>=0

Note

Before you solve this problem with Solver, you may want to attempt to solve this problem manually, by entering values in D12:F17 that minimize the shipping costs. And, of course, you need to make sure that all the constraints are met. Doing so may help you better appreciate Solver. ∎

Setting up the problem is the difficult part. For example, you must enter 27 constraints. When you have specified all the necessary information, click the Solve button to put Solver to work. Solver displays the solution shown in Figure 37.12.

Learning More about Solver

Solver is a complex tool, and this chapter barely scratches the surface. If you'd like to learn more about Solver, I highly recommend the Web site for Frontline Systems:

`www.solver.com`

Frontline Systems is the company that developed Solver for Excel. Its Web site has several tutorials and lots of helpful information, including a detailed manual that you can download. You can also find additional Solver products for Excel that can handle much more complex problems.

The total shipping cost is $55,515, and all the constraints are met. Notice that shipments to Miami come from both St. Louis and Boston.

FIGURE 37.12

The solution that was created by Solver.

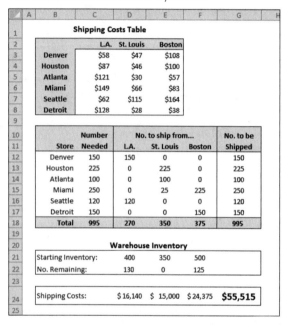

Allocating resources

The example in this section is a common type of problem that's ideal for Solver. Essentially, problems of this sort involve optimizing the volumes of individual production units that use varying amounts of fixed resources. Figure 37.13 shows an example for a toy company.

On the CD

This workbook is available on the companion CD-ROM. The file is named `allocating resources.xlsx`.

This company makes five different toys, which use six different materials in varying amounts. For example, Toy A requires 3 units of blue paint, 2 units of white paint, 1 unit of plastic, 3 units of wood, and 1 unit of glue. Column G shows the current inventory of each type of material. Row 10 shows the unit profit for each toy.

Using Solver to maximize profit when resources are limited.

	A	B	C	D	E	F	G	H	I
1					XYZ Toys Inc.				
2				Materials Needed					
3	Material	Toy A	Toy B	Toy C	Toy D	Toy E	Amt. Avail.	Amt. Used	Amt. Left
4	Red Paint	0	1	0	1	3	625	250	375
5	Blue Paint	3	1	0	1	0	640	250	390
6	White Paint	2	1	2	0	2	1,100	350	750
7	Plastic	1	5	2	2	1	875	550	325
8	Wood	3	0	3	5	5	2,200	800	1,400
9	Glue	1	2	3	2	3	1,500	550	950
10	Unit Profit	$15	$30	$20	$25	$25			
11	No. to Make	50	50	50	50	50			
12	Profit	$750	$1,500	$1,000	$1,250	$1,250			
13	Total Profit	$5,750							
14									

The number of toys to make is shown in the range B11:F11. These are the values that Solver determines (the changing cells). The goal of this example is to determine how to allocate the resources to maximize the total profit (B13). In other words, Solver determines how many units of each toy to make. The constraints in this example are relatively simple:

- **Ensure that production doesn't use more resources than are available.** This can be accomplished by specifying that each cell in column I is greater than or equal to 0 (zero).

- **Ensure that the quantities produced aren't negative.** This can be accomplished by specifying that each cell in row 11 be greater than or equal to 0.

Figure 37.14 shows the results that are produced by Solver. It shows the product mix that generates $12,365 in profit and uses all resources in their entirety, except for glue.

Solver determined how to use the resources to maximize the total profit.

	A	B	C	D	E	F	G	H	I
1					XYZ Toys Inc.				
2				Materials Needed					
3	Material	Toy A	Toy B	Toy C	Toy D	Toy E	Amt. Avail.	Amt. Used	Amt. Left
4	Red Paint	0	1	0	1	3	625	625	0
5	Blue Paint	3	1	0	1	0	640	640	0
6	White Paint	2	1	2	0	2	1,100	1,100	0
7	Plastic	1	5	2	2	1	875	875	0
8	Wood	3	0	3	5	5	2,200	2,200	0
9	Glue	1	2	3	2	3	1,500	1,353	147
10	Unit Profit	$15	$30	$20	$25	$25			
11	No. to Make	194	19	158	40	189			
12	Profit	$2,903	$573	$3,168	$1,008	$4,713			
13	Total Profit	$12,365							
14									
15									

Optimizing an investment portfolio

This example demonstrates how to use Solver to help maximize the return on an investment portfolio. A portfolio consists of several investments, each of which has a different yield. In addition, you may have some constraints that involve reducing risk and diversification goals. Without such constraints, a portfolio problem becomes a no-brainer: Put all your money in the investment with the highest yield.

This example involves a *credit union* (a financial institution that takes members' deposits and invests them in loans to other members, bank CDs, and other types of investments). The credit union distributes part of the return on these investments to the members in the form of *dividends*, or interest on their deposits.

This hypothetical credit union must adhere to some regulations regarding its investments, and the board of directors has imposed some other restrictions. These regulations and restrictions comprise the problem's constraints. Figure 37.15 shows a workbook set up for this problem.

FIGURE 37.15

This worksheet is set up to maximize a credit union's investments, given some constraints.

	A	B	C	D	E	F
1	Portfolio Amount:	$5,000,000				
2						
3						
4	Investment	Pct Yield	Amount Invested	Yield	Pct. of Portfolio	
5	New Car Loans	6.90%	1,000,000	69,000	20.00%	
6	Used Car Loans	8.25%	1,000,000	82,500	20.00%	
7	Real Estate Loans	8.90%	1,000,000	89,000	20.00%	
8	Unsecured Loans	13.00%	1,000,000	130,000	20.00%	
9	Bank CDs	4.60%	1,000,000	46,000	20.00%	
10	TOTAL		$5,000,000	$416,500	100.00%	
11						
12			Total Yield:	8.33%		
13						
14			Auto Loans	40.00%		
15						

On the CD

This workbook is available on the companion CD-ROM. The file is named `investment portfolio.xlsx`.

The following constraints are the ones to which you must adhere in allocating the $5 million portfolio:

- The amount that the credit union invests in new-car loans must be at least three times the amount that the credit union invests in used-car loans. (Used-car loans are riskier investments.) This constraint is represented as

  `C5>=C6*3`

- Car loans should make up at least 15 percent of the portfolio. This constraint is represented as

  D14>=.15

- Unsecured loans should make up no more than 25 percent of the portfolio. This constraint is represented as

  E8<=.25

- At least 10 percent of the portfolio should be in bank CDs. This constraint is represented as:

  E9>=.10

- The total amount invested is $5,000,000.

- All investments should be positive or zero. In other words, the problem requires five additional constraints to ensure that none of the changing cells goes below zero.

The changing cells are C5:C9, and the goal is to maximize the total yield in cell D12. Starting values of 1,000,000 have been entered in the changing cells. When you run Solver with these parameters, it produces the solution shown in Figure 37.16, which has a total yield of 9.25 percent.

FIGURE 37.16

The results of the portfolio optimization.

	A	B	C	D	E
1	Portfolio Amount:	$5,000,000			
2					
3					
4	Investment	Pct Yield	Amount Invested	Yield	Pct. of Portfolio
5	New Car Loans	6.90%	562,500	38,812	11.25%
6	Used Car Loans	8.25%	187,500	15,469	3.75%
7	Real Estate Loans	8.90%	2,500,000	222,500	50.00%
8	Unsecured Loans	13.00%	1,250,000	162,500	25.00%
9	Bank CDs	4.60%	500,000	23,000	10.00%
10	TOTAL		$5,000,000	$462,281	100.00%
11					
12			Total Yield:	9.25%	
13					
14			Auto Loans	15.00%	

Analyzing Data with the Analysis ToolPak

IN THIS CHAPTER

The Analysis ToolPak: An overview

Using the Analysis ToolPak

Meeting the Analysis ToolPak tools

Although Excel was designed primarily for business users, people in other disciplines, including education, research, statistics, and engineering, use it. One way how Excel addresses these nonbusiness users is with its Analysis ToolPak add-in. However, many features in the Analysis ToolPak are valuable for business applications as well.

The Analysis ToolPak: An Overview

The Analysis ToolPak is an add-in that provides analytical capability that normally isn't available.

Note

Prior to Excel 2007, the Analysis ToolPak add-in included many additional worksheet functions. These worksheet functions are built into Excel and no longer require the Analysis ToolPak add-in. ∎

These analysis tools offer many features that may be useful to those in the scientific, engineering, and educational communities — not to mention business users whose needs extend beyond the normal spreadsheet fare.

This section provides a quick overview of the types of analyses that you can perform with the Analysis ToolPak. This chapter covers each of the following tools:

- Analysis of variance (three types)
- Correlation

- Covariance
- Descriptive statistics
- Exponential smoothing
- F-Test
- Fourier analysis
- Histogram
- Moving average
- Random number generation
- Rank and percentile
- Regression
- Sampling
- t-Test (three types)
- z-Test

As you can see, the Analysis ToolPak add-in brings a great deal of functionality to Excel. These procedures have limitations, however, and in some cases, you may prefer to create your own formulas to do some calculations.

Installing the Analysis ToolPak Add-in

The Analysis ToolPak is implemented as an add-in. Before you can use it, though, you need to make sure that the add-in is installed. Click the Data tab. If you see an Analysis group, showing Data Analysis, the Analysis ToolPak is installed. If you can't access Data ➪ Analysis ➪ Data Analysis, install the add-in by following these steps:

1. **Choose File ➪ Options to display the Excel Options dialog box.**
2. **In the Excel Options dialog box, click the Add-Ins tab.**
3. **At the bottom of the dialog box, select Excel Add-Ins from the Manage drop-down list and then click Go.** Excel displays the Add-Ins dialog box.
4. **In the Add-Ins dialog box, place a check mark next to Analysis ToolPak.**
5. **Click OK to close the Add-Ins dialog box.**

Tip
Pressing Alt+TI is a much quicker way to display the Add-Ins dialog box. ∎

Using the Analysis Tools

Using the procedures in the Analysis ToolPak add-in is relatively straightforward as long as you're familiar with the particular analysis type. To use any of these tools, choose Data ➪ Analysis ➪ Data Analysis, which displays the dialog box shown in Figure 38.1. Scroll through the list until you find the analysis tool that you want to use and then click OK. Excel displays a dialog box specific to the procedure that you select.

Select your tool from the Data Analysis dialog box.

Usually, you need to specify one or more Input ranges, plus an Output range (one cell is sufficient). Alternatively, you can choose to place the results on a new worksheet or in a new workbook. The procedures vary in the amount of additional information required. In many dialog boxes, you may be able to indicate whether your Data range includes labels. If so, you can specify the entire range, including the labels, and indicate to Excel that the first column (or row) contains labels. Excel then uses these labels in the tables that it produces. Most tools also provide different output options that you can select, based on your needs.

Caution

The Analysis ToolPak isn't consistent in how it generates its output. In some cases, the procedures use formulas, so you can change your data, and the results update automatically. In other procedures, Excel stores the results as values, so if you change your data, the results don't reflect your changes. Make sure that you understand what Excel is doing. ■

Introducing the Analysis ToolPak Tools

This section describes each tool in the Analysis ToolPak and provides an example. Space limitations prevent a discussion of every available option in these procedures. However, if you need to use the advanced analysis tools, you probably already know how to use most of the options not covered here.

On the CD

The companion CD-ROM contains a workbook that shows output from all the tools discussed in this section. The file is named `atp examples.xlsx`.

Analysis of Variance

Analysis of Variance (sometimes abbreviated as *Anova*) is a statistical test that determines whether two or more samples were drawn from the same population. Using tools in the Analysis ToolPak, you can perform three types of analysis of variance:

- **Single-factor:** A one-way analysis of variance, with only one sample for each group of data

- **Two-factor with replication:** A two-way analysis of variance, with multiple samples (or replications) for each group of data

- **Two-factor without replication:** A two-way analysis of variance, with a single sample (or replication) for each group of data

Figure 38.2 shows the dialog box for a single-factor analysis of variance. Alpha represents the statistical confidence level for the test.

FIGURE 38.2

Specifying parameters for a single-factor analysis of variance.

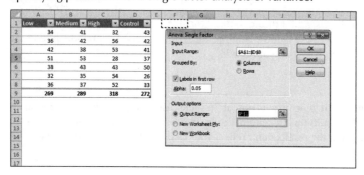

The output for this test consists of the means and variances for each of the samples, the value of F, the critical value of F, and the significance of F (P-value).

Correlation

Correlation is a widely used statistic that measures the degree to which two sets of data vary together. For example, if higher values in one data set are typically associated with higher values in the second data set, the two data sets have a positive correlation. The degree of correlation is expressed as a coefficient that ranges from –1.0 (a perfect negative correlation) to +1.0 (a perfect positive correlation). A correlation coefficient of 0 indicates that the two variables aren't correlated.

Figure 38.3 shows the Correlation dialog box. Specify the input range, which can include any number of variables, arranged in rows or columns.

FIGURE 38.3

The Correlation dialog box.

The output consists of a correlation matrix that shows the correlation coefficient for each variable paired with every other variable.

Note

The resulting correlation matrix doesn't use formulas to calculate the results. Therefore, if any data changes, the correlation matrix isn't valid. You can use the CORREL function to create a correlation matrix that changes automatically when you change data. ■

Covariance

The Covariance tool produces a matrix that is similar to the one generated by the Correlation tool. *Covariance*, like correlation, measures the degree to which two variables vary together. Specifically, *covariance* is the average of the product of the deviations of each data point pair from their respective means.

Because the Covariance tool does not generate formulas, you may prefer to calculate a covariance matrix using the COVAR function.

Descriptive Statistics

The Descriptive Statistics tool produces a table that describes your data with some standard statistics. Figure 38.4 shows some sample output.

FIGURE 38.4

Descriptive Statistics output.

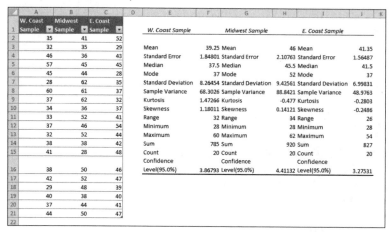

Because the output for this procedure consists of values (not formulas), you should use this procedure only when you're certain that your data isn't going to change; otherwise, you will need to re-execute the procedure. You can generate all these statistics by using formulas.

Exponential Smoothing

Exponential smoothing is a technique for predicting data that is based on the previous data point and the previously predicted data point. You can specify the *damping factor* (also known as a *smoothing constant*), which can range from 0 to 1. This factor determines the relative weighting of the previous data point and the previously predicted data point. You also can request standard errors and a chart.

The exponential smoothing procedure generates formulas that use the damping factor that you specify. Therefore, if the data changes, Excel updates the formulas.

F-Test (two-sample test for variance)

An *F-Test* is a commonly used statistical test that enables you to compare two population variances. Figure 38.5 shows a small data set and F-Test output.

The output for this test consists of the means and variances for each of the two samples, the value of F, the critical value of F, and the significance of F.

FIGURE 38.5

Output from the F-Test tool.

	A	B	C	D	E	F	G	H
1	Group 1	Group 2		F-Test Two-Sample for Variances				
2	96	39						
3	78	53			Group 1	Group 2		
4	72	51		Mean	75.44444	46.66667		
5	78	48		Variance	109.5278	25		
6	65	51		Observations	9	9		
7	66	42		df	8	8		
8	69	44		F	4.381111			
9	87	42		P(F<=f) one-tail	0.025855			
10	68	50		F Critical one-tai	3.438103			
11								
12								

Fourier Analysis

The Fourier Analysis tool performs a "fast Fourier" transformation of a range of data. Using the Fourier Analysis tool, you can transform a range limited to the following sizes: 1, 2, 4, 8, 16, 32, 64, 128, 256, 512, or 1,024 data points. This procedure accepts and generates complex numbers, which are represented as text string (not numerical values).

Histogram

The Histogram tool is useful for producing data distributions and histogram charts. It accepts an Input range and a Bin range. A *bin range* is a range of values that specifies the limits for each column of the histogram. If you omit the Bin range, Excel creates 10 equal-interval bins for you. The size of each bin is determined by the following formula:

```
=(MAX(input_range)- MIN(input_range))/10
```

Output from the Histogram tool is shown in Figure 38.6. As an option, you can specify that the resulting histogram be sorted by frequency of occurrence in each bin.

If you specify the Pareto (Sorted Histogram) option, the bin range must contain values and can't contain formulas. If formulas appear in the bin range, Excel doesn't sort properly, and your worksheet displays error values. The Histogram tool doesn't use formulas, so if you change any of the input data, you need to repeat the histogram procedure to update the results.

Cross-Reference

For other ways of generating frequency distributions, see Chapters 13 and 35. ■

FIGURE 38.6

Use the Histogram tool to generate distributions and graphical output.

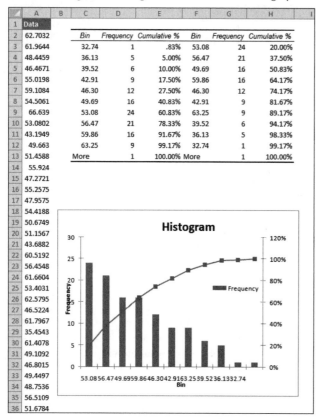

Moving Average

The Moving Average tool helps you smooth out a data series that has a lot of variability. This procedure is often used in conjunction with a chart. Excel does the smoothing by computing a moving average of a specified number of values. In many cases, a moving average enables you to spot trends that otherwise would be obscured by noise in the data.

Figure 38.7 shows a chart generated by the Moving Average tool. You can, of course, specify the number of values that you want Excel to use for each average. If you select the Standard Errors check box in the Moving Average dialog box, Excel calculates standard errors and places formulas for these calculations next to the moving average formulas. The standard error values indicate the degree of variability between the actual values and the calculated moving averages.

FIGURE 38.7

A chart produced by the Moving Average tool.

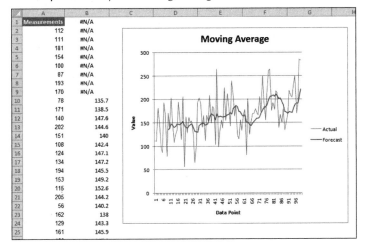

The first few cells in the output are #N/A because not enough data points exist to calculate the average for these initial values.

Random Number Generation

Although Excel contains built-in functions to calculate random numbers, the Random Number Generation tool is much more flexible because you can specify what type of distribution you want the random numbers to have. Figure 38.8 shows the Random Number Generation dialog box. The Parameters section varies, depending upon the type of distribution that you select.

FIGURE 38.8

This dialog box enables you to generate a wide variety of random numbers.

Number of Variables refers to the number of columns that you want, and Number of Random Numbers refers to the number of rows that you want. For example, if you want 200 random numbers arranged in 10 columns of 20 rows, you specify 10 and 20, respectively, in these fields.

In the Random Seed field, you can specify a starting value that Excel uses in its random number-generating algorithm. Usually, you leave this field blank. If you want to generate the same random number sequence, however, you can specify a seed between 1 and 32,767 (integer values only). You can create the following types of distributions via the Distribution drop-down list in the Random Number Generation dialog box:

- **Uniform:** Every random number has an equal chance of being selected. You specify the upper and lower limits.

- **Normal:** The random numbers correspond to a normal distribution. You specify the mean and standard deviation of the distribution.

- **Bernoulli:** The random numbers are either 0 or 1, determined by the probability of success that you specify.

- **Binomial:** This option returns random numbers based on a Bernoulli distribution over a specific number of trials, given a probability of success that you specify.

- **Poisson:** This option generates values in a Poisson distribution. A *Poisson distribution* is characterized by discrete events that occur in an interval, where the probability of a single occurrence is proportional to the size of the interval. The lambda parameter is the expected number of occurrences in an interval. In a Poisson distribution, lambda is equal to the mean, which also is equal to the variance.

- **Patterned:** This option doesn't generate random numbers. Rather, it repeats a series of numbers in steps that you specify.

- **Discrete:** This option enables you to specify the probability that specific values are chosen. It requires a two-column input range; the first column holds the values, and the second column holds the probability of each value being chosen. The sum of the probabilities in the second column must equal 100 percent.

Rank and Percentile

The Rank and Percentile tool creates a table that shows the ordinal and percentile ranking for each value in a range. You can also generate ranks and percentiles by using Excel functions (those that begin with RANK and PERCENTILE).

Regression

Use the Regression tool (see Figure 38.9) to calculate a regression analysis from worksheet data. You can use regression to analyze trends, forecast the future, build predictive models, and, often, to make sense out of a series of seemingly unrelated numbers.

Regression analysis enables you to determine the extent to which one range of data (the dependent variable) varies as a function of the values of one or more other ranges of data (the independent variables). This relationship is expressed mathematically, using values that Excel calculates. You can use these calculations to create a mathematical model of the data and predict the dependent variable by using different values of one or more independent variables. This tool can perform simple and multiple linear regressions and calculate and standardize residuals automatically.

FIGURE 38.9

The Regression dialog box.

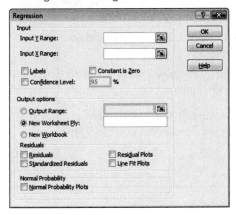

As you can see, the Regression dialog box offers many options:

- **Input Y Range:** The range that contains the dependent variable.
- **Input X Range:** One or more ranges that contain independent variables.
- **Confidence Level:** The confidence level for the regression.
- **Constant Is Zero:** If selected, forces the regression to have a constant of 0 (which means that the regression line passes through the origin; when the X values are 0, the predicted Y value is 0).
- **Residuals:** The four options in this section of the dialog box enable you to specify whether to include residuals in the output. *Residuals* are the differences between observed and predicted values.
- **Normal Probability:** Generates a chart for normal probability plots.

Sampling

The Sampling tool generates a random sample from a range of input values. The Sampling tool can help you to work with a large database by creating a subset of it.

This procedure has two options: periodic and random. If you choose a periodic sample, Excel selects every nth value from the Input range, where n equals the period that you specify. With a random sample, you simply specify the size of the sample you want Excel to select, and every value has an equal probability of being chosen.

t-Test

Use the t-Test tool to determine whether a statistically significant difference exists between two small samples. The Analysis ToolPak can perform three types of t-Tests:

- **Paired two-sample for means:** For paired samples in which you have two observations on each subject (such as a pretest and a post-test). The samples must be the same size.

- **Two-sample assuming equal variances:** For independent, rather than paired, samples. Excel assumes equal variances for the two samples.

- **Two-sample assuming unequal variances:** For independent, rather than paired, samples. Excel assumes unequal variances for the two samples.

Figure 38.10 shows output for the Paired Two Sample for Means t-Test. You specify the significance level (alpha) and the hypothesized difference between the two means (that is, the *null hypothesis*).

FIGURE 38.10

Output from the paired t-Test dialog box.

	A	B	C	D	E	F	G
1	Student#	Pretest	Posttest		t-Test: Paired Two Sample for Means		
2	1	71	69				
3	2	63	61			Pretest	Posttest
4	3	68	70		Mean	69.619048	71.09524
5	4	67	68		Variance	16.647619	48.79048
6	5	66	61		Observations	21	21
7	6	63	60		Pearson Correlation	0.962743	
8	7	76	83		Hypothesized Mean Difference	0	
9	8	70	72		df	20	
10	9	69	71		t Stat	-2.081522	
11	10	73	77		P(T<=t) one-tail	0.0252224	
12	11	71	72		t Critical one-tail	1.724718	
13	12	66	66		P(T<=t) two-tail	0.0504448	
14	13	70	71		t Critical two-tail	2.0859625	
15	14	78	86				
16	15	68	70				
17	16	75	78				
18	17	65	63				
19	18	67	68				
20	19	71	77				
21	20	74	78				
22	21	71	72				
23							

z-Test (two-sample test for means)

The t-Test is used for small samples; the z-Test is used for larger samples or populations. You must know the variances for both input ranges.

Part VI

Programming Excel with VBA

If you've ever wanted to do a bit more or automate routine operations so that you don't always have to perform boring, repetitious tasks manually, this part is for you. This part is also aimed at those Excel users who want to develop Excel-based applications for other users. VBA — Visual Basic for Applications — is the powerful programming language that you can use for these tasks as well as for more esoteric purposes, such as developing that specialized worksheet function that you simply can't find in Excel.

IN THIS PART

Chapter 39
Introducing Visual Basic for Applications

Chapter 40
Creating Custom Worksheet Functions

Chapter 41
Introducing UserForms

Chapter 42
Using UserForm Controls in a Worksheet

Chapter 43
Working with Excel's Events

Chapter 44
VBA Examples

Chapter 45
Creating Custom Excel Add-Ins

Introducing Visual Basic for Applications

This chapter is an introduction to the Visual Basic for Applications (VBA) macro language — a key component for users who want to customize and automate Excel. This chapter teaches you how to record macros and create simple macro procedures. Subsequent chapters expand upon the topics in this chapter.

IN THIS CHAPTER

Introducing VBA macros

Creating VBA macros

Recording VBA macros

More about recording VBA macros

Writing VBA code

Learning more about VBA

Introducing VBA Macros

In its broadest sense, a *macro* is a sequence of instructions that automates some aspect of Excel so that you can work more efficiently and with fewer errors. You may create a macro, for example, to format and print your month-end sales report. After the macro is developed, you can then execute the macro to perform many time-consuming procedures automatically.

You don't have to be a power user to create and use simple VBA macros. Casual users can simply turn on Excel's macro recorder: Excel records your actions and converts them into a VBA macro. When you execute this macro, Excel performs the actions again. More advanced users, though, can write code that tells Excel to perform tasks that can't be recorded. For example, you can write procedures that display custom dialog boxes, add new commands to Excel's menus, or process data in a series of workbooks.

What You Can Do with VBA

VBA is an extremely rich programming language with thousands of uses. The following list contains just a few things that you can do with VBA macros. (Not all of these tasks are covered in this book.)

- **Insert boilerplate text.** If you need to enter standard text into a range of cells, you can create a macro to do the typing for you.

- **Automate a procedure that you perform frequently.** For example, you may need to prepare a month-end summary. If the task is straightforward, you can develop a macro to do it for you.

- **Automate repetitive operations.** If you need to perform the same action in 12 different workbooks, you can record a macro while you perform the task once — and then let the macro repeat your action in the other workbooks.

- **Create a custom command.** For example, you can combine several Excel commands so that they're executed from a single keystroke or from a single mouse click.

- **Create a simplified "front end" for users who don't know much about Excel.** For example, you can set up a foolproof data-entry template.

- **Develop a new worksheet function.** Although Excel includes a wide assortment of built-in functions, you can create custom functions that greatly simplify your formulas.

- **Create complete macro-driven applications.** Excel macros can display custom dialog boxes and respond to new commands added to the Ribbon.

- **Create custom add-ins for Excel.** Most add-ins shipped with Excel were created with Excel macros. I used VBA exclusively to create my Power Utility Pak.

Displaying the Developer Tab

If you plan to work with VBA macros, you'll want to make sure that the Developer tab is present on the Excel Ribbon. The Developer tab, which does not appear by default, contains useful commands for VBA users. To display this tab

1. Choose File ⇨ Options.
2. In the Excel Options dialog box, select Customize Ribbon.
3. In the list box on the right, place a check mark next to Developer.
4. Click OK to return to Excel.

Figure 39.1 shows the Ribbon commands of the Developer tab.

The Developer tab.

About Macro Security

Macros have the potential to cause serious damage to your computer, such as erasing files or installing malware. Consequently, Microsoft has added macro-security features to help prevent macro-related problems.

Figure 39.2 shows the Macro Settings section of the Trust Center dialog box. To display this dialog box, choose Developer ➪ Code ➪ Macro Security.

The Macro Settings section of the Trust Center dialog box.

By default, Excel uses the Disable All Macros with Notification option. With this setting in effect, if you open a workbook that contains macros (and the file is not digitally "signed"), the macros will be disabled, and Excel displays a Security Warning above the Formula bar (see Figure 39.3). If you're certain that the workbook comes from a trusted source, click the Enable Content button in the security warning area, and the macros will be enabled. Excel remembers your decision; if you enable the macros, you will not see the Security Warning the next time you open that file.

Note

If the Visual Basic (VB) Editor window is open when you open a workbook that contains macros, Excel does not display the Security Warning above the Formula bar. Rather, it displays a dialog box with two buttons: Enable Macros and Disable Macros. ■

FIGURE 39.3

Excel displays a Security Warning if a workbook contains macros.

Rather than deal with individual workbooks, you may prefer to designate one or more folders as "trusted locations." All the workbooks in a trusted location are opened without a macro warning. You designate trusted folders in the Trusted Locations section of the Trust Center dialog box.

Saving Workbooks That Contain Macros

If you store one or more VBA macros in a workbook, you must save the file with an XLSM extension.

The first time you save a workbook that contains macros, the file format defaults to XLSX — and this format can't contain macros. Unless you change the file format to XLSM, Excel displays the warning shown in Figure 39.4. You need to click No, and then choose Excel Macro-Enabled Workbook (*.xlsm) from the Save As Type drop-down list in the Save As dialog box.

Note

Alternatively, you can save the workbook in the old Excel 97-2003 format (which uses an XLS extension). This file format can contain macros. ■

FIGURE 39.4

Excel warns you if your workbook contains macros and you attempt to save it in a nonmacro file format.

Two Types of VBA Macros

Before getting into the details of creating macros, you need to understand a key distinction. A *VBA macro* (also known as a *procedure*) can be one of two types: a Sub or a Function. The next two sections discuss the difference.

VBA Sub procedures

You can think of a Sub procedure as a new command that either the user or another macro can execute. You can have any number of Sub procedures in an Excel workbook. Figure 39.5 shows a simple VBA Sub procedure. When this code is executed, VBA inserts the current date into the active cell, applies a number format, makes the cell bold, and then adjusts the column width.

FIGURE 39.5

A simple VBA procedure.

On the CD

A workbook that contains this macro is available on the companion CD-ROM. It also includes a button that makes it easy to execute the macro. The file is named current date.xlsm.

Sub procedures always start with the keyword Sub, the macro's name (every macro must have a unique name), and then a pair of parentheses. (The parentheses are required; they're empty unless the procedure uses one or more arguments.) The End Sub statement signals the end of the procedure. The lines in between comprise the procedure's code.

What's New in the Visual Basic Editor?

In a word, nothing. Beginning with Excel 2007, Microsoft made many changes to Excel. However, the VB Editor has remained untouched. The VBA language has been updated to accommodate the new Excel features, but the VB Editor has no new features, and the toolbars and menus work exactly like they always have.

The `CurrentDate` macro also includes a comment. *Comments* are simply notes to yourself, and they're ignored by VBA. A comment line begins with an apostrophe. You can also put a comment in the same line as a statement. In other words, when VBA encounters an apostrophe, it ignores the rest of the text in the line.

You execute a VBA `Sub` procedure in any of the following ways:

- Choose Developer ➪ Code ➪ Macros to display the Macro dialog box. Select the procedure name from the list and then click Run. You can also access the Macro dialog box by pressing Alt+F8.
- Press the procedure's shortcut key combination (if it has one).
- If the VB Editor is active, move the cursor anywhere within the code and press F5.
- Execute the procedure by calling it from another VBA procedure.

VBA functions

The second type of VBA procedure is a function. A *function* always returns a single value (just as a worksheet function always returns a single value). A VBA function can be executed by other VBA procedures or used in worksheet formulas, just as you would use Excel's built-in worksheet functions.

Figure 39.6 shows a custom worksheet function. This function is named `CubeRoot`, and it requires a single argument. `CubeRoot` calculates the cube root of its argument. A `Function` procedure looks much like a `Sub` procedure. Notice, however, that function procedures begin with the keyword `Function` and end with an `End Function` statement.

On the CD

A workbook that contains this function is available on the companion CD-ROM. The file is named `cube root .xlsm`.

FIGURE 39.6

This VBA function returns the cube root of its argument.

Cross-Reference

Creating VBA functions that you use in worksheet formulas can simplify your formulas and enable you to perform calculations that otherwise may be impossible. Chapter 40 discusses VBA functions in greater detail. ∎

Some Definitions

If you're new to VBA, you may be overwhelmed by the terminology. I've put together some key definitions to help you keep the terms straight. These terms cover VBA and UserForms (custom dialog boxes) — two important elements that are used to customize Excel:

- **Code:** VBA instructions that are produced in a module sheet when you record a macro. You also can enter VBA code manually.

- **Controls:** Objects on a UserForm (or in a worksheet) that you manipulate. Examples include buttons, check boxes, and list boxes.

- **Function:** One of two types of VBA macros that you can create. (The other is a Sub procedure.) A function returns a single value. You can use VBA functions in other VBA macros or in your worksheets.

- **Macro:** A set of VBA instructions performed automatically.

- **Method:** An action taken on an object. For example, applying the `Clear` method to a `Range` object erases the contents and formatting of the cells.

- **Module:** A container for VBA code.

- **Object:** An element that you manipulate with VBA. Examples include ranges, charts, drawing objects, and so on.

- **Procedure:** Another name for a macro. A VBA procedure can be a Sub procedure or a Function procedure.

- **Property:** A particular aspect of an object. For example, a `Range` object has properties, such as `Height`, `Style`, and `Name`.

- **Sub procedure:** One of two types of Visual Basic macros that you can create. The other is a function.

- **UserForm:** A container that holds controls for a custom dialog box and holds VBA code to manipulate the controls. (Chapters 41 and 42 explain UserForms in depth.)

- **VBA:** Visual Basic for Applications. The macro language that is available in Excel, as well as in the other applications in Microsoft Office.

- **VB Editor:** The window (separate from Excel) that you use to create VBA macros and UserForms. Use Alt+F11 to toggle between Excel and the VB Editor.

Creating VBA Macros

Excel provides two ways to create macros:

- Turn on the macro recorder and record your actions.
- Enter the code directly into a VBA module.

The following sections describe these methods.

Recording VBA macros

In this section, I describe the basic steps that you take to record a VBA macro. In most cases, you can record your actions as a macro and then simply replay the macro; you needn't look at the code that's automatically generated. If simply recording and playing back macros is as far as you go with VBA, you don't need to be concerned with the language itself (although a basic understanding of how things work doesn't do any harm).

Recording your actions to create VBA code: The basics

The Excel macro recorder translates your actions into VBA code. To start the macro recorder, choose Developer ➪ Code ➪ Record Macro (or, click the Record Macro icon on the left side of the status bar). Excel displays the Record Macro dialog box, shown in Figure 39.7.

FIGURE 39.7

The Record Macro dialog box.

The Record Macro dialog box presents several options:

- **Macro Name:** The name of the macro. Excel proposes generic names, such as Macro1, Macro2, and so on.
- **Shortcut Key:** You can specify a key combination that executes the macro. The key combination always uses the Ctrl key. You can also press Shift when you enter a letter. For example, pressing Shift while you enter the letter *H* makes the shortcut key combination Ctrl+Shift+H.

Warning

Shortcut keys assigned to macros take precedence over built-in shortcut keys. For example, if you assign Ctrl+S to a macro, then you cannot use the key combination to save your workbook. ■

- **Store Macro In:** The location for the macro. Your choices are the current workbook, your Personal Macro Workbook (See "Storing macros in your Personal Macro Workbook," later in this chapter), or a new workbook.

- **Description:** A description of the macro (optional).

To begin recording your actions, click OK; your actions within Excel are converted to VBA code. When you finish recording the macro, choose Developer ➪ Code ➪ Stop Recording. Or, you can click the Stop Recording button on the status bar. This button replaces the Start Recording button while your macro is being recorded.

Note

Recording your actions always results in a new `Sub` procedure. You can't create a `Function` procedure by using the macro recorder. Function procedures must be created manually. ■

Recording a macro: A simple example

This example demonstrates how to record a very simple macro that inserts your name in the active cell.

To create the macro, start with a new workbook and follow these steps:

1. **Activate an empty cell.**

Note

Select the cell to be formatted *before* you start recording your macro. This step is important. If you select a cell while the macro recorder is turned on, the actual cell that you select will be recorded into the macro. In such a case, the macro would always format that particular cell, and it would not be a general-purpose macro. ■

2. **Choose Developer ➪ Code ➪ Record Macro.** Excel displays the Record Macro dialog box. (Refer to Figure 39.7.)

3. **Enter a new single-word name for the macro, to replace the default `Macro1` name.** A good name is MyName.

4. **Assign this macro to the shortcut key Ctrl+Shift+N by entering an uppercase N in the Shortcut Key field.**

5. **Click OK to close the Record Macro dialog box and begin recording your actions.**

6. **Type your name into the selected cell and then press Enter.**

7. **Choose Developer ➪ Code ➪ Stop Recording (or click the Stop Recording button on the status bar).**

Examining the macro

The macro was recorded in a new module named Module1. To view the code in this module, you must activate the VB Editor. You can activate the VB Editor in either of two ways:

- Press Alt+F11.
- Choose Developer ⇨ Code ⇨ Visual Basic.

In the VB Editor, the Project window displays a list of all open workbooks and add-ins. This list is displayed as a tree diagram, which you can expand or collapse. The code that you recorded previously is stored in Module1 in the current workbook. When you double-click Module1, the code in the module appears in the Code window.

Figure 39.8 shows the recorded macro, as displayed in the Code window.

FIGURE 39.8

The MyName procedure was generated by the Excel macro recorder.

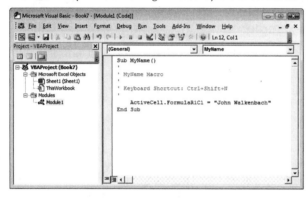

The macro should look something like this (with your name substituted for mine, of course):

```
Sub MyName()
'
' MyName Macro
'
' Keyboard Shortcut: Ctrl+Shift+N
'
    ActiveCell.FormulaR1C1 = "John Walkenbach"
End Sub
```

The macro recorded is a Sub procedure that is named MyName. The statements tell Excel what to do when the macro is executed.

Notice that Excel inserted some comments at the top of the procedure. These comments are some of the information that appeared in the Record Macro dialog box. These comment lines (which begin with an apostrophe) aren't really necessary, and deleting them has no effect on how the macro runs. If you ignore the comments, you'll see that this procedure has only one VBA statement:

```
ActiveCell.FormulaR1C1 = "John Walkenbach"
```

This single statement causes the name you typed while recording the macro to be inserted into the active cell. The `FormulaR1C1` part is a property of the `Range` object — but I'm getting ahead of myself.

Testing the macro

Before you recorded this macro, you set an option that assigned the macro to the Ctrl+Shift+N shortcut key combination. To test the macro, return to Excel by using either of the following methods:

- Press Alt+F11.
- Click the View Microsoft Excel button on the VB Editor toolbar.

When Excel is active, activate a worksheet. (It can be in the workbook that contains the VBA module or in any other workbook.) Select a cell and press Ctrl+Shift+N. The macro immediately enters your name into the cell.

Editing the macro

After you record a macro, you can make changes to it (although you must know what you're doing). For example, assume that you want your name to be bold. You could re-record the macro, but this modification is simple, so editing the code is more efficient. Press Alt+F11 to activate the VB Editor window. Then activate Module1 and insert the following statement before the End Sub statement:

```
ActiveCell.Font.Bold = True
```

The edited macro appears as follows:

```
Sub MyName()
'
' MyName Macro
'
' Keyboard Shortcut: Ctrl+Shift+N
'
    ActiveCell.FormulaR1C1 = "John Walkenbach"
    ActiveCell.Font.Bold = True
End Sub
```

Test this new macro, and you see that it performs as it should.

Another example

This example demonstrates how to record a time-stamp macro that inserts the current date and time into the active cell.

To create the macro, follow these steps:

1. **Activate an empty cell.**

2. **Choose Developer ⇨ Code ⇨ Record Macro.** Excel displays the Record Macro dialog box.

3. **Enter a new single-word name for the macro, to replace the default** `Macro1` **name.** A good name is TimeStamp.

4. **Assign this macro to the shortcut key Ctrl+Shift+T by entering an uppercase T in the Shortcut Key field.**

5. **Click OK to close the Record Macro dialog box.**

6. **Enter this formula into the selected cell:**

   `=NOW()`

7. **With the date cell selected, click the Copy button (or press Ctrl+C) to copy the cell to the Clipboard.**

8. **Choose Home ⇨ Clipboard ⇨ Paste ⇨ Values (V).** This step replaces the formula with static text so that the data and time do not update when the worksheet is calculated.

9. **Press Esc(ape) to cancel Copy mode.**

10. **Choose Developer ⇨ Code ⇨ Stop Recording (or click the Stop Recording button on the status bar).**

Running the macro

Activate an empty cell and press Ctrl+Shift+T to execute the macro. There's a pretty good chance that the macro won't work!

The VBA code that is recorded in this macro depends upon a setting on the Advanced tab of the Excel Options dialog box: namely, after Pressing Enter, Move Selection. If this setting is enabled, the recorded macro won't work as intended because the active cell was changed when you pressed Enter. Even if you reactivated the date cell while recording (in Step 7), the macro still fails.

Examining the macro

Activate the VB Editor and take a look at the recorded code. Figure 39.9 shows the recorded macro, as displayed in the Code window.

The procedure has five statements. The first inserts the NOW() formula into the active cell. The second statement selects cell C4 — an action I performed because the cell pointer moved to the next cell after I entered the formula.

FIGURE 39.9

The TimeStamp procedure was generated by the Excel macro recorder.

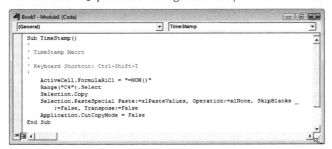

The third statement copies the cell. The fourth statement, which is displayed on two lines (the underscore character means that the statement continues on the next line), pastes the Clipboard contents (as a value) to the current selection. The fourth statement cancels the moving border around the selected range.

The problem is that the macro is hard-coded to select cell C4. If you execute the macro when a different cell is active, the code always selects cell C4. This is not what you intended, and it causes the macro to fail.

Note

You'll also notice that the macro recorded some actions that you didn't make. For example, it specified several options for the PasteSpecial operation. Recording actions that you don't specifically make is just a by-product of the method that Excel uses to translate actions into code. ■

Re-recording the macro

You can fix the macro in several ways. If you understand VBA, you can edit the code so it works properly. Or, you can re-record the macro using relative references.

Delete the existing TimeStamp procedure, and re-record it. Before you start recording, click the Use Relative References command in the Code group of the Developer tab. This control is a toggle, and it's turned off by default.

Figure 39.10 shows the new macro, recorded with relative references in effect.

This `TimeStamp` macro works correctly.

```
Sub TimeStamp()
    ActiveCell.FormulaR1C1 = "=NOW()"
    Selection.Copy
    Selection.PasteSpecial Paste:=xlPasteValues, Operation:=xlNone, SkipBlanks _
        :=False, Transpose:=False
End Sub
```

Testing the macro

When Excel is active, activate a worksheet. (It can be in the workbook that contains the VBA module or in any other workbook.) Select a cell and press Ctrl+Shift+T. The macro immediately enters the current date and time into the cell. You may need to widen the column to see the date and time. To widen the column automatically, just add this statement to the end of the macro (before the End Sub statement):

```
ActiveCell.EntireColumn.AutoFit
```

More about recording VBA macros

If you followed along with the preceding examples, you should have a better feel for how to record macros — and also a good feel for problems that might occur with even simple macros. If you find the VBA code confusing, don't worry. You don't really have to be concerned with it as long as the macro that you record works correctly. If the macro doesn't work, rerecording the macro rather than editing the code often is easier.

A good way to learn about what gets recorded is to set up your screen so that you can see the code that is being generated in the VB Editor windows. To do so, make sure that the Excel window isn't maximized; then arrange the Excel window and the VB Editor window so both are visible. While you're recording your actions, make sure that the VB Editor window is displaying the module in which the code is being recorded. (You may have to double-click the module name in the Project window.)

Tip

If you do a lot of work with VBA, consider adding a second monitor to your system. Then you can display Excel on one monitor and the VB Editor on the other. ∎

Absolute versus relative recording

If you're going to work with recorded macros, you need to understand the concept of *relative* versus *absolute* recording modes. In a previous example in this chapter, I showed how even a simple macro could fail because of an incorrect recording mode.

Normally, when you record a macro, Excel stores exact references to the cells that you select. (That is, it performs *absolute* recording.) If you select the range B1:B10 while you're recording a macro, for example, Excel records this selection as

```
Range("B1:B10").Select
```

This VBA statement means exactly what it says: "Select the cells in the range B1:B10." When you invoke the macro that contains this statement, the same cells are always selected, regardless of where the active cell is located.

Look in the Developer ⇨ Code group of the Ribbon for Use Relative References. When you click this control, Excel changes its recording mode from absolute (the default) to relative. When recording in relative mode, selecting a range of cells is translated differently, depending on where the active cell is located. For example, if you're recording in relative mode and cell A1 is active, selecting the range B1:B10 generates the following statement:

```
ActiveCell.Offset(0, 1).Range("A1:A10").Select
```

This statement can be translated as "From the active cell, move 0 rows down and 1 column right, and then treat this new cell as if it were cell A1. Now select what would be A1:A10." In other words, a macro that is recorded in relative mode starts out by using the active cell as its base and then stores relative references to this cell. As a result, you get different results, depending on the location of the active cell. When you replay this macro, the cells that are selected depend on the active cell. This macro selects a range that is 10 rows by 1 column, offset from the active cell by 0 rows and 1 column.

When Excel is recording in relative mode, the Use Relative Reference control appears depressed. To return to absolute recording, click the Use Relative Reference control again (and it displays its normal, undepressed state).

Storing macros in your Personal Macro Workbook

Most user-created macros are designed for use in a specific workbook, but you may want to use some macros in all your work. You can store these general-purpose macros in the Personal Macro Workbook so that they're always available to you. The Personal Macro Workbook is loaded whenever you start Excel. This file, named `personal.xlsb`, doesn't exist until you record a macro, using Personal Macro Workbook as the destination.

Note
The Personal Macro Workbook normally is in a hidden window (to keep it out of the way). ∎

To record the macro in your Personal Macro Workbook, select the Personal Macro Workbook option in the Record Macro dialog box before you start recording. This option is in the Store Macro In drop-down box.

If you store macros in the Personal Macro Workbook, you don't have to remember to open the Personal Macro Workbook when you load a workbook that uses macros. When you want to exit, Excel asks whether you want to save changes to the Personal Macro Workbook.

Assigning a macro to a shortcut key

When you begin recording a macro, the Record Macro dialog box gives you an opportunity to provide a shortcut key for the macro. Here's what to do if you'd like to change the shortcut key or provide a shortcut key for a macro that doesn't have one:

1. **Choose Developer ⇨ Code ⇨ Macros (or press Alt+F8) to display the Macro dialog box.**

2. **In the Macro dialog box, select the macro name from the list.**

3. **Click the Options button, and Excel displays its Macro Options dialog box.** See Figure 39.11.

4. **Specify the shortcut key.** Use a single letter (for a Ctrl+letter shortcut), or press Shift and enter an uppercase letter (for a Ctrl+Shift+letter shortcut).

5. **Click OK to return to the Macro dialog box.**

6. **Click Cancel to close the Macro dialog box.**

FIGURE 39.11

Use the Macro Options dialog box to add or change a shortcut key for a macro.

Assigning a macro to a button

After you record a macro and test it, you may want to assign the macro to a button placed in a worksheet. You can follow these steps to do so:

1. **If the macro is a general-purpose macro that you plan to use in more than one workbook, make sure that the macro is stored in your Personal Macro Workbook.**

2. **Choose Developer ⇨ Controls ⇨ Insert and then click the Button control from the Form Controls section (see Figure 39.12).** Move your mouse pointer over the icons, and you see a ToolTip that describes the control.

3. **Draw the button on the worksheet.** Excel displays the Assign Macro dialog box.

4. **In the Assign Macro dialog box, select the macro from the list.**

5. **Click OK to close the Assign Macro dialog box.**

6. **(Optional) Change the text that appears on the button to make it descriptive; right-click the button, choose Edit Text from the shortcut menu, and make your changes.**

After performing these steps, clicking the button executes the assigned macro.

FIGURE 39.12

Adding a button to a worksheet so that it can be used to execute a macro.

Tip

You can also assign a macro to a button on your Quick Access toolbar. Right-click the Quick Access toolbar and choose Customize Quick Access Toolbar from the shortcut menu. On the Quick Access Toolbar tab of the Excel Options dialog box that appears, select Macros from the drop-down list on the left. Then select your macro and click the Add button. To change the icon, click the Modify button. ■

Writing VBA code

As demonstrated in the preceding sections, the easiest way to create a simple macro is to record your actions. To develop more complex macros, however, you have to enter the VBA code manually — in other words, write a program. To save time, you can often combine recording with manual code entry.

Before you can begin writing VBA code, you must have a good understanding of such topics as objects, properties, and methods. And it doesn't hurt to be familiar with common programming constructs, such as looping and If-Then statements.

This section is an introduction to VBA programming, which is essential if you want to write (rather than record) VBA macros. It isn't intended to be a complete instructional guide. My book *Excel 2010 Power Programming with VBA* (Wiley) covers all aspects of VBA and advanced spreadsheet application development.

VBA Coding Tips

When you enter code in a module sheet, you're free to use indenting and blank lines to make the code more readable. In fact, this is an excellent habit.

After you enter a line of code (by pressing Enter), it's evaluated for syntax errors. If none are found, the line of code is reformatted, and colors are added to keywords and identifiers. This automatic reformatting adds consistent spaces (before and after an equal sign, for example) and removes extra spaces that aren't needed. If a syntax error is found, you receive a pop-up message, and the line is displayed in a different color (red, by default). You need to correct your error before you can execute the macro.

A single statement can be as long as you need. However, you may want to break the statement into two or more lines. To do so, insert a space followed by an underscore (_). The following code, although written as two lines, is actually a single VBA statement:

```
Sheets("Sheet1").Range("B1").Value = _
  Sheets("Sheet1").Range("A1").Value
```

You can insert comments freely into your VBA code. The comment indicator is an apostrophe single quote character ('). Any text that follows a single quote is ignored. A comment can be a line by itself, or it can be inserted after a statement. The following examples show two comments:

```
' Assign the values to the variables
Rate = .085   'Rate as of November 16
```

The basics: Entering and editing code

Before you can enter code, you must insert a VBA module into the workbook. If the workbook already has a VBA module, you can use the existing module sheet for your new code.

Use the following steps to insert a new VBA module:

1. **Press Alt+F11 to activate the VB Editor window.** The Project window displays a list of all open workbooks and add-ins.

2. **In the Project window, locate and select the workbook you're working in.**

3. **Choose Insert ➪ Module.** VBA inserts a new (empty) module into the workbook and displays it in the Code window.

A VBA module, which is displayed in a separate window, works like a text editor. You can move through the sheet, select text, insert, copy, cut, paste, and so on.

How VBA works

VBA is by far the most complex feature in Excel, and you can easily get overwhelmed. To set the stage for the details of VBA, here is a concise summary of how VBA works:

- **You perform actions in VBA by writing (or recording) code in a VBA module sheet and then executing the macro in any one of various ways.** VBA modules are stored in an Excel workbook, and a workbook can hold any number of VBA modules. To view or edit a VBA module, you must activate the VB Editor window. (Press Alt+F11 to toggle between Excel and the VB Editor window.)

- **A VBA module consists of procedures.** A *procedure* is basically computer code that performs some action. The following is an example of a simple Sub procedure called ShowSum, which adds 1 + 1 and displays the result:

```
Sub ShowSum()
  Sum = 1 + 1
  MsgBox "The answer is " & Sum
End Sub
```

- **A VBA module also can store function procedures.** A *function procedure* performs calculations and returns a single value. A function can be called from another VBA procedure or can even be used in a worksheet formula. Here's an example of a function named AddTwo. (It adds two values, which are supplied as arguments.)

```
Function AddTwo(arg1, arg2)
  AddTwo = arg1 + arg2
End Function
```

- **VBA manipulates objects.** Excel provides more than 100 classes of objects that you can manipulate. Examples of objects include a workbook, a worksheet, a range on a worksheet, a chart, and a rectangle shape.

- **Objects are arranged in a hierarchy and can act as containers for other objects.** For example, Excel itself is an object called Application, and it contains other objects, such as Workbook objects. The Workbook object can contain other objects, such as Worksheet objects and Chart objects. A Worksheet object can contain objects such as Range objects, PivotTable objects, and so on. The arrangement of all these objects is referred to as an *object model*.

- **Objects that are alike form a *collection*.** For example, the Worksheets collection consists of all worksheets in a particular workbook. The ChartObjects collection consists of all ChartObjects on a worksheet. Collections are objects in themselves.

- **You refer to an object in your VBA code by specifying its position in the object hierarchy, using a period as a separator.**

  For example, you can refer to a workbook named Book1.xlsx as

  ```
  Application.Workbooks("Book1.xlsx")
  ```

  This expression refers to the Book1.xlsx workbook in the Workbooks collection. The Workbooks collection is contained in the Application object (that is, Excel). Extending this to another level, you can refer to Sheet1 in Book1 as follows:

  ```
  Application.Workbooks("Book1.xlsx").Worksheets("Sheet1")
  ```

You can take it to still another level and refer to a specific cell as follows:

```
Application.Workbooks("Book1.xlsx").Worksheets("Sheet1"). _
    Range("A1")
```

- **If you omit specific references, Excel uses the *active* objects.** If `Book1.xlsx` is the active workbook, the preceding reference can be simplified as follows:

```
Worksheets("Sheet1").Range("A1")
```

If you know that Sheet1 is the active sheet, you can simplify the reference even more:

```
Range("A1")
```

- **Objects have properties.** A *property* can be thought of as a setting for an object. For example, a `Range` object has properties, such as `Value` and `Address`. A `Chart` object has properties such as `HasTitle` and `Type`. You can use VBA both to determine object properties and to change them.

- **You refer to properties by combining the object with the property, separated by a period.** For example, you can refer to the value in cell A1 on Sheet1 as follows:

```
Worksheets("Sheet1").Range("A1").Value
```

- **You can assign values to variables.** To assign the value in cell A1 on Sheet1 to a variable called `Interest`, use the following VBA statement:

```
Interest = Worksheets("Sheet1").Range("A1").Value
```

- **Objects have methods.** A *method* is an action that is performed with the object. For example, one of the methods for a `Range` object is `ClearContents`. This method clears the contents of the range.

- **You specify methods by combining the object with the method, separated by a period.** For example, to clear the contents of range A1:C12, use the following statement:

```
Worksheets("Sheet1").Range("A1:C12").ClearContents
```

- **VBA also includes all the constructs of modern programming languages, including variables, arrays, looping, and so on.**

The preceding describes VBA in a nutshell. Now you just have to learn the details, some of which are covered in the rest of this chapter.

Objects and collections

VBA is an *object-oriented language,* which means that it manipulates objects, such as `Ranges`, `Charts`, `Shapes`, and so on. These objects are arranged in a hierarchy. The `Application` object (which is Excel) contains other objects. For example, the `Application` object contains a number of objects, including the following:

- `AddIns` (a collection of `AddIn` objects)
- `Windows` (a collection of `Window` objects)
- `Workbooks` (a collection of `Workbook` objects)

Most of these objects can contain other objects. For example, a `Workbook` object can contain the following objects:

- `Charts` (a collection of `Chart` sheet objects)
- `Names` (a collection of `Name` objects)
- `Styles` (a collection of `Style` objects)
- `Windows` (a collection of `Window` objects in the workbook)
- `Worksheets` (a collection of `Worksheet` objects)

Each of these objects, in turn, can contain other objects. A `Worksheet` object, for example, can contain the following objects:

- `ChartObjects` (a collection of all `ChartObject` objects)
- `PageSetup` (an object that stores printing information)
- `PivotTables` (a collection of all `PivotTable` objects)

A *collection* consists of all like objects. For example, the collection of all `Workbook` objects is known as the `Workbooks` collection. You can refer to an individual object in a collection by using an index number or a name. For example, if a workbook has three worksheets (named Sheet1, Sheet2, and Sheet3), you can refer to the first object in the `Worksheets` collection in either of these ways:

```
Worksheets(1)
Worksheets("Sheet1")
```

Properties

The objects that you work with have *properties,* which you can think of as attributes of the objects. For example, a `Range` object has properties, such as `Column`, `Row`, `Width`, and `Value`. A `Chart` object has properties, such as `Legend`, `ChartTitle`, and so on. `ChartTitle` is also an object, with properties such as `Font`, `Orientation`, and `Text`. Excel has many objects, and each has its own set of properties. You can write VBA code to do the following:

- Examine an object's current property setting and take some action based on it.
- Change an object's property setting.

You refer to a property in your VBA code by placing a period (a dot) and the property name after the object's name. For example, the following VBA statement sets the `Value` property of a range named *frequency* to `15`. (That is, the statement causes the number `15` to appear in the range's cells.)

```
Range("frequency").Value = 15
```

Some properties are *read-only,* which means that you can examine the property, but you can't change the property. For a single-cell `Range` object, the `Row` and `Column` properties are read-only properties: You can determine where a cell is located (in which row and column), but you can't change the cell's location by changing these properties.

A Range object also has a `Formula` property, which is *not* read-only; that is, you can insert a formula into a cell by changing its `Formula` property. The following statement inserts a formula into cell A12 by changing the cell's `Formula` property:

```
Range("A12").Formula = "=SUM(A1:A10)"
```

Note
Contrary to what you may think, Excel doesn't have a `Cell` object. When you want to manipulate a single cell, you use the `Range` object (with only one cell in it). ■

At the top of the object hierarchy is the `Application` object, which is actually Excel, the program. The `Application` object has several useful properties:

- `Application.ActiveWorkbook`: Returns the active workbook (a `Workbook` object) in Excel.
- `Application.ActiveSheet`: Returns the active sheet (a `Sheet` object) of the active workbook.
- `Application.ActiveCell`: Returns the active cell (a `Range` object) object of the active window.
- `Application.Selection`: Returns the object that is currently selected in the active window of the `Application` object. This can be a `Range`, a `Chart`, a `Shape`, or some other selectable object.

You also should understand that properties can return objects. In fact, that's exactly what the preceding examples do. The result of `Application.ActiveCell`, for example, is a `Range` object. Therefore, you can access properties by using a statement such as the following:

```
Application.ActiveCell.Font.Size = 15
```

In this case, the `ActiveCell` property returns a `Range` object. The `Font` property returns a `Font` object, which is contained in the `Range` object. `Size` is a property of the Font object. The preceding statement sets the `Size` property to 15 — that is, it causes the font in the currently selected cell to have a size of 15 points (pt).

Tip
Because `Application` properties are so commonly used, you can omit the object qualifier (`Application`). For example, to get the row of the active cell, you can use a statement such as the following:

```
ActiveCell.Row
```

In many cases, you can refer to the same object in a number of different ways. Assume that you have a workbook named `Sales.xlsx` and it's the only workbook open. Furthermore, assume that this workbook has one worksheet, named Summary. Your VBA code can refer to the Summary sheet in any of the following ways:

```
Workbooks("Sales.xlsx").Worksheets("Summary")
Workbooks(1).Worksheets(1)
Workbooks(1).Sheets(1)
Application.ActiveWorkbook.ActiveSheet
ActiveWorkbook.ActiveSheet
ActiveSheet
```

The method that you use is determined by how much you know about the workspace. For example, if more than one workbook is open, the second or third method is not reliable. If you want to work with the active sheet (whatever it may be), any of the last three methods would work. To be absolutely sure that you're referring to a specific sheet on a specific workbook, the first method is your best choice.

Methods

Objects also have *methods*. You can think of a method as an action taken with an object. For example, Range objects have a Clear method. The following VBA statement clears a Range, an action that is equivalent to selecting the Range and then choosing Home ➪ Editing ➪ Clear ➪ Clear All:

```
Range("A1:C12").Clear
```

In VBA code, methods *look* like properties because they are connected to the object with a "dot." However, methods and properties are different concepts.

Variables

Like all programming languages, VBA enables you to work with variables. In VBA (unlike in some languages), you don't need to declare variables explicitly before you use them in your code (although doing so is definitely a good practice).

Note

If your VBA module contains an Option Explicit statement at the top of the module, then you must declare all variables in the module. Undeclared variables will result in a compile error, and your procedures will not run. ∎

In the following example, the value in cell A1 on Sheet1 is assigned to a variable named Rate:

```
Rate = Worksheets("Sheet1").Range("A1").Value
```

You then can work with the variable Rate in other parts of your VBA code. Note that the variable Rate is not a named range, which means that you can't use it as such in a worksheet formula.

Controlling execution

VBA uses many constructs that are found in most other programming languages. These constructs are used to control the flow of execution. This section introduces a few of the more common programming constructs.

The If-Then construct

One of the most important control structures in VBA is the If-Then construct, which gives your applications decision-making capability. The basic syntax of the If-Then structure is as follows:

```
If condition Then statements [Else elsestatements]
```

In plain English, if a condition is true, then a group of statement will be executed. If you include the Else clause, then another group of statements will be executed if the condition is not true.

The following is an example (which doesn't use the optional Else clause). This procedure checks the active cell. If it contains a negative value, the cell's color is changed to red. Otherwise, nothing happens.

```
Sub CheckCell()
   If ActiveCell.Value < 0 Then ActiveCell.Font.ColorIndex = 3
End Sub
```

For-Next loops

You can use a For-Next loop to execute one or more statements a number of times. Here's an example of a For-Next loop:

```
Sub SumSquared()
   Total = 0
   For Num = 1 To 10
     Total = Total + (Num ^ 2)
   Next Num
   MsgBox Total
End Sub
```

This example has one statement between the For statement and the Next statement. This single statement is executed 10 times. The variable Num takes on successive values of 1, 2, 3, and so on, up to 10. The variable Total stores the sum of Num squared, added to the previous value of Total. The result is a value that represents the sum of the first 10 integers squared. This result is displayed in a message box.

The With-End With construct

Another construct that you encounter if you record macros is the With-End With construct. This is a shortcut way of dealing with several properties or methods of the same object. The following is an example:

```
Sub AlignCells()
   With Selection
      .HorizontalAlignment = xlCenter
```

```
      .VerticalAlignment = xlCenter
      .WrapText = False
      .Orientation = xlHorizontal
   End With
End Sub
```

The following macro performs exactly the same operations but doesn't use the With-End With construct:

```
Sub AlignCells()
   Selection.HorizontalAlignment = xlCenter
   Selection.VerticalAlignment = xlCenter
   Selection.WrapText = False
   Selection.Orientation = xlHorizontal
End Sub
```

The Select Case construct

The Select Case construct is useful for choosing among two or more options. The following example demonstrates the use of a Select Case construct. In this example, the active cell is checked. If its value is less than 0, it's colored red. If it's equal to 0, it's colored blue. If the value is greater than 0, it's colored black.

```
Sub CheckCell()
   Select Case ActiveCell.Value
     Case Is < 0
       ActiveCell.Font.Color = vbRed
     Case 0
       ActiveCell.Font.Color = vbBlue
     Case Is > 0
       ActiveCell.Font.Color = vbBlack
   End Select
End Sub
```

Any number of statements can go below each Case statement, and they all get executed if the case is true.

A macro that can't be recorded

The following is a VBA macro that can't be recorded because it uses programming concepts that must be entered manually. This macro creates a list of all formulas on the active sheet. The list is stored on a new worksheet.

```
Sub ListFormulas()
' Create a range object
   Set InputRange = ActiveSheet.UsedRange
' Add a new sheet
   Set OutputSheet = Worksheets.Add
' Variable for the output row
   OutputRow = 1
' Loop through the range
```

```
      For Each cell In InputRange
        If cell.HasFormula Then
          OutputSheet.Cells(OutputRow, 1) = "'" & cell.Address
          OutputSheet.Cells(OutputRow, 2) = "'" & cell.Formula
          OutputRow = OutputRow + 1
        End If
      Next cell
    End Sub
```

On the CD

A workbook that contains this example is available on the companion CD-ROM. The file is named `list formulas.xlsm`.

Although this macro may look complicated, it's fairly simple when you break it down. Here's how it works:

1. The macro creates an object variable named `InputRange`. This variable corresponds to the used range on the active sheet (avoiding the need to check every cell).

2. It then adds a new worksheet and assigns the worksheet to an object variable named `OutputSheet`. The `OutputRow` variable is set to 1. This variable is incremented later on.

3. The `For-Next` loop examines each cell in the `InputRange`. If the cell has a formula, the cell's address and formula are written to the `OutputSheet`. The `OutputRow` variable is also incremented.

Figure 39.13 shows the result of running this macro — a handy list of all formulas in the worksheet.

FIGURE 39.13

The `ListFormulas` macro creates a list of all formulas in a worksheet.

	A	B	C	D
1	$G$2	=B9/2		
2	$A$8	=SUM(A2:A7)		
3	$B$8	=SUM(B2:B7)		
4	$C$8	=SUM(C2:C7)		
5	$D$8	=SUM(D2:D7)		
6	$A$9	=AVERAGE(A2:A7)		
7	$B$9	=AVERAGE(B2:B7)		
8	$C$9	=AVERAGE(C2:C7)		
9	$D$9	=AVERAGE(D2:D7)		
10	$E$9	=AVERAGE(E2:E7)		
11	$A$15	=RANDBETWEEN(1,1000)		
12	$B$15	=RANDBETWEEN(1,1000)		
13	$C$15	=RANDBETWEEN(1,1000)		
14	$D$15	=RANDBETWEEN(1,1000)		
15	$E$15	=RANDBETWEEN(1,1000)		
16	$A$16	=RANDBETWEEN(1,1000)		

As macros go, this example is okay, but it's certainly not perfect. It's not very flexible, and it doesn't include any error handling. For example, if the workbook structure is protected, trying to add a new sheet will cause an error.

Learning More

This chapter barely scratches the surface of what you can do with VBA. If this is your first exposure to VBA, you're probably a bit overwhelmed by objects, properties, and methods. I don't blame you. If you try to access a property that an object doesn't have, you get a run-time error, and your VBA code grinds to a screeching halt until you correct the problem. Fortunately, several good ways are available to learn about objects, properties, and methods.

- **Read the rest of the book.** Subsequent chapters in this section contain additional information and many more examples.

- **Record your actions.** The best way to become familiar with VBA is to turn on the macro recorder and record actions that you make in Excel. You can then examine the code to gain some insights regarding the objects, properties, and methods.

- **Use the Help system.** The main source of detailed information about Excel's objects, methods, and procedures is the VBA Help system. Help is very thorough and easy to access. When you're in a VBA module, just move the cursor to a property or method and press F1. You get help that describes the word that is under the cursor.

- **Get another book.** Several books are devoted exclusively to using VBA with Excel. My book, *Excel 2010 Power Programming with VBA* (Wiley), is one.

Creating Custom Worksheet Functions

A s mentioned in the preceding chapter, you can create two types of VBA procedures: Sub procedures and Function procedures. This chapter focuses on Function procedures.

Overview of VBA Functions

Function procedures that you write in VBA are quite versatile. You can use these functions in two situations:

- You can call the function from a different VBA procedure.
- You can use the function in formulas that you create in a worksheet.

This chapter focuses on creating functions for use in your formulas.

Excel includes hundreds of predefined worksheet functions. With so many from which to choose, you may be curious as to why anyone would need to develop additional functions. The main reason is that creating a custom function can greatly simplify your formulas by making them shorter, and shorter formulas are more readable and easier to work with. For example, you can often replace a complex formula with a single function. Another reason is that you can write functions to perform operations that would otherwise be impossible.

Note
This chapter assumes that you're familiar with entering and editing VBA code in the Visual Basic Editor (VB Editor). See Chapter 39 for an overview of the VB Editor. ■

IN THIS CHAPTER

Overview of VBA functions

About function procedures

Function procedure arguments

Debugging custom functions

Pasting custom functions

An Introductory Example

Creating custom functions is relatively easy after you understand VBA. Without further ado, here's an example of a VBA function procedure. This function is stored in a VBA module, which is accessible from the VB Editor.

A custom function

This example function, named NumSign, uses one argument. The function returns a text string of Positive if its argument is greater than 0 (zero), Negative if the argument is less than 0, and Zero if the argument is equal to 0. The function is shown in Figure 40.1.

A simple custom worksheet function.

You can, of course, accomplish the same effect with the following worksheet formula, which uses a nested IF function:

```
=IF(A1=0,"Zero",IF(A1>0,"Positive","Negative"))
```

Many would agree that the custom function solution is easier to understand and to edit than the worksheet formula.

Using the function in a worksheet

When you enter a formula that uses the NumSign function, Excel executes the function to get the result. This custom function works just like any built-in worksheet function. You can insert it in a formula by choosing Formulas ➪ Function Library ➪ Function Wizard, which displays the Insert Function dialog box. (Custom functions are listed in the User Defined category.) When you select the function from the list, you can then use the Function Arguments dialog box to specify the arguments for the function, as shown in Figure 40.2. You also can nest custom functions and combine them with other elements in your formulas.

Creating a worksheet formula that uses a custom function.

Analyzing the custom function

This section describes the NumSign function. Here again is the code:

```
Function NumSign(num)
    Select Case num
        Case Is < 0
            NumSign = "Negative"
        Case 0
            NumSign = "Zero"
        Case Is > 0
            NumSign = "Positive"
    End Select
End Function
```

Notice that the procedure starts with the keyword Function, followed by the name of the function (NumSign). This custom function uses one argument (num), and the argument's name is enclosed in parentheses. The num argument represents the cell or variable that is to be processed. When the function is used in a worksheet, the argument can be a cell reference (such as A1) or a literal value (such as -123). When the function is used in another procedure, the argument can be a numeric variable, a literal number, or a value that is obtained from a cell.

The NumSign function uses the Select Case construct (described in Chapter 39) to take a different action, depending on the value of num. If num is less than 0, NumSign is assigned the text Negative. If num is equal to 0, NumSign is Zero. If num is greater than 0, NumSign is Positive. The value returned by a function is always assigned to the function's name.

If you work with this function, you might notice a problem if the argument is non-numeric. In such a case, the function returns `Positive`. In other words, the function has a bug. Following is a revised version that returns an empty string if the argument is non-numeric. This code uses the VBA `IsNumeric` function to check the argument. If it's numeric, the code checks the sign. If the argument is not numeric, the `Else` part of the `If-Then-Else` structure is executed.

```
Function NumSign(num)
    If IsNumeric(num) Then
        Select Case num
          Case Is < 0
             NumSign = "Negative"
          Case 0
             NumSign = "Zero"
          Case Is > 0
             NumSign = "Positive"
        End Select
    Else
        NumSign = ""
    End If
End Function
```

About Function Procedures

A custom `Function` procedure has much in common with a `Sub` procedure. Function procedures have some important differences, however. Perhaps the key difference is that a function returns a *value* (which can be a number or a text string). When writing a `Function` procedure, the value that's returned is the value that has been assigned to the function's name when a function is finished executing.

To create a custom function, follow these steps:

1. Activate the VB Editor (press Alt+F11).

2. Select the workbook in the Project window.

3. **Choose Insert ➪ Module to insert a VBA module.** Or you can use an existing code module. However, it must be a standard VBA module.

4. **Enter the keyword Function followed by the function's name and a list of the arguments (if any) in parentheses.** If the function doesn't use an argument, the VB Editor adds a set of empty parentheses.

5. **Insert the VBA code that performs the work — and make sure that the variable corresponding to the function's name has the appropriate value when the function ends.** This is the value that the function returns.

6. **End the function with an** `End Function` **statement.**

Note

Step 3 is very important. If you put a function procedure in a code module for ThisWorkbook or a worksheet (for example, Sheet1), the function will not be recognized in a worksheet formula. Excel will display a #NAME? error. ■

Function names that are used in worksheet formulas must adhere to the same rules as variable names.

What a Function Can't Do

Almost everyone who starts creating custom worksheet functions using VBA makes a fatal mistake: They try to get the function to do more than is possible.

A worksheet function returns a value, and the function must be completely "passive." In other words, the function can't change anything on the worksheet. For example, you can't develop a worksheet function that changes the formatting of a cell. (Every VBA programmer has tried, and not one of them has been successful!) If your function attempts to perform an action that isn't allowed, the function simply returns an error.

VBA functions that aren't used in worksheet formulas can do anything that a regular Sub procedure can do — including changing cell formatting.

Executing Function Procedures

You can execute a Sub procedure in many ways, but you can execute a Function procedure in just two ways:

- Call it from another VBA procedure.
- Use it in a worksheet formula.

Calling custom functions from a procedure

You can call custom functions from a VBA procedure just as you call built-in VBA functions. For example, after you define a function called CalcTax, you can enter a statement such as the following:

```
Tax = CalcTax(Amount, Rate)
```

This statement executes the CalcTax custom function with Amount and Rate as its arguments. The function's result is assigned to the Tax variable.

Using custom functions in a worksheet formula

You use a custom function in a worksheet formula just like you use built-in functions. However, you must ensure that Excel can locate the function. If the function procedure is in the same workbook, you don't have to do anything special. If the function is defined in a different workbook, you may have to tell Excel where to find the function. The following are the three ways in which you can do this:

- **Precede the function's name with a file reference.** For example, if you want to use a function called CountNames that's defined in a workbook named MyFunctions, you can use a reference such as the following:

  `=MyFunctions.xlsm!CountNames(A1:A1000)`

  If the workbook name contains a space, you need to add single quotes around the workbook name. For example

  `='My Functions.xlsm'!CountNames(A1:A1000)`

  If you insert the function with the Insert Function dialog box, the workbook reference is inserted automatically.

- **Set up a reference to the workbook.** If the custom function is defined in a referenced workbook, you don't need to precede the function name with the workbook name. You establish a reference to another workbook by choosing Tools ➪ References (in the VB Editor). You are presented with a list of references that includes all open workbooks. Place a check mark in the item that refers to the workbook that contains the custom function. (Click the Browse button if the workbook isn't open.)

- **Create an add-in.** When you create an add-in from a workbook that has function procedures, you don't need to use the file reference when you use one of the functions in a formula; the add-in must be installed, however. Chapter 45 discusses add-ins.

Note

Function procedures don't appear in the Macro dialog box because you can't execute a function directly. As a result, you need to do extra, up-front work to test your functions while you're developing them. One approach is to set up a simple Sub procedure that calls the function. If the function is designed to be used in worksheet formulas, you can enter a simple formula that uses the function to test it while you're developing the function. ■

Function Procedure Arguments

Keep in mind the following about function procedure arguments:

- Arguments can be variables (including arrays), constants, literals, or expressions.
- Some functions do not have arguments.

- Some functions have a fixed number of required arguments (from 1 to 60).
- Some functions have a combination of required and optional arguments.

The following sections present a series of examples that demonstrate how to use arguments effectively with functions. Coverage of optional arguments is beyond the scope of this book.

On the CD

The examples in this chapter are available on the companion CD-ROM. The file is named VBA functions.xlsm.

A function with no argument

Functions don't necessarily use arguments. Excel, for example, has a few built-in worksheet functions that don't use arguments, such as RAND, TODAY, and NOW.

The following is a simple example of a function that has no arguments. This function returns the UserName property of the Application object, which is the name that appears in the Personalize section of the Excel Options dialog box. This function is very simple, but it can be useful because no other way is available to get the user's name to appear in a worksheet formula.

```
Function User()
' Returns the name of the current user
  User = Application.UserName
End Function
```

When you enter the following formula into a worksheet cell, the cell displays the name of the current user:

```
=User()
```

Like with Excel's built-in functions, when you use a function with no arguments, you must include a set of empty parentheses.

A function with one argument

The function that follows takes a single argument and uses the Excel text-to-speech generator to "speak" the argument.

```
Function SayIt(txt)
  Application.Speech.Speak (txt)
End Function
```

Note

To hear the synthesized voice, your system must be set up to play sound. ∎

For example, if you enter this formula, Excel will "speak" the contents of cell A1 whenever the worksheet is recalculated:

```
=SayIt(A1)
```

You can use this function in a slightly more complex formula, as shown here. In this example, the argument is a text string rather than a cell reference.

```
=IF(SUM(A:A)>1000,SayIt("Goal reached"),)
```

This formula calculates the sum of the values in Column A. If that sum exceeds 1,000, you will hear "Goal reached."

When you use the SayIt function in a worksheet formula, the function always returns 0 because a value is not assigned to the function's name.

Another function with one argument

This section contains a more complex function that is designed for a sales manager who needs to calculate the commissions earned by the sales force. The commission rate is based on the amount sold — those who sell more earn a higher commission rate. The function returns the commission amount, based on the sales made (which is the function's only argument — a required argument). The calculations in this example are based on the following table:

Monthly Sales	Commission Rate
0–$9,999	8.0%
$10,000–$19,999	10.5%
$20,000–$39,999	12.0%
$40,000+	14.0%

You can use any of several different methods to calculate commissions for various sales amounts that are entered into a worksheet. You could write a formula such as the following:

```
=IF(AND(A1>=0,A1<=9999.99),A1*0.08,IF(AND(A1>=10000,
A1<=19999.99), A1*0.105,IF(AND(A1>=20000,
A1<=39999.99),A1*0.12,IF(A1>=40000,A1*0.14,0))))
```

This approach isn't the best for a couple of reasons. First, the formula is overly complex and difficult to understand. Second, the values are hard-coded into the formula, making the formula difficult to modify if the commission structure changes.

A better solution is to use a lookup table function to compute the commissions; for example

```
=VLOOKUP(A1,Table,2)*A1
```

Using the VLOOKUP function requires that you have a table of commission rates set up in your worksheet.

Another option is to create a custom function, such as the following:

```
Function Commission(Sales)
'    Calculates sales commissions
     Tier1 = 0.08
     Tier2 = 0.105
     Tier3 = 0.12
     Tier4 = 0.14
     Select Case Sales
          Case 0 To 9999.99
             Commission = Sales * Tier1
          Case 1000 To 19999.99
             Commission = Sales * Tier2
          Case 20000 To 39999.99
             Commission = Sales * Tier3
          Case Is >= 40000
             Commission = Sales * Tier4
     End Select
End Function
```

After you define the Commission function in a VBA module, you can use it in a worksheet formula. Entering the following formula into a cell produces a result of 3,000. (The amount, 25,000, qualifies for a commission rate of 12 percent.)

```
=Commission(25000)
```

If the sales amount is in cell D23, the function's argument would be a cell reference, like this:

```
=Commission(D23)
```

A function with two arguments

This example builds on the previous one. Imagine that the sales manager implements a new policy: The total commission paid is increased by 1 percent for every year that the salesperson has been with the company. For this example, the custom Commission function (defined in the preceding section) has been modified so that it takes two arguments, both of which are required arguments. Call this new function Commission2:

```
Function Commission2(Sales, Years)
'     Calculates sales commissions based on years in service
      Tier1 = 0.08
      Tier2 = 0.105
      Tier3 = 0.12
      Tier4 = 0.14
      Select Case Sales
          Case 0 To 9999.99
            Commission2 = Sales * Tier1
          Case 1000 To 19999.99
            Commission2 = Sales * Tier2
          Case 20000 To 39999.99
            Commission2 = Sales * Tier3
          Case Is >= 40000
            Commission2 = Sales * Tier4
      End Select
      Commission2 = Commission2 + (Commission2 * Years / 100)
End Function
```

The modification was quite simple. The second argument (`Years`) was added to the `Function` statement, and an additional computation was included that adjusts the commission before exiting the function.

The following is an example of how you write a formula by using this function. It assumes that the sales amount is in cell A1, and that the number of years that the salesperson has worked is in cell B1.

```
=Commission2(A1,B1)
```

A function with a range argument

The example in this section demonstrates how to use a worksheet range as an argument. Actually, it's not at all tricky; Excel takes care of the details behind the scenes.

Assume that you want to calculate the average of the five largest values in a range named `Data`. Excel doesn't have a function that can do this calculation, so you can write the following formula:

```
=(LARGE(Data,1)+LARGE(Data,2)+LARGE(Data,3)+
LARGE(Data,4)+LARGE(Data,5))/5
```

This formula uses Excel's LARGE function, which returns the *n*th largest value in a range. The preceding formula adds the five largest values in the range named `Data` and then divides the result by 5. The formula works fine, but it's rather unwieldy. And, what if you need to compute the average of the top *six* values? You'd need to rewrite the formula and make sure that all copies of the formula also get updated.

Wouldn't it be easier if Excel had a function named `TopAvg`? For example, you could use the following (nonexistent) function to compute the average:

```
=TopAvg (Data,5)
```

This situation is an example of when a custom function can make things much easier for you. The following is a custom VBA function, named `TopAvg`, which returns the average of the top *n* values in a range:

```
Function TopAvg(Data, Num)
' Returns the average of the highest Num values in Data
  Sum = 0
  For i = 1 To Num
    Sum = Sum + WorksheetFunction.Large(Data, i)
  Next i
  TopAvg = Sum / Num
End Function
```

This function takes two arguments: `Data` (which represents a range in a worksheet) and `Num` (the number of values to average). The code starts by initializing the `Sum` variable to 0. It then uses a `For-Next` loop to calculate the sum of the *n*th largest values in the range. (Note that Excel's `LARGE` function is used within the loop.) You can use an Excel worksheet function in VBA if you precede the function with `WorksheetFunction` and a dot. Finally, `TopAvg` is assigned the value of `Sum` divided by `Num`.

You can use all Excel worksheet functions in your VBA procedures *except* those that have equivalents in VBA. For example, VBA has a `Rnd` function that returns a random number. Therefore, you can't use Excel's `RAND` function in a VBA procedure.

Debugging Custom Functions

Debugging a `Function` procedure can be a bit more challenging than debugging a `Sub` procedure. If you develop a function to use in worksheet formulas, an error in the `Function` procedure simply results in an error display in the formula cell (usually `#VALUE!`). In other words, you don't receive the normal run-time error message that helps you to locate the offending statement.

When you're debugging a worksheet formula, using only one instance of the function in your worksheet is the best technique. The following are three methods that you may want to use in your debugging:

- **Place `MsgBox` functions at strategic locations to monitor the value of specific variables.** Fortunately, message boxes in function procedures pop up when the procedure is executed. But make sure that you have only one formula in the worksheet that uses your function; otherwise, the message boxes appear for each formula that's evaluated.

- **Test the procedure by calling it from a** `Sub` **procedure.** Run-time errors display normally, and you can either fix the problem (if you know what it is) or jump right into the debugger.

- **Set a breakpoint in the function and then use the Excel debugger to step through the function.** Press F9, and the statement at the cursor becomes a breakpoint. The code will stop executing, and you can step through the code line by line (by pressing F8). Consult the Help system for more information about using VBA debugging tools.

Inserting Custom Functions

The Excel Insert Function dialog box is a handy tool from which you can choose a worksheet function; you even can choose one of your custom worksheet functions. After you select a function, the Function Arguments dialog box prompts you for the function's arguments.

Note
Function procedures that are defined with the `Private` keyword do not appear in the Insert Function dialog box. So, if you create a function that will be used only by other VBA procedures, you should declare the function by using the `Private` keyword. ∎

You also can display a description of your custom function in the Insert Function dialog box. To do so, follow these steps:

1. **Create the function in a module by using the VB Editor.**
2. **Activate Excel.**
3. **Choose Developer ➪ Code ➪ Macros.** Excel displays its Macro dialog box.
4. **In the Macro dialog box, type the name of the function (in the Macro Name field).** Notice that functions don't typically appear in this dialog box, so you must enter the function name yourself.
5. **Click the Options button.** Excel displays its Macro Options dialog box. (See Figure 40.3.)
6. **Enter a description of the function and then click OK.** The Shortcut key field is irrelevant for functions.

The description that you enter appears in the Insert Function dialog box.

FIGURE 40.3

Entering a description for a custom function. This description appears in the Insert Function dialog box.

Another way to provide a description for a custom function is to execute a VBA statement that uses the `MacroOptions` method. The `MacroOptions` method also lets you assign your function to a specific category, and even provide a description of the arguments. The argument descriptions display in the Function Arguments dialog box, which appears after you select the function in the Insert Function dialog box.

New Feature

The ability to provide a description of function arguments is new to Excel 2010. ■

Figure 40.4 shows the Function Arguments dialog box, which prompts the user to enter arguments for a custom function (`TopAvg`). This function appears in function category 3 (Math & Trig). I added the description, category, and argument descriptions by executing this `Sub` procedure:

```
Sub CreateArgDescriptions()
    Application.MacroOptions Macro:="TopAvg", _
        Description:="Calculates the average of the top n values in a range", _
        Category:=3, _
        ArgumentDescriptions:=Array("The range that contains the data", _
    "The value of n")
End Sub
```

The category numbers are listed in the VBA Help system. You execute this procedure only one time. After executing it, the description, category, and argument descriptions are stored in the file.

FIGURE 40.4

Using the Function Arguments dialog box to insert a custom function.

Learning More

The information in this chapter only scratches the surface when it comes to creating custom functions. It should be enough to get you started, however, if you're interested in this topic. See Chapter 44 for more examples of useful VBA functions. You may be able to use the examples directly or adapt them for your needs.

Creating UserForms

You can't use Excel very long without being exposed to dialog boxes. Excel, like most Windows programs, uses dialog boxes to obtain information, clarify commands, and display messages. If you develop VBA macros, you can create your own dialog boxes that work very much like those that are built in to Excel. These dialog boxes are known as UserForms.

IN THIS CHAPTER

Why create UserForms

UserForm alternatives

Creating UserForms: An overview

UserForm examples

More on creating UserForms

Why Create UserForms?

Some macros that you create behave exactly the same every time that you execute them. For example, you may develop a macro that enters a list of your sales regions into a worksheet range. This macro always produces the same result and requires no additional user input. You may develop other macros, however, that perform differently under different circumstances or that offer options for the user. In such cases, the macro may benefit from a custom dialog box.

The following is an example of a simple macro that makes each cell in the selected range uppercase (but it skips cells that have a formula). The procedure uses VBA's built-in `StrConv` function.

```
Sub ChangeCase()
  For Each cell In Selection
    If Not cell.HasFormula Then
      cell.Value = StrConv(cell.Value, vbUpperCase)
    End If
  Next cell
End Sub
```

This macro is useful, but it can be improved. For example, the macro would be more helpful if it could also change the cells to lowercase or *proper case* (only the first letter of each word is upper-case). This modification is not difficult to make, but if you make this change to the macro, you need some method of asking the user what type of change to make to the cells. The solution is to present a dialog box like the one shown in Figure 41.1. This dialog box is a UserForm that was created by using the Visual Basic (VB) Editor, and it is displayed by a VBA macro.

FIGURE 41.1

A UserForm that asks the user to select an option.

Another solution is to develop three macros, one for each type of text case change. Combining these three operations into a single macro and using a UserForm is a more efficient approach, how-ever. I discuss this example, including how to create the UserForm, in "Another UserForm Example," later in the chapter.

UserForm Alternatives

After you get the hang of it, developing UserForms isn't difficult. But sometimes using the tools that are built into VBA is easier. For example, VBA includes two functions (InputBox and MsgBox) that enable you to display simple dialog boxes without having to create a UserForm in the VB Editor. You can customize these dialog boxes in some ways, but they certainly don't offer the number of options that are available in a UserForm.

The InputBox function

The InputBox function is useful for obtaining a single input from the user. A simplified version of the function's syntax follows:

```
InputBox(prompt[,title][,default])
```

The elements are defined as follows:

- prompt: (Required) Text that is displayed in the input box
- title: (Optional) Text that appears in the input box's title bar
- default: (Optional) The default value

The following is an example of how you can use the `InputBox` function:

```
CName = InputBox("Customer name?","Customer Data")
```

When this VBA statement is executed, Excel displays the dialog box shown in Figure 41.2. Notice that this example uses only the first two arguments for the `InputBox` function and does not supply a default value. When the user enters a value and clicks OK, the value is assigned to the variable `CName`. Your VBA code can then use that variable.

FIGURE 41.2

This dialog box is displayed by the VBA `InputBox` function.

The MsgBox function

The VBA `MsgBox` function is a handy way to display information and to solicit simple input from users. I use the VBA `MsgBox` function in many of this book's examples to display a variable's value. A simplified version of the `MsgBox` syntax is as follows:

```
MsgBox(prompt[,buttons][,title])
```

The elements are defined as follows:

- `prompt`: (Required) Text that is displayed in the message box
- `buttons`: (Optional) The code for the buttons that are to appear in the message box
- `title`: (Optional) Text that appears in the message box's title bar

You can use the `MsgBox` function by itself or assign its result to a variable. If you use it by itself, don't include parentheses around the arguments. The following example displays a message and does not return a result:

```
Sub MsgBoxDemo()
  MsgBox "Click OK to continue"
End Sub
```

Figure 41.3 shows how this message box appears.

A simple message box, displayed with the VBA MsgBox function.

To get a response from a message box, you can assign the result of the MsgBox function to a variable. The following code uses some built-in constants (described in Table 41.1) to make it easier to work with the values that are returned by MsgBox:

```
Sub GetAnswer()
  Ans = MsgBox("Continue?", vbYesNo)
  Select Case Ans
   Case vbYes
' ...[code if Ans is Yes]...
   Case vbNo
' ...[code if Ans is No]...
   End Select
End Sub
```

When this procedure is executed, the Ans variable contains a value that corresponds to vbYes or vbNo. The Select Case statement determines the action to take based on the value of Ans.

You can easily customize your message boxes because of the flexibility of the buttons argument. Table 41.1 lists the built-in constants that you can use for the buttons argument. You can specify which buttons to display, whether an icon appears, and which button is the default.

Constants Used in the MsgBox Function

Constant	Value	Description
vbOKOnly	0	Displays OK button.
vbOKCancel	1	Displays OK and Cancel buttons.
vbAbortRetryIgnore	2	Displays Abort, Retry, and Ignore buttons.
vbYesNoCancel	3	Displays Yes, No, and Cancel buttons.
vbYesNo	4	Displays Yes and No buttons.

Constant	Value	Description
vbRetryCancel	5	Displays Retry and Cancel buttons.
vbCritical	16	Displays Critical Message icon.
vbQuestion	32	Displays Query icon (a question mark).
VBExclamation	48	Displays Warning Message icon.
vbInformation	64	Displays Information Message icon.
vbDefaultButton1	0	First button is default.
vbDefaultButton2	256	Second button is default.
vbDefaultButton3	512	Third button is default.

The following example uses a combination of constants to display a message box with a Yes button and a No button (vbYesNo), and a question mark icon (vbQuestion). The second button (the No button) is designated as the default button (vbDefaultButton2), which is the button that is executed if the user presses Enter. For simplicity, these constants are assigned to the Config variable, and Config is then used as the second argument in the MsgBox function.

```
Sub GetAnswer()
   Config = vbYesNo + vbQuestion + vbDefaultButton2
   Ans = MsgBox("Process the monthly report?", Config)
   If Ans = vbYes Then RunReport
   If Ans = vbNo Then Exit Sub
End Sub
```

Figure 41.4 shows how this message box appears when the GetAnswer Sub is executed. If the user clicks the Yes button the routine executes the procedure named RunReport (which is not shown). If the user clicks the No button (or presses Enter), the procedure is ended with no action. Because the title argument was omitted in the MsgBox function, Excel uses the default title (Microsoft Excel).

FIGURE 41.4

The second argument of the MsgBox function determines what appears in the message box.

The Sub procedure that follows is another example of using the MsgBox function:

```
Sub GetAnswer2()
    Msg = "Do you want to process the monthly report?"
    Msg = Msg & vbNewLine & vbNewLine
    Msg = Msg & "Processing the monthly report will take approximately"
    Msg = Msg & "15 minutes. It will generate a 30-page report for all"
    Msg = Msg & "sales offices for the current month."
    Title = "XYZ Marketing Company"
    Config = vbYesNo + vbQuestion
    Ans = MsgBox(Msg, Config, Title)
    If Ans = vbYes Then RunReport
    If Ans = vbNo Then Exit Sub
End Sub
```

This example demonstrates an efficient way to specify a longer message in a message box. A variable (Msg) and the concatenation operator (&) are used to build the message in a series of statements. vbNewLine is a constant that represents a break character. (Using two line breaks inserts a blank line.) The title argument is also used to display a different title in the message box. The Config variable stores the constants that generate Yes and No buttons and a question mark icon. Figure 41.5 shows how this message box appears when the procedure is executed.

FIGURE 41.5

A message box with a longer message and a title.

Creating UserForms: An Overview

The InputBox and MsgBox functions are adequate for many situations, but if you need to obtain more information, you need to create a UserForm.

The following is a list of the general steps that you typically take to create a UserForm:

1. **Determine exactly how the dialog box is going to be used and where it is to fit into your VBA macro.**

2. **Activate the VB Editor and insert a new UserForm.**

3. **Add the appropriate controls to the UserForm.**

4. **Create a VBA macro to display the UserForm.** This macro goes in a normal VBA module.

5. **Create event handler VBA procedures that are executed when the user manipulates the controls (for example, clicks the OK button).** These procedures go in the code module for the UserForm.

The following sections provide more details on creating a UserForm.

Working with UserForms

To create a dialog box, you must first insert a new UserForm in the VB Editor window. To activate the VB Editor, choose Developer ⇨ Visual Basic (or press Alt+F11). Make sure that the correct workbook is selected in the Project window and then choose Insert ⇨ UserForm. The VB Editor displays an empty UserForm, shown in Figure 41.6. When you activate a UserForm, the VB editor displays the Toolbox, which is used to add controls to the UserForm.

An empty UserForm.

Adding controls

The Toolbox, also shown in Figure 41.6, contains various ActiveX controls that you can add to your UserForm.

When you move the mouse pointer over a control in the Toolbox, the control's name appears. To add a control, click and drag it into the form. After adding a control, you can move it or change its size.

Table 41.2 lists the Toolbox controls.

TABLE 41.2

Toolbox Controls

Control	Description
Select Objects	Lets you select other controls by dragging.
Label	Adds a label (a container for text).
TextBox	Adds a text box (allows the user to type text).
ComboBox	Adds a combo box (a drop-down list).
ListBox	Adds a list box (to allow the user to select an item from a list).
CheckBox	Adds a check box (to control Boolean options).
OptionButton	Adds an option button (to allow a user to select from multiple options).
ToggleButton	Adds a toggle button (to control Boolean options).
Frame	Adds a frame (a container for other objects).
CommandButton	Adds a command button (a clickable button).
TabStrip	Adds a tab strip (a container for other objects).
MultiPage	Adds a multipage control (a container for other objects).
ScrollBar	Adds a scroll bar (to specify a value by dragging a bar).
SpinButton	Adds a spin button (to specify a value by clicking up or down).
Image	Adds a control that can contain an image.
RefEdit	Adds a reference edit control (lets the user select a range).

Cross-Reference

You can also place some of these controls directly on your worksheet. See Chapter 42 for details. ■

Changing the properties of a control

Every control that you add to a UserForm has several properties that determine how the control looks and behaves. You can change some of these properties (such as Height and Width) by clicking and dragging the control's border. To change other properties, use the Properties window.

To display the Properties window, choose View ➪ Properties Window (or press F4). The Properties window displays a list of properties for the selected control. (Each control has a different set of properties.) If you click the UserForm itself, the Properties window displays properties for the form. Figure 41.7 shows the Properties window for a CommandButton control.

To change a property, select the property in the Properties window and then enter a new value. Some properties (such as BackColor) enable you to select a property from a list. The top of the Properties window contains a drop-down list that enables you to select a control to work with. You can also click a control to select it and display its properties.

The Properties window for a CommandButton control.

When you set properties via the Properties window, you're setting properties at *design time*. You can also use VBA to change the properties of controls while the UserForm is displayed (that is, at *run time*).

A complete discussion of all the properties is well beyond the scope of this book — and it would indeed be very dull reading. To find out about a particular property, select it in the Properties window and press F1. The Help for UserForm controls is extremely thorough.

Handling events

When you insert a UserForm, that form can also hold VBA Sub procedures to handle the events that are generated by the UserForm. An *event* is something that occurs when the user manipulates a control. For example, clicking a button causes an event. Selecting an item in a list box control also triggers an event. To make a UserForm useful, you must write VBA code to do something when an event occurs.

Event-handler procedures have names that combine the control with the event. The general form is the control's name, followed by an underscore, and then the event name. For example, the procedure that is executed when the user clicks a button named MyButton is MyButton_Click.

Displaying a UserForm

You also need to write a procedure to display the UserForm. You use the Show method of the UserForm object. The following procedure displays the UserForm named UserForm1:

```
Sub ShowDialog()
    UserForm1.Show
End Sub
```

This procedure should be stored in a regular VBA module (not the code module for the UserForm). If your VB project doesn't have a regular VBA module, choose Insert ➪ Module to add one.

When the ShowDialog procedure is executed, the UserForm is displayed. What happens next depends upon the event-handler procedures that you create.

A UserForm Example

The preceding section is, admittedly, rudimentary. This section demonstrates, in detail, how to develop a UserForm. This example is rather simple. The UserForm displays a message to the user — something that can be accomplished more easily by using the MsgBox function. However, a UserForm gives you more flexibility in terms of formatting and layout of the message.

On the CD
This workbook is available on the companion CD-ROM. The file is named show message.xlsm.

Creating the UserForm

If you're following along on your computer, start with a new workbook. Then follow these steps:

1. **Choose Developer ⇨ Visual Basic (or press Alt+F11) to activate the VB Editor window.**

2. **In the VB Editor Project window, double-click your workbook's name to activate it.**

3. **Choose Insert ⇨ UserForm.** The VB Editor adds an empty form named `UserForm1` and displays the Toolbox.

4. **Press F4 to display the Properties window and then change the following properties of the `UserForm` object:**

Property	*Change To*
Name	AboutBox
Caption	About This Workbook

5. **Use the Toolbox to add a `Label` object to the UserForm.**

6. **Select the `Label` object. In the Properties window, enter any text that you want for the label's `Caption`.**

7. **In the Properties window, click the `Font` property and adjust the font.** You can change the typeface, size, and so on. The changes then appear in the form. Figure 41.8 shows an example of a formatted `Label` control. In this example, the `TextAlign` property was set to the code that center aligns the text.

   `2 - fmTextAlignCenter`

FIGURE 41.8

A `Label` control, after changing its `Font` properties.

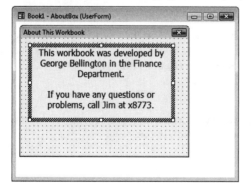

8. Use the Toolbox and add a `CommandButton` object to the UserForm, and use the Properties window to change the following properties for the `CommandButton`:

Property	Change To
Name	OKButton
Caption	OK
Default	True

9. **Make other adjustments so that the form looks good to you.** You can change the size of the form or move or resize the controls.

Testing the UserForm

At this point, the UserForm has all the necessary controls. What's missing is a way to display the UserForm. While you're developing the UserForm, you can press F5 to display it and see how it looks. To close the UserForm, click the X button in the title bar.

This section explains how to write a VBA `Sub` procedure to display the UserForm when Excel is active.

1. **Insert a VBA module by choosing Insert ⇨ Module.**

2. **In the empty module, enter the following code:**

    ```
    Sub ShowAboutBox()
        AboutBox.Show
    End Sub
    ```

3. **Activate Excel.** (Pressing Alt+F11 is one way.)

4. **Choose Developer ⇨ Code ⇨ Macros to display the Macros dialog box.** Or you can press Alt+F8.

5. **In the Macros dialog box, select ShowAboutBox from the list of macros and then click Run.** The UserForm then appears.

If you click the OK button, notice that it doesn't close the UserForm as you may expect. This button needs to have an event-handler procedure in order for it to do anything when it's clicked. To dismiss the UserForm, click the Close button (X) in its title bar.

Cross-Reference

You may prefer to display the UserForm by clicking a `CommandButton` on your worksheet. See Chapter 42 for details on attaching a macro to a worksheet `CommandButton`.

Creating an event-handler procedure

An *event-handler procedure* is executed when an event occurs. In this case, you need a procedure to handle the `Click` event that's generated when the user clicks the OK button.

1. **Activate the VB Editor.** (Pressing Alt+F11 is the fastest way.)

2. **Activate the `AboutBox` UserForm by double-clicking its name in the Project window.**

3. **Double-click the `CommandButton` control.** The VB Editor activates the code module for the UserForm and inserts some boilerplate code, as shown in Figure 41.9.

FIGURE 41.9

The code module for the UserForm.

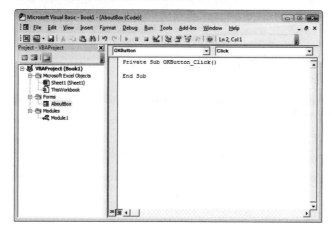

4. **Insert the following statement before the `End Sub` statement:**

```
Unload AboutBox
```

This statement simply dismisses the UserForm by using the `Unload` statement. The complete event-handler procedure is

```
Private Sub OKButton_Click()
    Unload AboutBox
End Sub
```

Another UserForm Example

The example in this section is an enhanced version of the ChangeCase procedure presented at the beginning of the chapter. Recall that the original version of this macro changes the text in the selected cells to uppercase characters. This modified version asks the user what type of case change to make: uppercase, lowercase, or proper case (initial capitals).

On the CD

This workbook is available on the companion CD-ROM. The file is change case.xlsm.

Creating the UserForm

This UserForm needs one piece of information from the user: the type of change to make to the text. Because only one option can be selected, OptionButton controls are appropriate. Start with an empty workbook and follow these steps to create the UserForm:

1. **Press Alt+F11 to activate the VB Editor window.**

2. **In the VB Editor, choose Insert ➪ UserForm.** The VB Editor adds an empty form named UserForm1 and displays the Toolbox.

3. **Press F4 to display the Properties window and then change the following property of the UserForm object:**

Property	Change To
Caption	Case Changer

4. **Add a CommandButton object to the UserForm and then change the following properties for the CommandButton:**

Property	Change To
Name	OKButton
Caption	OK
Default	True

5. **Add another CommandButton object and then change the following properties:**

Property	Change To
Name	CancelButton
Caption	Cancel
Cancel	True

6. **Add an** `OptionButton` **control and then change the following properties.** (This option is the default, so its `Value` property should be set to `True`.)

Property	Change To
Name	OptionUpper
Caption	Upper Case
Value	True

7. **Add a second** `OptionButton` **control and then change the following properties:**

Property	Change To
Name	OptionLower
Caption	Lower Case

8. **Add a third** `OptionButton` **control and then change the following properties:**

Property	Change To
Name	OptionProper
Caption	Proper Case

9. **Adjust the size and position of the controls and the form until your UserForm resembles the UserForm shown in Figure 41.10.** Make sure that the controls do not overlap.

FIGURE 41.10

The UserForm after adding controls and adjusting some properties.

Tip

The VB Editor provides several useful commands to help you size and align the controls. For example, you can make a group of selected controls the same size, or move them so they are all aligned to the left. Select the controls that you want to work with and then choose a command from the Format menu. These commands are fairly self-explanatory, and the Help system has complete details. ■

Testing the UserForm

At this point, the UserForm has all the necessary controls. What's missing is a way to display the form. This section explains how to write a VBA procedure to display the UserForm.

1. **Make sure that the VB Editor window is activated.**

2. **Insert a module by choosing Insert ⇨ Module.**

3. **In the empty module, enter the following code:**

   ```
   Sub ShowUserForm()
       UserForm1.Show
   End Sub
   ```

4. **Choose Run ⇨ Sub/UserForm (or press F5).**

The Excel window is then activated, and the new UserForm is displayed, as shown in Figure 41.11. The OptionButton controls work, but clicking the OK and Cancel buttons has no effect. These two buttons need to have event-handler procedures. Click the Close button in the title bar to dismiss the UserForm.

FIGURE 41.11

Displaying the UserForm.

Creating event-handler procedures

This section explains how to create two event-handler procedures: one to handle the `Click` event for the `CancelButton` CommandButton and the other to handle the `Click` event for the `OKButton` CommandButton. Event handlers for the OptionButton controls are not necessary. The VBA code can determine which of the three OptionButton controls is selected.

Event-handler procedures are stored in the UserForm code module. To create the procedure to handle the `Click` event for the CancelButton, follow these steps:

1. **Activate the UserForm1 form by double-clicking its name in the Project window.**
2. **Double-click the `CancelButton` control.** The VB Editor activates the code module for the UserForm and inserts an empty procedure.
3. **Insert the following statement before the `End Sub` statement:**

   ```
   Unload UserForm1
   ```

That's all there is to it. The following is a listing of the entire procedure that's attached to the `Click` event for the CancelButton:

```
Private Sub CancelButton_Click()
    Unload UserForm1
End Sub
```

This procedure is executed when the CancelButton is clicked. It consists of a single statement that unloads the UserForm1 form.

The next step is to add the code to handle the `Click` event for the `OKButton` control. Follow these steps:

1. **Select OKButton from the drop-down list at the top of the module.** The VB Editor begins a new procedure called `OKButton_Click`.
2. **Enter the following code.** The first and last statements have already been entered for you by the VB Editor.

   ```
   Private Sub OKButton_Click()
       Application.ScreenUpdating = False
   '   Exit if a range is not selected
       If TypeName(Selection) <> "Range" Then Exit Sub
   '       Upper case
       If OptionUpper Then
           For Each cell In Selection
           If Not cell.HasFormula Then
               cell.Value = StrConv(cell.Value, vbUpperCase)
   ```

```
                End If
            Next cell
        End If
'       Lower case
        If OptionLower Then
            For Each cell In Selection
            If Not cell.HasFormula Then
                cell.Value = StrConv(cell.Value, vbLowerCase)
            End If
            Next cell
        End If
'       Proper case
        If OptionProper Then
            For Each cell In Selection
            If Not cell.HasFormula Then
                cell.Value = StrConv(cell.Value, vbProperCase)
            End If
            Next cell
        End If
        Unload UserForm1
    End Sub
```

The macro starts by turning off screen updating, which makes the macro run a bit faster. Next, the code checks the type of the selection. If a range is not selected, the procedure ends. The remainder of the procedure consists of three separate blocks. Only one block is executed, determined by which OptionButton is selected. The selected OptionButton has a value of True. Finally, the UserForm is unloaded (dismissed).

Testing the UserForm

To try out the UserForm from Excel, follow these steps:

1. Activate Excel.

2. Enter some text into some cells.

3. Select the range with the text.

4. Choose Developer ⇨ Code ⇨ Macros (or press Alt+F8).

5. In the Macros dialog box, select ShowUserForm from the list of macros and then click OK. The UserForm appears.

6. Make your choice and click OK.

Try it with a few more selections. Notice that if you click Cancel, the UserForm is dismissed, and no changes are made.

Making the macro available from a worksheet button

At this point, everything should be working properly. However, you have no quick and easy way to execute the macro. A good way to execute this macro would be from a button on the worksheet. You can use the following steps:

1. **Choose Developer ⇨ Controls ⇨ Insert and click the** `Button` **control in the Form Controls group.**

2. **Click and drag in the worksheet to create the button.**

3. **Excel displays the Assign Macro dialog box.**

4. **In the Assign Macro dialog box, select ShowUserForm and then click OK.**

5. **(Optional) At this point, the button is still selected, so you can change the text to make it more descriptive.** You can also right-click the button at any time to change the text.

After performing the preceding steps, clicking the button executes the macro and displays the UserForm.

Cross-Reference
The button in this example is from the Form Controls group. Excel also provides a button in the ActiveX Controls group. See Chapter 42 for more information about the ActiveX Controls group. ∎

Making the macro available on your Quick Access toolbar

If you would like to use this macro while other workbooks are active, you may want to add a button to your Quick Access toolbar. Use the following steps:

1. **Make sure that the workbook containing the macro is open.**

2. **Right-click anywhere on the Ribbon and choose Customize Quick Access Toolbar from the shortcut menu.** The Excel Options dialog box appears, with the Quick Access Toolbar section selected.

3. **Choose Macros from the Choose Commands From drop-down menu on the left.** You'll see your macro listed.

4. **Select the macro's name and click Add to add the item to the list on the right.**

5. **(Optional) To change the icon, click Modify and choose a new image.** You can also change the Display Name.

6. **Click OK to close the Excel Options dialog box.** The icon appears on your Quick Access toolbar.

More on Creating UserForms

Creating UserForms can make your macros much more versatile. You can create custom commands that display dialog boxes that look exactly like those that Excel uses. This section contains some additional information to help you develop custom dialog boxes that work like those that are built in to Excel.

Adding accelerator keys

Custom dialog boxes should not discriminate against those who prefer to use the keyboard rather than a mouse. All Excel dialog boxes work equally well with a mouse and a keyboard because each control has an associated accelerator key. The user can press Alt plus the accelerator key to work with a specific dialog box control.

Adding accelerator keys to your UserForms is a good idea. You do this in the Properties window by entering a character for the `Accelerator` property.

The letter that you enter as the accelerator key must be a letter that is contained in the caption of the object. However, it can be *any* letter in the text — not necessarily the first letter). You should make sure that an accelerator key is not duplicated in a UserForm. If you have duplicate accelerator keys, the accelerator key acts on the first control in the tab order of the UserForm. Then, pressing the accelerator key again takes you to the next control.

Some controls (such as edit boxes) don't have a caption property. You can assign an accelerator key to a label that describes the control. Pressing the accelerator key then activates the next control in the tab order (which you should ensure is the edit box).

Controlling tab order

The previous section refers to a UserForm's *tab order*. When you're working with a UserForm, pressing Tab and Shift+Tab cycles through the dialog box's controls. When you create a UserForm, you should make sure that the tab order is correct. Usually, it means that tabbing should move through the controls in a logical sequence.

To view or change the tab order in a UserForm, choose View ⇨ Tab Order to display the Tab Order dialog box. You can then select a control from the list; use the Move Up and Move Down buttons to change the tab order for the selected control.

Learning More

Mastering UserForms takes practice. You should closely examine the dialog boxes that Excel uses to get a feeling for how dialog boxes are designed. You can duplicate many of the dialog boxes that Excel uses.

The best way to learn more about creating dialog boxes is by using the VBA Help system. Pressing F1 is the quickest way to display the Help window.

Using UserForm Controls in a Worksheet

IN THIS CHAPTER

Why use controls on a worksheet?

Using controls

The Controls Toolbox controls

Chapter 41 presents an introduction to UserForms. If you like the idea of using dialog box controls — but don't like the idea of creating a custom dialog box — this chapter is for you. It explains how to enhance your worksheet with a variety of interactive controls, such as buttons, list boxes, and option buttons.

Why Use Controls on a Worksheet?

The main reason to use controls on a worksheet is to make it easier for the user to provide input. For example, if you create a model that uses one or more input cells, you can create controls to allow the user to select values for the input cells.

Adding controls to a worksheet requires much less effort than creating a dialog box. In addition, you may not have to create any macros because you can link a control to a worksheet cell. For example, if you insert a CheckBox control on a worksheet, you can link it to a particular cell. When the CheckBox is checked, the linked cell displays TRUE. When the CheckBox is not checked, the linked cell displays FALSE.

Figure 42.1 shows an example that uses three types of controls: a Checkbox, two sets of OptionButtons, and a ScrollBar.

On the CD

This workbook is available on the companion CD-ROM. The file is named `mortgage loan.xlsm`.

FIGURE 42.1

This worksheet uses UserForm controls.

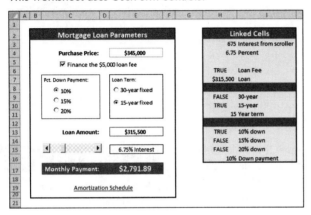

Adding controls to a worksheet can be a bit confusing because Excel offers two different sets of controls, both of which you access by choosing Developer ⇨ Controls ⇨ Insert.

- **Form controls:** These controls are unique to Excel.
- **ActiveX controls:** These controls are a subset of those that are available for use on UserForms.

Figure 42.2 shows the controls that appear when you choose Developer ⇨ Controls ⇨ Insert. When you move your mouse pointer over a control, Excel displays a ToolTip that identifies the controls.

To add to the confusion, many controls are available from both sources. For example, a control named ListBox is listed in both Forms controls and ActiveX controls. However, they are two entirely different controls. In general, Forms controls are easier to use, but ActiveX controls provide more flexibility.

Note

This chapter focuses exclusively on ActiveX controls. ■

A description of ActiveX controls appears in Table 42.1.

FIGURE 42.2

Excel's two sets of worksheet controls.

TABLE 42.1

ActiveX Controls

Button	What It Does
CommandButton	Inserts a CommandButton control (a clickable button)
ComboBox	Inserts a ComboBox control (a drop-down list)
CheckBox	Inserts a CheckBox control (to control Boolean options)
ListBox	Inserts a ListBox control (to allow the user to select an item from a list)
TextBox	Inserts a TextBox control (allows the user to type text)
ScrollBar	Inserts a ScrollBar control (to specify a value by dragging a bar)
SpinButton	Inserts a SpinButton control (to specify a value by clicking up or down)
OptionButton	Inserts an OptionButton control (to allow a user to select from multiple options)
Label	Inserts a Label control (a container for text)
Image	Inserts an Image control (to hold an image)
ToggleButton	Inserts a ToggleButton control (to control Boolean options)
More Controls	Displays a list of other ActiveX controls that are installed on your system. Not all these controls work with Excel.

Using Controls

Adding ActiveX controls in a worksheet is easy, but you need to learn a few basic facts about how to use them.

Adding a control

To add a control to a worksheet, choose Developer ⇨ Controls ⇨ Insert. From the Insert drop-down icon list, click the control that you want to use and then drag in the worksheet to create the control. You don't need to be too concerned about the exact size or position because you can modify those properties at any time.

Warning

Make sure that you select a control from the ActiveX controls — not from the Forms controls. If you insert a Forms control, the instructions in this chapter will not apply. ∎

About design mode

When you add a control to a worksheet, Excel goes into *design mode*. In this mode, you can adjust the properties of any controls on your worksheet, add or edit macros for the control, or change the control's size or position.

Note

When Excel is in design mode, the Design Mode icon in the Developer ⇨ Controls section appears highlighted. You can click this icon to toggle design mode on and off. ∎

When Excel is in design mode, the controls aren't enabled. To test the controls, you must exit design mode by clicking the Design Mode icon. When you're working with controls, you'll probably need to need to switch in and out of design mode frequently.

Adjusting properties

Every control that you add has various properties that determine how it looks and behaves. You can adjust these properties only when Excel is in design mode. When you add a control to a worksheet, Excel enters design mode automatically. If you need to change a control after you exit design mode, click the Design Mode icon in the Controls section of the Developer tab.

To change the properties for a control

1. Make sure that Excel is in design mode.
2. Click the control to select it.
3. If the Properties window isn't visible, click the Properties icon in the Controls section of the Developer tab. The Properties window appears, as shown in Figure 42.3.
4. Select the property and make the change.

The manner in which you change a property depends upon the property. Some properties display a drop-down list from which you can select from a list of options. Others (such as Font) provide a button that when clicked, displays a dialog box. Other properties require you to type the property value. When you change a property, the change takes effect immediately.

Tip

To find out about a particular property, select the property in the Properties window and press F1. ■

The Properties window has two tabs. The Alphabetic tab displays the properties in alphabetical order. The Categorized tab displays the properties by category. Both tabs show the same properties; only the order is different.

FIGURE 42.3

Use the Properties window to adjust the properties of a control — in this case, a CommandButton control.

Common properties

Each control has its own unique set of properties. However, many controls share properties. This section describes some properties that are common to all or many controls, as set forth in Table 42.2.

Note

Some ActiveX control properties are required (for example, the Name property). In other words, you can't leave the property empty. If a required property is missing, Excel will always tell you by displaying an error message. ■

TABLE 42.2

Properties Shared by Multiple Controls

Property	Description
AutoSize	If `True`, the control resizes itself automatically, based on the text in its caption.
BackColor	The background color of the control.
BackStyle	The style of the background (either transparent or opaque).
Caption	The text that appears on the control.
LinkedCell	A worksheet cell that contains the current value of a control.
ListFillRange	A worksheet range that contains items displayed in a `ListBox` or `ComboBox` control.
Value	The control's value.
Left and Top	Values that determine the control's position.
Width and Height	Values that determine the control's width and height.
Visible	If `False`, the control is hidden.
Name	The name of the control. By default, a control's name is based on the control type. You can change the name to any valid name. However, each control's name must be unique on the worksheet.
Picture	Enables you to specify a graphic image to display.

Linking controls to cells

Often, you can use ActiveX controls in a worksheet without using any macros. Many controls have a `LinkedCell` property, which specifies a worksheet cell that is "linked" to the control.

For example, you may add a `SpinButton` control and specify cell B1 as its `LinkedCell` property. After doing so, cell B1 contains the value of the `SpinButton`, and clicking the `SpinButton` changes the value in cell B1. You can, of course, use the value contained in the linked cell in your formulas.

Note

When specifying the `LinkedCell` property in the Properties window, you can't "point" to the linked cell in the worksheet. You must type the cell address or its name (if it has one). ∎

Creating macros for controls

To create a macro for a control, you must use the Visual Basic Editor (VB Editor). The macros are stored in the code module for the sheet that contains the control. For example, if you place an

ActiveX control on Sheet2, the VBA code for that control is stored in the Sheet2 code module. Each control can have a macro to handle any of its events. For example, a CommandButton control can have a macro for its Click event, its DblClick event, and various other events.

Tip
The easiest way to access the code module for a control is to double-click the control while in design mode. Excel displays the VB Editor and creates an empty procedure for the control's default event. For example, the default event for a CheckBox control is the Click event. Figure 42.4 shows the autogenerated code for a control named CheckBox1, located on Sheet1. ∎

FIGURE 42.4

Double-clicking a control in design mode activates the VB Editor and enters an empty event-handler procedure.

The control's name appears in the upper-left portion of the code window, and the event appears in the upper-right area. If you want to create a macro that executes when a different event occurs, select the event from the list in the upper-right area.

The following steps demonstrate how to insert a CommandButton and create a simple macro that displays a message when the button is clicked:

1. **Choose Developer ⇨ Controls ⇨ Insert.**
2. **Click the CommandButton tool in the ActiveX Controls section.**
3. **Click and drag in the worksheet to create the button.** Excel automatically enters design mode.

4. Double-click the button.

The VB Editor window is activated, and an empty Sub procedure is created.

5. Enter the following VBA statement before the End Sub statement:

MsgBox "Hello. You clicked the command button."

6. Press Alt+F11 to return to Excel.

7. (Optional) Adjust any other properties for the CommandButton, using the Properties window. Choose Developer ➪ Controls ➪ Properties if the Properties window isn't visible.

8. Click the Design Mode button in the Developer ➪ Controls section to exit design mode.

After performing the preceding steps, click the CommandButton to display the message box.

Note

You must enter the VBA code manually. You can't create macros for controls using the VBA macro recorder. However, you can record a macro and then execute it from an event procedure. For example, if you record a macro named FormatCells, insert Call FormatCells as a VBA statement. Or, you can copy the recorded code and paste it to your event procedure. ■

Reviewing the Available ActiveX Controls

The sections that follow describe the ActiveX controls that are available for use in your worksheets.

On the CD

The companion CD-ROM contains a file that includes examples of all the ActiveX controls. This file is named worksheet controls.xlsm.

CheckBox

A CheckBox control is useful for getting a binary choice: YES or NO, TRUE or FALSE, ON or OFF, and so on.

The following is a description of the most useful properties of a CheckBox control:

- Accelerator: A letter that enables the user to change the value of the control by using the keyboard. For example, if the accelerator is A, pressing Alt+A changes the value of the CheckBox control. The accelerator letter is underlined in the Caption of the control.

- LinkedCell: The worksheet cell that's linked to the CheckBox. The cell displays TRUE if the control is checked or FALSE if the control is not checked.

ComboBox

A ComboBox control is similar to a ListBox control. A ComboBox, however, is a drop-down box, and it displays only one item at a time. Another difference is that the user may be allowed to enter a value that does not appear in the list of items.

Figure 42.5 shows a ComboBox control that uses the range D1:D12 for the ListFillRange and cell A1 for the LinkedCell.

A ComboBox control.

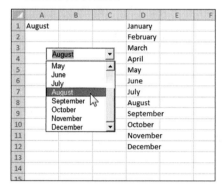

The following is a description of the most useful properties of a ComboBox control:

- BoundColumn: If the ListFillRange contains multiple columns, this property determines which column contains the returned value.
- ColumnCount: The number of columns in the list.
- LinkedCell: The worksheet cell that displays the selected item.
- ListFillRange: The worksheet range that contains the list items.
- ListRows: The number of items to display when the list drops down.
- ListStyle: Determines the appearance of the list items.
- Style: Determines whether the control acts like a drop-down list or a ComboBox. A drop-down list doesn't allow the user to enter a new value.

Cross-Reference

You can also create a drop-down list directly in a cell, by using data validation. See Chapter 25 for details. ■

CommandButton

A CommandButton control is used to execute a macro. When a CommandButton is clicked, it executes a macro with a name that is made up of the CommandButton name, an underscore, and the word *Click*. For example, if a CommandButton is named MyButton, clicking it executes the macro named MyButton_Click. This macro is stored in the code module for the sheet that contains the CommandButton.

Image

An Image control is used to display an image.

These are the most useful properties of an Image control:

- AutoSize: If TRUE, the Image control is resized automatically to fit the image.
- Picture: The path to the image file. Click the button in the Properties window, and Excel displays a dialog box so you can locate the image. Or, copy the image to the Clipboard, select the Picture property in the Properties window, and press Ctrl+V.

Tip

You can also insert an image on a worksheet by choosing Insert ➪ Illustrations ➪ Picture. In fact, using an Image control offers no real advantage. ■

Label

A Label control simply displays text. This control isn't a very useful for use on worksheets, and a TextBox control (described later in this list) gives you more versatility.

ListBox

A ListBox control presents a list of items, and the user can select an item (or multiple items). It's similar to a ComboBox. The main difference is that a ListBox displays more than one item at a time.

The following is a description of the most useful properties of a ListBox control:

- BoundColumn: If the list contains multiple columns, this property determines which column contains the returned value.
- ColumnCount: The number of columns in the list.

- `IntegralHeight`: This is TRUE if the height of the ListBox adjusts automatically to display full lines of text when the list is scrolled vertically. If FALSE, the ListBox may display partial lines of text when it is scrolled vertically.

- `LinkedCell`: The worksheet cell that displays the selected item.

- `ListFillRange`: The worksheet range that contains the list items.

- `ListStyle`: Determines the appearance of the list items.

- `MultiSelect`: Determines whether the user can select multiple items from the list.

Note

If you use a `MultiSelect` **ListBox, you can't specify a** `LinkedCell`**; you need to write a macro to determine which items are selected. ■**

OptionButton

`OptionButton` controls are useful when the user needs to select from a small number of items. OptionButtons are always used in groups of at least two.

The following is a description of the most useful properties of an `OptionButton` control:

- `Accelerator`: A letter that lets the user select the option by using the keyboard. For example, if the accelerator for an OptionButton is C, pressing Alt+C selects the control.

- `GroupName`: A name that identifies an OptionButton as being associated with other OptionButtons with the same `GroupName` property.

- `LinkedCell`: The worksheet cell that's linked to the OptionButton. The cell displays TRUE if the control is selected or FALSE if the control isn't selected.

Note

If your worksheet contains more than one set of `OptionButton` **controls, you must ensure that each set of OptionButtons has a different** `GroupName` **property. Otherwise, all OptionButtons become part of the same set. ■**

ScrollBar

A `ScrollBar` control is useful for specifying a cell value. Figure 42.6 shows a worksheet with three `ScrollBar` controls. These ScrollBars are used to change the color in the rectangle shape. The value of the ScrollBars determines the red, green, or blue component of the rectangle's color. This example uses a few simple macros to change the colors.

FIGURE 42.6

This worksheet has three `ScrollBar` controls.

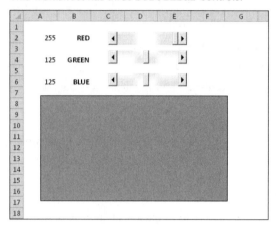

The following is a description of the most useful properties of a `ScrollBar` control:

- `Value`: The current value of the control
- `Min`: The minimum value for the control
- `Max`: The maximum value for the control
- `LinkedCell`: The worksheet cell that displays the value of the control
- `SmallChange`: The amount that the control's value is changed by a click
- `LargeChange`: The amount that the control's value is changed by clicking either side of the button

The `ScrollBar` control is most useful for selecting a value that extends across a wide range of possible values.

SpinButton

A `SpinButton` control lets the user select a value by clicking the control, which has two arrows (one to increase the value and the other to decrease the value). A SpinButton can display either horizontally or vertically.

The following is a description of the most useful properties of a `SpinButton` control:

- `Value`: The current value of the control.
- `Min`: The minimum value of the control.

- `Max`: The maximum value of the control.

- `LinkedCell`: The worksheet cell that displays the value of the control.

- `SmallChange`: The amount that the control's value is changed by a click. Usually, this property is set to 1, but you can make it any value.

TextBox

On the surface, a `TextBox` control may not seem useful. After all, it simply contains text — you can usually use worksheet cells to get text input. In fact, `TextBox` controls are useful not so much for input control but rather for output control. Because a TextBox can have scroll bars, you can use a TextBox to display a great deal of information in a small area.

Figure 42.7 shows a `TextBox` control that contains Lincoln's *Gettysburg Address*. Notice the vertical scroll bar, displayed using the `ScrollBars` property.

FIGURE 42.7

A `TextBox` control with a vertical scroll bar.

The following is a description of the most useful properties of a `TextBox` control:

- `AutoSize`: Determines whether the control adjusts its size automatically, based on the amount of text.

- `IntegralHeight`: If TRUE, the height of the TextBox adjusts automatically to display full lines of text when the list is scrolled vertically. If FALSE, the ListBox may display partial lines of text when it is scrolled vertically.

- `MaxLength`: The maximum number of characters allowed in the TextBox. If 0, no limit exists on the number of characters.

- `MultiLine`: If `True`, the TextBox can display more than one line of text.
- `TextAlign`: Determines how the text is aligned in the TextBox.
- `WordWrap`: Determines whether the control allows word wrap.
- `ScrollBars`: Determines the type of ScrollBars for the control: horizontal, vertical, both, or none.

ToggleButton

A `ToggleButton` control has two states: on or off. Clicking the button toggles between these two states, and the button changes its appearance. Its value is either `TRUE` (pressed) or `FALSE` (not pressed). You can often use a ToggleButton in place of a `CheckBox` control.

Working with Excel Events

IN THIS CHAPTER

Understanding events

Using workbook-level events

Working with worksheet events

Using non-object events

In the preceding chapters, I presented a few examples of VBA event-handler procedures. These procedures are the keys to making your Excel applications interactive. This chapter provides an introduction to the concept of Excel events and includes many examples that you can adapt to meet your own needs.

Understanding Events

Excel can monitor a wide variety of events and execute your VBA code when a particular event occurs. This chapter covers the following types of events.

- **Workbook events:** These occur for a particular workbook. Examples include Open (the workbook is opened or created), BeforeSave (the workbook is about to be saved), and NewSheet (a new sheet is added). VBA code for workbook events must be stored in the ThisWorkbook code module.

- **Worksheet events:** These occur for a particular worksheet. Examples include Change (a cell on the sheet is changed), SelectionChange (the cell pointer is moved), and Calculate (the worksheet is recalculated). VBA code for worksheet events must be stored in the code module for the worksheet (for example, the module named Sheet1).

- **Events not associated with objects:** The final category consists of two useful application-level events: OnTime and OnKey. These work differently from other events.

Entering Event-Handler VBA Code

Every event-handler procedure must reside in a specific type of code module. Code for workbook-level events is stored in the ThisWorkbook code module. Code for worksheet-level events is stored in the code module for the particular sheet (for example, the code module named Sheet1).

In addition, every event-handler procedure has a predetermined name. You can declare the procedure by typing it, but a much better approach is to let the VB Editor do it for you, by using the two drop-down controls at the top of the window.

Figure 43.1 shows the code module for the ThisWorkbook object. Select this code module by double-clicking it in the Project window. To insert a procedure declaration, select Workbook from the objects list in the upper left of the code window. Then select the event from the procedures list in the upper right. When you do, you get a procedure "shell" that contains the procedure declaration line and an End Sub statement.

FIGURE 43.1

The best way to create an event procedure is to let the VB Editor do it for you.

For example, if you select Workbook from the objects list and Open from the procedures list, the VB Editor inserts the following (empty) procedure:

```
Private Sub Workbook_Open()

End Sub
```

Your event-handler VBA code goes between these two lines.

Some event-handler procedures contain an argument list. For example, you may need to create an event-handler procedure to monitor the `SheetActivate` event for a workbook. (This event is triggered when a user activates a different sheet.) If you use the technique described in the previous section, the VB Editor creates the following procedure:

```
Private Sub Workbook_SheetActivate(ByVal Sh As Object)

End Sub
```

This procedure uses one argument (`Sh`), which represents the activated sheet. In this case, `Sh` is declared as an `Object` data type rather than a `Worksheet` data type because the activated sheet also can be a chart sheet.

Your code can, of course, make use of information passed as an argument. The following example displays the name of the activated sheet by accessing the argument's `Name` property. The argument becomes either a `Worksheet` object or a `Chart` object.

```
Private Sub Workbook_SheetActivate(ByVal Sh As Object)
    MsgBox Sh.Name & " was activated."
End Sub
```

Several event-handler procedures use a `Boolean` argument named `Cancel`. For example, the declaration for a workbook's `BeforePrint` event is

```
Private Sub Workbook_BeforePrint(Cancel As Boolean)
```

The value of `Cancel` passed to the procedure is `FALSE`. However, your code can set `Cancel` to `TRUE`, which cancels the printing. The following example demonstrates this:

```
Private Sub Workbook_BeforePrint(Cancel As Boolean)
    Msg = "Have you loaded the 5164 label stock? "
    Ans = MsgBox(Msg, vbYesNo, "About to print... ")
    If Ans = vbNo Then Cancel = True
End Sub
```

The `Workbook_BeforePrint` procedure executes before the workbook prints. This procedure displays a message box asking the user to verify that the correct paper is loaded. If the user clicks the No button, `Cancel` is set to `TRUE`, and nothing prints.

Using Workbook-Level Events

Workbook-level events occur for a particular workbook. Table 43.1 lists the most commonly used workbook events, along with a brief description of each. Keep in mind that workbook event-handler procedures must be stored in the code module for the `ThisWorkbook` object.

TABLE 43.1

Workbook Events

Event	Action That Triggers the Event
Activate	The workbook is activated.
AddinInstall	The workbook is installed as an add-in.
AddinUninstall	The workbook is uninstalled as an add-in.
BeforeClose	The workbook is about to be closed.
BeforePrint	The workbook (or anything in it) is about to be printed.
BeforeSave	The workbook is about to be saved.
Deactivate	The workbook is deactivated.
NewSheet	A new sheet is created in the workbook.
Open	The workbook is opened.
SheetActivate	Any sheet in the workbook is activated.
SheetBeforeDoubleClick	Any worksheet in the workbook is double-clicked. This event occurs before the default double-click action.
SheetBeforeRightClick	Any worksheet in the workbook is right-clicked. This event occurs before the default right-click action.
SheetCalculate	Any worksheet in the workbook is calculated (or recalculated).
SheetChange	Any worksheet in the workbook is changed by the user.
SheetDeactivate	Any sheet in the workbook is deactivated.
SheetFollowHyperlink	Any hyperlink in the workbook is clicked.
SheetSelectionChange	The selection on any worksheet in the workbook is changed.
WindowActivate	Any window of the workbook is activated.
WindowDeactivate	Any workbook window is deactivated.
WindowResize	Any workbook window is resized.

The remainder of this section presents examples of using workbook-level events. All the example procedures that follow must be located in the code module for the ThisWorkbook object. If you put them into any other type of code module, they will not work.

Using the Open event

One of the most common monitored events is a workbook's Open event. This event is triggered when the workbook (or add-in) opens and executes the Workbook_Open procedure. A Workbook_Open procedure is very versatile and is often used for the following tasks:

- Displaying welcome messages.

- Opening other workbooks.

- Activating a specific sheet.

- Ensuring that certain conditions are met; for example, a workbook may require that a particular add-in is installed.

Caution

Be aware that there is no guarantee that your `Workbook_Open` **procedure will be executed. For example, the user may choose to disable macros. And if the user holds down the Shift key while opening a workbook, the workbook's** `Workbook_Open` **procedure will not execute.** ■

The following is a simple example of a `Workbook_Open` procedure. It uses the VBA `Weekday` function to determine the day of the week. If it's Friday, a message box appears to remind the user to perform a file backup. If it's not Friday, nothing happens.

```
Private Sub Workbook_Open()
    If Weekday(Now) = 6 Then
        Msg = "Make sure you do your weekly backup!"
        MsgBox Msg, vbInformation
    End If
End Sub
```

What if you would like to activate a particular Ribbon tab automatically when a workbook is opened? Unfortunately, VBA can't do much at all with the Excel Ribbon, and there is no direct way to activate a particular Ribbon tab. The next example uses the `SendKeys` statement to simulate keystrokes. In this case, it sends Alt+H, which is the Excel's "keytip" equivalent of activating the Home tab of the Ribbon. Sending the F6 keystroke removes the keytip letters from the Ribbon.

```
Private Sub Workbook_Open()
    Application.SendKeys ("%h{F6}")
End Sub
```

The following example performs a number of actions when the workbook is opened. It maximizes the Excel window, maximizes the workbook window, activates the sheet named DataEntry, and selects the first empty cell in column A. If a sheet named DataEntry does not exist, the code generates an error.

```
Private Sub Workbook_Open()
    Application.WindowState = xlMaximized
    ActiveWindow.WindowState = xlMaximized
    Worksheets("DataEntry").Activate
    Range("A1").End(xlDown).offset(1,0).Select
End Sub
```

Using the SheetActivate event

The following procedure executes whenever the user activates any sheet in the workbook. The code simply selects cell A1. Including the On Error Resume Next statement causes the procedure to ignore the error that occurs if the activated sheet is a chart sheet.

```
Private Sub Workbook_SheetActivate(ByVal Sh As Object)
    On Error Resume Next
    Range("A1").Select
End Sub
```

An alternative method to handle the case of a chart sheet is to check the sheet type. Use the Sh argument, which is passed to the procedure.

```
Private Sub Workbook_SheetActivate(ByVal Sh As Object)
    If TypeName(Sh) = "Worksheet" Then Range("A1").Select
End Sub
```

Using the NewSheet event

The following procedure executes whenever a new sheet is added to the workbook. The sheet is passed to the procedure as an argument. Because a new sheet can be either a worksheet or a chart sheet, this procedure determines the sheet type. If it's a worksheet, it inserts a date and time stamp in cell A1.

```
Private Sub Workbook_NewSheet(ByVal Sh As Object)
  If TypeName(Sh) = "Worksheet" Then _
    Range("A1") = "Sheet added " & Now()
End Sub
```

Using the BeforeSave event

The BeforeSave event occurs before the workbook is actually saved. As you know, choosing Office ➪ Save sometimes brings up the Save As dialog box — for example, when the file has never been saved or was opened in read-only mode.

When the Workbook_BeforeSave procedure executes, it receives an argument that enables you to identify whether the Save As dialog box will appear. The following example demonstrates this:

```
Private Sub Workbook_BeforeSave _
  (ByVal SaveAsUI As Boolean, Cancel As Boolean)
    If SaveAsUI Then
        MsgBox "Use the new file-naming convention."
    End If
End Sub
```

When the user attempts to save the workbook, the `Workbook_BeforeSave` procedure executes. If the save operation brings up the Save As dialog box, the `SaveAsUI` variable is TRUE. The preceding procedure checks this variable and displays a message only if the Save As dialog box is displayed. In this case, the message is a reminder about how to name the file.

The `BeforeSave` event procedure also has a `Cancel` variable in its argument list. If the procedure sets the `Cancel` argument to TRUE, the file is not saved.

Using the BeforeClose event

The `BeforeClose` event occurs before a workbook is closed. This event often is used in conjunction with a `Workbook_Open` event handler. For example, use the `Workbook_Open` procedure to initialize items in your workbook, and use the `Workbook_BeforeClose` procedure to clean up or restore settings to normal before the workbook closes.

If you attempt to close a workbook that hasn't been saved, Excel displays a prompt that asks whether you want to save the workbook before it closes.

Caution
A problem can arise from this event. By the time the user sees this message, the `BeforeClose` event has already occurred. This means that the `Workbook_BeforeClose` procedure has already executed. ∎

Working with Worksheet Events

The events for a `Worksheet` object are some of the most useful. As you'll see, monitoring these events can make your applications perform feats that otherwise would be impossible.

Table 43.2 lists the more commonly used worksheet events, with a brief description of each. Remember that these event procedures must be entered into the code module for the sheet. These code modules have default names like Sheet1, Sheet2, and so on.

TABLE 43.2

Worksheet Events

Event	Action That Triggers the Event
`Activate`	The worksheet is activated.
`BeforeDoubleClick`	The worksheet is double-clicked.
`BeforeRightClick`	The worksheet is right-clicked.

continued

TABLE 43.2 (continued)	
Event	**Action That Triggers the Event**
Calculate	The worksheet is calculated (or recalculated).
Change	Cells on the worksheet are changed by the user.
Deactivate	The worksheet is deactivated.
FollowHyperlink	A hyperlink on the worksheet is clicked.
PivotTableUpdate	A PivotTable on the worksheet has been updated.
SelectionChange	The selection on the worksheet is changed.

Using the Change event

A Change event is triggered when any cell in the worksheet is changed by the user. A Change event is not triggered when a calculation generates a different value for a formula or when an object (such as a chart or SmartArt) is added to the sheet.

When the Worksheet_Change procedure executes, it receives a Range object as its Target argument. This Range object corresponds to the changed cell or range that triggered the event. The following example displays a message box that shows the address of the Target range:

```
Private Sub Worksheet_Change(ByVal Target As Excel.Range)
    MsgBox "Range " & Target.Address & " was changed."
End Sub
```

To get a feel for the types of actions that generate the Change event for a worksheet, enter the preceding procedure into the code module for a Worksheet object. After entering this procedure, activate Excel and, using various techniques, make changes to the worksheet. Every time the Change event occurs, a message box displays the address of the range that changed.

Unfortunately, the Change event doesn't always work as expected. For example

- Changing the formatting of a cell does not trigger the Change event (as expected), but choosing Home ➪ Editing ➪ Clear ➪ Clear Formats *does.*

- Pressing Delete generates an event even if the cell is empty at the start.

- Cells changed via Excel commands may or may not trigger the Change event. For example, sorting and goal seeking operations do not trigger the Change event. However, operations such as Find and Replace, using the AutoSum button, or adding a Totals row to a table *do* trigger the event.

- If your VBA procedure changes a cell, it *does* trigger the Change event.

Monitoring a specific range for changes

Although the Change event occurs when any cell on the worksheet changes, most of the time, you'll be concerned only with changes that are made to a specific cell or range. When the Worksheet_Change event-handler procedure is called, it receives a Range object as its argument. This Range object corresponds to the cell or cells that changed.

Assume that your worksheet has a range named InputRange, and you want to monitor changes to this range only. No Change event exists for a Range object, but you can perform a quick check within the Worksheet_Change procedure. The following procedure demonstrates this:

```
Private Sub Worksheet_Change(ByVal Target As Excel.Range)
    Dim VRange As Range
    Set VRange = Range("InputRange")
    If Union(Target, VRange).Address = VRange.Address Then
        Msgbox "The changed cell is in the input range."
    End if
End Sub
```

This example creates a Range object variable named VRange, which represents the worksheet range that you want to monitor for changes. The procedure uses the VBA Union function to determine whether VRange contains the Target range (passed to the procedure in its argument). The Union function returns an object that consists of all the cells in both of its arguments. If the range address is the same as the VRange address, Vrange contains Target, and a message box appears. Otherwise, the procedure ends, and nothing happens.

The preceding procedure has a flaw. Target may consist of a single cell or a range. For example, if the user changes more than one cell at a time, Target becomes a multicell range. Therefore, the procedure requires modification to loop through all the cells in Target. The following procedure checks each changed cell and displays a message box if the cell is within the desired range:

```
Private Sub Worksheet_Change(ByVal Target As Excel.Range)
    Set VRange = Range("InputRange")
    For Each cell In Target
      If Union(cell, VRange).Address = VRange.Address Then
          Msgbox "The changed cell is in the input range."
      End if
    Next cell
End Sub
```

On the CD

A workbook with this example is available On the CD-ROM the file is named monitor a range.xlsm.

Using the SelectionChange event

The following procedure demonstrates a `SelectionChange` event. It executes whenever the user makes a new selection on the worksheet:

```
Private Sub Worksheet_SelectionChange(ByVal Target _
    As Excel.Range)
        Cells.Interior.ColorIndex = xlNone
        With ActiveCell
            .EntireRow.Interior.ColorIndex = 35
            .EntireColumn.Interior.ColorIndex = 35
        End With
End Sub
```

This procedure shades the row and column of an active cell, making it easy to identify. The first statement removes the background color of all cells. Next, the entire row and column of the active cell is shaded light yellow. Figure 43.2 shows the shading.

On the CD

A workbook with this example is available On the CD-ROM. The file is named `selection change event.xlsm`**.**

FIGURE 43.2

Moving the cell cursor causes the active cell's row and column to become shaded.

Caution

You won't want to use this procedure if your worksheet contains background shading because the macro will erase it. However, if the shading is the result of a style applied to a table, the macro does not erase the table's background shading. ■

Using the BeforeRightClick event

Normally, when the user right-clicks in a worksheet, a shortcut menu appears. If, for some reason, you want to prevent the shortcut menu from appearing, you can trap the `RightClick` event. The following procedure sets the `Cancel` argument to `TRUE`, which cancels the `RightClick` event — and, thus, the shortcut menu. Instead, a message box appears.

```
Private Sub Worksheet_BeforeRightClick _
  (ByVal Target As Excel.Range, Cancel As Boolean)
    Cancel = True
    MsgBox "The shortcut menu is not available."
End Sub
```

Using Non-Object Events

So far, the events discussed in this chapter are associated with an object (`Application`, `Workbook`, `Sheet`, and so on). This section discusses two additional events: `OnTime` and `OnKey`. These events are not associated with an object. Rather, you access them by using methods of the `Application` object.

Note

Unlike the other events discussed in this chapter, you use a general VBA module to program the `On` events in this section. ■

Using the OnTime event

The `OnTime` event occurs at a specified time. The following example demonstrates how to program Excel to beep and then display a message at 3 p.m.:

```
Sub SetAlarm()
  Application.OnTime 0.625, "DisplayAlarm"
End Sub

Sub DisplayAlarm()
  Beep
  MsgBox "Wake up. It's time for your afternoon break!"
End Sub
```

In this example, the SetAlarm procedure uses the OnTime method of the Application object to set up the OnTime event. This method takes two arguments: the time (0.625, or 3 p.m., in the example) and the procedure to execute when the time occurs (DisplayAlarm in the example). In the example, after SetAlarm executes, the DisplayAlarm procedure is called at 3 p.m., bringing up the message.

Most people find it difficult to think of time in terms of Excel's time numbering system. Therefore, you may want to use the VBA TimeValue function to represent the time. TimeValue converts a string that looks like a time into a value that Excel can handle. The following statement shows an easier way to program an event for 3 p.m.: .

```
Application.OnTime TimeValue("3:00:00 pm"), "DisplayAlarm"
```

If you want to schedule an event that's relative to the current time — for example, 20 minutes from now — you can write an instruction like this:

```
Application.OnTime Now + TimeValue("00:20:00"), "DisplayAlarm"
```

You also can use the OnTime method to schedule a procedure on a particular day. Of course, you must keep your computer turned on, and Excel must be running.

Using the OnKey event

While you work, Excel constantly monitors what you type. As a result, you can set up a keystroke or a key combination that — when pressed — executes a particular procedure.

The following example uses the OnKey method to set up an OnKey event. This event essentially reassigns the PgDn and PgUp keys. After the Setup_OnKey procedure executes, pressing PgDn executes the PgDn_Sub procedure, and pressing PgUp executes the PgUp_Sub procedure. The next effect is that pressing PgDn moves down one row, and pressing PgUp moves up one row.

```
Sub Setup_OnKey()
   Application.OnKey "{PgDn}", "PgDn_Sub"
   Application.OnKey "{PgUp}", "PgUp_Sub"
End Sub

Sub PgDn_Sub()
   On Error Resume Next
   ActiveCell.Offset(1, 0).Activate
End Sub

Sub PgUp_Sub()
   On Error Resume Next
   ActiveCell.Offset(-1, 0).Activate
End Sub
```

Note

The key codes are enclosed in brackets, not parentheses. For a complete list of the keyboard codes, consult VBA Help. Search for OnKey. ■

Tip

The preceding examples used `On Error Resume Next` to ignore any errors generated. For example, if the active cell is in the first row, trying to move up one row causes an error. Furthermore, if the active sheet is a chart sheet, an error occurs because no such thing as an active cell exists in a chart sheet.

By executing the following procedure, you cancel the OnKey events, and the keys return to their normal functions.

```
Sub Cancel_OnKey()
    Application.OnKey "{PgDn}"
    Application.OnKey "{PgUp}"
End Sub
```

Caution

Contrary to what you may expect, using an empty string as the second argument for the OnKey method does *not* cancel the OnKey event. Rather, it causes Excel to ignore the keystroke and do nothing. For example, the following instruction tells Excel to ignore Alt+F4 (the percent sign represents the Alt key):

```
Application.OnKey "%{F4}", ""
```

VBA Examples

My philosophy about learning to write Excel macros places heavy emphasis on examples. Often, a well–thought-out example communicates a concept much better than a lengthy description of the underlying theory. In this book, space limitations don't allow describing every nuance of VBA, so I prepared many examples. Don't overlook the VBA Help system for specific details. To get help while working in the VB Editor window, press F1 or type your search terms into the Type a Question for Help field on the menu bar.

This chapter consists of several examples that demonstrate common VBA techniques. You may be able to use some examples directly, but in most cases, you must adapt them to your own needs. These examples are organized into the following categories:

- Working with ranges
- Working with workbooks
- Working with charts
- Programming techniques to speed up your VBA code

Working with Ranges

Most of what you do in VBA probably involves worksheet ranges. When you work with range objects, keep the following points in mind:

- Your VBA code doesn't need to select a range to do something with the range.
- If your code does select a range, its worksheet must be active.

- The macro recorder doesn't always generate the most efficient code. Often, you can use the recorder to create your macro and then edit the code to make it more efficient.

- I recommend that you use named ranges in your VBA code. For example, a reference such as Range ("Total") is better than Range ("D45"). In the latter case, you need to modify the macro if you add a row above row 45.

- When you record macros that select ranges, pay close attention to relative versus absolute recording mode (see Chapter 39). The recording mode that you choose can drastically affect the way the macro operates.

- If you create a macro that loops through each cell in the current range selection, be aware that the user can select entire columns or rows. In such a case, you need to create a subset of the selection that consists only of nonblank cells. Or, you can work with cells in the worksheet's used range (by using the UsedRange property).

- Be aware that Excel allows you to select multiple ranges in a worksheet. For example, you can select a range, press Ctrl, and then select another range. You can test for this in your macro and take appropriate actions.

The examples in the following sections demonstrate these points.

Copying a range

Copying a range is a frequent activity in macros. When you turn on the macro recorder (using absolute recording mode) and copy a range from A1:A5 to B1:B5, you get a VBA macro like this:

```
Sub CopyRange()
   Range("A1:A5").Select
   Selection.Copy
   Range("B1").Select
   ActiveSheet.Paste
   Application.CutCopyMode = False
End Sub
```

This macro works, but it's not the most efficient way to copy a range. You can accomplish exactly the same result with the following one-line macro:

```
Sub CopyRange2()
   Range("A1:A5").Copy Range("B1")
End Sub
```

This code takes advantage of the fact that the Copy method can use an argument that specifies the destination. Useful information about properties and methods is available in the Help system.

The example demonstrates that the macro recorder doesn't always generate the most efficient code. As you see, you don't have to select an object to work with it. Note that `CopyRange2` doesn't select a range; therefore, the active cell doesn't change when this macro is executed.

Copying a variable-size range

Often, you want to copy a range of cells in which the exact row and column dimensions are unknown.

Figure 44.1 shows a range on a worksheet. This range contains data that is updated weekly. Therefore, the number of rows changes. Because the exact range address is unknown at any given time, writing a macro to copy the range can be challenging.

FIGURE 44.1

This range can consist of any number of rows.

	A	B	C	D
1	Week Ending	Calls	Orders	
2	8/7/2009	452	89	
3	8/14/2009	546	102	
4	8/21/2009	587	132	
5	8/28/2009	443	65	
6	9/4/2009	609	156	
7	9/11/2009	592	92	
8	9/18/2009	487	95	
9	9/25/2009	601	105	
10	10/2/2009	515	133	
11	10/9/2009	540	122	
12				

The macro that follows demonstrates how to copy this range from Sheet1 to Sheet2 (beginning at cell A1). It uses the `CurrentRegion` property, which returns a `Range` object that corresponds to the block of used cells surrounding a particular cell. This is equivalent to choosing Home ➪ Editing ➪ Find & Select ➪ Go To, clicking the Special button, and then selecting the Current Region option.

```
Sub CopyCurrentRegion()
   Range("A1").CurrentRegion.Copy Sheets("Sheet2").Range("A1")
End Sub
```

On the CD

A workbook that contains this macro is available on the companion CD-ROM. The file is named `range copy.xlsm.`

Selecting to the end of a row or column

You probably are in the habit of using key combinations, such as pressing Ctrl+Shift+→ and Ctrl+Shift+↓, to select from the active cell to the end of a row or column. When you record these actions in Excel (using relative recording mode), you'll find that the resulting code works as you would expect it to.

The following VBA procedure selects the range that begins at the active cell and extends down to the last cell in the column (or to the first empty cell, whichever comes first). When the range is selected, you can do whatever you want with it — copy it, move it, format it, and so on.

```
Sub SelectDown()
    Range(ActiveCell, ActiveCell.End(xlDown)).Select
End Sub
```

Notice that the `Range` property has two arguments. These arguments represent the upper-left and lower-right cells in a range.

This example uses the `End` method of the `Range` object, which returns a `Range` object. The `End` method takes one argument, which can be any of the following constants: `xlUp`, `xlDown`, `xlToLeft`, or `xlToRight`.

On the CD

A workbook that contains this macro is available on the companion CD-ROM. The file is named `select cells.xlsm`.

Selecting a row or column

The macro that follows demonstrates how to select the column of the active cell. It uses the `EntireColumn` property, which returns a range that consists of a column:

```
Sub SelectColumn()
    ActiveCell.EntireColumn.Select
End Sub
```

As you may suspect, an `EntireRow` property also is available, which returns a range that consists of a row.

If you want to perform an operation on all cells in the selected column, you don't need to select the column. For example, when the following procedure is executed, all cells in the row that contains the active cell are made bold:

```
Sub MakeRowBold()
  ActiveCell.EntireRow.Font.Bold = True
End Sub
```

Moving a range

Moving a range consists of cutting it to the Clipboard and then pasting it to another area. If you record your actions while performing a move operation, the macro recorder generates code as follows:

```
Sub MoveRange()
  Range("A1:C6").Select
  Selection.Cut
  Range("A10").Select
  ActiveSheet.Paste
End Sub
```

As demonstrated with copying earlier in this chapter (see "Copying a range"), this method is not the most efficient way to move a range of cells. In fact, you can do it with a single VBA statement, as follows:

```
Sub MoveRange2()
 Range("A1:C6").Cut Range("A10")
End Sub
```

This statement takes advantage of the fact that the Cut method can use an argument that specifies the destination.

On the CD

A workbook that contains this macro is available on the companion CD-ROM. The file is named range move.xlsm.

Looping through a range efficiently

Many macros perform an operation on each cell in a range, or they may perform selective actions based on the content of each cell. These operations usually involve a For-Next loop that processes each cell in the range.

The following example demonstrates how to loop through all the cells in a range. In this case, the range is the current selection. In this example, Cell is a variable name that refers to the cell being processed. (Notice that this variable is declared as a Range object.) Within the For-Next loop, the single statement evaluates the cell. If the cell is negative, it's converted to a positive value.

```
Sub ProcessCells()
  Dim Cell As Range
  For Each Cell In Selection
    If Cell.Value < 0 Then Cell.Value = Cell.Value * -1
  Next Cell
End Sub
```

The preceding example works, but what if the selection consists of an entire column or an entire range? This is not uncommon because Excel lets you perform operations on entire columns or rows. In this case, though, the macro seems to take forever because it loops through each cell — even those that are blank. What's needed is a way to process only the nonblank cells.

You can accomplish this task by using the SelectSpecial method. In the following example, the SelectSpecial method is used to create a new object: the subset of the selection that consists of cells with constants (as opposed to formulas). This subset is processed, with the net effect of skipping all blank cells and all formula cells.

```
Sub ProcessCells2()
    Dim ConstantCells As Range
    Dim Cell As Range
'   Ignore errors
    On Error Resume Next
'   Process the constants
    Set ConstantCells = Selection.SpecialCells _
    (xlConstants, xlNumbers)
    For Each Cell In ConstantCells
        If Cell.Value < 0 Then Cell.Value = Cell.Value * -1
    Next Cell
End Sub
```

The ProcessCells2 procedure works fast, regardless of what is selected. For example, you can select the range, select all columns in the range, select all rows in the range, or even select the entire worksheet. In all these cases, only the cells that contain constants are processed inside the loop. This procedure is a vast improvement over the ProcessCells procedure presented earlier in this section.

Notice that the following statement is used in the procedure:

```
On Error Resume Next
```

This statement causes Excel to ignore any errors that occur and simply to process the next statement. This statement is necessary because the SpecialCells method produces an error if no cells qualify and because the numerical comparison will fail if a cell contains an error value. Normal error checking is resumed when the procedure ends. To tell Excel explicitly to return to normal error-checking mode, use the following statement:

```
On Error GoTo 0
```

On the CD

This macro is available on the companion CD-ROM. The file is named skip blanks while looping.xlsm.

Prompting for a cell value

As discussed in Chapter 41, you can take advantage of the VBA InputBox function to ask the user to enter a value. Figure 44.2 shows an example.

Using the VBA InputBox function to get a value from the user.

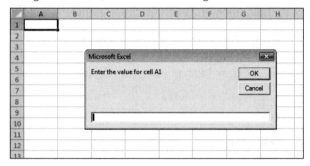

You can assign this value to a variable and use it in your procedure. Often, however, you want to place the value into a cell. The following procedure demonstrates how to ask the user for a value and place it into cell A1 of the active worksheet, using only one statement:

```
Sub GetValue()
    Range("A1").Value = InputBox("Enter the value for cell A1")
End Sub
```

Determining the type of selection

If your macro is designed to work with a range selection, you need to determine that a range is actually selected. Otherwise, the macro most likely fails. The following procedure identifies the type of object selected:

```
Sub SelectionType()
    MsgBox TypeName(Selection)
End Sub
```

On the CD

A workbook that contains this macro is available on the companion CD-ROM. The file is named
`selection type.xlsm.`

If a cell or a range is selected, the MsgBox displays Range. If your macro is designed to work only with ranges, you can use an If statement to ensure that a range is actually selected. The following is an example that displays a message and exits the procedure if the current selection is not a Range object:

```
Sub CheckSelection()
  If TypeName(Selection) <> "Range" Then
    MsgBox "Select a range."
    Exit Sub
  End If
' ... [Other statements go here]
End Sub
```

Another way to approach this task is to define a custom function that returns TRUE if the selection (represented by the sel argument) is a Range object, and FALSE otherwise. The following function does just that:

```
Function IsRange(sel) As Boolean
 IsRange = False
 If TypeName(sel) = "Range" Then IsRange = True
End Function
```

Here's a more compact version of the IsRange function:

```
Function IsRange(sel) As Boolean
   IsRange = (TypeName(sel) = "Range")
End Function
```

If you enter the IsRange function in your module, you can rewrite the CheckSelection procedure as follows:

```
Sub CheckSelection()
 If IsRange(Selection) Then
' ... [Other statements go here]
 Else
  MsgBox "Select a range."
  Exit Sub
 End If
End Sub
```

Identifying a multiple selection

Excel enables you to make a multiple selection by pressing Ctrl while you select objects or ranges. This method can cause problems with some macros; for example, you can't copy a multiple selection that consists of nonadjacent ranges. The following macro demonstrates how to determine whether the user has made a multiple selection:

```
Sub MultipleSelection()
  If Selection.Areas.Count > 1 Then
    MsgBox "Multiple selections not allowed."
    Exit Sub
  End If
' ... [Other statements go here]
End Sub
```

This example uses the Areas method, which returns a collection of all Range objects in the selection. The Count property returns the number of objects that are in the collection.

The following is a VBA function that returns TRUE if the selection is a multiple selection:

```
Function IsMultiple(sel) As Boolean
  IsMultiple = Selection.Areas.Count > 1
End Function
```

Counting selected cells

You can create a macro that works with the selected range of cells. Use the Count property of the Range object to determine how many cells are contained in a range selection (or any range, for that matter). For example, the following statement displays a message box that contains the number of cells in the current selection:

```
MsgBox Selection.Count
```

Caution

With the larger worksheet size introduced in Excel 2007, the Count property can generate an error. The Count property uses the Long data type, so the largest value that it can store is 2,147,483,647. For example, if the user selects 2,048 complete columns (2,147,483,648 cells), the Count property generates an error. Fortunately, Microsoft added a new property (CountLarge) that uses the Double data type, which can handle values up to 1.79+E^308.

For more on VBA data types, see upcoming Table 44.1.

Bottom line? In the vast majority of situations, the Count property will work fine. If there's a chance that you may need to count more cells (such as all cells in a worksheet), use CountLarge instead of Count.

If the active sheet contains a range named *data*, the following statement assigns the number of cells in the *data* range to a variable named `CellCount`:

```
CellCount = Range("data").Count
```

You can also determine how many rows or columns are contained in a range. The following expression calculates the number of columns in the currently selected range:

```
Selection.Columns.Count
```

And, of course, you can also use the `Rows` property to determine the number of rows in a range. The following statement counts the number of rows in a range named *data* and assigns the number to a variable named `RowCount`:

```
RowCount = Range("data").Rows.Count
```

Working with Workbooks

The examples in this section demonstrate various ways to use VBA to work with workbooks.

Saving all workbooks

The following procedure loops through all workbooks in the `Workbooks` collection and saves each file that has been saved previously:

```
Public Sub SaveAllWorkbooks()
    Dim Book As Workbook
    For Each Book In Workbooks
        If Book.Path <> "" Then Book.Save
    Next Book
End Sub
```

Notice the use of the `Path` property. If a workbook's `Path` property is empty, the file has never been saved (it's a new workbook). This procedure ignores such workbooks and saves only the workbooks that have a nonempty `Path` property.

Saving and closing all workbooks

The following procedure loops through the `Workbooks` collection. The code saves and closes all workbooks.

```
Sub CloseAllWorkbooks()
    Dim Book As Workbook
    For Each Book In Workbooks
        If Book.Name <> ThisWorkbook.Name Then
            Book.Close savechanges:=True
        End If
    Next Book
    ThisWorkbook.Close savechanges:=True
End Sub
```

The procedure uses an `If` statement within the `For-Next` loop to determine whether the workbook is the workbook that contains the code. This is necessary because closing the workbook that contains the procedure would end the code, and subsequent workbooks would not be affected.

Working with Charts

Manipulating charts with VBA can be confusing, mainly because of the large number of objects involved. To get a feel for working with charts, turn on the macro recorder, create a chart, and perform some routine chart editing. You may be surprised by the amount of code that's generated.

When you understand how objects function within in a chart, however, you can create some useful macros. This section presents a few macros that deal with charts. When you write macros that manipulate charts, you need to understand some terminology. An embedded chart on a worksheet is a `ChartObject` object, and the `ChartObject` contains the actual `Chart` object. A chart on a chart sheet, on the other hand, does not have a `ChartObject` container.

It's often useful to create an object reference to a chart (see "Simplifying object references," later in this chapter). For example, the following statement creates an object variable (`MyChart`) for the embedded chart named Chart 1 on the active sheet.

```
Dim MyChart As Chart
Set MyChart = ActiveSheet.ChartObjects("Chart 1")
```

The following sections contain examples of macros that work with charts.

On the CD
These macros are available on the companion CD-ROM. The file is named chart macros.xlsm**.**

Modifying the chart type

The following example changes the chart type of every embedded chart on the active sheet. It makes each chart an area chart by adjusting the `ChartType` property of the `Chart` object. A built-in constant, `xlColumnClustered`, represents a standard column chart.

```
Sub ChartType()
    Dim ChtObj As ChartObject
    For Each ChtObj In ActiveSheet.ChartObjects
        ChtObj.Chart.ChartType = xlColumnClustered
    Next ChtObj
End Sub
```

The preceding example uses a `For-Next` loop to cycle through all the `ChartObject` objects on the active sheet. Within the loop, the chart type is assigned a new value, making it an area chart.

The following macro performs the same function but works on all chart sheets in the active workbook:

```
Sub ChartType2()
    Dim Cht As Chart
    For Each Cht In ActiveWorkbook.Charts
        Cht.ChartType = xlColumnClustered
    Next Cht
End Sub
```

Modifying chart properties

The following example changes the legend font for all charts that are on the active sheet. It uses a `For-Next` loop to process all `ChartObject` objects and uses the `HasLegend` property to ensure that the chart has a legend. The code then adjusts the properties of the `Font` object contained in the `Legend` object:

```
Sub LegendMod()
    Dim ChtObj As ChartObject
    For Each ChtObj In ActiveSheet.ChartObjects
        ChtObj.Chart.HasLegend = True
        With ChtObj.Chart.Legend.Font
          .Name = "Arial"
          .FontStyle = "Bold"
          .Size = 8
        End With
    Next ChtObj
End Sub
```

Applying chart formatting

This example applies several different formatting types to the specified chart (in this case, Chart 1 on the active sheet):

```
Sub ChartMods()
    With ActiveSheet.ChartObjects("Chart 1").Chart
        .ChartType = xlArea
        .ChartArea.Font.Name = "Arial"
        .ChartArea.Font.FontStyle = "Regular"
        .ChartArea.Font.Size = 9
        .PlotArea.Interior.ColorIndex = 6
        .Axes(xlValue).TickLabels.Font.Bold = True
        .Axes(xlCategory).TickLabels.Font.Bold = True
    End With
End Sub
```

One way to learn about these properties is to record a macro while you apply various changes to a chart.

VBA Speed Tips

VBA is fast, but it's often not fast enough. This section presents programming examples that you can use to help speed your macros.

Turning off screen updating

You've probably noticed that when you execute a macro, you can watch everything that occurs in the macro. Sometimes, this view is instructive; but, after you get the macro working properly, it can be annoying and slow things considerably.

Fortunately, you can disable the normal screen updating that occurs when you execute a macro. Insert the following statement to turn off screen updating:

```
Application.ScreenUpdating = False
```

If, at any point during the macro, you want the user to see the results of the macro, use the following statement to turn screen updating back on:

```
Application.ScreenUpdating = True
```

Preventing alert messages

One benefit of using a macro is that you can perform a series of actions automatically. You can start a macro and then get a cup of coffee while Excel does its thing. Some operations cause Excel to display messages that must be attended to, however. For example, if your macro deletes a sheet, you see the message that is shown in the dialog box in Figure 44.3. These types of messages mean that you can't execute your macro unattended.

FIGURE 44.3

You can instruct Excel not to display these types of alerts while a macro is running.

To avoid these alert messages (and automatically choose the default response) , insert the following VBA statement:

```
Application.DisplayAlerts = False
```

To turn alerts back on, use this statement:

```
Application.DisplayAlerts = True
```

Simplifying object references

As you may have discovered, references to objects can get very lengthy — especially if your code refers to an object that's not on the active sheet or in the active workbook. For example, a fully qualified reference to a Range object may look like this:

```
Workbooks("MyBook.xlsx").Worksheets("Sheet1").Range("IntRate")
```

If your macro uses this range frequently, you may want to use the Set command to create an object variable. For example, to assign this Range object to an object variable named Rate, use the following statement:

```
Set Rate= Workbooks("MyBook.xlsx").Worksheets("Sheet1").Range("IntRate")
```

After this variable is defined, you can use the variable Rate instead of the lengthy reference. For example

```
Rate.Value = .0725
```

Besides simplifying your coding, using object variables also speeds your macros quite a bit. I've seen macros execute twice as fast after creating object variables.

Declaring variable types

Usually, you don't have to worry about the type of data that's assigned to a variable. Excel handles all these details behind the scenes. For example, if you have a variable named MyVar, you can assign a number of any type to it. You can even assign a text string to it later in the procedure.

If you want your procedures to execute as fast as possible, though, you should tell Excel in advance what type of data is going be assigned to each of your variables. Providing this information in your VBA procedure is known as *declaring* a variable's type.

Table 44.1 lists all the data types that are supported by VBA. This table also lists the number of bytes that each type uses and the approximate range of possible values.

TABLE 44.1

VBA Data Types

Data Type	Bytes Used	Approximate Range of Values
Byte	1	0 to 255
Boolean	2	True or False
Integer	2	–32,768 to 32,767
Long (long integer)	4	–2,147,483,648 to 2,147,483,647
Single (single-precision floating-point)	4	–3.4E38 to –1.4E–45 for negative values; 1.4E–45 to 4E38 for positive values
Double (double-precision floating-point)	8	–1.7E308 to –4.9E–324 for negative values; 4.9E–324 to .7E308 for positive values
Currency (scaled integer)	8	–9.2E14 to 9.2E14
Decimal	14	+/–7.9E28 with no decimal point
Date	8	January 1, 100 to December 31, 9999
Object	4	Any object reference
String (variable-length)	10 + string length	0 to approximately 2 billion
String (fixed-length)	Length of string	1 to approximately 65,400
Variant (with numbers)	16	Any numeric value up to the range of a Double
Variant (with characters)	22 + string length	Same range as for variable-length String
User-defined (using Type)	Number required by elements	Range of each element is the same as the range of its data type

If you don't declare a variable, Excel uses the `Variant` data type. In general, the best technique is to use the data type that uses the smallest number of bytes yet can still handle all the data assigned to it. An exception is when you're performing floating-point calculations. In such a case, it is always best to use the `Double` data type (rather than the `Single` data type) to maintain maximum precision. Another exception involves the `Integer` data type. Although the `Long` data type uses more bytes, it usually results in faster performance.

When VBA works with data, execution speed is a function of the number of bytes that VBA has at its disposal. In other words, the fewer bytes that are used by data, the faster VBA can access and manipulate the data.

To declare a variable, use the `Dim` statement before you use the variable for the first time. For example, to declare the variable `Units` as a `Long` data type, use the following statement:

```
Dim Units as Long
```

To declare the variable `UserName` as a string, use the following statement:

```
Dim UserName as String
```

If you declare a variable within a procedure, the declaration is valid only within that procedure. If you declare a variable outside of any procedures (but before the first procedure), the variable is valid in all procedures in the module.

If you use an object variable (as described in "Simplifying object references," earlier in this chapter), you can declare the variable as the appropriate object data type. The following is an example:

```
Dim Rate as Range
Set Rate = Workbooks("MyBook.xlsx").Worksheets("Sheet1").Range("IntRate")
```

To force yourself to declare all the variables that you use, insert the following statement at the top of your module:

```
Option Explicit
```

If you use this statement, Excel displays an error message if it encounters a variable that hasn't been declared. After you get into the habit of correctly declaring all your variables, you will find that it helps eliminate errors and makes spotting errors easier.

Creating Custom Excel Add-Ins

F or developers, one of the most useful features in Excel is the capability to create add-ins. This chapter discusses this concept and provides a practical example of creating an add-in.

IN THIS CHAPTER

Understanding add-ins

Converting a workbook to an add-in

What Is an Add-In?

Generally speaking, an *add-in* is something that's added to software to give it additional functionality. Excel includes several add-ins, including the Analysis ToolPak and Solver. Ideally, the new features blend in well with the original interface so that they appear to be part of the program.

Excel's approach to add-ins is quite powerful because any knowledgeable Excel user can create add-ins from workbooks. An Excel add-in is basically a different form of a workbook file. Any Excel workbook can be converted into an add-in, but not every workbook is a good candidate for an add-in.

What distinguishes an add-in form a normal workbook? Add-ins, by default, have an .xlam extension In addition, add-ins are always hidden, so you can't display worksheets or chart sheets that are contained in an add-in. But, you can access its VBA procedures and display dialog boxes that are contained on UserForms.

The following are some typical uses for Excel add-ins:

- **Store one or more custom worksheet functions.** When the add-in is loaded, you can use the functions like any built-in worksheet function.

- **Store Excel utilities.** VBA is ideal for creating general-purpose utilities that extend the power of Excel. The Power Utility Pak that I created is an example.

- **Store proprietary macros.** If you don't want end users to see (or modify) your macros, store the macros in an add-in and protect the VBA project with a password. A user can use the macros, but they can't view or change them unless the user knows the password. An additional benefit is that the add-in doesn't display a workbook window, which can be distracting.

As previously noted, Excel ships with several useful add-ins (see the sidebar "Add-Ins Included with Excel"), and you can acquire other add-ins from third-party vendors or the Internet. In addition, Excel includes the tools that enable you to create your own add-ins. I explain this process later in the chapter (see "Creating Add-Ins").

Working with Add-Ins

The best way to work with add-ins is to use the Excel Add-In Manager. To display the Add-In Manager

1. Choose File ⇨ Options.
2. In the Excel Options dialog box, select the Add-Ins category.
3. At the bottom of the dialog box, select Excel Add-Ins from the Manage list and then click Go.

Excel displays its Add-Ins dialog box, shown in Figure 45.1. The list box contains all the add-ins that Excel knows about. The add-ins that are checked are open. You can open and close add-ins from this dialog box by selecting or deselecting the check boxes.

Tip
Pressing Alt+TI is a much faster way to display the Add-Ins dialog box. ■

Caution
You can also open most add-in files by choosing File ⇨ Open. After an add-in is opened, however, you can't choose File ⇨ Close to close it. The only way to remove the add-in is to exit and restart Excel or to write a macro to close the add-in. Therefore, you're usually better off opening the add-ins by using the Add-Ins dialog box. ■

FIGURE 45.1

The Add-Ins dialog box.

The user interface for some add-ins (including those included with Excel) may be integrated into the Ribbon. For example, when you open the Analysis ToolPak add-in, you access these tools by choosing Data ➪ Analysis ➪ Data Analysis.

Add-Ins Included with Excel

The following table lists the add-ins included with Excel 2010. Some add-ins may not have been installed. If you try to use one of these add-ins and it's not installed, you receive a prompt asking whether you want to install it.

Add-In Name	What It Does	Where to Find It
Analysis ToolPak	Statistical and engineering tools. See Chapter 38.	Choose Data ➪ Analysis ➪ Data Analysis.
Analysis ToolPak — VBA	VBA functions for the Analysis ToolPak.	The functions in this add-in are used by VBA programmers, and they are not accessible from Excel.
Euro Currency Tools	Tools for converting and formatting the euro currency.	Choose Formulas ➪ Solutions ➪ Euro Conversion and Formulas ➪ Solutions ➪ Euro Formatting.
Solver Add-In	A tool that helps you to use a variety of numeric methods for equation solving and optimization.	Choose Data ➪ Analysis ➪ Solver.

Note

If you open an add-in created in a version prior to Excel 2007, any user interface modifications made by the add-in will not appear as they were intended to appear. Rather, you must access the user interface items (menus and toolbars) by choosing Add-Ins ➪ Menu Commands or Add-Ins ➪ Custom Toolbars. ∎

Tip

You can also download additional Excel add-ins from `http://office.microsoft.com`.

Why Create Add-Ins?

Most Excel users have no need to create add-ins. However, if you develop spreadsheets for others — or if you simply want to get the most out of Excel — you may be interested in pursuing this topic further.

Here are some reasons why you may want to convert your Excel workbook application to an add-in:

- **Avoid confusion.** If an end user loads your application as an add-in, the file isn't visible in the Excel window — and, therefore, is less likely to confuse novice users or get in the way. Unlike a hidden workbook, an add-in can't be unhidden.

- **Simplify access to worksheet functions.** Custom worksheet functions stored in an add-in don't require the workbook name qualifier. For example, if you have a custom function named MOVAVG stored in a workbook named `Newfuncs.xlsm`, you have to use a syntax such as the following to use this function in a different workbook:

  `=NEWFUNC.XLSM!MOVAVG(A1:A50)`

  However, if this function is stored in an add-in file that's open, the syntax is much simpler because you don't need to include the file reference:

  `=MOVAVG(A1:A50)`

- **Provide easier access.** After you identify the location of your add-in, it appears in the Add-Ins dialog box and can display a friendly name and a description of what it does.

- **Permit better loading control.** You can automatically open add-ins when Excel starts, regardless of the directory in which they're stored.

- **Omit prompts when unloading.** When an add-in is closed, the user never sees the Save Change In prompt because changes to add-ins aren't saved unless you specifically do so from the VB Editor window.

Creating Add-Ins

Technically, you can convert any workbook to an add-in. Not all workbooks benefit from this conversion, though. In fact, workbooks that consist only of worksheets (that is, not macros or custom dialog boxes) become unusable because add-ins are hidden.

Workbooks that benefit from conversion to an add-in are those with macros. For example, you may have a workbook that consists of general-purpose macros and functions. This type of workbook makes an ideal add-in.

These steps describe how to create an add-in from a workbook:

1. **Develop your application and make sure that everything works properly.**

2. **(Optional) Add a title and description for your add-in.** Choose File ➪ Info ➪ Properties ➪ Show Document Panel. When the Properties panel above your worksheet appears, enter a brief descriptive title in the Title field, and then enter a longer description in the Comments field. Although this step isn't required, it makes installing and identifying the add-in easier. To close the Document Properties panel, click its close button (X).

3. **(Optional) Lock the VBA project.** This step protects the VBA code and UserForms from being viewed. You do this in the VB Editor; choose Tools ➪ *projectname* Properties (where *projectname* corresponds to your VB project name). In the dialog box, click the Protection tab and select Lock Project for Viewing. If you like, you can specify a password to prevent others from viewing your code.

4. **Save the workbook as an add-in file by choosing File ➪ Save As and selecting Excel Add-In (*.xlam) from the Save as Type drop-down list.** By default, Excel saves your add-in in your AddIns directory. You can override this location and choose any directory you like.

Note

After you save the workbook as an add-in, the original (non–add-in) workbook remains active. You should close this file to avoid having two macros with the same name. ■

After you create the add-in, you need to install it:

1. **Choose File ➪ Options ➪ Add-Ins.**

2. **Select Excel Add-Ins from the Manage drop-down list and then click Go to display the Add-Ins dialog box.**

3. **In the Add-Ins dialog box, click the Browse button to locate the XLAM file that you created, which installs the add-in.** The Add-Ins dialog box uses the descriptive title that you provided in the Properties panel.

Note

You can continue to modify the macros and UserForms in the XLAM version of your file. Because the add-in doesn't appear in the Excel window, you save your changes in the VB Editor by choosing File ⇨ Save. ∎

An Add-In Example

This section discusses the steps to create a useful add-in from the `change case.xlsm` workbook I cover in Chapter 41. This workbook contains a UserForm that displays options that change the text case of selected cells (uppercase, lowercase, or proper case). Figure 45.2 shows the add-in in action.

FIGURE 45.2

This dialog box enables the user to change the case of text in the selected cells.

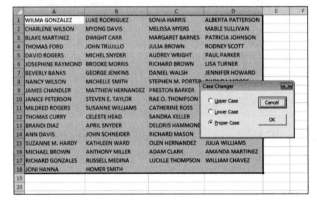

On the CD

This file is available on the companion CD-ROM and is named `change case.xlam`. The file is not locked, so you have full access to the VBA code and UserForm. ∎

Setting up the workbook

This workbook contains one worksheet, which is empty. Although the worksheet is not used, it must be present because every workbook must have at least one sheet.

Choose Insert ⇨ Module in the VB Editor to insert a VBA module (named Module1). Choose Insert ⇨ UserForm to insert a UserForm (named UserForm1).

Procedures in Module1

The two macros that follow are contained in the Module1 code module. The ShowUserForm procedure checks the type of selection. If a range is selected, the dialog box in UserForm1 appears. If anything other than a range is selected, a message box is displayed.

The ChangeCaseOfText procedure is a special callback procedure, with one argument, that is executed from a control on the Ribbon. See "Creating the user interface for your add-in macro," later in this chapter. This procedure simply executes the ShowUserForm procedure.

```
Sub ShowUserForm()
    If TypeName(Selection) = "Range" Then
        UserForm1.Show
    Else
        MsgBox "Select some cells."
    End If
End Sub

Sub ChangeCaseOfText(ByVal control As IRibbonControl)
    Call ShowUserForm
End Sub
```

About the UserForm

Figure 45.3 shows the UserForm1 form, which has five controls: three OptionButton controls and two CommandButton controls. The controls have descriptive names, and the Accelerator property is set so that the controls display an accelerator key (for keyboard users). The option button with the Upper Case caption has its Value property set to TRUE, which makes it the default option.

FIGURE 45.3

The custom dialog box.

The UserForm1 object contains the event-handler procedures for the two `CommandButton` objects that are on the form. The following procedure is executed when the OK button is clicked. This procedure does all the work:

```
Private Sub OKButton_Click()
    CaseChangerDialog.Hide
    Application.ScreenUpdating = False

'   Upper case
    If OptionUpper Then
        For Each cell In Selection
        If Not cell.HasFormula Then
            cell.Value = StrConv(cell.Value, vbUpperCase)
        End If
        Next cell
    End If
'   Lower case
    If OptionLower Then
        For Each cell In Selection
        If Not cell.HasFormula Then
            cell.Value = StrConv(cell.Value, vbLowerCase)
        End If
        Next cell
    End If
'   Proper case
    If OptionProper Then
        For Each cell In Selection
        If Not cell.HasFormula Then
            cell.Value = StrConv(cell.Value, vbProperCase)
        End If
        Next cell
    End If
    Unload UserForm1
End Sub
```

The following procedure is executed if the user clicks the Cancel button:

```
Private Sub CancelButton_Click()
    Unload UserForm1
End Sub
```

Testing the workbook

Before you convert this workbook to an add-in, test it when a different workbook is active to simulate what happens when the workbook is an add-in. Remember that an add-in is never the active workbook, and it never displays any of its worksheets.

To test it, save the workbook, close it, and then reopen it. With the workbook open, then activate a different workbook, select some cells that contain text, and then press Alt+F8 to display the Macros dialog box. Execute the ShowUserForm macro and try all the options.

Adding descriptive information

Adding descriptive information is recommended but not necessary. Choose File ➪ Info ➪ Properties ➪ Show Document Panel to display the Properties panel below the Ribbon. See Figure 45.4. Enter a title for the add-in in the Title field. This text appears in the Add-Ins dialog box. In the Comments field, enter a description. This information appears at the bottom of the Add-Ins dialog box when the add-in is selected.

Use the Document Properties panel to enter descriptive information about your add-in.

Protecting the project

In some situations (such as a commercial product), you may want to protect your project so that others can't see the source code. To protect the project, follow these steps:

1. **Activate the VB Editor.**
2. **In the Project window, click the project.**
3. **Choose Tools ➪ *project name* Properties.** The VB Editor displays its Project Properties dialog box.
4. **Click the Protection tab (as shown in Figure 45.5).**
5. **Select the Lock Project for Viewing check box.**
6. **Enter a password (twice) for the project.**
7. **Click OK.**

FIGURE 45.5

The Project Properties dialog box.

Creating the add-in

To save the workbook as an add-in, switch to the Excel window and activate your workbook. Then choose File ➪ Save As. Select Microsoft Excel Add-In (*.xlam) from the Save as Type drop-down list. Enter a name for the add-in file and then click OK. By default, Excel saves the add-in in your AddIns directory, but you can choose a different directory if you like.

Creating the user interface for your add-in macro

At this point, the add-in is created, but it's missing one key component: a way to execute the macro that displays the UserForm. Here are three ways to do this:

- Customize your Quick Access toolbar (or the Ribbon) to include a new command. See Chapter 23 for details.

- Create an old-style (pre–Excel 2007) CommandButton. See the sidebar, "Modify the User Interface the Old Way."

- Modify the add-in file so that it adds a new command to the Ribbon when the add-in is opened. I discuss this topic briefly in Chapter 23, but complete details are beyond the scope of this book.

Modify the User Interface the Old Way

Before Excel 2007, it was much simpler to provide a way to execute a macro in an add-in. It was done by using a `CommandBar` object, which display menus and toolbars. Excel 2010 still supports CommandBars for compatibility. All changes made to a `CommandBar` object are displayed in the Menu Commands or Custom Toolbars groups of the Add-Ins tab.

If you would like to modify `change case.xlsm` to use CommandBars, add these two procedures to the ThisWorkbook code module:

```
Private Sub Workbook_Open()
    Set NewMenuItem = Application.CommandBars("Worksheet Menu Bar") _
        .Controls("Tools").Controls.Add
    With NewMenuItem
        .Caption = "Change Case of Text..."
        .BeginGroup = True
        .OnAction = "ChangeCaseofText"
    End With
End Sub

Private Sub Workbook_BeforeClose(Cancel As Boolean)
    On Error Resume Next
    Application.CommandBars("Worksheet Menu Bar").Controls("Tools"). _
        Controls("Change Case of Text...").Delete
End Sub
```

When the add-in is opened, this code adds a new control to the Menu Commands group of the Add-Ins tab. When it's closed, the new control is removed. Simple and easy.

Installing the add-in

Now it's time to try the add-in. Choose File ➪ Excel Options ➪ Add-Ins. Select Excel Add-ins from the Manage drop-down list, and click Go.

Excel displays its Add-Ins dialog box. Click the Browse button and locate the `change case.xlam` add-in that you just created. After you do so, the Add-Ins dialog box displays the add-in in its list. Notice that the information that you provided in the Properties panel appears here. Click OK to close the dialog box and open the add-in.

Part VII

Appendixes

This part contains some very useful appendixes. Appendix A provides a complete reference of all the worksheet functions. Appendix B gives you the rundown on all the great sample files on the CD-ROM that accompanies this book. Appendix C contains some great additional Excel resources; discover Excel shortcut keys in Appendix D.

IN THIS PART

Appendix A
Worksheet Function Reference

Appendix B
What's on the CD-ROM

Appendix C
Additional Excel Resources

Appendix D
Excel Shortcut Keys

Worksheet Function Reference

This appendix contains a complete listing of Excel worksheet functions. The functions are arranged alphabetically by the categories displayed in the Insert Function dialog box.

For more information about a particular function, including its arguments, select the function in the Insert Function dialog box and then click Help on This Function.

On the CD

An interactive workbook that contains this information is available on the companion CD-ROM. The filename is `worksheet functions.xlsx`.

TABLE A.1

Compatibility Category Functions

Function	What It Does
BETADIST	Returns the cumulative beta probability density function.
BETAINV	Returns the inverse of the cumulative beta probability density function.
BINOMDIST	Returns the individual term binomial distribution probability.
CHIDIST	Returns the one-tailed probability of the chi-squared distribution.
CHIINV	Returns the inverse of the one-tailed probability of the chi-squared distribution.
CHITEST	Returns the test for independence.
CONFIDENCE	Returns the confidence interval for a population mean.
COVAR	Returns *covariance,* the average of the products of paired deviations.
CRITBINOM	Returns the smallest value for which the cumulative binomial distribution is less than or equal to a criterion value.
EXPONDIST	Returns the exponential distribution.
FDIST	Returns the F probability distribution.
FINV	Returns the inverse of the F probability distribution.
FTEST	Returns the result of an F-Test.
GAMMADIST	Returns the gamma distribution.
GAMMAINV	Returns the inverse of the gamma cumulative distribution.
HYPGEOMDIST	Returns the hypergeometric distribution.
LOGINV	Returns the inverse of the lognormal distribution.
LOGNORMDIST	Returns the cumulative lognormal distribution.
MODE	Returns the most common value in a data set.
NEGBINOMDIST	Returns the negative binomial distribution.
NORMDIST	Returns the normal cumulative distribution.
NORMINV	Returns the inverse of the normal cumulative distribution.
NORMSDIST	Returns the standard normal cumulative distribution.
NORMSINV	Returns the inverse of the standard normal cumulative distribution.
PERCENTILE	Returns the *k*th percentile of values in a range.

Function	What It Does
PERCENTRANK	Returns the percentage rank of a value in a data set.
POISSON	Returns the Poisson distribution.
QUARTILE	Returns the quartile of a data set.
RANK	Returns the rank of a number in a list of numbers.
STDEVP	Calculates standard deviation based on the entire population, ignoring text and logical values.
TDIST	Returns the Student's t-distribution.
TINV	Returns the inverse of the Student's t-distribution.
TTEST	Returns the probability associated with a Student's t-Test.
VAR	Estimates variance based on a sample, ignoring logical values and text.
VARP	Calculates variance based on the entire population, ignoring logical values and text.
WEIBULL	Returns the Weibull distribution.
ZTEST	Returns the two-tailed P-value of a Z-test.

The functions in the Compatibility category all have new versions in Excel 2010. The new versions are listed in the Statistical category. The old versions are still available for compatibility.

TABLE A.2

Cube Category Functions

Function	What It Does
CUBEKPIMEMBER*	Returns a key performance indicator name, property, and measure, and displays the name and property in the cell.
CUBEMEMBER*	Returns a member or tuple in a cube hierarchy.
CUBEMEMBERPROPERTY*	Returns the value of a member property in the cube.
CUBERANKEDMEMBER*	Returns the nth, or ranked, member in a set.
CUBESET*	Defines a calculated set of members or tuples by sending a set expression to the cube on the server.
CUBESETCOUNT*	Returns the number of items in a set.
CUBEVALUE*	Returns an aggregated value from a cube.

* Indicates a function introduced in Excel 2007.

TABLE A.3

Database Category Functions

Function	What It Does
DAVERAGE	Averages the values in a column of a list or database that match conditions you specify.
DCOUNT	Counts the cells that contain numbers in a column of a list or database that match conditions you specify.
DCOUNTA	Counts the nonblank cells in a column of a list or database that match conditions you specify.
DGET	Extracts a single value from a column of a list or database that matches conditions you specify.
DMAX	Returns the largest number in a column of a list or database that matches conditions you specify.
DMIN	Returns the smallest number in a column of a list or database that matches conditions you specify.
DPRODUCT	Multiplies the values in a column of a list or database that match conditions you specify.
DSTDEV	Estimates the standard deviation of a population based on a sample by using the numbers in a column of a list or database that match conditions you specify.
DSTDEVP	Calculates the standard deviation of a population based on the entire population, using the numbers in a column of a list or database that match conditions you specify.
DSUM	Adds the numbers in a column of a list or database that match conditions you specify.
DVAR	Estimates the variance of a population based on a sample by using the numbers in a column of a list or database that match conditions you specify.
DVARP	Calculates the variance of a population based on the entire population by using the numbers in a column of a list or database that match conditions you specify.

TABLE A.4

Date & Time Category Functions

Function	What It Does
DATE	Returns the serial number of a particular date.
DATEVALUE	Converts a date in the form of text to a serial number.
DAY	Converts a serial number to a day of the month.
DAYS360	Calculates the number of days between two dates, based on a 360-day year.
EDATE	Returns the serial number of the date that is the indicated number of months before or after the start date.
EOMONTH	Returns the serial number of the last day of the month before or after a specified number of months.
HOUR	Converts a serial number to an hour.

Function	What It Does
MINUTE	Converts a serial number to a minute.
MONTH	Converts a serial number to a month.
NETWORKDAYS	Returns the number of whole workdays between two dates.
NETWORKDAYS.INTL*	Returns the number of whole workdays between two dates (international version).
NOW	Returns the serial number of the current date and time.
SECOND	Converts a serial number to a second.
TIME	Returns the serial number of a particular time.
TIMEVALUE	Converts a time in the form of text to a serial number.
TODAY	Returns the serial number of today's date.
WEEKDAY	Converts a serial number to a day of the week.
WEEKNUM	Returns the week number in the year.
WORKDAY	Returns the serial number of the date before or after a specified number of work days.
WORKDAY.INTL*	Returns the serial number of the date before or after a specified number of work days (International version).
YEAR	Converts a serial number to a year.
YEARFRAC	Returns the year fraction representing the number of whole days between *start_date* and *end_date*.

* Indicates a function introduced in Excel 2010.

TABLE A.5

Engineering Category Functions

Function	What It Does
BESSELI	Returns the modified Bessel function In(x).
BESSELJ	Returns the Bessel function Jn(x).
BESSELK	Returns the modified Bessel function Kn(x).
BESSELY	Returns the Bessel function Yn(x).
BIN2DEC	Converts a binary number to decimal.
BIN2HEX	Converts a binary number to hexadecimal.
BIN2OCT	Converts a binary number to octal.
COMPLEX	Converts real and imaginary coefficients into a complex number.
CONVERT	Converts a number from one measurement system to another.

continued

TABLE A.5	*(continued)*
Function	**What It Does**
DEC2BIN	Converts a decimal number to binary.
DEC2HEX	Converts a decimal number to hexadecimal.
DEC2OCT	Converts a decimal number to octal.
DELTA	Tests whether two values are equal.
ERF	Returns the error function.
ERF.PRECISE*	Returns the error function.
ERFC	Returns the complementary error function.
ERFC.PRECISE*	Returns the complementary error function.
GESTEP	Tests whether a number is greater than a threshold value.
HEX2BIN	Converts a hexadecimal number to binary.
HEX2DEC	Converts a hexadecimal number to decimal.
HEX2OCT	Converts a hexadecimal number to octal.
IMABS	Returns the absolute value (modulus) of a complex number.
IMAGINARY	Returns the imaginary coefficient of a complex number.
IMARGUMENT	Returns the argument *theta,* an angle expressed in radians.
IMCONJUGATE	Returns the complex conjugate of a complex number.
IMCOS	Returns the cosine of a complex number.
IMDIV	Returns the quotient of two complex numbers.
IMEXP	Returns the exponential of a complex number.
IMLN	Returns the natural logarithm of a complex number.
IMLOG10	Returns the base-10 logarithm of a complex number.
IMLOG2	Returns the base-2 logarithm of a complex number.
IMPOWER	Returns a complex number raised to an integer power.
IMPRODUCT	Returns the product of complex numbers.
IMREAL	Returns the real coefficient of a complex number.
IMSIN	Returns the sine of a complex number.
IMSQRT	Returns the square root of a complex number.
IMSUB	Returns the difference of two complex numbers.
IMSUM	Returns the sum of complex numbers.
OCT2BIN	Converts an octal number to binary.
OCT2DEC	Converts an octal number to decimal.
OCT2HEX	Converts an octal number to hexadecimal.

* Indicates a function introduced in Excel 2010.

TABLE A.6

Financial Category Functions

Function	What It Does
ACCRINT	Returns the accrued interest for a security that pays periodic interest.
ACCRINTM	Returns the accrued interest for a security that pays interest at maturity.
AMORDEGRC	Returns the depreciation for each accounting period.
AMORLINC	Returns the depreciation for each accounting period. (The depreciation coefficient depends on the life of the assets.)
COUPDAYBS	Returns the number of days from the beginning of the coupon period to the settlement date.
COUPDAYS	Returns the number of days in the coupon period that contains the settlement date.
COUPDAYSNC	Returns the number of days from the settlement date to the next coupon date.
COUPNCD	Returns the next coupon date after the settlement date.
COUPNUM	Returns the number of coupons payable between the settlement date and maturity date.
COUPPCD	Returns the previous coupon date before the settlement date.
CUMIPMT	Returns the cumulative interest paid between two periods.
CUMPRINC	Returns the cumulative principal paid on a loan between two periods.
DB	Returns the depreciation of an asset for a specified period, using the fixed–declining-balance method.
DDB	Returns the depreciation of an asset for a specified period, using the double–declining-balance method or some other method that you specify.
DISC	Returns the discount rate for a security.
DOLLARDE	Converts a dollar price, expressed as a fraction, into a dollar price expressed as a decimal number.
DOLLARFR	Converts a dollar price, expressed as a decimal number, into a dollar price expressed as a fraction.
DURATION	Returns the annual duration of a security with periodic interest payments.
EFFECT	Returns the effective annual interest rate.
FV	Returns the future value of an investment.
FVSCHEDULE	Returns the future value of an initial principal after applying a series of compound interest rates.
INTRATE	Returns the interest rate for a fully invested security.
IPMT	Returns the interest payment for an investment for a given period.
IRR	Returns the internal rate of return for a series of cash flows.
ISPMT	Returns the interest associated with a specific loan payment.
MDURATION	Returns the Macauley modified duration for a security with an assumed par value of $100.

continued

TABLE A.6	(continued)
Function	**What It Does**
MIRR	Returns the internal rate of return where positive and negative cash flows are financed at different rates.
NOMINAL	Returns the annual nominal interest rate.
NPER	Returns the number of periods for an investment.
NPV	Returns the net present value of an investment based on a series of periodic cash flows and a discount rate.
ODDFPRICE	Returns the price per $100 face value of a security with an odd first period.
ODDFYIELD	Returns the yield of a security with an odd first period.
ODDLPRICE	Returns the price per $100 face value of a security with an odd last period.
ODDLYIELD	Returns the yield of a security with an odd last period.
PMT	Returns the periodic payment for an annuity.
PPMT	Returns the payment on the principal for an investment for a given period.
PRICE	Returns the price per $100 face value of a security that pays periodic interest.
PRICEDISC	Returns the price per $100 face value of a discounted security.
PRICEMAT	Returns the price per $100 face value of a security that pays interest at maturity.
PV	Returns the present value of an investment.
RATE	Returns the interest rate per period of an annuity.
RECEIVED	Returns the amount received at maturity for a fully invested security.
SLN	Returns the straight-line depreciation of an asset for one period.
SYD	Returns the sum-of-years' digits depreciation of an asset for a specified period.
TBILLEQ	Returns the bond-equivalent yield for a Treasury bill.
TBILLPRICE	Returns the price per $100 face value for a Treasury bill.
TBILLYIELD	Returns the yield for a Treasury bill.
VDB	Returns the depreciation of an asset for a specified or partial period using a double declining-balance method.
XIRR	Returns the internal rate of return for a schedule of cash flows that is not necessarily periodic.
XNPV	Returns the net present value for a schedule of cash flows that is not necessarily periodic.
YIELD	Returns the yield on a security that pays periodic interest.
YIELDDISC	Returns the annual yield for a discounted security, for example, a Treasury bill.
YIELDMAT	Returns the annual yield of a security that pays interest at maturity.

TABLE A.7

Information Category Functions

Function	What It Does
CELL	Returns information about the formatting, location, or contents of a cell.
ERROR.TYPE	Returns a number corresponding to an error type.
INFO	Returns information about the current operating environment.
ISBLANK	Returns TRUE if the value is blank.
ISERR	Returns TRUE if the value is any error value except #N/A.
ISERROR	Returns TRUE if the value is any error value.
ISEVEN	Returns TRUE if the number is even.
ISLOGICAL	Returns TRUE if the value is a logical value.
ISNA	Returns TRUE if the value is the #N/A error value.
ISNONTEXT	Returns TRUE if the value is not text.
ISNUMBER	Returns TRUE if the value is a number.
ISODD	Returns TRUE if the number is odd.
ISREF	Returns TRUE if the value is a reference.
ISTEXT	Returns TRUE if the value is text.
N	Returns a value converted to a number.
NA	Returns the error value #N/A.
TYPE	Returns a number indicating the data type of a value.

TABLE A.8

Logical Category Functions

Function	What It Does
AND	Returns TRUE if all its arguments are TRUE.
FALSE	Returns the logical value FALSE.
IF	Specifies a logical test to perform.
IFERROR*	Returns a different result if the first argument evaluates to an error.
NOT	Reverses the logic of its argument.
OR	Returns TRUE if any argument is TRUE.
TRUE	Returns the logical value TRUE.

* Indicates a function introduced in Excel 2007.

TABLE A.9

Lookup & Reference Category Functions

Function	What It Does
ADDRESS	Returns a reference as text to a single cell in a worksheet.
AREAS	Returns the number of areas in a reference.
CHOOSE	Chooses a value from a list of values.
COLUMN	Returns the column number of a reference.
COLUMNS	Returns the number of columns in a reference
GETPIVOTDATA	Returns data stored in a PivotTable.
HLOOKUP	Searches for a value in the top row of a table and then returns a value in the same column from a row you specify in the table.
HYPERLINK	Creates a shortcut that opens a document on your hard drive, a server, or the Internet.
INDEX	Uses an index to choose a value from a reference or array.
INDIRECT	Returns a reference indicated by a text value.
LOOKUP	Returns a value from either a one-row or one-column range or from an array.
MATCH	Returns the relative position of an item in an array.
OFFSET	Returns a reference offset from a given reference.
ROW	Returns the row number of a reference.
ROWS	Returns the number of rows in a reference.
RTD	Returns real-time data from a program that supports COM automation.
TRANSPOSE	Returns the transpose of an array.
VLOOKUP	Searches for a value in the leftmost column of a table and then returns a value in the same row from a column you specify in the table.

TABLE A.10

Math & Trig Category Functions

Function	What It Does
ABS	Returns the absolute value of a number.
ACOS	Returns the arccosine of a number.
ACOSH	Returns the inverse hyperbolic cosine of a number.
AGGREGATE**	Returns an aggregate in a list or database.
ASIN	Returns the arcsine of a number.

Function	What It Does
ASINH	Returns the inverse hyperbolic sine of a number.
ATAN	Returns the arctangent of a number.
ATAN2	Returns the arctangent from x and y coordinates.
ATANH	Returns the inverse hyperbolic tangent of a number.
CEILING	Rounds a number to the nearest integer or to the nearest multiple of significance.
CEILING.PRECISE**	Rounds a number up to the nearest integer or to the nearest multiple of significance, regardless of the sign of the number.
COMBIN	Returns the number of combinations for a given number of objects.
COS	Returns the cosine of a number.
COSH	Returns the hyperbolic cosine of a number.
DEGREES	Converts radians to degrees.
EVEN	Rounds a number up to the nearest even integer.
EXP	Returns e raised to the power of a given number.
FACT	Returns the factorial of a number.
FACTDOUBLE	Returns the double factorial of a number.
FLOOR	Rounds a number down, toward 0.
FLOOR.PRECISE**	Rounds a number down to the nearest integer or to the nearest multiple of significance, regardless of the sign.
GCD	Returns the greatest common divisor.
INT	Rounds a number down to the nearest integer.
ISO.CEILING**	Returns a number that is rounded up to the nearest integer or to the nearest multiple of significance.
LCM	Returns the least common multiple.
LN	Returns the natural logarithm of a number.
LOG	Returns the logarithm of a number to a specified base.
LOG10	Returns the base-10 logarithm of a number.
MDETERM	Returns the matrix determinant of an array.
MINVERSE	Returns the matrix inverse of an array.
MMULT	Returns the matrix product of two arrays.
MOD	Returns the remainder from division.
MROUND	Returns a number rounded to the desired multiple.
MULTINOMIAL	Returns the multinomial of a set of numbers.
ODD	Rounds a number up to the nearest odd integer.

continued

TABLE A.10 (continued)

Function	What It Does
PI	Returns the value of pi.
POWER	Returns the result of a number raised to a power.
PRODUCT	Multiplies its arguments.
QUOTIENT	Returns the integer portion of a division.
RADIANS	Converts degrees to radians.
RAND	Returns a random number between 0 and 1.
RANDBETWEEN	Returns a random number between the numbers that you specify.
ROMAN	Converts an Arabic numeral to Roman, as text.
ROUND	Rounds a number to a specified number of digits.
ROUNDDOWN	Rounds a number down, toward 0.
ROUNDUP	Rounds a number up, away from 0.
SERIESSUM	Returns the sum of a power series based on the formula.
SIGN	Returns the sign of a number.
SIN	Returns the sine of the given angle.
SINH	Returns the hyperbolic sine of a number.
SQRT	Returns a positive square root.
SQRTPI	Returns the square root of pi.
SUBTOTAL	Returns a subtotal in a list or database.
SUM	Adds its arguments.
SUMIF	Adds the cells specified by a given criteria.
SUMIFS*	Adds the cells specified by a multiple criteria.
SUMPRODUCT	Returns the sum of the products of corresponding array components.
SUMSQ	Returns the sum of the squares of the arguments.
SUMX2MY2	Returns the sum of the difference of squares of corresponding values in two arrays.
SUMX2PY2	Returns the sum of the sum of squares of corresponding values in two arrays.
SUMXMY2	Returns the sum of squares of differences of corresponding values in two arrays.
TAN	Returns the tangent of a number.
TANH	Returns the hyperbolic tangent of a number.
TRUNC	Truncates a number (you specify the precision of the truncation).

* Indicates a function introduced in Excel 2007.

** Indicates a function introduced in Excel 2010.

TABLE A.11

Statistical Category Functions

Function	What It Does
AVEDEV	Returns the average of the absolute deviations of data points from their mean.
AVERAGE	Returns the average of its arguments.
AVERAGEA	Returns the average of its arguments and includes evaluation of text and logical values.
AVERAGEIF*	Returns the average for the cells specified by a given criterion.
AVERAGEIFS*	Returns the average for the cells specified by multiple criteria.
BETA.DIST**	Returns the beta cumulative distribution function.
BETA.INV**	Returns the inverse of the cumulative distribution function for a specified beta distribution.
BINOM.DIST**	Returns the individual term binomial distribution probability.
BINOM.INV**	Returns the smallest value for which the cumulative binomial distribution is less than or equal to a criterion value.
CHISQ.DIST**	Returns the chi-square distribution
CHISQ.DIST.RT**	Returns the right-tailed probability of the chi-squared distribution.
CHISQ.INV**	Returns the inverse of the left-tailed probability of the chi-squared distribution
CHISQ.INV.RT**	Returns the inverse of the right-tailed probability of the chi-squared distribution.
CHISQ.TEST**	Returns the test for independence.
CONFIDENCE.NORM**	Returns the confidence interval for a population mean.
CONFIDENCE.T**	Returns the confidence interval for a population mean, using a student's t-distribution.
CORREL	Returns the correlation coefficient between two data sets.
COUNT	Counts how many numbers are in the list of arguments.
COUNTA	Counts how many values are in the list of arguments.
COUNTBLANK	Counts the number of blank cells in the argument range.
COUNTIF	Counts the number of cells that meet the criteria you specify in the argument.
COUNTIFS*	Counts the number of cells that meet multiple criteria.
COVARIANCE.P**	Returns covariance, the average of the products of paired deviations.
COVARIANCE.S**	Returns the sample covariance, the average of the products deviations for each data point pair in two data sets.
DEVSQ	Returns the sum of squares of deviations.
EXPON.DIST**	Returns the exponential distribution.
F.DIST**	Returns the F probability distribution.
F.DIST.RT**	Returns the F probability distribution.
F.INV**	Returns the inverse of the F probability distribution.
F.INV.RT**	Returns the inverse of the F probability distribution.

continued

TABLE A.11 *(continued)*

Function	What It Does
F.TEST**	Returns the result of an F-test.
FISHER	Returns the Fisher transformation.
FISHERINV	Returns the inverse of the Fisher transformation.
FORECAST	Returns a value along a linear trend.
FREQUENCY	Returns a frequency distribution as a vertical array.
GAMMA.DIST**	Returns the gamma distribution.
GAMMA.INV**	Returns the inverse of the gamma cumulative distribution.
GAMMALN.PRECISE**	Returns the natural logarithm of the gamma function, G(x).
GAMMALN	Returns the natural logarithm of the gamma function, G(x).
GEOMEAN	Returns the geometric mean.
GROWTH	Returns values along an exponential trend.
HARMEAN	Returns the harmonic mean.
HYPGEOM.DIST**	Returns the hypergeometric distribution.
INTERCEPT	Returns the intercept of the linear regression line.
KURT	Returns the kurtosis of a data set.
LARGE	Returns the *k*th largest value in a data set.
LINEST	Returns the parameters of a linear trend.
LOGEST	Returns the parameters of an exponential trend.
LOGNORM.DIST**	Returns the cumulative lognormal distribution.
LOGNORM.INV**	Returns the inverse of the lognormal cumulative distribution.
MAX	Returns the maximum value in a list of arguments, ignoring logical values and text.
MAXA	Returns the maximum value in a list of arguments, including logical values and text.
MEDIAN	Returns the median of the given numbers.
MIN	Returns the minimum value in a list of arguments, ignoring logical values and text.
MINA	Returns the minimum value in a list of arguments, including logical values and text.
MODE.MULT**	Returns a vertical array of the most frequently occurring, or repetitive values in an array or range of data.
MODE.SNGL**	Returns the most common value in a data set.
NEGBINOM.DIST**	Returns the negative binomial distribution.
NORM.DIST**	Returns the normal cumulative distribution.
NORM.INV**	Returns the inverse of the normal cumulative distribution.
NORM.S.DIST**	Returns the standard normal cumulative distribution.
NORM.S.INV**	Returns the inverse of the standard normal cumulative distribution.
PEARSON	Returns the Pearson product moment correlation coefficient.

Function	What It Does
PERCENTILE.EXC**	Returns the kth percentile of values in a range, where k is in the range 0 through 1, exclusive.
PERCENTILE.INC**	Returns the kth percentile of values in a range
PERCENTRANK.EXC**	Returns the rank of a value in a data set as a percentage (0 through 1, exclusive) of the data set.
PERCENTRANK.INC**	Returns the percentage rank of a value in a data set.
PERMUT	Returns the number of permutations for a given number of objects.
POISSON.DIST**	Returns the Poisson distribution.
PROB	Returns the probability that values in a range are between two limits.
QUARTILE.EXC**	Returns the quartile of the data set, based on percentile values from 0through1, exclusive.
QUARTILE.INC**	Returns the quartile of a data set.
RANK.AVG**	Returns the rank of a number in a list of numbers.
RANK.EQ**	Returns the rank of a number in a list of numbers.
RSQ	Returns the square of the Pearson product moment correlation coefficient.
SKEW	Returns the skewness of a distribution.
SLOPE	Returns the slope of the linear regression line.
SMALL	Returns the kth smallest value in a data set.
STANDARDIZE	Returns a normalized value.
STDEV.P**	Calculates standard deviation based on the entire population.
STDEV.S**	Estimates standard deviation based on a sample.
STDEVA	Estimates standard deviation based on a sample, including text and logical values.
STDEVPA	Calculates standard deviation based on the entire population, including text and logical values.
STEYX	Returns the standard error of the predicted y-value for each x in the regression.
T.DIST	Returns the Percentage Points (probability) for the student T-distribution.
T.DIST.2T**	Returns the Percentage Points (probability) for the Student T-distribution.
T.DIST.RT**	Returns the student's T-distribution.
T.INV**	Returns the t-value of the student's T-distribution as a function of the probability and the degrees of freedom.
T.INV.2T**	Returns the inverse of the student's T-distribution.
T.TEST**	Returns the probability associated with a student's T-test.
TREND	Returns values along a linear trend.
TRIMMEAN	Returns the mean of the interior of a data set.
VAR.P**	Calculates variance based on the entire population.
VAR.S**	Estimates variance based on a sample.
VARA	Estimates variance based on a sample, including logical values and text.

continued

TABLE A.11	(continued)
Function	**What It Does**
VARPA	Calculates variance based on the entire population, including logical values and text.
WEIBULL.DIST**	Returns the Weibull distribution.
Z.TEST**	Returns the one-tailed probability-value of a Z-test.

* Indicates a function introduced in Excel 2007.

** Indicates a function introduced in Excel 2010.

TABLE A.12

Text Category Functions

Function	**What It Does**
BAHTTEXT	Converts a number to Baht text.
CHAR	Returns the character specified by the code number.
CLEAN	Removes all nonprintable characters from text.
CODE	Returns a numeric code for the first character in a text string.
CONCATENATE	Joins several text items into one text item.
DOLLAR	Converts a number to text, using currency format.
EXACT	Checks to see whether two text values are identical.
FIND	Finds one text value within another (case-sensitive).
FIXED	Formats a number as text with a fixed number of decimals.
LEFT	Returns the leftmost characters from a text value.
LEN	Returns the number of characters in a text string.
LOWER	Converts text to lowercase.
MID	Returns a specific number of characters from a text string, starting at the position you specify.
PROPER	Capitalizes the first letter in each word of a text value.
REPLACE	Replaces characters within text.
REPT	Repeats text a given number of times.
RIGHT	Returns the rightmost characters from a text value.
SEARCH	Finds one text value within another (not case-sensitive).
SUBSTITUTE	Substitutes new text for old text in a text string.
T	Returns the text referred to by value.
TEXT	Formats a number and converts it to text.
TRIM	Removes excess spaces from text.
UPPER	Converts text to uppercase.
VALUE	Converts a text argument to a number.

What's on the CD-ROM

This appendix describes the contents of the CD that accompanies this book. For any last minute changes, please refer to the ReadMe file located at the root of the CD.

This appendix provides information on the following topics:

- System Requirements
- Using the CD
- Files and software on the CD
- Troubleshooting

System Requirements

Make sure that your computer meets these minimum requirements:

- A Windows PC with Microsoft Excel 2010 installed.
- A CD-ROM drive.

Using the CD

To install the items from the CD to your hard drive, follow these steps:

1. **Insert the CD-ROM into your computer's CD drive.**
2. **Read through the license agreement and then click the Accept button if you want to use the CD.**

Note

The interface won't launch if you have autorun (or autoplay) disabled. In that case, choose Start ➪ Run. In the dialog box that appears, type `D:\start.exe`. (Replace D with the proper letter if your CD drive uses a different letter. If you don't know the letter, see how your CD drive is listed under My Computer.) ∎

You can then view the directory structure on the CD.

What's on the CD

The following sections provide more details about the software and other materials available on the CD.

Applications

Adobe Reader

Adobe Reader is a freeware application for viewing files in the Adobe Portable Document format.

Freeware programs are copyrighted games, applications, and utilities that are free for personal use. Unlike shareware, these programs do not require a fee or provide technical support.

eBook version of *Excel 2010 Bible*

The complete text of the book you hold in your hands is provided on the CD in Adobe's Portable Document Format (PDF). You can read and quickly search the content of this PDF file by using Adobe's Acrobat Reader.

Sample files for *Excel 2010 Bible*

The files discussed in the book are organized by chapter. With a few exceptions, the files are all Excel 2010 files that have either of the following extensions:

- XLSX: An Excel workbook file
- XLSM: An Excel workbook file that contains VBA macros

When you open an XLSM file, Excel may display a Security Warning and tell you that macros have been disabled. To enable macros, click the Enable Content button in the Security Warning panel.

Because the files on this CD are from a trusted source, you may want to copy the files to your hard drive and then designate the folder as a trusted location. To do so, follow these steps:

1. **Open an Explorer window, and select the CD-ROM drive that contains the companion CD-ROM.**
2. **Right-click the folder that corresponds to the root folder for the samples files, and choose Copy from the shortcut menu.**
3. **Activate the folder on your hard drive where you'd like to copy the files.** Right-click the directory, and choose Paste from the shortcut menu.

The CD-ROM files will be copied to a subfolder in the folder you specified in Step 3. To designate this new folder as a trusted location:

1. **Start Excel and choose File ⇨ Options to display the Excel Options dialog box.**
2. **In the Excel Options dialog box, click the Trust Center tab.**
3. **Click the Trust Center Settings button.**
4. **In the Trust Center dialog box, click the Trusted Locations tab.**
5. **Click the Add New Location button to display the Microsoft Office Trusted Location dialog box.**
6. **In the Microsoft Office Trusted Location dialog box, click the Browse button and locate the folder that contains the files you copied from the CD-ROM.**
7. **Make sure that you select the option labeled Subfolders Of This Location Are Also Trusted.**

After performing these steps, when you open XLSM files from this location, the macros are enabled and you don't see the security warning.

Following is a list of the sample files, along with a brief description.

Note
Some chapters don't use any sample files. ■

Chapter 01
- `table and chart.xlsx`: An introductory hands-on example that creates a table and a chart.

Chapter 02
- `loan payment calculator.xlsx`: A workbook that demonstrates the difference between unformatted cells and formatted cells.
- `number formatting.xlsx`: A workbook with some examples of number formatting.

Chapter 04
- `budget.xlsx`: A simple multisheet budget workbook to demonstrate formatting across worksheets.

Chapter 05
- `real estate table.xlsx`: A workbook that contains a table of real estate listings for practice working with tables.

Chapter 06
- `background image.xlsx`: A workbook that contains a background image for a worksheet.
- `loan payments.xlsx`: A workbook that contains a range of data and formulas to demonstrate the effect of applying simple formatting.

- `text alignment.xlsx`: A workbook that demonstrates different types of horizontal text alignment.
- `theme examples.xlsx`: A workbook that contains a table, SmartArt, and a chart to demonstrate the effect of applying different document themes.

Chapter 10

- `cell references.xlsx`: A workbook used to demonstrate the effect of using different types of cell references when copying formulas.
- `circular reference.xlsx`: A workbook that demonstrates an intentional circular reference. When you open this workbook, you see a message informing you of the circular reference.
- `table formulas.xlsx`: A workbook used to demonstrate the use of formulas within a table.

Chapter 11

- `character set.xlsm`: A workbook that displays the characters available in any font installed on your system.
- `extract names.xlsx`: A workbook that contains formulas to extract first, middle, and last names.
- `text formula examples.xlsx`: A workbook that contains examples of advanced text formulas.
- `text histogram.xlsx`: A workbook that contains two examples of creating a histogram directly in a range.

Chapter 12

- `holidays.xlsx`: A workbook that demonstrates how to calculate the date for 10 U.S. holidays.
- `jogging log.xlsx`: A workbook that tracks time and distanced jogged. Demonstrates the use of times not associated with a time of day.
- `time sheet.xlsm`: A workbook that tracks hours worked during a week.
- `work days.xlsx`: A workbook that demonstrates how to calculate the number of work days between two dates (excluding weekends and holidays).
- `XDATE demo.xlsm`: A workbook that contains custom functions that allow you to work with dates prior to 1900.

Chapter 13

- `basic counting.xlsx`: A workbook that demonstrates basic counting formulas.
- `conditional sum.xlsx`: A workbook that demonstrates how to calculate conditional sums, using single and multiple criteria.
- `count unique.xlsx`: A workbook that demonstrates how to count unique (nonduplicated) items in a range.

- `counting text in a range.xlsx`: A workbook that demonstrates various ways to count text in a range.
- `cumulative sum.xlsx`: A workbook that demonstrates how to display a cumulative sum.
- `frequency distribution.xlsx`: A workbook that demonstrates four methods to create a frequency distribution.
- `multiple criteria counting.xlsx`: A workbook that demonstrates counting formulas that use multiple criteria.

Chapter 14

- `basic lookup examples.xlsx`: A workbook that demonstrates a variety of common lookup techniques.
- `specialized lookup examples.xlsx`: A workbook that demonstrates a variety of specialized lookup techniques.

Chapter 15

- `annuity calculator.xlsx`: A workbook that calculates interest on annuities.
- `credit card payments.xlsx`: A workbook that contains formulas to calculate credit card payments.
- `depreciation calculations.xlsx`: A workbook that demonstrates methods to calculate depreciation of an asset.
- `investment calculations.xlsx`: A workbook that demonstrates formulas to calculate interest on investments.
- `irregular payments.xlsx`: A workbook that calculates a loan with irregular payments.
- `loan amortization schedule.xlsx`: A workbook that calculates a loan amortization schedule.
- `loan data tables.xlsx`: A workbook that demonstrates how to use 1-way and 2-way data tables to calculate loan information.
- `loan payment.xlsx`: A workbook that contains formulas to calculate loan payments.

Chapter 16

- `array examples.xlsx`: A workbook that contains examples of array formulas.

Chapter 17

- `array formula calendar.xlsx`: A workbook that displays a calendar for any month by using a complex array formula.
- `multi-cell array formulas.xlsx`: A workbook that demonstrates a variety of multicell array formulas.
- `single-cell array formulas.xlsx`: A workbook that demonstrates a variety of single-cell array formulas.
- `yearly calendar.xlsx`: A workbook that displays monthly calendars for any year by using a complex array formula.

Chapter 18

- `area charts.xlsx`: A workbook that contains an area chart example.
- `bar charts.xlsx`: A workbook that contains bar chart examples.
- `bubble charts.xlsx`: A workbook that contains bubble chart examples.
- `column charts.xlsx`: A workbook that contains various types of column charts.
- `doughnut charts.xlsx`: A workbook that contains a doughnut chart example.
- `hands-on example.xlsx`: A workbook that contains data used in the hands-on charting example.
- `line charts.xlsx`: A workbook that contains bar chart examples.
- `pie charts.xlsx`: A workbook that contains pie chart examples.
- `radar charts.xlsx`: A workbook that contains radar chart examples.
- `six chart types.xlsx`: A workbook that shows a single range, displayed using six chart types.
- `stock charts.xlsx`: A workbook that contains stock chart examples.
- `surface charts.xlsx`: A workbook that contains a surface chart example.
- `xy charts.xlsx`: A workbook that contains XY chart examples.

Chapter 19

- `comparative histogram.xlsx`: A workbook that demonstrates how to create a comparative histogram chart.
- `conditional colors.xlsx`: A workbook that contains a chart that displays different color columns, based on the value.
- `function plot 2D.xlsx`: A workbook that demonstrates how to plot a function that uses one variable.
- `function plot 3D.xlsm`: A workbook that demonstrates how to plot a function that uses two variables.
- `gantt chart.xlsx`: A workbook that demonstrates how to create a simple Gantt chart for project planning.
- `gauge chart.xlsx`: A workbook that contains a chart that plots a single data point as a gauge.
- `log scale.xlsx`: A workbook that demonstrates a logarithmic scale on a chart.
- `picture charts.xlsx`: A workbook that demonstrates the use of pictures in charts.
- `thermometer chart.xlsx`: A workbook that contains a chart that plots a single data point as a thermometer.
- `weather combination chart.xlsx`: A workbook that demonstrates a combination chart with two value axes.

Chapter 20

- `color scale example.xlsx`: A workbook that demonstrates a conditional formatting color scale.
- `conditional formatting examples.xlsx`: A workbook that contains examples of various types of conditional formatting.
- `conditional formatting formulas.xlsx`: A workbook that demonstrates a variety of conditional formatting formulas.
- `data bars examples.xlsx`: A workbook that demonstrates conditional formatting data bars.
- `extreme color scale.xlsx`: A workbook that demonstrates a conditional formatting color scale in a large range.
- `icon set examples.xlsx`: A workbook that demonstrates a conditional formatting icon set.

Chapter 21

- `sparkline examples.xlsx`: A workbook that contains examples of Sparklines.

Chapter 22

- `photo styles.xlsx`: A workbook that contains examples of styles applied to a photo.
- `shape examples.xlsx`: A workbook that contains examples of shapes.
- `smartart demo xlsx`: A workbook that contains SmartArt.
- `smartart org chart.xlsx`: A workbook that contains an organizational chart created using SmartArt.
- `wordart examples.xlsx`: A workbook that contains examples of WordArt.

Chapter 24

- `number formats.xlsx`: A workbook that contains examples of many custom number formats.

Chapter 25

- `data validation examples.xlsx`: A workbook that contains examples that demonstrate data validation.

Chapter 26

- `outline example.xlsx`: A workbook that contains data suitable for an outline.

Chapter 27

- `dependent.xlsx`: A workbook used to demonstrate linking (uses `source.xlsx`).
- `region1.xlsx`: One of three workbooks used to demonstrate data consolidation.
- `region2.xlsx`: One of three workbooks used to demonstrate data consolidation.

- `region3.xlsx`: One of three workbooks used to demonstrate data consolidation.
- `source.xlsx`: A workbook used to demonstrate linking (uses dependent.xlsx).

Chapter 28
- `webpage.xlsx`: A workbook used to demonstrate HTML exporting.

Chapter 33
- `budget data.accdb`: A single-table Microsoft Access database file, used to demonstrate Microsoft Query.

Chapter 34
- `bank accounts.xlsx`: A workbook that contains data suitable for a pivot table.
- `normalized data.xlsx`: A workbook that demonstrates normalized data.

Chapter 35
- `calculated fields and items.xlsx`: A workbook that contains a pivot table that demonstrates calculated fields and calculated items.
- `county data.xlsx`: A workbook that contains a large table and a pivot table created from the table.
- `employee list.xlsx`: A workbook that contains a table to demonstrate the use of non-numeric data in a pivot table.
- `hourly readings.xlsx`: A workbook that contains time-based information to demonstrate grouping item by time.
- `income and expense.xlsx`: A workbook that contains a pivot table to demonstrate how to reference cells within a pivot table.
- `music list.xlsx`: A workbook that demonstrates how to create and format a pivot table report.
- `reverse pivot.xlsm`: A workbook that contains a VBA macro that converts a summary table into a 3-column database table.
- `sales by date.xlsx`: A workbook that contains time-based information to demonstrate grouping items by date.
- `sales by region pivot chart.xlsx`: A workbook that demonstrates how to create a pivot chart from a pivot table.
- `test scores.xlsx`: A workbook that demonstrates how to use a pivot table to create a frequency distribution.

Chapter 36
- `direct mail.xlsx`: A workbook that contains a profit model to demonstrate how to create a 2-way data table for what-if analysis.
- `mortgage loan.xlsx`: A workbook with input cells and formula cells to demonstrate what-if analysis.

- `mortgage loan data table.xlsx`: A workbook that demonstrate how to create a data 1-way data table for what-if analysis.
- `production model.xlsx`: A workbook to demonstrate the Scenario Manager.

Chapter 37

- `allocating resources.xlsx`: A workbook that contains a model to demonstrate how to allocate resources and maximize profit using Solver.
- `investment portfolio.xlsx`: A workbook that contains a model to demonstrate how to maximize the return on an investment portfolio using Solver.
- `linear equations.xlsx`: A workbook that demonstrates how to use Solver to solve a set of linear equations.
- `mortgage loan.xlsx`: A workbook with input cells and formula cells to demonstrate goal seeking.
- `shipping costs.xlsx`: A workbook that contains a model to demonstrate how to minimize shipping costs using Solver.
- `three products.xlsx`: A workbook that contains a simple profit model to demonstrate Solver.

Chapter 38

- `atp examples.xlsx`: A workbook that demonstrates the tools in the Analysis ToolPak add-in.

Chapter 39

- `cube root.xlsm`: A workbook that contains a VBA function to calculate the cube root.
- `current date.xlsm`: A workbook that contains a simple VBA macro to insert the current date into the active cell.
- `list formulas.xlsm`: A workbook that contains a VBA macro to generate a list of all formulas in a worksheet.

Chapter 40

- `vba functions.xlsm`: A workbook that contains examples of VBA functions used in worksheet formulas.

Chapter 41

- `change case.xlsm`: A VBA macro that uses a UserForm to enable the user to make a choice.
- `show message.xlsm`: A workbook that contains a UserForm that displays a message.

Chapter 42

- `mortgage loan.xlsx`: A workbook that demonstrates how to use ActiveX controls on a worksheet, with no macros.
- `worksheet controls.xlsm`: A workbook that contains examples of all ActiveX controls that can be used on a worksheet.

Chapter 43

- `monitor a range.xlsm`: A workbook that contains a VBA `Worksheet_Change` macro that monitors all changes made to a specific range.
- `selection change event.xlsm`: A workbook that contains a VBA `Selection_Change` macro that changes the color of the row and column of the active cell.

Chapter 44

- `chart macros.xlsm`: A workbook that contains VBA macros that manipulate charts.
- `range copy.xlsm`: A workbook that contains a VBA macro that copies a variable-sized range.
- `range move.xlsm`: A workbook that contains a VBA macro that moves a range of cells.
- `select cells.xlsm`: A workbook that contains VBA macros that demonstrate range selection techniques.
- `selection type.xlsm`: A workbook that contains a VBA macro that demonstrates how to identify the object type of the current selection.
- `skip blanks while looping.xlsm`: A workbook that contains a VBA macro that demonstrates how to loop through a range of cells efficiently.

Chapter 45

- `change case.xlam`: An add-in file, created from the change case.xlsm example in Chapter 41.

Troubleshooting

If you have difficulty installing or using any of the materials on the companion CD, try the following solutions:

- **Turn off any antivirus software that you may have running.** Installers sometimes mimic virus activity and can make your computer incorrectly believe that it is being infected by a virus. (Be sure to turn the antivirus software back on later.)
- **Close all running programs.** The more programs you're running, the less memory is available to other programs. Installers also typically update files and programs; if you keep other programs running, installation may not work properly.
- **Reference the ReadMe:** Refer to the ReadMe file located at the root of the CD-ROM for the latest product information (if any) at the time of publication.

Customer Care

If you have trouble with the CD-ROM, please call the Wiley Product Technical Support phone number at (800) 762-2974. Outside the United States, call 1(317) 572-3994. You can also contact Wiley Product Technical Support at **http://support.wiley.com**. John Wiley & Sons will provide technical support only for installation and other general quality control items. For technical support on the applications themselves, consult the program's vendor or author.

To place additional orders or to request information about other Wiley products, please call (877) 762-2974.

Additional Excel Resources

I f I've done my job, the information provided in this book will be very useful to you. The book, however, can't cover every conceivable topic about Excel. Therefore, I've compiled a list of additional resources that you may find helpful.

I classify these resources into four categories: Excel's Help System, Microsoft technical support, Internet newsgroups, and Internet Web sites.

The Excel Help System

Many users tend to forget about an excellent source of information: the Excel Help system. This Help information is available by clicking the question mark icon in the upper-right corner of Excel's window. Or, just press F1. Either method displays Excel Help in a new window. Type your search query and then click Search.

Note
The Search button is a drop-down control that lets you specify what and where to search. ∎

The Excel Help system isn't perfect — it often provides only superficial help and ignores some topics altogether — but, if you're stuck, a quick search of the Help system may be worth a try.

Microsoft Technical Support

Technical support is the common term for assistance provided by a software vendor. In this case, I'm talking about assistance that comes directly from Microsoft. Its technical support is available in several different forms.

Support options

The Microsoft support options are constantly changing. To find out what options are available (both free and fee-based), go to

    http://support.microsoft.com

Microsoft Knowledge Base

Perhaps your best bet for solving a problem may be the Microsoft Knowledge Base, which is the primary Microsoft product information source. This extensive, searchable database comprises tens of thousands of detailed articles containing technical information, bug lists, fix lists, and more.

You have free and unlimited access to the Knowledge Base via the Internet. To access the Knowledge Base, use the following URL and then click Search the Knowledge Base:

    http://support.microsoft.com/search

Microsoft Excel Home Page

The official home page of Excel is at

    http://www.microsoft.com/office/excel

This site contains a variety of material, such as tips, templates, answers to questions, training materials, and links to companion products.

Microsoft Office Home Page

For information about Office 2010 (including Excel), try this site:

    http://office.microsoft.com

You'll find product updates, add-ins, examples, and lots of other useful information.

Note

As you know, the Internet is a dynamic entity that changes rapidly. Web sites are often reorganized, so a particular URL listed in this appendix may not be available when you try to access it. ∎

Internet Newsgroups

Usenet is an Internet service that provides access to several thousand special interest groups that enable you to communicate with people who share common interests. A newsgroup works like a public bulletin board. You can post a message or questions, and (usually) others reply to your message.

Thousands of newsgroups cover virtually every topic you can think of (and many that you haven't thought of). Typically, questions posed on a newsgroup are answered within 24 hours — assuming, of course, that you ask the questions in a manner that makes others want to reply.

Accessing newsgroups by using a newsreader

You can use newsreader software to access the Usenet newsgroups. Many such programs are available, but you probably already have one installed: Microsoft Outlook Express, which is installed with Internet Explorer.

Microsoft maintains an extensive list of newsgroups, including quite a few devoted to Excel. If your Internet service provider (ISP) doesn't carry the Microsoft newsgroups, you can access them directly from the Microsoft's news server. (In fact, that's the preferred method.) You need to configure your newsreader software (not your Web browser) to access Microsoft's news server at this address:

```
msnews.microsoft.com
```

Accessing newsgroups by using a Web browser

As an alternative to using newsreader software, you can read and post to the Microsoft newsgroups directly from your Web browser. This option is often significantly slower than using standard newsgroup software and is best suited for situations in which newsgroup access is prohibited by network policies.

- Access thousands of newsgroups at Google Groups. The URL is

  ```
  http://groups.google.com
  ```
- Access the Microsoft newsgroups (including Excel newsgroups) from this URL:

  ```
  www.microsoft.com/communities/newsgroups/default.mspx
  ```

Table C.1 lists the most popular English-language Excel newsgroups found on the Microsoft news server (and also available at Google Groups).

TABLE C.1

The Microsoft.com Excel-Related Newsgroups

Newsgroup	Topic
`microsoft.public.excel`	General Excel topics
`microsoft.public.excel.charting`	Building charts with Excel
`microsoft.public.excel.interopoledde`	OLE, DDE, and other cross-application issues
`microsoft.public.excel.macintosh`	Excel issues on the Macintosh operating system
`microsoft.public.excel.misc`	General topics that don't fit one of the other categories
`microsoft.public.excel.newusers`	Help for newcomers to Excel
`microsoft.public.excel.printing`	Printing with Excel
`microsoft.public.excel.programming`	Programming Excel with VBA macros
`microsoft.public.excel.templates`	Spreadsheet Solutions templates and other Xlt files
`microsoft.public.excel.worksheet.functions`	Worksheet functions

Searching newsgroups

The fastest way to find a quick answer to a question is to search the past newsgroup postings. Often, searching past newsgroup postings is an excellent alternative to posting a question to the newsgroup because you can get the answer immediately. Unless your question is very obscure, there's an excellent chance that your question has already been asked and answered. The best source for searching newsgroup postings is Google Groups, at the following Web address:

```
http://groups.google.com
```

How does searching work? Suppose that you have a problem identifying unique values in a range of cells. You can perform a search using the following keywords: **Excel**, **Range**, and **Unique**. The Google search engine probably will find dozens of newsgroup postings that deal with these topics.

If the number of results is too large, refine your search by adding search terms. Sifting through the messages may take a while, but you have an excellent chance of finding an answer to your question. In fact, I estimate that at least 90 percent of the questions posted in the Excel newsgroups can be answered by searching Google Groups.

Tips for Posting to a Newsgroup

If you're new to online newsgroups, here are some pointers:

- Conduct a search to make sure that your question has not already been answered.

- Make the subject line descriptive. Postings with a subject line such as "Help me!" and "Another Question" are less likely to be answered than postings with a more specific subject, such as "Sizing a Chart's Plot Area."

- Specify the Excel version that you use. In many cases, the answer to your question depends on your version of Excel.

- For best results, ask only one question per message.

- Make your question as specific as possible.

- Keep your question brief and to the point but provide enough information so that someone can answer it adequately.

- Indicate what you've done to try to answer your own question.

- Post in the appropriate newsgroup, and don't cross-post to other groups unless the question applies to multiple groups.

- Don't type in all uppercase or all lowercase; check your grammar and spelling.

- Don't include a file attachment.

- Avoid posting in HTML format. Plain text is the preferred format.

- If you request an e-mail reply in addition to a newsgroup reply, don't use an "anti-spam" e-mail address that requires the responder to modify your address. Why cause extra work for someone doing you a favor?

Internet Web sites

The World Wide Web has dozens of excellent sites devoted to Excel. I list a few of my favorites here.

The Spreadsheet Page

This is my own Web site, which contains files to download, developer tips, spreadsheet jokes, an extensive list of links to other Excel sites, and information about my books. The URL is

```
http://spreadsheetpage.com
```

Daily Dose of Excel

This is a frequently updated weblog created by Dick Kusleika, with about a dozen contributors. It covers a variety of topics, and readers can leave comments. The URL is

```
http://dailydoseofexcel.com
```

Jon Peltier's Excel Page

Those who frequent the `microsoft.public.excel.charting` newsgroup are familiar with Jon Peltier. Jon has an uncanny ability to solve practically any chart-related problem. His Web site contains many Excel tips and an extensive collection of charting examples. The URL is

```
http://peltiertech.com/Excel
```

Pearson Software Consulting

This site, maintained by Chip Pearson, contains dozens of useful examples of VBA and clever formula techniques. The URL is

```
www.cpearson.com/excel.htm
```

Contextures

This site, maintained by Deborah Dalgleish, covers Excel and Access. The URL is

```
http://contextures.com
```

David McRitchie's Excel Pages

David's site is jam-packed with useful Excel information and is updated frequently. The URL is

```
www.mvps.org/dmcritchie/excel/excel.htm
```

Pointy Haired Dilbert

An interesting Excel blog by Chandoo. The URL is

```
http://chandoo.org/wp
```

Mr. Excel

Mr. Excel, also known as Bill Jelen, maintains an extensive site devoted to Excel. The site also features a message board. The URL is

```
www.mrexcel.com
```

Excel Shortcut Keys

M any users have discovered that using their keyboard can often be much more efficient than using their mouse. This appendix lists the most useful shortcut keys available in Excel. The shortcuts are arranged by context.

The keys listed assume that you're not using the Transition Navigation Keys, which are designed to emulate Lotus 1-2-3. You can select the Transition Navigation Keys option of the Advanced tab of the Excel Options dialog box. This option is in the Lotus Compatibility section.

Note

On the surface, the Ribbon interface appears to be designed for a mouse. However, you can access nearly all the Ribbon commands by using the keyboard. Press the Alt key, and Excel displays "keytips" next to each command. Just press the key that corresponds to the command you need. For example, the command to toggle worksheet gridlines is View ➪ Show ➪ Gridlines. The keyboard equivalent is Alt, followed by WVG. Note that you don't need to keep the Alt key depressed while you type the subsequent letters. ■

TABLE D.1

Moving through a Worksheet

Key(s)	What It Does
Navigation keys (←, →, ↑, ↓)	Moves left, right, up, or down one cell
Home	Moves to the beginning of the row
Home*	Moves to the upper-left cell displayed in the window
End*	Moves to the lower-left cell displayed in the window
Navigation keys*	Scrolls left, right, up, or down one cell
PgUp	Moves up one screen
PgDn	Moves down one screen
Ctrl+PgUp	Moves to the previous sheet
Ctrl+PgDn	Moves to the next sheet
Alt+PgUp	Moves one screen to the left
Alt+PgDn	Moves one screen to the right
Ctrl+Home	Moves to the first cell in the worksheet (A1)
Ctrl+End	Moves to the last nonempty cell of the worksheet
Ctrl+navigation key	Moves to the edge of a data block; if the cell is blank, moves to the first nonblank cell
Ctrl+Backspace	Scrolls to display the active cell
End, followed by Home	Moves to the last nonempty cell on the worksheet
F5	Prompts for a cell address to go to
F6	Moves to the next pane of a window that has been split
Shift+F6	Moves to the previous pane of a window that has been split
Ctrl+Tab	Moves to the next window
Ctrl+Shift+Tab	Moves to the previous window
Ctrl+F6	Moves to the next window
Ctrl+Shift+F6	Moves to the previous window

* With Scroll Lock on

TABLE D.2

Selecting Cells in the Worksheet

Key(s)	What It Does
Shift+navigation key	Expands the selection in the direction indicated.
Shift+spacebar	Selects the entire row(s) in the selected range.
Ctrl+spacebar	Selects the entire column(s) in the selected range.

Key(s)	What It Does
Ctrl+Shift+spacebar	Selects the entire worksheet.
Ctrl+Shift+spacebar	If the active cell is within a table. Selects the table without the header row and totals row. Pressing Ctrl+Shift+spacebar again selects the complete table. Pressing Ctrl+Shift+spacebar again selects the entire worksheet.
Shift+Home	Expands the selection to the beginning of the current row.
Ctrl+*	If the active cell is within a multicell range, selects the block of data surrounding the active cell.
F8	Extends the selection as you use navigation keys. Press F8 again to return to normal selection mode.
Shift+F8	Adds other nonadjacent cells or ranges to the selection; pressing Shift+F8 again ends Add mode.
F5	Prompts for a range or range name to select.
Ctrl+G	Prompts for a range or range name to select.
Ctrl+A	Selects the entire worksheet.
Ctrl+A	If the active cell is within a table. Selects the table without the header row and totals row. Pressing Ctrl+Shift+spacebar again selects the complete table. Pressing Ctrl+Shift+spacebar again selects the entire worksheet.
Shift+Backspace	Cancels a range selection and selects only the active cell.

TABLE D.3

Moving within a Range Selection

Key(s)	What It Does
Enter	Moves the cell pointer. The direction depends on the setting in the Edit tab of the Options dialog box.
Shift+Enter	Moves the cell pointer up to the preceding cell in the selection.
Tab	Moves the cell pointer right to the next cell in the selection.
Shift+Tab	Moves the cell pointer left to the preceding cell in the selection.
Ctrl+period (.)	Moves the cell pointer to the next corner of the current cell range.
Shift+Backspace	Collapses the cell selection to just the active cell.

TABLE D.4

Editing Keys in the Formula Bar

Key(s)	What It Does
F2	Begins editing the active cell
Navigation keys	Moves the cursor one character in the direction of the arrow

continued

TABLE D.4	*(continued)*
Key(s)	**What It Does**
Home	Moves the cursor to the beginning of the line
End	Moves the cursor to the end of the line
Ctrl+→	Moves the cursor one word to the right
Ctrl+←	Moves the cursor one word to the left
F3	Displays the Paste Name dialog box when you're creating a formula
Ctrl+A	Displays the Function Arguments dialog box (after you type a function name in a formula)
Del(ete)	Deletes the character to the right of the cursor
Ctrl+Del(ete)	Deletes all characters from the cursor to the end of the line
Backspace	Deletes the character to the left of the cursor
Esc	Cancels the editing

TABLE D.5

Formatting Keys

Key(s)	**What It Does**
Ctrl+1	Displays the Format dialog box for the selected object
Ctrl+B	Sets or removes boldface
Ctrl+I	Sets or removes italic
Ctrl+U	Sets or removes underlining
Ctrl+5	Sets or removes strikethrough
Ctrl+Shift+~	Applies the general number format
Ctrl+Shift+!	Applies the comma format with two decimal places
Ctrl+Shift+#	Applies the date format (day, month, year)
Ctrl+Shift+@	Applies the time format (hour, minute, a.m./p.m.)
Ctrl+Shift+$	Applies the currency format with two decimal places
Ctrl+Shift+%	Applies the percent format with no decimal places
Ctrl+Shift+&	Applies border to outline
Ctrl+Shift+_	Removes all borders

TABLE D.6

Other Shortcut Keys

Key(s)	What It Does
Ctrl+F1	Toggles the display of the Ribbon
Alt+=	Inserts the AutoSum formula
Alt+Backspace	Equivalent to Undo
Alt+Enter	Starts a new line in the current cell
Ctrl+;	Enters the current date
Ctrl+:	Enters the current time
Ctrl+0 (zero)	Hides columns
Ctrl+6	Cycles among various ways of displaying objects on a worksheet
Ctrl+8	Toggles the display of outline symbols
Ctrl+9	Hides rows
Ctrl+[	Selects direct precedent cells
Ctrl+]	Selects directly dependent cells
Ctrl+C	Equivalent to Home ⇨ Clipboard ⇨ Copy
Ctrl+D	Equivalent to Home ⇨ Editing ⇨ Fill ⇨ Down
Ctrl+F	Equivalent to Home ⇨ Editing ⇨ Find & Select ⇨ Find
Ctrl+H	Equivalent to Home ⇨ Editing ⇨ Find & Select ⇨ Replace
Ctrl+K	Equivalent to Insert ⇨ Links ⇨ Hyperlink
Ctrl+N	Creates a new workbook
Ctrl+O	Equivalent to File ⇨ Open
Ctrl+P	Equivalent to File ⇨ Print
Ctrl+R	Equivalent to Home ⇨ Editing ⇨ Fill ⇨ Fill Right
Ctrl+T	Equivalent to Insert ⇨ Tables ⇨ Table
Ctrl+Shift+T	Toggles the Total row in a table
Ctrl+Shift+L	Toggles the AutoFilter controls in a table
Ctrl+S	Equivalent to File ⇨ Save
Ctlr+Alt+V	Equivalent to Home ⇨ Clipboard ⇨ Paste ⇨ Paste Special
Ctrl+Shift+(	Unhides rows in the selection
Ctrl+Shift+)	Unhides columns in the selection
Ctrl+Shift+A	Inserts the argument names and parentheses for the function (after you type a valid function name in a formula)
Ctrl+V	Equivalent to Home ⇨ Clipboard ⇨ Paste
Ctrl+X	Equivalent to Home ⇨ Clipboard ⇨ Cut
Ctrl+Z	Undo

TABLE D.7

Function Keys

Key(s)	What It Does
F1	Displays Help
Alt+F1	Inserts default chart object that uses the selected range
Alt+Shift+F1	Inserts a new worksheet
F2	Edits the active cell
Shift+F2	Edits a cell comment
Alt+F2	Equivalent to File ⇨ Save As
Alt+Shift+F2	Equivalent to File ⇨ Save
F3	Pastes a name into a formula
Shift+F3	Pastes a function into a formula
Ctrl+F3	Equivalent to Formulas ⇨ Defined Names ⇨ Name Manager
Ctrl+Shift+F3	Equivalent to Formulas ⇨ Defined Names ⇨ Create From Selection
F4	Repeats the last action
Shift+F4	Repeats the last Find (Find Next)
Ctrl+F4	Closes the window
Alt+F4	Equivalent to File ⇨ Exit
F5	Equivalent to Home ⇨ Editing ⇨ Find & Select ⇨ Go To
Shift+F5	Equivalent to Home ⇨ Editing ⇨ Find & Select ⇨ Find
Ctrl+F5	Restores a minimized or maximized workbook window
Alt+F5	Refreshes active query or pivot table
F6	Moves to the next pane
Shift+F6	Moves to the previous pane
Ctrl+F6	Activates to the next window
Ctrl+Shift+F6	Activates the previous workbook window
F7	Equivalent to Review ⇨ Proofing ⇨ Spelling
Ctrl+F7	Allows moving the window with the arrow keys
F8	Extends a selection (toggle)
Shift+F8	Adds to the selection (toggle)
Ctrl+F8	Allows resizing the window with the arrow keys
Alt+F8	Equivalent to View ⇨ Macros ⇨ Macros, or Developer ⇨ Code ⇨ Macros
F9	Calculates all sheets in all open workbooks
Shift+F9	Calculates the active worksheet

Key(s)	What It Does
Ctrl+Alt+F9	Global calculation
Ctrl+F9	Minimizes the workbook
F10	Displays keytips for the Ribbon
Shift+F10	Displays a shortcut menu for the selected object (equivalent to right-clicking)
Ctrl+F10	Maximizes or restores the workbook window
F11	Creates a chart in a chart sheet
Shift+F11	Inserts a new worksheet
Ctrl+F11	Inserts an Excel 4.0 macro sheet
Alt+F11	Equivalent to Developer ⇨ Code ⇨ Visual Basic
F12	Equivalent to File ⇨ Save
Shift+F12	Equivalent to File ⇨ Save
Ctrl+F12	Equivalent to File ⇨ Open
Ctrl+Shift+F12	Equivalent to File ⇨ Print

Index

SPECIAL CHARACTERS AND NUMERICS

#DIV/0! error, 219, 653–654

#N/A error, 219, 360, 654–655

#NAME? error, 655

#NULL! error, 219, 655

#NUM! error, 219, 396–397, 655

#REF! error, 219, 656

#VALUE! error, 219, 656

& (ampersand), 234

* (asterisk) wildcard character, 77–78, 242, 568

@ (at) symbol, 217

= (equal sign), 203

(hash mark) character, 67, 218

? (question mark) wildcard character, 77, 242

~ (tilde) character, 78, 242

3 × 4 array constant, 361–362

3-D area chart, 428

3-D charts, 464–465

3-D clustered column chart, 421

3-D data point, 432

3-D line chart, 423

15-digit accuracy, 31

64-bit version, 4, 677

1900 date system, 250

1904 date system, 250

A

Above average conditional formatting rule, 481

ABS function, 274, 926

absolute references

    Data Validation dialog box, 575

    formulas and functions, 210–212

    problems with, 657

accelerator key, 19, 856

Accelerator property

    CheckBox control, 866

    OptionButton control, 869

Accept or Reject Changes dialog box, 635

Access database program

    versus Excel, 678

    importing tables, 679–680

Accounting format, Format Cells dialog box, 46–47, 554

Accounting Number Format button, Ribbon, 553

Accounting Number Format drop-down list, 44

ACCRINT function, 923

ACCRINTM function, 923

ACOS function, 926

ACOSH function, 926

actions, VBA, 813

Activate event, 876, 879

activating embedded chart, 405, 413

active area, worksheet, 172

active cell, 8–9

Active cell indicator, 6–7

active objects, VBA, 814

Active Sheets printing option, 178

active window, 51

active workbook, 50

ActiveX controls

    CheckBox, 866–867

    ComboBox, 867–868

    CommandButton, 868

    Image, 868

    Label, 868

    ListBox, 868–869

    OptionButton, 869

    overview, 861

    ScrollBar, 869–870

    SpinButton, 870–871

    TextBox, 871–872

    ToggleButton, 872

Add a Digital Signature command, Info pane, 155

Add button

    Consolidate dialog box, 601

    Customize Quick Access Toolbar, 41

Add Constraint dialog box, 767

Add operation, Paste Special dialog box, 599

Add Scenario dialog box, 755

Add to Dictionary button, Spelling dialog box, 672

Add View dialog box, 191

Index

`AddinInstall` event, 876
add-ins, 514. *See also* custom add-ins
Add-Ins dialog box
    installing add-ins, 913
    overview, 904–905
`AddIns` object, 814
Add-Ins tab, Ribbon, 11
`AddinUninstall` event, 876
address
    cell, 8–9, 69
    range, 69
`ADDRESS` function, 328, 385, 926
Advanced tab
    Excel Options dialog box, 36–38, 52, 439, 519, 806
    Share Workbook dialog box, 631–633
age, calculating, 265–266
`AGGREGATE` function, 201, 204–205, 380, 926
alert messages, 900
Align with Page Margins check box, 187
aligning objects, 523
Alignment tab
    Format Axis dialog box, 452
    Format Cells dialog box, 15, 122, 125
All Commands option, Choose Commands From drop-down
    list, 544
All Except Borders option, Paste Special dialog box, 88
All merging conditional formats option, Paste Special dialog
    box, 88
All Methods tab, Solver Options dialog box, 770–771
All option, Paste Special dialog box, 87
All References list box, Consolidate dialog box, 600
All Using Source Theme option, Paste Special dialog box, 88
`allocating resources.xlsx` sample file, 941
Allow drop-down list, Data Validation dialog box, 571
Allow Users to Edit Ranges dialog box, 641
Alphabetic tab, Properties window, 863
alternate-rows, shading, 497
Always Show Document Information Panel on Document
    Open and Initial Save check box, 151
`AMORDEGRC` function, 923
`AMORLINC` function, 923
ampersand (&), 234
Analysis ToolPak add-in
    `WORKDAY` function, 264
    counting formulas, 297–298
    installing, 298, 782
    overview, 781–782, 905
    tools
        Analysis of Variance, 784
        Correlation, 784–785

Covariance, 785
Descriptive Statistics, 785–786
exponential smoothing, 786
Fourier Analysis, 787
F-Test, 786–787
Histogram, 787–788
Moving Average, 788–789
overview, 783
Random Number Generation, 789–790
Rank and Percentile, 790
Regression, 790–791
Sampling, 791–792
t-Test, 792
z-Test, 792
using, 783
Analysis ToolPak—VBA add-in, 905
And criteria, 289–291, 305–307
`AND` function, 925
angled text, displaying, 125–126
animated border, 79
annuity, 348
`annuity calculator.xlsx` sample file, 937
ANSI character set, 231–232
Any Value option, Data Validation dialog box, 571
Application close button, 6–7
Application minimize button, 6–7
`Application` object, 814, 816
`Application.ActiveCell` property, 816
`Application.ActiveSheet` property, 816
`Application.ActiveWorkbook` property, 816
applications, on CD, 934
`Application.Selection` property, 816
Apply Names dialog box, 226
Apply These Changes to All Other Cells with the Same
    Setting check box, 572
area charts, 427–428
`area charts.xlsx` sample file, 938
`AREAS` function, 926
`Areas` method, 895
arguments
    formulas and functions, 201–202
    function procedure, 828–833
Arrange command, 521
Arrange Windows dialog box, 51
array, defined, 355
array argument, 316
`array examples.xlsx` sample file, 937
`array formula calendar.xlsx` sample file, 937
array formulas
    #VALUE! error, 656
    array constant elements, 360

array dimensions
    one-dimensional horizontal, 360–361
    one-dimensional vertical, 361
    two-dimensional, 361–362
creating array constants, 358–359
defined, 750
editing, 364–365
entering, 364
entry error, 650
multicell
    creating array constant from values in ranges, 367
    creating array from values in ranges, 366–367
    displaying calendar, 398–399
    expanding or contracting, 365–366
    generating array of consecutive integers, 370–371
    overview, 356–357
    performing operations on arrays, 368
    returning list of unique items, 396–398
    returning nonblank cells, 394–395
    returning only positive values, 394
    reversing order of cells, 395–396
    sorting range of values dynamically, 396
    transposing array, 369–370
    using functions with array, 369
naming array constants, 362–363
overview, 355–356
performing case-sensitive lookup, 320
selecting range, 364
single-cell
    computing averages that exclude zeros, 381–382
    counting characters in range, 371–372
    counting differences in two ranges, 384
    counting error values, 380–381
    counting text cells in range, 373–374
    determining closest values, 391
    determining whether particular values appears, 383–384
    determining whether range contains valid values, 386
    eliminating intermediate formulas, 374–376
    finding row of value's nth occurrence, 385
    overview, 357–358
    ranking data, 392–393
    removing non-numeric characters from strings, 390
    returning last value in columns, 391–392
    returning last value in rows, 392
    returning locations of maximum values, 384–385
    returning longest text, 385
    summing digits of integers, 386–387
    summing every nth value, 388–390
    summing ranges that contain errors, 379–380
    summing rounded values, 388
    summing smallest values in ranges, 372–373
        summing the n largest values, 381
        using arrays instead of range reference, 376–377
Artistic Effects feature, Office 2010, 533
ASIN function, 926
ASINH function, 927
Ask Me Which Changes Win option, Share Workbook dialog
        box, 633
asterisk (*) wildcard character, 77–78, 242, 568
at (@) symbol, 217
ATAN function, 927
ATAN2 function, 927
ATANH function, 927
atp examples.xlsx sample file, 941
Auditing tools
    background error-checking feature, 665–667
    fixing circular reference errors, 665
    Formula Evaluator feature, 667–668
    identifying cells of particular types, 661–662
    tracing cell relationships
        identifying dependents, 665
        identifying precedents, 664
        overview, 663–664
    tracing error values, 665
    viewing formulas, 662–663
AutoComplete feature, 39
AutoCorrect button, Spelling dialog box, 672
AutoCorrect dialog box, 40, 233, 672–674
AutoCorrect feature, 40, 672–674
AutoCorrect Options button, AutoCorrect feature, 40
AutoCorrect tab, AutoCorrect feature, 40
AutoFill feature
    copying to adjacent cells, 83
    generating series of dates, 260–261
    overview, 38–39
    worksheet data entry, 23
AutoFill handle, 38
autofiltering, 282
AutoFit Column Width option, 68
AutoFormat as You Type tab, AutoCorrect dialog box, 674
Automatic Calculation mode, 220
Automatic item grouping, pivot table, 717
automatic number formatting, 43–44, 552
automatic percent-entry feature, 44
Automatic Update option, Edit Links dialog box, 595
Automatically Every setting, Share Workbook dialog box, 632
Automatically Except for Data Tables option, 222
Automatically Insert a Decimal Point check box, Excel
        Options dialog box, 38
AutoRecover feature
    recovering unsaved work, 149–150
    recovering versions of current workbooks, 149

Index

`AutoSize` property
    defined, 864
    `Image` control, 868
    `TextBox` control, 871
auto-updating Sparklines, 513
Available Template screen
    My Templates icon, 165
    New from Existing option, 169
`AVEDEV` function, 929
`AVERAGE` function, 200, 375, 382, 929
Average summary formula, 108
`AVERAGEA` function, 929
`AVERAGEIF` function, 382, 929
`AVERAGEIFS` function, 929
averages, that exclude zeros, 381–382
axis
    categories, 452–455
    scaling, Sparkline graphics, 509–510
    value, 448–452
Axis Crosses At option, 452
Axis options tab, Format Axis dialog box, 448–449

B

`BackColor` property, 864
background error-checking feature, 665–667
background images
    displaying, 535
    printing, 185
    worksheet formatting, 130–131
`background image.xlsx` sample file, 935
Backstage view
    New page, 162
    Print tab, 179
    Share tab, 614
`BackStyle` property, 864
backups, 157
`BAHTTEXT` function, 932
Banded Columns check box, 107
Banded Rows check box, 107
`bank accounts.xlsx` sample file, 940
bar charts, 422
`bar charts.xlsx` sample file, 938
bar of pie chart, 425
`basic counting.xlsx` sample file, 936
`basic lookup examples.xlsx` sample file, 937
`BeforeClose` event, 876, 879
`BeforeDoubleClick` event, 879
`BeforePrint` event, 876
`BeforeRightClick` event, 883, 879

`BeforeSave` event, 876, 878–879
Bernoulli distribution option, Random Number Generation
    dialog box, 790
`BESSELI` function, 921
`BESSELJ` function, 921
`BESSELK` function, 921
`BESSELY` function, 921
Best Case scenario, Scenario Manager, 755
`BETADIST` function, 918
`BETA.DIST` function, 929
`BETAINV` function, 918
`BETA.INV` function, 929
bin range, 787
`BIN2DEC` function, 921
`BIN2HEX` function, 921
`BIN2OCT` function, 921
binding constraint, 769
`BINOMDIST` function, 918
`BINOM.DIST` function, 929
Binomial distribution option, Random Number Generation
    dialog box, 790
`BINOM.INV`, 929
bitmap image, 531
Bitmap paste option, Paste Special dialog box, 619
blank cells, counting formulas, 284–285
blank cells not blank error, 651–652
blank skipping, Paste Special dialog box, 89
Blanks option, Go to Special dialog box, 75
Bold button, Ribbon, 14
`book.xlt` template, 185
`Boolean` data type, 901
Border tab, Format Cells dialog box, 129, 484
borders, worksheet formatting, 128–129
Borders drop-down list, 128
Bottom vertical alignment option, 124
`BoundColumn` property
    `ComboBox` control, 867
    `ListBox` control, 868
breaking links, 620
Browse button, Consolidate dialog box, 601
bubble charts, 433
`bubble charts.xlsx` sample file, 938
`budget data.accdb` sample file, 940
`budget.xlsx` sample file, 935
built-in data form, 41
built-in date format, 566
buttons, assigning macros to, 810–811
buttons element, `MsgBox` function, 839
By Changing Cell field, Goal Seek dialog box, 763

By Changing Variable Cells field, Solver Parameters dialog
box, 767

By list box, Grouping dialog box, 720

`Byte` data type, 901

C

`Calculate` event, 880

calculated fields, 724–728

`calculated fields and items.xlsx` sample file, 940

calculated items, in pivot tables

creating, 724–725

inserting, 728–731

calculation mode, changing, 341

calendar, displaying in ranges, 398–399

Camera tool, 535

Cancel option, File in Use dialog box, 629

candlesticks, 434–435

Capitalize First Letter of Sentences option, AutoCorrect
dialog box, 672

Capitalize Names of Days option, AutoCorrect dialog box, 673

`Caption` property, 864

Cascading Style Sheets (CSS), 609

case

changing, 239–240

lookup formulas, 320–321

case sensitive password, 151

Categorized tab, Properties window, 863

category axis, 407, 452–455

Category field, database table, 698

`category_labels` argument, 459

CD

applications, 934

eBook version of Excel 2010 Bible, 934

sample files for Excel 2010 Bible, 934–942

system requirements, 933

troubleshooting, 942

using, 933–934

`CEILING` function, 927

`CEILING.PRECISE` function, 927

cell dependents, 663

`CELL` function, 925

cell precedents, 663

`cell references.xlsx` sample file, 936

Cell Styles command, 132

cells. *See also* ranges

blank, 317–318, 651–652

changing, 753, 765

comments

changing shape, 96

deleting, 98

editing, 98

formatting, 95

hiding and showing, 97

overview, 94–95

printing, 96–97

reading, 96

selecting, 97–98

conditional formatting

copying, 500

locating, 501

counting and summing, 281–283

counting characters in, 243

counting formulas, 283–285

counting occurrences of specific text, 292–293

counting occurrences of substrings in, 243–244

creating drop-down list, 573

Data Validation feature, 574–575

data-entry techniques

AutoComplete feature, 39

AutoCorrect feature, 40

AutoFill feature, 38–39

automatically moving the cell pointer, 37

Ctrl+Enter key combination, 38

current date or time, 42

decimal points, 38

forcing text to appear, 40

forms, 40–42

navigation keys, 37

numbers with fractions, 40

selecting range of input cells, 38

defined, 5

editing contents, 35–37

erasing contents, 35

filled with hash marks, 651

filling with repeating characters, 568

identifying particular type, 661–662

joining, 234–235

linking controls to, 864

look up address of values within range, 326

merging, 124–125

overview, 34, 69

printing gridlines, 183–184

prompting for values, 893

references in

changing types of, 212

from other workbooks, 213–214

from other worksheets, 212–213

overview, 209–210

relative, absolute, and mixed, 210–212

referencing within pivot tables, 733–735

replacing contents, 35

result, 759

reversing order of, 395–396

selecting

    complete rows and columns, 71

    multisheet ranges, 72–74

    noncontiguous ranges, 71–72

    ranges, 70

    by searching, 76–78

    special types of cells, 74–76

shortcuts for selecting in worksheet, 950–951

Sparkline, 507

summing all in range, 299–300

target, 765

tracing relationships

    identifying dependents, 665

    identifying precedents, 664

    overview, 663

unlocking, 639–640

Center across Selection horizontal alignment option, Format Cells dialog box, 123

Center command, Ribbon, 14

Center horizontal alignment option, Format Cells dialog box, 123

Center vertical alignment option, Format Cells dialog box, 124

Change All button, Spelling dialog box, 672

Change button, Spelling dialog box, 672

`change case.xlam` sample file, 942

`change case.xlsm` sample file, 941

Change Chart Type dialog box, 412, 465–466

Change event, 880

Change History option, Share Workbook dialog box, 632

Change Source button

    Edit Links dialog box, 595

    Links dialog box, 621

Change Source dialog box, 595

Change worksheet event, 880

`ChangeCaseOfText` procedure, 909

changing cells, 753, 765

Changing Cells field, Add Scenario dialog box, 756

`CHAR` function, 234, 932

character codes

    `CHAR` function, 231–233

    `CODE` function, 231

characters

    counting

        in cells, 243

        in ranges, 371–372

        in strings, 239

    extracting from strings, 240–241

    filling cells with repeating, 568

    removing from strings, 390

Chart Element drop-down control, 439–440

Chart Layouts option, 437

`chart macros.xlsm` sample file, 942

chart series feature, 439

chart sheet, 5, 49

Chart Styles option, 437

chart tip, 438

Chart Tools contextual tab, 405, 519, 621

Chart Tools control, 468

Chart type option, 437

`ChartObject` object, 897

`ChartObjects` object, 815

charts

    axis

        category, 452–455

        value, 448–452

    Chart Area, 443

    copying, 414

    creating and customizing

        choosing types, 409, 412

        data views, 411

        layouts, 409–411

        selecting data, 408–409

        styles, 412–413

    data series

        3-D charts, 464–465

        adding, 456–457

        changing, 457–460

        changing range by dragging range outline, 457–458

        combination charts, 465–468

        data labels, 460–461

        deleting, 456

        displaying data tables, 468–469

        Edit Series dialog box, 458

        editing Series formula, 459–460

        error bars, 461–463

        missing data, 461

        overview, 455–456

        trendlines, 463–464

    deleting, 414

    displaying colors in column, 474–475

    elements

        adding, 415

        Chart Element Control, selecting with, 439–441

        Format dialog box, 441–442

        formatting, 415–416

        keyboard, selecting with, 439

        Mini toolbar, 442

        moving and deleting, 415

        overview, 437–438

Ribbon feature, 442
    selecting with mouse, 438–439
embedded, 405
Gantt, 476–477
gauge, 473–474
gridlines, 448
histogram, 475–476
legends, 446–448
moving, 414
overview, 403–404
picture, 470–471
Plot Area, 444–445
plotting one variable mathematical functions, 477–478
plotting two variable mathematical functions, 479
printing, 416–417
resizing, 414
sheets, 406–407
templates, 469–470
thermometer, 472–473
titles, 445–446
types of
    area, 427–428
    bar, 422
    bubble, 433
    choosing, 417–419
    column, 419–421
    doughnut, 429–430
    line, 423–424
    pie, 424–426
    radar, 430–432
    stock, 433–436
    surface, 432–433
    XY (scatter), 426–427
using data bars instead of, 487
VBA macros and
    applying formatting, 899
    modifying properties, 898
    modifying type, 898
    overview, 897
`Charts` object, 815
Check Accessibility command, Info pane, 155
check boxes, Ribbon, 14
Check Compatibility command, Info pane, 156
Check for Issues button, 155
Check Mark icon
    Formula bar, 36
    New Formatting Rule dialog box, 491–492
`CheckBox` control, ActiveX, 844, 859, 861, 866–867
checkerboard shading, 497
Chi Square distribution, 201

`CHIDIST` function, 918
`CHIINV` function, 918
`CHISQ.DIST` function, 929
`CHISQ.DIST.RT` function, 929
`CHISQ.INV` function, 929
`CHISQ.INV.RT` function, 929
`CHISQ.TEST` function, 929
`CHITEST` function, 918
Choose Commands list, Customize Quick Access Toolbar, 41
Choose Data Source dialog box, 682, 684, 690
Choose Details dialog box, 152
`CHOOSE` function, 311, 926
Christmas Day, date functions, 271
Circle Invalid Data item, Data Validation drop-down list, 572
Circular Reference Warning message, 219
circular references, 219–220, 650, 665
`circular reference.xlsx` sample file, 936
`CLEAN` function, 239, 932
Clear All button, Office Clipboard, 85
Clear All command, 35
Clear button, Format Cells dialog box, 484
Clear Comments command, 35
Clear Contents command, 35
Clear Formats command, 35
Clear Hyperlinks command, 35
`Clear` method, 817
Clear Rules command, Conditional Formatting drop-down
        list, 483
`Click` event, 853
client-server network, 628
Clip Art task pane, 22, 531–532
ClipArt button, 470–471
Clipboard button, 470–471
Clipboards
    overview, 616–617
    replacing cell contents, 35
Close button, 50
closest values, determining, 391
closing
    all workbooks, VBA macros, 896–897
    Excel windows, 52–53
clustered column chart, 410, 419
`CODE` function, 932
codes
    entering and editing, 812
    for number formatting, 558–560
`col_index_num` argument, `VLOOKUP` function,
        312
`col_num` argument, `INDEX` function, 316
Collated option, 180

Index

collections, VBA macros, 814–815

colon operator, 225

color

    chart columns, 474–475

    charts, 430–432

    Sparkline graphics, 508

    worksheets, 127–128

Color Scale conditional formatting rule, 482

`color scale example.xlsx` sample file, 939

Color Scales command, Conditional Formatting drop-down
        list, 483

Columbus Day, date functions, 270

column chart, 418

`column charts.xlsx` sample file, 938

Column Differences option, Go to Special dialog box, 75

`COLUMN` function, 497–498, 926

column labels, pivot table, 704

column letters

    overview, 6–7

    replacing table headings, 63

Column Sparkline, 504

Column to Filter list, Query Wizard, 685–686

Column Width dialog box, 68

Column Widths option, Paste Special dialog box, 88

`ColumnCount` property

    `ComboBox` control, 867

    `ListBox` control, 868

columns. *See also* rows and columns

    defined, 99

    keeping visible while scrolling, 63

    selecting entire, 105

`COLUMNS` function, 926

`COMBIN` function, 927

combination chart, 407, 465–468

`ComboBox` control, ActiveX, 844, 861, 867–868

comma operator, 225

Comma Style button

    Number Format drop-down list, 44

    Ribbon, 553

`CommandBar` object, 913

`CommandButton` control, ActiveX, 844, 848, 861, 868

commands

    adding to Quick Access toolbar, 543–545

    Ribbon interface, 13–15

Commands Not in the Ribbon option, Choose Commands
        From drop-down list, 544

comments

    changing shape, 96

    deleting, 98

    editing, 98

    formatting, 95

    hiding and showing, 97

    overview, 94–95

    printing, 96–97

    reading, 96

    selecting, 97–98

    VBA code, 812

Comments option

    Add Scenario dialog box, 756

    Go to Special dialog box, 75

    Paste Special dialog box, 88

`comparative histogram.xlsx` sample file, 938

Compare Side by Side feature, 61

comparisons, chart, 417

compatibility

    checking, 157–159

    saving for use with older versions, 159–160

Compatibility Category Functions, 918–919

Compatibility Checker dialog box, 156–158

Compatibility Mode section, Info pane, 65, 154

`COMPLEX` function, 921

compound interest, calculating, 344–346

`CONCATENATE` function, 235, 932

concatenation operator, 234

`conditional colors.xlsx` sample file, 938

Conditional Formats option, Go to Special dialog box, 76

conditional formatting

    copying cells, 500

    deleting, 500

    formula-based rules

        formula examples, 496–499

        overview, 494–495

        relative and absolute references, 495–496

    graphics

        color scales, 487–490

        data bars, 485–487

        icon sets, 490–494

    loan amortization schedule, 337

    locating cells, 501

    making rules, 484–485

    managing rules, 499–500

    overview, 481–482

    types of, 483–484

Conditional Formatting command, Ribbon, 14

Conditional Formatting drop-down list, 483

`conditional formatting examples.xlsx` sample
        file, 939

conditional formatting formulas, 494

`conditional formatting formulas.xlsx` sample
        file, 939

Conditional Formatting Rules Manager dialog box, 483
conditional sums
    multiple criteria
        using And, 305–306
        using And and Or, 307
        using Or, 306–307
    single criterion
        only negative values, 303–304
        overview, 302–303
        values based on date comparisons, 305
        values based on different ranges, 304
        values based on text comparisons, 305
conditional sum.xlsx sample file, 936
CONFIDENCE function, 918
Confidence Level option, Regression dialog box, 791
CONFIDENCE.NORM function, 929
CONFIDENCE.T function, 929
confirmation message, saving references, 592
Connect button, Create New Data Source dialog box, 683
Connect Data Points with Line option, 461–462
consecutive integers, generating arrays of, 370–371
Consolidate command, consolidating worksheets, 600–601
Consolidate dialog box, 600
consolidating worksheets
    example of, 601–603
    overview, 597–598
    refreshing, 604
    using Consolidate command, 600–601
    using formulas, 598
    using Paste Special dialog box, 599
Constant Is Zero option, Regression dialog box, 791
Constants option, Go to Special dialog box, 75
Constraint Precision option, Solver Options dialog box, 771
constraints
    adding, 767–768
    binding, 769
    defined, 765
Constraints section, Solver Results dialog box, 769
contextual tabs, Ribbon interface, 13
Contextures, Web site, 948
contiguous range, 71
continuous compounding interest, 346–348
contracting multicell arrays, 365–366
controls
    defined, 801
    UserForm
        adding, 862
        adjusting properties, 862–863
        common properties, 863–864

        creating macros for, 864–866
        design mode, 862
        linking controls to cells, 864
        overview, 843–844, 861
Convert button, 154
CONVERT function, 921
Convert to Number option, Smart Tag, 230
converting
    charts to combination chart, 466–467
    tables to ranges, 113
Copy method, 888
Copy to New Sheet button, Compatibility Checker dialog box, 158
copying
    cells and ranges
        adjacent cells, 82–83
        drag-and-drop, 81–82
        Office Clipboard, 84–85
        to other sheets, 83
        overview, 78–79
        Paste Special dialog box, 87–89
        pasting, 85–86
        Ribbon commands, 79–80
        shortcut keys, 81
        shortcut menu commands, 80–81
    chart formatting, 447
    charts, 414
    from Excel to Word
        pasting links, 620–622
        pasting static information, 617–620
    with Office application, 615–617
    pivot tables, 708
    workbooks, in Word, 624–626
    worksheets, 56
Correct Accidental Use of cAPS LOCK key option, AutoCorrect dialog box, 673
Correct TWo INitial CApitals option, AutoCorrect dialog box, 672
CORREL function, 785, 929
Correlation dialog box, 785
Correlation tool, Analysis ToolPak add-in, 784–785
COS function, 927
COSH function, 927
Cost argument, 351
COUNT function, 282, 929
Count Numbers summary formula, 108
Count property, 895
Count summary formula, 108
count unique.xlsx sample file, 936
COUNTA function, 282, 285, 392, 929

Index

COUNTBLANK function, 282, 284–285, 929

COUNTIF function
    computing averages that excludes zeros, 382
    counting error values in range, 286
    counting text cells in range, 373
    formulas using, 287
    function of, 929
    overview, 282
    references, 576

COUNTIFS function, 282, 929

counting
    characters in strings, 239
    differences in two ranges, 384
    error values in ranges, 380–381
    number of words, 248
    occurrences of substrings in cells, 243–244
    specific characters in cells, 243
    text cells in range, 373–374

counting formulas
    blank cells, 284–285
    COUNTIF function, 287
    creating frequency distributions
        FREQUENCY function, 294–295
        using a pivot table, 298–299
        using formulas, 296–297
        using the Analysis ToolPak, 297–298
    error values in ranges, 286
    logical values, 286
    most frequently occurring entry, 291
    multiple criteria, 288–291
    nonblank cells, 285
    nontext cells, 285
    number of unique values, 293–294
    numeric cells, 285
    occurrences of specific text, 292–293
    overview, 281
    text cells, 285
    total number of cells, 283–284

counting text in a range.xlsx sample file, 937

CountLarge property, 895

county data.xlsx sample file, 940

COUPDAYBS function, 923

COUPDAYS function, 923

COUPDAYSNC function, 923

COUPNCD function, 923

COUPNUM function, 923

COUPPCD function, 923

COVAR function, 785, 918

Covariance tool, Analysis ToolPak add-in, 785

COVARIANCE.P function, 929

COVARIANCE.S function, 929

Create Chart dialog box, 736

Create from File tab, Object dialog box, 623, 626

Create Links to Source Data check box, Consolidate dialog box, 601–602, 604

Create Names from Selection dialog box, 92, 325

Create New Data Source dialog box, 682–683

Create New tab, Object dialog box, 623

Create New Theme Colors dialog box, 138–139

Create PivotTable dialog box, 701

Create Sparklines dialog box, 506

Create Table dialog box, 25, 102

credit card payment, calculating, 334–336

credit card payments.xlsx sample file, 937

credit union, 778

CRITBINOM function, 918

criteria argument
    COUNTIF function, 287
    SUMIF function, 302

Criteria pane, Microsoft Query, 690–691

Crop command, 535

CSS (Cascading Style Sheets), 609

Cube Category Functions, 919

cube root.xlsm sample file, 941

CUBEKPIMEMBER function, 919

CUBEMEMBER function, 919

CUBEMEMBERPROPERTY function, 919

CUBERANKEDMEMBER function, 919

CUBESET function, 919

CUBESETCOUNT function, 919

CUBEVALUE function, 919

CUMIPMT function, 332, 923

CUMPRINC function, 332, 923

cumulative sum, computing, 300–302

cumulative sum.xlsx sample file, 937

curly brackets, 284, 359, 362, 364

Currency data type, 901

Currency format, Format Cells dialog box, 46–47, 554

Current Array option, Go to Special dialog box, 75

Current Date button, 186

current date, displaying, 259

current date.xlsm sample file, 941

Current Region option, Go to Special dialog box, 75

Current Time button, 186

Curve and Scribble Shapes, 519

custom add-ins
    creating, 907–908
    defined, 903–904
    example of
        about UserForm, 909–910
        adding descriptive information, 911

creating user interface for add-in macros, 912–913
installing add-ins, 913
procedures in Module1, 909
protecting projects, 911–912
setting up workbooks, 908
testing workbook, 910–911
overview, 903–904
reasons for creating, 906
Custom category in the Number tab, Format Cells dialog box, 399
Custom conditional formatting rule, 482
Custom error bar, Format Error Bars dialog box, 462–463
Custom format, Format Cells dialog box, 46–47, 554
Custom Format option, 484
Custom option, Data Validation dialog box, 572
custom templates
changing workbook defaults, 166–167
changing worksheet defaults, 167–168
editing, 168
ideas, 170
overview, 165–166
resetting default settings, 168
saving, 170
Custom Value option, Sparkline group, 509
Custom Views feature, 587–588
Custom Views of worksheet, printing, 190–191
custom workbook template, 166
custom worksheet functions
debugging, 833–834
example of
analyzing, 825–826
custom function, 824
using function in worksheet, 824–825
function procedure arguments
function with no argument, 829
function with one argument, 829–831
function with range argument, 832–833
function with two arguments, 831–832
overview, 828–829
function procedures
calling custom functions from, 827
overview, 826–827
using custom functions in worksheet formulas, 828
inserting, 834–836
VBA functions, 823
customer list, 630
customer satisfaction charts, 413
Customize button, Customize Regional Options dialog box, 257
Customize Quick Access Toolbar
Add button, 41
Choose Commands list, 41

Form button, 41–42
New button, 42
Customize Regional Options dialog box, 257
Customize Ribbon tab, Excel Options dialog box, 548
customizing
charts, 408–413
Quick Access toolbar
adding new commands, 543–545
overview, 17–19, 541–542
Ribbon feature, 5, 546–549
SmartArt feature, 527–528
Sparkline graphics
adjusting axis scaling, 509–510
changing colors and line width, 508
changing type, 508
faking reference lines, 510–512
hidden or missing data, 508
highlighting certain data points, 509
sizing cells, 507
user interface
Quick Access toolbar, 541–546
Ribbon feature, 546–549
Cut method, 891

D

Daily Dose of Excel, Web site, 948
Dalgleish, Deborah, 948
damping factor, 786
Dark style category, tables, 103
data. *See also* entering and editing data
adding in outlines, 588
non-numeric, 715–717
for pivot tables, 698–701
preparing for outlines, 588
ranking with array formulas, 392–393
returned by Query
adjusting external data range properties, 688–689
changing, 690
deleting, 690
refreshing, 689–690
selecting from charts, 408–409
sharing with Office applications. *See* sharing data with Office applications
specifying location for, 687–688
transforming with formulas, 240
types of
formulas, 30–31
numeric values, 30
overview, 29
text entries, 30

Index

Data Analysis dialog box, 783
Data bar conditional formatting, 4, 485
data bars
    in pivot tables, 299
    simple, 486–487
    using instead of chart, 487
Data Bars command, Conditional Formatting drop-down list, 483
Data Bars conditional formatting feature, 237
Data bars conditional formatting rule, 482
data bars examples.xlsx sample file, 939
Data Consolidate feature, 600
Data field, database table, 698
data label
    adding to chart, 415
    selecting, 439
Data pane, Microsoft Query, 691, 693
data points, 407, 509
data relationships, comparing, 417
data series
    3-D charts, 464–465
    adding, 456–457
    changing
        by dragging range outline, 457–458
        by editing Series formulas, 459–460
        using Edit Series dialog box, 458
    combination chart, 407, 465–468
    data labels, 460–461
    deleting, 456
    displaying data tables, 468–469
    doughnut chart, 429
    error bars, 461–463
    line chart, 423
    missing data, 461
    overview, 455–456
    pie chart, 424
    trendlines, 463–464
data source, Query applications, 682–684
Data tab
    Analysis ToolPak add-in, 782
    Ribbon, 11
Data Table dialog box, 339, 749
Data Table feature, 338, 437
data tables
    one-input, 748–750
    one-way, 338–340
    overview, 747–748
    two-input, 750–753
    two-way, 340–341
Data Validation dialog box, 570–571, 574–575

data validation examples.xlsx sample file, 939
data validation feature
    adding comments to cells, 98
    cell references, 574–575
    creating drop-down lists, 573
    criteria types, 571–572
    formula examples
        accepting dates by day of week, 577
        accepting larger values than previous cell, 576
        accepting nonduplicate entries only, 576–577
        accepting only values that don't exceed total, 578
        accepting text only, 576
        accepting text that begins with specific characters, 577
        creating dependent lists, 578–579
        overview, 575
    overview, 569–570
    specifying criteria, 570–571
    using formulas, 574
Data Validation option, Go to Special dialog box, 76
data views, charts, 411
Database Category Functions, 920
database files, Query application, 681
Databases tab, Choose Data Source dialog box, 682
data-entry techniques
    AutoComplete feature, 39
    AutoCorrect feature, 40
    AutoFill feature, 38–39
    automatically moving the cell pointer, 37
    current date or time, 42
    decimal points, 38
    forcing text to appear, 40
    forms, 40–42
    navigation keys, 37
    numbers with fractions, 40
    selecting a range of input cells, 38
    using Ctrl+Enter, 38
Date & Time Category Functions, 920–921
date axis, Sparkline graphics, 512–513
Date category, 254
Date data type, 901
Date format category, 554
Date format, Format Cells dialog box, 46–47
DATE function
    calculating holiday dates, 268
    function of, 920
    overview, 258
    summing values based on date comparison, 305
    TIME function and, 273
date functions
    age calculation, 265–266
    converting nondate string to date, 261–262

current date, 259
date of most recent Sunday, 267
date's quarter, 271
day of week, 267
day of year, 266–267
displaying date, 259–260
first day of week after a date, 267–268
generating series of dates, 260–261
holiday dates
    Christmas Day, 271
    Columbus Day, 270
    Easter, 270
    Independence Day, 270
    Labor Day, 270
    Martin Luther King, Jr. Day, 269
    Memorial Day, 270
    New Year's Day, 269
    overview, 268–269
    Presidents' Day, 269
    Thanksgiving Day, 271
    Veterans Day, 270
last day of month, 271
leap year, 271
nth occurrence of day of week in month, 268
number of days between dates, 262
number of work days dates, 263–264
number of years between dates, 265
offsetting dates using only work days, 264
Date option, Data Validation dialog box, 570–572
DATEDIF function, 265–266
dates. See also date functions
    entering, 33–34, 42
    formatting, 566
    grouping in pivot tables, 719–721
DATEVALUE function, 258, 260, 920
DAVERAGE function, 920
David McRitchie's Excel Pages Web site, 948
DAY function, 258–259, 920
DAYS360 function, 258, 920
DB function, 350, 923
DCOUNT function, 282, 920
DCOUNTA function, 282, 920
DDB function, 350, 923
Deactivate event, 876, 880
dead formulas, 228
debugging custom worksheet functions, 833–834
DEC2BIN function, 922
DEC2HEX function, 922
DEC2OCT function, 922
Decimal data type, 901

decimal hours, 277–278
Decimal option, Data Validation dialog box, 571
decimal points, 38
Decrease Decimal Places button, Ribbon, 44, 553, 560
default element, InputBox function, 838
default number format, 556
default row height, 68
default templates, 166–168
Default Width command, 68
default workbook template, 166
default worksheet template, 166
DEGREES function, 927
Degrees spinner control, Format Cells dialog box, 126
Delete All Draft Versions command, Info pane, 156
Delete button, Consolidate dialog box, 601
Delete Columns option, Protect Sheet dialog box, 640
Delete command drop-down list, 35
Delete Rows option, Protect Sheet dialog box, 640
deleting
    chart elements, 415
    charts, 414
    comments in cells, 98
    conditional formatting, 500
    data series, 456
    queries, 690
    rows and columns, 66
    worksheets, 54
DELTA function, 922
dependent lists, 578–579
dependent variable, 791
dependent workbook
    defined, 589
    Save As command, 596
dependents, 665
Dependents option, Go to Special dialog box, 76, 665
dependent.xlsx sample file, 939
deposits, future value of
    compound interest, 344–346
    interest with continuous compounding, 346–348
    simple interest, 343–344
depreciation, calculating, 350–353
depreciation calculations.xlsx sample file, 937
Description option, Record Macro dialog box, 803
descriptive information, 151, 911
Descriptive Statistics tool, Analysis ToolPak add-in, 785–786
Design contextual tab, 13
Design Mode icon, 862
design mode, UserForm, 862
destination application, 615

Index

Developer tab
    displaying, 796–797
    Ribbon, 11
DEVSQ function, 282, 929
DGET function, 920
dialog box launcher, 15
dialog boxes
    navigating, 19–20
    tabbed, 20–21
Different First Page check box, 187
Different Odd & Even Pages check box, 187
digital IDs, 647
digital signatures, 646–648
Dim statement, 902
direct cell dependent, 663
direct cell precedent, 663
direct mail.xlsx sample file, 940
Disable All Macros with Notification option, Trust Center
        dialog box, 797
disabling Mini toolbar, 118
DISC function, 923
Discrete distribution option, Random Number Generation
        dialog box, 790
Display Options for This Workbook section, 174, 519
display preferences, files, 147
Display Unit as Millions settings, 451
Display Units settings, 451
displaying
    current time, 272–273
    data tables, 468–469
    icons in cells, 490
    image inside comment, 95
    Open dialog box, 143
    Page Setup dialog box, 653
    scenarios, 757
    time, 273
    UserForms, 846
    Win/Loss Sparkline goal achievement, 511
Distributed horizontal alignment option, Format Cells dialog
        box, 123
Distributed vertical alignment option, Format Cells dialog
        box, 124
Distribution drop-down list, Random Number Generation
        dialog box, 790
#DIV/0! error, 219, 653–654
dividends, 778
DMAX function, 920
DMIN function, 920

Document Information Panel dialog box, 151
Document Inspector dialog box, 646–647
Document Properties panel, 911
document theme
    applying, 137
    customizing, 138–139
    overview, 135–136
    Sparkline graphics color, 508
DOLLAR function, 236, 932
DOLLARDE function, 923
DOLLARFR function, 923
Don't Keep Change History button, Share Workbook dialog
        box, 632
Don't Move or Size with Cells option, 520
Don't Update option, 592
Double data type, 901
double-clicking charts, 415
"double-spaced" effect, 67
doughnut charts, 429–430
doughnut charts.xlsx sample file, 938
Down arrow key, 10
DPRODUCT function, 920
Draft Mode indicator, 440
draft versions, 149
drag-and-drop method
    versus cut and paste method, 81–82
        multiple windows, 60
        noncontiguous ranges, 72
Draw Border command, 128
Draw Border Grid command, 128
draw layer, 5
Drawing Tools contextual menu, WordArt, 530
Drawing Tools tab, Equation Editor, 536
drawings. See pictures and drawings
drop-down lists, data validation feature, 573
DSTDEV function, 920
DSTDEVP function, 920
DSUM function, 282, 920
duplicate rows, 109
Duplicate values conditional formatting rule, 482
DURATION function, 923
DVAR function, 920
DVARP function, 920
dynamic chart, 405
dynamic consolidation, 600
dynamic model, 745
dynamic ranges, Sparkline graphics, 514–515
dynamic updating, consolidation, 598

E

Easter, date functions, 270
eBook version, 934
EDATE function, 258, 920
Edit button
    Scenario Manager dialog box, 758
    Select Data Source dialog box, 446
Edit Criteria dialog box, 691
Edit Formatting Rule dialog box, 493
Edit Links dialog box, 593–594, 660
Edit mode
    multiple formatting styles in single cell, 121
    overview, 36
Edit Objects option, Protect Sheet dialog box, 640
Edit Scenarios option, Protect Sheet dialog box, 640
Edit Series dialog box
    charts, 458
    defined, 446
Edit Sparklines dialog box, 513
editing, 440. *See also* entering and editing data
Editing tab, Share Workbook dialog box, 631
EFFECT function, 923
element codes, headers and footers, 186–187
elements, of charts, 437–442
Else clause, If-Then-Else structure, 818
embedded chart
    activating, 405, 413
    changing data range, 457
embedding
    objects in worksheets
        non-Word documents, 623
        overview, 622
        Word documents, 623
    workbooks in Word
        copying, 624–626
        creating new Excel objects, 626
        saved workbooks, 626
employee list.xlsx sample file, 940
Enable Automatic Percent Entry check box, 44, 552
Enable Background Error Checking check box, 209, 665
Enable Content button
    Security Warning panel, 153, 934
    Trust Center dialog box, 797
Enable Iterative Calculation setting, 220
Encrypt Document dialog box, 150, 642
Encrypt with Password command, Info pane, 155
End Sub statement, 799
end_period argument

CUMIPMT function, 332
CUMPRINC function, 332
depreciation functions, 351
Engineering Category Functions, 921–922
entering and editing data
    array formulas, 364
    cell contents
        data-entry techniques, 37–42
        editing, 35–37
        erasing, 35
        overview, 34
        replacing, 35
    data types
        formulas, 30–31
        numeric values, 30
        overview, 29
        text entries, 30
    date values, 33–34
    number formatting
        automatic number formatting, 43–44
        custom number formats, 47–48
        Format Cells dialog box, 45–47
        overview, 42–43
        Ribbon interface, 44
        shortcut keys, 45
    text and values, 32–33
    time values, 33–34
Entire Workbook printing option, 178
EntireColumn property, 890
EntireRow property, 890
entry types, suppressing, 567
EOMONTH function, 258, 920
equal sign (=), 203
Equation Editor feature
    defined, 5
    general discussion, 535–537
Equation Tools tab, Equation Editor, 536
erasing cell contents, 35
ERF function, 922
ERFC function, 922
ERFC.PRECISE function, 922
ERF.PRECISE function, 922
Error Alert tab, Data Validation dialog box, 571, 574
error bars feature, 437, 461–463
Error Checking dialog box, 667
errors. *See also names of specific error*
    appropriate for Solver tool, 765
    AutoCorrect feature, 672–674

Index

errors *(continued)*

in formulas

#DIV/0! errors, 653–654

#N/A errors, 654–655

#NAME? errors, 655

#NULL! errors, 655

#NUM! errors, 655

#REF! errors, 656

#VALUE! errors, 656

absolute/relative reference problems, 657

actual versus displayed values, 658–659

blank cells not blank, 651–652

colors, 656

extra space characters, 652

floating point number errors, 659–660

formulas are not calculated, 658

hash mark filled cells, 651

mismatched parentheses, 650–651

operator precedence problems, 657–658

overview, 649–650

"phantom link" errors, 660

returning errors, 653

overview, 219

in ranges, 286

replacing information, 670

searching for formatting, 670–671

searching for information, 669–670

spell checking worksheets, 671–672

summing ranges containing, 379–380

tools for

background error-checking feature, 665–667

fixing circular reference errors, 665

Formula Evaluator feature, 667–668

identifying cells of particular type, 661–662

tracing cell relationships, 663–665

tracing error values, 665

viewing formulas, 662–663

ERROR.TYPE function, 925

Euro Currency Tools, 905

Evaluate button, Evaluate Formula dialog box, 668

Evaluate Formula dialog box, 390, 667

EVEN function, 927

events

defined, 846

entering event-handler VBA code, 874–875

non-object events

OnKey, 884–885

OnTime, 883–884

not associated with objects, 873

workbook

BeforeClose, 879

BeforeSave, 878–879

NewSheet, 878

Open, 876–877

SheetActivate, 878

worksheets

BeforeRightClick, 883

Change, 880

monitoring specific range for changes, 881

SelectionChange, 882–883

Evolutionary tab, Solver Options dialog box, 770

EXACT function, 234, 932

Excel Options dialog box

adding comments to cells, 94–95

Advanced tab, 36–38, 52, 439, 519, 806

Automatically Insert a Decimal Point check box, 38

Customize Ribbon tab, 548

Formulas tab, 665–666

Language tab, 127

Quick Access Toolbar section, 18

Reset button, 547

Reset Ignored Errors button, 666

Save Files in This Format option, 148

Selection option, 118

Set Precision as Displayed check box, 659

Set Precision as Displayed option, 551

Show Mini Toolbar on Selection option, 17

Transition Navigation Keys option, 949

Excel shortcut keys. *See* shortcut keys

EXP function, 927

expanding multicell arrays, 365–366

exploded view, pie chart, 425

EXPONDIST function, 918

EXPON.DIST function, 929

exponential smoothing tool, Analysis ToolPak add-in, 786

Export All Customization option, 546

exporting graphic objects, 525

Extended Date Functions add-in, 256

external cell references, 590

External Data Properties dialog box, 688–689

External Data Range Properties dialog box, 612–613

external database file data

data returned by Query

adjusting external data range properties, 688–689

changing, 690

deleting, 690

refreshing, 689–690

importing Access tables, 679–680

overview, 677–678

retrieving data
 database file, 681
 overview, 680
 selecting data source, 682–684
 specifying location for data, 687–688
 using Query Wizard, 684–687
 using without Wizard, 690–693
external reference formulas
 changing link source, 595
 changing startup prompt, 594
 creating link formulas by pointing, 591
 creating links to unsaved workbooks, 592
 link formula syntax, 590–591
 opening workbook with, 592–594
 pasting links, 591
 severing links, 595
 updating links, 594–595
extracting
 all but first word of strings, 245
 characters from strings, 240–241
 filenames from path specifications, 244
 first, middle, and last names, 245–247
 last word of strings, 244–245
`extreme color scale.xlsx` sample file, 939

F

`FACT` function, 927
`FACTDOUBLE` function, 927
Factor argument, 351
`FALSE` function, 925
Favorite Links list, 146
`FDIST` function, 918
`F.DIST` function, 929
`F.DIST.RT` function, 929
fence-post analogy, 262
field, database, 678
field buttons, pivot chart, 738
15-digit accuracy, 31
File Block Policy, 145
File button, 4, 6–7, 470–471
File in Use dialog box, 629
File Name button, 187
File Name field, Save As dialog box, 148
File Now Available dialog box, 629
File Path button, 187
File Tab option, Choose Commands From drop-down list, 544
files. *See also* workbooks
 AutoRecover feature, 149–150
 compatibility
  checking, 157–159
  saving for use with older versions, 159–160

display preferences, 147
Info options
 Compatibility Mode section, 154
 Permissions section, 154–155
 Prepare for Sharing section, 155–156
 Security Warning section, 153–154
 Versions section, 156
names of
 extracting from path specification, 244
 filtering, 146–147
organizing, 151–153
overview, 141–142
passwords, 150–151
reservations, 628–629
safeguarding, 157
fill handle, 23
Fill horizontal alignment option, Format Cells dialog box, 123
Fill tab, Format Cells dialog box, 484
Filter button, Name Manager dialog box, 660
Filter command, shortcut menu, 113
Filter Data dialog box, Query Wizard, 685
filtering
 data, Query Wizard, 685–686
 with slicers, 731–733
 tables, 112–113
final mark, workbooks, 646
financial application formulas. *See* formulas, for financial applications
Financial Category Functions, 923–924
financial functions, 4, 331
Find All button, Find and Replace dialog box, 669
Find and Replace dialog box, 76–77, 252, 501, 552, 668–671
Find Format dialog box, 670
`FIND` function, 242, 932
Finish button, Query Wizard, 686–687
`FINV` function, 918
`F.INV` function, 929
`F.INV.RT` function, 929
First Column check box, 107
First Point option, Sparklines, 509
`FISHER` function, 930
`FISHERINV` function, 930
fixed decimal–places option, 38
`FIXED` function, 932
fixed pitch font, 67
Fixed value error bar, Format Error Bars dialog box, 462–463
fixed-term investment, 344
floating point number errors, 659–660
`FLOOR` function, 927
`FLOOR.PRECISE` function, 927
Followed Hyperlink style, 611

Index

`FollowHyperlink` event, 880

Font tab, Format Cells dialog box, 120, 484

fonts
modifying in charts, 443
worksheet formatting, 119–122

footers. *See* headers and footers

`FORECAST` function, 371, 930

Form button, Customize Quick Access Toolbar, 41–42

Form controls, 860

Format Axis dialog box
Alignment tab, 452
Axis Options tab, 448–449
displaying, 415

Format button
Find What text box, 669
New Formatting Rule dialog box, 484–485

Format Cells dialog box
Alignment tab, 122
Border tab, 129, 484
Clear button, 484
Custom category in the Number tab, 399
Fill tab, 484
Font tab, 484
formatting numbers, 45–47, 554–555
Number tab, 254, 484
overview, 118–119
pivot tables, 703
Protection tab, 639
tabbed dialog boxes, 19–21

Format Cells option, Protect Sheet dialog box, 640

Format Chart Area dialog box, 189, 417

Format Columns option, Protect Sheet dialog box, 640

Format Comment dialog box, 95

Format contextual tab, 13

Format Data Labels dialog box, 460

Format Data Point dialog box, 456

Format Data Series dialog box
displaying, 456
Series Options tab, 425, 475

Format Data Table dialog box, 468–469

Format dialog box
charts, 441–442
Properties tab, 189

Format Error Bars dialog box, 462–463

Format Painter button, 131

Format Picture button, 187

Format Rows option, Protect Sheet dialog box, 640

Format Shape dialog box, 522

Format Trendline dialog box, 463–464

Formatted Text (RTF) paste option, Paste Special dialog box, 619

formatting
chart elements, 415–416
comments in cells, 95
conditional
copying cells, 500
deleting, 500
formula-based rules, 494–495
graphics, 485–494
locating cells, 501
making rules, 484–485
managing rules, 499–500
overview, 481–482
types of, 483–484
data, 693
dates and times, 254–255
numbers
automatic, 43–44, 552
creating, 555–560
custom, 47–48
examples of, 560–568
Format Cells dialog box, 45–47, 554–555
overview, 42–43, 551–552
Ribbon interface, 44, 552–553
shortcut keys, 45, 553
pivot tables, 703–705
searching for, 670–671
Shape images, 520–522
shortcut keys, 952
worksheets
background images, 130–131
borders and lines, 128–129
colors and shading, 127–128
document themes, 135–139
fonts, 119–122
named styles, 131–135
text alignment, 122–127
tools for, 115–119

Formatting (R) option, 86, 88

forms, data entry, 40–42

Formula Autocomplete feature, 204, 218

Formula AutoCorrect feature, 199, 651

Formula bar
array constants, 367
Check Mark icon, 36
defined, 32–33
editing keys, 951–952
overview, 6–7
using as calculator, 227
X icon, 36

formula data, 29–31

Formula Evaluator feature, 390, 667–668

`Formula` property, 816
Formula tab
    Excel Options dialog box, 230
    Ribbon, 11
Formula view, workbook, 662
formulas. *See also* array formulas; text formulas
    arguments, 201–202
    calculating amortization schedule, 338
    calculating loans with irregular payments, 342
    conditional sums using multiple criteria
        using And, 305–306
        using And and Or, 307
        using Or, 306–307
    conditional sums using single criterion
        only negative values, 303–304
        overview, 302–303
        values based on date comparison, 305
        values based on different range, 304
        values based on text comparison, 305
    consolidating worksheets, 598
    counting
        blank cells, 284–285
        `COUNTIF` function, 287
        creating a frequency distribution, 294–299
        error values in a range, 286
        logical values, 286
        most frequently occurring entry, 291
        multiple criteria, 288–291
        nonblank cells, 285
        nontext cells, 285
        number of unique values, 293–294
        numeric cells, 285
        occurrences of specific text, 292–293
        text cells, 285
        total number of cells, 283–284
        worksheet cells, 281–283
    creating conditional formatting rule, 496
    data validation feature
        accepting dates by day of week, 577
        accepting larger values than previous cell, 576
        accepting nonduplicate entries only, 576–577
        accepting only values that don't exceed total, 578
        accepting text only, 576
        accepting text that begins with specific characters, 577
        creating dependent lists, 578–579
        overview, 574
    editing, 209
    entering into worksheets
        inserting functions, 206–208
        manually, 203
        overview, 202–203
        pasting range names, 205–206
        by pointing, 203–205
        tips, 208–209
    errors
        `#DIV/0!` errors, 653–654
        `#N/A` errors, 654–655
        `#NAME?` errors, 655
        `#NULL!` errors, 655
        `#NUM!` errors, 655
        `#REF!` errors, 656
        `#VALUE!` errors, 656
        absolute/relative reference problems, 657
        actual versus displayed values, 658–659
        blank cells not blank, 651–652
        circular references, 219–220
        colors, 656
        extra space characters, 652
        floating point number errors, 659–660
        formulas are not calculated, 658
        hash mark filled cells, 651
        mismatched parentheses, 650–651
        operator precedence problems, 657–658
        overview, 218–219
        "phantom link" errors, 660
        returning errors, 653
        specifying when formulas are calculated, 220–222
    external reference
        changing link source, 595
        changing startup prompt, 594
        creating link formulas by pointing, 591
        creating links to unsaved workbooks, 592
        link formula syntax, 590–591
        opening workbook with, 592–594
        pasting links, 591
        severing links, 595
        updating links, 594–595
    for financial applications
        depreciation calculations, 350–353
        investment calculations, 343–350
        loan calculations, 330–343
        time value of money, 329–330
    formula-based rules
        formula examples, 496–499
        overview, 494–495
        relative and absolute references, 495–496
    hard-coding values, 746–747
    lookup
        calculating grade-point averages, 322–323
        case-sensitive, 320–321
        combining `MATCH` and `INDEX` functions, 316–318

formulas, lookup *(continued)*
  determining cell address of values within range, 326
  determining letter grades for test scores, 322
  exact values, 318–319
  HLOOKUP function, 313–314
  looking up values by using closest match, 327–328
  looking up values from multiple lookup tables, 321
  LOOKUP function, 314–315
  lookup relevant functions, 310–312
  overview, 309–310
  performing two-way lookup, 323–326
  values to left, 319–320
  VLOOKUP function, 312–313
making exact copies of, 227–228
naming techniques
  applying names to existing references, 226
  names for constants, 222–223
  names for formulas, 223–224
  range intersections, 224–226
overview, 30–31, 195–196, 281–282
selecting array formula range, 364
summing
  all cells in a range, 299–300
  computing a cumulative sum, 300–302
  "top *n*" values, 302
  worksheet cells, 281–283
syntax of, linking workbooks, 590–591
that use functions, 200–201
transforming data, 240
using cell references
  changing types of, 212
  from other workbooks, 213–214
  from other worksheets, 212–213
  overview, 209–210
  relative, absolute, and mixed, 210–212
using custom functions, 828
using functions in, 199–202
using in tables
  referencing data, 217–218
  summarizing data, 214–216
  within a table, 216–217
using operators in
  operator precedence, 197–199
  overview, 196–199
values
  converting to, 228
  hard-code, 227
viewing using Excel Auditing tools, 662–663
Formulas & Number Formatting option, 85, 88

Formulas option
  defined, 85
  Go to Special dialog box, 75, 661
  Paste Special dialog box, 87
Formulas tab
  Excel Options dialog box, 665–666, 764
  Function Library group, 206
For-Next loop
  looping through ranges, 891
  modifying chart properties, 898
  VBA macros, 818
Fourier Analysis tool, Analysis ToolPak add-in, 787
Fraction format category, 554
Fraction format, Format Cells dialog box, 46–47
fractions
  displaying, 564–565
  entering numbers with, 40
Frame control, 844
free-floating text, 445
FreeForm Shape, 519, 523
freeware programs, 934
Freeze First Column option, 63
Freeze Panes option, 63
Freeze Top Row option, 63
freezing panes, 62–64
frequency distributions
  creating, 722–724
  FREQUENCY function, 294–295
  using a pivot table, 298–299
  using formulas, 296–297
  using the Analysis ToolPak, 297–298
frequency distribution.xlsx sample file, 937
FREQUENCY function
  arrays and, 371
  counting formulas, 294–295
  function of, 930
  overview, 282
Frontline Systems company, 775
FTEST function, 918
F.TEST function, 930
F-Test tool, Analysis ToolPak add-in, 786–787
Full Screen mode, Quick Access toolbar, 541
Function Arguments dialog box
  displaying, 208
  inserting custom function, 835–836
  inserting functions into formulas, 206
  specifying arguments, 825
Function drop-down list, Consolidate dialog box, 600
Function keys, 954–955
Function Library group, 206

`function plot 2D.xlsx` sample file, 938
`function plot 3D.xlsm` sample file, 938
Function procedure, 800
functions
   custom worksheet
      debugging, 833–834
      example of, 824–826
      function procedure arguments, 828–833
      function procedures, 826–828
      inserting, 834–836
      VBA functions, 823
   date
      age calculation, 265–266
      converting nondate string to date, 261–262
      current date, 259
      date of most recent Sunday, 267
      date's quarter, 271
      day of week, 267
      day of year, 266–267
      displaying date, 259–260
      first day of week after a date, 267–268
      generating series of dates, 260–261
      holiday dates, 268–271
      last day of month, 271
      leap year, 271
      nth occurrence of day of week in month, 268
      number of days between dates, 262
      number of work days dates, 263–264
      number of years between dates, 265
      offsetting dates using only work days, 264
      overview, 258
   defined, 801
   time
      adding hours, minutes, or seconds, 278
      calculating difference between times, 274–275
      converting decimal hours, minutes, or seconds, 277–278
      converting from military time, 277
      displaying any time, 273
      displaying current time, 272–273
      non–time-of-day values, 279–280
      rounding time values, 279
      summing times that exceed 24 hours, 275–277
   using in worksheets, 824–825
   using with arrays, 369
Future Value (FV), defined, 330
FV function
   calculating compound interest, 347
   calculating final investment amounts, 345
   function of, 923

fv function argument, 331
FVSCHEDULE function, 923

G

GAMMADIST function, 918
GAMMA.DIST function, 930
GAMMAINV function, 918
GAMMA.INV function, 930
GAMMALN function, 930
GAMMALN.PRECISE function, 930
Gantt charts, 476–477
`gantt chart.xlsx` sample file, 938
Gaps option, 461–462
gauge charts, 473–474
`gauge chart.xlsx` sample file, 938
GCD function, 927
general array formula type, 374
General format, Format Cells dialog box, 46
General horizontal alignment option, Format Cells dialog box, 122
General number format category, 551, 554, 703
General Options dialog box, 643
GEOMEAN function, 930
GESTEP function, 922
GETPIVOTDATA function, 734–735, 926
Go To dialog box, 501
Go to Special dialog box
   Dependents option, 665
   identifying cells, 661
   Precedents option, 664
   selecting special types of cells, 74–76
Goal Seek tool, 761–764
grade-point averages, 322–323
Grand Total display
   defined, 704
   using calculated items in pivot table, 729
graphic object, exporting, 525
graphics
   conditional formats using
      color scale, 487–490
      data bars, 485–487
      icon sets, 490–494
   inserting, 532–533
   overview, 531
graphs. *See* charts
Greater than 10 conditional formatting rule, 481
GRG Nonlinear tab, Solver Options dialog box, 770–771
gridlines, charts, 448
Group mode, 73–74

Index

grouping
   automatically, 719–722
   manually, 717–722
   Shape images, 522
Grouping dialog box, 717, 720
GroupName property, 869
groups
   customizing on Ribbon, 546–547
   pivot table, defined, 704
GROWTH function, 371, 930

H

hands-on example.xlsx sample file, 938
hard drive, backing up, 157
hard-code values, 227, 746–747
HARMEAN function, 930
hash mark (#) character, 67, 218
hash mark filled cells, 651
HasLegend property, 898
Header Row, 110
Header Row check box, 107
Header/Footer tab, Page Setup dialog box, 185
headers and footers
   element codes, 186–187
   options, 187
   overview, 185–186
   predefined, 186
Height property, 864
Help button, 6–7
Help on This Function link, 206
Help option, 592
help resources
   Help system, 943
   Internet newsgroups
      accessing by newsreaders, 945
      accessing by Web browsers, 945–946
      searching, 946–947
   Internet Web sites
      contextures, 948
      daily dose of Excel, 948
      David McRitchie's Excel Pages, 948
      Jon Peltier's Excel page, 948
      Mr. Excel, 948
      Pearson Software Consulting, 948
      Pointy Haired Dilbert, 948
      spreadsheet page, 947
   Microsoft technical support
      Microsoft Excel home page, 944
      Microsoft Knowledge Base, 944

Microsoft Office Home page, 944–945
   options, 944
HEX2BIN function, 922
HEX2DEC function, 922
HEX2OCT function, 922
Hidden and Empty Cell Settings dialog box, 461, 508
hidden data, Sparkline graphics, 508
hiding
   comments, 97
   rows and columns, 66–67
   worksheets, 57–58
High Point option, Sparklines, 509
Highlight Changes dialog box, 633–634
Histogram tool, Analysis ToolPak add-in, 297–298, 787–788
histograms, 237–238, 475–476
HLOOKUP function, 311, 313–314, 327, 926
holidays
   Christmas Day, 271
   Columbus Day, 270
   Easter, 270
   Independence Day, 270
   Labor Day, 270
   Martin Luther King, Jr. Day, 269
   Memorial Day, 270
   New Year's Day, 269
   overview, 268–269
   Presidents' Day, 269
   Thanksgiving Day, 271
   Veterans Day, 270
holidays.xlsx sample file, 936
Home Tab option, 544
Home tab, Ribbon, 11–12, 116, 120
horizontal alignment options, 122–123
Horizontal Axis Crosses setting, 450–451
horizontal page-break line, 181
Horizontal scrollbar, 6–7
hot key, 19, 856
HOUR function, 272, 920
hourly readings.xlsx sample file, 940
hours, decimal, 277–278
HTML (HyperText Markup Language), 605–609
HTML Format paste option, Paste Special dialog box, 619
hundreds, displaying values in, 561
HYPERLINK function, 926
hyperlinks
   copying data from Excel to Word, 617
   inserting, 610–611
   pasting, 620–622
   selecting, 611
HyperText Markup Language (HTML), 605–609

`HYPGEOMDIST` function, 918
`HYPGEOM.DIST` function, 930
hypocycloid curve, 427

I

Icon Set conditional formatting rule, 482
`icon set examples.xlsx` sample file, 939
Icon Sets command, Conditional Formatting drop-down
    list, 483
identical strings, 233–234
IE (Internet Explorer), 609
`IF` function
    #DIV/0! errors, 654
    error values, 380
    formulas using, 200
    function of, 925
    hiding cumulative sums for missing data, 301
    Lookup formulas, 311–312
    returning location of maximum value in range, 384
`If` statement, 894
`IFERROR` function
    #DIV/0! errors, 654
    compatibility with older versions, 394
    extracting first word of string, 244–245
    function of, 925
    modified version, 380
    overview, 311
    testing for error results, 319
`If-Then` construct, VBA macros, 818
Ignore All button, Spelling dialog box, 672
Ignore Blank check box, Data Validation dialog box, 572
Ignore Error option, 666
Ignore Integer Constraints option, Solver Options dialog
    box, 771
Ignore Once button, Spelling dialog box, 672
Ignore Print Areas check box, 178
`IMABS` function, 922
`Image` control, ActiveX, 844, 861, 868
Image editing enhancements, 4
`IMAGINARY` function, 922
`IMARGUMENT` function, 922
`IMCONJUGATE` function, 922
`IMCOS` function, 922
`IMDIV` function, 922
`IMEXP` function, 922
`IMLN` function, 922
`IMLOG10` function, 922
`IMLOG2` function, 922
Import Customization File option, 546

Import Data dialog box, 687
Import/Export button, 545
importing, 679–680. *See also* external database file data
`IMPOWER` function, 922
`IMPRODUCT` function, 922
`IMREAL` function, 922
`IMSIN` function, 922
`IMSQRT` function, 922
`IMSUB` function, 922
`IMSUM` function, 922
Include in Personal View settings, 633
`income and expense.xlsx` sample file, 940
incomplete calculation error, 650
incorrect reference error, 649
Increase Decimal Places button, Ribbon, 44, 553, 560
Increase Font Size button, Ribbon, 14
Indent setting, 123
Independence Day, date functions, 270
independent variables, 791
`INDEX` function
    arrays, 363
    function of, 926
    general discussion, 316–318
    Lookup formulas, 311
    multiple forms, 208
    returning longest text in range, 385
indirect cell dependent, 663
indirect cell precedent, 663
`INDIRECT` function, 328, 371, 926
`INFO` function, 925
Info options
    Compatibility Mode section, 154
    Permissions section, 154–155
    Prepare for Sharing section, 155–156
    Security Warning section, 153–154
    Versions section, 156
information
    replacing, 670
    searching for, 669–670
Information Category Functions, 925
Information Rights Management (IRM), 638
Input Message tab, Data Validation dialog box, 571
Input X Range option, Regression dialog box, 791
`InputBox` function, 838–839, 893
Insert Calculated Field dialog box, 727
Insert Calculated Item dialog box, 729
Insert Chart Dialog box, 470
Insert Columns option, Protect Sheet dialog box, 640
Insert dialog box, 65–66

Index

Insert Function dialog box
    custom functions, 834–835
    overview, 202
    Search for a Function field, 207
    tips, 208
Insert Hyperlink dialog box, 610
Insert Hyperlinks option, Protect Sheet dialog box, 640
Insert Picture dialog box, 532
Insert Rows option, Protect Sheet dialog box, 640
Insert Shapes command, 6–7, 521
Insert shortcut menu, 106
Insert tab, Ribbon, 11
Insert Worksheet control, 54
inserting
    custom worksheet functions, 834–836
    rows and columns, 65–66
    WordArt graphic on worksheet, 530
Inspect Document command, Info pane, 155
inspecting workbook, 646
installing
    add-ins, 913
    Analysis ToolPak add-in, 298, 782
    Solver add-in, 765
INT function, 927
Integer data type, 901
integers
    generating arrays of, 370–371
    summing digits of, 386–387
IntegralHeight property
    ListBox control, 869
    TextBox control, 871
INTERCEPT function, 930
interest, calculating, 343–348
interest rate, 330
interface. *See* user interface
intermediary links, 597
Internet
    backup site, 157
    HTML, 605, 607, 609
    hyperlinks, 610–611
    newsgroups
        accessing by newsreaders, 945
        accessing by Web browsers, 945–946
        searching, 946–947
    Web formats
        creating HTML files, 607
        creating single file web pages, 607–609
        overview, 606
    Web queries, 612–613

Web sites
    contextures, 948
    daily dose of Excel, 948
    David McRitchie's Excel Pages, 948
    Jon Peltier's Excel Page, 948
    Mr. Excel, 948
    Pearson Software Consulting, 948
    Pointy Haired Dilbert, 948
    spreadsheet page, 947
Internet Explorer (IE), 609
intersection operator, 224
Interval between Labels setting, 453–454
INTRATE function, 923
investment calculations
    future value of series of deposits, 348–350
    future value of single deposit
        compound interest, 344–346
        interest with continuous compounding, 346–348
        simple interest, 343–344
investment calculations.xlsx sample file, 937
investment portfolio, optimizing, 778–779
investment portfolio.xlsx sample file, 941
invisible digital signature, 647
IPMT function, 332, 923
IrfanView, 531
IRM (Information Rights Management), 638
IRR function, 655, 923
irregular payment, calculating, 341–343
irregular payments.xlsx sample file, 937
ISBLANK function, 925
ISERR function, 286, 925
ISERROR function, 286, 925
ISEVEN function, 925
ISLOGICAL function, 925
ISNA function, 286, 925
ISNONTEXT function, 285, 925
ISNUMBER function, 925
ISO.CEILING function, 927
ISODD function, 925
ISPMT function, 923
ISREF function, 925
ISTEXT function, 925
item, pivot table, 705
Iterations option, Solver Options dialog box, 771

J

Jelen, Bill, 948
jogging log.xlsx sample file, 936

Jon Peltier's Excel Page, 948
Justify horizontal alignment option, Format Cells dialog box, 123
Justify vertical alignment option, Format Cells dialog box, 124

K

Keep Source Column Width (W) option, 85
Keep Source Formatting (K) option, 85
key field, 678
keyboard
    accessing Ribbon via, 15–16
    navigating with, 9–10
    selecting chart elements, 438–439
keyboard shortcuts, 587. *See also* shortcut keys
keytips pop-up, 15–16
KURT function, 930
Kusleika, Dick, 948

L

Label control, ActiveX, 844, 861, 868
Label Options tab, Format Data Labels dialog box, 460
Labor Day, date functions, 270
landscape orientation, 179
Language tab, Excel Options dialog box, 127
LARGE function
    function of, 930
    with range argument, 832
    summing values, 381
LargeChange property, 870
Last Cell option, Go to Special dialog box, 76
Last Column check box, 107
Last Custom Setting, Page Layout view, 180
Last Point option, Sparklines, 509
Layout contextual tab, 13
layouts
    of charts, 409–411
    of SmartArt diagram, 528
LCM function, 927
leap year, 255–256, 271
Left arrow key, 10
Left Column check box, Consolidate dialog box, 602
LEFT function
    extracting characters from string, 240–241
    function of, 932
Left horizontal alignment option, Format Cells dialog box, 122
Left property, 864
legend, chart, 407, 439, 442, 446–448
LEN function
    counting characters in string, 239
    function of, 932

letter grades for test scores, 322
levels, outline, 588
Life argument, 351
Light style category, tables, 103
line chart, 405, 418, 423–424
line charts.xlsx sample file, 938
Line Sparkline, 504
line width, Sparkline graphics, 508
linear equations, 771–773
linear equations.xlsx sample file, 941
lines, worksheet, 128–129
LINEST function
    function of, 930
    returning arrays, 371
Link to File check box, Object dialog box, 626
Linked Picture (I) option, 86
LinkedCell property
    CheckBox control, 867
    ComboBox control, 867
    defined, 864
    ListBox control, 869
    OptionButton control, 869
    ScrollBar control, 870
    SpinButton control, 871
linking workbooks
    external reference formulas
        changing link source, 595
        changing startup prompts, 594
        creating link formulas by pointing, 591
        creating links to unsaved workbooks, 592
        link formula syntax, 590–591
        opening workbook with, 592–594
        pasting links, 591
        severing links, 595
        updating links, 594–595
    overview, 589–590
    problem avoidance
        intermediary links, 597
        modifying source workbooks, 596–597
        overview, 595
        renaming or moving source workbooks, 596
        using Save As command, 596
Links dialog box, 621–622
list formulas.xlsm sample file, 941
List option, Data Validation dialog box, 571
ListBox control, ActiveX, 844, 861, 868–869
ListFillRange property
    ComboBox control, 867
    defined, 864
    ListBox control, 869

Index

`ListFormulas` macro, 820
`ListRows` property, `ComboBox` control, 867
list-separator character, 202
`ListStyle` property
    `ComboBox` control, 867
    `ListBox` control, 869
live preview, 132, 137
`LN` function, 927
`loan amortization schedule.xlsx` sample file, 937
loan calculations
    amortization schedule, 337–338
    credit card payments, 334–336
    data tables
        one-way, 338–340
        two-way, 340–341
    example of, 333–334
    `IPMT` function, 332
    irregular payments, 341–343
    `NPER` function, 333
    overview, 330
    `PMT` function, 331–332
    `PV` function, 333
    `RATE` function, 332
`loan data tables.xlsx` sample file, 937
`loan payment calculator.xlsx` sample file, 935
`loan payment.xlsx` sample file, 935, 937
locating functions, 828
`LOG` function, 927
`log scale.xlsx` sample file, 938
`LOG10` function, 927
`LOGEST` function
    function of, 930
    returning arrays, 371
Logical Category Functions, 925
logical error, 649
logical values
    counting formulas, 286
    `SUM` function, 300
`LOGINV` function, 918
`LOGNORMDIST` function, 918
`LOGNORM.DIST` function, 930
`LOGNORM.INV` function, 930
Long data type, 901
Look In drop-down list, 78, 669
Lookup & Reference Category Functions, 926
lookup formulas
    calculating grade-point averages, 322–323
    case-sensitive, 320–321
    combining `MATCH` and `INDEX` functions, 316–318
    determining cell address of values within range, 326

determining letter grades for test scores, 322
exact values, 318–319
`HLOOKUP` function, 313–314
looking up values by using closest match, 327–328
looking up values from multiple lookup tables, 321
`LOOKUP` function, 314–315
lookup relevant functions, 310–312
overview, 309–310
performing two-way lookup, 323–326
values to left, 319–320
`VLOOKUP` function, 312–313
`LOOKUP` function
    #N/A error, 655
    function of, 926
    general discussion, 314–315
    Lookup formulas, 311
`lookup_array` argument, `MATCH` function, 316
`lookup_value` argument
    `HLOOKUP` function, 314
    `LOOKUP` function, 315
    `MATCH` function, 316
    `VLOOKUP` function, 312
`lookup_vector` argument, `LOOKUP` function, 315
Lotus worksheet file, 255
Low Point option, Sparklines, 509
`LOWER` function
    changing text case, 239
    function of, 932

M

Macro Name option, Record Macro dialog box, 802
Macro Options dialog box, 810
Macro recorder indicator, 6–7
Macro Settings section, Trust Center dialog box, 797
macros. *See also* Visual Basic for Applications (VBA) macros
    creating, 864–866
    defined, 795, 801
    making available from worksheet button, 855
    making available on Quick Access toolbar, 855–856
    overview, 795–796
Macros option, Choose Commands From drop-down list, 544–545
Main Tabs, Customize Ribbon drop-down list, 548
major gridlines, 448
Major Tick Mark option, 451
malware, 145
Manage Rules command, Conditional Formatting drop-down list, 483

Manage Versions button, 156
Manual Calculation mode, 221
Manual item grouping, pivot table, 717
manual what-if analysis, 747
Manufacturing sheet tab, 73
"marching ants" border, 79
Margins tab, Page Setup dialog box, 181
Mark as Final option, Info pane, 155
Marker Color control, Sparklines, 509
Markers option, Sparklines, 509
Martin Luther King, Jr. Day, date functions, 269
master workbook, 135
Match Case check box
    Find and Replace dialog box, 78
    Find What text box, 669
Match Entire Cell Contents check box
    Find and Replace dialog box, 78
    Find What text box, 669
MATCH function
    function of, 926
    general discussion, 316–318
    Lookup formulas, 311
    returning longest text in range, 385
Match Style command, 443
match_type argument, MATCH function, 316
Math & Trig Category Functions, 926–927
Math AutoCorrect tab, AutoCorrect dialog box, 674
mathematical functions, plotting, 477–479
Max Feasible Solutions option, Solver Options dialog box, 771
MAX function
    formulas using, 200
    function of, 930
    returning longest text in range, 385
Max property
    ScrollBar control, 870
    SpinButton control, 871
Max Subproblems option, Solver Options dialog box, 771
Max summary formula, 108
Max Time option, Solver Options dialog box, 771
MAXA function, 930
Maximize (Restore) button, 50
Maximum Axis Value option, 450
MaxLength property, 871
MDETERM function, 927
MDURATION function, 923
MEDIAN function, 930
Medium style category, table, 103
Memorial Day, date functions, 270
Merge & Center control , Ribbon, 125

Merge Across option, 125
Merge Cells option, 125
Merge command, Ribbon, 14
Merge Conditional Formatting (G) option, 86
Merge Scenarios dialog box, 758–759
merging
    cells, 124–125
    name styles, 134–135
    scenarios, 758
metadata, 151, 911
methods
    defined, 801
    VBA, 814
Microsoft Excel Chart Object paste option, Paste Special
        dialog box, 619
Microsoft Excel Worksheet Object paste option, Paste Special
        dialog box, 619
Microsoft Office Graphic Object paste option, Paste Special
        dialog box, 619, 621
Microsoft Office Online, 161–162
Microsoft Query. See Query application
Microsoft technical support, 944–945
microsoft.public.excel newsgroup, 946
microsoft.public.excel.charting newsgroup, 946
microsoft.public.excel.interopoledde
        newsgroup, 946
microsoft.public.excel.macintosh newsgroup, 946
microsoft.public.excel.misc newsgroup, 946
microsoft.public.excel.newusers newsgroup, 946
microsoft.public.excel.printing newsgroup, 946
microsoft.public.excel.programming newsgroup,
        946
microsoft.public.excel.templates newsgroup, 946
microsoft.public.excel.worksheet.functions
        newsgroup, 946
MID function
    extracting characters from string, 240–241
    function of, 932
    summing integer digits, 386–387
military time, converting, 277
millions, displaying values in, 562–563
MIME HTML file, 606
MIN function
    function of, 930
    gauge charts, 473
    returning location of maximum value in range, 385
Min property
    ScrollBar control, 870
    SpinButton control, 870
Min summary formula, 108

Index

MINA function, 930
Mini toolbar, 17, 116–118, 439, 442
Minimize button, 50
Minimize Ribbon button, 6–7, 12
minor gridlines, 448
Minor Tick Mark option, 451
MINUTE function, 272, 921
minutes, decimal
    adding to a time, 278
    converting to a time, 277–278
MINVERSE function
    function of, 927
    returning arrays, 371
MIRR function, 924
mismatched parentheses, formula, 199
missing data, charts, 461
mixed references, 210–212, 300
MMULT function
    function of, 927
    returning arrays, 371
MOD function
    displaying alternate-row shading, 497–498
    function of, 927
    summing nth values in range, 389
modal dialog box, 19
MODE function
    counting frequently occurring entries, 291
    function of, 918
modeless dialog box, 19
MODE.MULT function, 930
MODE.SNGL function, 930
Modify Table Quick Style dialog box, 105
Module1 code module, 909
monitor a range.xlsm sample file, 942
Month argument, 351
MONTH function, 258, 921
More Controls option, Activex, 861
More Functions summary formula, 108
mortgage loan data table.xlsx sample file, 941
mortgage loan.xlsx sample file, 940–941
Most Likely scenario, Scenario Manager, 755
mouse
    navigating worksheets with, 10
    selecting chart element with, 438–439
Move and Size with Cells option, 520
Move But Don't Size with Cells option, 520
Move Chart dialog box, 406, 414
Move Down button, Ribbon, 549
Move or Copy dialog box, 56
Move Up button, Ribbon, 549

moving
    cells and ranges
        adjacent cells, 82–83
        drag-and-drop, 81–82
        Office Clipboard, 84–85
        to other sheets, 83
        overview, 78–79
        Paste Special dialog box, 87–89
        pasting, 85–86
        Ribbon commands, 79–80
        shortcut keys, 81
        shortcut menu commands, 80–81
    chart elements, 415
    charts, 414
    Excel windows, 51
    tables, 106–107
    worksheets, 56
Moving Average option, Format Trendline dialog box, 463–464
Moving Average tool, Analysis ToolPak add-in, 788–789
MP3 audio file, embedding, 623
Mr. Excel Web site, 948
MROUND function, 927
MsgBox function
    debugging custom functions, 833
    general discussion, 839–842
multi-cell array formulas.xlsx sample file, 937
multicell arrays
    creating array constant from values in ranges, 367
    creating array from values in ranges, 366–367
    expanding or contracting, 365–366
    formulas
        displaying calendar, 398–399
        overview, 356–357
        returning lists of unique items, 396–398
        returning nonblank cells, 394–395
        returning only positive values, 394
        reversing order of cells, 395–396
        sorting range of values dynamically, 396
    generating array of consecutive integers, 370–371
    performing operations on arrays, 368
    transposing array, 369–370
    using functions with array, 369
MultiLine property, 872
MULTINOMIAL function, 927
MultiPage control, 844
multiple copies, printing, 180
multiple criteria counting.xlsx sample file, 937
multiple database tables, 692–693
multiple formatted worksheet, 170
multiple windows, worksheet, 60–61

`MultiSelect` property, 869
multiuser application, 628
`music list.xlsx` sample file, 940
My Templates icon, Available Template screen, 165

N

N function, 925
`#N/A` error, 219, 360, 654–655
NA function, 925
Name box
    Excel screen, 6–7
    ranges, 70
`#NAME?` error, 219, 655
Name Manager dialog box
    Filter button, 660
    overview, 93
`Name` property, 864
Name text field, New Name dialog box, 91
named constant, 223
named styles
    applying, 132–133
    controlling with templates, 135
    creating, 134
    merging from other workbooks, 134–135
    modifying, 133
    overview, 131
names
    applying to existing references, 226
    assigning to cells and ranges
        Create Names from Selection dialog box, 91–92
        creating names, 90–92
        managing, 92–94
        Name box, 91
        New Name dialog box, 90–91
        overview, 89–90
    removing titles from, 247
    using for constants, 222–223
    using for formulas, 223–224
    of worksheets, changing, 54–55
`Names` object, 815
naming array constants, 362–363
Narrow setting, Page Layout view, 180
navigating tables, 105
navigation keys, 9–10, 32, 37, 439
negation operator, 658
Negative Points option, Sparklines, 509
negative signs, 565–566
negative times, 274–275
negative values, formula, 303–304

`NEGBINOMDIST` function, 918
`NEGBINOM.DIST` function, 930
nesting parentheses in formulas, 198
network server, 157
`NETWORKDAYS` function, 258, 263, 921
`NETWORKDAYS.INTL` function, 201, 258, 921
networks, 627
New button, Customize Quick Access Toolbar, 42
New Data Source option, Choose Data Source dialog box, 682
New dialog box, 165
New Formatting Rule dialog box
    customizing color scale, 489
    Edit Rule button, 491–492
    overview, 484–485
New from Existing option, Available Templates screen, 169
New Group button, Ribbon, 549
New Name dialog box
    creating arrays, 362–363
    creating names for cells and ranges, 91
    formulas, 223
    overview, 90–91
    Refers To box, 212
    Refers To field, 224
New page, Backstage view, 162
New Rule command, Conditional Formatting drop-down list, 483
New Tab button, Ribbon, 549
New Table Quick Style dialog box, 103–104
New Web Query dialog box, 612–613
New Year's Day, date functions, 269
newsgroups
    accessing by newsreaders, 945
    accessing by Web browsers, 945–946
    searching, 946–947
`NewSheet` event, 876, 878
newsreaders, 945
1900 date system, 250
1904 date system, 250
No Borders (B) option, 85
No Cell Icon, Edit Formatting Rule dialog box, 493–494
`No cells were found` message, 74
No Comments or Indicators option, 95
`No Switch` argument, 351
`NOMINAL` function, 924
nonblank cells
    counting, 285
    returning from ranges, 394–395
nondate, 250
None summary formula, 108
nonformula cells, unlocking, 169

Index

non-numeric characters
    pivot tables, 715–717
    removing from string, 390
non-object events
    OnKey, 884–885
    OnTime, 883–884
nonprinting characters, 239
nonrelative references, 212
nontext cells, 285
Normal distribution option, Random Number Generation
    dialog box, 790
Normal Font check box, 120
Normal mode formatting, 440
Normal Probability option, Regression dialog box, 791
Normal setting, Page Layout view, 180
Normal style, cells, 132–133
Normal view, workbooks, 662
normalized data, 700
`normalized data.xlsx` sample file, 940
`NORMDIST` function, 918
`NORM.DIST` function, 930
`NORMINV` function, 918
`NORM.INV` function, 930
`NORMSDIST` function, 918
`NORM.S.DIST` function, 930
`NORMSINV` function, 918
`NORM.S.INV` function, 930
`NOT` function, 925
Notify option, File in Use dialog box, 629
`NOW` function, 201, 258, 272, 829, 921
`NPER` function, 33, 924
`nper` function argument, 331
`NPV` function, 924
`#NULL!` error, 219, 655
null hypothesis, 792
`#NUM!` error, 219, 396–397, 655
Num Lock key, 9
Number Format drop-down control, 25, 44, 552
Number format, Format Cells dialog box, 46–47, 554
number format string, 556
`number formats.xlsx` sample file, 939
number formatting
    automatic, 43–44, 552
    creating
        format codes, 558–560
        overview, 555–557
        parts of format strings, 557–558
    custom, 47–48

    examples of
        dates and times, 566
        filling cells with repeating characters, 568
        fractions, 564–565
        leading zeros, 564
        negative signs on right, 565–566
        scaling values, 560–563
        suppressing entry types, 567
        text with numbers, 566–567
    Format Cells dialog box, 45–47, 554–555
    overview, 42–43, 551–552
    Ribbon interface, 44, 552–553
    shortcut keys, 45, 553
`number formatting.xlsx` sample file, 935
Number of Pages button, 186
Number of Random Numbers option, Random Number
    Generation dialog box, 790
Number of Variables option, Random Number Generation
    dialog box, 790
Number tab, Format Cells dialog box, 45–46, 254–255, 484, 554
numbers
    with fractions, 40
    ordinal, 247–248
    padding, 238–239
    serial
        dates, 249–250
        times, 252–253
numeric cells, 285
numeric values, 30

O

Object data type, 901
Object dialog box, 622–623
Object Linking and Embedding (OLE), 622
object references, 900–901
object-oriented language, 814
objects
    creating new in Word, 626
    defined, 801
    VBA, 813–815
Objects option, Go to Special dialog box, 75
`OCT2BIN` function, 922
ODBC (Open DataBase Connectivity), 678
`ODD` function, 927
`ODDFPRICE` function, 924
`ODDFYIELD` function, 924
`ODDLPRICE` function, 924
`ODDLYIELD` function, 924
Office applications. *See* sharing data with Office applications
Office ClipArt, 470–471

Office Clipboard
   cells and ranges, 84–85
   copying and pasting, 79–80
   versus Windows Clipboard, 616
Office Online Templates section, 161
OFFSET function
   function of, 926
   Lookup formulas, 311
   returning last value in column, 392
OLAP (OnLine Analytical Processing) cube, 678
OLAP Cubes tab, Choose Data Source dialog box, 682
OLE (Object Linking and Embedding), 622
On Error Resume Next statement, 878, 885
one-dimensional array
   horizontal, 360–361
   storing, 355
   vertical, 361
one-input data table, 748–750
one-way data table, 338–340
OnKey event, 884–885
OnLine Analytical Processing (OLAP) cube, 678
OnTime event, 883–884
Open and Repair option, Open dialog box, 146
Open as Copy option, Open dialog box, 146
Open DataBase Connectivity (ODBC), 678
Open dialog box
   compared to Save As dialog box, 148
   displaying, 143
   Open and Repair option, 146
   Open as Copy option, 146
   Open in Browser option, 146
   Open in Protected View option, 146
   Open option, 145
   Open Read-Only option, 145
   organizing files, 151
   resizing, 144
   Windows Vista, 144
Open event, 876–877
Open in Browser option, Open dialog box, 146
Open in Protected View option, Open dialog box, 146
Open option, Open dialog box, 145
Open Read-Only option, Open dialog box, 145
operand, 219
Operation section, Paste Special dialog box, 88
operator precedence, 197–199, 657–658
operators, 196–197
Option Explicit statement, 817
OptionButton control, ActiveX, 844, 861, 869
options
   headers and footers, 187
   tables, 107

Options button, Clipboard task pane, 84
Options dialog box. *See* Excel Options dialog box; Solver
      Options dialog box
Or criteria, formulas, 290–291, 306–307
OR function, 925
order argument, Series formula, 459
ordinal numbers, 247–248
organizing files, 151–153
orientation, chart data, 411
Other Charts category, 429–433
outliers, 417
outline example.xlsx sample file, 939
outlines
   adding data, 588
   creating, 584–587
   displaying levels, 587
   hiding symbols, 588
   overview, 581–584
   removing, 588
output
   Analysis ToolPak add-in, 783
   Descriptive Statistics tool, 785–786
   F-Test tool, 786–787
   Histogram tool, 787–788
   paired t-Test dialog box, 792
overriding
   positioning of category axis, 452
   time-based category axis, 454–455

P

padding numbers, 238–239
Page Break Preview, 172
page breaks, 173, 181–182
Page Layout tab, Ribbon, 11
Page Layout view, 27, 172
page margins, printing, 180–181
Page Number button, 186
page orientation, printing, 179
Page Setup dialog box
   displaying, 653
   Header/Footer tab, 185
   printing comments, 97
   Sheet tab, 183
page setup settings
   adjusting page margins, 180–181
   background images, 185
   changing page orientation, 179
   choosing printers, 178
   overview, 177–178

Index

page breaks
   inserting, 181–182
   removing, 182
printing
   cell gridlines, 183–184
   multiple copies, 180
   row and column headers, 185
   row and column titles, 182–183
scaling printed output, 183
specifying
   paper size, 179–180
   what to print, 178–179
Page View buttons, 6–7
`PageSetup` object, 815
Paired two-sample for means t-Test, 792
panes, worksheets, 62
paper size, printing, 179–180
Parameters section, Random Number Generation dialog box, 789
parentheses, mismatched, 650–651
Pareto option, Histogram tool, 787
Password dialog box, 642
passwords
   to open workbooks, 641–643
   protecting work, 637
   specifying, 150–151
Paste (P) option, 85
Paste All button, Clipboard task pane, 84
Paste button, Paste Special dialog box, 619
Paste command, 5
Paste Link (N) option, Paste Special dialog box, 86, 89, 619–620
Paste Name dialog box, 205–206
Paste Options Smart Tag, 617–618
Paste preview option, 5
Paste Special dialog box
   consolidating worksheets, 599
   copying formatting, 500
   copying from Excel to Word, 617–620
   mathematical operations without formulas, 88
   overview, 87–88
   skipping blanks, 89
   transposing a range, 89
Paste Special option, 86
`PasteSpecial` operation, 807
pasting
   cells and ranges, 85–86
   linking workbooks, 591
   with Office application, 616–617
   undoing, 79

pasting links, 590
`Path` property, 896
Patterned distribution option, Random Number Generation dialog box, 790
Payment (PMT), 330
PDF (Portable Document Format), 645
PDF files, 645–646
Pearson, Chip, 948
`PEARSON` function, 930
Pearson Software Consulting Web site, 948
peer-to-peer network, 628
`per` function argument, 331
Percent Style button
   Number Fromat drop-down list, 44
   Ribbon, 553
Percentage error bar, Format Error Bars dialog box, 462–463
Percentage format category, 554
Percentage format, Format Cells dialog box, 46–47
`PERCENTILE` function, 918
`PERCENTILE.EXC` function, 931
`PERCENTILE.INC` function, 931
`PERCENTRANK` function, 919
`PERCENTRANK.EXC` function, 931
`PERCENTRANK.INC` function, 931
period, interest, 330
`Period` argument, 351
periodic interest rate, 334
periodic sampling, 792
Permissions section, Info options, 154–155
`PERMUT` function, 931
Personal Macro Workbook, 809–810
PgDn key, 10
PgUp key, 10
"phantom link" errors, 660
`photo styles.xlsx` sample file, 939
`PI` function, 928
Pick from Drop-Down List, AutoComplete feature, 39
Picture (Enhanced Metafile) paste option, Paste Special dialog box, 619
Picture (GIF) paste option, Paste Special dialog box, 619
Picture (JPEG) paste option, Paste Special dialog box, 619
Picture (PNG) paste option, Paste Special dialog box, 619
Picture (U) option, 86
Picture (Windows Metafile) paste option, Paste Special dialog box, 619
Picture button, 187
picture charts, 470–471
`picture charts.xlsx` sample file, 938
Picture Fill tab, Format dialog box, 470

`Picture` property
  defined, 864
  `Image` control, 868
pictures and drawings
  Clip Art task pane, 531–532
  displaying worksheet background image, 535
  Equation Editor feature, 535–537
  graphics files
    inserting, 532–533
    overview, 531
  printing
    changing layout, 528
    changing style, 528–529
    customizing SmartArt feature, 527–528
    inserting SmartArt feature, 525–526
  screenshots, inserting, 533–535
  Shape images
    adding text to, 520
    aligning and spacing, 523
    formatting, 520–522
    grouping, 522
    inserting, 518–520
    overview, 517
    printing, 524
    reshaping, 523–524
  WordArt feature, 530
pie charts, 418, 424–426
`pie charts.xlsx` sample file, 938
pie of pie chart, 425
pivot charts
  example of, 736–738
  overview, 735
pivot tables
  appropriate data, 698–700
  calculated fields, 724–728
  calculated items, 724–725, 728–731
  counting formulas, 298–299
  creating
    formatting, 703–705
    laying out, 702–703
    modifying, 706–708
    specifying data, 701
    specifying location, 701–702
  creating frequency distributions, 722–724
  examples of, 696–698, 708–714, 739–741
  filtering with slicers, 731–733
  formatting option, 4
  grouping items automatically
    by date, 719–721
    by time, 722

grouping items manually, 717–718
  non-numeric data, 715–717
  overview, 695–696, 715–717
  pivot charts
    example of, 736–738
    overview, 735
  producing reports, 742–743
  referencing cells, 733–735
  versus worksheet outlines, 584
PivotTable Field List, 702
PivotTable Options dialog box, 705
`PivotTables` object, 815
`PivotTableUpdate` event, 880
Plot Area, charts, 444–445
plotting mathematical functions, 477–479
PMT (Payment), 330
`PMT` function
  calculating periodic loan payment, 334
  function of, 331–332, 924
`pmt` function argument, 331
pointer, data entry, 37
Pointy Haired Dilbert Web site, 948
Poisson distribution option, Random Number Generation
    dialog box, 790
`POISSON` function, 919
`POISSON.DIST` function, 931
Popular Commands option, Choose Commands From
    drop-down list, 544
Portable Document Format (PDF), 645
portfolios, optimizing investment, 778–779
positioning
  axis label, 452
  data label, 461
`POWER` function, 928
`PPMT` function, 924
pre-1900 dates, 256
precedents, 664
Precedents option, Go to Special dialog box, 76, 664
precision, adjusting, 764
Precision as Displayed option, Excel Options dialog box, 48
Prepare for Sharing section, Info options, 155–156
Present Value (PV), 330
Presidents' Day, date functions, 269
Preview box, Page Setup dialog box, 180
Preview Now button, Query Wizard, 684
`PRICE` function, 924
`PRICEDISC` function, 924
`PRICEMAT` function, 924
Print Area setting, 188

Index

Print button, Page Layout mode, 28
Print Preview, 173
Print tab, Backstage view, 179
Print Titles setting, 188
printing
    cell comments, 96–97
    charts, 416–417
    copying settings to other sheets, 188
    Custom Views of worksheet, 190–191
    headers and footers
        element codes, 186–187
        options, 187
        overview, 185
        predefined, 186
    one click, 171–172
    page setup settings
        adjusting page margins, 180–181
        background images, 185
        changing page orientation, 179
        choosing printer, 178
        overview, 177–178
        page breaks, inserting, 181–182
        page breaks, removing, 182
        printing cell gridlines, 183–184
        printing multiple copies, 180
        printing row and column headers, 185
        printing row and column titles, 182–183
        scaling printed output, 183
        specifying paper size, 179–180
        specifying what to print, 178–179
    page view
        Normal view, 173–174
        overview, 172–173
        Page Break Preview mode, 175–176
        Page Layout view, 174–175
    pictures and drawings
        changing layout, 528
        changing style, 528–529
        customizing SmartArt feature, 527–528
        inserting SmartArt feature, 525–526
        overview, 525–526
    preventing certain cells from being printed, 188–189
    preventing objects from being printed, 189
    Shape images, 524
Private keyword, 834
PROB function, 931
procedure
    defined, 801
    VBA module, 799, 813

procedure arguments
    function with no argument, 829
    function with one argument, 829–831
    function with range argument, 832–833
    function with two arguments, 831–832
    overview, 828–829
ProcessCells2 procedure, 892
PRODUCT function, 928
production model.xlsx sample file, 941
Project Properties dialog box, 912
project tracking, 630
Project window, VB Editor, 804
prompt element
    InputBox function, 838
    MsgBox function, 839
Proofing tab, AutoCorrect feature, 40
proper case, macro, 838
PROPER function, 200, 239–240, 932
properties
    adjusting, UserForm controls, 862–864
    VBA macros, 815–817
Properties dialog box, 178
Properties tab, Format dialog box, 189
Properties window, 845, 863
property
    defined, 801
    VBA, 814
Protect Current Sheet command, Info pane, 155
Protect Sheet dialog box, 19–20, 638
Protect Workbook button, 150, 154–155
Protect Workbook dialog box, 57, 644
Protect Workbook Structure command, Info pan, 155
Protected View mode, 5, 145
protection. See also passwords
    digital signatures
        getting digital ID, 647
        overview, 646–647
        signing workbooks, 647–648
    Information Rights Management (IRM), 638
    inspecting workbooks, 646
    marking workbooks as final, 646
    of projects using custom add-ins, 911–912
    safeguarding work, 157
    saving worksheet as PDF file, 645–646
    types of, 637
    VB Projects, 644–645
    workbooks
        protecting structures, 643–644
        protecting windows, 644
        requiring passwords to open, 641–643

worksheets
    assigning user permissions, 641
    overview, 638
    sheet protection options, 640
    unlocking cells, 639–640
Protection option
    Add Scenario dialog box, 756
    Style dialog box, 134
Protection tab, Format Cells dialog box, 639
Publish as PDF Or XPS dialog box, 645
Publish to Excel Services option, 614
pushpin icon, 144
PV (Present Value), 330
PV function
    function of, 924
    overview, 333

Q

quarters, determining, 271
QUARTILE function, 919
QUARTILE.EXC function, 931
QUARTILE.INC function, 931
Queries tab, Choose Data Source dialog box, 682
query, defined, 678
Query application
    data returned
        adjusting external data range properties, 688–689
        changing, 690
        deleting, 690
        refreshing, 689–690
    database files, 681
    overview, 680
    Query Wizard
        choosing columns, 684–685
        filtering data, 685–686
        Finish step, 686–687
        sort order, 686
    selecting data source, 682–684
    specifying location for data, 687–688
    using without Wizard
        adding and editing records in external database tables, 693
        creating query manually, 690–692
        formatting data, 693
        using multiple database tables, 692–693
question mark (?) wildcard character, 77, 242
Quick Access toolbar
    adding Camera tool to, 535
    adding command, 41
    customizing
        adding new commands, 543–545
        overview, 17–19, 541–542
    making macros available on, 855–856
    overview, 6–7
Quick Access Toolbar tab, Excel Options dialog box, 543–544
Quick Print icon, 171
QUOTIENT function, 928

R

radar charts, 419, 430–432
radar charts.xlsx sample file, 938
RADIANS function, 928
RAND function, 829, 928
RANDBETWEEN function, 228, 928
Random Number Generation dialog box, 789–790
Random Number Generation tool, Analysis ToolPak add-in, 789–790
random sampling, 792
Random Seed field, Random Number Generation dialog box, 790
range argument
    COUNTIF function, 287
    SUMIF function, 302
range copy.xlsm sample file, 942
range move.xlsm sample file, 942
Range object, 816
range_lookup argument
    HLOOKUP function, 314
    VLOOKUP function, 312
ranges
    adjusting external properties, 688–689
    appropriate for pivot tables, 700
    converting from table to, 113
    copying or moving
        adjacent cells, 82–83
        copying to other sheets, 83
        drag-and-drop, 81–82
        Office Clipboard, 84–85
        overview, 78–79, 888–889, 891
        Paste Special dialog box, 87–89
        pasting, 85–86
        Ribbon commands, 79–80
        shortcut keys, 81
        shortcut menu commands, 80–81
    copying variable-size, 889
    counting characters in, 371–372
    counting differences between, 384

Index

ranges (continued)
  counting error values in, 380–381
  determining whether contains valid values, 386
  displaying calendar, 398–399
  finding row of value's nth occurrence, 385
  intersections, 224–226
  looping through, 891–893
  naming
    Create Names from Selection dialog box, 91–92
    creating names, 90–92
    managing, 92–94
    Name box, 91
    New Name dialog box, 90–91
    overview, 89–90
    pasting into formulas, 205–206
  outline dragging, charts, 457–458
  picture effects, 534
  returning lists of unique items, 396–398
  returning locations of maximum values, 384–385
  returning longest text, 385
  returning nonblank cells from, 394–395
  sorting dynamically, 396
  summing smallest values in, 372–373
  summing the n largest values in, 381
  versus table, 101
  using references instead of arrays, 376–377
  VBA macros
    copying ranges, 888–889
    copying variable-size ranges, 889
    counting selected cells, 895–896
    determining type of selections, 893–894
    identifying multiple selections, 895
    looping through ranges, 891–893
    moving ranges, 891
    overview, 887–888
    prompting for cell values, 893
    selecting rows or columns, 890–891
    selecting to end of rows or columns, 890
Rank and Percentile tool, Analysis ToolPak add-in, 790
RANK function
  function of, 919
  overview, 392–393
RANK.AVG function, 931
RANK.EQ function, 931
RATE function
  #NUM! error, 655
  calculating loan information, 332
  function of, 924
rate function argument, 331
Read Only option, File in Use dialog box, 629

reading comments, cells, 96
ReadMe file, 942
read-only permission, 628
read-only property, 815–816
Read-Only Recommended check box, General Options dialog box, 643
real estate table.xlsx sample file, 935
rearranging
  Quick Access toolbar icons, 545
  worksheets, 56–57
RECEIVED function, 924
Recent Workbooks list, 143
Record Macro dialog box, 802–803, 809
recording VBA macros
  absolute versus relative, 808–809
  assigning to buttons, 810–811
  assigning to shortcut keys, 810
  basics, 802–803
  editing, 805
  examining, 804–805, 806–807
  example of, 803, 806
  re-recording, 807–808
  running, 806
  storing in Personal Macro Workbook, 809–810
  testing, 805, 808
records
  adding in external database tables, 693
  defined, 678
Recover Draft Versions command, 149, 156
recovering
  unsaved work, 149–150
  versions of current workbooks, 149
Redo tool, Quick Access toolbar, 542
#REF! error value, 219, 656
RefEdit control, 844
reference lines, faking, 510–512
reference operators, range, 225
Reference text box, Consolidate dialog box, 600
referencing
  cells within pivot tables, 733–735
  data in tables, 217–218
Refers To field, New Name dialog box, 91, 212, 224
refreshing
  consolidating worksheets, 604
  defined, 678
  pivot table, 705
  queries, 689–690
  Web query, 612
region1.xlsx sample file, 939
region2.xlsx sample file, 939

region3.xlsx sample file, 940
regional settings, data and time, 251
Regression dialog box, 791
Regression tool, Analysis ToolPak add-in, 790–791
relational database, 678, 691
relative cell reference, 574
relative comparisons, 417
relative references
    formulas and functions, 210–212
    problems, 657
Remove Duplicates dialog box, 109
removing
    Quick Access toolbar icons, 545
    titles from names, 247
Rename button, Ribbon, 549
Repeat button, Quick Access toolbar, 18
repeating characters, 236–237, 568
REPLACE function, 241–242, 932
Replace tab, Find and Replace dialog box, 670
Replace Text as You Type option, AutoCorrect dialog box,
    40, 673
replacing
    cell contents, 35
    within strings, 242–243
    text with other text, 241–242
report production, pivot tables, 742–743
Reports section, Solver Results dialog box, 769
REPT function, 236–237, 932
Reset button, Excel Options dialog box, 547
Reset Ignored Errors button, Excel Options dialog box, 666
Reset Only Selected Ribbon Tab option, 547
Reset to Match Style option, 416
resetting
    chart formatting, 443
    custom template default settings, 168
    Quick Access toolbar icons, 545
reshaping, Shape images, 523–524
Residuals option, Regression dialog box, 791
resizing
    charts, 414
    Name Manager dialog box, 93
    Open dialog box, 144
    Plot Area, 444
    windows, 51
resource allocation, Solver tool, 776–777
Rest All Customizations option, 547
Restore (Maximize) button, 50
Restrict Permission by People option, Info pane, 155
result cells, 759
result set, 678

result_vector argument, LOOKUP function, 315
returning errors, 653
reverse pivot table, 731
reverse pivot.xlsm sample file, 940
reversing actions, 19
reversing order of cells, 395–396
Review tab, Ribbon, 11
RGB components, chart, 430–432
Ribbon feature
    Accounting Number Format button, 553
    active chart sheets, 406
    charts, 442
    Comma Style button, 553
    copying ranges, 79–80
    customizing, 5, 546–549
    Decrease Decimal button, 553
    Home tab, 120
    interface
        accessing using keyboard, 15–16
        command types, 13–15
        contextual tabs, 13
        tabs, 11–12
    number formatting, 552–553
    overview, 6–7
    spinner control, 14–16
Right arrow key, 10
RIGHT function, 240–241, 932
Right horizontal alignment option, Format Cells dialog box, 123
Rights Management Services (RMS), 638
ripple effect, 219
ROMAN function, 928
rotating
    Shapes, 523
    text, 126
ROUND function
    defined, 48
    floating point number errors, 659
    function of, 928
    rounding time values, 279
ROUNDDOWN function, 928
ROUNDUP function, 928
Row Differences option, Go to Special dialog box, 75
ROW function
    displaying alternate-row shading, 497–498
    function of, 926
    generating array of consecutive integers, 370
Row Input Cell field, Data Table dialog box, 750
row labels, pivot table, 705
Row numbers, 6–7

Index

row_index_num argument, HLOOKUP function, 314
row_num argument, INDEX function, 316
rows and columns
    column width, changing, 67–68
    defined, 99
    deleting, 66
    headers, printing, 185
    height, changing, 67
    hiding, 66–67
    inserting, 65–66
    keeping visible while scrolling, 63
    returning last value in, 392
    row height, changing, 67
    selecting, 890–891
    selecting entire, 105
    selecting to end of, 890
    shading groups of, 498–499
    tables, 105–106
ROWS function, 926
RSQ function, 931
RTD function, 926
Rule of 72, 347–348
rules
    conditional formatting
        making, 484–485
        managing, 499–500
    formula-based, 494–499

S

sales by date.xlsx sample file, 940
sales by region pivot chart.xlsx sample file, 940
Salvage argument, 351
Sample box, Format Cells dialog box, 565
sample files, CD, 934–942
Sampling tool, Analysis ToolPak add-in, 791–792
Save As command, linking workbooks, 596
Save As dialog box
    compared to Open dialog box, 148
    Save As Type drop-down list, 798
    saving file for older version of Excel, 159
Save button, Quick Access toolbar, 18, 28
Save Chart Template dialog box, 469
Save Files in This Format option, Excel Options dialog box, 148
Save to SharePoint option, 614
Save to SkyDrive option, 614
Save tool, Quick Access toolbar, 542
saving
    custom templates, 170
    files for use with older versions, 159–160

workbooks
    containing macros, 798
    overview, 147–148, 896
    worksheets as PDF files, 645–646
Scale with Document check box, 187
scaling, printed output, 183
scaling values
    adding zeros, 563
    hundreds, 561
    millions, 562–563
    thousands, 560–561
scatter plots, 426
scattergrams, 426
Scenario Manager feature
    defined, 747
    defining scenarios, 754–756
    displaying scenarios, 757
    generating scenario reports, 758–759
    merging scenarios, 758
    modifying scenarios, 758
    overview, 753–754
Scenario Name field, Add Scenario dialog box, 756
Scenario PivotTable, 759
Scenario Summary dialog box, 759
Scenario Summary report, 759
Scenarios drop-down list, 757
Scientific format category, 554
Scientific format, Format Cells dialog box, 46–47
scope, 91
Screen capture tool, 4
screen updating, 899
screenshots, inserting, 533–535
ScreenTip button, Insert Hyperlink dialog box, 610
scroll box, 10
Scroll Lock key, 9
ScrollBar control, ActiveX, 844, 861, 869–870
scrollbars, 10
ScrollBars property, 872
Search button, Help system, 943
Search drop-down list, 669
Search for a Function field, Insert Function dialog box, 207
SEARCH function, 242, 932
searching
    formatting, 670–671
    information, 669–670
    newsgroups, 946–947
    selecting cells by, 76–78
    within strings, 242
SECOND function, 272, 921
seconds, decimal, 277–278

security, 797–798. *See also* protection
Security Warning, macros, 798
Security Warning section, Info options, 153–154
Select Case construct, Visual Basic for Applications (VBA)
   macros, 819
`select cells.xlsm` sample file, 942
Select Data Source dialog box
 defined, 446
 locating Access file, 679
Select Locked Cells option, Protect Sheet dialog box, 640
`Select Objects` control, 844
Select Unlocked Cells option, Protect Sheet dialog box, 640
Select Versions to Show button, Compatibility Checker
   dialog box, 158
Selected Table printing option, 178
selecting
 cells
  complete rows and columns, 71
  multisheet ranges, 72–74
  noncontiguous ranges, 71–72
  ranges, 70
  by searching, 76–78
  special types, 74–76
 comments, 97–98
 data from charts, 408–409
 multiple columns, 67
 parts of tables, 105
 rows and columns, 890–891
Selection and Visibility task pane, 521
`selection change event.xlsm` sample file, 942
Selection option, Excel Options dialog box, 118
Selection printing option, 178
`selection type.xlsm` sample file, 942
`SelectionChange` event, 880, 882–883
`SelectSpecial` method, 892
semantic error, 650
Send Using E-Mail option, 614
serial numbers
 dates, 249–250
 times, 252–253
Series formula, charts, 459–460
Series Options tab, Format Data Series dialog box, 425, 475
Series Overlap value setting, 475
`series_name` argument, `Series` formula, 459
`SERIESSUM` function, 928
Set Precision as Displayed check box, Excel Options dialog
   box, 48, 551, 659
Settings tab, Data Validation dialog box, 571
shading
 rows, 497–498
 worksheet formatting, 127–128

`shape examples.xlsx` sample file, 939
Shape images
 adding hyperlinks, 611
 adding text to, 520
 aligning and spacing, 523
 formatting, 520–522
 grouping, 522
 inserting, 518–520
 overview, 517
 printing, 524
 reshaping, 523–524
Share tab, Backstage view, 614
Share Workbook dialog box, 631–633
SharePoint server, 614
sharing data with Office applications
 copying and pasting, 615–617
 copying from Excel to Word
  pasting links, 620–622
  pasting static information, 617–620
 embedding objects in worksheets
  non-Word documents, 623
  overview, 622
  Word documents, 623
 embedding workbooks in Word
  copying, 624–626
  creating new Excel objects, 626
  saved workbooks, 626
sharing workbooks
 advanced sharing settings
  overview, 631–632
  resolving conflicting changes between users, 632–633
  tracking changes, 632
  updating changes, 632
 designating workbook as shared, 631
 overview, 629
 with yourself, 633
Sheet Name button, 187
sheet protection options, 640
Sheet settings, custom templates, 170
Sheet tab
 Excel screen, 6–7
 Page Setup dialog box, 183
`SheetActivate` event, 876, 878
`SheetBeforeDoubleClick` event, 876
`SheetBeforeRightClick` event, 876
`SheetCalculate` event, 876
`SheetChange` event, 876
`SheetDeactivate` event, 876
`SheetFollowHyperlink` event, 876
sheets, chart, 406–407
`SheetSelectionChange` event, 876

Index

shipping cost minimization, Solver tool, 773–776

`shipping costs.xlsx` sample file, 941

short date format, 251

Shortcut Key option, Record Macro dialog box, 802

shortcut keys
    assigning macros to, 810
    cells and ranges, 81
    number formatting, 553
    overview, 45, 949–955

shortcut menus
    commands, cells and ranges, 80–81
    overview, 16–17

Show All Properties Another option, 151

Show All Windows in the Taskbar option, 52

Show button, Scenario Manager dialog box, 757

Show Display Units Labels option, 451

Show Iteration Results option, Solver Options dialog box, 771

Show Margins option, Print Preview, 173

`show message.xlsm` sample file, 941

Show Mini Toolbar on Selection option, Excel Options dialog box, 17

Show Office Clipboard Automatically check box, 79, 84

Show Page Breaks check box, 174

Show Values As tab, Value Field Settings dialog box, 707

showing comments, cells, 97

`ShowUserForm` procedure, 909

Shrink to Fit option, 124

shrinking text, worksheet formatting, 124

side by side sheets, worksheets, 61

Sign dialog box, 647

`SIGN` function, 928

Signature Setup dialog box, 647

signatures, digital, 647–648

signing workbooks, 647–648

Simple buttons, Ribbon, 14

simple interest, 343–344

simultaneous linear equations, Solver tool, 771–773

`SIN` function, 928

`Single` data type, 901

Single File Web Page option, Save as Type drop-down list, 607

single file web pages, 607–609

single-cell array formulas
    computing averages that exclude zeros, 381–382
    counting characters in ranges, 371–372
    counting differences in two ranges, 384
    counting error values, 380–381
    counting text cells in ranges, 373–374
    determining closest values, 391
    determining whether particular values appears, 383–384
    determining whether range contains valid values, 386

eliminating intermediate formulas, 374–376
    finding row of value's nth occurrence, 385
    overview, 357–358
    ranking data, 392–393
    removing non-numeric characters from strings, 390
    returning last value in columns, 391–392
    returning last value in rows, 392
    returning locations of maximum values, 384–385
    returning longest text, 385
    summing digits of integers, 386–387
    summing every nth value, 388–390
    summing ranges that contain errors, 379–380
    summing rounded values, 388
    summing smallest values in ranges, 372–373
    summing the n largest values, 381
    using arrays instead of range references, 376–377

`single-cell array formulas.xlsx` sample file, 937

single-cell goal seeking, 762–764

Single-factor analysis of variance, 784

`SINH` function, 928

`six chart types.xlsx` sample file, 938

64-bit version, 4, 677

Size command, 521

`sizes` argument, `Series` formula, 459

sizing cells, Sparkline graphics, 507

`SKEW` function, 931

Skip Blanks option, Paste Special dialog box, 89

`skip blanks while looping.xlsm` sample file, 942

skipping blanks, Paste Special dialog box, 89

SkyDrive, 614

slicers, 4, 731–733

`SLN` function, 350, 924

`SLOPE` function, 931

`SMALL` function
    function of, 931
    nth smallest row number, 385
    summing values, 373

`SmallChange` property
    `ScrollBar` control, 870
    `SpinButton` control, 871

Smart Icon, 38–39

Smart Tag
    background error-checking, 665–666
    Convert to Number option, 230
    defined, 82
    Stop Automatically Creating Calculated Columns option, 217

Smart Tags tab, AutoCorrect dialog box, 674

`smartart demo xlsx` sample file, 939

SmartArt feature
    customizing, 527–528
    overview, 525–526
`smartart org chart.xlsx` sample file, 939
smoothing constant, 786
Solve button, Solver Parameters dialog box, 768
Solver Options dialog box, 770
Solver Parameters dialog box, 767
Solver Results dialog box, 768–769
Solver tool
    appropriate problems for, 765
    defined, 5
    examples using
        allocating resources, 776–777
        minimizing shipping costs, 773–776
        optimizing investment portfolios, 778–779
        overview, 765–769
        simultaneous linear equations, 771–773
    overview, 761, 764, 770–771, 905
Sort dialog box, 111–112
Sort option, Protect Sheet dialog box, 640
sort order, Query Wizard, 686
sorting
    range of values dynamically, 396
    tables, 110–112
source application, 615
source data, pivot table, 705
source workbook
    defined, 589
    modifying, 596–597
    Save As command, 596
`source.xlsx` sample file, 940
space character errors, 652
space operator, 225
spacing, Shape images, 523
Sparkline chart, 4, 403
`sparkline examples.xlsx` sample file, 939
Sparkline graphics
    auto-updating, 513
    creating, 505–507
    customizing
        adjusting axis scaling, 509–510
        changing colors and line width, 508
        changing type, 508
        faking reference lines, 510–512
        hidden or missing data, 508
        highlighting certain data points, 509
        sizing cells, 507
    displaying for dynamic ranges, 514–515

overview, 503
    specifying date axis, 512–513
    types of, 504–505
special characters, inserting, 233
Special format category, 554
Special format, Format Cells dialog box, 46–47
`specialized lookup examples.xlsx` sample file, 937
spell checking worksheets, 671–672
Spelling dialog box, 672
`SpinButton` control, ActiveX, 844, 861, 870–871
spinners, 14
Split button control, Ribbon, 14
splitting worksheet window into panes, 62
Spreadsheet Page, Web site, 947
SQL (Structured Query Language), 678
`SQRT` function, 928
`SQRTPI` function, 928
stacked area chart, 428
stacked column chart, 420, 430
Standard Deviation error bar, Format Error Bars dialog box, 462–463
Standard Errors check box, Moving Average dialog box, 788
`STANDARDIZE` function, 931
`start_period` argument
    `CUMIPMT` function, 332
    `CUMPRINC` function, 332
    depreciation functions, 351
Startup Prompt dialog box, 594
static consolidation, 600, 604
static information
    copying from Excel to Word, 617
    pasting, 617–620
Statistical Category Functions, 929–932
Status bar, 6, 8
StdDev summary formula, 108
`STDEVA` function, 931
`STDEVP` function, 919
`STDEV.P` function, 931
`STDEVPA` function, 931
`STDEV.S` function, 931
`STEYX` function, 931
stock charts, 433–436
`stock charts.xlsx` sample file, 938
Stop Automatically Creating Calculated Columns option, SmartTag, 217
Store Macro In option, Record Macro dialog box, 803
`StrConv` function, 837
String data types, 901

Index

strings
    converting from nondate to date, 261–262
    counting characters in, 239
    defined, 229
    extracting all but the first word of, 245
    extracting characters from, 240–241
    extracting the first word of, 244
    extracting the last word of, 244–245
    number formatting, 557–558
    removing non-numeric characters from, 390
    searching and replacing within, 242–243
    searching within, 242
    splitting without using formulas, 247
Structured Query Language (SQL), 678
Structures control, Equation Editor, 536
Style dialog box
    modifying named styles, 133
    Protection option, 134
Style Gallery, 611
`Style` property, `ComboBox` control, 867
Style settings, custom templates, 170
styles
    charts, 412–413
    named
        applying, 132–133
        controlling with templates, 135
        creating, 134
        merging from other workbooks, 134–135
        modifying, 133
        overview, 131
    pictures and drawings, 528–529
`Styles` object, 815
Sub procedure
    debugging custom functions, 834
    defined, 801
    general discussion, 799–800
    writing to display UserForm, 848
`SUBSTITUTE` function
    counting number of words in cells, 248
    function of, 932
    replacing text, 241
substrings, 243–244
`SUBTOTAL` function, 282, 928
subtotals, pivot table, 705
subtraction operator, 658
`SUM` formula, 371–372
`SUM` function
    array constants, 359
    counting differences in two ranges, 384
    displaying totals, 498–499

    function of, 928
    overview, 282
    ranges with error values, 379–380
    single array formula, 358
    summing all cells in range, 299–300
    "top *n*" values, 302
Sum summary formula, 108
`sum_range` argument, 302
`SUMIF` function
    arguments, 302
    function of, 928
    overview, 282
    summing values based on date comparison, 305
`SUMIFS` function, 282, 928
Summarize Values By tab, Value Field Settings dialog box, 707
summarizing formula data, 214–216
summary formulas
    consistency, 585
    Total Row, 108
summing
    digits of integers, 386–387
    every *n*th value, 388–390
    formulas
        all cells in a range, 299–300
        computing a cumulative sum, 300–302
        "top *n*" values, 302
    n largest values in ranges, 381
    ranges that contain errors, 379–380
    rounded values, 388
    smallest values in ranges, 372–373
`SUMPRODUCT` function, 282, 358–359, 928
`SUMSQ` function, 282, 928
`SUMX2MY2` function, 282, 928
`SUMX2PY2` function, 928
`SUMXMY2` function, 282, 928
surface charts, 432–433
`surface charts.xlsx` sample file, 938
switching, Excel windows, 52
`SYD` function, 351, 924
Symbol dialog box, 233
symbols, hiding in ouline, 588
Symbols control, Equation Editor, 536
Synchronous Scrolling toggle, 61
syntax
    `PMT` function, 331
    `PPMT` function, 331
    `HLOOKUP` function, 314
    `INDEX` function, 316
    `LOOKUP` function, 314
    `NPER` function, 333
    `PV` function, 333

`RATE` function, 332
`Series` formula, 459
syntax error, 649
system requirements, CD-ROM, 933

T

`T` function, 932
Tab list, 6, 8
tab order, UserForm, 856–857
tab scrolling controls, 53
tab split control, 53
`table and chart.xlsx` sample file, 935
Table Filter, pivot table, 705
`table formulas.xlsx` sample file, 936
table headings, 63
Table Style Options group, 107
`table_array` argument
    `HLOOKUP` function, 314
    `VLOOKUP` function, 312
tables. *See also* data tables; Pivot tables
    Access, importing, 679–680
    changing look of, 103–105
    converting back to ranges, 113
    creating, 102–103
    creating outlines, 585
    filtering, 112–113
    formulas within, 216–217
    moving, 106–107
    navigating, 105
    options, setting, 107
    overview, 99–102
    parts, selecting, 105
    referencing data, formulas, 217–218
    rows and columns
        adding, 105–106
        deleting, 106
        removing duplicate, 109
    selecting entire, 105
    sorting, 110–112
    summarizing formula data, 214–216
    Total Row feature, 107–109
Tables pane, Microsoft Query, 691, 693
tabs
    changing color, 55–56
    Ribbon interface, 11–12, 546–547
`TabStrip` control, 844
`TAN` function, 928
`TANH` function, 928
target cells, 765
task pane, 22
tasks, Query application, 681–682

`TBILLEQ` function, 924
`TBILLPRICE` function, 924
`TBILLYIELD` function, 924
`TDIST` function, 919
`T.DIST` function, 931
`T.DIST.2T` function, 931
`T.DIST.RT` function, 931
templates
    chart, 469–470
    creating workbooks from, 162–164
    custom
        changing workbook defaults, 166–167
        changing worksheet defaults, 167–168
        editing, 168
        ideas, 170
        overview, 165–166
        resetting default settings, 168
        saving, 170
    modifying, 164–165
    viewing, 161–162
Templates icon, 470
`test scores.xlsx` sample file, 940
testing
    custom number format, 565
    UserForms, 848, 852, 854–855
text
    adding to Shape images, 520
    alignment
        controlling the direction, 126–127
        displaying at an angle, 125–126
        horizontal alignment options, 122–123
        merging cells, 124–125
        vertical alignment options, 124
        wrapping or shrinking, 124
    case changing, 239–240
    counting occurrences of, 292–293
    counting text cells, 285
    displaying, 40
    entering and editing, 32–33
    entries, 30
    free-floating, 445
    number formatting, 566–567
    replacing with other text, 241–242
`text alignment.xlsx` sample file, 936
Text Axis option, 454
Text Category Functions, 932
text data, 29–31
Text Direction setting, 126
Text Filters option, 113
Text format category, 554

Index

Text format, Format Cells dialog box, 46–47
text formulas
    changing case of text, 239–240
    character codes, 231–233
    counting
        characters in strings, 239
        number of words, 248
        occurrences of substrings in cells, 243–244
        specific characters in cells, 243
    creating
        histograms, 237–238
        ordinal numbers, 247–248
    determining identical strings, 233–234
    displaying
        formatted currency values as text, 236
        formatted values as text, 235–236
    extracting
        all but first word of strings, 245
        characters from strings, 240–241
        filename from path specification, 244
        first word of strings, 244
        last word of strings, 244–245
        names, 245–247
    joining cells, 234–235
    overview, 229–230
    padding numbers, 238–239
    removing
        excess spaces and nonprinting characters, 239
        titles from names, 247
    repeating characters or strings, 236–237
    replacing text with other text, 241–242
    searching and replacing within strings, 242–243
    what is considered text, 229–230
TEXT function
    displaying formatted values as text, 235–236
    formatting numbers, 567
    function of, 932
text functions. *See* text formulas
text histogram.xlsx sample file, 936
Text Length option, Data Validation dialog box, 572
text string
    defined, 229
    splitting without using formulas, 247
TextAlign property, 872
TextBox control, ActiveX, 844, 861, 871–872
Texture Fill option, Format dialog box, 470
Thanksgiving Day, date functions, 271
The Changes Being Saved Win option, Share Workbook
        dialog box, 633
theme examples.xlsx sample file, 936

themes
    applying, 137
    customizing, 138–139
    overview, 135–136
thermometer charts, 472–473
thermometer chart.xlsx sample file, 938
thousands, number formatting, 560–561
three products.xlsx sample file, 941
3 × 4 array constant, 361–362
3-D area chart, 428
3-D charts, 464–465
3-D clustered column chart, 421
3-D data point, surface chart, 432
3-D line chart, 423
three-dimensional range, 72
three-part header, 186
tilde (~) character, 78, 242
Time category, 254
Time format category, 554
Time format, Format Cells dialog box, 46–47
TIME function, 921
time functions
    adding hours, minutes, or seconds to a time, 278
    calculating the difference between times, 274–275
    converting decimal hours, minutes, or seconds to a time,
        277–278
    converting from military time, 277
    displaying any time, 273
    displaying current time, 272–273
    non–time-of-day values, 279–280
    rounding time values, 279
    summing times that exceed 24 hours, 275–277
Time option, Data Validation dialog box, 571
time sheet.xlsm sample file, 936
time values
    entering and editing, 34
    of money, 329–330
    rounding, 279
times
    data entering, 42
    grouping in pivot tables, 722
    number formatting, 566
TimeStamp procedure, 807–808
TIMEVALUE function, 272–273, 884, 921
TINV function, 919
T.INV function, 931
T.INV.2T function, 931
title bar, Excel window, 6, 8
title element
    InputBox function, 838
    MsgBox function, 839

titles
    charts, 445–446
    removing from names, 247
TODAY function, 258–259, 829, 921
ToggleButton
    ActiveX control, 872
    Ribbon, 14
ToggleButton control, 844, 861
Tool Tabs, Ribbon, 548
Toolbox controls, 844
Tools control, Equation Editor, 536
Top Bottom Rules command, Conditional Formatting drop-down list, 483
"top *n*" values, formulas, 302
Top property, 864
Top Row check box, Consolidate dialog box, 602
Top vertical alignment option, Format Cells dialog box, 124
Total Row feature, tables, 107–109
tracking workbook changes
    reviewing, 635
    turning track changes on and off, 633–635
TRANPOSE function, 390
Transition Navigation Keys option, Excel Options dialog box, 949
Transpose (T) option, Paste Special dialog box, 86, 89
TRANSPOSE function
    arrays, 363
    function of, 926
    transposing arrays, 369–370
transposing
    arrays, 369–370
    ranges, Paste Special dialog box, 89
TREND function, 371, 931
trendlines, charts, 463–464
trial and error method, 455
TRIM function, 239, 652, 932
TRIMMEAN function, 931
troubleshooting, 942
TRUE function, 925
TRUNC function, 928
Trust Center dialog box, 797
TTEST function, 919
T.TEST function, 931
t-Test tool, Analysis ToolPak add-in, 792
Tufte, Edward, 505
two-dimensional array, 355, 361–362
Two-factor with replication analysis of variance, 784
Two-factor without replication analysis of variance, 784
two-input data tables, 750–753
Two-sample assuming equal variances t-Test, 792

Two-sample assuming unequal variances t-Test, 792
two-way data tables, 340–341
two-way lookup, 323–326
TYPE function, 925
type function argument, 331
Type Your Text Here window, SmartArt, 527

U

Undo command, Quick Access toolbar, 18–19
Undo tool
    pasting, 79
    Quick Access toolbar, 542
Unformatted Text paste option, Paste Special dialog box, 619
Unformatted Unicode Text paste option, Paste Special dialog box, 619
Unfreeze Panes option, 63
Unhide dialog box, 58
unhiding
    columns, 67
    rows, 67
    worksheets, 57–58
Uniform distribution option, Random Number Generation dialog box, 790
unique values, counting formulas, 293–294
unlocking
    cells, 639–640
    nonformula cells, 169
Unmerge Cells option, 125
Unprotect Workbook option, 643–644
Up arrow key, 10
up-bars, 434–435
Update Changes settings, Share Workbook dialog box, 632
Update Now button, Links dialog box, 621–622
Update Values dialog box, 592
updating
    changes when sharing workbooks, 632
    links, 594–595
    Sparklines, 513
UPPER function, 239, 932
U.S. English language date format, 249
USB drive, 157
Use AutoFilter option, Protect Sheet dialog box, 640
Use Automatic Scaling option, Solver Options dialog box, 771
Use Labels In check boxes, Consolidate dialog box, 601
Use PivotTable Reports option, Protect Sheet dialog box, 640
Use Relative References control, 809
Usenet, 945
user interface
    creating for add-in macros, 912–913
    customizations, 546

Index

user interface *(continued)*
  customizing
    Quick Access toolbar, 541–546
    Ribbon feature, 546–549
  modifying, 913
user permissions, 641
UserForms
  accelerator keys, 856
  ActiveX controls
    adding, 843–844, 862
    adjusting properties, 844–845, 862–863
    CheckBox, 866–867
    ComboBox, 867–868
    CommandButton, 868
    common properties, 863–864
    creating macros for, 864–866
    design mode, 862
    Image, 868
    Label, 868
    linking controls to cells, 864
    ListBox, 868–869
    OptionButton, 869
    overview, 861
    reasons for using, 859–861
    ScrollBar, 869–870
    SpinButton, 870–871
    TextBox, 871–872
    ToggleButton, 872
  alternatives to
    InputBox function, 838–839
    MsgBox function, 839–842
  controlling tab order, 856–857
  defined, 801
  displaying, 846
  examples of
    creating, 847–848, 850–852
    creating event-handler procedures, 849, 853–854
    overview, 846
    testing, 848, 852, 854–855
  handling events, 846
  macros
    making available from worksheet button, 855
    making available on Quick Access toolbar, 855–856
  overview, 837–838, 842–846, 909–910
  reasons for creating, 837–857

V

Validation option, Paste Special dialog box, 88
value axis, 407, 448–452

#VALUE! error value, 219, 656
Value Field Settings dialog box, 707
VALUE function, 932
Value property
  defined, 864
  ScrollBar control, 870
  SpinButton control, 870
values
  actual versus displayed errors, 658–659
  converting to, 228
  counting formulas, 286
  creating array constants from, 367
  creating arrays from, 366–367
  custom functions, 826
  displaying as text, 235–236
  entering and editing, 32–33
  formulas, 304–305
  looking up by using closest match, 327–328
  looking up from multiple lookup tables, 321
  lookup formulas, 318–320
  pie chart, 425
  returning only positive, 394
  sorting dynamically, 396
  summing, 388–390
  tracing errors with Excel Auditing tools, 665
Values (V) option, Paste Special dialog box, 86, 87
Values & Number Formatting (A) option, Paste Special
    dialog box, 86, 88
Values & Source Formatting (E) option, Paste Special dialog
    box, 86
Values area, pivot table, 705
values argument, Series formula, 459
Values in Reverse Order option, 450
VAR function, 919
Var summary formula, 108
variables
  declaring types, 901–902
  Visual Basic for Applications (VBA) macros, 817
Variant data types, 901
VARP function, 919
VAR.P function, 931
VARPA function, 932
Vary Colors by Point option, 474
VB Projects, protecting, 644–645
VBA (Visual Basic for Applications) functions, 800–801, 823
VBA (Visual Basic for Applications) macros. *See* Visual Basic
    for Applications macros
vba functions.xlsm sample file, 941
vbAbortRetryIgnore constant, MsgBox function, 840
vbCritical constant, MsgBox function, 841
vbDefaultButton1 constant, MsgBox function, 841

vbDefaultButton2 constant, MsgBox function, 841
vbDefaultButton3 constant, MsgBox function, 841
VBE (Visual Basic Editor). See Visual Basic Editor (VBE)
VBExclamation constant, MsgBox function, 841
vbInformation constant, MsgBox function, 841
vbOKCancel constant, MsgBox function, 840
vbOKOnly constant, MsgBox function, 840
vbQuestion constant, MsgBox function, 841
vbRetryCancel constant, MsgBox function, 841
vbYesNo constant, MsgBox function, 840
vbYesNoCancel constant, MsgBox function, 840
VDB function, 351, 924
vector-based image, 531
Versions section, Info options, 149, 156
vertical alignment options, worksheet, 124
vertical page break, 181–182
vertical scrollbar, 6, 8
Veterans Day, date functions, 270
View tab, Ribbon, 549
views
    chart data, 411
    page
        Normal view, 173–174
        overview, 172–173
        Page Break Preview mode, 175–176
        Page Layout view, 174–175
    templates, 161–162
    worksheets
        freezing panes, 62–64
        multiple windows, 60–61
        overview, 58
        side by side sheets, 61
        splitting window into panes, 62
        Watch Window, 64–65
        zooming, 59–60
Visible Cells Only option, Go to Special dialog box, 76
visible digital signature, 647
Visible property, 864
Visual Basic Editor (VBE)
    creating macros for controls, 864–865
    defined, 801
    disabling Mini toolbar, 118
    Project window, 804
    sizing and aligning controls, 852
    window, 798
Visual Basic for Applications (VBA) functions, 800–801, 823
Visual Basic for Applications (VBA) macros
    charts
        applying formatting, 899
        modifying properties, 898
        modifying type, 898
    displaying Developer tab, 796–797

    overview, 795–796
    ranges
        copying, 888–889
        copying variable-size, 889
        counting selected cells, 895–896
        determining type of selections, 893–894
        identifying multiple selections, 895
        looping through, 891–893
        moving, 891
        overview, 887–888
        prompting for cell values, 893
        selecting rows or columns, 890–891
        selecting to end of rows or columns, 890
    recording
        absolute versus relative, 808–809
        assigning to buttons, 810–811
        assigning to shortcut keys, 810
        basics, 802–803
        editing, 805
        examining, 804–807
        example of, 803, 806
        re-recording, 807–808
        running, 806
        storing in Personal Macro Workbook, 809–810
        testing, 805, 808
    saving with .xlsx file extension, 148
    saving workbooks
        all, 896
        closing and, 896–897
        containing macros, 798
    security, 797–798
    speed tips
        declaring variable types, 901–902
        preventing alert messages, 900
        simplifying object references, 900–901
        turning off screen updating, 899
    Sub procedures, 799–800
    writing VBA code
        entering and editing, 812
        event-handler procedures, 874–875
        For-Next loops, 818
        how VBA works, 812–814
        If-Then construct, 818
        macro that can't be recorded, 819–821
        methods, 817
        objects and collections, 814–815
        overview, 811
        properties, 815–817
        Select Case construct, 819
        variables, 817
        With-End With construct, 818–819

Index

Visual Basic (VB) protection, 637
VLOOKUP function
    function of, 926
    general discussion, 312–313
    looking up values, 327
    Lookup formulas, 311

W

Watch Window
    formula results, 747
    worksheets, 64–65
watermark, 184
weather combination chart.xlsx sample file, 938
Web formats
    HTML files, 607
    overview, 606
    single file web pages, 607–609
Web Options dialog box, 608
Web pages, 607–609
Web queries, 612–613
Web sites
    contextures, 948
    daily dose of Excel, 948
    David McRitchie's Excel Pages, 948
    Jon Peltier's Excellge, 948
    Mr. Excel, 948
    Pearson Software Consulting, 948
    Pointy Haired Dilbert, 948
    spreadsheet page, 947
webpage.xlsx sample file, 940
WEEKDAY function, 258, 267, 577, 921
WEEKNUM function, 258, 921
WEIBULL function, 919
WEIBULL.DIST function, 932
What You See Is What You Get (WYSIWYG) mode, 406
what-if analysis
    creating data tables
        one-input, 748–750
        two-input, 750–753
    example of, 745–747
    goal seeking and Solver tools, 761
    manual, 747
    Scenario Manager feature
        defining scenarios, 754–756
        displaying scenarios, 757
        generating scenario reports, 758–759
        merging scenarios, 758
        modifying scenarios, 758
        overview, 753–754
    types of, 747

When File Is Saved setting, Share Workbook dialog box, 632
Whole Number option, Data Validation dialog box, 571
Wide setting, Page Layout view, 180
Width property, 864
wildcard characters, 77–78
Window Close button, 6, 8
Window Maximize/Restore button, 6, 8
Window Minimize button, 6, 8
WindowActivate event, 876
WindowDeactivate event, 876
WindowResize event, 876
windows
    closing, 52–53
    moving, 51
    overview, 49–51
    resizing, 51
    splitting, 62
    switching, 52
Windows Clipboard, 79–80, 616
Windows Control Panel
    adjusting date and time, 42
    Regional and Language Options, 251
    specifying two-digit years, 257
Windows object, 814, 815
Windows Vista, 144
Win/Loss Sparkline
    displaying goal achievement, 511
    overview, 504
With-End With construct, VBA macros, 818–819
Within drop-down list, 669
Word documents
    copying from Excel, 617–622
    embedding, 624–626
wordart examples.xlsx sample file, 939
WordArt feature, 530
WordArt Styles command, 521
Words that contain X conditional formatting rule, 482
WordWrap property, 872
work days, date fuctions, 263–264
work days.xlsx sample file, 936
Workbook Connections dialog box, 689
Workbook events, 873
workbook file, 5
Workbook_BeforeClose procedure, 879
Workbook_BeforePrint procedure, 875
Workbook_BeforeSave procedure, 878–879
Workbook_Open procedure, 876–877, 879
workbooks
    adding digital signatures, 646
    changing default number of worksheets, 55
    closing, 156

creating
  overview, 141–143
  from templates, 162–164
defined, 49
embedding when saved, 626
events
  BeforeClose, 879
  BeforeSave, 878–879
  NewSheet, 878
  Open, 876–877
  overview, 875–876
  SheetActivate, 878
inspecting, 646
linking
  avoiding potential problems, 595–597
  external reference formulas, 590–595
  overview, 589–590
marking as final, 646
opening
  with external reference formulas, 592–594
  Favorite Links list, 146
  file display preferences, 147
  filtering filenames, 146–147
  overview, 143–146
overview, 5–8
protecting
  overview, 637
  requiring passwords to open, 641–643
  structures, 643–644
  windows, 644
referencing from, 213–214
renaming or moving source, 596
saving
  containing macros, 798
  overview, 147–148, 896
setting up, 908
sharing
  advanced sharing settings, 631–633
  designating workbook as shared, 631
  overview, 629
  with yourself, 633
signing, 647–648
source workbooks, 596–597
templates, 168
testing custom add-ins, 910–911
tracking changes in, 633–635
VBA macros, 896–897
Workbooks object, 814–815
WORKDAY function, 258, 264, 921
WORKDAY.INTL function, 201, 258, 921

workgroups
  file reservations, 628–629
  sharing workbooks
    advanced sharing settings, 631–633
    designating workbook as shared, 631
    overview, 629
    with yourself, 633
  tracking workbook changes
    reviewing, 635
    turning track changes on and off, 633–635
  using on networks, 627
worksheet button, making macros available, 855
worksheet controls.xlsm sample file, 941
Worksheet events, 873
Worksheet_Change procedure, 880
worksheets
  activating, 53
  adding to workbook, 54
  changing sheet tab color, 55–56
  consolidating
    example of, 601–603
    overview, 597–598
    refreshing, 604
    using Consolidate command, 600–601
    using formulas, 598
    using Paste Special dialog box, 599
  creating
    appearance, 25
    creating charts, 26
    formatting numbers, 24–25
    month names, 23
    printing, 27–28
    sales data, 23–24
    saving, 28
    starting, 22–23
    summing values, 25–26
  custom functions
    debugging, 833–834
    example of, 824–826
    function procedure arguments, 828–833
    function procedures, 826–828
    inserting, 834–836
    using in formulas, 828
    VBA functions, 823
  Custom Views of worksheet, printing, 190–191
  defined, 49
  deleting, 54
  entering formulas, 203–205
  events
    BeforeRightClick, 883
    Change, 880

Index

worksheets, events *(continued)*
  monitoring specific range for changes, 881
  overview, 879–880
  SelectionChange, 882–883
formatting
  background images, 130–131
  borders and lines, 128–129
  colors and shading, 127–128
  document themes, 135–139
  fonts, 119–122
  named styles, 131–135
  text alignment, 122–127
  tools for, 115–119
function references, 917–932
hiding/unhiding, 57–58
inserting functions into formulas, 206–208
naming, 54–55
navigating, 9–10, 950
overview, 5–10
pasting range names into formulas, 205–206
protecting
  assigning user permissions, 641
  overview, 637–638
  sheet protection options, 640
  unlocking cells, 639–640
rearranging, 56–57
referencing from, 212–213
rows and columns
  changing height, 67–68
  changing width, 67–68
  deleting, 66
  hiding, 66–67
  inserting, 65–66
saving as PDF file, 645–646
spell checking, 671–672
views
  multiple windows, 60–61
  overview, 58
  panes, freezing, 62–64
  side by side sheets, 61
  splitting windows into panes, 62
  Watch Window, 64–65
  zooming, 59–60
windows
  closing, 52–53
  moving, 51
  overview, 49–51
  resizing, 51
  switching, 52

Worksheets object, 815
Worst Case scenario, Scenario Manager, 755
Wrap Text option, 124
wrapping text, worksheet formatting, 124
WYSIWYG (What You See Is What You Get) mode, 406

X

X icon
  Formula bar, 36
  New Formatting Rule dialog box, 491–492
XDATE demo.xlsm sample file, 936
XIRR function, 924
XLSA format, 159
XLSB format, 159
XLSK format, 159
XLSM format, 159, 934
XLStart folder, 135, 147
XLSX format, 159, 934
XLTM format, 159
XLTX format, 159
XML files, 159
XNPV function, 924
XPS format, 645
XY charts, 426–427
xy charts.xlsx sample file, 938

Y

YEAR function, 258, 265, 921
YEARFRAC function, 258, 265, 921
yearly calendar.xlsx sample file, 937
years between dates, calculating, 265
YIELD function, 924
YIELDDISC function, 924
YIELDMAT function, 924

Z

Zero option, 461–462
zeros, 563–564
Zip-compressed text files, 159
Zoom control, 6, 8
Zoom to Page option, Print Preview, 173
zooming, worksheets, 59–60
ZTEST function, 919
z.TEST function, 932
z-Test tool, Analysis ToolPak add-in, 792

John Wiley & Sons, Inc.
End-User License Agreement

5. **Limited Warranty.**

    (a) WILEY warrants that the Software and Software Media are free from defects in materials and workmanship under normal use for a period of sixty (60) days from the date of purchase of this Book. If WILEY receives notification within the warranty period of defects in materials or workmanship, WILEY will replace the defective Software Media.

    (b) WILEY AND THE AUTHOR(S) OF THE BOOK DISCLAIM ALL OTHER WARRANTIES, EXPRESS OR IMPLIED, INCLUDING WITHOUT LIMITATION IMPLIED WARRANTIES OF MERCHANTABILITY AND FITNESS FOR A PARTICULAR PURPOSE, WITH RESPECT TO THE SOFTWARE, THE PROGRAMS, THE SOURCE CODE CONTAINED THEREIN, AND/OR THE TECHNIQUES DESCRIBED IN THIS BOOK. WILEY DOES NOT WARRANT THAT THE FUNCTIONS CONTAINED IN THE SOFTWARE WILL MEET YOUR REQUIREMENTS OR THAT THE OPERATION OF THE SOFTWARE WILL BE ERROR FREE.

    (c) This limited warranty gives you specific legal rights, and you may have other rights that vary from jurisdiction to jurisdiction.

6. **Remedies.**

    (a) WILEY's entire liability and your exclusive remedy for defects in materials and workmanship shall be limited to replacement of the Software Media, which may be returned to WILEY with a copy of your receipt at the following address: Software Media Fulfillment Department, Attn.: Excel 2010 Bible, John Wiley & Sons, Inc., 10475 Crosspoint Blvd., Indianapolis, IN 46256, or call 1-800-762-2974. Please allow four to six weeks for delivery. This Limited Warranty is void if failure of the Software Media has resulted from accident, abuse, or misapplication. Any replacement Software Media will be warranted for the remainder of the original warranty period or thirty (30) days, whichever is longer.

    (b) In no event shall WILEY or the author be liable for any damages whatsoever (including without limitation damages for loss of business profits, business interruption, loss of business information, or any other pecuniary loss) arising from the use of or inability to use the Book or the Software, even if WILEY has been advised of the possibility of such damages

    (c) Because some jurisdictions do not allow the exclusion or limitation of liability for consequential or incidental damages, the above limitation or exclusion may not apply to you.

7. **U.S. Government Restricted Rights.** Use, duplication, or disclosure of the Software for or on behalf of the United States of America, its agencies and/or instrumentalities "U.S. Government" is subject to restrictions as stated in paragraph (c)(1)(ii) of the Rights in Technical Data and Computer Software clause of DFARS 252.227-7013, or subparagraphs (c) (1) and (2) of the Commercial Computer Software - Restricted Rights clause at FAR 52.227-19, and in similar clauses in the NASA FAR supplement, as applicable.

8. **General.** This Agreement constitutes the entire understanding of the parties and revokes and supersedes all prior agreements, oral or written, between them and may not be modified or amended except in a writing signed by both parties hereto that specifically refers to this Agreement. This Agreement shall take precedence over any other documents that may be in conflict herewith. If any one or more provisions contained in this Agreement are held by any court or tribunal to be invalid, illegal, or otherwise unenforceable, each and every other provision shall remain in full force and effect.

The keys to your new Office.

Unlock the full potential of Microsoft Office 2010 with our comprehensive Bibles from expert authors. These are the books you need to succeed!

978-0-470-59184-0

978-0-470-47487-7

978-0-470-59186-4

978-0-470-47534-8

978-0-470-59185-7